Computer-aided modelling and simulation

International Lecture Series in Computer Science

These volumes are based on the lectures given during a series of specially funded chairs. The International Chair in Computer Science was created by IBM Belgium in co-operation with the Belgium National Foundation for Scientific Research. The holders of each chair cover a subject area considered to be of particular relevance to current developments in computer science.

The Correctness Problem in Computer Science (1981)
R. S. BOYER and J. STROTHER MOORE

Computer-aided Modelling and Simulation (1982)
J. A. SPRIET and G. C. VANSTEENKISTE

Computer-aided modelling and simulation

By

Jan A. Spriet and Ghislain C. Vansteenkiste

Department of Applied Mathematics and Biometrics
University of Ghent
Belgium

1982

ACADEMIC PRESS
A Subsidiary of Harcourt Brace Jovanovich, Publishers
London · New York
Paris · San Diego · San Francisco · São Paulo · Sydney · Tokyo · Toronto

ACADEMIC PRESS INC. (LONDON) LTD.
24–28 Oval Road
London NW1 7DX

U.S. Edition published by
ACADEMIC PRESS INC
111 Fifth Avenue
New York, New York 10003

Copyright © 1982 by
ACADEMIC PRESS INC. (LONDON) LTD.

All Rights Reserved

No part of this book may be reproduced in any form by photostat, microfilm, or any
other means, without written permission from the publishers

British Library Cataloguing in Publication Data

Spriet, J. A.
   Computer-aided modelling and simulation.
   1. Computer simulation
   I. Title   II. Vansteenkiste, G. C.
   001.42′4   QA76.9.C65

   ISBN 0-12-659050-8

   LCCN 81-68976

Typeset by Preface Ltd, Salisbury, Wilts.
Printed in Great Britain by the St. Edmundsbury Press

QA
76.9
C65S67
1982

Preface

Management and control of the behaviour of complex systems are becoming more and more of a challenge. Model-making appears to be an essential feature of human thinking. Therefore, the impact of simulation on innovative decision-making is proving to be substantial and extremely valuable.

We had the unique opportunity at the University of Ghent of establishing an international chair in simulation, during the academic year 1979–80. In order that all aspects of modelling and simulation should be comprehensively covered, five experts representing different areas of the field were selected to hold the chair.

Walter J. Karplus provided new directions in continuous systems simulation. Peter C. Young was particularly interested in identification and estimation of simulation models. Bernard P. Zeigler developed multifacetted system simulation methodology. Wolfgang K. Giloi designed architecture of interactive programming systems. Leendert Dekker discussed parallel simulation.

This book is a synthesis of the contributions made through the lectures, discussions and informal conversations held during the year. Various research staff from the University of Ghent contributed to this exchange of ideas (J. L. Willems, E. H. D'Hollander) as also did visitors from the Delft University of Technology (J. C. Zuidervaart, H. J. Sips, R. W. Sierenberg, E. J. H. Kerckhoffs). The authors are aware that in synthesizing, assembling, expanding, adding and writing the text, they had to impose their personal views; they take full responsibility for the content of the book.

Throughout, modelling and simulation are considered together. After an introduction, modelling-oriented topics are considered first. Basic and required knowledge is covered in chapter two. The definition of "model" is based on the lectures of B. P. Zeigler; we have added the fundamentals of modelling and have tried to give a complete picture of the future based on the personal opinions of the contributors. Modelling methodology for ordinary differential equations (chapter three) and for partial differential

v

equations (chapter four) is considered next. Chapter three contains sections on system identification and recursive parameter estimation which are based on parts of the lecture course given by P. C. Young. A more complete treatment of the subject including practical examples will be available in two forthcoming books by P. C. Young: "An Introduction to Recursive Estimation" to be published by Springer-Verlag in their "Lecture Notes in Control and Information Sciences" series, and "Recursive Estimation and Time-Series Analysis" to be published by Marcel Dekker. In particular Sections 3.2.3 to 3.2.6 on the instrumental variable estimation approach, were promoted by P. C. Young. We have highlighted many other modelling issues, including basic considerations on modelling power, identifiability concepts, general ideas on parameter estimation, other estimation procedures, structure characterization techniques, hints on experimental design, frame definition and model validation. Chapter four contains Section 4.2 on the deductive approach to partial differential equation model-building from W. J. Karplus, and discusses inductive methods as well. Chapter five is at the crossroads between modelling and simulation. It discusses advanced simulation software based on system theoretical concepts and is an adaptation of the presentations from B. P. Zeigler. Zeigler's contributions to Chapters 2 and 5 will appear in expanded form in a forthcoming book "Multifacetted System Modelling Methodology" to be published by Academic Press, London. Chapters six and seven are devoted to simulation aspects respectively in software and hardware. Section 6.2.2 and large parts of Chapter seven are adaptations of a chapter of a forthcoming book "Digital Computer Treatment of Partial Differential Equations" by V. Vemuri and W. J. Karplus, Prentice-Hall, Inc., to whom we are greateful for permission to use this material. Chapter eight considers trends in simulator developments in the future. This is based upon ideas presented by L. Dekker; the iterative software treatment (Section 8.4) and Section 6.3.3 are adaptations of the contribution of W. K. Giloi. A more elaborate treatise on the latter topic can be found in "Architecture of Interactive Software" available from the Technical University of Berlin, FB Informatik, Tech. Report 80-15.

The literature in the area of modelling and simulation has previously been fragmented in a number of diverse publications. This volume attempts a real synthesis of the field. Moreover it is probably one of the first to address all important issues that follow from a partnership between man and machine. It is indeed realized nowadays that a powerful simulator bears the promise of becoming an important aid to the model-builder in carrying modelling activities through. Certainly, it has not been the intention to give a complete picture of all existing methodological tools available. However, the scope of the text is sufficiently general as to present to the reader a more comprehensive picture of the major options and facilities that concern the model-builder. In that respect the book is thought to break new grounds. We hope that it will be of use not only to those currently involved in simulation, but also to students approaching the subject for the first time. A basic knowledge of linear algebra, probablity and estimation theory, differential calculus and control theory is required. The material is presented in discussion format rather than a theorem–proof format and results are often developed in an intuitive manner.

The greatest appreciation is expressed to IBM Belgium, the Belgian National Science Research Foundation and the University of Ghent for making this volume possible. The authors are also grateful to Annie Gevaert for the extensive typing, to Jan De Backer for the artwork and to everyone who was indirectly involved in all aspects arising from the establishing of this chair.

Jan A. Spriet
Ghislain C. Vansteenkiste

November 1981

Contents

1. Introduction and outline

1.1 MODELLING AND SIMULATION

1.1.1 The Scientific-engineering Approach to Reality

Since the very early days of his existence, man has been urged to interact with his environment to fulfil his essential needs. With time, the "modes" of interaction he has relied upon, have become more varied and more sophisticated. More specifically, his scientific and engineering endeavour is one of the more mature forms of interaction with the real world. Although its use has sometimes been questioned, there cannot be any doubt about its value; at least, if one is prepared to be fair in assessing the achievements so far attained. It has to be recognized that the scientific engineering approach to reality, has endowed man with a remarkable amount of power over his environment. It is not the objective to go into philosophical discussions in order to analyse the nature of this success. Of more importance here is the stimulating effect that the remarkable results of the approach have produced: a systematic search to improve methodological skills.

In recent years, research in methodology has intensified for different reasons. It seems now, that the computer, which has been helpful from the very beginning of its existence, has opened new perspectives. The machine can play a still more important role to relieve man of certain tedious burdens: this is the major theme of this book. It intends to present recent advances in the modelling and simulation field, with an emphasis on the useful partnership between model-builder and machine. To clarify this point further, a closer view of the "scientific-engineering mode" of interaction will be helpful.

1.1.2 Modelling as an Age-old Human Activity

Human-world interaction based on a "scientific-engineering" approach seems to have a "formal" model or an abstract representation as a key to power. A large part of scientific work, and some people believe all scientific work, consists in formalization and model-building. Through

1

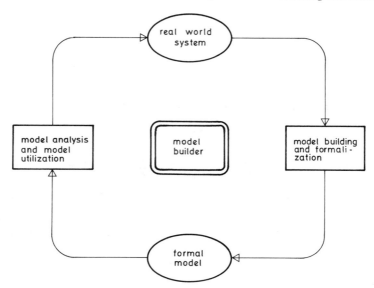

FIG. 1.1   Scientific-engineering interaction between man and reality

observation and experimentation the scientist attempts to create abstract
representations and laws that formalize verified hypotheses concerning
real world phenomena. The formal "models" are only useful if they succeed in "seizing" the essential features of the real life system. They permit
extrapolation, analysis and design; so in a sense they provide us with
manipulative power.

It is important to realize that the special type of human-world interaction
under study here, entails two different steps (Fig. 1.1). First of all, there is
always a model-building or formalization step, which yields a model of the
real world system. This stage is clearly scientifically oriented, in the sense
that one tries to gain sufficient understanding of the phenomena by constructing an abstract representation. In a second stage, the formal model is
analysed, and utilized in order to learn how the real system can be manipu-
lated for man's own purposes: clearly this has an engineering flavour. The
role of the computer becomes more apparent if the human skill in performing the stages is considered.

1.1.3   Skill Imbalance in the Major Interaction Stages

For proper interaction it is essential that the model-building step and the
model-analysis step can be properly carried through. Unfortunately, a successful performance in one stage is no guarantee for success in other stages.

In fact, in many cases, although one of the steps could be properly done, lack of skill in the other phase has hampered global interaction. In the mathematical modelling field, good examples exist to illustrate the point. The Schrödinger wave equations, for instance, are the result of a difficult model-building problem on certain physical phenomena. The model is available now, but its utilization is often very difficult. To a large extent mathematical skills for analysing the equations, except for very easy configurations, are inadequate. On the other hand, it may happen that proper model use would have been possible whenever a sufficiently valid model could have been produced.

It may be a pity that, at a given point, certain human ends cannot be met with a scientific-engineering approach because of the limitations of the nature of interaction. However, it is frustrating to recognize that other objectives cannot be met because of an imbalance in man's skills to proceed through both interaction stages. One may hope that, with time, some problems will be solved as those skills mature, but it has to be recognized that man has his own limits and that these limits set bounds on his achievements. This fact was recognized very early in the domain of human sensory perception, and it was soon realized that measurement instruments could be of invaluable help in extending the human senses, as well as in obtaining observations through means far beyond human capabilities. For the act of modelling, human capabilities may also have their limits. A human being is apt in making abstractions: he is skilful in recognizing patterns and making associations, he can perform calculations, he has a memory, etc; *so*, it is to be expected that the modelling approach he uses is the result of the specific "blend" of his capabilities. His limits, on the other hand, will also restrict the modelling achievements and it is natural to look for "instruments" and "devices" which may be of help in overcoming these restrictions. It is in this context that the role of computers has to be evaluated.

1.1.4 Simulation to the Rescue

Almost as soon as computers were born, it became clear that the new machines carried an exceptional promise for solving many problems. In the beginning, their role in the context of man's scientific-engineering activities was limited. They were essentially used as powerful, fast, though rather dumb, computing machines. In those early days the word "simulation" was coined. Since then the role of the computer has gradually increased while the machine has become more sophisticated and better "educated". Table 1.1 provides a schematic survey of the evolution in the modelling and simulation field [250].

TABLE 1.1   Brief survey of historical developments in modelling and simulation

Historical perspective
1600–1940 : Modelling in the physical sciences
1940 : Advent of the electronic computer
1955 : Simulation in the aerospace industry
1960 : Simulation of industrial operations scheduling
1970 : Simulation of large scale systems including economic, social and environmental factors
1975 : Systems and simulation merge
1975 : Systems simulation and higher level decision making

The precise meaning of the word "simulation" is, even at the present, a point of debate. In loose terms, most people understand simulation to be the act of running a program which represents an abstract model in order to study the real system's behaviour. Simulation under these terms can be of as much value in the model-building stage as in the model-analysis stage of the scientific-engineering approach to reality. The fact that simulation is used in different branches of the complete process has often led to confusion. It is easy to see, however, that in both cases, simulation is used as a means to overcome the existing imbalance between the major interaction stages.

Instead of the simple representation of Fig. 1.1, a more complex diagram is required to clarify the relationships and important entities for "modelling and simulation", as in Fig. 1.2. The model-builder, who previously stood in the centre of the overall process, now has the computer as a partner to support him. The model-builder himself relies on an abstract model in order to "function" adequately. By analogy it is easy to understand that the computer needs a proper "language" in order to operate. Basically, the machine works on programs and it is the model-builder who chooses and implements these programs with the help of suitable software tools. The programs relate to the formal model and the computing and simulation activity of the machine directly influences and supports the basic activities: model-building and model-analysis.

A word of caution is appropriate here. Here, the computer has been directly introduced as the suitable partner in the scientific-engineering approach. Though few persons may question this choice, it has to be recognized that other devices like small-scale physical models or "maquettes" have also been used and are still in use to assist the model-builder. There are electric network analogons, electrolytic tanks for solving electric field problems, "maquettes" for analysing aerodynamic properties, and so on.

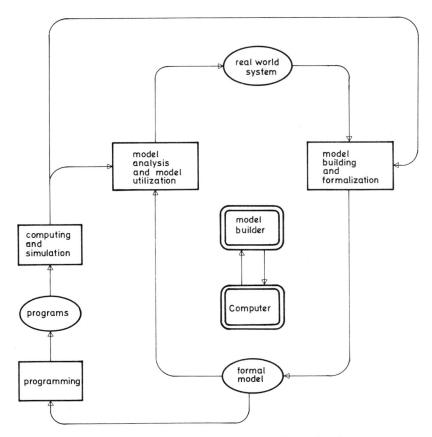

FIG. 1.2   Interaction between man, machine and reality

These types of simulation activity are not considered in this text. The authors focus on computer-aided modelling and simulation, though the adjective computer-aided will often be dropped in the sequel.

It is appropriate now to reconsider the meaning one can attribute to the concept of "simulation". In fact, one could view all computing that supports model-building and model-analysis as simulation activities. In order to distinguish this type of simulation activity from the classic one, it could be termed "simulation in the large". Consequently, the box "computing and simulation" on Fig. 1.2 could have been labelled "simulation in the large". Notice that the meaning of simulation in the title of the book is the more general one. Often the rather cumbersome "in the large" will be dropped whenever the meaning of the word follows directly from the context.

1.1.5   Scope of the Book

In this book, methodology for modelling and simulation is considered. Certainly it is not the intention to give a complete picture of all possible methodological tools available to the engineer or scientist. Such an enterprise would be so gigantic that even thinking of it engenders considerable mental resistance and awe. The topics for the presentation have been selected along two lines of thought. First, the level of generality of the issues concerning modelling and simulation plays an important role. Broadly, one can distinguish four levels of generality. At the lowest level of generality, considerations related to a specific topic or problem area in a scientific branch are relevant to the methodological approach. At a second level, the issues arise from properties typical for a scientific area. At a third level of specialization, only the types of models, the nature of the modelling context, or the special features of computation are important. Finally, at the highest level it is the mathematical language itself as formalization tool, that specifies the issues in methodology. This book only discusses methodology at the two higher levels of specialization and do not enter specific scientific disciplines.

The second line of thought is much more restrictive. It is close to the special interests of the authors and their perception of the needs and promises of the field. Consequently, although an attempt has been made to set the topics under discussion into a more general perspective, it is only claimed that advances in the field are presented. A topical outline follows as a guide to the reader.

1.2   TOPICAL OUTLINE

A presentation of the different subjects of the book is given in this section. They are inherently related to the important steps displayed in Fig. 1.2. In order to gain a better insight into the relationships between different topics to be considered in the text, it is useful to rethink the diagram of Fig. 1.2. Formerly, a text on scientific-engineering interaction methodology would have focused on methods that belong to the realm of human mathematical thinking and reasoning. Nowadays, the presence of a computer, which enhances the overall performance of the process, has resulted in a more complex situation, especially from a methodological point of view. Though the burden is shared, adequate "team-work" between model-builder and machine is still needed. Despite the fact that the computer is a product of the human mind, its manner of operation is substantially different from that of the mind. Consequently communication is not always easy. There is a strong belief nowadays that an increased "symbiosis", or a better organized partnership between model-builder and machine, will enhance the overall efficiency on scientific-engineering interactions. The precise nature of such enhanced partnership is not yet established, although a better understanding of the important issues are available.

Fig. 1.3 shows a more detailed build-up of a human being as model-builder in relation to a computer as simulator. At the extreme left and the extreme right, one finds the "hardware" of both partners: for man it is the human body which supports activities, for the machine it is the computer hardware. At the next level one has the human mind which is the controlling part and which carries the thinking process. For the simulator there is low-level computer software which provides means for utilizing the hardware: included are the operating system, the drivers and the machine instructions. Another level comprises respectively the human thinking process itself, which is the very base of all abstract work; and general high level computer software, which permits easy execution of programming and system utilization in general, now including higher level languages, editors, etc. . . Finally, the level of human modelling methodology is reached. There should be an equivalent level in the machine, in the form of modelling and simulation special-purpose software, designed for assisting the

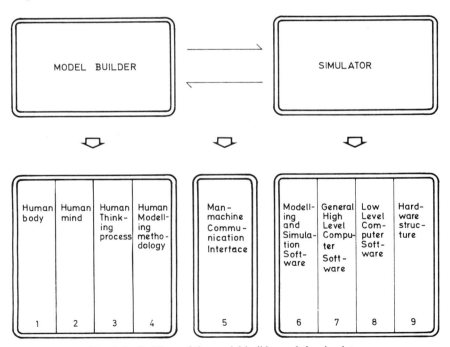

Fig. 1.3   Build-up of the model-builder and the simulator

model-builder in specific model-building and utilization tasks. The two highest levels need provisions for efficient man–machine communication. If all levels are properly integrated a more uniform and powerful approach will be available to attack all kind of problems.

A large part of the text is devoted to topics in human modelling methodology, level 4. In chapter 2 a major part of the fundamental concepts required for the subsequent chapters is provided. The mathematical model itself stands central to the overall approach. It is important to have a clear idea concerning the meaning and the nature of a formal model. Attention is restricted to state–space models. No attempt has been made to be very rigorous but it is necessary to ponder many of the ideas for quite a while in order to get sufficient insight and feeling. The material concerning the model nature, though basic, is not new and references to more advanced and elaborate books are given. A much more original part concerns general principles and facts on the process of mathematical model-building itself. These principles are simple but they are rarely mentioned. It is not claimed that the way of presentation and the interpretations are unique and some experts may disagree on the relevance of certain concepts, because they touch philosophical issues which still may be matters of debate. An effort has been made to take an "average" and impartial standpoint. In a final part of the chapter the issue of the adequacy and usefulness of the mathematical modelling approach in different disciplines is considered. Different opinions on the issue of future developments are presented, which reflect the interests of the authors. They are the fruits of personal experience and though they are in a sense controversial, they are by no means the result of lighthearted thoughts. The discussion can be seen as a "state-of-the-art" review. One of its roles is to justify to a certain level the material presented in the following three chapters.

Chapter 3 considers model-building methodology for (ordinary) difference and differential equations. The equations are not primarily discussed from a mathematical standpoint. They are seen much more as descriptive tools for real-world objects and processes. They are certainly not the only type of formal models for dynamic systems, but they have a long tradition dating back to the time of Newton and Leibniz and have been used in numerous ways to describe a wide variety of real-world systems. Emphasis in the chapter is on "building" such models. For that purpose the mathematical object is thought to be composed of different elements: the frame, the structure and the parameters. Methodology is provided to assemble these model components. The traditional approaches for obtaining the model constituent parts are not mentioned. For finding physical constants in a system description an often used procedure is to look for a related real-world situation, which bears enough resemblance to the original system so that one of the parameters is also an element of its description, and is sufficiently simple for experimentation to yield directly the value of the constant. Such technique is in the tradition of scientific work and is not considered in the chapter. On the contrary, procedures are given which focus directly on the system under study and its model, in the sense that model elements are inferred from experiments on the system itself. In such circumstances, a machine can be helpful in two ways. First, it may provide means for solving the difference and differential equations that are analytically intractable. Second, it may make enough computing power available to utilize techniques that would otherwise be unfeasible.

Though the computer will rarely be mentioned, its existence and availability is an inherent assumption of almost all the computational schemes that will be discussed. The major part of the chpater is devoted to parameter estimation and more specifically to recursive parameter estimation, where the data elements are handled one at a time. The last decade has witnessed a boom in research on that topic and many fundamental issues are explored. The subject is treated in considerable depth so that modelbuilders may design their own computational schemes tailored to their specific modelling needs. After methodology for parameter estimation, methodology for finding another constituent part of the model called the "structure" is presented. Here too it is assumed that a powerful computing machine is at one's disposition. The topic is still an area of research and it may be expected that a considerable amount of basic work remains to be done. The other issues which play a role in building differential and difference equation models are briefly touched on in a closing section of the chapter.

In chapter 4 another type of model description, based on partial differential equations, is under scrutiny. The model type is more involved and model building methodology has not yet advanced to the same level as for the differential equations model. It is, however, often used in many branches of science and engineering. The chapter is in the same vein as the previous one in the sense that human modelling methodology is discussed. The impact of the simulator is larger here. Analytical techniques for solving differential equations are limited and numerical solutions are so computationally demanding that even present-day computers may sometimes be overwhelmed. For model construction too, computational requirements are on the average much more stringent than for ordinary differential equations. The excessive computational loads are responsible for the fact that less attention has been paid to the subject. As a consequence, the most efficient method for constructing partial differential equations models remains based on the traditional deductive approach. The model type is used in many disciplines but, irrespective of the origin, general rules seem to exist to deduce a suitable model for a given process. A large part of the chapter addresses the following issues: which disciplines use partial differential equations? Are there general approaches in building the model and how do they proceed? Which types of partial differential equations mostly arise? A final section deals with the problem of constructing the model in a manner similar to the one presented for ordinary differential equations and comparisons are made in order to understand how the type of model may influence the modelling methodology.

Chapter 5 serves a dual purpose, with attention gradually shifting to the simulator aspects. Referring to Fig. 1.3, it is meant to develop concepts for construction of an upper layer of modelling and simulation software. Such a layer has to be closely matched to human modelling methodology so that communication between the model-builder and the machine can be very effective. Therefore, the contents of chapter 2 remain the basis for this chapter. Though a good match between human modelling procedures and modelling and simulation software seems to be a straightforward requirement, the subject has only been studied very recently and a considerable amount of work remains to be done. One of the major tasks of such an upper layer would consist in the organization of information concerning the real-world system under investigation. For comparison, it is fruitful to consider the human case. Human scientific knowledge is organized hierarchically from the specific at the lower end towards the general at the upper end. The process of organization of such knowledge, which is closely related to the construction of scientific theories, in the human mind is difficult and takes a considerable amount of effort. Proper organization of information concerning real-world systems in a computer with provisions for activities which organize and relate that information in a suitable way, may turn out to be of invaluable help, not only to achieve adequate communication between man and machine but to provide an information base that is capable of supporting intensively the model-building activity. The chapter deals with the concepts that underly computer-based storage of data, models and modelling goals. For the purpose of illustration a third type of model, the discrete event system description model, is used.

Chapter 6 relates to better established modelling and simulation software. This leaves the subject of model-building almost completely and turns to simulation tools. Simulation languages and packages are especially designed to solve or run models on the computer, without burdening the model-builder with so much programming that the whole model construction and model usage project is brought into jeopardy. Essentially, a survey is given of existing languages according to the model type that can be simulated: ordinary differential equations, partial differential equations and discrete event models. As will be seen, the existing software focuses on simulation with its restricted meaning of running models. Clearly, extension is required with software that provides simple means of carrying through many model-building procedures like those mentioned in Chapters 3 and 4.

Chapter 7 deals with the simulator hardware and with level 9 on Fig. 1.3. The computer has been developed primarily for computation, but its nature has gradually changed under pressure of new needs and new advances in technology. As the machine has been designed by man, it can be modified according to his wishes. As soon as the computer is considered as a partner in carrying through scientific-engineering interactions, there is no reason why it should not be modified as to enhance the overall capability. Though software may alleviate certain hardware deficiencies, the ultimate goal is to find a hardware structure that is suited in an optimal way to one's purpose. The chapter reviews new developments in the hardware of computing machines and evaluates the impact from the viewpoint of simulation.

The final chapter builds a dream for the future. It proposes an ideal partner for modelling and simulation. The future simulator is thought to have a parallel structure: requirements, its build-up and related issues are discussed. An amount of attention is also paid to the communication interface between the model-builder and the future simulator.

2. Mathematical models and modelling generalities

2.1 INTRODUCTION

In this chapter generalities about mathematical models and modelling methodology are introduced. It is hoped that they will provide the reader with sufficient background so that the rest of the information in this book can be more readily understood. Moreover, it is meant to set the material in a proper perspective and, in particular, to indicate how the subject matters of other chapters frame contemporary research in the field of modelling and simulation.

A mathematical model is seen here as a tool that can be useful for reaching certain goals, so the purpose of mathematical representation is discussed first. It is shown how such a representation can be utilized for objectives that can be mainly classified under two attitudes towards reality. Later it will become clear that emphasis on the modelling goal may be important in building a suitable model.

Next, the nature of the model is analysed. This part is certainly more abstract and requires more thought. In order to avoid a heavy load of details that might obscure the main ideas, mathematical sophistication has been kept to a minimum. It is tried to convey to the reader a proper feeling about the meaning of a mathematical representation. Basically, such a model is an abstract "image" of a small part and a few aspects of reality based on the notion of "system". The system point of view permits the real-world process to be "encoded" at different hierarchically structured levels of detail. Therefore it is interesting to be able to relate different models to each other. The relationships between model representations are mathematically involved. In the text, only the concept of isomorphism and homomorphism are introduced, which are the basic relationships occurring between equivalent model representations that are for studying a certain real-world process behaviour.

It is a fact of life that a wide variety of model representations are used in practice. They are all special cases of a general model form, which unfortu-

12

nately is too general to be directly practical in specific circumstances. An example of "model form taxonomy" serves as an illustration. The proper use of the general model introduced here, or one of its "short-hand" representations, as an "image" for real systems, depends on a number of assumptions. An informal discussion on the assumptions for partial decomposability and state-existence is given.

After a presentation of the essence of the mathematical model itself, modelling methodology is considered next: how does one build a mathematical representation? How does one form a suitable abstract image of a real-world object or process? Modelling has long been thought of as an "art" and has only more recently been subjected to more detailed analysis. In fact, model-building is a very complex human skill. It is by no means certain, or even probable, that the human modelling process, which relies on a blend of logic, intuition, abstraction, association and skill, could be analysed in a systematic way. It is useful, however, to discover the basic framework of the process as it provides a better understanding of which issues are most important. Here the model "image" is seen as an entity that encodes information. Modelling thus consists of condensing information coming from the modeller's environment. The sources of model information are presented and a general discussion about the implications of "tapping" from these sources is given. The attitude of the model-builder towards these information sources gives rise to different modelling philosophies. The quality of the model image is then discussed under the heading of "validation". Finally, with the help of such analysis and on the basis of a decomposition of the mathematical model itself, it is possible to give a complete picture of the modelling process.

In the final section of this chapter, the success and usefulness of mathematical model-building is investigated. The ideas are a blend of facts and personal viewpoints. Consequently, they are subject to updating even, perhaps, in the near future. The power of mathematical representation seems, on average, to depend on the field of human knowledge, to which it is applied. An investigation into the reasons for this observation is made. The analysis is certainly a controversial issue and has been included to project the content of the other chapters into present-day research in the field and, more importantly, to advocate new research activities on subjects now scarcely touched but of the utmost relevance.

2.2 MATHEMATICAL MODELS: DUALITY IN GOALS

Mathematical models have many applications and they can be of benefit as well in pure science as in engineering. As mentioned before, Section 2.1, they provide increased domination over real-world phenomena. In a first approximation, this domination can be of a more "passive" nature, in the sense that increased insight into the phenomena, or a hint for constructing new experiments are satisfactory results; but it can also be of a more "active" form, namely, in raising one's capability for decision-making or intervention. For each of these general goals three levels of importance can be mentioned (Fig. 2.1).

For insight purposes, in order of increasing domination, communication, thought and understanding can be distinguished. A mathematical representation permits a precise and unambiguous form of communication. It limits the chance for misunderstanding when information is passed to other persons. Besides clear communication, it is an appreciable aid to thought when different questions concerning the system are studied or alternative hypotheses considered. As soon as the models are integrated in a set of axioms and laws, they provide a better understanding of real-world phenomena.

In the same manner, for increased decision-making capability three broad levels of intervention can be distinguished: management, control and design. Management connotes a limited power to intervene: one can set goals and determine broad courses of action, but these policies cannot be spelled out in full detail. Their execution must thus be delegated to, and interpreted at, subordinate levels; so the link between intention and implementation is ambiguous. In the control context, however, action is deterministically related to policy. Still, constraints remain on the scope of intervention, in that control action is limited to the selection of alternatives within fixed extant domains. In contrast, design connotes greater scope for choice in that the designer expects to augment, or replace a part of, the existing reality. Implementation of a design is relatively expensive and

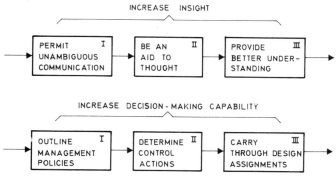

FIG. 2.1   Role of mathematical models

infrequent, while control and management are continual "on-line" activities.

From the point of view of these goals, one can think of a real-world system as being composed in the first case, of an observable and unobservable part; in the second case, of a controllable and uncontrollable part (Fig. 2.2). The observable part refers to all aspects of the system which can be distinguished, followed, observed and measured; the controllable part, to all aspects which are within one's means to modify, alter, steer and influence. The other part refers to whatever is left, usually most of the system, i.e. the aspects which are not observable or controllable. It will later become clear that what is taken to be the real system and its decomposition is not fixed for all time, but depends on perception and viewpoint as well as on the objective situation. Naturally, observation and intervention must be limited, respectively, to the observable and controllable part of the system.

The effect of speculative action, or control action, is uncertain due to the existence of the unobservable and uncontrollable sections which interact with the remaining part. The greater the knowledge of the latter, the greater the certainty one can have in assessing success in understanding or in intervening.

Up to now the purpose of the modelling effort has been clearly divided into two categories. The fact that a mathematical representation can serve a dual goal bears special consequences. Though in a given circumstance the modelling exercise may have been undertaken for gaining insight, the model will provide us with an opportunity to intervene at some level. Similarly, a model built for control will enhance one's insight into the system. Models encode knowledge: their *sine qua non* is their ability to integrate sets of disconnected relationships whose point implications would

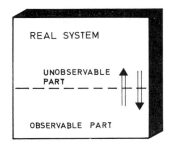
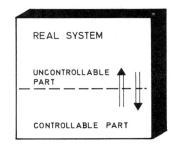

FIG. 2.2   Real-world system build-up according to modelling goals

otherwise be difficult to draw. They are especially useful to the extent that they enable extrapolation beyond the data so far acquired.

Though mathematical modelling can serve many purposes, it would be foolish to conclude that this special representation procedure is useful for all goals. This point has seldom been stressed. It may well happen that quantitative analysis is too cumbersome and mathematical rigour too precise.

The general objectives for modelling have so far been discussed. In practical circumstances their purposes will be stated in more precise and concrete terms. It is very important to realize that these purposes are the driving forces that orient the whole modelling effort, as will become more evident as the discussion progresses.

2.3 MATHEMATICAL MODELS: THEIR NATURE AND ASSUMPTIONS

2.3.1 Definition and Relationship to Systems

2.3.1.1 *Abstraction: the approach*

As the mathematical model plays a very central role in the approach to manipulate real-world phenomena in accordance with our wishes, the very essence and the inherent assumptions of a mathematical formulation are discussed in more detail before proceeding to techniques and tools. Therefore, a brief outline is given of some of the basic concepts and formalisms of system theory.

One of the most striking relationships between a model and the real world process is abstraction. The abstraction process is fundamental to the modelling process. An example will clarify the point. When considering the trajectories of objects, such as spacecrafts and planets in space, the laws of motion can be applied. In this process, the detailed nature of the objects is not important. After abstraction, they are essentially thought of as a mass quantity at the centre of gravity.

In mathematics, the concept of "set" is also based on abstraction. Set operations allow us to manipulate abstractions without having to specify their detailed nature. Because modelling and set theory both rely on abstraction, the latter is very useful to the modelling enterprise. It is shown in the sequel that commonly used mathematical models can be seen as constructs on sets. To prove the point, some elementary notions of set theory are required.

Some commonly employed sets are finite sets such as the digits $\{0, 1, 2, 3, 4, 5, 6, 7, 8, 9\}$ or the alphabet $\{a, b, \ldots, z\}$ and infinite sets such as the integers $I = \{0, \pm 1, \pm 2, \ldots\}$ and the real numbers R. Subsets of these sets are also important: $I^+ = \{1, 2, 3, \ldots\}$ is the subset of positive integers; $I_0^+ = I^+ \cup \{0\} = \{0, 1, 2, 3, \ldots\}$ is the subset of non-negative integers. Adding the infinity concept we get: $I_{0,\infty}^+ = I_0^+ \cup \{\infty\}$, the set of non-negative integers together with the symbol ∞. R^+, R_0^+ and $R_{0,\infty}^+$ denote the analogous sets in the case of the reals.

A fundamental set operation is the cross-product. Let A and B be arbitrary sets. Then $A \times B = \{(a, b) \mid a \in A, b \in B\}$. Note how the detailed nature of the elements in A and B need not be known in order to form pairs of these elements. This is the power to manipulate abstractions that we just referred to. Similarly one can define tuples, quartuples, . . . , and in general n-tuples. Furthermore sets of n-tuples with different n-values can be combined. $A^+ = \{(a_1, a_2, \ldots, a_n) \mid a_i \in A, n \in I^+\}$ is the set of all n-tuples of elements of A, we may also identify the tuple $(a_1, a_2, \ldots, a_n)$ with the sequence or string $a_1 a_2 \ldots a_n$. With Λ the empty string, a new set can be defined $A^* = A^+ \cup \{\Lambda\}$.

Manipulating such abstractions becomes interesting when one forms set structures by not accepting all the combinations in a cross-product. The simplest such set structure is a binary relation $R \subseteq A \times B$. A function or mapping is a relation $F \subseteq A \times B$ in which there is at most one pair involving any member of A, i.e. $(a, b) \in F$ and $(a, b') \in F \Rightarrow b = b'$. In this case we also write $F : A \to B$ and $F(a)$ to mean the unique b for which $(a, b) \in F$. An example of such functional relationship is a segment. It is a map of the form ω: $\langle t_0, t_1 \rangle \to F$ where for instance $\langle t_0, t_1 \rangle \subset R$ and $F \in R^p - \langle$ stands for [or (. The elements of the map constitute a segment set. Below other set structures are formed on these principles.

The very few set-theoretic concepts suffice to draw a picture of the model-building process. When setting up a mathematical representation, a number of abstractions are made. By this is meant defining sets: input, output and state variables are chosen as representatives of physical properties and they take numerical values. Further on, compound set structures on these abstractions are built: more specifically, functional relationships are defined. The process can be seen as *theory construction*.

Going in the other direction from model to real-world process, which is necessary eventually to apply such set structures to the world, the abstractions must be connected to real objects. This poses a fundamental axiom that there exists a sufficiently complex abstract model, with a lot of detail, that faithfully represents the system. Under such assumptions, we go in the direction of connecting abstractions to real objects by adding detail to these abstractions. We call this *process concretization*: making the abstract more concrete.

So, theory construction consists in building set structures on sufficiently abstract concepts for the model to gain a wider range and applicability. Concretization amounts to adding detail by replacing abstracts sets by set structures. So both theory construction and its concretization involve building structures, but in opposite directions.

Having analysed the relationships between sets, abstractions and mathematical models, it is interesting to show how the familiar concept of a system ties in with the previous arguments.

2.3.1.2   Systems: the fundamental ideas

Man nowadays perceives parts of the real world as systems. A system is a composition of interacting component systems. From this innocent looking definition much follows. Obeying the recursion implicit in the definition, we find that a system is a composition of systems, each of which in turn is another composition of systems, . . . , and so on, ad infinitum. But to be useful such a decomposition process must be allowed to stop. We must therefore have a concept of system which allows us to treat it as atomic when we wish to stop decomposing, but also allows us to continue decomposing when we wish to do so. If we consider systems from the above point of view, it follows quite naturally that set theory is just the right tool for this, since what we require is a definition of a system as an abstract set structure with the property that it can always be concretized by replacing it with a composition of structures of the same kind.

To consider the implications of the last thought: since a system may be a component of a larger system, it must be provided with an interface i.e., a means to interact with other systems. The interface should represent the potential events which can occur at the system boundary. What goes on at this boundary is determined both by the system, within the boundary, and its environment, outside the boundary. The system's role in this arises from the constraints it imposes on the interface i.e., by what is called its internal structure. It is this internal structure which must be allowed either to leave abstractly described, so as to stop decomposition, or to concretize, to continue decomposition, as desired.

To concretize faithfully the internal structure it must be able to be reconstituted by combining the separate constraints which the internal structure of all the component systems places on their mutual interfaces. A system submits to a decomposition if such a reconstitution is possible with this decomposition.

So far the relationship between mathematical model, system and real-world process has been discussed, in very general terms. Below, the general notions on models are presented in more precise mathematical terms, so as to come to the models commonly used by system analysts in practice, e.g.

differential equations, difference equations and discrete event models, which can be seen as special model formalisms. By doing so, one can learn how these model formalisms embody the notions of interface, internal structure and recursive decomposability.

To start with, a yet general form of formalism which is useful in the modelling and simulation context is stated.

2.3.1.3 Systems modelling formalism

A system may conceptually be defined as a set structure:

$$S = \langle T, X, \Omega, Q, Y, \delta, \lambda \rangle$$

where T is the *time base*
  X is the *input set*
  Ω is the *input segment set*
  Q is the *internal state set*
  Y is the *output set*
  δ is the *state transition function*
  λ is the *output function*.

What are the interpretations and restrictions put on these elements?

Time base

T is a set which represents clock time and serves to order events. Common choices for T are I the integers or R the reals; S is said to be a discrete time respectively, continuous time system accordingly.

Input set

X is a set representing that part of the interface through which the environment affects the system, e.g. through the inflow of information or material. Thus the system is viewed as being subjected at any time to inputs from the set X, over which it has no direct control: a common choice for X is R^n, for some $n \in I^+$, representing n real valued, input variables. Another common choice is $X_M \cup \{\phi\}$ where X_M represents a set of external events and ϕ represents the non-event.

Input segment set

An input segment describes a pattern of inputs to the system over some time period. When embedded in a larger system such a pattern is determined by the system's environment. When the system is isolated, by cutting its input wires so to speak, these wires are free and the environment is replaced by a set of segments, which for reconstitutability should include all the patterns receivable by S as a component in the larger system.

Thus, an input segment is a particular segment as defined in Section 2.3.1.1 and a map of the form $\omega : \langle t_0, t_1 \rangle \to X$ where $\langle t_0, t_1 \rangle$ is an interval of the time base between t_0 (the initial instant) and t_1 (the final instant). The set of all such input segments is called (X, T). The input segment set Ω is a subset of (X, T).

A common choice for Ω is the set of piecewise continuous segments; in this case $T = R$ and $X = R^n$. A second choice is the set of discrete event segments over X_M (a set of external events) and $T = R$. Such a discrete event segment is a mapping $\omega : \langle t_0, t_1 \rangle \to X_M \cup \{\phi\}$ such that $\omega(t) = \phi$ except possibly for a finite set of event times $\{\tau_1, \ldots, \tau_n\} \subseteq \langle t_0, t_1 \rangle$. Finally when $T = I$, Ω is, in effect, a set of finite sequences.

Internal state set

The set Q of internal states represents the memory of the system, i.e. the residue of its past history which will affect its present and future response. This is the heart of the modelling of internal structure which was referred to earlier.

State transition function

The state transition function is a map $\delta : Q \times \Omega \to Q$. Its interpretation is that when the system is in state q at time t_0 and an input segment $\omega : \langle t_0, t_1 \rangle \to X$ is applied, then $\delta(q, \omega)$ is the state of the system at time t_1. Thus the internal state at any time and the input segment from that time on, uniquely determine the state of the end of the segment.

For every $q \in Q$, $\omega \in \Omega$, and t in the domain of ω (the interval on which it is defined)

$$\delta(q, \omega) = \delta[\delta(q, \omega_{t)}), \omega_{(t}] \qquad \text{(semi-group-axiom)}$$

where $\omega_{t)} = \omega \mid \langle t_0, t \rangle$ (the part of ω between t_0 and t) and $\omega_{(t} = \omega \mid \langle t, t_1 \rangle$ (the part between t and t_1). This requires that the state $q_t = \delta(q, \omega_{t)})$ pertaining at any time t summarizes necessary previous history, so that continuing the experiment from this state results in the same final state as would otherwise be the case.

Based on the definition of a state given, the choice of the state set is not unique and even its dimensionality is not fixed. Finding a proper and useful state space, i.e. a state space permitting the composition property, of a system is not a trivial matter. But once done it enables one to replace the past by an abstract quantity in the present. This formulation of internal structure greatly simplifies the ability to deal with decomposition (concretization of internal structure) and simulation (relation to other systems).

It should be clear that the state set is mainly a modelling concept. Nothing in the real system needs to correspond directly to it. One should also realize that the input segment set, state set and state transition function specify together a state segment set (see the concept of state trajectory below).

Output set

Y is a set representing that part of the interface through which the system affects the environment. The interpretation is the same as that for the input value set except for direction. Embedded in a larger system the input (output) of a system component is the output (input) of its environment.

Output function

In its simplest form the output function is a map $\lambda : Q \to Y$, which relates the hypothetical internal state of the system to the effect of the system on its environment. Such an output map, however, does not permit direct influence from the inputs on the outputs. A more general output function is a map $\lambda : Q \times X \times T \to Y$. In other words $\lambda(q, x, t)$ is what can be sensed by the environment when the system is supposed to be in state q and when the present input to the system is X; furthermore, the output function need not to be time–invariant. Often, λ is a many to one mapping, so that the state cannot be directly observed. The output function gives rise to an output segment set.

Based on the formalism defined above, it is possible to specify the notion of system behaviour. The behaviour of a system is the external manifestation of its internal structure, i.e. the relation it imposes on the crossproduct $(X, T) \times (Y, T)$.

This relation is computed as follows. With every state $q \in Q$ and input segment $\omega : \langle t_0, t_1 \rangle \to X$ in Ω there is associated a unique state trajectory

$$STRAJ_{q,\omega} : \langle t_0, t_1 \rangle \to Q$$

such that

$$STRAJ_{q,\omega}(t_0) = q$$

and

$$STRAJ_{q, \omega}(t) = \delta(q, \omega_{t)})$$

for

$$t \in \langle t_0, t_1 \rangle.$$

Such a state trajectory is the result of an analytical solution or is computed during a computer simulation run. The observable projection of this trajectory is the output trajectory associated with $q \in Q$ and $\omega \in \Omega$,

$$OTRAJ_{q,\omega} : \langle t_0, t_1 \rangle \to Y$$

In the case of the simple output function $\lambda(q)$, for instance:

$$OTRAJ_{q,\omega}(t) = \lambda(STRAJ_{q,\omega}(t)).$$

The behaviour of the system is then represented by its input–output relation R_S:

$$R_S = \{(\omega, \rho) \,|\, \omega \in \Omega, \rho = OTRAJ_{q,\omega} \qquad \text{for some } q \in Q\}$$

Each element $(\omega, \rho) \in R_S$ is called an input–output segment pair and represents the result of an observation or experiment on the system in which ω is the input to the system and ρ is the output observed. Because the system could have been in any one of its states initially, there may be many output segments ρ associated with the same input segment ω.

2.3.1.4   Levels of representation

A real-life process can be seen as a system which is decomposed to a certain level of detail. There exists a mathematical representation procedure for describing the decomposed system at any such required level. It is useful for subsequent chapters, and especially for the subject of validation, to consider some of these levels of system descriptions (Fig. 2.3).

1. Behaviour level   At this level one describes a system as if one were viewing it as a black box and recording measurements done on it in their chronological order. For this one needs, at minimum, a "time base" which is usually a subinterval of the reals (continuous time) or the integers (discrete time). An elementary descriptive unit is a "trajectory", which is a mapping from a subinterval of the time base to some set of values representing possible observation results. A "behavioural" description consists of a set of such trajectories. Such a description may also be called the "behaviour" of the system.

Typically, in a simulation context, an orientation is placed on the black box such that some variables are considered as input, i.e. not under control of the box itself, and the others as output, i.e. externally perceivable to the experimenter or to the environment outside the system boundary represented by the box.

The behaviour level is important because experimentation on the real-world process addresses that level. Some thought reveals that this descriptive level is of a simpler nature than the set structure description presented in the previous section.

2. State structure level   At this level one describes a system as if one were providing a mechanism for its internal working. Such a description is sufficient to generate, by iteration over time, a set of trajectories, i.e. a

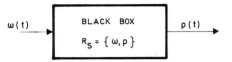

(a) *System at the behaviour level*

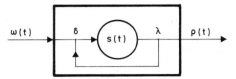

(b) *System at the state structure level*

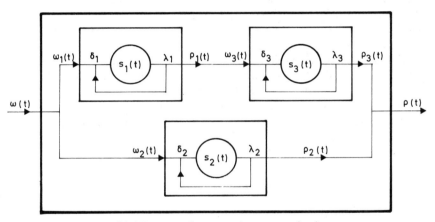

(c) *System at the composite structure level*

FIG. 2.3   Description levels of systems

behaviour. The basic device which enables such iteration is the "state set", which represents the possible configurations at any time, and the "state transition function" which provides the rule for computing the future state given the current state. Moreover, as we have seen, an output function is required in order to map the state set, which is not directly observable, to the observable output set. A description at the state structure level is typically of the type presented before. We mention that the state set should be sufficient to account for the behaviour of the system.

3. Composite structure level   At this level one describes a system as if one were specifying how to construct it by connecting together more elementary black boxes. Such a description may also be called a network description. The elementary black boxes are called components and each must be given a system description at the state structure level. Moreover, each component must have identified "input variables" and "output variables". A "coupling specification" must be given which determines the interconnection of the components and the interfacing of the input with the output variables. One can continue to further decompose the system and attain higher level descriptions.

A cardinal rule concerning different descriptions is that, given a system specification at a certain level, one can associate, at most one specification at the next lower level. Thus a meaningful composite structure description has a unique state structure description (whose state set, for example, is obtained by performing set operations on the state sets of the individual components). The state structure description itself has a unique behavioural description. In this case, one and the same system can be considered as having a network structure, a state structure and a behaviour.

In the previous sections the essence of a mathematical model as a system has been presented in general terms. The concepts have been introduced in order to convey to the reader the important characteristics of such a description. Mathematical details were disregarded on purpose. Interested readers are referred to more advanced texts on the subject [117, 163, 251].

2.3.2   Specific Modelling Formalisms

2.3.2.1   Definition

In the previous section a yet more general definition of a system as a set structure is given. However, in practical situations, one never starts from so general a structure. Usually a more specific "modelling formalism" is used. Here, a formalism is a set of conventions for specifying a subset of system description.

Once such formalism is laid down, then this is also the case for the information common to the subclass of systems being referred to. As a consequence, to express a model in such a formalism, one need only give the information necessary to distinguish this model from the others in the class. In this manner, one can regard a special model formalism as providing a shorthand way of specifying a subclass of systems. A model expressed in a formalism is a system specification, i.e. it indirectly selects a particular system from the set of all systems.

Ören [170] has provided a classification of modelling formalisms based upon the type of trajectories produced by the models in the formalism class. The classification is reproduced in table form (Table 2.1).

TABLE 2.1 Classification of model formalism

Trajectory of model's descriptive variables	Time set of model	Modelling formalism	Range of variables	
			Cont.	Discr.
CONTINUOUS [-CHANGE] MODEL	CONTINUOUS-TIME MODEL	Partial differential equation	√	
DISCONTINUOUS [-CHANGE] MODEL		Ordinary differential equation	√	
COMBINED [-CHANGE] MODEL	DISCRETE-TIME MODEL	Activity scanning	√	√
		Difference equation	√	√
		Finite-state machine		√
DISCRETE [-CHANGE] MODEL		Markov chain		√
	CONTINUOUS-TIME MODEL	Discrete event	√	√
		Process interaction	√	√

(Attributes within [ ] may be omitted)

2.3.2.2 Examples

A few model formalisms are presented and used in subsequent chapters. It is shown how they agree with, and specify, the general set structure.

Time invariant, continuous-time, lumped model (ordinary differential equations)

$M_1 : \langle U, X, Y, \underline{f}, \underline{g} \rangle$

$\underline{u} \in U$: set of inputs $\underline{\dot{x}} = \underline{f}(\underline{x}, \underline{u})$
$\underline{x} \in X$: set of states $\underline{y} = \underline{g}(\underline{x}, \underline{u})$
$\underline{y} \in Y$: set of outputs
$\underline{f}$: rate of change function $\underline{f}$: satisfies Lipschitz
$\underline{g}$: output function   conditions

$$(2.1)$$

Such a model formalism is clearly a special case of the set structure defined in 2.3.1.3. In fact $M_1 \equiv S_1$ with

$$S_1 : \langle T, X, \Omega, Q, Y, \delta, \lambda \rangle$$

where $t \in T : [t_0, \infty) \subset R$
$\quad\quad X \equiv U : R^m \quad m \in I^+$
$\quad\quad Q \equiv X : R^n \quad n \in I^+$
$\quad\quad Y \equiv Y : R^p \quad p \in I^+$

$\quad\quad\quad\quad \Omega : \{\underline{\omega} : [t_0, t_0 + \tau] \to U$ bounded almost everywhere and continuous function, $\tau > 0\}$

$\quad\quad\quad\quad \delta$: supposes that the differential model (2.1) has a unique solution $\underline{\Phi}(t)$ so that $\underline{\Phi}(0) = \underline{q}_0$

$$\frac{d\,\underline{\Phi}(t)}{dt} = \underline{f}(\underline{\Phi}(t), \underline{\omega}(t))$$

then the map $\delta \quad Q \times \Omega \to Q$ can be set up with the solutions $\underline{\Phi}(t)$.

The conditions for the transition function (2.3.1.3) can easily be shown to hold.

$$\lambda = \underline{g}$$

Stochastic continuous-time lumped model

For many applications, one likes to have the option of specifying unmeasurable and random inputs. These disturbances can, for instance, be seen as the impact of the uncontrollable or unobservable part of the real world on the part modelled (see Section 2.2). The procedure should permit a more representative model behaviour to be obtained.

$$M_2 : \langle U, V, W, X, Y, \underline{f}, \underline{g} \rangle$$

$$\underline{\dot{x}} = \underline{f}(\underline{x}, \underline{u}, \underline{w}, t) \tag{2.2}$$

$$\underline{y} = \underline{g}(\underline{x}, \underline{v}, t)$$

The additional vectors $\underline{w}$ and $\underline{v}$ are random model disturbances. Conditions for existence of a solution and interpretation rules for the stochastic differential equation have to be provided.

If $\underline{v}$ and $\underline{w}$ are random or stochastic vector processes, then $\underline{x}$ and $\underline{y}$ will be such processes too. Whether such a model formalism is compatible with the set structure defined in 2.3.1.3, which postulates the existence of a state, remains a matter of research and debate.

Formally, the problem can be avoided by considering the $\underline{w}$ and $\underline{v}$ vectors as inputs. The stochastic properties of these vectors do not belong then to the model specification. For a given $\underline{v}$ and $\underline{w}$, (2.2) can be seen as a set structure:

$$M_2 \equiv S_2$$

$$S_2 : \langle T, X, \Omega, Q, Y, \delta, \lambda \rangle$$

where $t \in T$ $: [t_0, \infty) \subset R$

   $X \equiv U \cup W \cup V : R^{m+m_1+m_2}$

$m \in I^+$

$m_1 \in I^+$

$m_2 \in I^+$

$Q \equiv X$	$: R^n$	$n \in I^+$
$Y \equiv Y$	$: R^p$	$p \in I^+$
Ω	$:$	
δ	$:$	defined in the same way as above
$\lambda \equiv \underline{g}$		: the general output map $X \times Q \times T \to Y$

As there exist many realizations for $\underline{v}$ and $\underline{w}$, a "stochastic" model is then a family of deterministic set structures.

Discrete event model

In some cases, and especially in management and operational research, the real-world process can be thought to be made up of a collection of events. Even the state changes at specific time instants. A mathematical description takes the form of a discrete event model M_3

$$M_3 : \langle X_M, S_M, Y_M, \delta_M, \lambda_M, \tau_M \rangle$$

where X_M : set of external events

   S_M : set of sequential discrete event states

   Y_M : set of outputs

   δ_M : quasi-transition function

     this function is specified by two other ones

     δ_M^{ϕ} : map $S_M \to S_M$; it says to which state the system will evolve from a given state if no external events occur.

     δ_M^{ex} : map $X_M \times S_M \times T \to S_M$, it tells what happens if the system is in state s, and an external event x happens at a time e since the last state transition occurred.

   λ_M : output function: map $Q_M \to Y_M$

   τ_M : time advance function, it is a map $S_M \to R_{0,\infty}^+$ and specifies how long the system will remain in state s before a new transition occurs under the hypothesis that no external event disturbs the process.

Such a system specification may look awkward for control specialists but it is well known to researchers in other fields. Here too, one can proof that $M_3 \equiv S_3$

$S_3 : \langle T, X, \Omega, Q, Y, \delta, \lambda \rangle$

$T : [t_0, \infty) \subset R$

$X : X_M \cup \{\Phi\}$

Ω : set of discrete event segments

$\Omega : \{\omega \,|\, \omega : \langle t_0, t_1 \rangle \to X, \; \omega(t) \neq \phi$ for at most a finite subset of $\langle t_0, t_1 \rangle\}$

Q : the actual state set is constructed from the sequential set S_M and the time advance function τ_M as follows:

$\tau_M : S \to R_{0,\infty}^+$

$Q : \{(s, e) \,|\, s \in S, \; 0 \leq e \leq \tau_M(s)\}$

Thus a total state is a pair (s, e) where s is a sequential state and e the time elapsed in this state.

δ : is constructed from δ_M

map $Q \times X \to Q$ such that for each τ the state results from

$\delta(s, e, \Phi) = s \qquad\qquad e < \tau_M(s)$

$\delta(s, \tau_M(s), \Phi) = \delta_M{}^\Phi$

$\delta(s, e, x) = \delta_M{}^{ex}(s, e, x)$

$\lambda : \lambda_M$

Distributed model (partial differential equation)

Many real-world systems have properties that vary continuously in space. Distributed models take that fact into account. A general formalism for partial differential equations has never been popular. The following description could be given

$M_4 : \langle U, \Phi, Y, \underline{f}', \underline{b}, \underline{g} \rangle$

$$0 = \underline{f}'(\Phi, \frac{\partial\Phi}{\partial t}, \frac{\partial\Phi}{\partial z_i}, \underline{u}, \underline{z}, t) \qquad \underline{z} \in Z$$

$$0 = \underline{b}(\Phi, \underline{z}, t) \qquad\qquad \underline{z} \in \delta Z \qquad\qquad (2.3)$$

$$\underline{y} = \underline{g}(\Phi, \underline{z}, t) \qquad\qquad \underline{z} \in Z$$

Besides an independent variable t, the space coordinates $\underline{z}$ are introduced. Φ is the vector of dependent variables which may vary in space and time. The equations hold in a spatial domain Z while conditions are provided on the boundary of the domain δZ. There are inputs $\underline{u}$ and output $\underline{y}$. Though the model is much more complex than the ones presented before, it can be proved that it fits into the set structure concept under suitable regularity conditions for existence and uniqueness. The most important feature of such equivalent set structure is the infinite dimensionality of the state set Q. The set depends on $\underline{\Phi}$ which at a certain time instant is a function of the spatial variables. The boundary conditions have a role in the choice of a state too.

2.3.3 Relations Between System Representations

The essence of modelling is to establish a relation between a pair of systems. The essence of simulation is also a relation between such a pair: the model and the simulation program. Since systems have both internal structure and external behaviour, these are two fundamental levels at which they can be related.

At the behavioural level the basic relation is that of equivalence. Systems S and S' are behaviourally equivalent or $R_S = R_{S'}$, or they have exactly the same input/output relation. Equivalent systems are indistinguishable as far as any observer or the environment can tell.

At the structural level one has the notion of homomorphism and of isomorphism. Consider two systems S and S' which have the same T, X, Ω and Y sets, but possibly different internal structures, i.e. Q, δ, λ and Q', δ', λ', respectively. A homomorphism from S to S' is a map h from the state set Q of S onto the state set Q' of S', such that the following hold:

Preservation of transition function

For all $\omega \in \Omega$, $q \in Q$

$$h[\delta(q, \omega)] = \delta'[h(q), \omega].$$

Preservation of output function

For all $q \in Q$

$$\lambda(q) = \lambda'[h(q)].$$

An isomorphism is a homomorphism in which the map h is a one–one correspondence of the states.

It can be shown that if there is a homomorphism from S to S' then they are behaviourally equivalent. Thus the homomorphic image S' could be much simpler (have fewer states) than the pre-image S and yet be indistinguishable from it in behaviour. Isomorphism, on the other hand, is an equivalence relation on systems which equivalences two systems, if they have the same internal structure as far as can be told from the state abstraction. Isomorphism implies behavioural equivalence but the converse is not true. For other relations and more details one can consult Zeigler [251].

The concepts of homomorphism and isomorphism are useful in many instances. Consider the linear system (2.4)

$$S \quad \dot{\underline{x}} = A\underline{x} + B\underline{u}$$
$$\underline{y} = C\underline{x} + D\underline{u} \tag{2.4}$$
$$\text{dimension } (\underline{x}) = n; \ S \text{ controllable and observable.}$$

Using Laplace transforms it is easy to obtain an input–output description

$$\underline{y}(s) = [C(Is - A)^{-1} B + D] \underline{u}(s) \tag{2.5}$$

Linear system theory learns that the same input–output relationship (2.5) can be obtained with the following alternative model descriptions:

$$S_1 \quad \dot{\underline{x}}_1 = A_1\underline{x}_1 + B_1\underline{u}$$
$$\underline{y} = C_1\underline{x}_1 + D_1\underline{u}$$
$$\text{dimension } (\underline{x}_1) > n$$
$$A_1H = HA$$
$$B_1 = HB$$
$$C_1H = C$$
$$D_1 = D$$

or

$$S_2 \quad \dot{\underline{x}}_2 = A_2\underline{x}_2 + B_2\underline{u}$$
$$\underline{y} = C_2\underline{x}_2 + D_2\underline{u}$$
$$\text{dimension } (\underline{x}_2) = n$$
$$A_2T = TA$$
$$B_2 = TB$$
$$C_2T = C$$
$$D_2 = D$$

For a suitable H (max. rank) a homomorphism exists between S and S_2, because the relation between the states is 'onto'. For $\det(T) \neq 0$, an isomorphism exists between S and S_1; in fact there is a one-to-one relation between the states of S and those of S_1.

2.3.4 Basic assumptions in the systems approach

It is clear that a model is in fact only a poor image of the real-world object, in the sense that only a few components and a few aspects are captured in the abstract sets which underly the mathematical representation. Fortunately, the model has also a limited purpose and may thus suffice.

However, it remains a basic assumption that the whole world, the processes studied, and the objects modelled, are at least "partially decomposable" as soon as they are focused on with a particular purpose in mind. There are a number of analogies which clarify the notion.

Consider the "bowl of spaghetti" analogy: an indecomposable system would be one in which one could not pull on any one strand without pulling out the whole mass of spaghetti. A fully decomposable system, on the other hand, would allow one to extract any one strand without at all disturbing the rest.

Real systems seem to be somewhere between these two extremes, that is they are partially decomposable. They are well-cooked spaghetti bowls in which one can get some distance by tugging on a strand (how far may depend on which strand one pulls) but eventually other strands will start to interfere with further progress. In such a bowl, the strands represent facets or aspects and the tangle represents the fact that ultimately "everything is linked to everything else", a commonly expressed view concerning biological and higher systems on the organized complexity scale. Tugs on the strands represent purposes or objectives and the ability to narrow one's interest in the system to one of its facets.

In a partially decomposable system there is a marked use for such narrowing. However, only in a totally decomposable system would it be possible to ignore completely other strands. Specialized disciplines in today's sciences assume high decomposability. Decision-makers who must solve problems that cut across many disciplines are more aware of the limited ability of each speciality to contribute relevant non-contingent information.

There is an important way in which the analogy of a spaghetti bowl fails. It suggests that the strands, or facets, are inherent features of the real system. This may be true only in part. The situation is more like a bowl of clay in which one is free to string out one's own strands subject to the constraints imposed by the clay. Each such "spaghettization" represents a decomposition of the system. What may be tangled in one decomposition may be separable in another.

The analogies suggest that the modeller should perceive the systems as "multifacetted", as having many aspects. It is the modelling goal which should determine the crucial "facets" and, as long as the real system is partially decomposable in the modeller's frame, the systems point of view is applicable and models can be built.

The ideas mentioned throw some light on a long-standing controversy in science between the "reductionists" and the "holists". The former claim that all phenomena can be broken down into physico-chemical elements and understood on the basis of the laws of physics. The latter deny that this is possible and assert that most interesting systems must be understood as indivisible wholes.

According to the analogies, both could be right. A holistic point of view is essential if the "spaghettization" is completely entangled and decomposition is impossible; while reductionism is applicable whenever the "spaghetti bowl" is loose and decomposition is achievable. In practice, decomposability will be partial and a careful mix of holism and reductionism is appropriate.

An example of the partial decomposability according to purposes, is given in Table 2.2. The real-world object is man-made: a business firm. A short list of categories relevant to the operation of the firm are outlined. An all-inclusive model would be able to provide the basis for decision-making in each of these categories. However, the impediments to constructing such a comprehensive model make it a near impossibility for the foreseeable future. Instead we can envisage a collection of partial models, each oriented to one or more objectives.

TABLE 2.2. The firm as a multifacetted system

Objectives	Need model of:
Manpower requirements	Plant operations: timings, routings, etc.
Location of plant	Environment: availability of resources, energy, personnel, impact
Layout of plant	Plant machinery: sizes, routings, etc.
Marketing	Environment: consumer tastes, competition
Safety assurance	Material characteristics: alarms, escape routes, etc.
Quality control	Material characteristics: production process, etc.
Customer satisfaction	Customer interface: waiting, routing, etc.
Inventory control	Environment: customers, orders. Firm: purchasing, production, delivery departments
Corporate planning	Environment: investment capital, long-term trends, etc. Firm: unused capacity, growth potential
Research and development	Projects: interactions, likely pay-offs

Besides decomposability, another basic assumption is the existence of a state. It is assumed that the state captures all of the system's past history necessary to compute what it will do in the future or, at least, what the outputs will be under the assumption of known inputs. The existence of a state is a fundamental assumption, that has shown to be applicable under many circumstances. For certain mathematical formalisms the dimension of the state set is finite. That need not be always the case. Partial differential equations for instance, can be shown to have an infinite state. Still, the fundamental question remains whether all real-world systems can be adequately described by a state mechanism, be it infinite.

2.4   MATHEMATICAL MODELLING METHODOLOGY

2.4.1   A Quest for a Systematic Methodology

There exists no clear-cut technique for building mathematical models for a broad spectrum of real-world processes. In the past, the activity of constructing a mathematical representation was left to the specialist in a certain discipline where particular techniques were known to be helpful. From this point of view a model-builder is bound to have more success if:

(a) he is well acquainted and has experience with the field, the process belongs to;

(b) starting from "easy" projects, he developed skill in modelling of similar processes;

(c) he has the required intuition and ingenuity for the specific problem under study.

In recent years the overall picture has changed:

(a) the computer has endowed a modeller with new capabilities;

(b) modelling projects may cut through many disciplines: as it is difficult to be an expert in all fields, the task has grown more complicated;

(c) many projects are set up under pressure of real needs so that a relatively fast answer is required.

The new circumstances have urged systems analysts to look at the modelling process itself in a more systematic and rigorous way. Just as statistics gathers in a systematic way the procedures required to apply the tenets of the theory of probability to the real world, so will the field of "modelling and simulation" form an interface between the real-world processes and the field of General Systems Theory.

2.4.2   Information Sources for the Modelling Process

In order to understand better the paths followed to build mathematical
models, it is useful to ponder the "sources" feeding the modelling activity.
It is easily realized that the modelling activity itself is an ongoing, never-
ending set of activities. Practical constraints, however, are responsible for
the fact that, at a given point in time, the modelling process takes the form
of a "modelling project". Within cost and time constraints scientific work
will be carried out taking into account a set of objectives, funds and personnel. In the project system, analysts will apply their skill and use techniques on information "tapped" from different sources, until a satisfactory a
posteriori result is achieved. A very schematic representation can be drawn
(Fig. 2.4).

Three major information sources can be identified:

Goals and purposes

As mentioned in Section 2.3.4, a mathematical model gives in fact a very
restrictive image of a real process. The same real system may be subject to
a multiplicity of objectives (see Section 2.3.4). These objectives orient the
modelling process. They can help determine such factors as the system
boundaries by partitioning reality into a part to be focused on, and a part

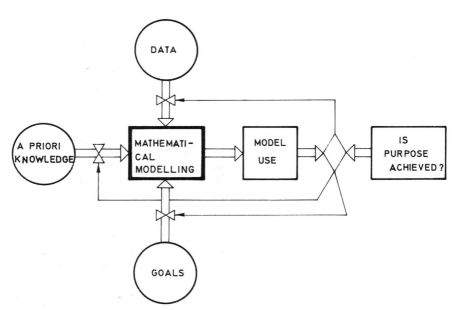

Fig. 2.4   Information sources for mathematical modelling

whose effect on the former is to be represented by input variables and/or boundary conditions; other factors are the components of relevance, and even sometimes the level of detail at which the latter ones are represented.

A priori knowledge

At the initiation of the modelling project, the processes under study will often have been looked upon by other persons before, most probably in another context. Usually, as time progresses, knowledge about a "class of phenomena" has been grouped and integrated in a branch of science, where a number of "laws", principles and models have been identified. Isaac Newton's "If I see far, it is because I stand on the shoulders of giants" means that we now make progress by standing on the foundations built by such people as Leonardo da Vinci, Galileo, Newton, Gauss and Einstein. The same idea applies to the modelling process tapping from the a priori knowledge source. One person's reasoning may provide a starting point for another in the search for a solution to a problem. Besides scientific experience, the same or related processes may have been analysed by modellers for similar or related purposes. In more delicate circumstances, the model-builder may have plausible "beliefs", originating from experience with similar or analogous real-life systems. This synergism is represented by the information source: a priori knowledge.

Experimental data

During the project, information about the process can also be gathered through experimentation and measurements on the phenomena. Judicious quantitative observation is another means of approaching the modelling problem.

2.4.3 Approaches to Modelling

The art of modelling resides in a successful use of the above-mentioned information sources in constructing a model that achieves the goals for which it was built. History has shown that there remains freedom in choosing a "proper" blend of the information categories mentioned.

"Deductive modellers" tend to rely on a priori information. If theory is lacking, they postulate hypotheses and principles and then try to find the model through mathematical and logical deductions. They go, in fact, from the general to the specific and see a model as a result of deductions from a set of premises. Experimental data is used to confirm or reject the principles that were at the origin.

The deductive approach has its existential problems. A complete set of axioms will lead to a unique model. The choice of the premises themselves may be a matter of debate, but the deductive approach faces another fundamental problem: substantially different a priori axioms may lead to very similar models. Einstein has clearly been faced with the fundamental problem mentioned. Newtonian axioms are different from the principles of relativity; yet for most everyday experimental conditions both axiom sets lead to extremely similar results [60].

"Inductive modellers" start with observed behaviour and try to induce higher level knowledge compatible with the observations, by going from the specific to the general.

Inductive methodology starts at the lowest level of the systems representation hierarchy (see Section 2.3.1.4) and tries to infer higher level information. In general, such choices are not unique. The problem can be stated from another point of view. The available data set is always finite and often scarce. Any representation is, in fact, an extrapolation on the data as the model will suggest data sets that are not available at the moment of model construction. One may argue that such extrapolation should be performed by adding a minimal amount of additional information. This guideline may be valid, but it is hardly useful for specific problems as it does not tell how and when such minimal amount of information is obtained.

"Pragmatic modellers" take an extreme engineering point of view and tend to focus on purposes. They see the model basically as a means towards an end. Pragmatism focuses directly on the specific goals of the project. It is not always easy to bring the objectives into play when modelling. Another drawback is that the goals may be so specific that the model has a very limited scope and turns out to be insignificant.

Pure forms of these approaches will seldom yield acceptable results and most often a proper mix is required. Arguments and controversy concerning a "good" mix are usually matters of emphasis and degree.

As the way to a satisfactory model is not clear-cut and is fed, especially during the modelling phase itself, by subjective action from the model-builder, the process has to be checked for validity over and over again. The act of investigating the "trustworthiness" of a mathematical representation is called validation.

2.4.4 Model Validation

Validation itself is a complex procedure depending partly on the kind of mathematical model, partly on the model-constructing process. The model itself can be set on trial at different levels and so one can distinguish a hierarchy of validity levels. In increasing order of strength and difficulty to achieve, a model may be valid:

(a) at the behavioural level, i.e. the model is able to reproduce the behaviour of the real system;

(b) at the state-structure level, i.e. the model is able to be synchronized with the real system into a state, from which unique prediction of future behaviour is possible;

(c) at the composite structure level, i.e. the model can be shown to uniquely represent the internal workings of the real system.

These levels of validity are sometimes called replicative, predictive and structural, respectively. A way to look at this situation is to regard each level as making a claim to knowledge about a real system. With each ascending "epistemological" level, the claims made become stronger, i.e. they assert more, but are less credible: they are more in need of justification.

Regardless of the levels of validity under study, validation considerations are pertinent during all modelling phases and also afterwards. One has to consider the following.

Validation in deduction

It is straightforward that deductive analysis should be carried out in a logical, correct and a mathematically rigorous manner. Under these circumstances the validity of the representation will depend on the validity of a priori knowledge. Unfortunately, the available a priori knowledge is stratified as well in exactitude as in generality. The commonly used and widely accepted procedures for reporting scientific results in the literature does not facilitate making an estimate about the exactitude and generality of such information. An assessment of basic assumptions is difficult too. Apart from these difficulties, validation can be done in two ways:

(i) Any investigation into the exactitude of the premises validates the model itself. Little is known, though, about the degree of validation such action is encompassing.

(ii) A check on other consequences of the premises, validates that information and consequently the model.

Validation in induction

First it can be checked whether the induction procedure has been carried through in a mathematical and logical correct way. All further validation reduces to comparison of model and real system behaviour.

In that respect it is useful to consider the real system as a source of data, which one obtains by input–output measurements. This means that one is concerned with the input–output relation of the real system, represented by $R_{\overline{r.s}}$. As available experimental data is limited, at a certain time t only a portion of all potentially obtainable data elements will be available denoted by $R_{\overline{r.s}}^{t}$.

The model itself is also a source of such data $R_{\overline{m}}$. A valid model at a certain point in time means $R_{\overline{r.s}}^{t} = R_{\overline{m}}^{t}$ where the equality sign has to be specified. In practice, one has to choose a metric, distance measure, which inevitably reflects a certain weighting of features of the behaviour. Validity can be ascertained as long as deviations of the model data and the real-world data are close, with respect to the chosen metric.

A second choice must be made if the real system data is believed to be stochastically generated and/or if the model is taken to represent a stochastic process. In this case, statistical tests must be chosen in order to assess the probability that the degree of agreement found between model and real system with the finite amount of data available is truly representative of the stochastic processes from which the data was sampled.

Validation in purpose

An often used adage is "the proof of the pudding is in the eating". From a practical point of view, a model is sufficiently valid if its goal can be obtained. A model is really under fire from the moment it has to serve its purpose.

In Section 2.2, modelling purposes have been discussed in general. A truly valid model would be a model that permits all possible objectives that can be set to meet. Some goals are easier to attain than others. Interpolation, for instance, is easier to obtain than prediction. Little, however, is known as to how a limited objective allows for less stringent validity requirements.

2.4.5   An Overview

A summary of the modelling process is given in Fig. 2.5.

More specific techniques for model-building cannot be provided without choosing a certain model formalism. Specific procedures according to different formalisms will be discussed in subsequent chapters. When considering a model at the state structure level, it is possible to give a more detailed overview of the overall modelling process. In fact, up to now no use has been made of the definition of a mathematical model as stated in Section 2.3.1.3.

It is difficult to obtain a system set structure as a whole. Most often modelling procedures focus on a part of the description. Useful decompositions of the mathematical representation are shown in Fig. 2.6.

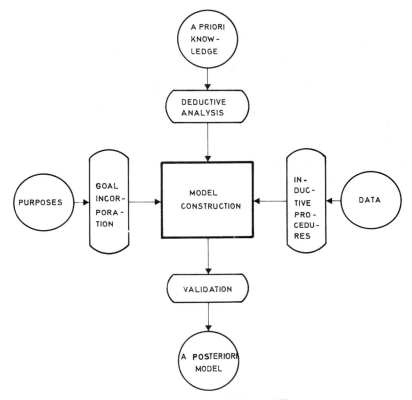

FIG. 2.5   Schematic overview of the modelling process

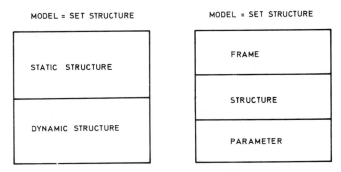

FIG. 2.6   Model decompositions

A first decomposition yields:

(a) a static structure; the static structure is composed of the sets X, Y, Q and the output function λ

(b) a dynamic structure; the dynamic components of the set structure are the sets T, Ω and the transition function δ.

A second decomposition sees a model as being composed of a frame, a structure and the parameters. The definitions depend slightly on the kind of description that is under study

(a) a frame : input–output behavioural model: the sets X, Y, T, Ω and the boundaries of the system;

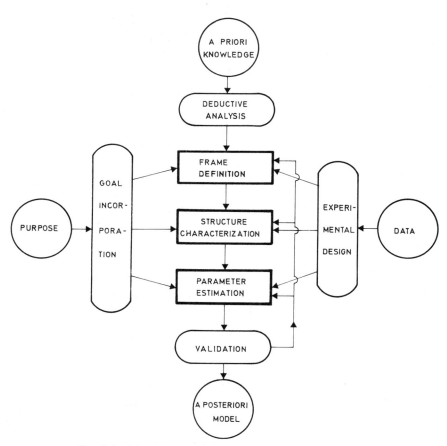

FIG. 2.7 Schematic representation of the modelling process

state structure model: the sets X, Y, T, Ω, Q and the system boundaries;

(b) a structure : state structure model: the functional relationships f, g without knowledge of intrinsic constants;
   input–output model: the same components as above augmented with an arbitrary state set;
(c) parameters : the constants that occur in the model definition; they may or may not have a physical meaning.

Model descriptions are in fact not fully decomposable. By permitting zero constants, it is possible to modify a structure through parametrization. In the same way, decompositions however remain useful as they allow the modeller to concentrate on a more simple problem than finding the model as a whole. They also play a useful role in discussing methodological techniques. On the basis of the last decomposition a more complete picture of the modelling process can be provided (Fig. 27.7).

2.5 USEFULNESS OF MATHEMATICAL MODELS ACCORDING TO SCIENTIFIC DISCIPLINES

2.5.1 Generalities

Not only mathematical models, but even the mathematical "language" in general, have proven very effective in physics and classical engineering, where physical phenomena form the basis for a variety of machines, devices and processes useful for mankind. It has to be recognized, however, that mathematics was applied in other branches of science, too. In the past, the activity of constructing a mathematical framework was left to the specialist scientist or engineer in a certain discipline where, by tradition, a certain level of mathematical sophistication was felt to be adequate.

The advent of modern computing devices has dramatically altered this situation by enhancing the status of mathematical representation. Simulation, in fact, permits investigation into mathematical structures that before were analytically intractable. Through computation, the scientist can explore consequences of certain mathematical formulations and the engineer can perform more complex design tasks. Physics and the traditional engineering branches have benefited quite rapidly from the advantages offered by the electronic computer. It was thought for some time that the mathematical skills of the specialists were the major reason for the success and the usefulness of the modelling and simulation approach in these fields. As a consequence, it could be expected that mathematical models were bound to be successful in other disciplines like biology, economics and, eventually, sociology and psychology.

In the mid-seventies, systems analysts studying water resources and environmental systems [119, 225], began to realize that the kind of systems in which they were involved, were difficult to describe in precise mathematical terms. Furthermore, a final description did not always turn out to be useful for practical means. In the field of mathematical modelling methodology the concept of "greyness" or "softness" was introduced. It was realized that the "background" knowledge available in certain scientific disciplines to build a mathematical representation might be less adequate, and that the lack of suitable a priori information entailed the need for extensive experimentation. These findings were, and still are, certainly applicable to a whole spectrum of systems ranging from the chemical, biochemical and biological ones to those in economics, sociology and biology.

Later on still other limitations became evident. In that respect, the terminology of ill-definition and ill-defined systems [206, 242] was chosen as an indication for the overall problems that arise when a mathematical description for phenomena belonging to the "soft" fields had to be developed. Nowadays, there seems to exist a certain consensus about the usefulness and power of mathematical representations. It is believed that, at the present, they are most useful in the physical sciences and less useful in the human-related disciplines. This quite surprising broad range is an invitation to look into the reasons of the "state of the art", which is the next subject.

2.5.2   The Modelling Process and its Environment

In order to make a proper diagnosis concerning the causes of "unsatisfactory" achievements of the mathematical modelling approach in some fields, a closer study of the relationships between real-world system, scientific knowledge and the modelling activity is required (see Fig. 2.8).

One has to admit that a modelling activity that is started at a given point in time, bears heavily on the results of similar projects which were performed earlier by other researchers, most probably for other purposes. Such results have often been properly incorporated into a consistent body of knowledge: a scientific theory. Especially if the real-world system is made up of natural phenomena, these may have been studied for long periods by scientists with their only purpose being an increased understanding of the processes. A new project on the system, however, will be characterized by a new objective so that some degree of effort, skill and creativity is required to obtain satisfactory results. Nevertheless, the model

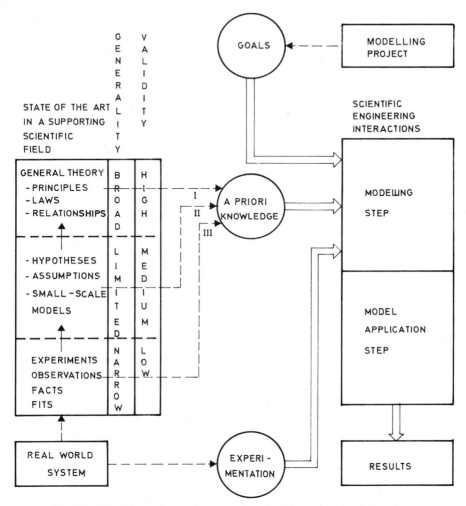

FIG. 2.8   The information environment for scientific-engineering interactions

builder will rely on the associated scientific discipline or body of knowledge, to minimize his effort. It is rarely taken into account that the knowledge available in the field under study never has a uniform structure: some
statements have more validity and generality than others.

All scientific endeavour starts with fact finding, observations and experiments, often followed by fitting curves and simple mathematical relationships. Taking into consideration the difficulties and uncertainties of that

initial work, there is no doubt that most of the data and facts have low validity and narrow generality. As more evidence is gathered, one is able to make assumptions, to draw conclusions, to posit hypotheses and to generate small-scale models. Some deeper understanding is gained and pieces of information are available that may be considered of medium validity and limited generality. The most difficult, but most gratifying, step is to assemble all pieces into a general theory. The principles, laws and relationships that form the theory necessarily have a broad generality and high validity. As the theory is able to explain a wide variety of phenomena it is considered to be the truth at a certain point in time. The model builder who tries to solve his particular problem can draw a priori knowledge from any of these categories along route I, II or III according to Fig. 2.8.

As explained in Section 2.4.2, the modelling effort will further be guided by the specific goals of the model-builder. Moreover information will often be gathered through direct experimentation on the real-world system.

2.5.3 Physical Systems Versus Other Systems

It is now extremely relevant to compare the state of the art in the physical sciences with the situation in the other fields. Many physical phenomena have been well isolated and studied in detail. In many sub-fields, a mature general theory is available stating its principles and laws in mathematical and, hence, quantitative terms. As an example, consider electro-magnetic phenomena. They can be generated and freely isolated in a laboratory. Precise and sophisticated measurement techniques are available. The theory is well developed. Maxwell's laws with their relativistic interpretation form a firm basis for explanations of a wide variety of processes. As a consequence, the model-builder will draw almost all a priori information from route I. He has an adequate modelling methodology and consequently, his model will have high validity. In many cases, linear system theory, which is best understood and best developed, is applicable. Under such circumstances, it is understandable that his modelling activity can yield exceptional results.

The modelling activity on the so-called "softer" processes, using mathematical tools, has been less successful. It is sufficient to examine the same diagram (Fig. 2.8) to discover the deficiencies responsible for the less successful mathematical models and their lower performance. These deficiencies can be classified into three groups.

2.5.3.1 *Deficiencies in the general scientific theory: softness or greyness*

As long as the process includes physical phenomena, the general theory explaining these phenomena can be used (tapped along route I). For the typical softer areas, however, the general theory is not so well developed and is seldom expressed in mathematical terms. Consequently, the model-builder has to use routes II, and even III, to assemble the necessary a priori information: information that is, unfortunately, of more dubious validity.

To illustrate the deficiencies in the general theory, a few examples are given. Species interaction is of key importance in the study of ecological systems. According to Darwin, interactions are dictated by the law of survival of the fittest, while changes in genetic structure occur at random. The law is widely accepted, but in verbal form. Furthermore, details are missing and it is impossible to give the law a precise mathematical repre-sentation. At last, although the theory has been considered for a long time as having broad generality and high validity, more and more biologists have started to question the usefulness, the relevance and even the trust-worthiness of the theory [227]. Another important principle in biology is the fact that organisms may be divided into classes depending on morph-ology, growth form, and their mode of reproduction [70]. Here, the validity is well established but, again, the rule is qualitative and its impact on models is poorly understood. In short, one has to conclude that the theo-retical foundations in biology for instance, have not reached the level of abstraction of certain other fields. The deficiency in scientific background can be a first obstacle and, consequently, the methodology of the system analyst will often produce less valid representations.

2.5.3.2 Difficult separability, complexity and low accessibility of soft systems: ill-definition

Soft systems themselves may have a number of properties which make a quantitative approach cumbersome and difficult to carry out in a rigorous way. Ill-definition is a generic term for these undesirable properties.

The processes are often of an intricate nature. On average, the number of meaningful interconnections will be larger than in physical disciplines. A cell, for instance, has a large number of highly integrated sub-systems. Another aspect of complexity is the multifacetted character of such sys-tems. One recognizes that the same process can be approached from a large multiplicity of objectives. In terms of a previous analogy: the "spaghettizations" are manifold and entangled.

As a second feature, it can be mentioned that soft systems may be difficult to separate in space as well as in scale, and often in time. Illustra-tions can easily been found in the biological field. One of the major princi-ples states that the activities of an organism and the rates at which it carries on those activities are dependent, not only on the organism itself, but on the organism's environment [70]. It is, therefore, difficult to define clearly the boundaries of the system, and separation for experimentation is almost unfeasible without substantially altering the phenomena. It is, for instance, well known that *in vivo* processes are often impossible to reproduce *in vitro*.

Difficult spatial separability is not the only hindrance. Scale differences are also small so that it is sometimes not clear which level is appropriate. Again, comparison with physical phenomena is helpful. For electromagnetism, for example, a microscopic theory is available which explains the phenomena at the atomic or subatomic level. There exists also a macroscopic theory, represented by the Maxwell equations, which describes larger objects. For the latter theory, microscopic events have been averaged over an appropriate region. Scale differences between microscopic entities: electrons, nuclei, etc. (<1 Å) and the macroscopic systems ($>10^8$ Å) are impressive and they explain, for a part, the extremely accurate results obtained for such systems. Chemical models are another example. Chemical concentrations assume a large number of molecules within a tiny space and a macroscopic point of view is acceptable.

However, if one considers size differences between an organism (10^8–10^9 Å), a cell (10^4–10^5 Å), and a macromolecule (10^2–10^3 Å), it is seen that the different hierarchical levels are less far apart from each other, and determination of an appropriate level is consequently less evident. For a population of cells, e.g. it is difficult to decide whether modelling at the cell level or a macroscopic population-oriented approach is better, or adequate, for a particular purpose. This fundamental question is still largely unsolved. An illustrative example is the state-of-the-art in modelling biomass for fermentation processes. A classification of mathematical models of microbial populations has been made by Tsuchiya, Fredrickson and Aris [222] (see Fig. 2.9). Segregated models consider individual cells and therefore start from a lower scale level than non-segregated models, where the biophase has been lumped through averaging. In both categories, the

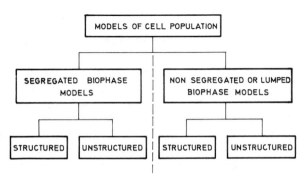

FIG. 2.9   Models of cell population [222]

biophase can be given some structure but this is a matter of modelling detail and aggregation. The first classification is more fundamental. The major problem remains as how to indicate which models are adequate for given engineering purposes.

Beside scale differences, time separation may also be difficult. In electromagnetic theory, a quasi-stationary theory permits easy analysis for relatively "slow" phenomena. Electrical eigen-frequencies are much higher than "surrounding" mechanical, chemical or thermal frequencies. Conversely, in biology for instance, all time constants are usually of the same order of magnitude, which makes the separation difficult.

Finally, a low accessibility to the soft systems has to be recognized. For almost all such processes, experimentation is a pain, not only because of the processes being difficult to separate, but because of measurement techniques being inadequate and/or very expensive. Some facets of low accessibility can be summarized as follows:

(a) Many measurement techniques are based on complex procedures (e.g. chemical analysis for biological processes or huge complex data gathering in economy). Such an approach requires a lot of manipulative action and is prone to a wide variety of biases and errors.

(b) In the case of animals, ethical considerations may set limitations on experimental set-ups and for human beings those restrictions are even much more severe.

(c) The inherent variability between different processes of the same kind limits drastically the advantages of consecutive or parallel experiments.

All these aspects of soft systems, which makes them ill-defined, form the second important stumbling block for a systematic and well performing modelling approach.

2.5.3.3 Inadequacy in methodology

The main step in reaching the project goal is the construction of a specific mathematical representation and the application of system theoretical results on that representation. Historically, system analysis originated from pure mathematics, and the theory has been built up around linear systems because of their analytic tractability. It happened to be that the tools developed were adequate for the study of many physical processes. Soft systems, on the contrary, are highly non-linear and adaptive. This last feature, for instance, is even one of the major principles in biology, and it is usually stated as: the current phenotype, state, or constitution, of an organism depends not only on its genotype, but also on the past history of environments seen by that organism. Mathematical formulations with such properties are not always well understood. Another aspect of biological entities is their variability. This can be taken into account by postulating stochastic models, the theoretical foundations of which are, even in the non-linear case, better established. Practical application methodology is, however, lacking. The Monte Carlo approach, a brute force technique, is still the only general method available. Besides problems in model application, the first stage, model-building, poses problems too. The modelling methodology that has mainly been advocated up to now, consists in a largely deductive approach forming an interface between a priori knowledge and the parameter estimation or calibration and validation stages, as the two major and most important inductive steps in the overall procedure (Fig. 2.10). The techniques for these latter two steps often assume large data sets. This global approach in fact assumes implicitly that the a priori knowledge is of good quality: general and exact; and, therefore, referring to Fig. 2.8, that the knowledge is drawn along route I from a comprehensive and powerful scientific theory. Furthermore, the iterative loop requires the possibility of easy experimentation. It is clear that the properties of softness and ill-definition violate the implicit assumptions present in the modelling procedure.

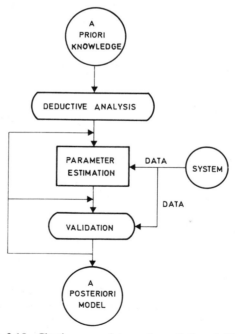

FIG. 2.10 Classic approach to mathematical modelling

Summarizing, it can be stated that for soft systems there are three "weak" points in the diagram of Fig. 2.8: the non-availability of a comprehensive general theory, the ill-defined character of the systems themselves, and a badly-adapted methodology. The analysis made can be supplemented with other arguments and facts and, as mentioned above, there has grown a certain consensus among modelling specialists about these major causes of the limited success of mathematical models in the soft disciplines. Much more open to speculation are the conclusions that can be drawn out of such an analysis as they depend on personal points of view. A few interpretations are presented below.

2.5.4 Interpretations

If one scrutinizes the analysis made above and summarizes the opinions given by specialists concerning future developments, one can lay out three scenario's that indicate the domains on which research activities should next be conducted.

2.5.4.1 *Scenario I: mismatch between systems and formal methods*

From this point of view, it is believed that application of mathematical modelling and simulation techniques has already reached a more mature level. Certainly future developments in the softer domains will occur, but they will arise most probably along the traditional qualitative lines. The role of the formal mathematical representation methods will not significantly increase.

This scenario is not without grounds, but based on inferences from experiences in Artificial Intelligence. As very "soft" examples, the areas of natural language translation and of speech recognition are particularly illuminating.

During the 1950s one of the exciting frontiers of computer-oriented research was the development of computer programs for language translation. When large digital computers became generally available, few observers doubted that it was only a matter of time before it would be possible to perform automatic translations from one natural language to another, for example from English to Russian and vice versa. Apparently adequate formal methods had been gradually developed by mathematical linguists, most notably Dr Noam Chomsky, and these tools have been eminently successful in the development of programming languages designed to facilitate man–computer communication.

A basic element of the mathematical linguistic method was a careful separation of semantics and syntax. Syntactic analysis involves the phrase structure approach. Each word in a sentence to be translated is assigned a so-called non-terminal symbol, such as noun, article, verb, etc. Groups of these non terminals are then recognized as forming a phrase, e.g. a noun phrase, verb phrase, etc., and these phrases are then combined to form other more general phrases until, finally, the entire sentence is completely represented. A language translator program requires two major components: the syntactic analyser/synthesizer and the dictionary. The syntactic analyser should be able to parse progressively more complex sentences and then be able to reassemble the components according to the grammatical structure of the target language into which the original sentence is to be translated. At the same time, the dictionary should list equivalent word pairs in the two languages. It was recognized of course that some problems with synonyms and shades of meanings would be encountered, but it was generally expected that most texts would eventually be able to be translated by this approach. After many years of intensive, expensive and disappointing efforts it was recognized this expectation was unrealistic.

It gradually became apparent that ambiguities at many different levels make it virtually impossible to perform a satisfactory translation without understanding the meaning of the sentence, i.e. the semantic component. These ambiguities involve not only the meaning of specific words, but also the non-terminal symbol to be applied to each word. For example, the sentence "Time flies" can be interpreted in at least two ways depending upon which of the two words is considered to be the noun and which the verb. As a rule, there is insufficient information in any given sentence to resolve successfully all inherent ambiguities. It is necessary to consider the meaning of the sentence, i.e. to understand. If possible at all, this can only be accomplished by considering the context in which the sentence resides, other sentences forming the text, the source and the purpose of the text, etc.

Translation is generally impossible without an understanding of the semantic component of a text; it therefore requires the reader to possess a wealth of contextual insights and auxiliary information; even then there is considerable possibility of misinterpretation. Chomsky subsequently introduced the notion of deep structure as a tool for linguistic analysis. This approach to linguistic analysis was for a time held to have considerable promise in extending the power of the phrase structure method, but more recently the interest of linguists has shifted elsewhere.

Although it may theoretically be possible to provide a set of algorithms and a vast computerized data base to mimic a human reader's utilization of contextual information, it is evident that this is several orders of magnitude more difficult than the phrase structure approach. The general translation of natural language text is now generally accepted to be far outside the range of our technical capabilities. This once promising field has therefore virtually been abandoned.

Another area, also falling under the general heading of artificial intelligence, involves the recognition of human speech. Here too during the heady days of the 1950s it was thought that it would eventually be possible to digitize the acoustic signals generated in human speech and to employ a digital computer to provide a printed version of the speech or to take various actions in accordance with the verbal message received. This too is a task which humans, even of relatively low intelligence, can be taught to do with considerable reliability. Accordingly, a considerable amount of research and development has been devoted to various speech recognition projects. The general approach is based on the observation that acoustic information is comprised of a hierarchy of progressively more complex sounds. At the simplest level are the phonemes, including 16 vowels and 22 consonants in English; these phonemes are combined in speech to form syllables which, in turn, are combined to form words; words are combined to form word groups until full sentences and messages are created. In examining recordings of different types of speakers, conversing under many different conditions, a surprising non-uniformity and complexity of speech patterns is observed. Of particular difficulty in the recognition of speech signals is the tendency of most speakers to fail to pause between words, to swallow or to fail to pronounce portions of words or entire words, and to utilize changes in pitch and loudness to convey information.

Eventually it was concluded that, just as in the case of the translation of natural languages, the acoustic signals received by a listener are in themselves insufficient to permit the understanding of speech. Rather, a listener is forced to make use of a variety of contextual data to aid him in interpreting what he hears. This contextual information includes a knowledge of the syntax of the speaker's language, a general knowledge of the subject of the spoken message, observations of events occurring while the speech is taking place, and a suitable interpretation of variations in the pitch, stress and rapidity of the spoken words. Even then frequent mistakes are made. While there is no fundamental reason why a computer could not be programmed so as to be able to make contextual interpretations of acoustic data, the actual magnitude of such a task is far out of the range of present-day technology. As a result, most recent projects in the speech recognition area content themselves with very limited objectives.

Under scenario I it would appear that the problem of devising formal models and mathematical representations for soft systems has much in common with the above two examples. A large mass and wide varieties of data, often of limited quality, are available from measurements of system inputs and outputs. A human being in charge of such a system usually makes use of only a small portion of this available information. When faced with a decision to take, he includes a large amount of contextual information which would be very difficult if not impossible to include in a systematic way. This information includes his awareness of the historical, social, and even political environment; it also includes a general knowledge of the behaviour of other similar systems.

If one continues along the lines of the scenario presented, future effort should concentrate on relaxing the basic attributes of the formalism described in Section 2.3.1.3. A key characteristic of all formal methods discussed so far in this text is that they are inherently unambiguous and their manipulation follows rigorous rules which lead to unambiguous solutions. Recognizing that such rigour is not feasible, or even desirable, in many situations involving human judgement, L. Zadeh introduced the notion of "fuzzy sets". Fuzzy descriptions of systems permit the inclusion of such imprecise concepts as "slightly polluted" or "very heavy". Such expressions are highly meaningful and significant to human observers, but they are absent in classical formal methods. Zadeh has developed a calculus for manipulating expressions containing fuzzy variables in a manner which permits the treatment of problems that cannot be treated by classical methods, even when probabilistic measures are employed. In this way "fuzzy sets" can be highly illuminating in viewing real-life systems.

At present, little experience is available concerning the success of the fuzzy formalism in real-world problems. It remains an area of research to investigate how such formalism can meet the objectives.

2.5.4.2 Scenario II: computer-based general theory

The premise of a second scenario is that the process of systems modelling can be made much more effective, reliable and greatly speeded up by interactive computer assistance. The potentialities of computer technology are far from being exploited to their full extent in the field of modelling.

As mentioned before, for problems in many soft areas knowledge is extremely scattered and fragmented. In other words, there is no systematic and quantitative general theory available. Such a highly exact consistent theory is very important for all small-scale modelling projects [119]. Building such a theory is a feat which has only been achieved in certain branches of the physical sciences by a few superbly skilful minds. Whether such a quantitative general theory will be developed at all in the softer field, may be a matter of much debate. In many instances, however, a large amount of data, observations, and small-scale models of narrow or limited generality and low or medium exactitude may be available. As a specific example, the modelling of energy generation and consumption by society could be given. The problem is presented in more detail in Chapter 5.

For the discussion here, it is sufficient to stress that information about the subject is of the type mentioned in this section. Conditions are changing so fast that it may happen that general principles would be outdated at the moment of discovery. It is within the present technological capabilities, however, to gather all such information in a systematic way into computer data bases.

It is believed now that computer support could be developed first, for maintenance of a multiplicity of partial models in an environment in which the real system boundaries and its facets of interest are constantly evolving; and second, for integration of such models to a consistent whole. Such a computer support system would "in a sense" provide an alternative to the general theory concept mentioned in Section 2.5.2. In fact, the system would provide the model-builder with the opportunity to draw information from available a priori knowledge in a faster and much more reliable way. The hope of the success of such an approach is based on the remarkable achievements that have been obtained with related data base systems for simple information retrieval.

2.5.4.3   *Scenario III: towards advanced methodology*

From another point of view, it is thought that the mathematical modelling methodology is badly adapted to the nature of the soft or ill-defined systems. Classic mathematical modelling techniques are badly adapted to the structure of the information sources for the modelling process.

The impact on the modelling procedure of the information sources mentioned for the engineering problems in the physical sciences, show a specific pattern (Fig. 2.11). The importance of a priori knowledge is overwhelming. Data is useful, but quite often easily obtainable. As the model is

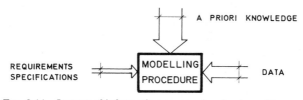

FIG. 2.11   Impact of information sources for classic problems

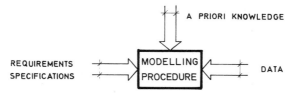

FIG. 2.12   Impact of information sources for soft problems

a valid and faithful representation of the system, a large variety of engineering goals can be met and, therefore, engineering specifications only have a limited influence on the total process.

For the systems encountered in other disciplines, however, the a priori knowledge is of less good quality due to greyness and softness, and so its role is reduced. The vacuum which is left has to be filled with information from the other sources. Data from experiments could be extremely valuable but ill-definition limits its supply. As its gathering may not be easy and straightforward, special attention paid to experimental design and set-up may be very useful (Fig. 2.12). It is to be expected that the validity and generality of the models obtained are likely to be of a lesser extent. To reach a final goal within time and cost resources, it may not only be convenient, but also necessary, to incorporate goal specifications and requirements during the modelling process. As the importance of "data" and "requirement" sources is increased, more advanced techniques which are able to "tap" efficiently from these sources are required (see Fig. 2.7) and these procedures will form interfaces between these sources and the modelling process much in the same way as deductive reasoning forms an interface between a priori knowledge and the equation constructing process in Fig. 2.10.

2.6 CONCLUSIONS

Faced with the real world, one may choose to approach it with mathematical tools. It was tried to reveal that the essence of such approach and its basic assumptions, far from being trivial, are the methods available to obtain a mathematical description. A certain philosophical point of view may guide the model-builder, but here it has been attempted to give, in simple terms, a more objective picture of the basic entities and considerations that guide the modelling process. What does one use in order to forge a mathematical representation? What does one need to find in order to obtain a complete picture? Is the description acceptable on logical grounds?

Unfortunately, nowadays, a mathematical model is sometimes less useful than one has hoped. Personal points of view exist on the causes of this often observed fact of life. The mathematical language itself may be questioned. This is by far the most drastic attack, but the most difficult to yield tangible results. A whole new way of perceiving reality has to be developed and its relevance tested and proved. Within the basic tenets of the conventional mathematical approach, improvements are believed to be possible.

First, the methodological tools should be better adapted to what could be called the modelling context or the precise nature of the modelling problem. It has been shown that this context could be described by evaluating the nature of the information sources that will feed the modelling process. It is necessary to gain a better insight into the most appropriate techniques and their limits. To gain that insight, there is still a long way to go. The next two chapters intend to present available techniques for specific model formalisms: Chapter 3 treats ordinary difference and differential equations and Chapter 4 partial differential equations. In Chapter 3 inductive or "data-processing" techniques are emphasized, mainly because efficient extraction of model information from measurements, where a priori information is lacking, remains a difficult problem. The choice of the techniques is certainly guided by present-day research trends and the personal interests of the authors. Besides providing advanced methodology it is intended to introduce new concepts that may be useful in future research and to reveal new research areas in methodology, which bear promise for improved models. In Chapter 4, methodology is presented for a more complex model formalism: partial differential equations. By comparing the state of the art for the latter formalism with the former one, it can be seen how the same modelling issues may take other dimensions and play other roles.

Another road to better models and more faithful descriptions consists in developing improved structures for gathering and manipulating model information. As mentioned, scientific theories are highly effective means towards well structuring objective information. Other methods, however, could be useful too, especially when theory is still lacking. Chapter 5 introduces concepts and techniques to structure, and eventually properly condense prior modelling results in order to ensure that the modelling efforts are cumulative. In that manner more faithful representations can probably be obtained. In short it can be said that the subsequent three chapters will address in more detail the modelling issues mentioned only generally so far.

3. Model-building methodology for difference and differential equations

3.1 INTRODUCTION

3.1.1 Generalities

In the previous chapter, it has been said that a model representation could be seen as a piece of condensed information related to a real world object or process. From that point of view, model building is nothing else than gathering information and condensing it in an appropriate form. Methodology has been discussed in general terms in Section 2.4. As mentioned there, specific techniques cannot be presented without choosing a model formalism. In this chapter, ordinary difference and differential equations are used as model representations.

It is by no means the objective here to present a complete overview of existing techniques for constructing such models. The enterprise would be too gigantic. The choice of subjects has been large influenced by the considerations of Section 2.4. It was argued that one of the reasons for the difficulties in obtaining a valid representation for certain real systems could be traced down to a badly adapted methodology. The analysis started from the observation that there are, in fact, three information sources that feed the modelling process (see Section 2.4.2). The modelling effort, as well as the methodology, depends on the relative use of these sources, and on their information structure. Techniques are presented that are useful when relatively little a priori information is available. A more precise circumscription will be given in the sequel.

The elements of the diagram in Fig. 2.7 are taken as the main subjects for this chapter. First, the model itself is presented in Section 3.1.2. The strong and weak points of the formalism in the model-building context are briefly mentioned, and a few special model forms that have been studied in more detail, are given.

In building these models, a number of methodological issues may rise, some of which have drawn much more attention than others. It is to be hoped that the manner of presentation in this book will convince the reader that certain subjects really deserve more research, which should be beneficial to the status and usefulness of mathematical modelling. The space allocated to the different subjects reflects, however, the present state of the art.

Section 3.2. presents the parameter estimation problem. The set of parameters is an important part of the mathematical model. Techniques for parameter estimation assume that a model frame and structure are available. Parameter determination selects a final unique model from a set of candidate models. The candidate set is a subset of the more general set of models specified by the model formalism, and the subset is defined by frame and structure. The importance of the parameter estimation step is heavily dependent on the purpose of the model. In adaptive control, the knowledge of the exact parameter values may be only secondary. In other cases, the parameters may themselves be the goal of the modelling process, especially if they embody physical constants, whose precise numerical values are looked for. During modelling itself, parameter estimation is often required to investigate other modelling issues. Because of its importance, considerable attention is paid to the problem. Recursive on-line techniques, which have been studied in more detail in the last decade, are emphasized. Quite a number of ready-to-use algorithms are presented, as well as general concepts concerning the problem and the methodology, so that new schemes can be developed and new issues investigated.

In Section 3.3., the structure characterization problem is discussed. For a given frame, model structures define subsets of models (Section 2.4.5). The subsets may have different relations with each other. The mathematical study of structural relationships is by no means easy. The choice of a suitable structure is most easily done deductively, because theory and the system build-up quite often lead directly to a structure, so that purely mathematical issues can be avoided. If a priori knowledge is lacking, inductive characterization techniques are required. The methodology is less developed, and only recently has the subject become more popular. Here special attention is given to concepts that may be helpful in gaining insight and developing new techniques.

Finally, Section 3.4 briefly considers the remaining issues. Which are the ways to define a suitable frame? Is it possible to plan data collection in order to obtain model parts in an optimal way within given constraints? Once the model is built, how can one perform additional checks on the validity? How does one effectively bring the modelling goals into play during the different modelling stages?

3.1.2   The model formalism

3.1.2.1   The general case

The model definition

A popular mathematical modelling formalism for dynamic systems is the well-known, non-linear, state space continuous-time model, mentioned in Section 2.3.2.2, equation 2.1. The more general form, equations 3.1–4, is termed ODESS, ordinary differential equation system specification.

$$\dot{\underline{x}} = \underline{f}(\underline{x}, \underline{u}, \underline{p}, t) \tag{3.1}$$

$$\underline{y} = \underline{g}(\underline{x}, \underline{u}, \underline{p}, t) \tag{3.2}$$

$$\underline{x}(t_0) = \underline{x}_0 \tag{3.3}$$

Using the mathematical more sophisticated but more precise, terminology of Section 2.3.2.2., these equations define a set structure and they consequently imply a number of assumptions about the variables used, e.g. $\underline{x} \in R^n$. In practical circumstances, it often happens that the variable and parameter sets are constrained. In order to be unambiguous, one should specify such constraints, for instance by providing a set of inequalities:

$$0 \leqslant \underline{h}(\underline{x}, \underline{u}, \underline{p}, t) \tag{3.4}$$

As before, $\underline{x}$ is the n-dimensional state vector, $\underline{u}$ the m-dimensional input vector, $\underline{y}$ the p-dimensional output vector, and $\underline{p}$ a vector of n_p unknown constants, termed parameters.

The vector functions $\underline{f}$, $\underline{g}$, $\underline{h}$ are nominally non-linear, non-stationary. The continuous-time formulation is chosen because many physical relationships, such as mass or energy conservation relationships, are stated more naturally in continuous time; thus it is likely that a priori knowledge and a priori assumptions will fit more easily within the continuous–time framework.

A disadvantage of the model (3. 1–4) is its deterministic aspects. Almost everywhere in real-world applications uncertainty is an inherent part of the phenomena. Sometimes such "noise" patterns can be neglected or averaged out, but often a description that takes these uncertainties into account is more realistic. A natural extension of the model form presented above is given by the following equations with $\underline{w}$ and $\underline{v}$ noise processes.

$$\dot{\underline{x}} = \underline{f}(\underline{x}, \underline{u}, \underline{w}, \underline{p}, t) \tag{3.5}$$

$$\underline{y} = \underline{g}(\underline{x}, \underline{u}, \underline{v}, \underline{p}, t) \tag{3.6}$$

$$\underline{x}(t_0) = \underline{x}_0 \tag{3.7}$$

$$0 \leqslant \underline{h}(\underline{x}, \underline{u}, \underline{p}, t) \tag{3.8}$$

Having introduced random process vectors in the equations, the $\underline{x}$- and $\underline{y}$-vectors become random processes. The mathematical implications are very complex. Special calculus, e.g. Itô-calculus, may be required. The theoretical aspects of stochastic differential equations have been studied [54, 162].

As the practical implications from the viewpoint of model-building are for a part unknown, and the state concept difficult to define, the approach mentioned in Section 2.3.2.2 is adopted. The mathematical sophisticated machinery required for handling continuous random processes is obviated. As here practical model-building is under scrutiny, the theoretical issues are not discussed.

The model properties

Before proceeding, the model formalism's relevance as a mathematical representation for a real-world system is discussed, as well as its practicality in utilization.

The "descriptive power" of equations (3. 1–4) is high. A wide variety of system behaviour may be observed. Well known is the linear time-invariant case, which also serves as a tool for investigating non-linear cases. The non-linear case is a very rich descriptive source. In fact, though the model description has been used for centuries, interest into the behavioural patterns of specific descriptions still exist. Recent studies, for instance, are the contributions from Thom [218] and Zeeman [249] based on "Catastrophe Theory". The theory investigates the relationship between "types of catastrophes" and mathematical description. Based upon this, models for heart beat and nerve impulse were presented. Another development is the analysis by May [155] and Hassel [91] of non-linear differential equations which show deterministic, but chaotic, behaviour. Such examples illustrate that the descriptive potentiality of equations (3. 1–4) is far from being exhausted. On the other hand, the differential equation model has its limitations. Time is the only independent variable. Spatial features have to be "discretized" or "lumped". If the approximation is too crude, one has to turn towards partial differential equations (Chapter 4).

The "analytical tractability" of ODESS is limited. Classic techniques exist for soiving ordinary differential equations, but in many circumstances a closed form solution is difficult to find even in some rather simple-looking cases. An example is the Tessier-model for bacterial growth:

$$\frac{dx}{dt} = \mu_M\left(1 - \exp\left[-\frac{(x_M - x)}{T}\right]\right)x \tag{3.9}$$

Thanks to numerical computer techniques, analytical intractable models are manageable during model-building as long as their complexity, i.e. the number of equations, is acceptable. Circumstances remain where numerical approximation techniques constitute a problem in itself, e.g. "stiff" models, with special "mode" configurations.

The most important issue here is the ease with which a model of the type mentioned can be built, under the assumption that such a model is sufficiently valid for the purpose at hand: "modelling tractability". In general, one could say that, due to long use in history, methodological tools are available. Static models are easier to handle, but they have a much more limited descriptive power. Partial differential equations are much more involved, while the computational requirements are very stringent.

In the context of model-building, too little attention has been paid to the fact that the degree of modelling difficulty has a very wide range. Some modelling exercises are rather straightforward, while others require very careful and imaginative scientific work.

A first consideration is the precise nature of the ODESS to be expected: are the model sets $\underline{u}$, $\underline{x}$, $\underline{y}$, large; are the relationships $\underline{f}$, $\underline{g}$ and $\underline{h}$ complex; are there major non-linear effects? In assessing the modelling effort that will be required, the modelling context may be more important than the features of the model formalism.

The modelling context concerns the sources that will feed the model-building process. In Section 2.4.2., it was showed how three "information sources" were involved. The level of difficulty of a modelling task is determined for a large part by the special characteristics of the information sources. What is the specific purpose of the model? Prediction, for instance, requires a more faithful model than some control tasks. How much a priori information is available and what is the quality of that information, exactitude and generality? How much measurement and data can be collected? Are planned experiments possible? What is the signal –to–noise ratio of the measurements? Modelling techniques should be classified according to the specific information patterns that underly the modelling exercise.

The modelling context

As mentioned in Chapter 2, typically in the physical sciences the a priori information is often rather complete and it is almost always of high validity and broad generality. Modelling methodology is even better established.

This chapter, discusses techniques for problems that have a different information pattern in the sense that the amount of a priori knowledge available is smaller and less adequate. The techniques will therefore be more useful for disciplines where quantitative scientific theory is less developed and less trustworthy. One could mention hydrology, biology and the environmental sciences. More specifically, the following conditions specify in an average manner the situation for which the methodology is useful.

Because of limited a priori knowledge, experimental data is assumed to be available. Measurements of all the major input and output variables are available. Parts of the data set may be the result of planned experiments, while operational records may provide additional information. The amount of data required depends on its quality. Average noise levels are characterized by signal-to-noise ratios between 1 and 10. Examples for sample sizes will be given later on. There is, however, an order of magnitude more data needed whenever large parts of the structure have to be inferred, compared with cases where only straightforward parameter estimation on a known system structure is required.

It is assumed that the frame, Section 2.4.5, of the model can be deduced from a priori knowledge and goal considerations. As a last resort trial and error could be used. Often the structure is supposed to be partly known. For many techniques the structure is required to be linear, or what is called linear, in the parameters. So they are useful if the structure is truly linear, or if the goal permits linearization around working conditions, or else if one is in an initial modelling stage where linear analysis is a first step towards more complex representations.

The requirement for a "linear" situation arises because ODESS is inherently complex in the sense that problems can result at all phases of model-building. At the present, there is no simple unified theory for non-linear systems. The basic modelling theory developed here is developed for a linear system specification. It will be possible however to "detect" certain non-linear behavioural patterns starting from a linearized version of the model. Some techniques only require linearity in the parameters so that in fact, certain non-linear problems can also be treated. The linear version of the ordinary differential equation model now follows.

3.1.2.2 The linear case

Linearization and discretization

The process for linearization for small perturbations is well known and has been used as the basis for dynamic analysis in many different areas of research. The details of the linearization procedure are not considered here, but note that it is possible to describe the small perturbation behaviour of the system by a set of linear differential equations: LODESS.

$$\delta \underline{\dot{x}} = \Phi\ (\underline{p},t)\ \delta\underline{x} + \Gamma\ (\underline{p},t)\ \delta\underline{u} \qquad (3.10)$$

$$\delta\underline{y} = \Pi\ (\underline{p},t)\ \delta\underline{x} + \Lambda\ (\underline{p},t)\ \delta\underline{u} \qquad (3.11)$$

where $\delta\underline{x} = \underline{x} - \underline{x}^*$ and $\delta\underline{y} = \underline{y} - \underline{y}^*$ are respectively the deviations of the state and output vectors from some defined equilibrium values $\underline{x}^*$, $\underline{y}^*$; $\delta\underline{u}$ are the input perturbations about the values appropriate to the chosen equilibrium solution and $\Phi(\underline{p},t)$, $\Gamma(\underline{p},t)$, $\Pi(\underline{p},t)$, $\Lambda(\underline{p},t)$ are suitably dimensioned coefficient matrices. It may be useful in the modelling context to let these matrices have elements which vary in time. Time variability may be a specific property of the real-world system or it may be a clue to non-linear behaviour, in the sense that parametric variation may be a function of other variables affecting the system both internally or externally. The constraints (3.4) can be linearized, but they often do not need to be.

So far all system descriptions mentioned have been of the continuous type, for reasons mentioned already. At this point, however, it is useful to introduce discrete-time versions of the models. Ordinary difference equations may be models in their own right and be good representations for certain real life systems. There is, however, another reason why discrete-time models are useful.

Chapter 1 mentioned the extremely large impact that computation technology has produced in the field of model-building. Nowadays for a number of reasons which have little connection with the important issues in modelling theory, digital machines have emerged as the main computational tools. This implies that, as soon as one intends to capitalize on computational power, one has to use discretization techniques. For that reason discrete versions of LODESS are especially useful. If a uniform sampling period of T time units is assumed, equations (3.10) and (3.11) can be approximated, for instance by a set of discrete-time equations (3.12) (3.13):

$$\underline{x}_k = F(k-1,\underline{p})\, \underline{x}_{k-1} + G(k-1,\underline{p})\, \underline{u}_{k-1} \qquad (3.12)$$

$$\underline{y}_k = H(k,\underline{p})\, \underline{x}_k + E(k,\underline{p})\, \underline{u}_k \qquad (3.13)$$

where $\underline{x}_k$, $\underline{u}_k$, $\underline{y}_k$ are the sampled values of the small perturbation variables $\delta\underline{x}$, $\delta\underline{u}$, $\delta\underline{y}$ respectively, at the k-th sampling instant. For ease of notation the matrix dependence on $\underline{p}$ will not always be mentioned.

Linear stochastic versions

As mentioned before, a purely deterministic and discrete LODESS has its limitations. The introduction of "white noise" components that represent uncertainties, poses, in contrast with the continuous-time case, no special mathematical problems. A more faithful representation will be obtained if the discrete LODESS is completed with stochastic terms $\underline{w}(k)$ and $\underline{v}(k)$:

$$\underline{x}_k = F(k-1)\underline{x}_{k-1} + G(k-1)\underline{u}_{k-1} + D(k-1)\underline{w}_{k-1} \qquad (3.14)$$

$$\underline{y}_k = H(k)\underline{x}_k + E(k)\underline{u}_k + \underline{v}_k \tag{3.15}$$

$$E[\underline{w}(k)] = 0 \qquad\qquad E[\underline{w}(k) \cdot \underline{w}^T(j)] = Q\,\delta_{kj}$$

$$E[\underline{v}(k)] = 0 \qquad\qquad E[\underline{v}(k) \cdot \underline{v}^T(j)] = R\,\delta_{kj}$$

$$E[\underline{v}(k) \cdot \underline{w}^T(j)] = S\,\delta_{kj}$$

Some remarks concerning model (3.14) and (3.15) are appropriate here. Though less complex than the more general non-linear model (3.5–8), the state space model (3.14–15) has a wide variety of applications in different branches of science. It plays an important role in a large part of engineering endeavour; it is used in biology under the heading of compartmental analysis and it is utilized as a prediction tool in the environmental, earth and economic sciences. Its mathematical properties have been thoroughly studied in systems and control theory. Throughout this chapter many of its properties important in the model-building context will be quoted. The reader is also referred to standard texts in control theory [49, 168] for details and proofs.

Modelling implications

It is important to be fully aware of the fact that equations (3.14) and (3.15) are a model specification at the state structure level. A first case arises whenever a model correspondence with reality is required at that level: an isomorphism. The state vector is then defined in the frame (see Section 2.4.5). In this linear case, the structure then consists in specifying the zero and non-zero entries in the matrices. As a priori knowledge about the mechanistic build-up of the real system is needed to be able to specify the state set, this case does not correspond with the problem formulation, the modelling context, that was presented here.

Often the model (3.14), (3.15) is used to define an input–output relationship R_S. Then the choice of the state set is a problem of structure characterization. Unfortunately, such a description is not unique in the sense that an infinite number of LODESS are possible; in other words, the modelling problem has no unique solution. Furthermore, for certain solutions it will not be possible to infer all the parameters from the input–output data, even under noiseless conditions. These, perhaps rather surprising, statements have been the subject of important theoretical considerations in the system theoretical branch of mathematics. The correct way of proceeding from this point is by no means straightforward. One option would be to refuse to continue unless more information about the state structure could be obtained by studying the real system in more detail, conducting other experiments on different variables etc. Engineering experience has learned however that it is possible to continue the model-building process and obtain meaningful results for the goals set in this paragraph.

To do so the general principle of simplicity or parsimony [19] is invoked. From all solutions to the modelling problem it is postulated that the most simple one is bound to be the most appropriate. What is meant with "most simple" is in fact still a matter of debate. It is certainly true that the state concept is central in the mathematical model concept (Section 2.3). Quite naturally, a model with a low dimension for the state is simpler than another with a large dimensional state vector. This evident interpretation of the simplicity principle does not solve the uniqueness problem. With a fixed number of states there remain an infinite number of parametrizations (Section 2.3.3).

Another issue concerns the manner of specifying stochastic terms. In the system description (3.14) and (3.15) a white noise sequence w(k) is added in a linear fashion in the state transition part of the model, standing for disturbances and process uncertainties and another sequence v(k) independent of the former is introduced in the output function, representing measurement noise. These noise terms are unmeasurable and it is known that they cannot be recovered independently. The theory learns that, from the point of view of the input–output relationships, an equivalent representation for (3.14) and (3.15) is provided by what is called the steady-state Kalman filter representation:

$$\underline{\hat{x}}(k) = F(k-1)\,\underline{\hat{x}}_{k-1} + G(k-1)\,\underline{u}_{k-1} + K(k-1)\,\underline{e}_{k-1} \tag{3.16}$$

$$\underline{y}(k) = H(k)\,\underline{\hat{x}}_k + E(k)\,\underline{u}_k + \Sigma(k)\,e_k \tag{3.17}$$

$$E\,[\underline{e}_k] = 0 \quad E\,[\underline{e}_k\,\underline{e}^{\mathrm{T}}_j] = I\,\delta_{kj}$$

Σ and K are not independent but related by a set of equations.

Although the specification of disturbances looks natural, other options are possible. We discuss the issue here for the time-invariant SISO case.

An alternative model representation

The input–output relationship can explicitly be computed by using the backward shift operator z^{-1}.

$$I_x(k) = Fz^{-1}\underline{\hat{x}}(k) + Gz^{-1}u(k) + Kz^{-1}e(k)$$

$$y(k) = H(I - Fz^{-1})^{-1}Gz^{-1}u(k) + Eu(k) + (H(I - Fz^{-1})^{-1}Kz^{-1} + \Sigma)e(k) \tag{3.18}$$

Equation (3.18) has the general form

$$(1 + a_1z^{-1} + a_2z^{-2} + \ldots + a_nz^{-n})y(k)$$

$$= (b_0 + b_1z^{-1} + b_2z^{-2} + \ldots + b_nz^{-n})u(k)$$

$$+ (d_0 + d_1z^{-1} + d_2z^{-2} + \ldots + d_nz^{-n})e(k) \qquad (3.19)$$

or with a straightforward polynomial notation

$$A(z^{-1})y(k) = B(z^{-1})u(k) + D(z^{-1})e(k) \qquad (3.20)$$

(3.20) is termed a transfer-function model or ARMAX-model [19]: Auto-Regressive Moving Average model with exogeneous inputs. Without u(k) one speaks of an ARMA-model.

In short, an n-th order time-invariant SISO state representation is equivalent with a transfer function representation of the type (3.20). A more pictorial representation is given on Fig. 3.1a. In a sense, the output can be seen as the sum of a deterministic answer x(k) that should be obtained if no disturbances occurred and a cumulative noise term $\xi(k)$. Properties are defined by a transformation on a white noise sequence by a transfer function with the same denominator as the deterministic part of the real system.

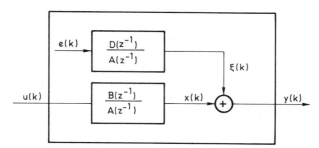

(a) ARMAX-model in transfer function notation

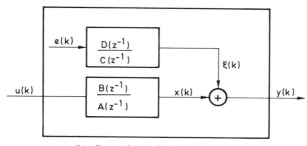

(b) General transfer function model

FIG. 3.1   Different transfer function models

The rationale is that, though noise effects enter the deterministic system at different points, the total impact on the output can be summarized under the form of a coloured noise sequence $\xi(k)$ added to a noise-free output. Clearly, this consideration is based on the superposition principle. It is interesting to recognize that the spectral components of the colour are partly defined by the characteristics of the system: the denominators of both transfer functions on Fig. 3.1a are the same.

It is not difficult in the transfer function formalism to find a more general representation by "decoupling" spectral properties of noise and system. One finds the model (3.21), represented in Fig. 3.1b:

$$y(k) = \frac{B(z^{-1})}{A(z^{-1})} u(k) + \frac{D(z^{-1})}{C(z^{-1})} e(k) \qquad (3.21)$$

Though (3.21) is more general, it can also be brought in state-space form; (3.22) has the same form as (3.20), but then the state vector is larger.

$$A(z^{-1})C(z^{-1})y(k) = C(z^{-1})B(z^{-1})u(k) + A(z^{-1})D(z^{-1})e(k) \qquad (3.22)$$

It has to be extended to provide means to "colour" the noise appropriately.

If a real-world systems has a known deterministic structure, then the transfer function representation (3.21) may be more adequate from a purely descriptive point of view as it clearly separates noise from deterministic system; while for the corresponding state-space description, the state vector is a combination of the features of the deterministic part and the stochastic part. The example shows how adding white process and measurement noise to the equations (3.12) and (3.13) is but one technique for making a specific deterministic system stochastic.

To conclude with a few considerations on the role of formalisms: in the present case the two different representations were mathematically equivalent in the sense that representations, when properly interpreted, cover the same information. For the purpose of relating the elements of the representation with reality, however, one formalism could be more useful than the other. In the same manner, the choice of representation may influence analytical tractability or computational precision. Model formalisms should be looked upon from this point of view: they allow for alternative problem formulations so that the problem can be solved more easily or in a more precise way.

3.1.3   Modelling methodology

The modelling methodology consists of all concepts and all techniques that are related and can be used to derive a mathematical description of the type presented in this chapter. For convenience, the methods can be classified on the basis of the diagram presented in Chapter 2. Different problem areas are defined dependent on the part of the mathematical representation that has to be obtained and the source of information that is utilized.

Complete coverage of the present state of the art is far beyond the authors' capabilities and much too extensive to be presented in full detail in this book. The methodology for deductive reasoning, which uses a priori information in order to find parts of the modelling representation, is the most classical part of the theory. According to the discipline of origin, such as circuit theory, mechanical systems, compartmental systems etc., clear presentations concerning the use of general laws and principles in order to deduce model equations, have been available [37, 110]. A more unified presentation could be given, in the sense that the fundamental procedures common to all or most, disciplines could be gathered in order to identify a more basic deductive approach. As for lumped systems most of it is better known and well established, so the subject will not be treated here. In the next chapter, because of the nature of the formalism, deductive approaches are more crucial and a more thorough discussion is presented.

The use of both other sources will now be discussed in more detail. In fact one of the themes of the book is the belief that more adequate use of these sources may provide better models. The strategy here will be to present a few well-established and well-documented techniques, which can be applied immediately to a practical problem for certain important model representations; and then to give a more general overview of the remaining issues, with emphasis on those areas requiring further development. In fact, as briefly hinted at in the introduction, in the last two decades the amount of study analysis and investigation of techniques for modelling, though extensively pursued, have been very unequally spread over the different modelling stages.

An overview of the efforts made in other modelling stages is summarized in Fig. 3.2. Clearly, most attention has been paid to the parameter estimation patterns while certain issues such as the use of the modelling goal in guiding the modelling effort have been neglected.

From a systematic point of view one should first discuss the procedures for choosing a frame, then continue with techniques for obtaining a structure and, finally, present schemes for parameter estimation. This appears to be logical in the sense that a frame has to be available before a structure can be found, and a structure has to be at one's disposition before estimating the parameters. Unfortunately, for many modelling problems, the exercise is not so straightforward, certainly with the present state of the art and as indeed is shown in Fig. 2.7, the process works in "feedback". It may be necessary to start with parameter estimation on a hypothetical structure and then, after having analysed all results, continue with other stages.

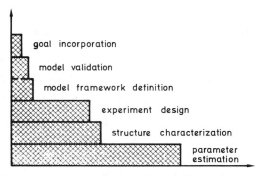

FIG. 3.2   Research efforts in techniques for the different modelling stages

Because of the better developed nature of the parameter estimation discipline, and also because of the fact that the problem is more straightforward, parameter estimation is discussed first. Furthermore, the presentation will provide a sufficient background to enable subsequent discussion of the other aspects of the modelling problem.

3.2   PARAMETER ESTIMATION

3.2.1   Introduction

Parameter estimation is defined as the experimental determination of the values of the parameters or the constants that arise in a mathematical description, assuming that the structure of the process model, in other words the relationships between variables and parameters are explicitly known. The definition is not so innocent as it looks. In fact, it is difficult to draw a sharp borderline between structure and the parameter set. The change of a parameter value from a non-zero to a zero value may represent a simplification in the structure, since a "branch" in the model may be deleted. For convenience, it is assumed that all parameters have non-zero values and it is the structure which specifies how many constants are required. In mathematical terms, the problem can be formulated in the following way. Given the model (3. 1–4), or in the stochastic case (3. 5–8), and a data set of inputs and outputs, find the unknown parameter vector $\underline{p}$. Initial conditions for the state may be known, and either completely or partly included in the unknown parameter vector.

How well posed is the problem? Is it mathematically possible to find the parameter values or, in other words, are the parameters identifiable? Terminology is confusing here. Statisticians use the term: estimability, while identification addresses the problem of inferring structural knowledge. In the control literature identification means the same, but identifiability stands for estimability, which is in fact misleading. Here the word identifiability means the same as estimability but identification is not used; instead structure characterization stands for structure identification. As soon as the problem is consistent parameter estimation schemes can be applied.

Methods for determining parameters are far from being a unified field and certainly more than one complete volume could be dedicated to the subject. A wealth of techniques are presented in the work of Eykhoff [65]. Classification of the algorithms is often done according to several aspects,

(a) the model formalism	: continuous-time, discrete-time;
	linear or non-linear;
	deterministic, stochastic.
(b) the modelling context	: type of measurements;
	a priori knowledge;
	purpose of the model.
(c) the estimation philosophy	: the criterion;
	the numerical procedure;
	the computational approach.

In the late sixties the field could be seen as a "bag of tricks". During the last decade a considerable effort has been made to unify and to give structure. However, more work is required before a more cohesive theory can be generally accepted.

The oldest and most straightforward estimation techniques address the problem of parameter estimation, when measurements can be easily performed and the noise level of the data is low. One can mention: step and impulse response techniques, simple frequency response techniques, "moment" methods, etc. These techniques are even better known and are not considered here. Attention is focused on the case characterized by more heavy noise contamination. The problem of determining parameters under such conditions can be attacked in the time domain, as well as in the frequency domain. In both domains, sophisticated techniques are available and a recent study compares the approaches [145]. It is argued that the methods are complementary. Spectral analysis seems to be most adequate, either if the goal of the modelling exercise requires spectral characteristics, or if engineering insight has to be applied in the initial analysis phases of model-building. It is believed that spectral analysis methods often give good insights into the properties of the data and the system. Such information may be very valuable in the beginning. Time domain methods relate more directly to the model formalism itself. Consequently, for most modelling purposes they seem to be the natural approach, in the sense that the model obtained can be easily validated and used for the purpose for which it was meant. Another advantage resides in the often superior statistical properties of the estimates. If accuracy is strived for, parameter estimation schemes in the time domain seem to be more adequate.

This work is restricted to time domain methods and stress the on-line recursive techniques. Two roads are followed. First, after some initial considerations on computational schemes, an intuitive approach is used to introduce the recursive least squares and instrumental variable estimation algorithms. Emphasis is on practical usefulness. In fact, almost all techniques have proved to be useful to practitioners in the field of model-building. Statistical and more theoretical considerations are provided only to give the reader more confidence and a better understanding of the many formulas throughout the text. The starting point is the least squares approach for static models. Parameter estimation is seen as a minimization problem. The solution can be given en bloc for off-line computation or in recursive form for on-line processing. As the models grow more complex, bias in the estimates is avoided by introducing instrumental variables. Subsequent developments lead to the basic IV-AML parameter estimation scheme. Further refinements require a statistical point of view and, based on a theoretical analysis, prefilters are added to the algorithm. Extensions, modifications and practical problems are discussed. Multiple input–multiple output systems, for example, and time-varying parameter problems are considered. It is hoped that the gradual build-up towards still more complex algorithms will provide the reader with basic terminology, some important principles and insight into the fundamental issues. However, the presentation remains limited in scope; therefore, a second road is followed afterwards and the parameter problem is considered in more general terms. The basic elements that characterize parameter estimation methods are given and examples provided. Then a general recursive estimator is presented. It is shown how from this estimator, a wide variety of recursive estimators can be derived. A first class contains the prediction error estimators; a second class the pseudo-linear regression schemes. So all these estimation algorithms are very similar.

The reader will obtain a broader view and become acquainted with an approach to build and derive new algorithms that suit his specific needs. At the same time, interesting new areas of research are indicated and concludes the section on parameter estimation.

3.2.2   Identifiability concepts

The identifiability concept has been a matter of debate during most of the seventies. Only more recently [52] has terminology been presented in a more unified fashion.

3.2.2.1 The deterministic case
Definitions

The following definitions can be given for a model, with a known structure:

(1) The single parameter p_i of the model (3. 1–4) is said to be identifiable on $[t_0, T]$ if there exists a finite number of solutions for p_i from these relationships. The single parameter is unidentifiable if there exists an infinite number of solutions for p_i from these relationships.

(2) The model description is system identifiable, if all parameters are identifiable. It is system unidentifiable as soon as one parameter is unidentifiable. If the parameter space for the unknown parameters is a subset of R^p, a finite number of solutions means that, locally, in a small region around a solution, that solution will be unique. One finds in the literature [17, 86] the term "locally identifiable", which bears the same meaning as system identifiability.

(3) The single parameter p_i is said to be uniquely identifiable on $[t_0, T]$ if there exists a unique solution for p_i from the model relationships with the given input available.

(4) The model specification is parameter identifiable on $[t_0, T]$ if all parameters are uniquely identifiable, it is also said to be globally identifiable [38, 248].

It is seen that the parameter estimation problem is ill posed as soon as a parameter is unidentifiable. However, if the model is system unidentifiable, there will always be identifiable combinations of parameters. The definitions, presented in terms of a continuous-time, lumped parameter model, apply also for discrete-time system models. They are sufficient to describe all identifiability conditions that may arise. However, they do not tell how identifiability can be checked. It is important to understand that system and parameter identifiability depend on two factors:

(i) The specific input applied and the initial conditions: non-zero initial conditions $\underline{x}_0$ can be handled efficiently in identifiability analysis by explicitly incorporating them into the system dynamical equations as appended impulse inputs, $\underline{x}_0 \delta(t)$. Initial conditions are important as system and parameter identifiability may depend on its particular values. It may happen that for a given system the input segment set can be divided into several categories. Some may encompass a type of identifiability, while others may yield unidentifiable problems. The latter inputs are almost always "special" in the sense that they only make a part of the whole system respond, while the remaining part is not excited.

(ii) The structure of the equations and the constraints (3, 1–4): these are important as they may be crucial in achieving identifiability. Some structures may be identifiable if suitable inputs are provided, while others are unidentifiable regardless of the inputs chosen.

A simple example illustrates the concepts. Consider the linear SISO system (3.23). Suppose that the model is a description at the state structure level. The state vector, thus, has a physical meaning:

$$
\begin{vmatrix} \dot{x}_1 \\ \dot{x}_2 \end{vmatrix} = \begin{vmatrix} a_{11} & a_{12} \\ a_{21} & a_{22} \end{vmatrix} \begin{vmatrix} x_1 \\ x_2 \end{vmatrix} + \begin{vmatrix} b_1 \\ b_2 \end{vmatrix} u
$$

$$
y = |c_1 \quad c_2| \begin{vmatrix} x_1 \\ x_2 \end{vmatrix}
$$

(3.23)

The transfer function has the following form:

$$
\frac{y(s)}{u(s)} = \frac{(b_1c_1 + b_2c_2)s + a_{12}b_2c_1 + a_{21}b_1c_2 - a_{11}b_2c_2 - a_{22}c_1b_1}{s^2 - (a_{11} + a_{22})s + a_{11}a_{22} - a_{12}a_{21}}
$$

(3.24)

Comparing (3.24) with (3.25):

$$
\frac{y'(s)}{u'(s)} = \frac{b'_1 s + b'_2}{s^2 + a'_1 s + a'_2}
$$

(3.25)

From input–output measurements only, the coefficients b'_1, b'_2, a'_1, a'_2 or four parameters can be identified if the input function is sufficiently "rich".

Case I— all parameters in (3.23) are unknown.

(3.23) is system unidentifiable. In fact there are four relationships (3.26) and eight unknowns:

$$
\begin{aligned}
b'_1 &= b_1c_1 + b_2c_2 \\
b'_2 &= a_{12}b_2c_1 + a_{21}b_1c_2 - a_{11}b_2c_2 - a_{22}c_1b_1 \\
a'_1 &= -(a_{11} + a_{22}) \\
a'_2 &= a_{11}a_{22} - a_{12}a_{21}
\end{aligned}
$$

(3.26)

Case II— if $a_{22} = 0$ $a_{12} = 1$ $c_1 = 1$ $c_2 = 0$

then (3.26) becomes (3.27):

$$
\begin{aligned}
b'_1 &= b_1 \\
b'_2 &= b_2 \\
a'_1 &= -a_{11} \\
a'_2 &= -a_{21}
\end{aligned}
$$

(3.27)

The system is parameter identifiable or globally identifiable if the input is sufficiently elaborate.

Case III— $b_1 = c_1$ $b_2 = c_2$ $a_{11} = a_{22}$ $a_{12} = 1$

Equations (3.26) yield:

$$
a_{11} = -\frac{1}{2} a'_1
$$

$$
a_{21} = \frac{1}{4} a'^2_1 - a'_2
$$

$$b_1^2 + b_2^2 = b'_1$$

$$b_1 b_2 = \left(b'_2 - \frac{a'_1 b'_1}{2}\right) \bigg/ \left(1 - a'_2 + \frac{1}{4} a'^2_1\right)$$

Though a_{11} and a_{21} are uniquely identifiable, b_1 and b_2 are in general not uniquely identifiable. This is a case where the system is system identifiable while it is not parameter identifiable if $b_1 = \alpha$ and $b_2 = \beta$ are solutions then $b_1 = -\alpha$ and $b_2 = -\beta$ or $b_1 = \beta$ and $b_2 = \alpha$ are solutions too.

All the above examples assume that all parameters in the transfer function can be identified. This is only true for a sufficiently rich input. In the case of a single sinusoid, the output will be a sinusoid with modified amplitude and phase, and therefore not all the parameters of (3.25) can be found. With an input of that type all cases considered are system unidentifiable.

Identifiability analysis

For the general model (3.1–4), identifiability analysis can be performed using a sensitivity study. Consider an inherently local parameter perturbation $\Delta \underline{p}$, the output perturbation is related to $\Delta \underline{p}$ by (3.28):

$$\Delta \underline{y} = S(\underline{p}, t)\Delta \underline{p}$$

(3.28)

$$S_{ij} = \frac{\partial y_i}{\partial p_j}$$

Local parameter identifiability or system identifiability requires that (3.28) can be solved uniquely for $\Delta \underline{p}$; so the rank of S must be equal to the dimension of the parameter vector. This condition can be checked by computing a determinant (3.29).

$$\det (S^T S) \neq 0$$

(3.29)

It has been shown [51, 185] that, for constant coefficient linear systems, condition (3.29) can be derived in the following way. Set up the Markov parameter matrix

$$M(p) = \begin{vmatrix} C(p) & B(p) & \\ C(p) & A(p) & B(p) \\ & \cdot & \\ & \cdot & \\ & \cdot & \\ C(p) & A^{2n-1}(p) & B(p) \end{vmatrix}$$

then condition (3.29) becomes:

$$
\det \left[\frac{\partial M}{\partial \underline{p}} \right]^{\mathsf{T}} \left[\frac{\partial M}{\partial \underline{p}} \right] \neq 0 \tag{3.30}
$$

This condition ensures system identifiability at some p_0, for which it holds. If $\partial M/\partial \underline{p}$ is parameter independent then conditions (3.29) and (3.30) encompasses global or parameter identifiability. Note that in (3.30) the input does not appear; it has to be sufficiently rich to stimulate all modes. For linear time-invariant systems the computation of (3.30) may be complicated. Another procedure consists in transforming the system description into its frequency form. In fact, as shown in the example above, system and parameter identifiability can be easily checked on the transfer function representation. This property has led, in the early seventies, to the concept of transfer function identifiability [82]. However, as it is only applicable for special systems, it was abandoned as a general concept later on.

The identifiability concepts show whether or not a parameter estimation problem is "well posed". The technique requires a known structure. If the structure is unknown, or partly unknown, any structure chosen, deduced or inferred, or any candidate structure tentatively proposed, must be identifiable. However, structure analysis is more involved than simply checking whether the estimation problem is well posed and the identifiability question is part of a larger problem addressed by realization theory. This subject is briefly discussed in Section 3.3.2.6.

3.2.2.2   *The stochastic case*

The identifiability concept for stochastic systems is by no means so straightforward as for the deterministic case. As the output sequences are stochastic processes, the problem is compounded with the requirement of obtaining the parameters from one realization of the process. Ljung [142] has argued that the problem of identifiability can now be split up in three parts. Identifiability will depend on:

(1) *The structure*, which relates the parameters with each other and with the inputs and outputs. As in the deterministic case, unidentifiability may be caused by the specific structural relationships. The structural aspect of identifiability is the same as in the deterministic case.

(2) *The inputs*, certain of which may be too "poor" to achieve identifiability. As above, the inputs must first excite the system in an adequate manner, but, in addition, excitation must be long enough to permit the estimation algorithm to converge, i.e. the excitation must be persistent.

(3) *The estimation procedure*: it must be possible to recover the parameters with the estimation algorithm chosen; in other words, the estimates

must be consistent in the sense that they converge to the true parameter values in the limit, for the number of data points going to infinity.

System identifiability requires the existence of a consistent estimator whose estimate converges to one of a finite number of allowable parameter vectors. Parameter identifiability requires the same, but the allowable parameter vector is unique. The definitions in the stochastic case are more stringent than in the deterministic case. Consider the linear time-invariant model, which can be written as follows:

$$\underline{y}(z^{-1}) = G(z^{-1})\,\underline{u}(z^{-1}) + \underline{\xi}(z^{-1}) \qquad G(z^{-1}) = A^{-1}(z^{-1})B(z^{-1}) \qquad (3.31)$$

In addition to the requirements for identifiability without the noise term $\underline{\xi}$, stability of the system has to be ensured in order to guarantee a consistent estimate; therefore, the solutions of det $A(z^{-1}) = 0$ must be outside the unit circle (for the z^{-1}-plane). The noise $\underline{\xi}$ is thought to have a rational spectral density, and thus to be the output of a linear time-invariant system excited by white noise:

$$\underline{\xi}(z^{-1}) = H(z^{-1})\,\underline{e}(z^{-1}) \qquad H(z^{-1}) = C^{-1}(z^{-1})\,D(z^{-1})$$

Estimating the noise characteristics reduces to estimating the coefficients of the noise filter $H(z^{-1})$, the problem is somewhat different from the case of estimating the parameters in $G(z^{-1})$ in the sense that, for the latter, the input is known while, for the former, it is only specified that the input has white noise properties without providing the actual noise values. Identifiability here is related to the "spectral factorization theorem". The transfer function $H(z^{-1})$ must have following properties:

- $\displaystyle\lim_{z^{-1}\to 0} H(z^{-1}) = I$
- roots of det $C(z^{-1}) = 0$ outside the unit circle
- roots of det $D(z^{-1}) = 0$ on or outside the unit circle.

The requirement for a persistently exciting input can be brought in the following form (see Ljung [142]).

$$U_M(k) = [\underline{u}(k), \underline{u}(k-1), \ldots, \underline{u}(k-M)]$$

$$\delta I < \frac{1}{N}\sum_{k=1}^{N} U_M(k)U_M(k)^T < \frac{1}{\delta}I \quad \text{for} \quad N > N_0 \qquad (3.32)$$

M sufficiently large (related to the order of the system)

From the above, it must be clear that the requirements for identifiability in the stochastic case are quite more stringent than in the deterministic case. From the practical point of view, Young [240] has argued that these identifiability conditions may be too restrictive, as they rely purely on asymptotic characteristics. Before leaving the subject of identifiability, therefore, it is worth noting the following points:

(a) Though certain signals may not be persistently exciting, e.g. a single step input, this does not mean that sensible estimates of the system parameters cannot be obtained when using such signals. It merely means that when the signal no longer continues to excite the system, no more information will be received and the estimates will not improve beyond that point, i.e.

$$\lim_{N \to \infty} (\hat{a}_k - a) \neq 0$$

Nevertheless, the estimates obtained upto the point where the input signal loses its persistent excitation property, may well be good enough for the purposes of the experiment.

(b) Again, while a stable system is certainly necessary to prevent the matrices becoming asymptotically unbounded, it may still be possible to obtain estimates of an unstable system provided sufficient estimation accuracy is achieved before the matrices "blow up".

(c) It is true that it is not possible to fully identify a non-minimum phase noise process: solutions of $\det D(z^{-1}) = 0$ inside the unit circle, since the covariance generating function is the same for both the non-minimum and equivalent minimum phase systems. However, this does not mean that the equivalent minimum phase model that can be estimated from the data, is not sufficient for the problem under study.

These remarks show that, for low noise levels, identifiability in the deterministic sense may be more appropriate than the same concept in the stochastic sense. It is the modelling context which must help the systems analyst to decide which identifiability concepts are appropriate.

3.2.3   Estimation of static and quasi-static models

3.2.3.1   Computational approaches to parameter estimation

The basic computational schemes

When a parameter has to be estimated, different computational approaches can be taken. Three modes of computation can be distinguished. Estimating the mean of a random variable when N samples are given, will serve as an illustration.

(1) The 'en bloc', non-recursive or single iteration method

All the measurements are assumed to be available at the time of computation and straight calculations are used to obtain the quantities required. Such 'en bloc' procedure for estimating the mean is defined as follows:

$$\bar{y}_N = \frac{1}{N} \sum_{i=1}^{N} y_i \tag{3.33}$$

In a straightforward way, all measurements are added and the result is divided by the number of samples.

(2) The recursive method

Typical for the 'recursive' approach is the fact that the pieces of information—the samples—are digested one at a time. This requires that the data points are ordered. The most widely used order is that based on time evolution. Computing recursively means basically two things:

(a) the data base is expanding during computation;
(b) intermediate estimates of the quantity one desires, are available and these values tend to the 'en bloc' solution as computation proceeds.

A recursive specification of the sample mean is the following:

$$\hat{a}_0 = 0$$

$$\hat{a}_k = \hat{a}_{k-1} - \frac{1}{k} (\hat{a}_{k-1} - y_k) \tag{3.34}$$

compute for k increasing from 0 to N.

Note that the algorithm shows the major features of recursivity.

First during computation the amount of data used increases:

for k = 1 : data base $\{y_1\}$
for k = 2 : data base $\{y_1, y_2\}$
$\vdots$
for k = N : data base $\{y_1, y_2, \ldots, y_N\}$

Second a sequence of numbers is obtained:

$$\hat{a}_1, \hat{a}_2, \hat{a}_3, \ldots, \hat{a}_N$$

It remains to be proved that $\hat{a}_N$ equals $\bar{y}_N$. This could be done formally. It is more useful for further developments to show how the recursive estimate can be deduced from the en bloc solution. One proceeds as follows:

Write the en bloc solution for $k - 1$, and k samples

$$\hat{a}_{k-1} = \frac{1}{k-1} \sum_{i=1}^{k-1} y_i$$

$$\hat{a}_k = \frac{1}{k} \sum_{i=1}^{k} y_i = \frac{1}{k} \left(\sum_{i=1}^{k-1} y_i + y_k \right)$$

eliminate $\sum\limits_{i=1}^{k-1} y_i$ and obtain

$$\hat{a}_k = \frac{k-1}{k}\,\hat{a}_{k-1} + \frac{1}{k}\,y_k = \hat{a}_{k-1} - \frac{1}{k}\,(\hat{a}_{k-1} - y_k) \qquad (3.35)$$

The validity of the recursive procedure follows by induction.

While the "en bloc" (non-recursive or single iteration) method of determining the mean value is well known, the recursive algorithm is comparatively little known. And yet the algorithm is significant in a number of ways: not only is it elegant and computationally attractive, but it also exposes, in a most vivid manner, the physical nature of the estimate for increasing sample size, and so provides insight into a mechanism which is useful in many more general problems. Referring to equation (3.35), the estimate of the mean after k samples is equal to the previous estimates $\hat{a}_{k-1}$ obtained after k-1 samples with a correction term which is the product of 1/k and the difference between the new sample observation y_k and $\hat{a}_{k-1}$. In effect, therefore, the previous estimate $\hat{a}_{k-1}$ is modified in proportion to the error between the observation of the random variable and the latest estimate of its mean value.

(3) The iterative method

The last computational technique to be discussed is the iterative method. Here the whole set of data is used sequentially to obtain a solution. Just as in the case of recursive computation a sequence of solutions is produced which converges to the en bloc solution:

$$\hat{a}^1_N, \hat{a}^2_N, \dots, \hat{a}^1_N$$

However, in the case of recursion, the sequence arises because the data set grows during the computational process. In the iterative case, all samples are available but the "en bloc" solution cannot be computed directly and it has to be approximated by successive calculations on the whole data set. At each iterative step the estimated variable only is modified and no data elements are added or left out.

For the simple example of estimating the mean, iterative computation is by no means necessary. To illustrate the point, let us suppose that the machine, which will compute the sample mean, is very crude in carrying out divisions. To calculate (3.33), it will divide 1 by N approximately and then multiply $\sum_{i=1}^N y_i$. "En bloc" computation will yield an approximate value: $\hat{a}_N = \alpha/N.\sum_{i=1}^N y_i$. Iterative processing can be used to increase the precision of the sample mean estimate. Consider the following function:

$$f(x) = xN - \sum_{i=1}^N y_i$$

For $x = \underline{y}_N$, $f(\underline{y}_N) = 0$. An iterative scheme for finding a zero of a function is the Newton-Raphson procedure:

$$x_{k+1} = x_k - \alpha \frac{f(x_k)}{f'(x_k)} \quad \text{with} \quad 0 < \alpha < 2 \tag{3.36}$$

For the problem at hand

$$\hat{a}_N^{\,1} = \frac{\alpha}{N} \sum_{i=1}^{N} y_i$$

$$\hat{a}_N^{\,k+1} = \hat{a}_N^{\,k} - \frac{\alpha}{N} \left(\hat{a}_N^{\,k} \cdot N - \sum_{i=1}^{N} y_i \right) \tag{3.37}$$

where α/N represents the approximate division.

The algorithm generates a set of approximations which converge to a precise value. Note that the complete data base is available and that only the estimate is updated. For a proper use of iterative schemes a suitable stopping rule has to be provided; for example

$$\bar{y}_N = \hat{a}_N^{\,l} \text{ for } l \text{ such that } |\hat{a}_N^{\,l} - \hat{a}_N^{\,l-1}| < \varepsilon \tag{3.38}$$

For the purpose of parameter estimation, all the computational procedures presented in this section will be useful.

Useful notational conventions

Time has learned that a clear presentation of recursive algorithms requires rigour in notation. Such a notation is now introduced and presented with the arithmetic mean estimate utilized previously, as an example.

Any recursive algorithm, that will be discussed in this text can be brought in the following form:

$$\hat{a}_k = p_k\, b_k \tag{3.39}$$

With the sample mean as an estimate of the mean value

$$p_k = \frac{1}{k}$$

$$b_k = \sum_{i=1}^{k} y_i$$

It is easily seen that p_k and b_k are related to their previous values p_{k-1} and b_{k-1} by the equations

$$\frac{1}{p_k} = \frac{1}{p_{k-1}} + 1 \tag{3.40}$$

$$b_k = b_{k-1} + y_k \tag{3.41}$$

After simple manipulation, (3.40) yields

$$p_k = \frac{p_{k-1}}{1 + p_{k-1}} \tag{3.42}$$

$$= p_{k-1} - \frac{p_{k-1}^2}{1 + p_{k-1}} \tag{3.43}$$

Introducing the new notation

$$k_k = \frac{p_{k-1}}{1 + p_{k-1}}$$

and in view of (3.42)

$$k_k = p_k \tag{3.44}$$

Equation (3.43) results in

$$p_k = p_{k-1} - k_k \, p_{k-1} \tag{3.45}$$

As in the previous section the objective is to obtain $\hat{a}_k$, the estimate at the k-th instant, as a function of quantities obtained at the $(k - 1)$th instant:

$$\hat{a}_k = p_k \, b_k$$

with (3.41) and (3.44)

$$= p_k \, b_{k-1} + p_k \, y_k = p_k \, b_{k-1} + k_k \, y_k$$

with (3.45)

$$= p_{k-1} \, b_{k-1} - k_k \, p_{k-1} \, b_{k-1} + k_k \, y_k$$

$$\hat{a}_k = \hat{a}_{k-1} - k_k \, (\hat{a}_{k-1} - y_k) \tag{3.46}$$

The sequence of derivations (3.39), (3.40), (3.41) by the way of (3.42), (3.43), (3.44) and (3.45) to (3.46) will often arise in further developments, as will be seen soon. With a high degree of analogy, the details of equation (3.46) and thus its build-up will be similar for different estimation tasks, independent of the degree of complexity.

3.2.3.2 *Estimating the mean value: interpretations*

In the previous paragraph only the computational aspects of estimating the mean have been presented, without specifying why equation (3.33) was proposed. The choice follows from classic estimation theory, which will not be discussed in detail here. The use of computational schemes for model-building purposes requires, however, insight into their meaning. In this section the basic background for such insight is introduced.

Statistical interpretation

If the random variable is Gaussian and if the samples are independent observations, then it can be proved that (3.33) is an optimal estimator in the sense that it has no bias and that its variance is smaller than for any other computational procedure. Under the conditions mentioned, the formula (3.33) can be found as the maximum likelihood estimate. The recursive estimate (3.46) embodies a Bayesian point of view in the sense that with a priori knowledge of $\hat{a}_{k-1}$, a new sample y_k brings us to an a posteriori estimate $\hat{a}_k$. For details on estimation concepts refer to a standard text [50, 156].

Minimizing a cost

(3.33) can be seen as the minimum of a cost:

$$J = \sum_{i=1}^{N} [y_i - \bar{a}]^2 \tag{3.47}$$

If one ponders the meaning of (3.47), it is easily understood that it is looking for a value that is in the centre of the samples, on the basis of a "square" measure. Note that no statistical assumptions are required here; all samples contribute to the cost. The gradient per sample, also termed instantaneous gradient, is $2 (y_i - \bar{a})$. Equation (3.46) the recursive estimator, can thus be viewed as a "gradient algorithm" in which the estimate $\hat{a}_{k-1}$ is updated in a direction defined by the gradient of the instantaneous cost and with a magnitude of stepsize dictated by k_k; a weighting factor that is not constant but, in fact is inversely proportional to the size of the data base at computation time. Thus as the algorithm proceeds and confidence in the estimate increases, less and less notice is taken of the gradient measure, since it is more likely to arise from the noise than from an error in the previous estimate of the mean value.

A filtering point of view

Equation (3.46) can be interpreted as a digital filter. With z^{-1} the "backward shift" operator so that $z^{-1} \hat{x}_k = \hat{x}_{k-1}$, a block diagram of the algorithm can be constructed (Fig. 3.3).

The diagram can be thought to represent a digital low-pass filter with variable gain—k_k in the forward path changes with time—. The term "low-pass" is applied because the filter in its fixed gain form $k_k = K$ "passes" low frequency variations in the input signal y_k, but attenuates and thus "filters off" high frequency changes. Note that the transfer function is:

$$\frac{k_k}{1 - (1 - k_k)z^{-1}}$$

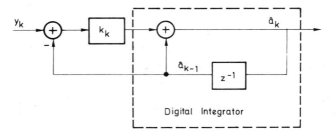

FIG. 3.3   A recursive estimator presented as a digital filter

As k_k is made a strictly decreasing function of time, the effect is simply to reduce sequentially the "pass band" of the filter until $k_k = 0$ and the output of the integrator remains fixed at the final estimate. It is meaningful to use the "filtering" point of view as a heuristic technique to gain insight into recursive algorithms, the least squares approach allows new schemes to develop, while remaining intuitively transparent. Purely statistical methods are more precise but much more difficult to apply.

3.2.3.3   Estimating a single unknown parameter

The model: a regression relationship

Consider the case where the measurements are related to a parameter in the following way:

$$y_i = x_i\, a + e_i \qquad i: 1, 2, 3, \ldots, N \tag{3.48}$$

Assumptions are:
  − x_i : values perfectly known
  − e_i : zero mean errors

The problem

Estimate the unknown parameter a using the available measurements.

The "en bloc" solution

The "en bloc" solution can easily be obtained by minimizing the quadratic cost

$$J = \sum_{i=1}^{N} [y_i - x_i\hat{a}]^2 = \sum_{i=1}^{N} e'^2_i \tag{3.49}$$

One obtains

$$\left[\sum_{i=1}^{N} x_i^2 \right] \hat{a} = \sum_{i=1}^{N} x_i y_i \tag{3.50}$$

Once again, the great simplicity of the least squares formulation (3.49) is demonstrated. Its simplicity appealed to Gauss and it has appealed to almost everyone concerned with the analysis of observations ever since.

The recursive solution

With the notational conventions introduced in Section 3.2.3.1., it is now a more easy matter to develop the recursive estimation procedure. Note that with

$$\hat{a}_k = p_k \, b_k$$

according to (3.50):

$$p_k = \left[\sum_{i=1}^{k} x_i^2 \right]^{-1}$$

$$b_k = \sum_{i=1}^{k} x_i y_i$$

Proceeding in a similar manner to that used in the case of the recursive estimation of the mean:

$$\frac{1}{p_k} = \frac{1}{p_{k-1}} + x_k^2 \tag{3.51}$$

$$b_k = b_{k-1} + x_k y_k \tag{3.52}$$

Out of (3.51) is obtained

$$p_k = \frac{p_{k-1}}{1 + p_{k-1} x_k^2} \tag{3.53}$$

Simple manipulation of this equation gives

$$p_k = p_{k-1} - p_{k-1}^2 \, x_k^2 \, [1 + p_{k-1} \, x_k^2]^{-1} \tag{3.54}$$

$$= p_{k-1} - p_k \, p_{k-1} \, x_k^2 \tag{3.55}$$

Here too, k_k can be introduced

$$k_k = p_{k-1} \, x_k \, [1 + p_{k-1} \, x_k^2]^{-1} \tag{3.56}$$

Comparing (3.56) with (3.53):

$$k_k = p_k \, x_k \tag{3.57}$$

So one obtains

$$p_k = p_{k-1} - p_{k-1} \, k_k \, x_k.$$

Equipped with these results the estimate can be computed as follows:

$$\hat{a}_k = p_k \, b_k = p_k \, (b_{k-1} + x_k \, y_k) = p_k \, b_{k-1} + p_k \, x_k \, y_k$$

Utilizing (3.55) and (3.57)

$$\hat{a}_k = \hat{a}_{k-1} - k_k \, [x_k \, \hat{a}_{k-1} - y_k] \tag{3.58}$$

Remarks

The estimation algorithm given by equations (3.54), (3.56) or (3.57) and (3.58), is the required recursive version of equation (3.50). The similarity with the recursive algorithm for estimating the mean value is obvious on inspection: the reader can easily verify that (3.58) is a discrete-step gradient algorithm, as before, with the weighting factor or gain k_k, a strictly decreasing function of k. The initiation of the gradient algorithm is again rather obvious: a_1 and p_1 can be computed easily from the non-recursive relationship in (3.50) and then the recursive algorithm can be used thereafter.

Here too a number of statistical considerations can be made. If the errors have besides zero mean finite and equal variance σ^2, and if they are serially uncorrelated and independent of the variables x_i, then the least squares estimate (3.50) is the best (minimum variance) linear unbiased estimate. The variance is

$$p^* = \sigma^2 \left[\sum_{i=1}^{N} x_i^2 \right]^{-1}.$$

The general σ^2 is not known but an estimate is also available:

$$\hat{\sigma}_N^2 = \frac{1}{N-1} \sum_{i=1}^{N} e'^2_i.$$

Note that the final value $p_N = p^*/\sigma^2$. Under the supplementary assumption of a Gaussian probability distribution for the noise, the least squares estimate is the best unbiased estimate and also the maximum likelihood estimate.

To go further and assume that prior information on the mean and covariance matrix is available in the form of the initial estimates $\hat{\underline{a}}_0$ and p^*_0 the algorithm can be considered as a Bayesian estimator. Indeed, the algorithm can be viewed as the physical embodiment of Bayesian estimation: at each recursive step from the first, the a priori estimates are modified with the help of the new information imparted by the latest data sample $\{y_k, x_k\}$ and the resultant calculation of the k-th innovation (recursive residual e'_k) to yield a posteriori estimates which, in turn, become the a priori estimates for the next recursive step.

The relationship between recursive estimation and the Bayesian interpretation suggests another strategy for choosing "initial" values $\hat{\underline{a}}_0$ and p^*_0. In fact, if no a priori knowledge is available, $\hat{\underline{a}}_0$ may be set to zero and p^*_0 to infinity.

3.2.3.4 Estimating the parameters in a linear regression

The model: multiple linear regression

The measurements are related to the parameters by the way of a "linear regression" form:

$$y_i = a_1 x_{1i} + \ldots + a_j x_{ji} + \ldots + a_n x_{ni} + e_i \qquad i = 1,2,3, \ldots, N \quad (3.59)$$

Assumptions are:

$\underline{x}_j$: values perfectly known and linearly independent.

e_i : zero mean errors.

The problem

Estimate the unknown parameters a_j, using the available measurements.

The "en bloc" solution

Here too, the "en bloc" solution can be obtained by minimizing a cost

$$J = \sum_{i=1}^{N} \left[\sum_{j=1}^{n} x_{ji} \hat{a}_j - y_i \right]^2 = \sum_{i=1}^{N} e'^2_i \quad (3.60)$$

Now, however, a set of n linear, simultaneous algebraic equations that are sometimes termed the "normal equations" are obtained.

A simple and concise statement of the least squares results in the multi-parameter case being obtained by using a vector–matrix formulation:

(3.59) becomes : $y_i = \underline{x}^T_i \underline{a} + e_i$ and

(3.60) becomes : $J = \sum_{i=1}^{N} [\underline{x}_i^T \underline{a} - y_i]^2$

With these notations the normal equations are:

$$\left[\sum_{i=1}^{N} \underline{x}_i \underline{x}_i^T \right] \hat{\underline{a}} - \sum_{i=1}^{N} \underline{x}_i y_i = 0 \quad (3.61)$$

The recursive solution

When vectors and matrices are used, the similarity with the equivalent scalar analysis can be retained.

$$\hat{\underline{a}}_k = P_k \underline{b}_k \quad (3.62)$$

with

$$P_k = \left[\sum_{i=1}^{k} \underline{x}_i \underline{x}_i^T \right]^{-1}$$

$$\underline{b}_k = \sum_{i=1}^{k} \underline{x}_i y_i \qquad (3.63)$$

(3.62) and (3.63) imply:

$$P_k^{-1} = P_{k-1}^{-1} + \underline{x}_k \underline{x}_k^T \qquad (3.64)$$

$$\underline{b}_k = \underline{b}_{k-1} + \underline{x}_k y_k \qquad (3.65)$$

One has to be more careful in manipulating matrices and vectors. Pre-multiplication of (3.64) by P_k and post-multiplication with P_{k-1} give a form equivalent with (3.55)

$$P_k = P_{k-1} - P_k \underline{x}_k \underline{x}_k^T P_{k-1} \qquad (3.66)$$

A straightforward elimination of P_k in the second part of the equation would provide an acceptable formula for the matrix P_k as a function of P_{k-1}. A more careful approach, however, yields a recursive algorithm which is computationally more advantageous, in the sense that direct matrix inversion can be avoided. (3.66) is post-multiplied by $\underline{x}_k$; then terms in $P_k \underline{x}_k$ are collected. After post-multiplication with $[1 + \underline{x}_k P_{k-1}\underline{x}_k]^{-1} \underline{x}_k^T P_{k-1}$ and elimination of $P_k \underline{x}_k \underline{x}_k^T P_{k-1}$ with (3.66), the following equation, which is often termed the "matrix inversion lemma", is obtained

$$P_k = P_{k-1} - P_{k-1} \underline{x}_k [1 + \underline{x}_k^T P_{k-1} \underline{x}_k]^{-1} \underline{x}_k^T P_{k-1} \qquad (3.67)$$

As $1 + \underline{x}_k^T P_{k-1} \underline{x}_k$ is a scalar, the recursive forms will offer an advantage over the en bloc solution (3.61) where a matrix inversion is required. One proceeds as follows:

$$\underline{k}_k = P_{k-1} \underline{x}_k [1 + \underline{x}_k^T P_{k-1} \underline{x}_k]^{-1} \qquad (3.68)$$

or with (3.67) and (3.66)

$$\underline{k}_k = P_k \underline{x}_k \qquad (3.69)$$

and

$$\underline{\hat{a}}_k = P_k \underline{b}_k = P_k(\underline{b}_{k-1} + \underline{x}_k y_k) = P_k \underline{b}_{k-1} + P_k \underline{x}_k y_k \qquad (3.70)$$

and with (3.67) and (3.69) after substitution in (3.70)

$$\underline{\hat{a}}_k = \underline{\hat{a}}_{k-1} - \underline{k}_k [\underline{x}_k^T \underline{\hat{a}}_{k-1} - y_k] \qquad (3.71)$$

Here again (3.67) (3.68) or (3.69) and (3.71) constitute the least squares algorithm, now for general regression-type problems.

Remarks

All the remarks for the scalar case carry over to the vector problem, more specifically, if the errors e_i are zero mean, serially uncorrelated and have constant variance σ^2, and if they are independent of x_{ji}, the problem presented above is known as the General Linear Regression Model (GLR). The estimate is unbiased with covariance matrix:

$$\mathbf{P}^* = \sigma^2 \left[\sum_{i=1}^{N} \underline{x}_i \underline{x}_i^T \right]^{-1}$$

So at sample k : $\mathbf{P}_k = \dfrac{1}{\sigma^2} \mathbf{P}^*_k$. As an estimate for σ^2, one can utilize

$$\frac{1}{k-n} \sum_{i=1}^{k} e_i'^2$$

Under Gaussian conditions the maximum likelihood and Bayesian interpretation can be given too.

3.2.3.5 Extensions: varying parameters

The model: linear in varying parameters

The measurements are related to the parameters by the way of a linear regression form:

$$y_i = \underline{x}_i^T \underline{a} + e_i \qquad i = 1,2,3, \ldots ,N \qquad (3.72)$$
$$\underline{a} \text{ varies with the index } i$$

Assumptions are:

$\underline{x}_j$: values perfectly known and linearly independent.
e_i : zero mean errors.

The problem

Estimate or track the parameter vector $\underline{a}$.

Solution I: weighting the past

The classic least squares algorithm is not suited because the procedure will average out the eventually slow or rare variations in $\underline{a}$, which may be quite important as "time" evolves. On the other hand there are stretches in the data where $\underline{a}$ remains approximately constant. So intuitively, one can deduce that the estimate must take sufficient samples into account to remove the noise pattern but on the other hand forget "obsolete" data, so as to be able to follow the variations in a.
Instead of minimizing (3.60), the following form could be proposed

where only the last M samples are taken into account

$$J = \sum_{i=k-M+1}^{k} (y_i - \underline{x}_i^T \underline{a})^2 \tag{3.73}$$

Using the techniques developed in the previous paragraph it is straightforward to obtain the "en bloc" solution as well as the recursive algorithm. Note that (3.73) can be brought in the following form

$$J = \sum_{i=1}^{k} w_i (y_i - \underline{x}_i^T \underline{a})^2 \tag{3.74}$$

where

$$w_i = 1 \qquad i \in [k - M + 1, k]$$
$$w_i = 0 \qquad \text{otherwise}$$

One sees that a "window" is applied to the cost in order to "forget" the past. Developing a recursive algorithm is easy if one realizes that, thanks to superposition, incrementing k can be done in two steps: first utilizing (3.64) and (3.65) to add a new sample to the data base and obtain in that way intermediate values P'_k and $\underline{\hat{a}}'_k$, second utilizing the same equations to remove an old sample—change plus into minus and $\underline{x}_k$, y_k into $\underline{x}_{k-M}$, y_{k-M} and find P_k and $\underline{\hat{a}}_k$. The details are left as an exercise for the reader.

Another less abrupt approach is to weight the cost another way:

$$J = \sum_{i=1}^{k} w_i (y_i - \underline{x}_i^T \underline{a})^2 \tag{3.75}$$

where $w_i = \gamma(1 - \gamma)^{k-i}$.

For the "en bloc" solution at a sample k one finds

$$\left[\sum_{i=1}^{k} w_i \underline{x}_i \underline{x}_i^T \right] \underline{\hat{a}}_k - \sum_{i=1}^{k} w_i \underline{x}_i y_i = 0 \tag{3.76}$$

with $\underline{\hat{a}}_k = P_k \underline{b}_k$

$$P_k^{-1} = (1 - \gamma) P_{k-1}^{-1} + \gamma \underline{x}_k \underline{x}_k^T$$

and

$$\underline{b}_k = (1 - \gamma) \underline{b}_{k-1} + \gamma \underline{x}_k y_k$$

Note that: for $\gamma = 1$, the past is completely forgotten;
                for $\gamma = 0$, only the past is believed to be trustworthy.
In a similar approach the window is defined as $w_i = \alpha^{k-i}$; one then finds:

$$P_k^{-1} = \alpha P_{k-1}^{-1} + \underline{x}_k \underline{x}_k^T$$
$$\underline{b}_k = \alpha \underline{b}_{k-1} + \underline{x}_k y_k$$

with for $\alpha = 0$: the past is forgotten
    and $\alpha = 1$: the classic recursive least squares algorithm (RLS).
Straightforward calculation yields for the recursive algorithm:

$$\mathbf{P}_k = \frac{1}{1-\gamma}\,\mathbf{P}_{k-1} - \frac{\gamma}{(1-\gamma)^2}\,\mathbf{P}_{k-1}\underline{x}_k\left[1 + \frac{\gamma}{1-\gamma}\,\underline{x}_k{}^T\mathbf{P}_{k-1}\underline{x}_k\right]^{-1}\underline{x}_k{}^T\mathbf{P}_{k-1}$$

$$(3.77)$$

$$\underline{k}_k = \frac{1}{1-\gamma}\,\mathbf{P}_{k-1}\underline{x}_k\left[1 + \frac{\gamma}{1-\gamma}\,\underline{x}_k{}^T\mathbf{P}_{k-1}\underline{x}_k\right]^{-1} \qquad\qquad (3.78)$$

$$\underline{k}_k = \mathbf{P}_k\underline{x}_k \qquad\qquad (3.79)$$

$$\underline{\hat{a}}_k = \underline{\hat{a}}_{k-1} - \gamma\underline{k}_k\left[\underline{x}_k{}^T\underline{\hat{a}}_{k-1} - y_k\right] \qquad\qquad (3.80)$$

Observation on the results of the operation of this algorithm on particular problems shows that the physical effect of the factor γ is simply to prevent the P-matrix elements from becoming too small, so that new data continues to have some effect on the estimates. In this way, any modification to the measured gradient caused by the parameter variation can be detected and used to update the parameter estimates. Of course, the approach has the disadvantage that noise influence is not filtered away as well.

Practical considerations

Due to the noise, γ will have to be chosen fairly small (< 0.1). In practice it was found that initial convergence of the algorithm is intolerably slow. To start the algorithm, the following procedure has been shown to be suitable:

compute $\underline{\hat{a}}_1$, $\mathbf{P}_1$ using the classic RLS;
for $k > 1$ use a variable $\gamma : \gamma_k$ so that

$$\gamma_k = \frac{\gamma}{1 - (1-\gamma)^k}$$

(note that for $k \to \infty\ \gamma_k \to \gamma$, but for small $k : \gamma_k > \gamma$ and stability is better)

Remarks

The simple scheme for tracking parameter changes has a major deficiency. Most often the rate of change will vary from parameter to parameter. Unfortunately, the recursive algorithm presented above accepts only one tunable quantity : γ. If it is adapted to the most rapidly changing parameter, estimation accuracy for the other ones is limited. Therefore, another solution to the problem addressed is useful.

Solution II: modelling the parameter variations

Suppose at first that some linear model for the parameter variations is available:

$$\underline{a}_k = \Phi(k, k-1)\, \underline{a}_{k-1} + \Gamma(k, k-1)\, \underline{q}_{k-1} \qquad (3.81)$$

$\Phi(k, k-1) : n \times n$ transition matrix

$\Gamma(k, k-1) : n \times m$ input matrix

$\underline{q}_{k-1}$: $m \times 1$ vector of serially independent random variables with zero mean and covariance matrix Q.

In the sequel, the abbreviations Φ and Γ will be used. Clearly, equation (3.81) summarizes a priori knowledge about the parameter variations which could be exploited to update the estimate. This is completely in accordance with the Bayesian interpretation of the RLS algorithm. In the classic algorithm (3.67) (3.68) (3.69) (3.71), the best estimates available at instant k to feed these equations are $\hat{\underline{a}}_{k-1}$ and P_{k-1}. In the present case, this statement is no longer true as one knows that $\underline{a}_{k-1}$, for instance, will have undergone changes predicted by equation (3.81). This information is to be used to obtain better entries $\hat{\underline{a}}_{k/k-1}$ and $P_{k/k-1}$ for the RLS estimate. Having available $\hat{\underline{a}}_{k-1}$ an estimate $\hat{\underline{a}}_{k/k-1}$ of $\hat{\underline{a}}_k$ based on the knowledge at time $k - 1$ is:

$$\hat{\underline{a}}_{k/k-1} = \Phi(k, k-1)\, \hat{\underline{a}}_{k-1} + \Gamma(k, k-1)\, \underline{q}_{k-1} \qquad (3.82)$$

Unfortunately $\underline{q}_{k-1}$ is not known and, thus, the prediction formula has to be based on expectations:

$$E\,[\hat{\underline{a}}_{k/k-1}] = \Phi(k, k-1) . E\,[\hat{\underline{a}}_{k-1}] + 0 \qquad (3.83)$$

Remember (Section 3.2.3.4) that

$$E\,[\,(\hat{\underline{a}}_{k-1} - E\,(\hat{\underline{a}}_{k-1}))\,(\hat{\underline{a}}_{k-1} - E\,(\hat{\underline{a}}_{k-1}))^{\mathrm{T}}] = E\,(\tilde{\underline{a}}_{k-1}\, \tilde{\underline{a}}_{k-1}^{\mathrm{T}})$$
$$= P_{k-1}^{*} = \sigma^2\, P_{k-1}$$

Define now:

$$P_{k/k-1}^{*} \triangleq E\,(\tilde{\underline{a}}_{k/k-1} . \tilde{\underline{a}}_{k/k-1}^{\mathrm{T}})$$

With the help of (3.82) and (3.83) and taking into account that the estimates are independent of new noise terms $\underline{q}_{k-1}$, one obtains

$$P_{k/k-1}^{*} = \Phi\, P_{k-1}^{*}\, \Phi^{\mathrm{T}} + \Gamma\, Q\, \Gamma^{\mathrm{T}} \qquad (3.84)$$

or

$$P_{k/k-1} = \Phi\, P_{k-1}\, \Phi^{\mathrm{T}} + \Gamma\, \frac{Q}{\sigma_{k-1}^2}\, \Gamma^{\mathrm{T}} \qquad (3.85)$$

(3.84), (3.85) and the following equations then constitute the complete algorithm:

$$P_k = P_{k/k-1} - P_{k/k-1} \underline{x}_k [1 + \underline{x}^T_k P_{k/k-1} \underline{x}_k]^{-1} \underline{x}^T_k P_{k/k-1} \quad (3.86)$$

$$\underline{k}_k = P_k \underline{x}_k = P_{k/k-1} \underline{x}_k [1 + \underline{x}^T_k P_{k/k-1} \underline{x}_k]^{-1} \quad (3.87)$$

$$\hat{\underline{a}}_k = \hat{\underline{a}}_{k/k-1} - \underline{k}_k [\underline{x}^T_k \hat{\underline{a}}_{k/k-1} - y_k] \quad (3.88)$$

At this point it may well be argued that, while the algorithm has theoretical appeal, it may be difficult to specify the parameter variation model. Fortunately, such understandable pessimism is not fully justified in this case. A random walk model (3.89), is often an acceptable way to account for parameter variations:

$$\underline{a}_k = \underline{a}_{k-1} + \underline{q}_{k-1} \quad (3.89)$$

It is then only necessary to specify the covariance matrix Q of the random parameter variations between samples. If parameter values vary slowly, Q can be chosen to be diagonal with elements selected to reflect the expected rate of variation.

$$q_{ii} = (\triangle a_i)^2$$

This is inherently more flexible than the alternative, exponentially weighted past approach because different expected rates of change can be specified for different parameters. If overall variation in the estimated parameters for any specified covariance matrix Q, accompanied by greater "smoothing" of the short-term variations is required, the integrated random walk (3.90) or a smoothed version (3.91) can be applied

$$\underline{a}_k = \underline{a}_{k-1} + \underline{\delta}_{k-1}$$
$$\underline{\delta}_k = \underline{\delta}_{k-1} + \underline{q}_{k-1} \quad (3.90)$$

or

$$\underline{a}_k = (1 - \alpha) \underline{a}_{k-1} + \alpha \underline{\delta}_{k-1}$$
$$\underline{\delta}_k = \underline{\delta}_{k-1} + \underline{q}_{k-1} \quad (3.91)$$

If the parameter variations are expected to be correlated in time, and so are fairly smooth, a first order Gauss-Markov model appears to have fairly wide applicability.

$$\underline{a}_k = B \underline{a}_{k-1} + \underline{q}_{k-1} \quad (3.92)$$

B : diagonal and $-1 < \beta_{ii} < 1$

The general model (3.81) is likely to be less useful in practical terms since it requires much more a priori information. Nevertheless, it may be useful if such a priori knowledge is available and the model then provides means to summarize and incorporate such knowledge into an estimating procedure.

Remarks

The equations developed here are closely related to the Kalman filter for state estimation. In the present context the unknown "parameters" can be considered as the state of a dynamic process which is responsible for the parameter variations. They are considered here as parameters because they are supposed to be fairly constant over certain intervals. In the light of the above discussion, the problem could equally well have been considered as one of state estimation and solved by application of Kalman's approach.

3.2.3.6 Cautionary comments

Regression analysis is probably the most widely used yet, at the same time, the most widely abused statistical tool in both the physical and social sciences. Of the many caveats which should be issued to the unwary user of regression analysis, we will mention only two which are particularly pertinent to the subject of the present book.

(a) Multiple collinearity

Although, as we have pointed out, the regressors or "independent variables" x_{ji} that compose the vector $\underline{x}_i$ should be linearly independent, it will often be impossible to pose the estimation problem such that they are orthogonal. It may happen that there is a tendency towards at least partial linear dependence then it can be shown [25] that the estimates will have high estimation error variance, even though the sum of squares of the residuals e'_i may be small and indicative of a good fit or explanation of the data. The reader should be wary of this problem, particularly in general practical applications of regression analysis, and should note that a check on the existence of problems of this type is available by using Multiple Correlation Analysis [5, 113].

More is said on the topic of multiple collinearity in a time-series context later on. It is worth noting here, however, that the physical effect of multiple correlation problems in RLS analysis is for the various recursive estimates apparently to converge slowly and "wander about" often in sympathy with each other. This is a consequence of the high correlation between regressors tending to drive the data matrix

$$\sum_{i=1}^{k} \underline{x}_i \, \underline{x}^T_i$$

towards singularity, so that the elements of its inverse P_k assume correspondingly high values. Given the relationship between P_k and the error covariance matrix P^*_k, we can see that this will imply high parametric estimation error variance [26].

From a geometric standpoint [237] multiple collinearity can also be interpreted as a tendency towards the development of valley-like phenomena in the hypersurface associated with the cost function J in the parameter–cost function hyperspace. Thus, there is no clearly defined minimum in the surface and the estimates wander along the elongated, valley-like bottom in some partial relationship with each other: this leads to low residual errors but some ambiguity about the parameter values, as indicated by the high estimation error variance. In the case of exact linear dependence, there will, of course, be an exact linear relationship between the regressors, a true valley in the cost function hypersurface and complete ambiguity. In theory, P_k will be indeterminate: in practice, however, the recursive matrix inversion lemma will yield an inverse with very large elements indicative of the high level of uncertainty about the resulting parameter estimates.

(b) Errors-in-variables and the structural model

Up to this point, only a particular form of linear estimation model has been considered; namely the regression model, in which the variables associated with the unknown parameters are exactly known quantities. In practice, a number of different estimation models are encountered and the techniques described here may need to be modified in some manner. This whole topic is discussed fully in a book by Graybill [85], in which he treats all the major possibilities in considerable detail. In the present context, it will suffice to mention one of the most important models met in practical situations, the "structural model".

In the structural model, the basic relationship between the parameters is still in the form shown in (3.59) but the elements of $\underline{x}$ are no longer exactly known quantities and can only be observed in error. In other words, the observed value of $\underline{x}$ is $\underline{z}$ where

$$\underline{z} = \underline{x} + \underline{\varepsilon} \tag{3.93}$$

and $\underline{\varepsilon}$ is an n vector of measurement noise associated with the observation of $\underline{x}$. In the context of regression analysis, it is worth noting that the presence of errors-in-variables of the above type induces an asymptotic bias on the parameter estimates which is a function of the signal/noise ratio on the signals and is zero only when there is no noise, i.e. $\underline{\varepsilon} \equiv 0$. In other words, no matter how many data are utilized to estimate the parameters in $\underline{a}$, the resultant estimates $\hat{\underline{a}}_k$ will always be biased away from the true values, i.e.

$$\underset{k \to \infty}{\text{p lim.}} \; \hat{\underline{a}}_k \neq \underline{a}$$

where p lim. is the "probability in the limit".

The importance of the asymptotic bias on the parameter estimates will depend upon the application of the regression analysis. If it is being used merely for forecasting the dependent variable y_k on the basis of the noisy dependent variables $\underline{z}_k$, then the results may be acceptable, since it can be shown that the "forecast" $\hat{y}_k = \underline{z}_k^T\hat{\underline{a}}$ is unbiased in most situations, provided the noise is stationary and retains those statistical characteristics it possessed in the data used to obtain the estimate $\hat{\underline{a}}$ [6]. But if the parameters or regression coefficients in $\underline{a}$ are important in their own right and, for example, have physical significance, then the problem can assume major proportions.

To provide the reader with a feeling for the observations above, an example is worked out for the case of wide-sense stationary data from which the mean has been removed. First, in relation to the linear regression problem, in a situation of a structural model the normal equations must be formulated as

$$\left[\sum_{i=1}^{N} \underline{z}_i\underline{z}_i^T\right]\hat{\underline{a}} = \sum_{i=1}^{N} \underline{z}_iy_i \tag{3.94}$$

Substituting equations (3.93) and (3.59) in (3.94) and dividing by N one obtains

$$\frac{1}{N}\sum_{i=1}^{N}(\underline{x}_i + \underline{\varepsilon}_i)(\underline{x}_i + \underline{\varepsilon}_i)^T\hat{\underline{a}} = \frac{1}{N}\sum_{i=1}^{N}(\underline{x}_i + \underline{\varepsilon}_i)((\underline{x}_i)^T\underline{a} + e_i)$$

The following elements can be defined for $N \to \infty$:

$$\frac{1}{N}\sum_{i=1}^{N}\underline{x}_i\underline{x}_i^T = R_{\underline{x}}$$

$$\frac{1}{N}\sum_{i=1}^{N}\underline{\varepsilon}_i\underline{\varepsilon}_i^T = R_{\underline{\varepsilon}}$$

$$\frac{1}{N}\sum_{i=1}^{N}\underline{x}_i\underline{\varepsilon}_i^T = \frac{1}{N}\sum_{i=1}^{N}\underline{\varepsilon}_i\underline{x}_i^T = 0:$$ "structural" noise is uncorrelated with the signal.

$$\frac{1}{N}\sum_{i=1}^{N}\underline{x}_ie_i = 0$$: e_i are uncorrelated with the components of the $\underline{x}$ vector.

$$\frac{1}{N}\sum_{i=1}^{N}\underline{\varepsilon}_ie_i = 0$$: the measurement noise e_i is uncorrelated with the structural noise.

In the limit

$$(R_{\underline{x}} + R_{\underline{\varepsilon}})\,\hat{\underline{a}} = R_{\underline{x}}\,\underline{a}$$

and $\underline{\hat{a}}$

$$(R_{\underline{x}} + R_{\underline{\varepsilon}})^{-1} R_{\underline{x}} \underline{a} \tag{3.95}$$

There are a number of ways of solving the structural model problem. If the noise statistics are known a priori for example, then there is no real problem since it is possible to compensate directly for the bias [137], although the estimates can be highly sensitive to errors in the a priori assumptions. If one is prepared to resort to non-linear estimation, then it is possible to use more sophisticated procedures such as maximum likelihood, which provide a good, but usually more complicated, general approach to the problem. Probably the simplest approach of this type is the "suboptimal" estimation procedure suggested by James, Souter and Dixon [138] which involves the iterative application of the linear least squares solution, with modifications to allow for the estimation and removal of bias effects. If one wishes to retain the simplicity of linear least squares estimation, however, there seems to be only one real possibility: this is the method of Instrumental Variables (IV) [55, 125].

The IV method is an extremely simple technique which retains the single iteration, linear least squares-like solution and is particularly attractive because it does not require detailed a priori information on the noise statistics to yield consistent, asymptotically unbiased estimates. As said before, a naive estimation procedure would be to solve equation (3.94). This solution is now modified, for the purposes of estimation, to yield the following "IV normal equations":

$$\left[\sum_{i=1}^{N} \underline{\hat{x}}_i \underline{z}_i^T\right] \underline{\hat{a}} - \sum_{i=1}^{N} \underline{\hat{x}}_i y_i = 0 \tag{3.96}$$

so that the IV estimate is obtained as

$$\underline{\hat{a}}_N = \left[\sum_{i=1}^{N} \underline{\hat{x}}_i \underline{z}_i^T\right]^{-1} \sum_{i=1}^{N} \underline{\hat{x}}_i y_i \tag{3.97}$$

or, in relation to equation (3.61)

$$\underline{\hat{a}}_N = [\hat{X}^T Z]^{-1} \hat{X}^T \underline{y} \tag{3.98}$$

where $\hat{X}$ is an $N \times n$ matrix with rows $\underline{\hat{x}}_i^T$ and Z a similarly dimensioned matrix with elements $\underline{z}_i^T$, $i = 1, 2, \ldots, N$.

In equation (3.97) $\underline{\hat{x}}_i$ is a vector of instrumental variables which are chosen to be as highly correlated as possible with the equivalent variables in the noise-free vector $\underline{x}_i$ but totally statistically independent of the noise $\underline{\varepsilon}$, i.e.,

$$E[\underline{\hat{x}}_i \underline{x}_j^T] \neq 0 ; \quad \text{and} \quad E[\underline{\hat{x}}_i \underline{\varepsilon}_j^T] = 0, \text{ for all } i, j \tag{3.99}$$

To demonstrate the effectiveness of the IV modification, the same analysis as above can be performed. In the limit one finds

$$R_{\hat{x}x}\hat{\underline{a}} = R_{\hat{x}x}\underline{a}$$

The troublesome bias is eliminated while the existence of a solution is preserved.

However, though consistency is guaranteed, the statistical efficiency of the solution is dependent upon the degree of correlation between $\hat{x}_i$ and x_i; in particular the most efficient estimates are obtained only when $\hat{x}_i = x_i$, i.e. when the $\hat{x}_i$ are equal to the hypothetical and nominally unavailable noise-free variables x_i.

The major problem with the IV method is the generation of suitable instrumental variables. In general, the difficulty in obtaining such variables has acted as a strong deterrent to the use of the IV method, as evidenced by the paucity of literature on the application of the method to the analysis of real data. Fortunately, the difficulty can be overcome fairly easily when dealing with time series as will be shown in the sequel.

Taking such an IV approach, the "en bloc" solution for k samples can be written in the form

$$\hat{\underline{a}}_k = \hat{P}_k \hat{\underline{b}}_k$$

$$\hat{P}_k = \left[\sum_{i=1}^{k} \hat{\underline{x}}_i \underline{z}_i^T \right]^{-1}$$

$$\hat{\underline{b}}_k = \sum_{i=1}^{k} \hat{\underline{x}}_i y_i$$

As a result it is a simple matter to obtain a recursive IV algorithm using an approach similar to that employed in the RLS case. Performing completely similar steps to those in Section 3.2.3.4 the following equations can be readily derived.

$$\hat{P}_k = \hat{P}_{k-1} - \hat{P}_{k-1} \hat{\underline{x}}_k [1 + \underline{z}_k^T \hat{P}_{k-1} \hat{\underline{x}}_k]^{-1} \underline{z}_k^T \hat{P}_{k-1} \qquad (3.100)$$

$$\underline{k}_k = \hat{P}_{k-1} \hat{\underline{x}}_k [1 + \underline{z}_k^T \hat{P}_{k-1} \hat{\underline{x}}_k]^{-1} \qquad (3.101)$$

$$\underline{k}_k = \hat{P}_k \hat{\underline{x}}_k \qquad (3.102)$$

$$\hat{\underline{a}}_k = \hat{\underline{a}}_{k-1} - \underline{k}_k [\underline{z}_k^T \hat{\underline{a}}_{k-1} - y_k] \qquad (3.103)$$

In the case of the RLS-scheme, the P matrix was directly related to the covariance matrix P^* of the estimate. Knowledge about this matrix is important as it gives us an indication concerning the degree of confidence we can have in the parameter estimates. Although here a P-matrix is available, its relationship with the parameter covariance matrix is not so straightforward. Therefore in equations (3.100–103) the computational matrix has been given a new notation $\hat{P}$. Useful results about the relationship between $\hat{P}$ and P^* can only be obtained when more details are available concerning the structural model.

3.2.4 Estimation of dynamic models: the SISO case

3.2.4.1 *Dynamic single input—single output models*

In Section 3.2.3, only static and quasi-static models have been discussed mainly for the purpose of introducing the basic algorithms that can be used for on-line parameter estimation. There is now enough background and insight to tackle the parameter estimation problem for more ambitious models: dynamic system representations. The basic SISO model treated in the following section can be represented by the following equations:

$$y_k + a_1 y_{k-1} + a_2 y_{k-2} + \ldots + a_n y_{k-n}$$
$$= b_o u_k + b_1 u_{k-1} + \ldots + b_n u_{k-n} + \xi_k + \ldots + a_n \xi_{k-n} \quad (3.104)$$

$$\xi_k + c_1 \xi_{k-1} + c_2 \xi_{k-2} + \ldots + c_n \xi_{k-n}$$
$$= e_k + d_1 e_{k-1} + \ldots + d_n e_{k-n} \quad (3.105)$$

with e_k random variables: $E(e_k) = 0$, $E(e_k e_j) = \sigma^2 \delta_{jk}$

Using a backward shift operator z^{-1}, these equations become

$$A(z^{-1})y(k) = B(z^{-1})u(k) + A(z^{-1})\xi(k) \quad (3.106)$$
$$C(z^{-1})\xi(k) = D(z^{-1})e(k)$$

with

$$A(z^{-1}) = 1 + a_1 z^{-1} + \ldots + a_n z^{-n}$$
$$B(z^{-1}) = b_0 + b_1 z^{-1} + \ldots + b_n z^{-n}$$
$$C(z^{-1}) = 1 + c_1 z^{-1} + \ldots + c_n z^{-n}$$
$$D(z^{-1}) = 1 + d_1 z^{-1} + \ldots + d_n z^{-n}$$

See Section 3.1.2.2 for a discussion concerning the generality of the representation in relation with other linear stochastic difference equation system representations. Here it is simply stated that the n-th order linear deterministic system is thought to be corrupted by noise that has a rational spectral density.

3.2.4.2 *A special case: autoregressive-type models*

Consider the model presented above with, for the noise description,

$C(z^{-1}) = A(z^{-1})$ and $D(z^{-1}) = 1$. Equations (3.104–105) reduce to

$$y_k = \underline{z_k}^T \underline{a} + e_k \qquad\qquad (3.107)$$

One notes that $\underline{z_k}^T = [-y_{k-1}, -y_{k-2} \ldots -y_{k-n}, u_k \ldots u_{k-n}]$ and $\underline{a}^T = [a_1, a_2, \ldots, a_n, b_0, b_1, \ldots, b_n]$ and so, as u_k is a deterministic input sequence, the model is an extension of the simple autoregressive time series model. The question arises whether the problem of estimating $\underline{a}$ is a regression problem of the type mentioned in Section 3.2.3.4. The $\underline{z_k}^T$ vectors are perfectly known and with a suitable input the components may be sufficiently linearly independent. However, they are not statistically independent of the noise. It is well known in the literature [154] that the RLS algorithm yields an estimate with the following properties:

(a) biased but consistent;
(b) asymptotically efficient with a Gaussian noise assumption for e_k.

If one is satisfied with the asymptotic properties, the estimation schemes presented above can be applied without modification. Little attention has otherwise been paid to the finite sample case.

3.2.4.3   *The general case: problems of bias*

In the general case, equations (3.104) and (3.105) yield

$$y(k) = \frac{B(z^{-1})}{A(z^{-1})} u(k) + \frac{D(z^{-1})}{C(z^{-1})} e(k)$$

A straightforward technique to reduce the general case to the former one would be to multiply by $C(z^{-1})/D(z^{-1})$ obtaining

$$\frac{C(z^{-1})}{D(z^{-1})} y(k) = \frac{C(z^{-1})B(z^{-1})}{D(z^{-1})A(z^{-1})} u(k) + e(k)$$

or

$$A^*(z^{-1})y(k) = B^*(z^{-1})u(k) + e(k)$$

with

$$A^*(z^{-1}) = C/D \quad \text{and} \quad B^*(z^{-1}) = CB/DA.$$

Note that polynomials A^* and B^* will mostly have an infinite number of parameters. Practical experience has shown that, for a good fit, quite a large number of parameters may be required. As the data available is finite, the procedure is lengthy and the estimation results poor.

Consider equation

$$y_k = \underline{z_k}^T \underline{a}_k + \eta_k \qquad\qquad (3.108)$$

Though of the same type as (3.107), it is not a classic regression model. Not only are the noise values correlated with the components of z_k as before, but η_k is far from white as it is serially correlated. Application of RLS yields biased estimates, even in the limit for $N \to \infty$.

The problem has given rise to a vast amount of research on procedures to eliminate the bias, even in the field of recursive estimators. At present, there is still no coherent theory able to reveal all advantages and disadvantages of these techniques. The instrumental variable approach, described in Section 3.2.3.6., will be presented in full detail. Other parameter estimation techniques, will be mentioned later.

Having made an option for an instrumental variable approach to the problem inherent in equation (3.108), algorithms of different complexity can be proposed. All have their use dependent on the purpose of the model-builder. The schemes are based on the recursive algorithms presented in the previous sections. Each can be developed in two versions, an iterative one, where the computations are performed stagewise, and an on-line version, which is completely recursive. The algorithms are presented in increasing order of complexity. The problem of process dynamics parameter estimation is addressed first.

3.2.4.4   The instrumental variable approach

The basic principles

It may happen that one is not concerned with the detailed nature of the noise. It is considered merely as interfering. Such cases arise if the deterministic process itself is a matter of concern. Under such circumstances the important equation is (3.104). Due to the nature of the equation, RLS is of little use. The instrumental variable approach discussed in Section 3.2.3.6., can be applied.

The biased "en bloc" solution

$$\left[\sum_{i=1}^{N} \underline{z}_i \underline{z}_i^T \right] \underline{\hat{a}} = \sum_{i=1}^{N} \underline{z}_i y_i$$

has to be modified with an instrumental variable $\underline{\hat{x}}_k$:

$$\left[\sum_{i=1}^{N} \underline{\hat{x}}_i \underline{z}_i^T \right] \underline{\hat{a}} = \sum_{i=1}^{N} \underline{\hat{x}}_i y_i \tag{3.109}$$

The true output of the system x_k is free of any relation to the noise; unfortunately, these values are not directly available. Any variables that are correlated with the outputs will also serve. It is obvious that the inputs, and quantities suitably derived from them are correlated with these outputs. These considerations are the basis for a number of proposals for an instrumental vector. Note that ideally:

$$\hat{\underline{x}}_k^{T} = \underline{x}_k^{T} = [-x_k, \ldots, -x_{k-n}, u_k, \ldots, u_{k-n}]$$

As an instrumental vector one could use

$$\hat{\underline{x}}_k^{T} = [u_{k\delta}, \ldots, u_{k-\delta n}, u_k, \ldots, u_{k-n}]$$

where ideally δ can be chosen to maximize the degree of correlation with the previous vector. Pursuing this line of reasoning one step further, it is possible to obtain instrumental variables that are even more highly correlated with x_k: instead of using u_k directly, one can use the input to activate an "auxiliary model" of the process, whose output $\hat{\underline{x}}_i$ $i = k - 1, \ldots, k - n$, is used to define an IV vector of the form:

$$\hat{\underline{x}}_k^{T} = [-\hat{x}_{k-1}, \ldots, -\hat{x}_{k-n}, u_k, \ldots, u_{k-n}]$$

It makes sense to construct this auxiliary model in the same form as the model, i.e.

$$\hat{A}[z^{-1}]\hat{x}_k = \hat{B}[z^{-1}]u_k \tag{3.110}$$

where

$$\hat{A}[z^{-1}] = 1 + \alpha_1 z^{-1} + \ldots + \alpha_n z^{-n}$$
$$\hat{B}[z^{-1}] = \beta_0 + \beta_1 z^{-1} + \ldots + \beta_n z^{-n}$$

The coefficients α_i, β_i are the auxiliary model parameters chosen in some sensible manner. Clearly, the closer the parameters are to the actual, but unknown, process parameters a_i, b_i, the more highly correlated are $\hat{\underline{x}}_k$ and $\underline{x}_k$ and the lower the variance of the IV estimates; in particular, if $\alpha_i = a_i$, $\beta_i = b_i$ for all i then $\hat{\underline{x}}_k = \underline{x}_k$ and the optimum IV estimates are obtained. The principles mentioned above can be worked out to yield an iterative IV-procedure or a purely on-line procedure. Both are presented below in more detail

The iterative IV-procedure: I—IV

As discussed in Section 3.2.3.1, an iterative computation performs stage calculations on the whole data set. A complete specification of the scheme requires a description of

  (a) the initial computational stage;
  (b) the j-th computational stage;
  (c) a stopping rule.

For the purpose of the presentation the general j-th computational stage is described first.

  Having obtained a final estimate at the $(j-1)$-th stage: $\hat{\underline{a}}_N^{j-1}$, an auxiliary model based on these estimates can be built: $\hat{B}^{j-1}/\hat{A}^{j-1}$. That model is fed with the input u_k and a sequence $\hat{x}_k^{j-1}$ can be generated. The u_k, y_k and $\hat{x}_k^{j-1}$ sequences can be used to solve the instrumental variable equations. It has been argued before that the recursive form has many desirable features. Based on the equations presented in section 3.2.3.6, one obtains

$$\hat{\underline{a}}_k^j = \hat{\underline{a}}_{k-1}^j - \underline{k}_k^j[\underline{z}_k^T\hat{\underline{a}}_{k-1}^j - y_k] \qquad (3.111)$$

$$\underline{k}_k^j = \hat{P}_k^j\,\hat{\underline{x}}_k^{j-1} \qquad (3.112)$$

$$\hat{P}_k^j = \hat{P}_{k-1}^j - \hat{P}_{k-1}^j\hat{\underline{x}}_k^{j-1}[1 + \underline{z}_k^T\hat{P}_{k-1}^j\hat{\underline{x}}_k^{j-1}]^{-1}\underline{z}_k^T\hat{P}_{k-1}^j \qquad (3.113)$$

Completeness requires a description of the start and the end of the computational stage. Initial conditions can be chosen as follows:

$$\hat{\underline{a}}_0^j = \hat{\underline{a}}_N^{j-1}$$

with

$$\hat{P}_0^j = \hat{P}_M^{j-1} \qquad (3.114)$$

Note that $M = N$ could be chosen. Remember that $\hat{P}$ is related to the covariance matrix of $\hat{\underline{a}}$, but it is in itself an estimate. Choosing the final value of $\hat{P}$ at the previous run may be overly optimistic.

In practice it has been found that a more realistic choice is an intermediate value of $\hat{P}$, e.g. $M = N/J$ with J the number of iterations required.

For $k = 1$ a vector $\underline{z}_1$ must be available. Two possibilities arise.

(i) it is known that the real system was at rest before excitation with an input

$$\underline{z}_1^T = [0, 0, 0, \ldots, u_1, 0, 0, \ldots, 0]$$

(ii) Inputs and outputs are unknown before the first sampling moment. Then one has to start from the $n+1$-th sample and use

$$\underline{z}_1^T = [-y_n, -y_{n-1}, \ldots, -y_1, u_{n+1}, u_n, \ldots, u_1]$$

In that case $N + n$ samples are required to be able to make N recursive estimates with the algorithm of Fig. 3.4. At the end of the run the auxiliary model has to be updated for the next run. The estimate $\hat{\underline{a}}_N^j$ will be used. However as these coefficients will only be estimates of the true values, it is required to check for stability. An unstable auxiliary model is certainly unacceptable. To test stability the Jury or Shur-Cohn criteria can be applied [116]. If the new model is stable updating consists in a simple substitution of old values by the new ones.

In the case of instability, the most simple approach is to freeze the model parameters at their previous stable values until a stable update is obtained. A more complicated approach provides a facility to compute the poles and

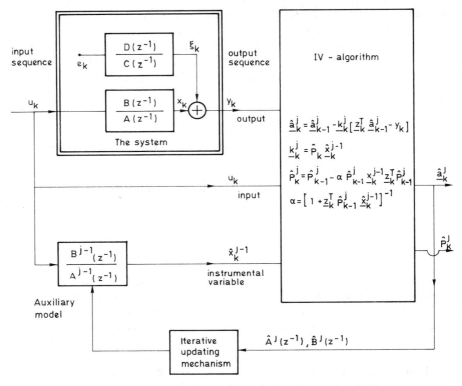

FIG. 3.4   The basic IV-algorithm; the iterative version: I-IV

to "mirror" unstable poles into stable positions, relative to the unit circle in the z-plane. With a suitable auxiliary model, the instrumental variables $\hat{x}_k^j$ have to be computed. Therefore, the filter needs to be assigned initial values, which is more complicated here. These can be computed if it is known that the system was at rest before excitation; otherwise one has to set the initial values either to zero, to the measured output or to some other suitable values.

The first run cannot be carried out according to the procedure described above, because no auxiliary model is available. There are a number of options.

(i) substitute the IV-algorithm by the simple RLS algorithm. The theoretical argument which makes such a procedure acceptable has been mentioned before: though the model parameters will have biased estimates, the predictions $\hat{x}_k^1$ of the model output are unbiased and will be sufficient for the next iterative run.

(ii) use an instrumental variable of the type:

$$[u_{k-\delta}, \ldots, u_{k-\delta-n}, u_k, u_{k-1}, \ldots, u_{k-n}]$$

where δ is chosen in a way to minimize correlations with the output. This is more cumbersome but may help whenever the previous approach yields unacceptable unstable models.

A stopping rule is easy to construct based on the changes of the parameter vector and/or the auxiliary model outputs.

Practical applications have shown that the number of iterative steps is small. Often convergence occurs after the third stage and more than six runs are very seldom required.

The on-line IV-procedure: OL—IV

With the on-line version of the IV-algorithm, the auxiliary model is continuously updated so that only one pass through the data is made; essentially the same block diagram as Fig.3.4 can be retained. The main difference resides in the fact that now the updating mechanism and the instrumental variable computation occur parallel with the computation of the IV equations, which are themselves on-line estimation procedures. The special features of the on-line approach thus are all concerned with the auxiliary model behaviour. Start-up of the algorithm poses some problems. In fact, the on-line version is only fully justified if an initial estimate of the auxiliary model is available, for instance from a priori knowledge or previous experience; or, if sufficient data is available to use a first batch to obtain an initial estimate with such a procedure presented for the start-up of I–IV, e.g. the RLS algorithm. Having at one's disposition a suitable initial parameter vector $\hat{\underline{a}}_0$, which defines the auxiliary model, the updating part of the OL–IV takes usually the form shown in Fig. 3.5.

Experience has shown that, in order to ensure that the auxiliary model is well behaved and that the instrumental variables satisfy their validity condition, it is necessary to update the parameters of the auxiliary model in a special way. A modified low-pass filter compensates for the fact that the estimate $\hat{\underline{a}}_k$ is correlated with the noise ξ_k at the same instant, by passing it through a special form of time delay and a discrete low-pass filter. One first chooses two integers K_1 and K_2; K_2 is the most important and it specifies $\hat{\underline{a}}_k$ (t.d):

$$\hat{\underline{a}}_k(t.d) = \hat{\underline{a}}_k(k - K_2)$$

It has to be taken in such a manner that ξ_{k-K_2} and ξ_k can be assumed to be essentially independent. The purpose of the time delay is to uncorrelate the instrumental variables as much as possible from the noise. An acceptable choice is K_2 just larger than n, the order of the process. As any digital filter

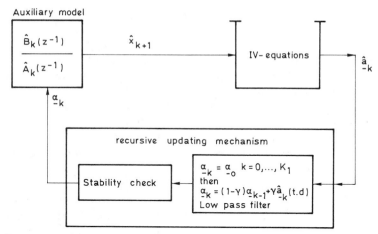

FIG. 3.5   Updating mechanism for the on-line instrumental variable algorithm

has a transient, it is safe to choose a K_2 value – $K_2 > K_1$, so that the auxiliary model parameters are kept at their initial values $\underline{\alpha}_0$ in the start-up period of K_2 samples. The choice of the design parameter K_2 does not appear to be crucial.

Then to avoid rapid changes in the auxiliary model parameters, the delayed estimate $\hat{a}_k(t.d)$ is low-pass filtered (3.115).

$$\hat{\underline{\alpha}}_k = (1 - \gamma)\,\hat{\underline{\alpha}}_{k-1} + \gamma\,\hat{\underline{a}}_k\,(t.d) \qquad\qquad (3.115)$$

$\gamma = 1/T$, where T is the exponential smoothing time constant in sampling intervals. A few such intervals will do the job.

Finally, as in the previous algorithm, it is safe to add a procedure for checking stability.

3.2.4.5   The approximate maximum likelihood method (AML)

In the previous paragraphs, only the first equation (3.104) of the complete model has been used. As will be seen in the sequel, it may be useful to have some idea about the characteristics of the noise.

Practical and simulation experience with the IV-algorithm indicates that the instrumental variable output of the auxiliary model quickly becomes indistinguishable from the output of a similar model constructed with a statistical, more elaborated, procedure, such as the maximum likelihood technique. In fact, convergence in that sense is nearly always faster than convergence in a purely parametric sense. For this reason, it is possible to generate a rapidly convergent estimate $\hat{\xi}_k$ of the noise ξ_k from the relationship

$$\hat{\xi}_k = y_k - \hat{x}_k \tag{3.116}$$

This time series generated from (3.116) will represent a good estimate of the noise time series, ξ_k. In the iterative case such a noise sequence will be available at each iteration stage. In the on-line case, each new value $\hat{x}_k$ will yield an estimate $\hat{\xi}_k$.

In a first approximation it is assumed that the statistical properties of $\hat{\xi}_k$ closely resemble those of ξ_k. The equation (3.105) is replaced by an approximation (3.117).

$$\hat{\xi}_k = \hat{\underline{n}}_k^T \cdot \underline{c} + e_k \tag{3.117}$$

$$\hat{\underline{n}}_k^T = [-\hat{\xi}_{k-1}, \ldots, -\hat{\xi}_{k-n}, e_{k-1}, \ldots, e_{k-n}]$$

(3.105) is a pure ARMA-model. Here too, straightforward linear regression analysis is bound to yield biased estimates as the noise is correlated with the $\hat{n}_k$ vector.

One could attempt to use here again the IV approach. Unfortunately, in this case, no known input is available. An instrumental variable could be constructed on the basis of delayed versions of the $\hat{\xi}_k$ values. The approach has been found to be of little value [239].

A better solution is to use a recursive Approximate Maximum Likelihood (AML) procedure that owes much in conceptual terms to the Maximum Likelihood procedure of Aström and Bohlin [10]. In order to understand the motivation behind the method, it is necessary to consider the ARMA model (3.105). If the $e_{k-1}, \ldots, e_{k-n}$ could be measured then the problem is similar to the autoregressive model case (see Section 3.2.4.2). An approximate solution is possible by substituting noise inputs by estimates of these noise terms: $\hat{e}_{k-1}, \ldots, \hat{e}_{k-n}$ in the vector $\hat{\underline{n}}_k$.

$$\check{\underline{n}}_k^T = [-\hat{\xi}_{k-1}, \ldots, -\hat{\xi}_{k-n}, \hat{e}_{k-1}, \ldots, \hat{e}_{k-n}]$$

The algorithm proceeds as follows:
Collect the first n values for $\hat{\xi}$
Define $\check{\underline{n}}_{n+1}^T = [-\hat{\xi}_n, -\hat{\xi}_{n-1}, \ldots, -\hat{\xi}_1, 0, 0, \ldots, 0]$
With $\underline{c}_n = 0$ and $\check{P}_n = \infty I$ use the common RLS algorithm for $k = n + 1$

$$\hat{\underline{c}}_k = \hat{\underline{c}}_{k-1} - \check{\underline{k}}_k [\check{\underline{n}}_k^T \hat{\underline{c}}_{k-1} - \hat{\xi}_k] \tag{3.118}$$

$$\check{\underline{k}}_k = \check{P}_k \cdot \check{\underline{n}}_k \tag{3.119}$$

$$\check{P}_k = \check{P}_{k-1} - \check{P}_{k-1} \check{\underline{n}}_k [1 + \check{\underline{n}}_k^T \check{P}_{k-1} \check{\underline{n}}_k]^{-1} \check{\underline{n}}_k^T \check{P}_{k-1} \tag{3.120}$$

Compute $\hat{e}_k = \hat{\xi}_k - \check{\underline{n}}_k^T \hat{\underline{c}}_k$ for $k = n + 1$ \tag{3.121}

Update $\check{\underline{n}}_k$ to obtain $\check{\underline{n}}_{k+1}$

$$\check{\underline{n}}_{k+1}^T = [\, -\hat{\xi}_{n+1} - \hat{\xi}_n \ldots - \hat{\xi}_2, \hat{e}_k, 0, 0, \ldots\,]$$

Return to (3.118) with $k = n+2$ and continue till all data points have been processed.

A block diagram of the AML estimate is shown in Fig. 3.6. Equation (3.121) consists in making a prediction for the noise with the help of an "inverse" noise filter $\hat{C}(z^{-1})/\hat{D}(z^{-1})$. The filter is updated recursively. It is prudent to provide an updating mechanism and a stability check may be useful. More complex data processing of the type mentioned for the on-line IV-algorithm, may be provided too.

The AML technique can easily be combined with both IV algorithms.

I-IV-AML : at each iteration stage a sequence $\hat{x}_k$ is obtained which can be used to generate a sequence $\hat{\xi}_k$. The AML algorithm is

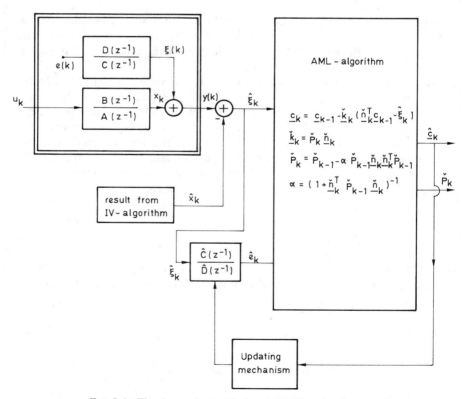

FIG. 3.6   The Approximate Maximum Likelihood estimator

then applied from the first sample point where n ξ-values are available.

OL-IV-AML : here each time a new IV value $\hat{x}_k$ is obtained an AML computation step is performed. The complete alogorithm alternates between an IV step and an AML step at each measurement, while in the previous case alternation occurs at the iteration stage level.

3.2.4.6 Practical and statistical considerations

Practical considerations

Identifiability

The question whether the parameter estimation problem is well posed has been addressed in general terms in Section 3.2.2.1. The deterministic part as well as the stochastic part of the model has been described with a transfer function formalism. As a consequence, identifiability from the purely structural point of view is guaranteed in the sense that all parameters can be found, as long as complete freedom in choosing inputs and identification schemes exists.

Program interaction

Actual implementation of the algorithms does not pose major problems. However, it is important to realize that the techniques are not foolproof, in the sense that conditions may occur which will lead to poor results or even a breakdown of the program, e.g. failure of the data to provide stable auxiliary models. The most elegant implementation procedure should provide ample opportunity for human interactive intervention, so that "tuning" parameters can be freely changed or computational options chosen by the model builder according to intermediate results obtained and displayed, for convenience, during the computational session itself.

Statistical considerations

Generalities on consistency and efficiency

The most important question is that of consistency. Do the algorithms yield unbiased estimates in the limit for N, the number of points going to infinity? This problem has been studied by Söderström and Stoica [202] for IV-algorithms. As long as the problem is well posed, the IV-algorithm is consistent in a generic sense, or in other words, the IV scheme is almost always consistent. It may however occasionally happen that a particular input sequence causes inconsistency. The input itself needs to be the output of a filter, whose parameters are matched in a special way to the parameters of the real-world system, when a given auxiliary model is in use. If a white noise input sequence is used, no problems can occur.

Another important issue is the efficiency or accuracy for limiting circumstances. Söderström and Stoica prove that the technique is not so efficient as the Maximum Likelihood technique. Young has found that the estimates are not efficient, but often acceptable. The asymptotic covariance for the parameter vector is reached reasonably fast, if the number of data points is increased. For higher efficiency, the techniques of the following sections is required. In short, the IV-algorithm is a "quick and dirty", computationally simple, parameter estimation scheme, especially useful in exploratory phases of the modelling process. The AML technique, on the other hand, is not so trustworthy. Söderström has shown that for certain cases consistency is not a property of the algorithms. Furthermore, convergence of the parameters may be much slower and the efficiency is lower. However, the algorithm normally exhibits good performance.

Parameter error covariance matrices

As discussed in Section 3.2.3.6, it is in fact difficult to reveal the precise meaning of the $\hat{P}$- and $\check{P}$-matrices. At this point, only some heuristic arguments can be given. After discussion of the move advanced parameter estimation schemes, these arguments will be easier to evaluate.

For the IV-part, one could mention that for a sufficiently large number of points, bearing the analysis of Section 3.2.3.6 in mind, $(1/k)\hat{P}_k$ will approximate $(1/k)[\underline{x}_k{}^T\underline{x}_k]^{-1}$ and thus, if the ξ_k are serially independent, the error covariance matrix P^* could be approximated by.

$$P^{*1} \approx \hat{\sigma}^2.\hat{P}_N \tag{3.122}$$

As soon as the ξ_k are correlated, the noise covariance matrix may play a certain role. Young proposed (238), based on an analysis that ran parallel with the same developments in the case of simple least squares, a more refined equation.

$$P^{*1} \approx \hat{P}_N{}^T.\hat{X}_N{}^T.\hat{W}.\hat{X}_N.\hat{P}_N \tag{3.123}$$

$\hat{W}$: covariance of the noise

For the purpose of easy computation (3.122) could be retained as long as one need only an approximate value of the estimation accuracy. In other cases, the more refined approach discussed in the following sections should be applied.

For the AML, the same consideration as above apply and for an approximate estimate one can use

$$P^{*2} \approx \hat{\sigma}^2\check{P}_N \tag{3.124}$$

3.2.4.7   Refined instrumental variable — approximate maximum likelihood schemes

Theoretical development

The basic algorithms presented so far are useful but do not provide the most efficient estimates. If high precision is needed, more refined versions of the techniques are required. The question arises how more elaborate techniques can be developed. Up to now, in estimation theory, the best that can be done is to strive for an asymptotically unbiased minimum variance estimator under Gaussian assumptions for the noise in the system. An estimator which is known to possess such properties is the maximum likelihood estimator. In order to upgrade the IV–AML estimator it may be useful to compare it with an ML approach. Indeed Young [241] has shown that a relationship between these estimators exists, on the basis of which a refined algorithm can be derived. The basic derivations are presented below.

Relationships between ML and IV–AML

The maximum likelihood approach consists in choosing the parameters in the polynomials A,B,C,D and in characterizing the input noise in such a manner as to maximize the probability of obtaining the actual measurements. As will be seen in the sequel the relationship between ML and IV–AML and an improvement of the latter can be obtained by decomposition of the ML problem in a manner shown in Fig. 3.7.

Consider the model of Section 3.2.4.1 with the following assumptions

$$\underline{e}^T = [e_1, e_2, \ldots, e_N] \qquad \underline{e} = N(0, \sigma^2 I)$$

where $N(\underline{a}, B)$ is a Gaussian distribution with mean $\underline{a}$ and covariance B.

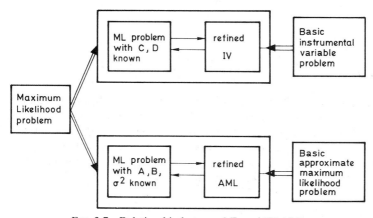

FIG. 3.7   Relationship between ML and IV-AML

Many textbooks [11, 83] learn that the logarithm of the maximum likelihood takes the form of equation (3.125). In fact, the formula is related to the conditional maximum likelihood, as 2n initial conditions are needed. These initial conditions have no effect on asymptotic results and for the presentation here the more simple conditional maximum likelihood is adequate.

$$\log p\,(\underline{y}\,|\,\underline{a},\,\underline{b},\,\sigma^2,\,\underline{u}) = L(\underline{a},\,\underline{b},\,\sigma^2,\,\underline{y},\,\underline{u}) =$$

$$\frac{(N-2n)}{2}\log(2\pi) - \frac{(N-2n)}{2}\log\sigma^2 - \frac{1}{2\sigma^2}\cdot\sum_{k=2n+1}^{N}\left[\frac{C}{D}y_k\right.$$
$$\left. - \frac{BC}{AD}u_k\right]^2 \qquad (3.125)$$

A,B,C,D are polynomials in z^{-1}, the backward shift operator; when the C, D coefficients are known, the ML estimates for $\underline{a},\underline{b}$ and σ^2 maximize (3.125) and thus they are solutions of the set of equations:

$$\frac{\partial L}{\partial a_i} = 0,\ \frac{\partial L}{\partial b_i} = 0,\ \frac{\partial L}{\partial \sigma^2} = 0$$

More specifically, they satisfy

$$\frac{\partial L}{\partial a_i} = \frac{1}{\hat{\sigma}^2}\sum_{k=2n+1}^{N}\left[\frac{C}{D}y_k - \frac{\hat{B}.C}{\hat{A}.D}u_k\right]\frac{\hat{B}.C}{\hat{A}^2.D}z^{-i}u_k = 0 \quad i = 1, 2\ldots n$$

$$(3.126)$$

$$\frac{\partial L}{\partial b_i} = \frac{1}{\hat{\sigma}^2}\sum_{k=2n+1}^{N}\left[\frac{C}{D}y_k - \frac{\hat{B}.C}{\hat{A}.D}u_k\right]\frac{C}{\hat{A}.D}z^{-i}u_k = 0 \quad i = 0, 1, 2\ldots n$$

$$(3.127)$$

$$\frac{\partial L}{\partial \sigma^2} = -\frac{(N-2n)}{2\hat{\sigma}^2} + \frac{1}{2\hat{\sigma}^4}\sum_{k=2n+1}^{N}\left[\frac{C}{D}y_k - \frac{\hat{B}.C}{\hat{A}.D}u_k\right]^2 = 0 \qquad (3.128)$$

The equations are highly non-linear in the a_i and b_i parameters but are linear in the b_i for a given a_i and they are linear in the σ^2. Solving (3.126–128) directly requires non-linear programming techniques. These same equations take a more familiar look, if one introduces a set of new variables, which will be called "prefiltered" variables as they are the result of passing available variables through linear filters.

$$y^*_k = \frac{C}{\hat{A}.D}y_k \qquad (3.129)$$

$$u^*_k = \frac{C}{\hat{A}.D} u_k \tag{3.130}$$

$$\hat{x}^*_k = \frac{\hat{B}}{\hat{A}} u^*_k = \frac{C.\hat{B}}{\hat{A}^2.D} u_k \tag{3.131}$$

After substitution in (3.126–127), one finds:

$$\sum[\hat{A}y_k^* - \hat{B}u_k^*]\hat{x}^*_{k-i} = 0 \qquad i = 1, 2, \ldots, n \tag{3.132}$$

$$\sum[\hat{A}y_k^* - \hat{B}u_k^*]u^*_{k-i} = 0 \qquad i = 0, 1, 2, \ldots, n \tag{3.133}$$

Recall (Section 3.2.4.4) that the IV solution to parameter estimation of the process dynamics took the form:

$$\left[\sum_k \hat{\underline{x}}_k z_k^T \right] \hat{a} - \sum_k \hat{\underline{x}}_k y_k = 0 \tag{3.134}$$

with

$$\hat{a}^T = [\hat{a}_1, \ldots, \hat{a}_n, \hat{b}_0, \hat{b}_1, \ldots, \hat{b}_n]$$

$$\hat{x}_k^T = [-\hat{x}_{k-1}, \ldots, -\hat{x}_{k-n}, u_k, \ldots, u_{k-n}]$$

$$z_k^T = [-y_{k-1}, \ldots, -y_{k-n}, u_k, \ldots, u_{k-n}]$$

(3.134) is a vector-matrix notation for $2n+1$ equations. It is a simple matter to write them out:

$$\sum_k [\hat{A}y_k - \hat{B}u_k]\hat{x}_{k-i} = 0 \quad i = 1, 2, \ldots, n \tag{3.135}$$

$$\sum_k [\hat{A}y_k - \hat{B}u_k]u_{k-i} = 0 \quad i = 0, 1, 2, \ldots, n \tag{3.136}$$

All crucial equations are now available. If one breaks the ML problem down into two parts, the first one yields equations (3.132, 3.133). These are similar in structure as the basic IV equations (3.135, 3.136) in the sense that, for the latter, easily obtainable quantities y_k, u_k, $\hat{x}_k$ are used instead of prefiltered variables y_k^*, u_k^*, $\hat{x}_k^*$. This could be seen by writing the ML equations (3.126) and (3.127) under a special form (3.132), (3.133). It will be seen later that a refinement of the basic IV-estimator can be obtained by proposing a algorithm based on (3.132) and (3.133).

So far the upper path of Fig. 3.7 has been successfully clarified. The lower path can be discussed in much the same fashion. Under the assumption of known A, B and σ^2, the derivatives of (3.125) are

$$-\frac{\partial L}{\partial c_i} = \frac{1}{\sigma^2} \sum_{k=2n+1}^{N} \left[\frac{\hat{C}}{\hat{D}} y_k - \frac{B.\hat{C}}{A.\hat{D}} u_k \right] \left[\frac{1}{\hat{D}} z^{-i} y_k - \frac{B}{A.\hat{D}} z^{-i} u_k \right] = 0$$

$$i = 1, 2, \ldots, n$$

(3.137)

$$-\frac{\partial L}{\partial d_i} = \frac{1}{\sigma^2} \sum_{k=2n+1}^{N} \left[\frac{\hat{C}}{\hat{D}} y_k - \frac{B.\hat{C}}{A.\hat{D}} u_k \right] \left[-\frac{\hat{C}}{\hat{D}^2} z^{-i} y_k \right.$$

$$\left. + \frac{B.\hat{C}}{A.\hat{D}^2} z^{-i} u_k \right] = 0 \quad i = 1, 2, \ldots, n$$

(3.138)

or with

$$\xi_k = y_k - \frac{B}{A} u_k$$

and

$$e_k = \frac{\hat{C}}{\hat{D}} \xi_k$$

$$\sum_k \left[\frac{\hat{C}}{\hat{D}} y_k - \frac{B.\hat{C}}{A.\hat{D}} u_k \right] \frac{1}{\hat{D}} z^{-i} \xi_k = 0 \quad i = 1, 2, \ldots, n \qquad (3.139)$$

$$\sum_k \left[\frac{\hat{C}}{\hat{D}} y_k - \frac{B.\hat{C}}{A.\hat{D}} u_k \right] \frac{1}{\hat{D}} z^{-i} e_k = 0 \quad i = 1, 2, \ldots, n \qquad (3.140)$$

Note also that

$$\frac{\hat{C}}{\hat{D}} y_k - \frac{B.\hat{C}}{A.\hat{D}} u_k = \frac{\hat{C}}{\hat{D}} \left(y_k - \frac{B}{A} u_k \right) = \frac{\hat{C}}{\hat{D}} \xi_k = e_k$$

By definition

$$e_k = \xi_k + c_1 \xi_{k-1} + \ldots + c_n \xi_{k-n} - d_1 e_{k-1} - \ldots - d_n e_{k-n}$$

$$= C\xi_k - D^* e_k$$

(3.141)

when $D^* = D^*(z^{-1}) = d_1 z^{-1} + d_2 z^{-2} + \ldots + d_n z^{-n}$

Equations (3.139) and (3.140) become with (3.141)

$$\sum_k [\hat{C}\xi_k - \hat{D}^* e_k]\xi^*_{k-i} = 0 \quad i = 1, 2, \ldots, n \qquad (3.142)$$

$$\sum_k [\hat{C}\xi_k - \hat{D}^* e_k] e^*_{k-i} = 0 \quad i = 1, 2, \ldots, n \tag{3.143}$$

with

$$\xi^*_k = \frac{1}{\hat{D}} \xi_k \tag{3.144}$$

$$e^*_k = \frac{1}{\hat{D}} e_k \tag{3.145}$$

Thus once again a set of linear equations in the unknown parameters have been obtained by defining certain prefiltered variables. Less straightforward is that ξ_k and e_k are not available while y_k and u_k in (3.129) and (3.130) are measured variables. Recall that the AML solution (Section 3.2.4.5) consists of:

$$\hat{\xi}_k = y_k - \hat{x}_k$$
$$\underline{\check{n}}_k = [-\hat{\xi}_{k-1}, \ldots - \hat{\xi}_{k-n}, \hat{e}_{k-1}, \ldots \hat{e}_{k-n}]$$
$$\hat{e}_k = \hat{\xi}_k - \underline{\check{n}}_k^T \underline{\hat{c}}_k$$

and $\underline{\hat{c}}_k$ is the solution of the equation

$$\left(\sum_k \underline{\check{n}}_k \cdot \underline{\check{n}}_k^T \right) \underline{\hat{c}}_k - \sum_k \underline{\check{n}}_k \hat{\xi}_k = \underline{0} \tag{3.146}$$

It is also found that (3.146) can be brought into the following form:

$$\sum_k [\hat{C}\hat{\xi}_k - \hat{D}^* \hat{e}_k] \hat{\xi}_{k-i} = 0 \quad i = 1, 2, \ldots, n \tag{3.147}$$

$$\sum_k [\hat{C}\hat{\xi}_k - \hat{D}^* \hat{e}_k] \hat{e}_{k-i} = 0 \quad i = 1, 2, \ldots, n \tag{3.148}$$

If one uses the same procedure of substituting estimates $\hat{\xi}_k$ and $\hat{e}_k$ into (3.142) and (3.143), it can be concluded that the AML differs from a second part of the ML problem by using throughout estimated variables $\hat{\xi}_k$ and $\hat{e}_k$, instead of a more proper use of filtered variables $\hat{\xi}_k^*$ and $\hat{e}_k^*$. This now forms a complete picture of the relationship between ML and IV–AML.

3.2.4.8 *The refined IV–AML algorithms, R–IV–AML: implementations*

The iterative refined IV–AML algorithm: IR–IV–AML

On the basis of the previous discussions, it may be hoped that an algorithm based on equations (3.132), (3.133) and (3.142), (3.143) will be more efficient. A complete picture is given in Fig. 3.8. Basically the difference

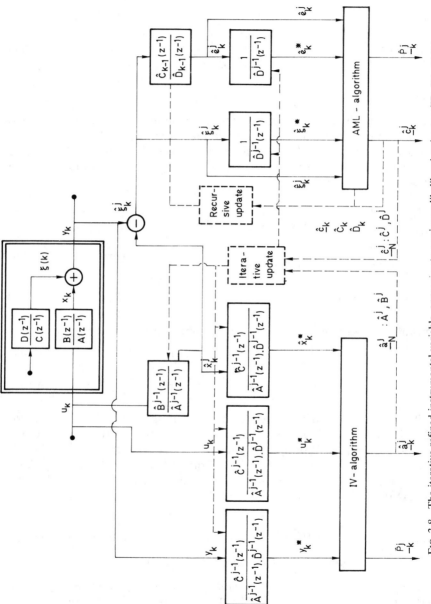

FIG. 3.8 The iterative refined instrumental variable, approximate maximum likelihood estimator (IR–IV–AML)

between IR–IV–AML and I–IV–AML consists in the addition of a number of prefilters, one of the type

$$\frac{\hat{C}(z^{-1})}{\hat{A}(z^{-1})\hat{D}(z^{-1})}$$

for the IV part, and another of the type $(1/\hat{D})$ in the AML part. The role of these prefilters can be intuitively understood. They only pass these frequencies to the estimation algorithms that matter for parameter determination. The filters try to reduce the deleterious effects of the noise, by eliminating frequency bands which are of no avail; in other words, they feed the basic estimation algorithms with signals that have a higher signal to noise ratio. With these remarks, the diagram in Fig. 3.8, and the previous sections it should be possible to derive the complete algorithm. For the sake of completeness the major features are specified.

Having at one's disposition the results of the computations at the (j-1)th stage, the algorithm proceeds as follows:

(a) With an iterative update mechanism of the type described in Section 3.2.4.4, essentially a stability check, the auxiliary model is updated yielding $\hat{B}^{j-1}(z^{-1})/\hat{A}^{j-1}(z^{-1})$ and the prefilters also giving $\hat{C}^{j-1}(z^{-1})/\hat{A}^{j-1}(z^{-1})$. $\hat{D}^{j-1}(z^{-1})$.

(b) Then, for the whole sequence, u_k is fed into the auxiliary model to yield $\hat{x}_k$ and y_k, u_k, $\hat{x}_k$ are fed into the prefilters to result in sequences y^*_k, u^*_k, $\hat{x}^*_k$. The start-up is done as discussed in Section 3.2.4.4, depending on the conditions that existed before exciting the real system at the time of experimentation.

(c) The sequences y^*_k, u^*_k and $\hat{x}^*_k$ are recursively processed by the classic algorithm:

$$\hat{P}_k^j = \hat{P}_{k-1}^j - \hat{P}_{k-1}^j \hat{\underline{x}}^*_k [1 + \underline{z}^{*T}_k \hat{P}_{k-1}^j \hat{\underline{x}}^*_k]^{-1} \underline{z}^{*T}_k \hat{P}_{k-1}^j \tag{3.149}$$

$$\underline{k}_k^j = \hat{P}_k^j \hat{\underline{x}}^*_k \tag{3.150}$$

$$\hat{\underline{a}}_k^j = \hat{\underline{a}}_{k-1}^j - \underline{k}_k^j [\underline{z}^{*T}_k \cdot \hat{\underline{a}}_{k-1}^j - \underline{y}^*_k] \tag{3.151}$$

when

$$\underline{z}^{*T}_k = [-y^*_{k-1}, -y^*_{k-2}, \ldots, -y^*_{k-n}, u^*_k, \ldots, u^*_{k-n}]$$

and

$$\underline{\hat{x}}^{*T}_k = [-\hat{x}^*_{k-1}, \ldots, -\hat{x}^*_{k-n}, u^*_k, \ldots, u^*_{k-n}]$$

The initial conditions are: $\hat{\underline{a}}_0^j = \hat{\underline{a}}_N^{j-1}$

$$\hat{P}_0^j = \hat{P}_M^{j-1}$$

where the choice of M was discussed before (M = N/J : J number of iterations).

(d) The final result $\underline{\hat{a}}_N{}^j$ is kept for initial condition and updating purposes in the following stage, while an intermediate value $\hat{P}_M{}^j$ is also stored as for the next stage.

Then computation proceeds with the refined AML-algorithm which is completely recursive.

(a) A sequence of error estimates is generated:

$$\hat{\xi}_k{}^j = y_k - \hat{x}_k{}^j$$

(b) Here too, the iterative updating mechanism will set the prefilters $1/\hat{D}^{j-1}(z^{-1})$ with the help of the parameters obtained at the previous stage. This is not the case for the filter $\hat{C}_{k-1}(z^{-1})/\hat{D}_{k-1}(z^{-1})$, which is part of the recursive algorithm.

(c) With initial conditions $\underline{\hat{c}}_0{}^j = \underline{\hat{c}}_N{}^{j-1}$ and $\check{P}_0{}^j = \check{P}^{j-1}$, for each data point, thus recursively the following steps are performed.

$$\check{P}_k{}^j = \check{P}_{k-1}^j - \check{P}_{k-1}^j \underline{\hat{m}}^*{}_k [1 + \underline{\check{n}}_k{}^T \check{P}_{k-1} \underline{\hat{m}}^*{}_k]^{-1} \underline{\check{n}}_k{}^T \check{P}_{k-1}^j \qquad (3.152)$$

$$\underline{\check{k}}_k{}^j = \check{P}_k{}^j \underline{\hat{m}}^*{}_k \qquad (3.153)$$

$$\underline{\hat{c}}_k{}^j = \underline{\hat{c}}_{k-1}^j - \underline{\check{k}}_k{}^j \{\underline{\check{n}}_k{}^{jT} \underline{\hat{c}}_{k-1}^j - \hat{\xi}_k{}^j\} \qquad (3.154)$$

with

$$\underline{\check{n}}_k{}^T = [-\hat{\xi}_{k-1}^j, \ldots - \hat{\xi}_{k-n}^j, \hat{e}_{k-1}^j, \ldots, \hat{e}_{k-n}^j]$$

$$\underline{\hat{m}}^*{}_k{}^T = [-\hat{\xi}_{k-1}^*, \ldots - \hat{\xi}_{k-n}^*, \hat{e}_{k-1}^*, \ldots, \hat{e}_{k-n}^*]$$

with the $\hat{\xi}^*{}_k$ and $\hat{e}^*{}_k$, values being the result of prefiltering $\hat{\xi}_k{}^j$ and $\hat{e}_k{}^j$ with $1/\hat{D}^{j-1}(z^{-1})$

$$\hat{e}_k{}^j = \hat{\xi}_k{}^j - \underline{\check{n}}_k{}^T \underline{\hat{c}}_k{}^j \qquad (3.155)$$

It is more cautious here to use a $\hat{c}_k{}^j$ which is the output of a recursive updating mechanism as presented in Section 3.2.4.4.

(iv) The final result $\underline{\hat{c}}_N{}^j$ is kept for the next stage as well as a value $\check{P}_M{}^j$

(v) Assigning initial values can be done in many ways, the most careful manner is to precede the IR–IV–AML with an I–IV–AML estimation session. One obtains an $\underline{\hat{a}}_0$, $\underline{\hat{c}}_0$ and values for the auxiliary model and prefilters. It is meaningful to keep $\hat{P}_0$ and $\check{P}_0$ at infinity. A quicker and often satisfactory technique is to use the first step of the I–IV–AML only for start-up.

The recursive or on-line form of the refined IV–AML:OLR–IV–AML

The iterative version of the refined IV–AML described above includes recursive parameter estimation at each iteration, but this recursive solution does not involve recursive updating of the prefilter and the auxiliary model parameters. A fully recursive solution, which does include such operations, is clearly feasible however, and it has maximum potential utility in on-line applications such as forecasting and adaptive control. In such a recursive algorithm auxiliary model parameters are updated in the same manner as in the iterative version, but updating takes place after each recursive step.

The algorithm has almost the same block diagram as the IR–IV–AML (Fig 3.8). Now the iterative update mechanism has to be replaced by a recursive update mechanism of the type described in Section 3.2.4.4. Then for each data point y_k, first the R–IV and then the R–AML algorithms are referred to. One has to start with an RLS period as before. It may be advisable to proceed then with an OL–IV–AML period before continuing with the full refined algorithm. If one considers the recursive updating mechanism, it becomes clear that quite a number of parameters have to be specified. Choosing these parameters is termed "tuning". In order to obtain good results, experience has shown that tuning sometimes has to be done carefully and the updating schemes may even need modifications – like introducing a fading memory factor.

Recent advances: the modified refined IV–AML procedure

In all the algorithms mentioned above the IV and AML computations remain the same. They differ in the choice of auxiliary model, prefilters and updating mechanisms. Taking into consideration, recent theoretical developments [204, 205] based on the fundamental work of Ljung [139], it would appear that certain improvements to the basic estimation procedure described above are possible. In the equations mentioned above, the P-matrix is not necessarily symmetric. Advantage may be obtained when the P-matrix is forced to be symmetric. Instead of (3.149–151) the following equations are used:

$$\hat{P}_k = \hat{P}_{k-1} - \hat{P}_{k-1}\underline{\hat{x}}^*_k[1 + \underline{\hat{x}}^*_k{}^T\hat{P}_{k-1}\underline{\hat{x}}^*_k]^{-1}\underline{\hat{x}}^*_k{}^T\hat{P}_{k-1} \tag{3.156}$$

$$\underline{k}_k = \hat{P}_k\underline{\hat{x}}^*_k \tag{3.157}$$

$$\underline{\hat{a}}_k = \underline{\hat{a}}_{k-1} - \underline{k}_k[\underline{z}^*_k{}^T.\underline{\hat{a}}_{k-1} - y^*_k] \tag{3.158}$$

And in the same way

$$\check{P}_k = \check{P}_{k-1} - \check{P}_{k-1}\underline{\hat{m}}^*_k[1 + \underline{\hat{m}}^*_k{}^T\check{P}_{k-1}\underline{\hat{m}}^*_k]^{-1}\underline{\hat{m}}^*_k{}^T\check{P}_{k-1} \tag{3.159}$$

$$\underline{k}_k = \check{P}_k\underline{\hat{m}}^*_k \tag{3.160}$$

$$\underline{\hat{c}}_k = \underline{\hat{c}}_{k-1} - \underline{k}_k[\underline{\check{n}}_k{}^T.\underline{\hat{c}}_{k-1} - \hat{\xi}_k] \tag{3.161}$$

With these equations one can build iterative modified refined IV–AML schemes (IMR–IV–AML) as well as on-line versions (OLMR–IV–AML).

3.2.4.9   *Practical and statistical considerations*

Practical considerations

The practical implementation issues are the same as for the IV–AML algorithm. Some comments are added on the average sample sizes that can be handled with the estimation schemes. These sizes are most easily expressed in terms of the number of parameters in the model. Low sample sizes have 1–25 times as many points as there are unknown model parameters. Intermediate sample sizes have 25–75 times as many points and high sample sizes more than 75–80 times as many points. These numbers serve as a reference for subsequent discussions concerning the properties of the algorithms.

Statistical considerations

Generalities on consistency and efficiency

Of importance here are the results of Pierce, Söderström, Ljung, Holst, Young and Jakeman [93, 181, 244]. Where the estimation problem is well posed in the sense mentioned in Section 3.2.2.2, non-consistency of the R–IV will be extremely rare, the R–AML scheme will fail in certain rare circumstances to converge completely on the true values. The MR–IV, and especially the MR–AML, should have superior convergence properties. In short, refined algorithms improve convergency and modified ones do even better. From the point of view of efficiency a Monte Carlo analysis indicates that the results are almost always an improvement on the equivalent IV–AML results, though these improvements are sometimes quite small and rarely large. The experiments suggest that the R–IV–AML does not perform so well, with regard to the estimation of the noise model parameters, as it does for the process model parameters. For small and moderate sample size, the estimates quite often appear to be biased and the minimum error variance is not achieved; indeed it is only for large sample sizes that the algorithm seems to achieve anything like optimum performance. The modified refined IV–AML shows an average superior performance with regard to the statistical properties of the estimates. It is necessary, however, to give a caveat for the modified version. In practice, problems have occurred when the sample size to the number of unknown parameters is very low (< 5). When there is a paucity of data the classic algorithm may out-perform the modified form.

All the findings apply to the iterative case, the on-line case has not yet been studied in detail.

The parameter error covariance matrix

As mentioned in Section 3.2.4.6, it is always useful to have an estimate for the precision with which the parameters have been obtained. For the IV–AML estimates, only a heuristic argument could be given for a relationship between the parameter error covariance matrices and the $\hat{P}$, respectively $\check{P}$ matrices. Fortunately, Pierce [181] has provided a theorem which yields a better insight.

Theorem: Given the model under study here with

e_k: independent and identically distributed random variables with mean zero, variance σ^2, skewness κ_1, and kurtosis κ_2.

Suppose the estimation problem is well posed (see section 3.2.2.2) then the ML estimates $\hat{a}_N$, $\hat{c}_N$, $\hat{\sigma}_N^2$ obtained from a data set of N samples possess the following properties:

1—The limiting distribution of the estimates is Gaussian

2—The mean for $\hat{\underline{a}}_N$, $N \rightarrow \infty$ is $\underline{a}$, the covariance

$$P^{*1} = \frac{\sigma^2}{N} \left[\lim_p \frac{1}{N} \sum \hat{\underline{x}}^*_k \hat{\underline{x}}^{*T}_k \right]^{-1}$$

3—The estimate $\hat{\underline{C}}_N$ is asymptotically independent of $\hat{\underline{a}}_N$, its mean for $N \rightarrow \infty$ is $\underline{c}$, the covariance

$$P^{*2} = \frac{\sigma^2}{N} [E\{\hat{\underline{m}}^*_k \hat{\underline{m}}^{*T}_k\}]^{-1}$$

4—The estimate $\hat{\sigma}^2$ has a mean value σ^2 and variance $(2\sigma^4/N(1 + 1/2\ \kappa_2))$ and is independent of $\hat{\underline{c}}$ and $\hat{\underline{a}}$, if $\kappa_1 = 0$

Remark: $\hat{\underline{x}}^*_k$, $\hat{\underline{m}}^*_k$ are the values obtained whenever the auxiliary model, the inverse noise model and the prefilter parameters were all set at values based on the true model parameters $\underline{a}$ and $\underline{c}$.

It is seen that in the limit

$$P^{*1} \approx \hat{\sigma}^2 \hat{P} \tag{3.162}$$

$$P^{*2} \approx \hat{\sigma}^2 \check{P} \tag{3.163}$$

In case of a finite sample size, the best procedure to obtain a good estimate for P^{*1}, P^{*2} is to set all filters to the final parameter values and perform a last run with the MR–IV–AML and $\hat{P}_0 = I_\infty$, $\check{P}_0 = I_\infty$ as initial conditions. Monte Carlo analysis has shown that (3.162) is fairly correct, even for smaller sample sizes as well as for R–IV–AML as MR–IV–AML. For the noise model (3.163) will only hold for rather large sample sizes. In the other cases (3.163) is only an approximation, however, almost always $\hat{\sigma}^2 \check{P}$ is larger than P^{*2} and so the estimate is a safe one. For on-line purposes equations (3.162), (3.163) can be computed on-line, but they will provide crude estimates as long as the algorithm proceeds through the early estimation phase.

3.2.4.10   Extensions

Varying parameters

The whole parameter estimation scheme assumes the validity of a linear stochastic model of the type presented in Section 3.2.4.1. In initial stages of the model-building process, the choice of such a model may be hypothetical. As mentioned before, the recursivity concept may at least be used to check the hypothesis by scrutinizing the appearance of the function representing the parameter estimates. The IV–AML algorithms are not directly applicable for that purpose, as they have been derived under the assumption of constant parameters.

It is possible to account in a heuristic manner for varying parameters. The core of the IV and AML computational technique is a RLS-type set of equations. It is straightforward to replace these equations by the modified forms presented in section 3.2.3.5. Solutions presented there can easily be incorporated in the algorithms presented here. These modified algorithms have not been analysed theoretically, but experience has indicated their usefulness.

Careful readers will come up with an important implementation question. They will have observed that the algorithms advocated in the present section can only be directly implemented with the OL–IV–AML scheme. Indeed the auxiliary model and the inverse noise model require to be continuously updated as the parameters are allowed to vary. It is, however, conceivable to work in an iterative manner, while parameter profiles are prepared at the end of each iteration for the next run. As far as is known by the authors, up to now no iterative procedures have been suggested in that context.

3.2.5   Estimation of Dynamic Systems: the MIMO Case

Multi-input–multi-output systems are inherently more difficult to handle. The basic reason is the structurally more complex nature of the models. This means that it is much more difficult to propose a suitable model form so that the parameters can be estimated, while their number is kept minimal in order to achieve high parameter estimation efficiency. The parameter estimation algorithms themselves can easily be extended to the multivariable case. For straightforward multivariable model forms the Refined Instrumental Variable–Approximate Maximum Likelihood Estimators will be presented.

3.2.5.1   The MIMO-models

A straightforward extension of the model (3.21) is the following

$$A(z^{-1})\ \underline{x}_k = B(z^{-1})\ \underline{u}_k$$
$$C(z^{-1})\underline{\xi}_k = D(z^{-1})\underline{e}_k \qquad\qquad (3.164)$$
$$\underline{y}_k = \underline{x}_k + \underline{\xi}_k$$

with $\underline{y}_k$, $\underline{x}_k$, $\underline{\xi}_k$, $\underline{e}_k$: p-dimensional vectors

$\qquad \underline{u}_k \qquad\qquad$: m-dimensional input vector

$\qquad A(z^{-1}) = I + A_1 z^{-1} + A_2 z^{-2} + \ldots + A_n z^{-n}$

$\qquad B(z^{-1}) = B_0 + B_1 z^{-1} + B_2 z^{-2} + \ldots + B_n z^{-n}$

$\qquad C(z^{-1}) = I + C_1 z^{-1} + C_2 z^{-2} + \ldots + C_n z^{-n}$

$\qquad D(z^{-1}) = I + D_1 z^{-1} + D_2 z^{-2} + \ldots + D_n z^{-n}$

$\qquad A_i, C_i, D_i$: pxp-matrices; B_i : pxm-matrices.

Another useful MIMO model is the ARMAX model characterized by $C(z^{-1}) = I$. A discussion concerning the relationship between the ARMAX model and model (3.164) is similar as in the SISO case (Section 3.1.2.2.).

3.2.5.2   The multivariable R–IV–AML-algorithm

For the model (3.164), the refined instrumental variable, approximate maximum likelihood approach can be easily developed. The major effort goes into building the appropriate vectors. Any of the matrices of the model can be thought to be built up of vectors: $B_i = [\underline{b}_{i1}, \underline{b}_{i2}, \underline{b}_{i3}, \ldots, \underline{b}_{im}]$. Then two vectors $\underline{a}$ and $\underline{c}$ are made by stacking all the vectors which define the matrices:

$$\underline{a}^T = [a_{11}{}^T, a_{12}{}^T, \ldots, a_{1p}{}^T, a_{21}{}^T, \ldots, a_{np}{}^T, b_{o1}{}^T, \ldots, b_{om}{}^T, b_{11}{}^T, \ldots,$$
$$b_{1m}{}^T, \ldots, b_{nm}{}^T]$$

$$\underline{c}^T = [c_{11}{}^T, c_{12}{}^T, \ldots, c_{1p}{}^T, c_{21}{}^T, \ldots, c_{np}{}^T, d_{11}{}^T, d_{12}{}^T, \ldots, d_{1p}{}^T,$$
$$d_{21}{}^T, \ldots, d_{np}{}^T]$$

These vectors have to be multiplied with the proper delayed values of the outputs, inputs, etc. In order to be able to use suitable shorthand notations, matrices are defined:

$$Y_k = I_p \oplus \underline{y}_k{}^T$$
$$U_k = I_p \oplus \underline{u}_k{}^T$$
$$\hat{X}_k = I_p \oplus \underline{\hat{x}}_k$$

$\oplus$ is the Kronecker product: each element of the second matrix is replaced by the first matrix multiplied by the element itself. An example clarifies the definition. Suppose

$$p = 2 \text{ and } \underline{y}_k^T = [y_k^1, y_k^2] \text{ then } I_p \oplus \underline{y}_k^T \text{ is:}$$

$$[I_p y_k^1 \quad I_p y_k^2] = \begin{bmatrix} y_k^1 & 0 & y_k^2 & 0 \\ 0 & y_k^1 & 0 & y_k^2 \end{bmatrix}$$

$\hat{x}_k$ is defined as the output of an auxiliary filter:

$$\hat{A}(z^{-1})\underline{\hat{x}}_k = \hat{B}(z^{-1})\underline{u}_k$$

Filtered variables are defined too:

$$\underline{y}^*_k : \hat{A}(z^{-1})\,\tilde{\underline{y}}_k = \underline{y}_k \quad \hat{D}(z^{-1})\,\underline{y}^*_k = \hat{C}(z^{-1})\,\tilde{\underline{y}}_k$$

$$\underline{u}^*_k : \hat{A}(z^{-1})\,\tilde{\underline{u}}_k = \underline{u}_k \quad \hat{D}(z^{-1})\,\underline{u}^*_k = \hat{C}(z^{-1})\,\tilde{\underline{u}}_k$$

$$\underline{\hat{x}}^*_k : \hat{A}(z^{-1})\,\tilde{\underline{x}}_k = \underline{\hat{x}}_k \quad \hat{D}(z^{-1})\,\underline{\hat{x}}^*_k = \hat{C}(z^{-1})\,\tilde{\underline{x}}_k$$

Out of these, one constructs:

$$Y^*_k = I_p \oplus \underline{y}^*_k$$
$$U^*_k = I_p \oplus \underline{u}^*_k$$
$$\hat{X}^*_k = I_p \oplus \underline{\hat{x}}^*_k$$

Then still larger matrices are built:

$$Z^*_k{}^T = [-Y^*_{k-1} - \ldots - Y^*_{k-n}, U^*_k \ldots U^*_{k-n}]$$

$$\hat{X}^*_k = [-\hat{X}^*_{k-1} - \ldots - \hat{X}^*_{k-n}, U^*_k \ldots U^*_{k-n}]^T$$

It can be shown [243] that, if Q is the covariance matrix of the white noise, the refined IV-solution to estimate $\underline{a}$ is given by

$$\left[\sum_k \hat{X}^*_k Q^{-1} Z^*_k{}^T\right]\underline{\hat{a}} = \sum_k \hat{X}^*_k Q^{-1}\underline{y}^*_k$$

It is by no means difficult to deduce that a suitable recursive estimation algorithm has the form

$$\underline{\hat{a}}_k = \underline{\hat{a}}_{k-1} - \hat{P}^{*1}_{k-1} \cdot \hat{X}^*_k [\hat{Q}_{k-1} + Z^*_k{}^T \cdot \hat{P}^{*1}_{k-1} \cdot \hat{X}^*_k]^{-1}(Z^*_k{}^T \cdot \underline{\hat{a}}_{k-1} - \underline{y}^*_k)$$

$$\hat{P}^{*1}_k = \hat{P}^{*1}_{k-1} - \hat{P}^{*1}_{k-1} \cdot \hat{X}^*_k[\hat{Q}_{k-1} + Z^*_k{}^T \cdot \hat{P}^{*1}_{k-1} \cdot \hat{X}^*_k]^{-1}Z^*_k{}^T \cdot \hat{P}^{*1}_{k-1}$$

$$(3.165)$$

$$\hat{Q}_k = \hat{Q}_{k-1} + \frac{1}{k}[\hat{e}_k \cdot \hat{e}_k{}^T - \hat{Q}_{k-1}]$$

Note that a matrix inversion is now required; the dimension of this matrix is small compared to the dimension of the $\hat{P}^{*1}$ matrix. Notice also that modified versions can easily be written down.

In a similar way, the estimation of the noise model can be considered. Define

$$\Xi_k = I_p \oplus \underline{\xi}_k^T$$
$$E_k = I_p \oplus \underline{e}_k^T$$
$$\hat{D}^{-1}(z^{-1})\underline{\xi}_k = \underline{\xi}^*_k$$
$$\hat{D}^{-1}(z^{-1})\underline{e}_k = \underline{e}^*_k$$
$$\Xi^*_k = I_p \oplus \underline{\xi}^*_k{}^T$$
$$E^*_k = I_p \oplus \underline{e}^*_k{}^T$$
$$N_k^T = [-\Xi_k, \ldots -\Xi_{k-n}, E_{k-1}, \ldots, E_{k-n}]$$
$$M_k = [-\Xi^*_k, \ldots -\Xi^*_{k-n}, E^*_{k-1}, \ldots, E^*_{k-n}]^T$$

The $\underline{c}$ vector, defined in a similar manner as the $\underline{a}$ vector, can be estimated as follows:

$$\left(\sum_k M_k Q^{-1} N_k^T\right) \hat{\underline{c}} = \sum_k M_k Q^{-1} \underline{\xi}_k \tag{3.166}$$

A recursive estimator can be obtained with estimates for its components

$$\hat{\underline{\xi}}_k = \underline{y}_k - \hat{\underline{x}}_k$$
$$\hat{D}(z^{-1})\hat{\underline{e}}_k = \hat{C}(z^{-1})\hat{\underline{\xi}}_k \text{ or } \hat{\underline{e}}_k = \hat{\underline{\xi}}_k - \hat{N}_k^T \hat{\underline{c}}_k$$
$$\hat{\underline{c}}_k = \hat{\underline{c}}_{k-1} - \hat{P}^{*2}_{k-1} \cdot \hat{M}_k [\hat{Q}_{k-1} + \hat{N}_k^T \cdot \hat{P}^{*2}_{k-1} \cdot \hat{M}_k]^{-1} \{\hat{N}_k^T \cdot \hat{\underline{c}}_{k-1} - \hat{\underline{\xi}}_k\}$$
$$\hat{P}^*_k{}^2 = \hat{P}^{*2}_{k-1} - \hat{P}^{*2}_{k-1} \cdot \hat{M}_k [\hat{Q}_{k-1} + \hat{N}_k^T \cdot \hat{P}^{*2}_{k-1} \cdot \hat{M}_k]^{-1} \hat{N}_k \cdot \hat{P}^{*2}_{k-1}$$
$$\hat{Q}_k = \hat{Q}_{k-1} + \frac{1}{k} [\hat{\underline{e}}_k \hat{\underline{e}}_k^T - \hat{Q}_{k-1}] \tag{3.167}$$

In the same way as for the SISO case, an iterative version as well as a purely recursive or on-line version of the algorithm can be obtained. Estimation algorithms for the ARMAX model can be obtained by simplifying the estimation equations.

3.2.5.3 *Properties and discussions*

From the parameter estimation point of view, the results are very similar to the SISO case. The results of Pierce [181] can be extended to the multivariable situation:

(a) the asymptotic covariance matrix of the estimation errors for the

ML-estimate $\hat{\underline{a}}$ of the parameter vector $\underline{a}$ is of the form

$$P^{*1} = \frac{1}{T}\left[\lim\left\{\frac{1}{T}\sum_k X^*_k Q^{-1}X^*_k{}^T\right\}\right]^{-1}$$

(b) the asymptotic covariance matrix of the estimation errors associated with the ML estimate $\hat{\underline{c}}$ of the parameter vector $\underline{c}$ is of the form:

$$P^{*2} = \frac{1}{T}[E\{M_k Q^{-1}M_k{}^T\}]^{-1}$$

Here X^*_k and M_k are defined as the values of these variables which would result if the auxiliary model, inverse noise model and prefilter parameters were all set to values based on the true model parameters $\underline{a}$ and $\underline{c}$. The significance of these results are obvious if the refined IV–AML converge to the ML estimates, then $\hat{P}^{*1}_k$ and $\hat{P}^{*2}_k$ will provide good estimates of the covariance matrices P^{*1} and P^{*2} respectively. Monte Carlo simulations have been performed by Young and Jakeman [111]. For small and moderate sample sizes, the basic system model parameters are estimated very well. The predictions for the standard errors on the parameter estimates may be twice as large as the values computed on theoretical grounds especially in the small sample case. The parameters of the noise model are not so well estimated. Bias may occur, the estimates of the variances are often too large, and, as can be expected, in the large sample case the estimates are better.

At first sight it may appear that for the multivariable case the parameter estimation problem is solved in a satisfactory manner, at least from the practical point of view. In fact, this is only approximately true. Questions remain related to the choice of the MIMO model. The models presented here, are straightforward extensions of the SISO models. Unfortunately, they are seldom parametrically efficient. The number of parameters may be unnecessarily large as the degrees of the polynomials grow. As a consequence, accuracy of the estimates based on a finite sample size may be in jeopardy. Basically the problem of suitable model representation is a structural one and will be discussed later. Only recently has parameter estimation for MIMO systems been seen in the light of efficient model structures, and new developments can still be expected here.

3.2.6 Continuous-time models

For certain applications, a model may be discrete-time, even if the real-life system is continuous-time. This is often the case in engineering applications, where the model is to be used in a digital computer. In other cases, the continuous-time features of the real system cannot be completely neglected. There are basically two ways that can be followed. Continuous-time versions of estimation schemes are developed so that the algorithms match the nature of the system. Comparatively little research has been done on this approach. The other procedure is to process the data in a discrete-time manner, while somewhere the translation of continuous-time to discrete-time is done. A limited amount of research seems to have been conducted on the most appropriate manner to carry out the discrete-time step. We briefly state some useful techniques, always assuming that eventual sampling has been performed at frequencies higher ($\approx 10x$ or more) than the Shannon frequency (twice the highest frequency component in the signal), but not so high that numerical problems occur.

A first technique consists in writing the state–space representation of the model and approximating the derivative by a suitable difference formula. The parameters of the true model will relate to those of the discrete-time version and the latter ones can be estimated with the techniques mentioned in this chapter.

A more careful approach is to derive the discrete-time model which yields the same output as the sampled output of the continuous-time model. Consider for example the state–space model

$$\dot{\underline{x}} = A\underline{x} + B\underline{u}$$
$$\underline{y} = C\underline{x}$$
(3.168)

The solution of (3.168) is

$$\underline{x}(t) = e^{A(t-t_0)} \cdot \underline{x}_0 + \int_{t_0}^{t} e^{A(t-\tau)}B\underline{u}(\tau)\, d\tau$$

Take $t = t_{k+1}$, $t_0 = t_k$, then

$$\underline{x}(t_{k+1}) = e^{A(t_{k+1}-t_k)}\underline{x}(t_k) + \int_{t_k}^{t_{k+1}} e^{A(t-\tau)}B\underline{u}(\tau)\, d\tau$$

$$y(t_{k+1}) = C\underline{x}(t_{k+1})$$

If the input is constant between sampling intervals and the sampling interval is T:

$$\underline{x}_{k+1} = e^{AT}\underline{x}_k + \int_{t_k}^{t_k+T} e^{A(t-\tau)}B\, d\tau \cdot \underline{u}_k = A'\underline{x}_k + B'\underline{u}_k$$

$$\underline{y}_{k+1} = C\underline{x}_{k+1}$$
(3.169)

(3.169) is a discrete version of the initial model.

A second approach sticks to the continuous model to a certain point, but performs the typical estimation algorithms in discrete time. It is sometimes referred to as continuous-discrete analysis. Young gives an implementation for the refined IV–AML technique.

It is assumed that input and output y(t) and u(t) are available in continuous-time form. A suitable sampling frequency is chosen. The model is thought to be made up of a continuous-time deterministic part $X(s)/U(s) = A(s)/B(s)$ and a discrete-time noise model part $\xi/e = D(z^{-1})/C(z^{-1})$. In that manner analytical problems with continuous white noise are avoided. The R–AML part of the estimator remains the same. The R–IV part is similar to its discrete counterpart with the exception of the definition of z^*_k and $\hat{x}^*_k$. These vectors are not made up of delayed samples of input and output. Instead they are:

$$\underline{z}^{*\,T}_k = [-y^*_{1k}, -y^*_{2k}, \ldots -y^*_{nk}, u^*_{0k}, \ldots, u^*_{nk}]$$
$$\underline{\hat{x}}^{*\,T}_k = [-\hat{x}^*_{1k}, -\hat{x}^*_{2k}, \ldots -\hat{x}^*_{nk}, u^*_{0k}, \ldots, u^*_{nk}]$$

where y_{ij} means the value of the i-th derivative of y at the j-th sampling instant.

To obtain these values the data-filtering shown on Fig. 3.9 is required. The auxiliary model and the filter part $1/A(s)$ work in continuous time. This means that integration is performed in the digital machine with sufficiently small steps. At the same time the derivatives are generated. The obtained variables are $\tilde{u}_0, \tilde{u}_1, \ldots, \tilde{u}_n, \tilde{y}_0, \tilde{y}_1, \ldots, \tilde{y}_n, \tilde{x}_0, \ldots, \tilde{x}_n$, with $\sim$ meaning partly filtered. These variables are sampled and then fed into the discrete-time part of the prefilters $\hat{C}(z^{-1})/\hat{D}(z^{-1})$. From there on everything is carried on in discrete time. Young reports practical application results [246].

As far as is known, little analysis has been done to investigate how the discrete-time procedure is most appropriately done. The principles are applicable for the multivariate case too.

3.2.7 Parameter estimation in general

3.2.7.1 Introduction

There are different approaches to the parameter estimation problem. The purely statistical point of view is the classic one. It sets the problem in a framework that reveals the relationships between many different techniques. Unfortunately, the approach is theoretically quite involved, it requires a considerable number of assumptions, and it does not consider the aspects of computation and approximation. From a more modern point of view, parameter determination is looked upon as an optimization of well-defined cost functions. The optimum is said to be the best approximation and the computational aspects of finding extremes are even better known.

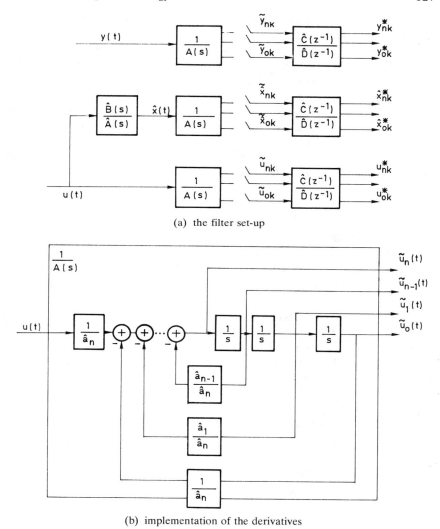

(a) the filter set-up

(b) implementation of the derivatives

FIG. 3.9 Data filtering for the R–IV on continuous-time models

Clearly, both approaches seem to complement one another. Here the second one will be stressed as the problem is looked upon by a mathematical model-builder. For him, the goal of the modelling effort is particularly important. The cost function that is optimized in order to find the parameters, should be related, albeit in an indirect way, to the goals of the modelling enterprise. It will further be assumed that the reader has sufficient statistical background to be able to grasp the statistical aspects of the estimation procedures.

Up to now, specific modelling goals have never been taken directly into account. It is believed that a useful model is a model which faithfully represents the real-world system. Therefore, an error function $\varepsilon(\underline{p}, k)$ is chosen, which is thought to reflect the discrepancy between representation and real system. A cost or objective function is then a function of the error and the best choice of the parameters is a choice which makes the objective function extreme.

The various estimation techniques can be classified according to the choice of the error and objective function.

3.2.7.2   The objective function

A very general definition proceeds as follows:

Define a function l from $R \times R_{n_p} \times R_{n_\varepsilon} \rightarrow r \times r$ symmetric matrices; n_p is the number of parameters and n_ε the dimension of the error.

Form a matrix Q_N

$$Q_N(\underline{p}) = \frac{1}{N} \sum_{k=1}^{N} l(k, \underline{p}, \varepsilon(\underline{p}, k)) \tag{3.170}$$

Note that (3.170) holds for the discrete case. It is straightforward to define a continuous-time version of (3.170).

Finally the cost or objective function is a scalar function of Q_N:

$$J(\underline{p}) = h(Q_N(\underline{p})) \tag{3.171}$$

One is not completely free in choosing the functions l and h. They have to be defined in such a way that the parameter estimation problem remains well posed and meaningful. Ljung [141] has investigated these conditions. For $h(\cdot)$, it often must hold that

$$\text{trace } Q > 0 \Rightarrow h(\Lambda + Q) > h(\Lambda) \tag{3.172}$$

with Q : symmetric positive semidefinite
     Λ : strictly positive definite

$h(Q) = \det Q$ satisfies condition (3.172).

A somewhat stronger condition is:

$$h(A) > h(B) \Leftrightarrow \text{trace } (A) > \text{trace } (B) \tag{3.173}$$

A, B : symmetric positive semidefinite

$h(Q) = \text{trace } (Q)$ satisfies (3.173), but $h(Q) = \det Q$ does not satisfy the latter condition.

The conditions on l are more involved. They depend on the distribution of the errors $\underline{\varepsilon}(p, k)$. There are however some common choices for l.

A quadratic objective function

$$l(k, \underline{p}, \underline{\varepsilon}) = \underline{\varepsilon}^T(k, \underline{p}) \cdot \underline{\varepsilon}(k, \underline{p}) \text{ and } h(Q) = Q \qquad (3.174)$$

$$l(k, \underline{p}, \underline{\varepsilon}) = \underline{\varepsilon}(k, \underline{p}) \cdot \underline{\varepsilon}^T(k, \underline{p}) \text{ and } h(Q) = \text{trace } (Q) \qquad (3.175)$$

A weighted norm objective function

$$l(k, \underline{p}, \underline{\varepsilon}) = \underline{\varepsilon}^T(k, \underline{p}) \cdot R(k) \cdot \underline{\varepsilon}(k, \underline{p}) \qquad h(Q) = Q \qquad (3.176)$$

An objective function derived from the maximum likelihood under Gaussian conditions

$$l(k, \underline{p}, \varepsilon) = \underline{\varepsilon}^T(k, \underline{p}) \cdot \Lambda(\underline{p}) \cdot \underline{\varepsilon}(k, \underline{p}) + \log \det \Lambda(\underline{p}) \qquad h(Q) = Q$$
$$(3.177)$$

A robust objective function

$$l(k, \underline{p}, \varepsilon) = \alpha(\underline{\varepsilon}^T(k, \underline{p}) \cdot \underline{\varepsilon}(k, \underline{p})) \qquad h(Q) = Q \qquad (3.178)$$
$$\alpha(k)/k \to 0 \qquad k \to \infty$$

It is simple to reformulate these definitions for the continuous-time case.

If the errors are assumed to be Gaussian with zero mean and covariance $\Lambda(\underline{p})$, maximizing the likelihood corresponds to minimizing (3.171) with (3.177). If $\Lambda(\underline{p}) \equiv \sigma^2 I$, criterion (3.177) reduces to (3.174), known as the least squares criterion; (3.176) is the generalized least squares criterion.

For certain modelling problems it may happen that the errors are not normally distributed and that the distribution function is known. Under such conditions, the maximum likelihood principle may be used to derive a proper objective function that is fitted to the case in hand. In most cases, the precise nature of the error distribution will not be known. It may happen, however, that certain characteristics of the error distribution can be derived a priori. Suppose that the distribution has heavy tails when compared with the normal distribution. It may then be expected that, compared to a Gaussian random vector, some samples behave like "outliers". The objective function of type (3.174–177) may yield poor estimation results. A statistically more sensible approach consists in using a more robust objective function (3.178), which will prevent the "outliers" from causing trouble.

3.2.7.3 The error

Some often occurring definitions for the error are

The output error

Output error methods define the error in a way shown on Fig. 3.10 for the SISO case.

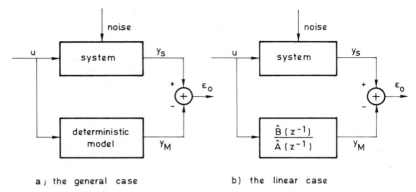

a) the general case   b) the linear case

FIG. 3.10   The output error for a SISO-system

The system output $y_S(t)$ or $y_S(k)$ is compared with the output of a deterministic model: $y_M(t)$ or $y_M(k)$. For the linear discrete-time case:

$$y_M(k) = \frac{\hat{B}(z^{-1})}{\hat{A}(z^{-1})} u_k \qquad (3.179)$$

The output error definition is extremely natural, in the sense that one expects the model output to behave like the system output. Minimizing a cost based on the output error is not a simple matter, as the unknown parameters will, even in the linear case, appear in a non-linear fashion in the objective function. Nevertheless, the approach has attracted a wide number of investigators (see Young [245]). Convergence of the estimation schemes has been thoroughly studied. Unfortunately, the approach has its limitations. It is most useful in the deterministic case when the noise level is considered low or in the stochastic case without process noise and with white observation noise. If the noise is of a more general nature as for the models (3.20) and (3.21), output error identification schemes will yield biased parameter estimates, even under Gaussian noise. Thus the output error methods have to be avoided or used with care.

The equation error

The use of an equation error follows from the observation that a linear relationship between the parameters and the error can be extremely useful from the computational point of view. This is because linear regression techniques are simple and well known.

To obtain such suitable error, the input and the output are transformed by model parts (Fig. 3.11). For the linear SISO case:

$$\varepsilon_k = \hat{A}(z^{-1}) y_k - \hat{B}(z^{-1}) u_k \qquad (3.180)$$

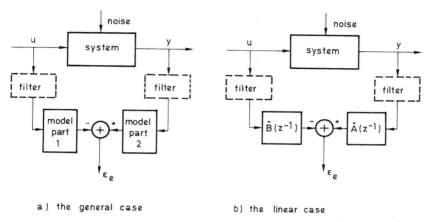

a) the general case   b) the linear case

Fig. 3.11   The equation-error for a SISO system

The set-up will require differentiation of the signals in the continuous–time case. As this operation is hazardous under noisy conditions, filters are added. One generally speaks of a "generalized equation error". The equation error approach may be often useful: it is computationally advantageous but will result in biased estimates as soon as the noise is of a more general nature that does not correspond with a "white" equation error. That will be the case for models (3.20) and (3.21).

The prediction error

In many cases the white noise sequence does not simply add to the output or to the model equation. One has to consider not only the deterministic part of the system description, but the complete stochastic model. A suitable error results from the prediction of the output based on the total model (Fig. 3.12a). For the linear model, the prediction error ε_p is shown in Fig. 3.12b; the output error ε_0 and equation error ε_c are also indicated.

$$\varepsilon_p = \frac{\hat{C}(z^{-1})}{\hat{D}(z^{-1})}\, y_k - \frac{\hat{C}(z^{-1})}{\hat{D}(z^{-1})}\, \frac{\hat{B}(z^{-1})}{\hat{A}(z^{-1})}\, u_k \qquad (3.181)$$

Other errors

Previously mentioned errors have, or could have, been chosen on purely heuristic grounds. A more theoretical approach towards a useful error is based on statistical or theoretical information grounds. The maximum likelihood technique is by far the most popular method for estimating parameters in dynamic systems. The precise nature of the important errors

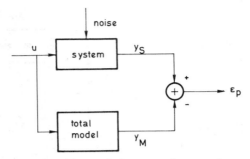

FIG. 3.12a   The prediction error: the general case

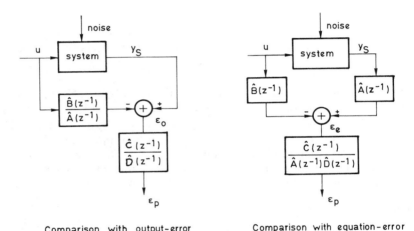

Comparison with output-error   Comparison with equation-error

FIG. 3.12b   The prediction error: the linear case

and the objective function depend on the kind of model and the assumptions concerning the distribution of the noise.

3.2.7.4   *Off-line parameter estimation methods*

A parameter estimation method is completely defined by:
 – an error function;
 – an objective function;
 – an optimization scheme.
In some very special cases the optimization can be done at least for a part analytically. In most cases a numerical procedure is required. In the off-line approach all data points are available at computation time. Though the measurements can be processed recursively, they can also be treated en

bloc. If no analytical en bloc solution is available, numerical techniques are required to optimize the objective function. This is the basic problem addressed by the applied mathematical branch of non-linear programming.

The available algorithms are manifold: random search, shooting methods, relaxation techniques, steepest descent, conjugate directions, Newton–Raphson, etc. An interested reader should refer to the literature [109, 151]. The en bloc approach may be interesting if rather few data points are available, or if one intends to try out several objective functions. This text focuses on recursive algorithms for parameter estimation. Of course, the recursive approach can also be applied off-line.

3.2.8 Recursive parameter estimation methods in general

Recursive estimation has developed in a separate domain. The algorithms have different origins. Some have been obtained from an off-line parameter estimation scheme. This is the approach adopted in Sections 3.2.3–3.2.4. Another source of useful algorithms has been the field of "stochastic approximation" [56]. Finally, a number of schemes have been developed in the context of non-linear filtering. Recently Ljung [147] has given a more unified treatment of recursive parameter estimation in general.

3.2.8.1 *A numerical technique for optimizing a cost*

In Section 3.2.3.1, a simple numerical technique was given for finding a zero of a function. This same technique can be used to optimize a cost. Consider for simplicity a function of one variable $x : t(x)$. A necessary condition for an optimum is:

$$f(x) = \frac{dt(x)}{dx} = 0$$

As seen before, a numerical scheme for finding a zero of $f(x)$ is given by

$$x_{k+1} = x_k - \alpha \frac{f(x_k)}{f'(x_k)} = x_k - \alpha f'^{-1}(x_k)f(x_k)$$

In terms of the function to be minimized, one has:

$$x_{k+1} = x_k - \alpha t''^{-1}(x_k)t'(x_k) \qquad (3.182)$$

For the multi-dimensional case (3.182) becomes:

$$\underline{x}_{k+1} = \underline{x}_k - \alpha H^{-1}(\underline{x}_k)\underline{g}(\underline{x}_k) \qquad (3.183)$$

$H(\underline{x}_k)$: Hessian or matrix of second derivatives.
$\underline{g}(\underline{x}_k)$: gradient.

Algorithm (3.183) is known as a Newton–Raphson algorithm for optimizing a function. Computation of the Hessian may be very difficult and often an approximation is used for this matrix. A particular approximation gives rise to algorithms known as Gauss–Newton algorithms. It is shown in the sequel that almost all recursive identification schemes are of the Gauss–Newton type.

3.2.8.2   A basic scheme: the Gauss–Newton algorithm

In search of consistency and convergence results, Ljung has performed pioneering work in unifying different recursive parameter estimation schemes [143, 144, 148].

A first class of such algorithms are the prediction error schemes. The basic idea consists in seeing a mathematical representation as a means towards prediction of the future. A model permits an educated guess for an output to come, based on the available past history. More specifically, at a certain instant k, one will observe an output $y(k)$. Before the actual observation, one has available all previous inputs $\underline{u}(k-1)$, $\underline{u}(k-2)$, ..., $\underline{u}(0)$ and all previous outputs $y(k-1)$, $y(k-2)$, ...,$y(0)$. This whole past, and eventually the present input $\underline{u}(k)$, can be used to make, with the help of a model, a prediction for the output $y(k)$ at time k. This prediction is represented by $\hat{y}(k)$ or $\hat{y}_k$. In fact, the prediction $\hat{y}_k$, could be a complicated function of y_{k-1}, y_{k-2}, ..., y_0, $\underline{u}_{k-1}$, ..., $\underline{u}_0$.

In the context of model-building, it may be assumed that there exists a relationship between input and output. Then this relationship or model can be used to make a prediction. In the sequel, the model will be thought to be linear. As a consequence, the prediction itself can be seen as the output of the following linear filter

$$\underline{\varphi}(k+1, \underline{p}) = A(\underline{p})\underline{\varphi}(k, \underline{p}) + B(\underline{p}) \left(\begin{matrix} y(k) \\ \underline{u}(k) \end{matrix} \right) \tag{3.184}$$

$$\hat{y}(k, \underline{p}) \qquad = C(\underline{p})\underline{\varphi}(k, \underline{p}) \tag{3.185}$$

This will become more clear as soon as some specific examples are worked out in detail.

As for off-line estimation algorithms, a recursive estimation technique is defined by an objective function, a suitable error and a numerical optimization scheme. Prediction error methods are characterized by an error of the type:

$$\underline{\varepsilon}(k, \underline{p}) = \underline{y}(k) - \hat{\underline{y}}(k, \underline{p}) = \underline{y}_k - \hat{\underline{y}}_k$$

A suitable cost will be a function of $\underline{\varepsilon}(k, \underline{p})$ according to the considerations of Section 3.2.7.2. An algorithm for optimizing the objective function is derived from the Newton–Raphson procedure (3.183), which for the unknown parameter vector becomes:

$$\underline{p}_{k+1} = \underline{p}_k - \alpha(k)H^{-1}(\underline{p}_k)\underline{g}(\underline{p}_k)$$

A major problem is the determination of the H and $\underline{g}$ functions.

A number of well known and familiar recursive estimation algorithms follow from the classic quadratic cost:

$$l(k, \underline{p}, \underline{\varepsilon}) = \underline{\varepsilon}^T(k, \underline{p}) \cdot \underline{\varepsilon}(k, \underline{p})$$

They differ in the choice and implementation of H and $\underline{g}$. With these considerations, it is seen that they are all basically similar: they have the same cost and the same numerical scheme.

For ease in presentation, the objective function J($\underline{p}$) is defined as:

$$J(\underline{p}) = 1/2 \, E(\underline{\varepsilon}^T \cdot \underline{\varepsilon}) \tag{3.186}$$

It is easy to see that (3.174) is an approximation of (3.186). The particular choice for J(p) is not essential. The derivative can be computed.

$$\frac{\partial J}{\partial \underline{p}} = E\left[\frac{\partial \underline{\varepsilon}^T}{\partial \underline{p}} \cdot \underline{\varepsilon}\right] = -E\left[\frac{\partial \hat{\underline{y}}^T(k, \underline{p})}{\partial \underline{p}} \cdot \underline{\varepsilon}(k, \underline{p})\right]$$

$$\left(\frac{\partial \hat{\underline{y}}_k^T}{\partial \underline{p}}\right)^T = \left[\frac{\partial \hat{\underline{y}}}{\partial p_1}, \frac{\partial \hat{\underline{y}}}{\partial p_2}, \ldots, \frac{\partial \hat{\underline{y}}}{\partial p_{n_p}}\right] = \left[\underline{\psi}_1, \underline{\psi}_2, \underline{\psi}_3, \ldots\right] = \Psi_k^T \tag{3.187}$$

For the stochastic version of (3.187), the gradient can be taken to be

$$\underline{g}(\underline{p}_k) = -\Psi_k \underline{\varepsilon}_k \tag{3.188}$$

The matrix of second derivatives is

$$\frac{\partial^2 J}{\partial \underline{p} \cdot \partial \underline{p}^T} = \frac{\partial}{\partial \underline{p}}\left(\frac{\partial J}{\partial \underline{p}^T}\right) = -E\left[\frac{\partial}{\partial \underline{p}}\left(\underline{\varepsilon}^T \cdot \frac{\partial \hat{\underline{y}}}{\partial \underline{p}^T}\right)\right]$$

$$= E\left[\frac{\partial \hat{\underline{y}}^T}{\partial \underline{p}} \cdot \frac{\partial \hat{\underline{y}}}{\partial \underline{p}^T} - \underline{\varepsilon}^T \cdot \frac{\partial^2 \hat{\underline{y}}}{\partial \underline{p} \cdot \partial \underline{p}^T}\right] \tag{3.189}$$

A Newton–Raphson scheme would require the use of the Hessian (3.189). In a Gauss–Newton scheme, the Hessian is approximated. In particular, the second term in (3.189) is dropped. Neglecting this factor is acceptable, as one of its elements $\underline{\varepsilon}$ is the residual and its value should be small compared with the other terms. One thus sets:

$$H(\underline{p}_k) \approx \Psi_k \cdot \Psi_k^T \tag{3.190}$$

As the expectation has been dropped, the instantaneous values of (3.190) may fluctuate in an unacceptable way. In actual algorithms a smoothed Hessian is used.

One is now able to give a general form for a recursive prediction error estimator based on a quadratic cost and a Gauss–Newton iteration algorithm:

$$\underline{p}_k = \underline{p}_{k-1} + \alpha(k)R^{-1}(k)\Psi(k)\underline{\varepsilon}(k) \tag{3.191}$$

$$\underline{\varepsilon}_k = \underline{y}_k - \hat{\underline{y}}_k \tag{3.192}$$

$$R_k = R_{k-1} + \alpha(k)(\Psi_k \cdot \Psi_k^T - R_{k-1}) \tag{3.193}$$

A full specification of the algorithm still requires means to compute the predicted output $\hat{\underline{y}}_k$ and its derivatives $\partial\hat{\underline{y}}_k^T/\partial p$.

In general terms, such specification can be given using the canonical sensitivity system based on the model (3.184–185). From these equations, one obtains after differentiation to the i-th component of the parameter vector

$$\underline{\psi}_i = \frac{\partial\hat{\underline{y}}}{\partial p_i} = C(\underline{p})\frac{\partial\varphi}{\partial p_i} + \frac{\partial C(\underline{p})}{\partial p_i} \cdot \underline{\varphi}$$

$$\frac{\partial\underline{\varphi}}{\partial p_i} = A(\underline{p})\frac{\partial\varphi}{\partial p_i} + \frac{\partial A(\underline{p})}{\partial p_i} \cdot \underline{\varphi} + \frac{\partial B(\underline{p})}{\partial p_i}\begin{pmatrix} y_k \\ u_k \end{pmatrix}$$

Define the vectors

$$\underline{\eta}^T(\underline{p}) = \left(\underline{\varphi}^T(\underline{p}), \frac{\partial\underline{\varphi}^T}{\partial p_1}, \frac{\partial\underline{\varphi}^T}{\partial p_2}, \ldots, \frac{\partial\underline{\varphi}^T}{\partial p_i}, \ldots\right)$$

$$\underline{\psi}^T(\underline{p}) = (\underline{\psi}_1^T, \underline{\psi}_2^T, \ldots, \underline{\psi}_i^T, \ldots)$$

Then the canonical sensitivity sytem is given by:

$$\underline{\eta}_{k+1} = A'(\underline{p})\underline{\eta}_k + B'(\underline{p})\begin{pmatrix} y_k \\ u_k \end{pmatrix} \tag{3.194}$$

$$\begin{pmatrix} \hat{y}_k \\ \underline{\psi}_k \end{pmatrix} = C'(\underline{p})\underline{\eta}_k \tag{3.195}$$

Note that (3.194) and (3.195) require the availability of $\underline{p}$. One substitutes $\underline{p}$ by its current estimate $\underline{p}_k$. Herewith (3.191–193) and (3.194–195) specify a complete recursive algorithm shown in Fig. 3.13, where an updating mechanism is specified. This mechanism is necessary to maintain proper behaviour. Remember that all IV–AML schemes presented before were provided with suitable updating procedures. This is because convergence can only be guaranteed as long as the canonical sensitivity system

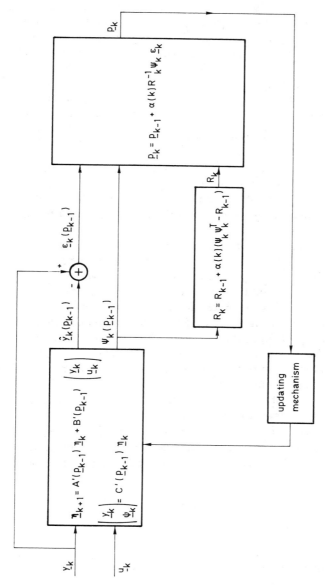

FIG. 3.13 Stochastic Gauss–Newton recursive parameter estimator for linear finite dimensional models

remains stable. In control theory, it is well known that the sensitivity system has the same stability properties as the basic system (3.184–185). During iteration the stability of the system will depend on the current estimate of the parameter vector p. There is no inherent property in the Gauss–Newton computation algorithms that warrants a stable prediction system. In order to ensure convergence, a suitable updating mechanism has to be provided, so that "unruly" poles are kept within stable regions of the complex plane.

A few remarks are also appropriate concerning the scalar function $\alpha(k)$. A typical choice is $\alpha(k) = 1/k$. It is required that $\lim_{k\to\infty} k\alpha(k) = \mu_c > 0$. Determining more elaborate $\alpha(k)$ functions is called "tuning of the algorithm".

Ljung [147] indicates that the general algorithms (3.191–195) with a suitable updating mechanism and a proper scalar function $\alpha(k)$ converge to a local minimum of the objective function. This result means that recursive estimation yields in the limit the same result as off-line estimators for the same cost.

Given the general recursive estimator and its derivation, it is possible now to derive other general schemes based on other choices for the objective function. In particular, robust recursive estimators could be worked out and convergence properties checked. The beauty of the general representation in Fig. 3.13 resides in the fact that different estimation schemes, apparently suggested on ad hoc grounds, can be deduced from it.

A first class of algorithms follows the general set-up of the Gauss–Newton scheme presented in this section. These schemes are rather complex as they require the canonical sensitivity system or a related construct. They are termed here "true prediction error techniques". As an effort is made to obtain correct values for the derivatives, the algorithms converge. This class is discussed first.

A second class tries to avoid the canonical sensitivity system by approximation procedures. The algorithms are, in fact, computationally simpler than the former. However, they often have convergence problems and will be discussed next.

3.2.8.3   Prediction error algorithms

The basic equation

A number of algorithms can be related to each other in a simple way. Consider for the SISO case the general model

$$F(z^{-1})y_k = \frac{B(z^{-1})}{A(z^{-1})} u_k + \frac{D(z^{-1})}{C(z^{-1})} e_k \qquad (3.196)$$

This is a slightly more complex form than (3.21). To keep the discussion general, the following definitions hold for the polynomials

$$A(z^{-1}) = 1 + a_1z^{-1} + a_2z^{-2} \ldots a_{n_a}z^{-n_a}$$
$$B(z^{-1}) = b_1z^{-1} + b_2z^{-2} \ldots b_{n_b}z^{-n_b}$$
$$C(z^{-1}) = 1 + c_1z^{-1} + c_2z^{-2} \ldots c_{n_c}z^{-n_c}$$
$$D(z^{-1}) = 1 + d_1z^{-1} + d_2z^{-2} \ldots d_{n_d}z^{-n_d}$$
$$F(z^{-1}) = 1 + f_1z^{-1} + f_2z^{-2} \ldots f_{n_f}z^{-n_f}$$

Note that e_k is white with zero mean, its estimate ε_k will be the residual, so from (3.196) is obtained:

$$y_k - \hat{y}_k = \frac{C(z^{-1})}{D(z^{-1})} F(z^{-1})y_k - \frac{C(z^{-1})}{D(z^{-1})} \frac{B(z^{-1})}{A(z^{-1})} u_k$$

The best one-step-ahead prediction becomes

$$\hat{y}_k = \left(1 - \frac{C(z^{-1})}{D(z^{-1})} F(z^{-1})\right)y_k + \frac{C(z^{-1})}{D(z^{-1})} \frac{B(z^{-1})}{A(z^{-1})} u_k \tag{3.197}$$

It can easily be seen that the right hand side of (3.197) does not contain y_k and u_k. Before proceeding it is useful to introduce a number of intermediate variables

$$\mu_k = \frac{B(z^{-1})}{A(z^{-1})} u_k \tag{3.198}$$

$$v_k = F(z^{-1})y_k - \mu_k \tag{3.199}$$

$$\varepsilon_k = y_k - \hat{y}_k = \frac{C(z^{-1})}{D(z^{-1})} v_k = \frac{C(z^{-1})}{D(z^{-1})} (F(z^{-1})y_k - \mu_k) \tag{3.200}$$

In the previous paragraphs the prediction of the output was given by a model in state–space form. In order to relate the model (3.196) with its counterpart (3.184–185), it has to be brought in a state–space form. Define

$$\underline{\varphi}_k^T = (-y_{k-1}, -y_{k-2}, \ldots, -y_{k-n_f}, u_{k-1}, \ldots, u_{k-n_b}, -\mu_{k-1}, \ldots -\mu_{k-n_a},$$
$$\varepsilon_{k-1}, \ldots, \varepsilon_{k-n_d}, -v_{k-1}, \ldots, -v_{k-n_c})$$
$$C(\underline{p}) = (f_1, \ldots, f_{n_f}, b_1, \ldots, b_{n_b}, a_1, \ldots, a_{n_a}, d_1, \ldots, d_{n_d}, c_1, \ldots c_{n_c})$$

Using (3.198–200) it is easy to see that

$$\hat{y}_k = C(\underline{p}) \cdot \underline{\varphi}_k$$

Setting up the matrices $A(\underline{p})$, $B(\underline{p})$ is straightforward; most elements in these matrices are zero or one, only a few rows contain parameters. These rows are for the elements v_k, ε_k, μ_k in $\underline{\varphi}_{k+1}$ and their precise definition follows from (3.198–200) too.

Instead of setting up the complex canonical sensitivity system, simply specify the derivatives. Again with equations (3.198–200) one finds easily

$$\frac{\partial \varepsilon_k}{\partial a_i} = \frac{C(z^{-1})}{D(z^{-1})A(z^{-1})} \mu_{k-i} \qquad (3.201)$$

$$\frac{\partial \varepsilon_k}{\partial b_i} = -\frac{C(z^{-1})}{D(z^{-1})A(z^{-1})} u_{k-i} \qquad (3.202)$$

$$\frac{\partial \varepsilon_k}{\partial f_i} = \frac{C(z^{-1})}{D(z^{-1})} y_{k-i} \qquad (3.203)$$

$$\frac{\partial \varepsilon_k}{\partial c_i} = \frac{1}{D(z^{-1})} v_{k-i} \qquad (3.204)$$

$$\frac{\partial \varepsilon_k}{\partial d_i} = -\frac{1}{D(z^{-1})} \varepsilon_{k-i} \qquad (3.205)$$

The gradient vector ψ_k is obtained by linear filtering operations, which are unfortunately dependent on the parameter vector. Clearly, up to here nothing especially difficult has been done, all variables important for recursive estimation have been derived for a special model form (3.196). It turns out that many well-known recursive estimation schemes are themselves concretizations of the Gauss–Newton scheme for model forms that can be derived from (3.196).

The RLS-algorithm (Recursive Least Squares)

Set $A(z^{-1}) = C(z^{-1}) = D(z^{-1}) = 1$

- $\hat{y}_k \quad = (1 - F(z^{-1}))y_k + B(z^{-1})u_k$

- $\varepsilon_k \quad = v_k$

- $v_k \quad = F(z^{-1})y_k - B(z^{-1})u_k$

- $\mu_k \quad = B(z^{-1})u_k$

- $\varphi_k^T \quad = (-y_{k-1}, -y_{k-2}, \ldots, -y_{k-n_f}, u_{k-1}, \ldots, u_{k-n_b})$

- $C(\underline{p}) = (f_1, f_2, \ldots, f_{n_f}, b_1, b_2, \ldots, b_{n_b})$

$$\frac{\partial \varepsilon_k}{\partial f_i} = y_{k-i}$$

$$\frac{\partial \varepsilon_k}{\partial b_i} = -u_{k-i}$$

thus $\underline{\psi} = \underline{\varphi}$

One thus has

$$\underline{p}_k = \underline{p}_{k-1} + \alpha(k)R_k^{-1}\underline{\varphi}_k\varepsilon_k$$
$$\varepsilon_k = y_k - \hat{y}_k = y_k - \underline{p}_{k-1}^T\underline{\varphi}_k \qquad (3.206)$$
$$R_k = R_{k-1} + \alpha(k)(\underline{\varphi}_k \cdot \underline{\varphi}_k^T - R_{k-1})$$

This is the classic RLS-algorithm of Section 3.2.3.4, but with other notations. Substitute $\underline{p}_k$ by $\underline{a}_k$, $\underline{\varphi}_k$ by $\underline{x}_k$, $\alpha(k)$ by $1/k$, and $k \cdot R_k$ by P_k^{-1} and (3.206) becomes

$$\underline{a}_k = \underline{a}_{k-1} - P_k\underline{x}_k(\underline{x}_k^T\underline{a}_{k-1} - y_k) \qquad (3.207)$$
$$P_k^{-1} = P_{k-1}^{-1} + \underline{x}_k\underline{x}_k^T \qquad (3.208)$$

Note that the second equation has been modified for computational purposes to

$$P_k = P_{k-1} - P_{k-1}\underline{x}_k(1 + \underline{x}_k^TP_{k-1}\underline{x}_k)^{-1}\underline{x}_k^TP_{k-1} \qquad (3.209)$$

In the present context the former equation is more useful.

If one intends to use the RLS or other schemes presented in this section, it is important to be aware of the fact that (3.209) is equivalent but computationally more advantageous than (3.208).

Based on previous considerations it is noted that the RLS scheme will converge, even if the true system does not correspond with the simple model chosen here. Unfortunately, convergence does not guarantee consistency and, if the model is too simple, biased estimates will result. This is in agreement with previously mentioned results on the RLS scheme.

The RML-algorithm (Recursive Maximum Likelihood)

Another linear model is now to be considered: $A(z^{-1}) = C(z^{-1}) = 1$. This is the so-called **ARMAX** model. Its general nature was discussed in Section 3.1.2.2.

$$\hat{y}_k = \left(1 - \frac{F(z^{-1})}{D(z^{-1})}\right)y_k + \frac{B(z^{-1})}{D(z^{-1})}u_k$$

$$\mu_k = B(z^{-1})u_k$$

$$v_k = F(z^{-1})y_k - B(z^{-1})u_k$$

$$\varepsilon_k = \frac{1}{D(z^{-1})}v_k$$

$$\underline{\varphi}_k^T = (-y_{k-1}, -y_{k-2}, \ldots, -y_{k-n_f}, u_{k-1}, u_{k-2}, \ldots, u_{k-n_b},$$
$$\varepsilon_{k-1}, \ldots, \varepsilon_{k-n_d})$$

$$C(\underline{p}) = (f_1, f_2, \ldots, f_{n_f}, b_1, b_2, \ldots, b_{n_b}, d_1, d_2, \ldots, d_{n_d})$$

$$\frac{\partial \varepsilon_k}{\partial b_i} = -\frac{1}{D(z^{-1})} u_{k-i}$$

$$\frac{\partial \varepsilon_k}{\partial f_i} = \frac{1}{D(z^{-1})} y_{k-i} \qquad\qquad \text{thus } \underline{\psi}_k = \frac{1}{D(z^{-1})} \underline{\varphi}_k$$

$$\frac{\partial \varepsilon_k}{\partial d_i} = -\frac{1}{D(z^{-1})} \varepsilon_{k-i}$$

The recursive algorithm takes the form:

$$\underline{p}_k = \underline{p}_{k-1} - \alpha(k) R_k^{-1} \underline{\psi}_k (\underline{p}_{k-1}^T \cdot \underline{\varphi}_k - y_k)$$

$$R_k = R_{k-1} + \alpha(k)(\underline{\psi}_k \cdot \underline{\psi}_k^T - R_{k-1})$$

$$\underline{\psi}_k + d_1\underline{\psi}_{k-1} + d_2\underline{\psi}_{k-2} + \ldots + d_{nd}\underline{\psi}_{k-nd} = \underline{\varphi}_k \qquad\qquad (3.210)$$

Algorithm (3.210) is known as the "recursive maximum likelihood method". For finite sample sizes, it gives of course only approximate off-line maximum likelihood estimates. Convergence is guaranteed and consistency follows as soon as the correct orders for the polynomials are known. Experience has shown that initial convergence is slow if $\alpha(k) = 1/k$. Therefore $\alpha(k)$ is often taken to be $(1/k)\beta(k)$, where $\beta(k)$ increases to 2–3 over the first couple of hundred steps and then decreases to unity.

These findings correspond with what has been said in Section 3.2.4.9. In fact, the modified approximate maximum likelihood method of Section 3.2.4.8, is the RML method (3.210).
Take $B(z^{-1}) \equiv 0$, then

$$\underline{\varphi}_k^T = [-y_{k-1}, -y_{k-2}, \ldots, -y_{k-nf}, \varepsilon_{k-1}, \ldots, \varepsilon_{k-nd}]$$

corresponds with $\underline{\hat{n}}_k^T$ if $y_k = \hat{\xi}_k$ and $\varepsilon_k = \hat{e}_k$ and $\underline{\psi}_k^T$ follows from filtering $\underline{\varphi}_k^T$ through a filter $1/D(z^{-1})$: see (3.152–155);
hence $\underline{\psi}_k^T = [-y_{k-1}^*, -y_{k-2}^*, \ldots, -y_{k-n}^*, \varepsilon_{k-1}^*, \ldots, \varepsilon_{k-nd}^*]$ and $\underline{\psi}_k^T$ corresponds with $\underline{m}_k^T$ if $y_k^* = \hat{\xi}_k^*$ and $\hat{\varepsilon}_k^* = \hat{e}_k^*$.
It is a simple matter to relate (3.210) with equations (3.159–161) with $\alpha(k) = 1/k$ and $k.R_k = \check{P}_k^{-1}$.

As discussed in Section 3.2.4.9, the modified AML is consistent but problems may occur with low sample sizes. In the latter case, the estimator is in its initial convergence zone and, as mentioned, convergence is slow. A suitable $\alpha(k)$ function could be tried out in order to improve small sample behaviour.

The RIV-variant (Recursive Instrumental Variable)

Choose $F(z^{-1}) = 1$ and the model (3.196) reduces to the model (3.104–105) used in the discussion on the instrumental variable technique.

Here

$$\hat{y}_k = \left(1 - \frac{C(z^{-1})}{D(z^{-1})}\right)y_k + \frac{B(z^{-1}) \cdot C(z^{-1})}{A(z^{-1}) \cdot D(z^{-1})}u_k$$

$$\mu_k = \frac{B(z^{-1})}{A(z^{-1})}u_k$$

$$v_k = y_k - \frac{B(z^{-1})}{A(z^{-1})}u_k$$

$$\varepsilon_k = \frac{C(z^{-1})}{D(z^{-1})}v_k = \frac{C(z^{-1})}{D(z^{-1})}\left(y_k - \frac{B(z^{-1})}{A(z^{-1})}u_k\right) \qquad (3.211)$$

$$\underline{\varphi}_k{}^T = (u_{k-1}, \ldots, u_{k-n_b}, -\mu_{k-1}, \ldots, -\mu_{k-n_a}, \varepsilon_{k-1}, \ldots, \varepsilon_{k-n_d}, -v_{k-1}, \ldots, -v_{k-n_c})$$

$$C(\underline{p}) = (b_1, b_2, \ldots, b_{n_b}, a_1, a_2, \ldots, a_{n_a}, d_1, d_2, \ldots, d_{n_d}, c_1, c_2, \ldots, c_{n_c})$$

$$\frac{\partial\varepsilon_k}{\partial b_i} = -\frac{C(z^{-1})}{D(z^{-1})A(z^{-1})}u_{k-i}$$

$$\frac{\partial\varepsilon_k}{\partial a_i} = \frac{C(z^{-1})}{D(z^{-1})A(z^{-1})}\mu_{k-i}$$

$$\frac{\partial\varepsilon_k}{\partial c_i} = \frac{1}{D(z^{-1})}v_{k-i}$$

$$\frac{\partial\varepsilon_k}{\partial d_i} = -\frac{1}{D(z^{-1})}\varepsilon_{k-i}$$

To proceed more easily some changes in terminology and minor modifications are useful.

$$\hat{x}_k = \mu_k$$

$$\hat{\xi}_k = v_k$$

$$\hat{e}_k = \varepsilon_k$$

$$\begin{aligned}
\underline{\tilde{\varphi}}_k{}^T &= (-\mu_{k-1}, \ldots, -\mu_{k-n_a}, u_{k-1}, \ldots, u_{k-n_b}, -v_{k-1}, \ldots, -v_{k-n_c}, \\
&\quad \varepsilon_{k-1}, \ldots, \varepsilon_{k-n_d}) \\
&= (-\hat{x}_{k-1}, \ldots, -\hat{x}_{k-n_a}, u_{k-1}, \ldots, u_{k-n_b}, -\hat{\xi}_{k-1}, \ldots, -\hat{\xi}_{k-n_c}, \\
&\quad \hat{e}_{k-1}, \ldots, \hat{e}_{k-n_d}) \\
&= (\underline{\hat{x}}_k{}^T, \underline{\check{n}}_k{}^T)
\end{aligned}$$

$$\begin{aligned}
C(\underline{p}) &= (a_1, \ldots, a_{n_a}, b_1, \ldots, b_{n_b}, c_1, \ldots, c_{n_c}, d_1, \ldots, d_{n_d}) \\
&= (\underline{a}^T, \underline{c}^T)
\end{aligned}$$

Thus $\hat{y}_k = \underline{a}^T \cdot \underline{\hat{x}}_k + \underline{c}^T \cdot \underline{\check{n}}_k = \underline{\hat{x}}_k{}^T \cdot \underline{a} + \underline{\check{n}}_k{}^T \cdot \underline{c}$

Furthermore

$$\hat{x}^*_k = \frac{C(z^{-1})}{D(z^{-1}) \cdot A(z^{-1})} \hat{x}_k \qquad \hat{\xi}^*_k = \frac{1}{D(z^{-1})} \xi_k$$

$$u^*_k = \frac{C(z^{-1})}{D(z^{-1}) \cdot A(z^{-1})} u_k \qquad \hat{e}^*_k = \frac{1}{D(z^{-1})} \hat{e}_k$$

and

$$\underline{\hat{x}}^{*T}_k = (-\hat{x}^*_{k-1}, \ldots, -\hat{x}^*_{k-n_a}, u^*_{k-1}, \ldots, u^*_{k-n_b})$$

$$\underline{\hat{m}}^{*T}_k = (-\hat{\xi}^*_{k-1}, \ldots, -\hat{\xi}^*_{k-n_c}, \hat{e}^*_{k-1}, \ldots, \hat{e}^*_{k-n_d})$$

Then

$$\underline{\psi}^T_k = (\underline{\hat{x}}^{*T}_k, \underline{\hat{m}}^{*T}_k).$$

The notations have been brought to correspond to those used in the previous sections concerning the R–IV–AML-algorithm.

For a matter of convenience, R_k is subdivided:

$$R_k = \begin{pmatrix} R_k^{11} & R_k^{12} \\ R_k^{21} & R_k^{22} \end{pmatrix}$$

Consider first the recursion formula for R_k

$$R_k = R_{k-1} + \frac{1}{k}\left(\begin{pmatrix}\underline{\hat{x}}^*_k \\ \underline{\hat{m}}^*_k\end{pmatrix}(\underline{\hat{x}}^{*T}_k, \underline{\hat{m}}^{*T}_k) - R_{k-1}\right) \tag{3.212}$$

The formula computes recursively the following en bloc matrix

$$R_N = \frac{1}{N}\sum_{k=1}^{N}\begin{pmatrix}\underline{\hat{x}}^*_k \cdot \underline{\hat{x}}^{*T}_k & \underline{\hat{x}}^*_k \cdot \underline{\hat{m}}^{*T}_k \\ \underline{m}^*_k \cdot \underline{\hat{x}}^{*T}_k & \underline{m}^*_k \cdot \underline{\hat{m}}^{*T}_k\end{pmatrix}$$

The off-diagonal terms are estimates of the cross-correlation between $\underline{\hat{x}}^*_k$ and $\underline{\hat{m}}^*_k$. Note that by virtue of the model build-up, these vectors are uncorrelated and it is that property which permits the instrumental variable approach to work. For sufficiently large N:

$$\underline{\hat{x}}^*_k \cdot \underline{\hat{m}}^{*T}_k \approx 0 \qquad \underline{m}^*_k \cdot \underline{\hat{x}}^{*T}_k \approx 0$$

As a consequence, the equation (3.212) can be written as two separate ones:

$$R_k^{11} = R_{k-1}^{11} + \frac{1}{k}(\underline{\hat{x}}^*_k \cdot \underline{\hat{x}}^{*T}_k - R_{k-1}^{11})$$

$$R_k^{22} = R_{k-1}^{22} + \frac{1}{k}(\underline{\hat{m}}^*_k \cdot \underline{\hat{m}}^{*T}_k - R_{k-1}^{22})$$

The estimates are

$$\begin{pmatrix} \hat{\underline{a}}_k \\ \hat{\underline{c}}_k \end{pmatrix} = \begin{pmatrix} \hat{\underline{a}}_{k-1} \\ \hat{\underline{c}}_{k-1} \end{pmatrix} + \frac{1}{k} R_k^{-1} \begin{pmatrix} \hat{\underline{x}}^*_k \\ \hat{\underline{m}}^*_k \end{pmatrix} \varepsilon_k$$

With the approximation of above

$$R_k^{-1} = \begin{pmatrix} (R_k^1)^{-1} & 0 \\ 0 & (R_k^2)^{-1} \end{pmatrix} \quad \text{with} \quad \begin{aligned} R_k^1 &= R_k^{11} \\ R_k^2 &= R_k^{22} \end{aligned}$$

and two separate equations can be written:

$$\hat{\underline{a}}_k = \hat{\underline{a}}_{k-1} + \frac{1}{k} (R_k^1)^{-1} \hat{\underline{x}}^*_k \cdot \varepsilon_k \tag{3.213}$$

$$\hat{\underline{c}}_k = \hat{\underline{c}}_{k-1} + \frac{1}{k} (R_k^2)^{-1} \hat{\underline{m}}^*_k \cdot \varepsilon_k \tag{3.214}$$

With the proper interpretation for $k \cdot R_k^1$ and $k \cdot R_k^2$, the equations (3.158) and (3.161) of the modified refined IV–AML procedure are found as soon as the residual ε_k is appropriately defined.

$$\varepsilon_k = y_k - \hat{y}_k = y_k - \hat{\underline{a}}_{k-1}^T \cdot \hat{\underline{x}}_k - \hat{\underline{c}}_{k-1}^T \cdot \check{\underline{n}}_k = \xi_k - \hat{\underline{c}}_{k-1}^T \cdot \check{\underline{n}}_k \tag{3.215}$$

From (3.211)

$$\begin{aligned} \varepsilon_k &= \frac{\hat{C}(z^{-1})}{\hat{D}(z^{-1}) \cdot \hat{A}(z^{-1})} (\hat{A}(z^{-1})y_k - \hat{B}(z^{-1})u_k) \\ &= \frac{\hat{C}(z^{-1})}{\hat{D}(z^{-1}) \cdot \hat{A}(z^{-1})} (y_k - \hat{\underline{a}}_{k-1}^T \cdot \underline{z}_k) = y^*_k - \hat{\underline{a}}_{k-1}^T \cdot \underline{z}^*_k \end{aligned} \tag{3.216}$$

(3.215) and (3.216) complete the proof. Asymptotically, the modified IV–AML procedure is obtained. Clearly for a finite and rather small sample size, decomposition is not possible and in this section a more complex IV scheme is obtained.

The RML-variant and RGLS (Recursive Generalized Least Squares)

Choose $A(z^{-1}) = D(z^{-1}) = 1$ and the model becomes

$$F(z^{-1})y_k = B(z^{-1})u_k + \frac{e_k}{C(z^{-1})} \tag{3.217}$$

Instead of the simple model $F(z^{-1})y_k = B(z^{-1})u_k + e_k$, which leads to the RLS scheme, a more complex noise term ξ_k is allowed. $C(z^{-1})\xi_k = e_k$, thus ξ_k is of the autoregressive type. An estimator which follows from (3.217) is called "generalized least squares" because the noise term in the equation is allowed to be more general than in the simple white noise case.

One finds:

$$\hat{y}_k = (1 - C(z^{-1}) \cdot F(z^{-1}))y_k + C(z^{-1}) \cdot B(z^{-1})u_k$$

$$\mu_k = B(z^{-1})u_k$$

$$v_k = F(z^{-1})y_k - B(z^{-1})u_k$$

$$\varepsilon_k = C(z^{-1})v_k$$

$$\varphi_k^T = (-y_{k-1}, \ldots, -y_{k-n_f}, u_{k-1}, \ldots, u_{k-n_b}, -v_{k-1}, \ldots, -v_{k-n_c})$$

$$C(\underline{p}) = (f_1, f_2, \ldots, f_{n_f}, b_1, b_2, \ldots, b_{n_b}, c_1, c_2, \ldots, c_{n_c})$$

$$\frac{\partial \varepsilon_k}{\partial b_i} = -C(z^{-1})u_{k-i}$$

$$\frac{\partial \varepsilon_k}{\partial f_i} = C(z^{-1})y_{k-i}$$

$$\frac{\partial \varepsilon_k}{\partial c_i} = v_{k-i}$$

A full development of the algorithm leads to a variant recursive maximum likelihood method. Better known is the recursive generalized least squares, which block diagonalizes the R-matrix. Define

$$u^*_k = C(z^{-1})u_k$$
$$y^*_k = C(z^{-1})y_k$$

Then one has

$$\underline{\psi}^T = (u^*_{k-1}, u^*_{k-2}, \ldots, u^*_{k-n_b}, -y^*_{k-1}, \ldots, -v_{k-1}, \ldots, -v_{k-n_c})$$

It is useful to distinguish two components in ψ

$$\underline{\psi}^T = (\underline{u}^*_k{}^T, \underline{v}_k^T) \qquad \underline{v}_k^T = (-v_{k-1}, \ldots, -v_{k-n_c})$$

$$\underline{u}^*_k{}^T = (u^*_{k-1}, u^*_{k-2}, \ldots, u^*_{k-n_b}, -y^*_{k-1}, \ldots, -y^*_{k-n_f})$$

The recursive relation for the approximation to the Hessian becomes

$$R_k = R_{k-1} + \frac{1}{k}\left[\begin{pmatrix} \underline{u}^*_k \\ \underline{v}_k \end{pmatrix} (u^*_k{}^T, \underline{v}_k^T) - R_{k-1} \right] \tag{3.218}$$

Suppose one takes that in the limit

$$\frac{1}{N}\sum_{k=1}^{N} \underline{u}^*_k \cdot \underline{v}_k^T \to 0 \qquad \frac{1}{N}\sum_{k=1}^{N} \underline{v}_k \cdot \underline{u}^*_k{}^T \to 0$$

then (3.218) can be thought to be made up of two equations

$$R_k^1 = R_{k-1}^1 + \frac{1}{k}(\underline{u}^*_k \cdot \underline{u}^*{_k}^T - R_{k-1}^1)$$

$$R_k^2 = R_{k-1}^2 + \frac{1}{k}(\underline{v}_k \cdot \underline{v}{_k}^T - R_{k-1}^2) \tag{3.219}$$

The parameter vector can be thought to consist of two parts

$$\underline{p}^T = (\underline{b}^T, \underline{c}^T) \quad \text{with} \quad \underline{c}^T = (c_1, c_2, \ldots, c_{n_c})$$

The parameter update is done as follows

$$\begin{pmatrix} \underline{b}_k \\ \underline{c}_k \end{pmatrix} = \begin{pmatrix} \underline{b}_{k-1} \\ \underline{c}_{k-1} \end{pmatrix} + \frac{1}{k}\begin{pmatrix} (R_k^1)^{-1} & 0 \\ 0 & (R_k^2)^{-1} \end{pmatrix}\begin{pmatrix} \underline{u}^*_k \\ \underline{v}_k \end{pmatrix}\varepsilon_k \tag{3.220}$$

$$\varepsilon_k = C(z^{-1})v_k = C(z^{-1})(y_k - \underline{b}^T \cdot \underline{u}_k) = y^*_k - \underline{b}^T \cdot \underline{u}^*_k \tag{3.221}$$

$$\varepsilon_k = C(z^{-1})v_k = v_k - \underline{c}^T \cdot \underline{v}_k \tag{3.222}$$

Equations (3.219–222) yield the recursive generalized least squares method:

$$\underline{b}_k = \underline{b}_{k-1} + \frac{1}{k}(R_k^1)^{-1}\underline{u}^*_k(y^*_k - \underline{u}^*{_k}^T \cdot \underline{b}_{k-1})$$

$$R_k^1 = R_{k-1}^1 + \frac{1}{k}(\underline{u}^*_k \cdot \underline{u}^*{_k}^T - R_{k-1}^1)$$

$$\underline{c}_k = \underline{c}_{k-1} + \frac{1}{k}(R_k^2)^{-1}\underline{v}_k(v_k - \underline{v}{_k}^T \cdot \underline{c}_{k-1})$$

$$R_k^2 = R_{k-1}^2 + \frac{1}{k}(\underline{v}_k \cdot \underline{v}{_k}^T - R_{k-1}^2)$$

This is a second example where a rather large parameter vector is split up into two parts to yield a more simple algorithm.

3.2.8.4 *Pseudo-linear regression techniques*

The general equations

As in the previous paragraph, we start for the SISO-case from the general model (3.196), with the same definitions for the polynomials as above

$$F(z^{-1})y_k = \frac{B(z^{-1})}{A(z^{-1})}u_k + \frac{D(z^{-1})}{C(z^{-1})}e_k \tag{3.223}$$

Here too, the best one step ahead prediction is used

$$\hat{y}_k = (1 - \frac{C(z^{-1})}{D(z^{-1})} F(z^{-1}))y_k + \frac{C(z^{-1})}{D(z^{-1})} \frac{B(z^{-1})}{A(z^{-1})} u_k \qquad (3.224)$$

In order to indicate the relationship with linear regression analysis the same intermediate variables are useful:

$$\mu_k = \frac{B(z^{-1})}{A(z^{-1})} u_k \qquad (3.225)$$

$$v_k = F(z^{-1})y_k - \mu_k \qquad (3.226)$$

$$\varepsilon_k = y_k - \hat{y}_k = \frac{C(z^{-1})}{D(z^{-1})} v_k = \frac{C(z^{-1})}{D(z^{-1})} (F(z^{-1})y_k - \mu_k) \qquad (3.227)$$

In Section 3.2.8.3, it was shown that the one step ahead predictions $\hat{y}$ could be seen as the output of a linear filter

$$\hat{y}_k \quad = C(\underline{p})\underline{\varphi}_k \qquad (3.228)$$

$$\underline{\varphi}_k^T \quad = (-y_{k-1}, -y_{k-2}, \dots, -y_{k-n_f}, u_{k-1}, \dots, u_{k-n_b}, -\mu_{k-1}, \dots,$$
$$\qquad -\mu_{k-n_a}, \varepsilon_{k-1}, \dots, \varepsilon_{k-n_d}, -v_{k-1}, \dots, -v_{k-n_c})$$

$$C(\underline{p}) = (f_1, f_2, \dots, f_{n_f}, b_1, \dots, b_{n_b}, a_1, \dots, a_{n_a}, d_1, \dots, d_{n_d},$$
$$\qquad c_1, \dots, c_{n_c})$$

If one takes $\underline{p}^T = C(\underline{p})$, equation (3.228) can be written as follows:

$$\hat{y}_k = \underline{p}^T \cdot \underline{\varphi}_k = \underline{\varphi}_k^T \cdot \underline{p} \qquad (3.229)$$

(3.229) would be a linear regression relationship, were it not that $\underline{\varphi}_k$, in fact, is dependent on $\underline{p}$ itself through the matrices $A(\underline{p})$, $B(\underline{p})$. In fact, (3.229) should be written

$$\hat{y}_k = \underline{p}^T \cdot \underline{\varphi}_k(\underline{p}) = \underline{\varphi}_k^T(\underline{p}) \cdot \underline{p} \qquad (3.230)$$

The pseudo-linear regression technique consists in neglecting the dependence of $\underline{\varphi}_k$ on $\underline{p}$. Then for the derivatives one obtains a very simple form:

$$\frac{d\varepsilon_k}{d\underline{p}} = - \frac{d\hat{y}_k}{d\underline{p}} = -\underline{\varphi}_k$$

Of course, the approach is an approximation, and so the prefix "pseudo-" is used.

The Gauss–Newton algorithm becomes:

$$\underline{p}_k = \underline{p}_{k-1} + \alpha(k)R^{-1}(k)\underline{\varphi}_k \cdot \varepsilon_k$$
$$\varepsilon_k = y_k - \underline{p}^T \cdot \underline{\varphi}_k = y_k - \underline{\varphi}_k^T \cdot \underline{p} \qquad (3.231)$$
$$R_k = R_{k-1} + \alpha(k)(\underline{\varphi}_k \cdot \underline{\varphi}_k^T - R_{k-1})$$

Clearly, the recursive estimator (3.231) is simple. A number of algorithms are apparently based on the pseudo-linear regression approach. As in the case of the prediction error schemes, they differ in their choice of model, which in fact has little to do with parameter estimation itself.

The ELS-scheme (Extended Least Squares)

Suppose $A(z^{-1}) = C(z^{-1}) = 1$.
The model is of the ARMAX type

$$F(z^{-1})y_k = B(z^{-1})u_k + D(z^{-1})e_k$$

$$\varphi_k^T = (-y_{k-1}, \dots, -y_{k-n_f}, u_{k-1}, \dots, u_{k-n_b}, \varepsilon_{k-1}, \dots, \varepsilon_{k-n_d})$$

$$\underline{p}^T = C(\underline{p}) = (f_1, \dots, f_{n_f}, b_1, \dots, b_{n_b}, d_1, \dots, d_{n_d})$$

It is easy to see why the name 'Extended Least Squares' is used. Basically (3.231) is the recursive least squares approach, but the data and parameter vectors are extended. As the true noise terms $e_{k-1}, \dots, e_{k-n_d}$ are not known, they are substituted by estimates $\varepsilon_{k-1}, \dots, \varepsilon_{k-n_d}$. Without input, one recognizes the so-called AML method, Section 3.2.4.5. As mentioned before, the technique is not foolproof. Ljung [148] points out that convergence can only be guaranteed when the following relationship holds:

$$|D(e^{j\omega}) - 1| < 1 \qquad \text{for all } \omega$$

Landau's scheme

Choose $F(z^{-1}) = C(z^{-1}) = D(z^{-1}) = 1$.
    The model is

$$y_k = \frac{B(z^{-1})}{A(z^{-1})} u_k + e_k \tag{3.232}$$

The system representation is natural in the sense that the output of a deterministic system is contaminated with white noise. One easily finds

$$\hat{y}_k = \frac{B(z^{-1})}{A(z^{-1})} u_k$$

$$\mu_k = \hat{y}_k$$

$$\varphi_k^T = (u_{k-1}, \dots, u_{k-n_b}, -\mu_{k-1}, \dots, -\mu_{k-n_a})$$

$$\underline{p}^T = (b_1, b_2, \dots, b_{n_b}, a_1, \dots, a_{n_a})$$

In the original scheme, the φ_k and $\underline{p}_k$ vectors were rearranged so that a-parameters come before the b-parameters. The recursive estimator is then given by (3.231), and has also been termed "the model reference output error estimator". The method is guaranteed to be convergent if

$$|A(e^{j\omega}) - 1| < 1 \qquad \text{for all } \omega$$

Landau's modified scheme

Here $F(z^{-1}) = D(z^{-1}) = 1$.

The model is

$$y_k = \frac{B(z^{-1})}{A(z^{-1})} u_k + \frac{1}{C(z^{-1})} e_k$$

This is a generalization of the previous case in the sense that the deterministic model part is now contaminated with autoregressive-type noise instead of white noise.

$$\mu_k = \frac{B(z^{-1})}{A(z^{-1})} u_k$$

$$v_k = y_k - \mu_k$$

$$\varepsilon_k = C(z^{-1})v_k = C(z^{-1})(y_k - \mu_k)$$

$$\underline{\varphi}_k{}^T = (u_{k-1}, u_{k-2}, \ldots, u_{k-n_b}, -\mu_{k-1}, \ldots, -\mu_{k-n_a}, -v_{k-1}, \ldots, -v_{k-n_c})$$

$$\underline{p}^T = (b_1, \ldots, b_{n_b}, a_1, \ldots, a_{n_a}, c_1, \ldots, c_{n_c})$$

Note that an auxiliary model is used to find the μ_k. The estimator is given by (3.231).

The EMM method (Extended Matrix Method)

For $A(z^{-1}) = 1$, another pseudo-linear regression estimator can be derived which is called the Extended Matrix Method. The details are left to the reader. Convergence is not guaranteed in general.

3.2.8.5 Conclusions

It is quite interesting to note that the previous discussion shows how many apparently different estimation schemes do not differ in essence from each other. They all have the same cost function, they all consider the prediction error and they all use a Gauss–Newton scheme as computational tool. The different appearances stem from the a priori choice of the model structure. It is seen here that parameter estimation cannot be fully decoupled of structure characterization step during modelling as the structure indicates which estimation model is appropriate. From discussions in Section 3.1.2.2 concerning the generality of certain model structures, it appears that the RML and RIV schemes are the most generally applicable, while the others are more restricted in utility. In day-to-day modelling other specific cases may arise. So it is useful to be able to design one's proper specific estimation algorithm, the methodology for which has been illustrated in Section 3.2.8.

Another important question relates to the convergence of the techniques. For the prediction error methods, this property is the same and so, why bother about a specific choice? In practical cases, however, other issues are also important, such as convergence rate and small sample properties. These properties may differ from algorithm to algorithm and research remains to be done into these properties. Practical experience is still quite relevant and therefore the early sections, with their detailed presentations on IV-related algorithms, show their utility and relevance.

3.3 STRUCTURE CHARACTERIZATION

3.3.1 Introduction

The process of building a mathematical representation has been described in Section 2.4. Based on the concepts introduced in Chapter 2, the process can also be described as follows. In an initial phase a tentative model formalism is chosen. The choice restricts the candidate descriptions to a subset of all possible set structures. Then other considerations lead to a proper frame and the candidate representations are further restricted. A subsequent step will result in the choice of a structure. At that point, calibration or parameter estimation will yield a final unique mathematical description. Structure characterization addresses the question of choosing a suitable structure.

In Section 3.3.2, a more detailed discussion of the meaning of structure is given and an overall approach for structure characterization is discussed. It is argued that characterizing a structure is often done in steps. The problem has many wide-ranging aspects and only a few will be discussed here. In order to relate the modelling stage with others such as estimation and validation, a perspective is given next. Then in view of the general concepts introduced in Chapter 2, the role of the different modelling information sources for characterization is evaluated. Armed with these more general considerations, the problem is looked upon in more detail. The guiding principles are fundamental. They embody some very simple and elementary considerations concerning model-building and useful models. It will be seen later on that structure characterization methods try to give a quantitative expression to these principles. After a discussion of guidelines some preliminary mathematical definitions are given. Characterization is described as model class selection between candidate classes. For later reference, some commonly occurring characterization problems are presented. Finally, some useful results concerning maximum likelihood estimates are given.

In Section 3.3.3, a number of characterization procedures are given. First, more established methods are discussed. Their origin and philosophy is considered, together with an understanding of their usefulness in the light of the general considerations of Section 3.3.2. Advantages and disadvantages will be discussed, then more recent methods will be presented and the improvements they bring, compared with the more traditional procedures. Though the field is still in its infancy, there are still a large number of techniques. However, the objective is not to cover all existing procedures but only the most interesting ideas which show promise for further research, or embody in a striking way the major characterization principles.

Finally, in Section 3.3.4, a suggestive framework is presented. The viewpoint of structure characterization as a problem in pattern recognition seems to be useful to enhance one's insight into the problem. All characterization problems can be formulated in the framework. In an easy manner important issues concerning characterization can be discovered. As theoretical results in the field are still lacking, the pattern recognition approach is useful in practical terms since, for specific problems, more accurate characterization schemes can be designed. Therefore, the methodology of the pattern recognition field can be utilized. This concludes Section 3.3.

3.3.2 Structure and structure characterization: general concepts

3.3.2.1 *The structure of a mathematical description: the O.D.E. case*

There is not yet a general agreement on the precise definition of "structure" of ordinary differential and difference equations. The confusion arises because one group of authors think of a model as a representation of a real-world system, at least at the state-structure level; whereas a second group perceives the model as a representation of the input–output behaviour.

For the former class, the state in the system representation should correspond with physical considerations. As a consequence, though there may still be different choices for the state vector, its dimensionality is directly related to the descriptive level of detail of the mathematical representation and it can thus be considered as a part of the system frame. The structure then consists of the functional relationships between the variables; more specifically, see equations (3.1–4). This specification of structure will be called the structure at the state descriptive level. As an example, consider an electric network. For a wide range of modelling goals a macroscopic lumped model will suffice, provided the frequencies of importance are sufficiently low. A number of currents and voltages related to the network components that store energy, form a suitable state vector with physical meaning. The structure will depend on the component interconnections and the component behaviour.

In certain modelling situations there is often no a priori knowledge that favours a certain class of states. The model-builder is in search of an input–output relationship. He is aware of the fact, however, that a state concept may underly that input–output relationship and therefore he is looking for a set structure. Unfortunately, there are many set structures that may model the input–output relationship. The functional relationships are now tied to the choice of the state and its dimension. In these circumstances the proper choice of a state set is considered to be part of the model structure.

3.3.2.2 Structure characterization: the overall approach

As follows from the definitions, the model structure represents a large amount of information. There does not exist yet a systematic procedure or even a complete set of well-established guidelines to help assemble the complete structure. Nowadays, approaches seem to exist and the model-builder chooses the approach which is most adequate for the purpose of the modelling exercise; based on ad hoc grounds, on personal experience or on professional judgement.

Before going into more details, it is possible to give an overview of the structure characterization process. At the outset, the choice of a model formalism and a model frame specifies a large set of possible mathematical representations: M_{in}. After characterization, one is still left with a set of models M_{out}. The candidate models now only differ by the numerical values of their parameters. Structure characterization consists in reducing the initial large set of models M_{in}, to a much smaller set, M_{out}. For ordinary differential equation models, and in fact for most other more complex model formalisms, this is seldom done in one stage. Usually, structure characterization proceeds in steps. The procedure is shown on Fig. 3.14. A number of propositions are assembled. The decision concerning each proposition reduces the initial model set to a smaller model set. As can be seen, during characterization the remaining candidate model set is still further restricted: $M_4 \subset M_3 \subset M_2 \subset M_1 \subset M_0 = M_{in}$. The procedure stops as soon as a parametrized model set is obtained. Modelling then enters the parameter estimation stage.

With the characterization process in mind, it can be concluded that basically two bodies of knowledge are required. Firstly, structural knowledge concerns the mathematical properties of the model set that

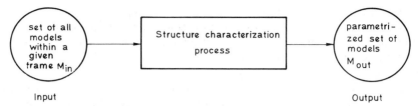

(a) *The purpose of structure characterization*

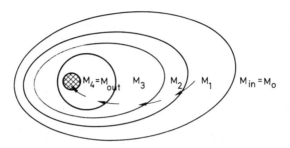

(b) *Hierarchically proceeding characterization process*

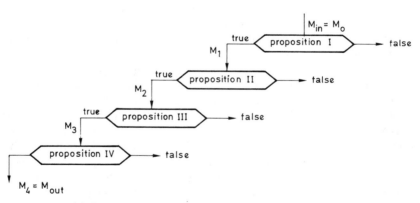

(c) *Decision network of the structure characterization process*

FIG. 3.14   Representation of the structure characterization process

results from a decision for a proposition. Clearly, studying the structural concepts and properties of model sets is a purely mathematical question dependent on the model formalism; it is often called realization theory. It is however of utmost importance. It provides the model-builder with insight into the descriptive power of the model set. It is also the basic knowledge required to be able to define further useful propositions.

Secondly, knowledge on characterization methodology is required so that decisions concerning propositions can be made in a plausible manner, based on the modelling sources. The latter knowledge truly belongs to the theory of mathematical modelling methodology. In order to clarify the more general considerations made up so far, consider a case in model-building, where the model formalism has been chosen to be an ordinary differential equation set: an ODESS, continuous time. The frame specifies a single input, a single output, a basically deterministic system within well-specified system borders. Measurements are taken discretely and it is known that the measurement procedure on the output introduces considerable noise. Table 3.1 gives a number of propositions, chosen during the characterization stage and the answers given. The model set defined by formalism and frame has been reduced to the following set, given in transfer function notation:

$$M_{out} : \frac{y(s)}{u(s)} = \frac{b_3 s^3 + b_2 s^2 + b_1 s + b_0}{s^3 + a_2 s^2 + a_1 s + a_0}$$

$$y_k = y(t_k) + e_k \quad E(e_k) = 0 \quad E(e_k e_j) = \sigma^2 \delta_{kj}$$

$$u_k = u(t_k)$$

The choice of the correct propositions is dictated by the modelling context and also by the results of realization theory. The theory shows, for instance, that deterministic, linear, SISO, black-box models without pure time delays have the model order as the most important structural property. The same theory indicates when a linear model is expected to be a good approximation of an eventual non-linear model. It also states that in the case of coloured noise, states may have to be assigned for modelling the uncertainties, etc.

Useful modelling methodology, are here, techniques that permit the establishment of answers on the propositions required for complete characterization. How can whiteness of noise be ascertained, how is linearity established, how is a model order chosen, etc.? Because one of the major themes of the book is modelling, structure characterization methods

TABLE 3.1 Propositions during characterization in a simple modelling exercise

Step	Proposition	Answer
1	There is little a priori knowledge: black-box case.	True
2	The measurement errors are essentially white.	True
3	The behaviour of the model is linear.	True
4	There are no pure time delays.	True
5	The model order is three.	True

is focused on, and results of realization theory are stated when required; assuming the reader has sufficient a priori knowledge in systems theory or the willingness to consult an adequate textbook on the subject.

3.3.2.3   Characterization vs. estimation and validation

In the present context it is useful to compare the characterization stage with other modelling stages, especially parameter estimation and model validation.

As mentioned before, it is not possible to separate completely structural issues from parameter estimation ones. Often, different structures can be combined to yield a more general structure so that the original ones follow from it by setting certain parameters to zero. In that manner the structure selection problem could be solved by estimating the parameters and deciding whether or not the crucial parameters are zero. Though such an approach may be used to a certain extent, it has only a limited applicability. First, under noisy conditions, establishing the zero value for a parameter is by no means straightforward and needs very accurate estimation. Second, as the sample size is finite, adding unnecessary parameters to the parameter vector is penalized with added uncertainty. If the total modelling activity is seen as a successive and stepped restriction of a set structure to a final unique mathematical description, then it may be argued precisely at which candidate model set parameter estimation will succeed structure characterization. However, it is bad policy to try to solve all structure characterization issues with pure parameter estimation.

A more subtle issue concerns the difference between structure characterization and model validation, though here too, at the extremes there is no difficulty. True validation techniques involve the use of a new data set to check the mathematical description while characterization methods compare model classes in order to select the most appropriate candidate class. Validation is, however, often used in a less "extreme" sense and it means checking the model adequacy of a description, on the same data set used for modelling. One looks for inconsistencies or contradictions by comparing model and data. To achieve this goal in practice, a property sometimes is tested against its alternative. Then, in fact, two model classes are compared and the technique may be seen as a structure characterization problem whenever the property is a structural entity. Here a distinction only exists in purpose. The boundary is fuzzy and is easily understood if one realizes that structure characterization validates the candidate selected against its opponents. It must be recognized that certain characterization methods may be useful in the validation stage, while an established validation technique may be reshaped in a characterization procedure. The ambiguity, however, is partly due to lack of insight into certain procedures: structure selecting procedures should have correct decision capability while validation methods should be oriented towards finding critical flaws without rejecting too readily a model where considerable effort has been put into its construction. As knowledge is not that far advanced, the choice of characterization methods here is, for a part, subjective.

3.3.2.4   *The role of the different information sources*

In order to obtain the model structure, one can rely on the information sources that are available to the model-builder (Section 2.4.2). For structure characterization, their impact is rather different.

High quality a priori knowledge under the form of laws and principles presented by a scientific discipline, is highly effective in characterizing the structure. Here one goes from the general to the specific. In many instances, the structural characterization problem has a unique solution. Using such a priori knowledge for model-building is called white-box modelling. Examples of the power of deduction and the beauty of the derivations will be given in the next chapter on partial differential equations, where the complexity of the model further interferes with inductive work.

Experimental data can also be used to obtain structural properties of a model. The process is much more complicated. It may be that only the model frame is known, while no a priori information about the structure is available. One speaks of black-box modelling. The problem is of considerable theoretical importance as the impact of one of the major information sources, a priori knowledge, is reduced to a bare minimum. In practice, the data set is finite. It is well known, that the characterization problem based on a finite data set alone has no unique solution [16, 226], in the sense that an infinite number of models exist that will fit the arbitrary data closely. The sensible approach is to look for the most adequate model, keeping in mind the limited information available in the data set.

The final information source: the model purpose, may sometimes be of help in determining a structure. Unfortunately, only guiding principles are available and will be subsequently discussed.

For structure characterization the following picture could be drawn. First, the purpose of the model shall give some clues concerning the requirements on the structure choice. Clearly, certain modelling goals can be more easily met than others. In Section 2.2, the goals have been discussed in order of increasing degree of difficulty. For simple descriptive or management purposes, the choice of a suitable structure can be straightforward. Suppose a number of almost noiseless observations are given; for interpolation purposes a static polynomial structure may be adequate. For the more ambitious modelling goals, the use of well-established a priori knowledge is preferable by far; but it will require professional skill from the model-builder to deduce the structure. Unfortunately, white-box modelling is not always possible. In most cases, "gray" boxes are encountered. Inductive characterization techniques are far less reliable. Though the precise "colour" of the system will completely depend on the specific case, Karplus [120] has given an average picture on the degree of induction that can be expected to be required. Mechanical, optical and electrical systems permit extensive use of deduction. An increased amount of induction is needed as one goes from chemical and structural processes via mass and heat transfer, hydrological phenomena and pollution processes, to biological systems like physiological and ecological phenomena. Finally, economical, social and psychological systems are very difficult to approach from a deductive point of view. This is a very approximate statement, but it is useful to make a rapid appraisal of the modelling effort that may be required, and eventually the success that will be obtained.

3.3.2.5 Guiding principles for structure characterization

It may happen in the characterization stage, that neither on the basis of deduction from a priori knowledge, nor on the basis of the data, can a unique choice for the structure be made. It has been argued, for instance, that it is not possible to find a unique structure from a finite data set. Clearly, the structure should be taken which serves the purpose of the model in the most acceptable way. Little is known about the relationship between specific modelling goals and structural properties; nevertheless, guiding principles have often been applied.

Physicality

A model that bears the most resemblance with reality is to be chosen. It is meant here that a priori knowledge should prevail.

Fit

The model structure has to be chosen in a manner that permits an acceptable representation of the data available. Basically, the experimental data must be explained by the model as well as possible.

Identifiability

It has to be remembered that the characterization stage will be followed by parameter estimation. A structure for which the parameters cannot be estimated, is useless. Since a final unique model is required, a model structure which is not system identifiable should be reconsidered in order to achieve an identifiable form. Concepts of identifiability have been proposed in Section 3.2.2.

Parsimony

A model structure is believed to be most effective and plausible if it is simple. Clearly, the model with the least number of parameters is most adequate for the parameter estimation stage. The principle goes further: it is accepted that a simple explanation for phenomena has to be preferred to a complex one.

Balanced accuracy

The model is the sum of frame, structure and parameter set. If limited information sets a limit to model accuracy, the most useful model is often a balanced compromise. There is little sense in retaining an eventually more valid structure, if the parameters in it can only be poorly estimated. An approximate structure with more precise parameter values may be more adequate. It is not sure yet whether this principle is as important as the others.

It is clear that the mathematical problems which arise during modelling, must remain well posed. This is inherent to the whole model-building approach. The other principles, however, are all sensible more or less to the same degree but as they may be in competition with each other, a suitable trade-off has to be found. The major efforts in the characterization field concern a search for a quantitative trade-off between the principles, and it may turn out that the specific trade-off is dependent on the model objective. However, final answers are not yet available.

3.3.2.6 Structure characterization: mathematical formulation and examples

In view of the definition of the structure, it could be expected that techniques for finding a model structure would be formulated from a mathematical framework with provision for functionals; in fact, one searching for functional relationships. It is possible to draw an analogy with optimal control, where one looks directly for an optimal input function instead of for a finite set of numbers. Unfortunately, the field does not seem to have developed to that point. Almost all characterization methods are based on a choice between model sets. The problem can be formulated as follows.

Given a finite set $\mathscr{L}$ of candidate model sets M_j:

$$\mathscr{L} : \{M_a, M_b, \ldots, M_l\}$$

choose the most appropriate model set.

As mentioned above, the complete characterization is done through a number of characterization problems of the type defined here. The propositions of Section 3.3.2.5 are nothing other than property specifications which partition the model set $\mathscr{L}$ in order to generate a specific characterization problem by defining candidate model classes. For example:

$\mathscr{L}$: {M_a, M_b}

M_a : set of models that behave linearly;

M_b : set of models that behave non-linearly;

Choose M_a or M_b.

If the choice in a characterization problem is to be done on the basis of measurements or data, one recognizes a problem of hypothesis testing or a problem pertaining to decision theory. In a subsequent section, a slightly more suggestive framework will be chosen.

A number of frequently encountered characterization problems, that have been studied in more detail, are now specified. They will be referred to in other sections and go from the specific to the general.

Autoregressive models: CP1

A model representation that has a very simple structure, is the autoregressive model class. An autoregressive model of order i is given by the following equation:

$$M_i : y_k + a_1 y_{k-1} + a_2 y_{k-2} + \ldots + a_i y_{k-i} = e_k$$

$$E(e_k) = 0 \qquad E(e_k e_j) = \sigma^2 \delta_{kj}$$

The complete structure is specified when it is known which parameters a_j are non-zero. The structurally most important parameter is a_i as it determines the so-called order of the model. For autoregressive black-box models, structure characterization is order selection, while resolving the remaining uncertainty is left to the parameter estimation phase. It is easily seen that $M_1 \subset M_2 \subset M_3 \ldots \subset M_l$. The structure characterization problem is then:

$\mathscr{L}$: {$M_1, M_2, M_3, \ldots, M_l$}

M_i : autoregressive model of order i : $a_i \neq 0$

Notice that the number of parameter $n_p = i + 1$. Besides the a_i coefficients, the variance σ^2 is usually unknown. The characterization problem CP1 has been extremely important in design and analysis of characterization procedures. It can easily be extended to the multi-output case. Then the parameters a_i, σ^2 become parameter matrices.

Single input–single output linear systems: CP2

A slightly more general case considers SISO linear deterministic systems with observation noise.

$$\mathscr{L} : \{M_1, M_2, \ldots, M_l\}$$

$$M_i : x_k + a_1 x_{k-1} + a_2 x_{k-2} + \ldots + a_i x_{k-i} = b_0 u_k + b_1 u_{k-1} + \ldots + b_i u_{k-i}$$

$$y_k = x_k + e_k \quad E(e_k) = 0 \quad E(e_k \cdot e_j) = \sigma^2 \delta_{kj}$$

In the time-series analysis context M_i is often thought to have two structural parameters and so in fact one should have $M_{i1,i2}$ — i1: maximum delay in x_k, i2: maximum delay in u_k. In systems theory, it is argued that the state dimension is the most important structural parameter and so the basic form remains M_i. Here too: $M_1 \subset M_2 \subset M_3 \ldots M_l$. It is more difficult properly to partition the total set M_l. Now $a_i \neq 0$ does not guarantee the model to be of order i: the parameter of the polynomials in x_k and u_k may be so that a zero of the y_k polynomial, often termed pole, cancels with a zero of the u_k polynomial. In the parameter space, there are generalized surfaces which correspond with lower order models.

In the stochastic case, different possibilities arise: see Section 3.1.2.2. If a state–space form is chosen one will obtain the following problem:

$$\mathscr{L} : \{M_1, M_2, \ldots, M_l\}$$

$$M_i : x_k + a_1 x_{k-1} + \ldots + a_i x_{k-i} = b_0 u_k + b_1 u_{k-1} + \ldots + b_i u_{k-i} + e_k$$
$$+ c_1 e_{k-1} + \ldots + c_i e_{k-i}$$

$$E(e_k) = 0 \quad E(e_k \cdot e_j) = \sigma^2 \delta_{kj}$$

Basically, the order remains the fundamental problem. If transfer function models are taken, it can be postulated that the order of the noise transfer function is equal to the order of the deterministic part and the characterization problem remains the same. It could be conceived that in a more general framework, the order of both the deterministic part and the stochastic part, assume different values. Then a more general problem follows.

Multiple input–multiple output linear systems: CP3

Multiple input–multiple output systems have a much more complicated structure. Consequently it is more difficult to give a complete specification useful in the modelling context. In general, one can write, for instance, based on a transfer function notation:

$$\mathscr{L} : \{M_1, M_2. \ldots, M_l\}$$

$$M_i : \underline{x}_k = G(z^{-1}) \underline{u}_k$$

$$\underline{y}_k = \underline{x}_k + \underline{e}_k \quad E(\underline{e}_k) = \underline{0} \quad E(\underline{e}_k \cdot \underline{e}_j^T) = \Lambda \delta_{kj}$$

$G(z^{-1})$: matrix with rational entries.

A straightforward approach would be to specify the order of the rational entries as i. Unfortunately, the procedure is not efficient parametrically, in the sense that, for a given structure, too many parameters are available.

Realization theory shows that the dimension of the state vector n, is not the only important structural parameter. If the model is considered from the point of view of adequate observation, then there is a structural parameter for each output variable. For p outputs, the choice of an integer set $(\kappa_1, \kappa_2, \ldots, \kappa_p)$ where $\sum_{j=1}^{p} \kappa_j = n$, permits the finding of a unique parametrization with a minimum number of parameters. The number of parameters depends on the values of the κs. At most, there are $n(p + m)$ parameters. There are a number of ways of defining the κs resulting in different so-called canonical forms. For more details, refer to the literature [32, 48, 234] and simply see its relevance in the context of model-building.

For SISO systems, the order specifies a unique parametrization that is most easily written down by using a transfer function notation, e.g. (3.20). For the MIMO case and for a given system order n, there may be many model forms, even when a transfer function notation is used. They depend on the definition of the κs and on their precise values. A very approximate picture of the situation is given in Fig. 3.15. Suppose that for a given definition of the κs, the most general description having $n(p + m)$ parameters is taken. Then a small number of systems will be described badly or not at all; these systems are in the shaded regions on Fig. 3.15. For instance, system $M(\hat{\underline{p}}_1)$ is adequately described, system $M(\hat{\underline{p}}_2)$ is not. If

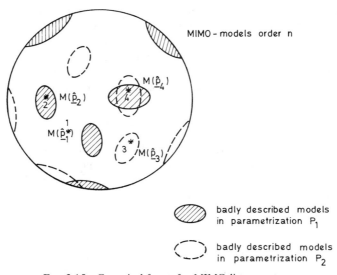

FIG. 3.15   Canonical forms for MIMO-linear systems

another definition for the κs was taken and the most general description with that particular definition is considered, then system $M(\hat{p}_2)$ is properly represented but now system $M(\hat{p}_3)$ is not. There may be systems: $M(\hat{p}_4)$, where both model representations fail. The trouble is that, besides the dimensionality of the state, other information is required in order to find a suitable parametrization. The problem is still an area of intensive research and the reader is referred to the literature for more details [89, 140, 224].

For the more general stochastic case, the same remarks can be given as for the SISO case. A characterization problem can be formulated in the following way:

$$\mathscr{L} : \{M_1, M_2, \ldots, M_l\}$$
$$M_i : \underline{y}_k = G(z^{-1})\underline{u}_k + H(z^{-1})\underline{e}_k$$
$$G(z^{-1}), H(z^{-1}) : \text{matrices with rational entries}$$
$$E(\underline{e}_k) = \underline{0} \qquad E(\underline{e}_k \cdot \underline{e}_j^T) = \Lambda\delta_{kj}$$

Note that identifiability conditions are implicitly assumed.

Prediction error models: CP4

A more general class of models is given by the prediction error formulation. Because there are special parameter estimation methods for this class, it is useful to consider them separately.

$$\mathscr{L} : \{M_1, M_2, \ldots, M_l\}$$
$$M_i : \underline{y}_k = \underline{f}_i(\underline{p}, k, \underline{y}_{k-i}, \ldots, \underline{u}_{k-i}, \ldots) + \underline{e}_k$$
$$E(\underline{e}_k) = \underline{0} \qquad E(\underline{e}_k \cdot \underline{e}_j^T) = \Lambda\delta_{kj}$$

The structure characterization problem is difficult in the non-linear case. For linear systems, canonical state space or transfer function models are available but for non-linear ones, the choice of a model structure is generally unclear. Still on the basis of a priori knowledge, of expansions, or of other approaches a characterization problem of the type mentioned may arise.

The general case: CP5

The most general case occurs when the candidate model sets are of type (3.1–4) for deterministic descriptions or of type (3.5–8) for the stochastic descriptions.

Some important characterization methods are related to the parameter estimation step. It may happen that such a method requires the parameter estimation to be performed in a specific manner, or the structure choice and the parameter estimate may be combined in one single problem. In those cases, very often the maximum likelihood estimates are referred to.

For later reference, the main results and properties concerning the maximum likelihood approach are reviewed and summarized here.

Consider the prediction error models. Suppose that the innovations, or the residuals, are identically distributed, independent and Gaussian. The logarithm of the (conditional) likelihood function is given by:

$$L(\underline{p}) = \log l(\underline{p}) = \log p(\underline{y}_1, \underline{y}_2, \ldots, \underline{y}_N)$$

$$= -\left(\frac{N \cdot p}{2} \log 2\pi + \frac{N}{2} \log \det \Lambda + \frac{1}{2} \sum_{k=1}^{N} \underline{\varepsilon}_k^T \Lambda^{-1} \underline{\varepsilon}_k\right) \qquad (3.233)$$

$\Lambda = E(\underline{e}_k \cdot \underline{e}_k^T)$: covariance of the white noise sequence

N   : number of samples

p   : number of outputs

Maximization of L(p) is most easily done if Λ is completely known or if Λ is completely unknown. The latter case is more useful in the modelling context and the maximum likelihood estimates $\underline{\hat{p}}^*_N$ and $\hat{\Lambda}^*_N$ are obtained as follows:

$$\underline{\hat{p}}^*_N = \min_{\underline{p}} \{V_N(\underline{p})\} = \det\left(\frac{1}{N} \sum_{k=1}^{N} \underline{\varepsilon}_k \cdot \underline{\varepsilon}_k^T\right) \qquad (3.234)$$

$$\hat{\Lambda}^*_N = \frac{1}{N} \sum_{k=1}^{N} \underline{\varepsilon}_k \cdot \underline{\varepsilon}_k^T \qquad (3.235)$$

The maximum of L(p) is:

$$L(\underline{\hat{p}}^*_N) = -\left(\frac{N \cdot p}{2}(1 + \log 2\pi) + \frac{N}{2} \log \det \hat{\Lambda}^*_N\right) \qquad (3.236)$$

It is known that the estimate $\hat{p}_N$ has the following properties, subject to mild regularity and stationary conditions:

* consistent $\lim_{N\to\infty} E[\underline{\hat{p}}^*_N] = \underline{p}$ p: true parameter

* asymptotically normal;

* asymptotically efficient: smallest covariance under the unbiased estimates;

$$* \quad \lim_{N\to\infty} E[(\underline{\hat{p}}^*_N - \underline{p})(\underline{\hat{p}}^*_N - \underline{p})^T] = \lim_{N\to\infty} \frac{2}{N}\left[\frac{\partial^2 \log \det \Lambda}{\partial \underline{p}^T \partial \underline{p}}\right]^{-1}$$

$$= \lim_{N\to\infty} Q_N(\underline{\hat{p}}^*) \qquad (3.237)$$

Other forms for (3.237) are:

$$\lim_{N \to \infty} \frac{2}{N} \left\{ \frac{\partial^2 \log \det \Lambda}{\partial \underline{p}^T \partial \underline{p}} \right\}^{-1} = \lim_{N \to \infty} \frac{2}{N} \det \hat{\Lambda}^*_N \left\{ \frac{\partial^2 \det \Lambda}{\partial \underline{p}^T \partial \underline{p}} \right\}^{-1}$$

$$= \frac{1}{N} \left\{ E\left[\left(\frac{\partial \varepsilon}{\partial \underline{p}}\right)^T \Lambda^{-1} \left(\frac{\partial \varepsilon}{\partial \underline{p}}\right) \right] \right\}^{-1} \qquad (3.238)$$

Notice that for $N \to \infty$ $\qquad \hat{\Lambda}^*_\infty = \Lambda$ and $\hat{\underline{p}}^*_N = \underline{p}$

By virtue of the estimate being the maximum of the likelihood:

$$\frac{\partial L}{\partial \underline{p}} \bigg|_{\underline{p}=\hat{\underline{p}}^*} = \frac{\partial V}{\partial \underline{p}} \bigg|_{\underline{p}=\hat{\underline{p}}^*} = 0 \qquad (3.239)$$

The random variable

$$-\frac{1}{2} (\underline{p} - \hat{\underline{p}}^*_N)^T \frac{\partial^2 L}{\partial \underline{p}^T \partial \underline{p}} \bigg|_{\hat{\underline{p}}^*_N} (\underline{p} - \hat{\underline{p}}^*_N)$$

or

$$-\frac{N}{2} \left[(\underline{p} - \hat{\underline{p}}^*_N)^T \frac{\partial^2 V}{\partial \underline{p}^T \partial \underline{p}} \bigg|_{\hat{\underline{p}}^*_N} (\underline{p} - \hat{\underline{p}}^*_N) \right] (V)^{-1} \qquad (3.240)$$

is distributed in the limit for $N \to \infty$ as $\chi^2(n_p)$ and thus its mean is n_p and the variance $2n_p$. For a proof see [203], but an intuitive insight can be obtained by considering (3.240) in the light of (3.237).

Often the distribution of the innovations will not be known; they are, however, white and identically distributed. If (3.234) and (3.235) are kept as estimators, again under mild regularity and stationarity conditions, all asymptotic results are carried over except the asymptotic efficiency. This means that the maximum likelihood estimate is still of use even if the Gaussian assumption does not hold.

3.3.2.7 *Classification of techniques*

At present, no general theory exists which would allow a really meaningful classification of the techniques. Historically, the end of the sixties were a turning-point.

Before 1970 research activity on the subject was limited. There were three traditional fields of interest. The statistical literature contained the most elaborate methods, though they had their defects, typical of which is "fit" as the most important principle, while parsimony is taken into account in very rudimentary ways. There are also the optimum cost techniques, Wilks' method and simple hypothesis testing. In control theory, simple methods for linear systems were available: the pole–zero cancellation technique is presented as an example. In the simulation field heuristic test quantities were used, often "tailored" to the practical case under study.

After 1970 the activity in the field has increased considerably, partly because identification became popular in systems theory. Several trends can be distinguished related to important questions such as, what is the most suitable trade-off between fit and complexity given a finite data set? A prediction error approach and an improved likelihood approach are compared. Are there other theoretical concepts that could be useful for structure characterization? New developments seem to indicate that information theory can be of help. Is it possible to find structure indicating quantities which relate directly to well-known parameter estimation techniques? Because of the attention paid in this work to the instrumental variable approach, this specific case is investigated. Can one get a measure of confidence for the structure choice? A method which takes a Bayesian point of view is useful here.

Derivations will be kept to a minimum. Interested readers are referred to the literature referenced in subsequent sections.

3.3.3   Early structure characterization techniques

3.3.3.1   *Model response characteristics*

A very crude, intuitive approach to characterization is based on model response characteristics. The technique is related to the very human approach to recognition: looking for typical discriminating characteristics. In its simple form, the candidate structures are mathematically analysed in order to find a salient unique property of the response. Then the measurements are visually inspected and, if the noise levels are not too high, it may happen that recognition of a property points to the most appropriate candidate. A historically famous characterization problem of type CP5 is an example.

In search of a suitable mathematical description for bacterial growth, Monod compared, at a given stage of his research, two candidate models [165]. Both had the general form:

$$\frac{dx}{dt} = \mu(x, S) \cdot x$$

$$\frac{dS}{dt} = -\frac{1}{Y}\frac{dx}{dt}$$

$$y(t) = x(t) + e(t)$$

x   = biomass concentration as a measure for population density.

S   = substrate concentration as a measure for available food.

The difference in the models came from the choice of $\mu(x, S)$

$$M_1 : \mu(x, S) = \mu_V\left(1 - \frac{x}{x_M}\right) \quad x_M = x_0 + yS_0$$

$$M_2 : \mu(x, S) = \mu_M S/(k_M + S)$$

The models are both non-linear. If the response $x(t)$ is analysed, it can be mathematically found that it is S-shaped and non-decreasing. M_1 has an inflection point halfway between zero and the maximum value x_M. The model M_2 has an inflection point, dependent on parameter values, somewhere in the upper half of the curve. By inspection of the experimental curves, Monod found inflection points close to the maximum value x_M, so the model M_1 could be rejected immediately.

The approach of specifying typical response characteristics is popular in the field of simulation. Though it is very rudimentary, it shows all important features of characterization methods and it is therefore useful for gaining intuitive insight into many issues that concern structure characterization. It will be used to define a framework which unifies many procedures. As specified here, it is difficult to use as soon as the noise levels are high. A number of less noise-prone techniques have their origin in the field of statistics and are discussed next.

3.3.3.2 Optimum cost techniques

In Section 3.2.7, parameter estimation was presented as an optimization problem on a cost or objective function. If several structures are candidates for the final model, each model representation can be completed by carrying through the parameter estimation phase. In that way, for each candidate model the cost will have been optimized. It appears natural to choose as the most representative, the model with the more favourable optimum cost. In a sense, it can be said that the final mathematical representation has the most appropriate structure as it optimizes a measure for adequacy: the objective function. The utilization of the cost is basically very general and widely applicable. The technique depends on the choice of the cost, as shown by the following two special cases most often encountered.

Consider the first case where the cost is defined as follows:

$$l(k, \underline{p}, \underline{\varepsilon}) = \underline{\varepsilon}_k^T \cdot \underline{\varepsilon}_k$$

$$V_N = Q_N = \frac{1}{N} \sum_{k=1}^{N} l(k, \underline{p}, \underline{\varepsilon})$$

Then for a characterization problem of the following type, $\mathscr{L}: \{M_1, M_2, \ldots, M_l\}$ one shall compute: $\{V_N^1, V_N^2, \ldots, V_N^l\}$ and take $M_{opt} = M_i$, so that $V_N^i = \underset{j}{opt}\{V_N^j\}$.

Though often applied, the procedure has a serious flaw. In fact, the cost measures the "fit" of the model to the data and, consequently, the choice of the structure is based on the "fit" principle, Section 3.3.2.5. If the number of parameters is allowed to increase, the fit can be made arbitrarily good. Thus models of high complexity with many parameters will be favoured. Unfortunately, complex models turn out to be useless. It is seen that the characterization technique does not take into account the principle of parsimony. The unsatisfactory behaviour of complex models can be understood heuristically: as the sample size is finite, increasing the number of parameters will yield better fit, but the estimates will necessarily be less precise. At a certain point, these estimates are so bad that the model loses all representative value.

There has been a very early attempt to take parsimony into account based on the concept of degrees of freedom. Consider the scalar case, when

$$\frac{1}{N} \sum_{k=1}^{N} \varepsilon_k^2$$

is an estimate of the noise variance. It is well-known to statisticians that the estimate is biased. An unbiased estimate is available:

$$\hat{\sigma}^2 = \frac{1}{N - n_p} \sum_{k=1}^{N} \varepsilon_k^2 \tag{3.241}$$

N : number of samples

n_p : number of estimated parameters in the model.

The role of the fit principle is now even more apparent: the best model is the model with the smallest estimated noise variance. For further reference (3.241) is modified. As the $\log(\cdot)$ function is ever-increasing, the choice can be based on $\log \hat{\sigma}^2$:

$$\log \hat{\sigma}^2 = \log \frac{1}{N - n_p} \sum_{k=1}^{N} \varepsilon_k^2 = \log V_N + \log \left(\frac{N}{N - n_p} \right) \tag{3.242}$$

The last term in (3.242) can be expanded for $N \to \infty$

$$\log \hat{\sigma}^2 = \log V_N + \frac{n_p}{N} + \text{higher order terms in } \frac{n_p}{N} \tag{3.243}$$

In (3.243), there are basically two terms: the first $\log V_N$ is a measure of fit and will decrease as the number of parameters grows, the second is a linear function of the parameter dimension, with which it will increase. A minimum will occur when the increase in fit is too small to compensate for the increase of the second term. Thus, fit is traded against complexity.

Unfortunately, the trade-off is almost certainly bad, as shall be seen in the sequel.

A second important case arises when the likelihood is chosen as objective function. Under the assumption of Gaussian prediction errors, with zero mean and covariance matrix Λ, the logarithm of it is given by equation (3.233), see Section 3.3.2.5. The precise value of the likelihood is not known, but usually $\underline{p}$ is estimated to maximize (3.233) and instead of $L(\underline{p})$, $L(\underline{\hat{p}}^*_N)$ is used where $\hat{p}^*_N$ stands for the maximum likelihood estimate of the parameter vector. It is a well-known result (3.236) that:

$$L(\underline{\hat{p}}^*_N) = -\frac{N \cdot p}{2}(1 + \log 2\pi) - \frac{N}{2} \log \det\left(\frac{1}{N}\sum_{k=1}^{N} \varepsilon_k \cdot \varepsilon_k^T\right) \qquad (3.244)$$

For the scalar output case (3.244) becomes:

$$L(\underline{\hat{p}}^*_N) = -\frac{N}{2}(1 + \log 2\pi) - \frac{N}{2} \log \frac{1}{N}\sum_{k=1}^{N} \varepsilon_k^2 \qquad (3.245)$$

The first term is model independent and the second is only a measure for the fit. When only two candidate models are considered, the procedure is called the likelihood ratio test, because a ratio is used as test quantity:

$$\Lambda = \frac{L_{M_2}(\underline{\hat{p}}^*_N{}^2)}{L_{M_1}(\underline{\hat{p}}^*_N{}^1)} \qquad (3.246)$$

The major defect in (3.245) stems from its independence from factors related to parsimony. It will be shown later that $L(\hat{p}^*_N)$ is a biased estimate of $L(\underline{p})$ so that criterium (3.245) can be improved.

Another important consideration concerns the nature of the test quantities, which are all random variables. Certain data sets will be more adequate to obtain structural knowledge from it than other ones. The quality of the data may influence the decision itself and will certainly influence the confidence with which a choice can be made. At least a rough idea would be helpful. In the context of the most favourable cost, little attention has been paid to this still important aspect. For the test statistic (3.241), it is known that $(\hat{\sigma}^2/\sigma^2)(N - n_p)$ is distributed according to $\chi^2(N - n_p)$ under suitable assumptions for the residuals.

To sum up, it can be noted that the optimum of the objective function used for estimation can be used for structure characterization. The early versions of the method are inadequate whenever the models have differing complexity, because no provisions are made to take into account the additional freedom stemming from more parameters; this is the case for problems CP1–CP3. Furthermore, it is difficult to get even a rough idea about the strength of any choice. The following technique seems to be more adequate from the latter point of view.

3.3.3.3   *The Wilks' method*

A statistically more elaborate and still general technique is the method introduced by Wilks. As in the previous case, all candidate models are fitted to the data by estimating the parameters as accurately as possible. Instead of focusing on the optimized cost, the model outputs $\hat{y}_k^j$, k-th sample of the j-th candidate, are compared with the actual measurements $\underline{y}_k$ by relating them through a linear equation:

$$\underline{y}_k = \sum_{j=1}^{1} q_j \hat{\underline{y}}_k^j + \underline{e}_k \tag{3.247}$$

Then (3.247) is treated as a linear regression model and the q_j are estimated under a constraint $\Sigma_{j=1}^{1} q_j = 1$. This is a slightly more general case than the problem considered in Section 3.2.3.4. Equation (3.247) can be handled as follows:

$$\sum_{i=1}^{1} q_j \underline{y}_k - \sum_{j=1}^{1} q_j \hat{\underline{y}}_k^j - \underline{e}_k = \underline{0}$$

$$\sum_{j=1}^{1} q_j \underline{\varepsilon}_k^j - \underline{e}_k = \underline{0}$$

And with an obvious matrix notation, one obtains:

$$\mathbf{E}_k \underline{q} - \underline{e}_k = 0 \tag{3.248}$$

A straightforward least squares estimate can only be obtained if the variance of the noise Λ is known. Unfortunately, for the purpose here, that will seldom be the case. Suppose first that Λ is given, a suitable cost is:

$$J = \sum_{k=1}^{N} \underline{q}^T \mathbf{E}_k^T \Lambda \mathbf{E}_k \underline{q} + 2\lambda(\underline{e}^T \cdot \underline{q} - 1)$$

where the first part evaluates the weighted square of the errors and the second part is provided in order to take care of the constraint. λ is a Lagrange multiplier. Setting the appropriate derivatives of J to zero, one obtains:

$$\left(\sum_{k=1}^{N} \mathbf{E}_k^T \Lambda \mathbf{E}_k \right) \underline{q} + \lambda \underline{e} = \underline{0}$$

$$\underline{e}^T \cdot \underline{q} \qquad\qquad = 1$$

It is a simple matter to solve these equations:

$$\hat{\lambda} = - |\underline{e}^T \Upsilon^{-1} \underline{e}|^{-1} \tag{3.249}$$

$$\hat{\underline{q}} = |\underline{e}^T \Upsilon^{-1} \underline{e}|^{-1} \Upsilon^{-1} \underline{e} \tag{3.250}$$

where for notational convenience

$$\Upsilon = \sum_{k=1}^{N} E_k^T \Lambda E_k$$

It is known that if $\underline{q}$ is known, an estimate for $\hat{\Lambda}$ can be found:

$$\hat{\Lambda} = \frac{1}{N} \sum_{k=1}^{N} \underline{\varepsilon}_k \cdot \underline{\varepsilon}_k^T = \frac{1}{N} \sum_{k=1}^{N} E_k \underline{q} \cdot \underline{q}^T E_k^T \qquad (3.251)$$

In the realistic case when neither Λ nor $\underline{q}$ are known, an estimate can be found by alternating between (3.249–250) and (3.251). One can start with $\Lambda = I$, compute $\hat{\lambda}_1$, $\hat{\underline{q}}_1$, then evaluate $\hat{\Lambda}_1$ with (3.251) and iterate till convergence.

Once the vector $\hat{\underline{q}}$ is obtained, the characterization method is as follows. From $\mathscr{L} : \{M_1, M_2, \ldots, M_l\}$, choose M_i so that $q_i = \max_j\{|q_j|\}$.

The advantage of Wilks' method resides in the fact that an approximation for the covariance matrix of the $\underline{q}$ vector can be computed. Hosten [95] proposes

$$E[(\hat{\underline{q}} - \underline{q})(\hat{\underline{q}} - \underline{q})^T] = \Upsilon^{-1}[I - (\underline{e}^T \Upsilon^{-1} \underline{e})^{-1} \underline{e} \cdot \underline{e}^T \Upsilon^{-1}] \qquad (3.252)$$

Based on simplifications for $\hat{\Lambda}$, one could even utilize the existing statistical methods for testing the meaningfulness of the differences between q-values, in order to evaluate the relevance of the characterization experiment.

However, such techniques are probably of limited value. An underlying hypothesis of the complete regression approach is the linear independence of the regressors, $\hat{y}_k^j$. Furthermore, these quantities should be perfectly known. Unfortunately, in this context, the regressors are the result of parameter estimation procedures on a unique data set. They are thus random variables. This is contrary to the hypotheses mentioned. A more careful study is required in order to evaluate the equations presented here.

In summary, it can be said that the Wilks method has a very general applicability. A measure for the statistical spread on the decision vector is available. The next approach sees the characterization problem directly as a test of hypotheses.

3.3.3.4 *Methods derived from hypothesis testing*

Another technique, coming from the statistical field, is based on hypothesis testing. The rationale of the procedure is sound, but it has been under fire in the last decade, so the advantages and disadvantages will be discussed.

The classic theory of hypothesis testing is applicable for comparing only two classes: $\mathscr{L} : \{M_1, M_2\}$, when $M_1 \subset M_2$ or M_1 is the smaller model and can be obtained from M_2 by simplification. A test quantity F is computed:

$$F = \frac{V_N^1 - V_N^2}{V_N^2} \frac{N - n_{p1}}{n_{p2} - n_{p1}} \tag{3.253}$$

where

$$V_N^i = \frac{1}{N} \det\left(\frac{1}{N} \sum \varepsilon_k^i \cdot \varepsilon_k^{iT}\right)$$

n_{p1} = number of parameters in M_1.
n_{p2} = number of parameters in M_2.

It is assumed that the maximum likelihood technique is used to estimate the parameters and to obtain the residuals. Then for

$F \leq \eta_0$ choose M_1
$F > \eta_0$ choose M_2

For static linear regression, it can be proved that the distribution of F is given by $F(N - n_{p2}, n_{p2} - n_{p1})$. For autoregressive models the statement can still be proved. By a generalizing argument it can be proposed or conjectured that the F-statistic holds at least asymptotically [182].

The major problem resides in choosing the quantity η_0. It is related in tables of the F-distribution to π_1: the probability of the so-called Type I errors, rejecting M_1 when in spite of the extreme value of F, the model M_1 holds. Unfortunately, the authors have no idea about the probability of Type II errors: accepting M_1 when M_2 was the actual model.

The procedure is difficult to generalize for more than two models. Several problems are encountered.

(a) The decision rule is not transitive, i.e., model M_1 may be preferred to M_2, M_2 to M_3 and M_3 to M_1: the answer is inconsistent.

(b) It is not easy to choose the risk levels π. It is clear that there is not the same risk in selecting a second order model when the first order model is the true one, as there is in selecting a fifth order if the first order model is adequate.

Application of the test for multiple classes remains a heuristic procedure.

3.3.3.5   Pole–zero cancellations

If all the candidate models are linear, the problem of characterization has special features. In the linear case there is a very special relationship between model parameters and model structure: variables are multiplied by parameters. This special relationship explains why special characterization techniques may exist for that type of problem.

One of the well-known examples is the pole–zero cancellation test. It is based on the fact that linear models with too high an order have zeros that coincide with poles. After pole–zero cancellation, a simpler model is obtained, which is the basic idea. A systematic procedure can be given for comparison of the two model structures where $M_1 \subset M_2$:

(a) Fit the model M_2, obtain an estimate $\hat{\underline{p}}^*_2$ (the maximum likelihood estimate is chosen here) and compute a covariance estimate $\hat{\Lambda}^*_N$.

(b) Suppose that, in fact, the model M_1 holds and find a relationship $\underline{p}_2 = \underline{f}(\underline{p}_1)$. The function $\underline{f}$ can be found by requiring that by pole–zero cancellation the M_2 models reduces to M_1.

(c) Estimate a $\hat{\underline{p}}_1$ parameter so that (3.254) is minimized:

$$J_p(\underline{p}_1) = [\underline{f}(\underline{p}_1) - \hat{\underline{p}}^*_2] \Lambda^{*-1}_N [\underline{f}(\underline{p}_1) - \hat{\underline{p}}^*_2] \tag{3.254}$$

(d) If $J_p(\underline{p}_1)$ is sufficiently small, consider M_1 as the true model.

The procedure is simple, but like the hypothesis testing procedures discussed in Section 3.3.3.4, it is difficult to extend it in a consistent manner for cases where more than two models have to be compared. Notice that the fit principle is also used.

3.3.3.6 Conclusions

After the evaluation of early structure characterization techniques, a number of important issues typical for the field can be identified.

A decision is made always based on a criterion. The choice of such a criterion can be very specific as in the case of response characteristics; related to a wide class of systems as for linear model representations, or it can be more general. Often the criterion measures fit. Unfortunately, if the principle of parsimony is not accounted for, erroneous results may be obtained. The criterion itself is always a statistical variable, so is interesting if a measure of decision confidence can be given. For the early methods, at most a confidence interval is available if the true system is supposed to be in the candidate set.

Though many basic ideas can be found in the early techniques, they are rather primitive and ad hoc. In the next paragraph, more recent methods will be presented which focus on a particular aspect of the characterization problem and bring an improvement, when compared with the techniques already described. They try to find a more firm basis from which to suggest or validate an approach; try to obtain better decision criteria, or else try to better evaluate the confidence with which a candidate can be selected.

3.3.4 Recent techniques for structure characterization

3.3.4.1 *The final prediction error FPE* [1]

When comparing different structures, a measure of the prediction error is under conditions of ergodicity:

$$V_\infty(\underline{p}_\infty) = E[(y_k - \hat{y}(k, \underline{p}_\infty)^2] = \lim_{N \to \infty} \frac{1}{N} \sum_{k=1}^{N} (y_k - \hat{y}(k, \underline{p}_\infty))^2 \qquad (3.255)$$

It supposes, for instance, that a maximum likelihood estimate $\hat{p}^*_\infty$ is done on an infinite number of points and that an estimate of the mean squared error is performed. Notice that in Section 3.3.3.2, equation (3.241) yields an unbiased estimate for it and thus (3.255) tells nothing new. Some careful thought indicates that in fact $V_\infty(\underline{p}_\infty)$ is unrealistic: since a model is going to be built from a finite set of data, $V_\infty(\underline{p}_\infty)$ has little meaning. A better measure for the prediction capability with which the model will be able to operate, is given by $V_\infty(\hat{\underline{p}}_N)$: it is the prediction efficiency that can be attained with a parameter estimate $\hat{\underline{p}}_N$. In order to evaluate the prediction capability in a proper way, an infinite amount of data is needed; this explains the index of the function V. The reasoning invokes in essence the principle of "balanced accuracy". If the model complexity grows, the parameter estimate on a finite sample will be less precise and $V_\infty(\hat{\underline{p}}_N)$ can be expected to deteriorate. Fit remains the major issue, but the finite sample size is taken directly into account. As $\hat{\underline{p}}_N$ is a stochastic vector, $V_\infty(\hat{\underline{p}}_N)$ is a stochastic variable and an average value $E[V_\infty(\hat{\underline{p}}_N)]$ is appropriate. To obtain the decision quantity, the following derivation is necessary. A Taylor expansion yields:

$$V_\infty(\hat{\underline{p}}_N) = V_\infty[\underline{p}_\infty + (\hat{\underline{p}}_N - \underline{p}_\infty)] = V_\infty(\underline{p}_\infty) + \left. \frac{\partial V_\infty}{\partial \underline{p}} \right|_\infty (\hat{\underline{p}}_N - \underline{p}_\infty)$$

$$+ \frac{1}{2} (\hat{\underline{p}}_N - \underline{p}_\infty)^T \left. \frac{\partial^2 V_\infty}{\partial \underline{p}^T \cdot \partial \underline{p}} \right|_\infty (\hat{\underline{p}}_N - \underline{p}_\infty)$$

$$+ \text{ higher order terms} \qquad (3.256)$$

If a maximum likelihood estimation scheme is used, then $(dV/d\underline{p})_\infty = 0$, remember (3.239); and so from (3.256):

$$V_\infty(\hat{\underline{p}}^*_N) = V_\infty(\underline{p}_\infty) + Q(\hat{\underline{p}}^*_N, \underline{p}_\infty) = V_\infty(\underline{p}_\infty)\left(1 + \frac{Q(\hat{\underline{p}}^*_N, \underline{p}_\infty)}{V_\infty(\underline{p}_\infty)}\right)$$

Taking expectations on both sides, one thus finds with the result (3.240)

$$E[V_\infty(\underline{p}_N)] = V_\infty(\underline{p}_\infty)\left(1 + \frac{n_p}{N}\right) \qquad (3.257)$$

Unfortunately, $V_\infty(p_\infty)$ is not known. The unbiased estimate (3.241) is used as a substitute and the final prediction error test quantity is obtained.

$$\text{FPE} = V_N(\hat{\underline{p}}^*{}_N)\frac{N + n_p}{N - n_p} = \hat{\sigma}^2\frac{N + n_p}{N - n_p} \tag{3.258}$$

Some remarks are appropriate:

(a) For the multivariate case $\hat{\sigma}^2$ has to be replaced by $\det \hat{\Lambda}(\hat{\underline{p}}^*{}_N)$. The parameter estimate should be a maximum likelihood estimate. If conditional maximum likelihood estimates are used, care should be taken in choosing initial conditions. They have to be similar for all the models, otherwise (3.258) is not an estimate of the final prediction error. A standard approach is to take them all zero.

(b) For the purpose of comparison, it can be stated that the structure choice can be made on log FPE: for large N, the criterion can be simplified further:

$$\log \text{FPE} = \log V_N(\hat{\underline{p}}^*{}_N) + \log\left(\frac{1 + \dfrac{n_p}{N}}{1 - \dfrac{n_p}{N}}\right) \approx \log V_N(\hat{\underline{p}}^*{}_N) + \frac{2n_p}{N} \tag{3.259}$$

(c) Though the final prediction error is estimated without bias, that does not mean that the procedure is consistent in the sense that the true model order will be found if the number of observations grows beyond limit. This means, e.g. for the characterization problem CP1, that even with an unlimited amount of data the procedure sometimes will indicate a model with a wrong order, in fact too high an order. This phenomenon is discussed in more detail later, but Akaike [1] was aware of this and he suggested another form:

$$\text{FPE}^\beta = V_N(\hat{\underline{p}}^*{}_N)\frac{1 + \dfrac{n_p}{N^\beta}}{1 - \dfrac{n_p}{N}} \tag{3.260}$$

$$0 < \beta < 1$$

Unfortunately, the test quantity (3.260) has lost its interpretation. Furthermore, based on simulation, Akaike preferred the FPE criterion to $\text{FPE}^{1/4}$.

(d) In the scalar output case and under suitable normal assumptions $N\hat{\sigma}^2/\sigma^2$ is distributed as $\chi^2(N - n_p + 1)$. An approximation for the dispersion of FPE thus is

$$\text{FPE}\sqrt{\frac{2}{N - n_p}}$$

To conclude, equation (3.259) is compared with equation (3.241). For large samples, they have the same appearance. For the FPE criterion, the second term is twice as large as the second term in (3.241). The factor which has to induce parsimony is more heavily weighted. The main contribution of the FPE method to the field consists in better trading fit for efficient parametrization. More detailed discussion is postponed until the AIC method is explained.

3.3.4.2   *The AIC procedure*

Akaike recognized the relevance of information-theoretical concepts in the model-building context and introduced the AIC criterion for model selection [3]. The authors first derive the criterion in a more direct way [121] and then consider the interpretation from the point of view of information theory.

One of the early characterization methods is based on the maximum likelihood $l(\hat{\underline{p}}^*_N)$: the probability of getting the specific observations when a given model is accepted to be true. The technique described in Section 3.3.3.2 computes the logarithm of this likelihood by inserting the maximum likelihood parameter estimate which introduces bias. In fact, instead of $L(\hat{\underline{p}}_N^\infty)$, it is $L(\hat{\underline{p}}_\infty^\infty)$ which should be considered, as it represents the likelihood with the most appropriate parameter vector $\hat{\underline{p}}^*$, based on an infinite data set. A Taylor expansion for $L(\hat{\underline{p}}^*_\infty)$ can be written:

$$L(\underline{p}_\infty) = L(\hat{\underline{p}}^*_N) + \left.\frac{\partial L}{\partial \underline{p}}\right|_{\hat{\underline{p}}^*_N} (\hat{\underline{p}}_\infty - \hat{\underline{p}}^*_N)$$

$$+ \frac{1}{2}(\hat{\underline{p}}_\infty - \hat{\underline{p}}^*_N)^T \left.\frac{\partial^2 L}{\partial \underline{p}^T \cdot \partial \underline{p}}\right|_{\hat{\underline{p}}^*_N} (\hat{\underline{p}}_\infty - \hat{\underline{p}}^*_N) + \text{higher order terms}$$

Due to the maximum likelihood parameter estimate $\hat{\underline{p}}^*_N$, the second term disappears, see (3.239), and the third term is considered in (3.240). Taking expectations on both sides of condition of $\hat{\underline{p}}^*_N$, one obtains a more appropriate likelihood.

$$\log l(\hat{\underline{p}}_\infty) \approx \log l(\hat{\underline{p}}^*_N) - n_p$$

Using equation (3.236), and dropping the structure independent term, one obtains the AIC criterion for the single output case:

$$\text{AIC} = N \log \frac{1}{N} \sum_{k=1}^{N} \varepsilon_k^2 + 2n_p \qquad (3.261)$$

The selection technique is often stated as follows:

For $\mathscr{L}$ $\{M_1, M_2, \ldots, M_1\}$

Compute $\{AIC_1, AIC_2, \ldots, AIC_1\}$ $AIC = N \log \hat{\sigma}^2 + 2n_p$

Take M_i so that $AIC_i = \min_j \{AIC_j\}$

The derivation immediately indicates the asymptotic equivalence between FPE and AIC. It is not difficult to extend the procedure to the multi-variable case; det $\hat{\Lambda}^*_N$ comes instead of $\hat{\sigma}^2$. The importance of AIC derives from its linkage with system theoretical concepts.

Akaike [2] was the first to try to give a structure characterization technique information-theoretical meaning. As model-building can be seen as information reduction and processing, the approach is conceptually important. Furthermore, it allows the characterization problem to be seen as a problem in approximation instead of a decision problem, under the knowledge that the true system belongs to the set. This is an important step towards a better understanding of the problem.

Suppose that the observations y_k are independent and identically distributed with probability density $d_m(y)$. If a model is used to describe y_k, its outputs $\hat{y}_k$ have a probability density $d_s(y/\hat{p})$, conditional on a choice for the parameter vector. Information theory shows that the logarithm of the probability of getting the sample realization y_k by using the density $d_s(y/\hat{p})$, is asymptotically given by $NS(d_m, d_s)$, $S(d_m, d_s)$ being known as the generalized entropy.

$$S(d_m, d_s) = \int d_m(y) \log \frac{d_s(y/\hat{p})}{d_m(y)} \, dy \qquad (3.262)$$

It is quite natural to choose $\hat{p}$ in such manner that (3.262) is maximized. In a way, a best approximation is looked after. The meaning of (3.262) can be made more clear by seeing it as the difference between two terms:

$$S(d_m, d_s) = \int d_m(y) \log \frac{1}{d_m(y)} \, dy - \int d_m(y) \log \frac{1}{d_s(y/\hat{p})} \, dy \qquad (3.263)$$

Information theorists will recognize the Shannon entropy in the first term: the average amount of information required to resolve the uncertainty in the random variable y. The second term is an analogous measure, it represents the amount of uncertainty left in y once $\hat{p}$ is chosen. The second term should be as small as possible and S as large as possible. $I(d_m, d_s) = -S(d_m, d_s)$ is known as the Kullback–Leibner information matrix and it is a measure of the difference between two probability densities. It should be minimized:

$$I(d_m, d_s) = \int d_m(y) \log d_m(y) - \int d_m(y) \log d_s(y/\underline{p}) \, dy \qquad (3.264)$$

Minimizing (3.264) requires maximizing the second term, as the first one cannot be influenced. Notice that $d_m(y)$ is not known, so an estimate for the second term in (3.264) has to be chosen. As it represents nothing else but $E[\log d_s(y/\hat{p})]$ the classic estimate of the mean can be taken.

$$E[\log d_s(y/\underline{\hat{p}})] = \frac{1}{N} \sum_{k=1}^{N} \log d_s(y/\underline{\hat{p}}) \tag{3.265}$$

The right side is the log-likelihood, and so the maximum likelihood estimate seems to bring the information coming from the model into agreement with the information in the data. It can thus be concluded that in the limit for $N \to \infty$, minimizing the Kullback–Leibner measure is done by utilizing the maximum likelihood for the parameter estimates, while the choice of the structure is based on AIC. The argument can be extended to the more general case, where the y_k values are not independent and identically distributed. In the same way as above, AIC can be derived, which is in fact an average information measure. The gain in the information-theoretical approach is that one need not directly assume that the true structure is within the candidate set. The procedure tries to find the candidate which yields most information concerning the observation.

The AIC procedure has often been applied and it has suggested new research directions. As can be seen from (3.261), it is an improvement on the early likelihood approach in the sense that a better balance between fit and parsimony has been obtained. The asymptotical equality between AIC and FPE seems to strengthen the confidence in this quantitative balance. Unfortunately, analysis has shown that the procedure has its drawbacks.

The characterization problem for autoregressive scalar models, CP1, has been analysed in more detail with the AIC criterion [123, 196]. The method was found to be inconsistent, in the sense that for $N \to \infty$ the probability of choosing a model with an order that is higher than the true order, does not vanish. The study has also brought more insight in adequacy of other approaches. It shows that for the procedure (3.241), the probability of obtaining the correct order can be made arbitrarily small for $N \to \infty$! This is an important result. The fit–parsimony balance is thus poor for (3.241) and, though FPE and AIC are improvements that have a considerable amount of justification, they still remain in a certain way unsatisfactory balances. The inconsistency of the AIC rule has prompted more research. The procedure can be generalized yielding a test quantity given by equation (3.266):

$$DQ = N \log \hat{\sigma}^2 + f(n_p, N) \tag{3.266}$$

Kashyap [123] has shown that consistency for the CP1 problem is attained if $f(n_p, N) = n_p f^*(N)$ and

$$f^*(N) > 0; \qquad \lim_{N \to \infty} f^*(N) = \infty; \qquad \lim_{N \to \infty} \frac{f^*(N)}{N} = 0 \qquad (3.267)$$

It can be easily checked that the AIC-rule does not fulfil these conditions, but that FPE^β is consistent.

The section is concluded with a discussion on the statistical properties of the AIC procedure. Consider the single-output case and a selection problem between two models. It is readily established with (3.261) and (3.236) that

$$AIC_2 - AIC_1 = 2 \log \frac{l_1(\hat{\underline{p}}^*_1)}{l_2(\hat{\underline{p}}^*_2)} + 2(n_{P2} - n_{P1}) \qquad (3.268)$$

For the case where $M_1 \subset M_2$, and under certain restrictions [83], minus the first term on (3.268) is asymptotically χ^2 distributed with $(n_{P2} - n_{P1})$ degrees of freedom. It then follows:

$$var(AIC_2 - AIC_1) = 2(n_{P2} - n_{P1}) \qquad (3.269)$$

(3.269) may be used to obtain a rough idea about the confidence, one may have in the actual choice of the model class.

3.3.4.3 *The maximum entropy approach*

The AIC procedure is easily interpreted as a balance between fit and parsimony. A more complex trade-off, between the principles of fit, parsimony and balanced accuracy, can be obtained from another information-theoretical approach: the maximum entropy approach [189, 190]. The procedure, in fact, treats the parameter estimation and structure characterization problems as a whole, but again a relationship with the maximum likelihood estimate can be found.

The development starts from the observation that during modelling, not only a parameter vector but also residuals are estimated and the joint probability of $\hat{\underline{p}}$ and $\underline{\varepsilon}_1, \underline{\varepsilon}_2, \ldots, \underline{\varepsilon}_N$ is to be considered. For notational convenience, a new vector is defined: $\underline{\varepsilon}_t^T : \{\underline{\varepsilon}_1^T, \underline{\varepsilon}_2^T, \ldots, \underline{\varepsilon}_N^T\}$.

By standard rules of probability, one can decompose the joint probability:

$$d(\hat{\underline{p}}, \underline{\varepsilon}_t) = d_\varepsilon(\underline{\varepsilon}_t/\hat{\underline{p}}) - d_p(\hat{\underline{p}}) \qquad (3.270)$$

The decomposition is natural in the modelling context because the parameter estimate must be available before the residuals can be evaluated. A fundamental assumption is made: it is postulated for convenience that the mean and covariance matrices are the relevant statistics under consideration:

$$E[\hat{\underline{p}}_N] = \underline{p}^0 \qquad E[(\hat{\underline{p}}_N - \underline{p}^0)(\hat{\underline{p}}_N - \underline{p}^0)^T] = Q_N$$
$$E[\underline{\varepsilon}_t] = \underline{0} \qquad E[\underline{\varepsilon}_k\underline{\varepsilon}_k^T] = \Lambda_N$$

The information-theoretical concept of entropy of a random variable $\underline{x}$ with density $d_x(\underline{x})$ is utilized:

$$H_x(\underline{x}) = -\int d_x(\underline{x})\log d_x(\underline{x}) \, d\underline{x} \qquad (3.271)$$

As mentioned before $H_x(\underline{x})$ is the average information required to resolve the uncertainty in $\underline{x}$. By standard rules, one obtains:

$$H(\hat{\underline{p}}, \, \underline{\varepsilon}_t) = H_{\varepsilon_t}(\underline{\varepsilon}^t/\hat{\underline{p}}) + H_p(\hat{\underline{p}}) \qquad (3.272)$$

The definition (3.271) clearly shows that the quantitative value of the entropy is dependent on the shape of the probability distribution. Here one can proceed in two ways: either assume normal densities based on the asymptotic properties of existing estimators, e.g. the maximum likelihood estimate or invoke Jaynes' Principle of Minimum Prejudice [112] which says: "the minimally prejudiced assignment of probabilities is that which maximizes the entropy subject to given information about the situation". In this context d_ε and d_p are to be taken so that the entropies are maximized under the constraint of available first and second moments. By a theorem due to Shannon [195], the random variables are independent and normally distributed. It is simple to check that for a density

$$((2\pi)^m \det \Sigma)^{-1/2} \exp(-1/2(\underline{x} - \underline{\mu})^T\Sigma^{-1}(\underline{x} - \underline{\mu})),$$

the entropy H_x is given by:

$$H_x = 1/2m(\log 2\pi + 1) + 1/2 \log \det \Sigma \qquad (3.273)$$

One thus can take ε_t independent from $\hat{p}$ and the vectors $\underline{\varepsilon}_k$ and $\underline{\varepsilon}_t$ independent of each other. (3.272) then becomes with (3.273) in mind and under suitable stationary conditions:

$$\max H(\hat{\underline{p}} - \underline{p}^0, \, \underline{\varepsilon}_t) = 1/2n_p(\log 2\pi + 1) + 1/2 \log \det Q_N$$
$$+ N/2(p(\log 2\pi + 1) + \log \det \Lambda_N) \qquad (3.274)$$

Now the parameters and the structure should be chosen, in such a manner that uncertainty left in the measurement is minimum. In an average manner, this is attained by minimizing (3.274). Note also that:

$$\min[\max H(\hat{\underline{p}} - \underline{p}^0, \, \underline{\varepsilon}_t)] = \min[1/2(N \log \det \Lambda_N + n_p(1 + \log 2\pi)$$
$$+ \log \det Q_N)] \qquad (3.275)$$

Asymptotically, the parameter estimate based on (3.274) will be the maximum likelihood estimate whenever this estimate is efficient. Clearly, part of (3.274) is the minimum value of the log-likelihood and under efficiency log det Q_N is minimized too, see Section 3.3.2.5. Equation (3.275) can now be used as a selection criterion for structure characterization. Note that the accuracy of parameter estimation now enters directly into equation (3.275). So, it is seen that a trade-off is looked for between fit, complexity, and accuracy.

It is important to realize that in deriving (3.275) several assumptions have been made, which are more or less arbitrary. There is also an unsatisfactory aspect to (3.275): its value is dependent on the choice of the parameter vector and thus dependent on the scaling of these parameters. Proper use of (3.275) requires parameters which have statistical meaning.

The major contribution, however, of the maximum entropy approach resides in its suggestion for a decision rule of the following type:

$$DR = N \log \det \Lambda_N + f_1(n_p, N) + f_2[N, \text{norm}[\det Q_N]] \qquad (3.276)$$
$$\text{norm}[\cdot] : \text{normalized quantity of det } Q_N$$

It remains a fundamental problem in structure characterization whether or not the estimation accuracy has to enter explicitly into the decision rule.

3.3.4.4 Special methods for linear systems

As mentioned before, the special relationship between structure and parametrization in linear systems has resulted in techniques that rely on that kind of relationship. The best known technique is based on the sample correlations and related quantities. Refer to the work of Box and Jenkins [19] for a detailed discussion and a recent development [247]. Because of the special emphasis on the instrumental variable approach, a procedure related to it will be presented here.

The determinant ratio and related test

These tests are based on a simple observation that too high a model order induces linear dependence in certain matrices.

The observation of Lee [149]

Suppose there is no noise, thus $\xi(k) = 0$.

The en bloc linear least squares solution is developed in Section 3.2.3.4 and can be written in matrix notation:

$$\underline{p} = [\Phi^T(y, u)\Phi(y, u)]^{-1}\Phi^T(y, u)\underline{y}$$
$$\text{with } \underline{y}^T : [y_{n+1}, y_{n+2}, \ldots, y_N]$$
$$\Phi^T : [\underline{\varphi}_{n+1}, \underline{\varphi}_{n+2}, \ldots, \underline{\varphi}_N]$$

Φ is written as $\Phi(y, u)$ to show explicitly its dependence on y and u values.

A useful observation is the following: under the assumption that the model order n is larger than the true model order n_0, the element $-y_{k-1}$ in φ will be a linear combination of the other elements; this is directly seen from (3.104) for $n = n_0$. As a consequence, there is at least one row in Φ which is a linear combination of the other ones. In fact, the rank of Φ is n_0 and thus:

$$\det Q_n = \det(\Phi^T(y, u)\Phi(y, u)) = 0$$

The structure characterization rule is

 —compute Q_n for $n = 1, 2, \ldots, n_{max}$
 —choose $n = \hat{n}_0$ so that $Q_{\hat{n}_0+1} = 0$.

The Woodside determinant ratio test [235]

In the presence of white noise $\xi(k) = e(k) \neq 0$, $\det Q_n$ for $n > n_0$ will no longer be zero. Woodside advocated the use of a ratio:

$$DR(n) = \frac{\det Q_n}{\det Q_{n+1}} \tag{3.277}$$

He provided a technique for easy computation of the ratio. A large jump in the determinant ratio $DR(n)$ will indicate the order of the system.

  The important question concerning the test is how fast the noise deteriorates the determinant ratio. From simulation experiments, Woodside concluded that the test could only be used for noise levels with a dispersion of 5% of the signal in the large sample case.

The Wellstead instrumental product matrix [230]

In order to enhance the test, Wellstead proposed to modify the procedure by defining a new matrix Δ_n, the instrumental product matrix, instead of the matrix Q_n.

 $\Delta_n = \Phi^T(\hat{x}, u)\Phi(y, u)$

 $\hat{x}_n$: instrumental variable associated with the problem; an estimate of
  the noise-free output.

The value of Δ_n, stems from its limiting properties as the number of samples goes to infinity:

$$\lim_{N \to \infty} \frac{1}{N} \Phi^T(\hat{x}, u)\Phi(y, u) = \lim_{N \to \infty} \frac{1}{N} \Phi^T(x, u)\Phi(x, u)$$

In other words, for large sample sizes, the IPM used will provide a good estimate for the noise-free matrix. The decision on the model order can now be based on the instrumental determinant ratio:

$$IDR(n) = \frac{\det \Delta_n}{\det \Delta_{n+1}} \tag{3.278}$$

Though the procedure looks similar, it is in fact more complicated because parameter estimation has to precede the test on model order. An approximate auxiliary model could be used; however, the better the instrumental variable approaches the deterministic output, the more powerful will be the test.

The error variance norm [247]

The IDR test makes no reference to the type of parameter estimation scheme that is used. If recursive instrumental variable type algorithms are applied, it is computationally advantageous to develop another test. Young, Jakeman and McMurtrie [247], mention a test based on an error variance norm.

In the IV-algorithms, the matrix Λ_n is not computed directly. To avoid matrix inversion in the algorithm, a P-matrix is defined. From the discussion in Section 3.2.3.6, it can be seen that

$$P = [\Delta_n]^{-1} = (\text{Adj} \cdot \Delta_n)/\det(\Delta_n) \tag{3.279}$$

In this situation, it would be convenient to construct an order test that could be applied directly to P or an equivalent. In computing the inverse of Δ_n, its determinant comes in the denominator and, as a consequence, there are elements in P which will be very large. In order to get a single characteristic value, some overall norm of P can be used: 1/n trace (P), the geometric mean or the largest eigen-value of the matrix. Because of the fact that the diagonal elements of the P-matrix are related to the error covariance matrix of the parameter estimates, the test value is called error variance norm.

Practical experience is reported in [247]. It is seen that the error variance norm is a useful indicator. For one of the simulation examples, averages over ten large samples (1000 points, 4–6 parameters) are given. This indicates that for structure characterization a lot of data is required. Signal-to-noise ratios as low as two were used. Notice also that in the IV or R–IV context, the noise $\xi(k)$ may have a more complicated nature.

The major conclusion of the simulation study was that a single criterion for deciding on structure problems is not sufficient. It is useful if other criteria can be computed as additional clues. Young [247] suggests the use of a measure of fit: the total correlation coefficient defined by:

$$R_T^2 = 1 - \frac{\hat{\sigma}^2}{\sigma^{*2}}$$

$$\hat{\sigma}^2 = \frac{1}{N} \sum_{k=1}^{N} \varepsilon_k^2$$

$$\sigma^{*2} = \frac{1}{N} \sum_{k=1}^{N} y_k^2 \tag{3.280}$$

If the fit is good, R_T^2 will be close to 1, otherwise it will be close to zero. Notice that the parsimony principle is not incorporated in (3.280). Finally, the multiple correlation coefficients may also be useful. They are defined as follows:

$$R_{p_i}^2 = 1 - \frac{1}{\hat{p}_{ii}\Sigma s_k^2} \tag{3.281}$$

p_i : i-th parameter in $\underline{p}$
$\hat{p}_{ii}$: corresponding diagonal element in $\hat{P}$
Σs_k^2 : sum of the squares of the signal components
$\Sigma s_k^2 = \Sigma y_k^2$: for a-parameters
$\Sigma s_k^2 = \Sigma u_k^2$: for b-parameters

If any of the multiple correlation coefficients tend to 1, there may be over-parametrization while, if they all are less than unity, it is indicative that the current order model is a better candidate than any of the lower order models.

It has to be noted that one must be careful in utilizing these indicators. The estimates of the correlation coefficients are biased. So an overall approach is to look for a candidate model set with the following properties:

(a) The error variance norm attains or is close to its minimum value.

(b) R_T^2 should be consistent with the degree of model fit expected. An idea is here required about the noise levels that may occur. This information may come from a priori knowledge. For further increase in model order, the quantity should "plateau".

(c) The multiple correlation coefficients may give clues to over-parametrization if one of them tends to unity.

3.3.4.5 *A characterization method based on a Bayesian viewpoint*

Kashyap [122] recognized in the class selection problem all the features of a decision problem. He developed a decision rule based on classic decision theoretical methods.

Consider the scalar output: y_k; for an experiment with N samples a vector $\underline{y_N}^T = [y_1, y_2, \ldots, y_N]$ can be defined. In an N-dimensional space, an experiment with outcome $\underline{y_N}$ corresponds with a single point. Structure characterization for a problem $\mathscr{L} : \{M_1, \ldots, M_l\}$ can then be seen as a partitioning of the space in l regions, while each region is assigned to a model class M_i. If $\underline{y_N}$ belongs to region i, the model class is said to be M_i.

Within this formulation, the crux of the problem is to subdivide the sample space, by minimizing an expected "loss". In a sense, the idea is extremely straightforward and provides, at the same time, a measure for the quality of the decision. The loss function is defined as follows:

$$L_S(M_i, M_j \text{ is chosen}) = 0 \qquad M_i = M_j$$
$$= \omega_{ij} > 0 \qquad M_i \neq M_j \qquad (3.282)$$

The selection of the correct model does not encompass any loss, but wrong choices are penalized by a fixed quantity. This may be not entirely satisfactory and may be elaborated on in the future. The partitioning of the observation space is then based on the requirement of minimizing the expected loss. It requires the a posteriori probabilities: $P(M_i/\underline{y}_N)$, the probability of a true system M_i when $\underline{y}_N$ was observed. Subdividing the sample space follows from the decision rule:

$$M = M_i : C_i = \min_j \{ C_j = \sum_{k=1}^{1} \omega_{kj} P(M_j/\underline{y}_N) \} \qquad (3.283)$$

A very popular loss is obtained when $\omega_{ij} = 1$. Then C_i is the probability of error. The fundamental concept which conveys to the model-builder an idea about the confidence he can have in the actual selection, is in fact the error probability. It is easily computed from (3.283):

$$\text{Probability (error)} = 1 - \max_j P(M_j/\underline{y}_N) \qquad (3.284)$$

Fundamental to the solution of the overall problem is the computation of the a posteriori probabilities $P(M_i/\underline{y}_N)$. It is to be remembered that the parameter vector is not known at this point of the analysis. Standard rules in probability show:

$$P(M_j/\underline{y}_N) = d_y(\underline{y}_N/M_i) P\{(M_i)/d_y(\underline{y}_N))$$

$$= \int d_y(\underline{y}_N/\underline{p}, M_i) \, d_p(\underline{p}/M_i) \, \frac{P(M_i)}{d_y(\underline{y}_N)} \, d\underline{p} \qquad (3.285)$$

$$\underline{p}^T = [\underline{p}^*, \sigma^2]$$

Kashyap has computed (3.285) for a certain class of systems under a number of assumptions. The model class is a special case of the prediction error model:

$$f(y_k) = g(y_k, y_{k-1}, \ldots, y_{k-n}, u_{k-1}, \ldots, u_{k-n}, k, \underline{p}^*) + e(k) \qquad (3.286)$$

$f(\cdot)$: differentiable function with unique inverse;
$g(\cdot)$: linear in the parameter $\underline{p}^*$;
$e(k)$: white Gaussian sequence.

The Bayesian point of view requires a number of a priori probabilities $P(M_i)$, which can be chosen equal for instance. Furthermore, in order to be able to compute the probabilities, special densities have to be chosen for the first n measurements: the initial conditions for the estimation algorithm, and for the parameter vector $\underline{p}$. With these assumptions, the a posteriori probability is given by (3.287):

$$P[M_i/\underline{y}_N] = C \exp[1/2h^i(\underline{y}_N)] \tag{3.287}$$

$$h^i(\underline{y}_N) = h_1^i(\underline{y}_N) + h_2^i(\underline{y}_N) + h_3^i(\underline{y}_N) + h_4^i(\underline{y}_N) + 0(1/N) \tag{3.288}$$

$$0\left(\frac{1}{N}\right) = \frac{C_1}{N} \qquad C_1 : \text{constant}$$

These are four terms in $h(\underline{y}_N)$:

$$h_1^i(\underline{y}_N) = 2 \sum_{k=1}^{N} \log\left[\frac{df^i}{dy}\right]_{y=y_k} \tag{3.289}$$

(3.289) relates to the non-linear transformation to which the measurements have to be submitted in order to obtain a white noise residual e_k. It can be seen as an indication of model complexity. If for all the candidate model sets the f-transformations are equal, then this term will disappear:

$$h_2^i(\underline{y}_N) = -(N - n_i)\log[\hat{\sigma}_i^2 + (\sigma^*{}_i^2 - \hat{\sigma}_i^2)/N] \tag{3.290}$$

n_i : order of the model

$$\hat{\sigma}_i^2 = \frac{1}{N - n_i} \sum_{k=n+1}^{N} (\varepsilon_k^i)^2$$

$$\sigma^*{}_i^2 = \frac{1}{N} \sum_{k=1}^{N} [f^i(y_k)]^2$$

It is useful to decompose (3.287) into two parts:

$$h_2^i(\underline{y}_N) = -(N - n_i)\log \hat{\sigma}_i^2 - (N - n_i)\log\left(1 + \left(\frac{\sigma^*{}_i^2}{\hat{\sigma}_i^2} - 1\right)/N\right) \tag{3.291}$$

The first part of (3.291) is the classic measure for degree of fit. The second part is meant to limit the fit per sample. $\sigma^*{}_i^2/\hat{\sigma}_i^2$ is the signal to noise ratio and thus $(\sigma^*{}_i^2/\hat{\sigma}_i^2 - 1)/N$ is a measure for the amount of modelling done on the measurements per sample. This amount has to be constrained, otherwise the noise pattern typical for the measurement sequence is modelled too. This is a very drastic way to induce parsimony and balanced accuracy.

$$h_3^i(\underline{y}_N) = -n_{p_i} \log N \tag{3.292}$$

(3.289) is clearly a direct measure for parsimony. Notice that it fulfils the conditions (3.267).

$$h_4^i(\underline{y}_N) = n_i - \left(\frac{1}{\sigma^*{}_i^2}\right) \sum_{k=1}^{n_i} f^i(y_k) - n_i \log \sigma^*{}_i^2 + 2 \log P(M_i) \tag{3.293}$$

(3.293) is directly related to the initial conditions and it can be neglected whenever N is sufficiently large.

The procedure mentioned in this section is quite general, though moving average terms may not occur. It can usually be considerably simplified for special characterization problems. Consider for instance CP1, then a minimum error probability choice will result in a model selection M_i, so that (3.294) is minimized:

$$DR = N \log \hat{\sigma}_i^2 + n_{p_i} \log N \qquad (3.294)$$

In (3.287) N is supposed to be large enough for terms depending on n_i ($\equiv n_{p_i}$) to vanish. In a simpler context, Schwarz [194] derived equation (3.294). The decision rule (3.287) has many useful properties: it is consistent under certain regularity conditions, it is transitive and the probability of error can be computed; it certainly deserves more interest.

3.3.4.6 Conclusions

After the presentation of recent techniques, some concluding remarks can now be made. Early techniques have been extended in various ways. First, decision criteria which formerly were only computed approximately, are now estimated more adequately: a beautiful example is the maximum likelihood. Furthermore, there has been an extensive search towards a technique which balances in a proper way the important characterization principles: fit, parsimony and eventual balanced accuracy. A final answer does not seem to be available yet. There has been a tendency to refine existing methods in order to make them more adequate: an example is the developments around the determinant ratio test. New basic philosophies have been tried out. Information theory especially seems to offer a fruitful feeding ground. Finally, an appropriate measure for the quality of the decision has been looked after and the probability of error or a related quantity seem to be most adequate.

Upto now, little comparative work has been performed. The most extensive survey is that by Genesio and Milanese [75]. Söderström found a similarity between FPE, AIC, pole–zero cancellation and suitable adaptations of the F-test. Equivalence is used only asymptotic and for the case of a choice between two model classes $M_1 \subset M_2$.

For most methods, simulation studies indicate that small and medium-size sample properties differ widely from asymptotic results. The problem should be looked at in more detail.

The present state of the art suggests that a general frame of thought may be useful in order to gain insight into the many aspects of structure characterization. In the next section, such a framework is suggested.

3.3.5 A general framework for structure characterization

3.3.5.1 Introduction

When considering the techniques presented in the previous sections, it immediately becomes clear that a wide variety of approaches can be adopted. This may stem from the quite diversified kind of problems, that may arise in the structure characterization context. It is still true that, for the same type of problems, methods ranging from simple visual clues on the measurements to sophisticated trade-offs between fit, complexity and accuracy can be applied. The appearance, origin and computational details of these techniques are so diversified, that it is difficult to evaluate similarities and dissimilarities. A frame of thought that easily reveals the characteristics of the methods, would be useful for the purpose of comparison. The framework would be more worthwhile if it provided a sufficiently broad view, so that even new, still untried methods were suggested.

All techniques serve a common purpose. Besides their superficial details, their usefulness will largely depend on properties that evaluate their adequacy for structure characterization. For parameter estimation, such properties have yet to be established. Estimators are classified according to characteristics like: unbiasedness, consistency, efficiency, computational and statistical robustness, computational requirements, etc. An analogous set of properties is needed for the characterization problem too, and a suitable framework may suggest some of these properties. It then must be sufficiently powerful to provide means of evaluating these properties, even for more heuristic techniques. It is a pity that certain methods have to be rejected because of a lack of methodology for evaluating their characteristics.

In today's world, computational power increases much more rapidly than our analytical capabilities. It is by no means unrealistic to conceive an approach that tailors a characterization technique to a specific problem and to specific needs, in order to achieve adequate performance. It may thus be useful if the framework would permit such an approach.

3.3.5.2 Structure characterization as a pattern recognition task

When looking for a frame for structure characterization, one could start out from a statistical point of view. Unfortunately, the field of statistics is so general that, though it provides tools, it is not suggestive enough to engender useful ideas. In that respect, the more restricted area of decision theory would be more adequate. This point of view was helpful in deriving the Bayesian characterization procedure described in Section 3.3.4.5. As characterization is seen as model class selection, the adequacy of decision theory is apparent. Decisions are made, however, on the basis of decision criteria. Unfortunately, the decision framework does not give any clues concerning the choice of useful criteria. Therefore, the slightly different framework of pattern recognition is advocated here.

Its appeal stems from an analogy between human recognition tasks and structure characterization. Consider the human act of recognizing a letter of the alphabet, e.g. the letter "a". Recognition is based on typical features which distinguish the letter from other letters of the alphabet. It must be said that the appearance of the letter may vary in size, orientation, and even shape. Thus, the properties belonging to a written letter may be differentiated in two categories: the first pertaining to the casual circumstances, the second relating to the definition of the letter itself. It is the latter category which is important for recognition, and man seems to be especially skilful in "filtering" trivial properties which do not concern the discriminating task. In the same way, it could be hypothesized that the structure of a model class induces special properties in the measurements. The parametrization could then be compared with the "size" and "orientation features" of the previous example. Structure characterization would consist in recognizing those features, which are typical for the model class and do not concern the parametrization. Useful decision criteria are those which pertain to structure differences and not to parametrization effects. The analogy is certainly only partially acceptable, but it may suggest useful approaches. The advantage consists in the fact that the body of knowledge that is available in that field, which moreover borrows heavily from statistics and decision theory, can be used and applied for the purpose of structure characterization.

The idea of using pattern recognition techniques for structure characterization has originated in the last decade. At first, it was suggested by Karplus [118] and Simundich [200], and probably independently by Saridis and Hofstadter [193], Thiga and Gough [217], as an alternative for classical characterization techniques. Recently, Spriet [207] considered it as a general framework to analyse the characterization problem and compare the techniques. The framework has permitted the treatment of the topics mentioned in Section 3.3.5.1.

3.3.5.3 *A general pattern recognizer for selecting a model class*

It is well known that a pattern recognizer can be, for a matter of convenience, thought to be built up of three parts: a preprocessor, a feature extractor and a classifier (Fig. 3.16).

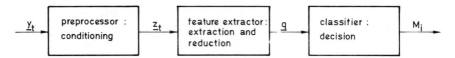

FIG. 3.16   Structure of a general pattern recognizer

The algorithms serve different purposes:

—the *preprocessor* is a set of algorithms that collect measurements $\underline{y}_t$ from the sensors and recondition them for further processing.
—the *feature extractor* is a group of schemes that condense incoming information $\underline{z}_t$ into a number of important decision criteria $\underline{q}$.
—the *classifier* concerns algorithms that actually select the best model based on the decision quantities.

Structure characterization schemes can always be seen in the light of the sequence presented: data conditioning, information extraction and reduction, followed by classification through decision-making. Spriet [207] has shown that the feature extractor itself can be further split up into different parts (Fig. 3.17). One can distinguish:

—a *data selector* which orders the output of the preprocessor for further processing;
—an *intermediate feature extractor*; in general the data is processed in two steps, in the first of which quite a large number of intermediate features are still extracted;
—a *feature concentrator:* the many intermediate features are sometimes condensed into one or a few decision criteria.

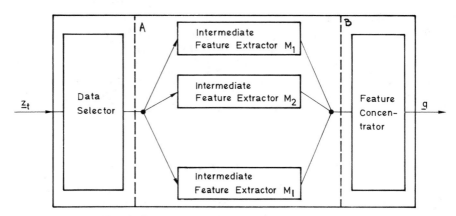

FIG. 3.17   A decomposition of the feature extractor

In the most general set-up, the feature extractor is a parallel bank of as many selectors, extractors and concentrators, as there are candidate model sets. Almost always however, a common data selector and feature concentrator are used, so one usually finds the set-up shown in Fig. 3.17.

It is a simple exercise to bring all characterization schemes into the frame presented here. Consider as an example, the use of the AIC-rule for the characterization problem CP1. The complete procedure can be seen to consist of several parts:

—the preprocessor: no special algorithm, though an outlier test might be useful to perform. Remember that the Kullback–Leibner information measure, which is an expectation, was approximated by a sample mean. This is only optimal under Gaussian conditions.
—the feature extractor:
  –the data selector; remove outliers.
  –the intermediate feature extractor for M_j: compute the maximum likelihood estimate for the parameter vector under Gaussian assumptions and compute the one step ahead predictors $\hat{y}_k^j$ and the residuals ε_k^j.
  –the feature concentrator: reduce the intermediate features ε_k^j to a single decision quantity AIC_j:

$$AIC_j = N \log \det \hat{\Lambda}_N^j + 2n_p^j$$

—the classifier; select as follows:

$$M_i : AIC_i = \min_j \{AIC_j\}$$

3.3.5.4 *Similarities and dissimilarities of characterization methods*

If, in the light of a pattern recognizer, one compares techniques like the cost-related approach, the method of Wilks, hypothesis testing, the FPE and AIC-rules and the Bayesian method, it then becomes clear that they all are similar, in the sense that the intermediate features are mainly residuals. They differ in the choice of a feature concentrator and thus in the choice of the decision criteria. Up to level B on Fig. 3.17, all those methods have the same characteristics. From this point of view, quite different structure characterization techniques would be obtained if the intermediate features belonged to the parameter space instead of to the observation space. The maximum entropy approach is one of the few techniques that incorporate information concerning the parameter estimates into the feature concentrator.

New characterization techniques need to be designed on the basis of multiple parameter estimates and, in fact, attempts have been made to obtain such techniques. They are based on the idea that if multiple estimates for the parameters are available, structure defects will induce an increased amount of variability within these estimates. To obtain more than one parameter estimate, one can proceed in different ways:

(1) divide the measurement record in a small number of batches; estimate the parameter vector from each batch;
(2) estimate the parameters recursively and utilize the recursive estimates;
(3) use a minimum number of data points for calculating the parameters algebraically.

All options have been tried out. To be especially mentioned is the work of Whitehead, Young [232] and Black [15] with option 2, and the work of Simundich [200] and Spriet [207] with option 3. The techniques are promising, but difficult to analyse. We refer to the literature for more detail.

Multiple parameter estimates are not the only alternative to residuals for obtaining intermediate features; one could conceive useful intermediate characteristics in the frequency domain.

3.3.5.5 *Important issues in structure characterization*

Inherent in the pattern recognition point of view is the assumption that discriminating features exist in the sensor outputs, so that the recognition task is well posed. This important issue seems to have been neglected almost completely in the characterization field. For parameter estimation a considerable amount of analysis has gone into the concept of identifiability (see Section 3.2.2). A concept as characterizability is required in the context of inductive structure selection. Characterizability will depend on:

— the model formulation; the model classes have to be disjunct. Kashyap [122] paid attention to this issue.
— the model frame; the outputs must allow the model builder to discover the structural patterns.
— the inputs; the experiment must reveal these patterns.

A preliminary study on the concept has been done by Spriet [207].

The *sine qua non* is how well posed the problem is; once this is ascertained, structure characterization methods can be applied. Questions related to their usefulness can be analysed with the performance standards set for pattern recognizers. The final step in the recognition task is a classification. Classifiers are designed with decision theory. The overall performance of the algorithm is its expected loss (see Section 3.3.4.5). The loss function should ideally be related to the purpose of the modelling effort, which is almost always difficult. Most often the performance index is the probability of error. In the context of structure characterization, it can thus be said that the most adequate techniques are those which have the lowest probability of making a wrong model selection. Based on that ultimate measure, heuristic techniques may be quite useful. It is possible to implement them and, conceptually, it is possible to evaluate through simulation their degree of applicability.

It is now possible, still within the pattern recognition framework, to look for useful properties for characterization, so that the techniques may be compared more easily. Still, the ultimate measure would be the expected loss or the probability error, but certain related intermediate properties which influence the probability of error, may be interesting. It is easy to consider the decision space of the pattern recognizer: a vector of decision criteria q can be thought to be a point in a Euclidean space; dependent on the model class, the decision vector will occupy different locations in the decision space (Fig. 3.18). The decision rule simply partitions the decision space into l subregions.

In relation with the loss, the following properties are important:

(a) the discriminating power of the features: how "typical" are the decision criteria; and how well do they discriminate between model classes? This property has to do with the separation of the decision quantities in the decision space under different hypotheses for the model classes. Trivial scaling is, of course, to be ruled out.

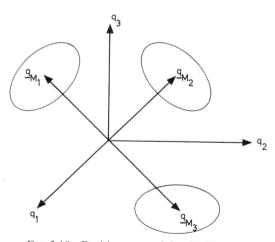

FIG. 3.18   Decision space of the classifier

(b) efficiency: how large is the spread on the decision criteria due to the noise? This will certainly influence the probability of error.

Other important aspects are:

(c) computational robustness: how serious is the degradation in discriminating power due to computations?

(d) statistical robustness: how dependent is the error probability on statistical assumptions concerning the noise patterns?

(e) computational requirement: how expensive are the procedures in computational terms?

Finally, to mention properties related to the sample size:

(f) consistency of the choice,

(g) small sample size behaviour.

As an example of the use of these concepts, consider the determinant ratio test. With little or no noise, discriminating power and efficiency are high. As soon as the signal to noise ratio lowers, bias occurs on the ratio, and the stochastic spread on the test quantity becomes more important; as a consequence, the error probability will grow and the test may become useless. Quantitative knowledge concerning such questions is still lacking. More research is needed to acquire an insight into the mentioned properties, useful for the structure characterization field.

A last remark that can be made when considering structure characterization in the light of pattern recognition, concerns the computational load of the different operations that are actually made. The "overall" performance, like the probability of error, will depend on all algorithms that are used to obtain the final decision. Characterization methods, however, emphasize the feature extractor. Elaborate parameter estimation schemes are used to obtain the residuals. Comparatively little attention is paid to the preprocessor and the classifier. As the global result is dependent on all the parts, it may pay off to invest more in preprocessor and classifier design, and perhaps reduce a little the computational requirements for the feature extractor.

3.3.5.6 *Characterization method design through simulation*

One could wonder whether it is possible to design or tailor a characterization technique to a particular problem. Given a finite sample size, a certain noise level, and a given characterization problem, the existing techniques may be unsatisfactory; or, with a given technique, it may be interesting to obtain an idea about the error probability. Under such circumstances, the theory of pattern recognition provides techniques to design or tune an algorithm based on computation.

One could start from a given criterion which is partly unknown, e.g. (3.266), (3.276), then with artificial data coming from simulation results, it is possible to "train" the classifier. This is a problem known in the literature as supervised training, and a number of procedures are available [28, 43]. Another option would be to "augment" the decision space and combine many different criteria. In that way, it is even possible to evaluate the additional gain that one obtains by adding a new feature.

In a similar way, the loss or the error probability can be estimated: techniques are known as, for instance, the "resubstitution" method, the "hold-out" method, the "leave one out" method, etc. We refer to the pattern recognition literature [124, 221]. The main point here is that the pattern recognition framework is useful for suggesting procedures for research in, and design of, structure characterization procedures.

3.4 OTHER MODELLING METHODOLOGY ISSUES

3.4.1 Introduction

There are a number of modelling methodology issues that have not been discussed yet; in particular model frame definition, experiment design, validation, and goal incorporation. Though these issues may be extremely important in certain cases, much less attention has been paid to them (see Section 3.1.3). All the topics deserve further research, and because we believe that none of the areas has reached a mature level, we only briefly review the subjects. We simply introduce the topic, then give some indication concerning the important issues, especially from the point of view of the model-building activity. Rarely are results presented; however, references are given that are themselves keys to a more extensive literature. This section concludes the chapter on modelling methodology for ordinary differential and difference equations.

3.4.2 Model frame definition

The definition of a frame consists in choosing the level of detail of the system representation, and then specifying the boundaries of the part of the real world that is under study, the inputs and outputs, and eventually a representative state set. In fact, the choice of an acceptable model formalism is also a part of the frame definition. It is obvious that the very act of defining a system frame is totally dependent on the basic axioms of systems theory discussed in Chapter 2: separability of a part of the real world from its environment, decomposability of that part at a suitable level, and existence of a state that relates the past, via the present, with the future.

In this early stage of modelling, experience, intuition, analogies, and trial and error, seem to be the only resources left to man. Sometimes the choice of a frame is an easy and almost trivial matter. The goal directly points to desirable outputs; known causal chains indicate the inputs of relevance and the states of importance; the level of decomposition can be easily determined, and a given formalism has proven to be suitable. In such cases the frame can be derived from goal considerations and a priori information. For an amplifier, for instance, the outputs are currents or voltages at terminals which will be connected to other devices, while the inputs are the sources applied. As a man-made object the boundaries are well defined. The kind of approximations that can be made, and the level of detail that is required for proper modelling are well known; so the differential equation formalism will be adequate.

The important issue in model frame definition is expressed in the following question. Is it possible to use data in order to infer information concerning the frame? A straightforward approach is to follow a procedure that is used for structure characterization too: catch the uncertainty in a number of candidate frames, perform the whole modelling exercise for each candidate, and finally choose a suitable mathematical representation on the basis of a validation test.

Recently, a drastically different procedure has been advocated. Promoted by Ivakhnenko and co-workers, the fundamental principle of parsimony is rejected. An analogy is made with the brain. It is argued that a very complex structure can adapt itself, or better organize itself, to perform a certain task. Consequently, it is sufficient to provide organizing principles to a very complex but general system representation, so that after training the model is suitable for being used for the purpose for which it is required. To paraphrase a statement of Ivakhnenko [108]: for the discovery of mathematical-laws it is not necessary for the human operator (the model-builder), to specify the set of independent variables, the input and output variables, the control variables, the disturbances, etc. All of this is done by the computer. The GMDH (general method of data handling) only assumes that a complete list of variables, which is given with a large margin, contains all the variables that are important for the model. It is evident from the text that such an approach could be useful to resolve uncertainties concerning the model frame. Whether the GMDH-method is as powerful as claimed, remains to be seen. The contributions of Ivakhnenko and co-workers can be traced in the literature [4, 105, 106, 107]. Recently, the technique has been reviewed by Mehra [160]. It is argued that theoretical comparison of the methods with other approaches is extremely difficult, due to the complexity and the heuristic nature of the GMDH. The success of the method will be judged from its applications and so further research is required.

3.4.3 Design of experiments

3.4.3.1 Generalities

As mentioned in Chapter 2, data are one of the main information sources for modelling. They result from experiments conducted on the real-world system or a model implemented on a simulator. As the data are used to extract model information, the question arises as to how to "do" the experiments in order to make the data as rich in suitable information as possible. If experimentation is easy, and the cost of data collection is low, the design of experiments may be straightforward and a few principles may suffice. However, experiments are expensive and difficult to conduct (see Chapter 2) and it is interesting in such cases to investigate whether the experiment can be planned in a manner that is optimal for the purpose at hand.

A list of important issues are summarized in Table 3.2. The "hardware", or physical requirements, relate directly to the type of real world system and the practical circumstances. The "software", or mathematical issues, relate to the model and the model-building procedures. Most often there will be limitations on the experimental conditions and thus a suitable experimental set-up is subject to constraints. Such constraints that might be

TABLE 3.2 Important issues for the experimental set-up.

"Software" and Mathematical Issues	"Hardware" and Physical Issues
Choice of inputs to be excited and outputs to be measured.	Equipment for input segment generation.
Choice of control conditions on the system.	Sensor devices.
Selection of the input segments.	
Sampling rate.	Storage equipment for the measurements.
Sampling period.	Filters for signal conditioning.
Representation of the behaviour of the sensors.	
Design of digital filters.	

met in practice follow from availability conditions of transducers, filters and actuators, from amplitude or power limitations on inputs, outputs or internal variables, from the time period available for the experiment, and from the extent of financial resources.

There is a rather restricted amount of literature available on the experiment design problem for dynamic systems. We do not completely discuss the subject here. As the topic deserves more attention, an elementary survey is given, and the interested reader is referred to the references.

The design problem should be related directly to the goal of the modelling enterprise. This is not always easy and therefore suitability is usually evaluated against a step in the modelling process.

3.4.3.2   *Experiment design for parameter estimation*

In this section the question is treated whether an experiment is better than another one in order to obtain precise parameter values. Recall from Section 3.2.2 that parameter estimation can only be successful if identifiability holds. Minimum requirements on the experiment thus relate to conditions for identifiability. For linear systems, it can be said that in the case of a deterministic representation the inputs have to excite all modes, while in the case of a stochastic representation the inputs have to ensure sufficient persistent excitation. The non-linear case has drawn much less attention. We are only aware of a practical study by Mehra and Wang [159] on a class of non-linear systems that can be treated with catastrophe theory. It is shown through simulation that the inputs must cause catastrophic events to occur, if certain parameters which weight the non-linearities are expected to be estimated with reasonable precision.

Within the class of experiments that result in identifiability for the parameters of interest to the model builder, there are often designs that yield better estimates than others. The quality of parameter estimates is expressed in terms of the bias and the covariance properties of the estimates. These properties depend on the parameter estimator, and the experiment design problem is linked to the parameter estimation problem. Usually, for input design purposes one assumes that an unbiased and efficient estimator is used, so that the optimal input designs can be carried out independently of the estimator. This leads to great simplifications. We close the topic by mentioning that pseudo-random binary sequences are often acceptable inputs, and refer for more details on the subject to a few key texts [83, 157, 158].

3.4.3.3 *Experiment design for structure characterization*

Data may be needed to discriminate between competing candidate structures. Here, too the experiment must ensure characterizability (see Section 3.3.5.5). As soon as the experiments enable one model to be distinguished from another, experiments can be looked for which minimize the probability of decision error, or another related cost. A few techniques, which are not very satisfactory are available for the case of static models [18, 99, 186]. Almost no work has been done on the subject for the dynamic case, which forms an interesting domain for further research.

3.4.4 Model validation

Model validation may occur during the whole modelling process. A few fundamental ideas were presented in Section 2.4.4. After having built a version of the mathematical representation on the basis of a priori knowledge, data and model goal considerations, it is useful to set the model under heavy fire. Mehra [159] distinguishes data based model validation and theory based validation.

Validation based on data can be done by looking for inconsistencies between the model outputs and the measurements. The most adequate approach is to design new experiments and check whether the new data is adequately described by the model available at that point. If new experiments cannot be done, or if they are too expensive, two ways remain to check a model. The first is to do the modelling on a subset of the data and then check the model on the remaining measurements. Little attention has been paid to this procedure. The other approach is to model on the complete data set and simply check whether there are any remaining inconsistencies between data set and the system representation. To do this, there are again two methods.

The first is to investigate whether initial model assumptions are properly satisfied. Often the most important assumption concerns the nature of the noise sequence: zero mean, white and, eventually, Gaussian distributed. Hypothesis testing is used to check such assumptions. In particular, one can do tests for a zero mean, for the absence of sinusoidal terms for serial independence, or for normality.

The other technique consists in comparing characteristics of the model output such as correlograms, spectral densities, and extreme value characteristics, with the corresponding characteristics of the empirical data. To compare these characteristics, the various statistical properties of the model output can be obtained either by analysis, or by simulation. Acceptance of the model is done if the discrepancy between the two sets of characteristics is within one or two standard deviations of the corresponding reference ones. The two approaches are thought to be more or less complementary. More details on the subject of validation can be found in the work by Box and Jenkins [19] and Kashyap and Rao [121].

Validation based on theory consists in analysing the theoretical properties of the estimated model. Here the model builder capitalizes on his mathematical skills—eventually supported by simulation tools—in order to investigate whether the properties of the mathematical description are in correspondence with the expected characteristics of the system. Notice that such characteristics may come from the global body of a priori information. Mehra [159] mentions as key properties: the sensitivity and the modal behaviour. Basically two kinds of sensitivity can be distinguished. The first is sensitivity towards changes in certain model components:

Parameter sensitivity: how do certain outputs change if the parameters vary? Herewith one can investigate whether certain parametric aspects are relevant or not.
Structure sensitivity: do certain structural properties influence the outputs?
Frame sensitivity: here several types can be considered as follows:
Input sensitivity: how important are certain inputs for the outputs? It may be interesting to know how variations on the inputs cause fluctuations on the outputs.
Level of detail sensitivity: suppose that the level of detail is coarsened or refined, what is the result on the input–output behaviour?
Formalism sensitivity: is the choice of the formalism adequate for the purpose at hand?

A second type of sensitivity is towards the information taken from the modelling sources. The most important question is related to *data sensitivity*: how sensitive is the model or the model output to errors on the data? It is seen that such sensitivity analysis is nothing more than a reassessment of decisions made during the modelling process.

Besides sensitivity questions, key properties of the model are related to the "modes" or "eigenvalues" of the system. These concepts are especially useful in the linear case but are also applicable in a non-linear context. The qualitative dynamic properties of systems can be inferred to a large extent from modal analysis: stability properties, cyclic and non-cyclic behaviour, bifurcation, jump and limit cycle behaviour, etc., can be evaluated from a systematic computation of the eigenvalues and eigenvectors. References on this subject are provided in [159].

3.4.5 Goal incorporation

The role of the modelling goal has not been emphasized in the literature on modelling methodology. It was, and still is, believed that a "good" model is able to serve a wide variety of purposes. The general question can be raised whether a limited scope of the model, in the sense that the modelling exercise is undertaken for a particular goal, can be exploited at the expense of certain desirable properties like physicality, faithful representation, or even parsimony.

That the modelling goal is a driving force in the modelling process is beyond doubt. Clearly, the choice of inputs, outputs, and system boundaries is often made in accordance with the goal of the model-builder. This is a straightforward example of goal incorporation. Recall from Section 2.2 that models may serve many objectives. One then can wonder whether a specific objective may influence the modelling process. The issue has many aspects:

(a) Are certain identification, characterization and model framework definition techniques more advantageous than others for specific applications like control or prediction?

(b) Can the model building process be influenced by criteria that help reach the final goal more easily?

(c) What is, for a specific objective, the required validity, generality and physicality of the mathematical representation?

Interest in these important issues has been weak. Recent developments concern the study of adaptive and learning systems. The basic idea is as follows. A final model can eventually be seen as the result of "training" a class of models on a data set. For a given objective, the training should be pursued in a manner that enhances the model capabilities for that objective. Training happens according to certain guiding principles proposed by a teacher. The field of goal incorporation should be able to provide the guiding principles for training. Notice that the general principles in Section 3.3.2.5 for structure characterization can be seen as guiding principles. It is believed, however, that more principles should be available to match the model more closely to the objective. Research on training principles in the context of model-building has been done by Ivakhnenko and co-workers [4, 105, 106, 107]. A few examples follow.

Consider the case of N samples that are divided into two sets N_A and N_B. For interpolation purposes a criterion called "regularity criterion", should be helpful in "training" a mathematical representation class. For a scalar output y_k, the measurements are first normalized:

$$y_k^n = \frac{y_k - \bar{y}}{\bar{y}} \qquad \bar{y} = \frac{1}{N} \sum_{j=1}^{N} y_j \qquad (3.295)$$

$$y_k{}^n = \frac{y_k - y_{min}}{y_{max} - y_{min}} \tag{3.296}$$

Regularity expressed as a percentage is given by:

$$R = \frac{\sum\limits_{k=1}^{N_B} (y_k{}^n - \hat{y}_k{}^n)^2}{\sum\limits_{k=1}^{N_B} (y_k{}^n)^2} \cdot 100 \tag{3.297}$$

In the equations, $y_k{}^n$ stands for normalized measurements and $\hat{y}_k{}^n$ for normalized predictions, on the basis of a model built on the training set. How do we choose the training and testing set? For each time instance a statistic D_k is computed:

$$D_k = \frac{1}{m+1}\left[y_k{}^2 + \sum_{j=1}^m x_j{}^2 \right] \tag{3.298}$$

The time points are sorted in descending order of magnitude. The data at times where D_k is large go into the training set. The heuristic justification is that a larger information matrix is obtained for modelling.

For the objective of detecting relationships with a more general validity the unbiasedness criterion is proposed. A model class is trained on the data set N_A, the data set N_B, and on the whole set N. Unbiasedness is evaluated as follows:

$$U = \frac{\sum\limits_{k=1}^{N} [\hat{y}_{N_A}{}^n(k) - \hat{y}_{N_B}{}^n(k)]^2}{\sum\limits_{k=1}^{N} [\hat{y}_N{}^n(k)]^2} \tag{3.299}$$

For prediction the "Balance of Variables" measure is proposed [108]. It is obvious that such criteria are still very heuristic and more research or experience is required to evaluate their usefulness.

Another recent result is related to the field of self-tuning regulators [12]. Recently [66, 84], indications have been found that, for linear systems, certain specific control objectives can be achieved without unique specification of the model order, or the systems parameters. This means that in an adaptive environment, structure characterization does not have to be considered in detail, and that the parameter estimation problem can be attacked with simple algorithms. There is hope that, for certain specific tasks, the impact of goal considerations on the model-building process can be so important that the modelling task is considerably simplified and that even certain model stages can be bypassed.

The next chapter deals with modelling methodology for another model formalism: partial differential equations. It will be seen that the formalism itself has a certain impact on methodology.

4. Model-building methodology for partial differential equations

4.1 INTRODUCTION

4.1.1 Generalities

After having presented modelling methodology for ordinary differential equations (ODESS), with an emphasis on the needs for sharper techniques in order to infer a maximum of information from the available modelling information sources, this chapter is devoted to another model formalism: the partial differential equations system specification, PDESS.

It will be argued that, from the modelling point of view, a PDE-formalism is more "natural" than an ODE-formalism. Nevertheless, the system theoretical and statistical literature, which together should provide the basic knowledge and theory about the formalism, have avoided the subject. One often hears the customary remark that very few papers have been written about PDE-systems mainly because the representation is much more involved and difficult than the ODE-representation.

In part, the main ideas about modelling methodology run parallel with those presented in the previous chapter. There are, however, a number of points which are specifically dependent on the formalism itself. Though the ODE-formalism is similar and thus close to the PDE-formalism, the most crucial problem areas in the context of modelling differ considerably. It will be seen for instance that computational aspects and approximation issues deserve much more attention for PDESS than for ODESS.

Besides the intention to provide the reader with methodological tools to attack a modelling problem using a PDE-formalism, the chapter is meant to illustrate how the choice of the formalism is by no means without consequences for the modelling task itself. By tradition, PDE-models have been built largely on the basis of a priori knowledge, while the ability to use other information sources is still limited. For the PDE-formalism, it is very clear that more advanced methodology could be of substantial help in achieving the goals that are believed to be attainable with a mathematical representation. In the rest of Section 4.1, the PDESS is defined in general terms, the main features of the formalism (descriptive power, analytical and modelling tractability) are discussed, and a few introductory comments on methodology are given.

In Section 4.2 deductive formulation procedures of PDEs from a priori knowledge are dealt with. A few universal principles and laws seem to govern the manner of derivation of PDEs in almost all branches of science. Only the nature of certain constituent elements seems to vary. Based upon such considerations, the types of PDEs that seem to occur most frequently are introduced and discussed. Because a priori information is the main source of modelling information here, a brief survey of analytical solution techniques is presented. Ample reference is made to different physical disciplines, so that the relevance and appropriateness of the mathematical descriptions can be ascertained. As PDEs seem to play a rather important role in many disciplines oriented to physical phenomena and engineering systems, it can be expected that the formalism can be of help in the "softer" areas of science. The final paragraph is devoted to the appearance of PDEs as descriptive tools for environmental systems. Attention is paid to problems related to water, air, and land resources.

The final section of Chapter 4 concerns inductive techniques that may be useful in building partial differential equations. Only a few aspects are touched upon. Parameter estimation, structure characterization, and experimental design are discussed briefly. We have tried to reveal which kinds of problem are direct consequences of the specific properties of the partial differential equation model formalism.

4.1.2 The model formalism

4.1.2.1 The model definition

The complexity of a partial differential equation model or system specification (PDESS) is apparent as soon as one considers the mathematical representation itself. Agreement on that matter is by no means so complete as for the ODESS. Using only first-order differentials, a form which arises directly from deduction on a priori knowledge is as follows for the deterministic case (4.1–5):

$$F_0(\underline{\phi}, \underline{p}, \underline{z}, t) \frac{\partial \underline{\phi}}{\partial t} + \sum_{i-1}^{k} F_i(\underline{\phi}, \underline{p}, \underline{z}, t) \frac{\partial \underline{\phi}}{\partial z_i} = f(\underline{\phi}, \underline{p}, \underline{u}, \underline{z}, t) \qquad (4.1)$$

$$\underline{b}\,(\underline{\phi}, \underline{p}, \underline{z}, t) = 0 \text{ for } \underline{z} \in \delta\,Z \qquad (4.2)$$

$$\underline{\phi}\,(\underline{z}, 0) = \underline{\phi}^0(\underline{z}) \qquad (4.3)$$

$$\underline{y}(t) = \int_{Z_s(t)} \underline{g}'(\phi, \underline{p}, \underline{z}, t)\, d\underline{z} \quad \text{or} \quad \underline{y}(\underline{x}, t) = \underline{g}(\phi, \underline{p}, \underline{z}, t) \tag{4.4}$$

$$0 \leqslant \underline{h}(\phi, \underline{u}, \underline{p}, \underline{z}, t) \tag{4.5}$$

The model (4.1–5) needs some clarifications. It is made up of:

—*Independent variables*: ordinary differential equations (ODE) have only one independent variable viz. time. Partial differential equations (PDE) on the contrary, also have spatial independent variables, such as,
(a) a time variable : $t \in T : (t_1, t_2) \subset R$
(b) spatial variables : $\underline{z} \in Z \subset R^k$
The open connected set Z is called the field.

—*Input variables*: $\underline{u} \in U \subset R^m$.

—*An input segment set*: map $Z \times T \to U : \underline{u}(\underline{z}, t)$.

—*Dependent variables*: $\phi \in \Phi \subseteq R^n$; through (4.1) the dependent variables are functions of $\underline{z}$ and t.

—*Parameters*: $\underline{p}$ is a vector of unknown quantities, which we take here to be constant and thus independent of the variables $\underline{z}$, t. Many authors allow for $\underline{z}$ and t dependence and so arrive at infinite dimensional parameter spaces. This is clearly adequate from a physical point of view, where certain system properties, then called system parameters, may be distributed in space and time. For model-building, we prefer the model parameters to be truly constant and we include the functional relationships into the structure.

—*The PDE* (4.1) consists of a number of operators relating the partial derivatives:
$F_0, F_1, \ldots, F_k$ and $\underline{f}$ are respectively matrix maps and a vector map on $\phi \times Z \times T$.

—*Boundary conditions* (4.2) specify the values of ϕ over time at the boundary of the field: $\underline{z} \in \delta Z$ (δZ boundary of Z).

—*Initial conditions* (4.3) specify the value of ϕ over the field at the initial time t.

—*Output variables*: $\underline{y} \in Y \subseteq R^p$; these variables could be functions of space and time. In general however, sensors do not cover the complete field and moreover they produce an averaging activity over a spatial domain $Z_s(t)$ which may vary in time: consequently the explicit form of the output equation depends on the type of sensor, see (4.4).

—*Constraints*: a set of constraints (4.5) which incorporate a priori knowledge concerning the parameters.

A few pertinent remarks are required here. It can be argued that the PDESS is basically of the same nature as the set structure defined in Chapter 2. Then one of the most important conclusions is that the state-vector must have infinite dimensionality. Recall that the state at a given point in time contains all past information required to produce the of past experience now requires more than a finite set of numbers. In fact, this can easily be seen heuristically from the PDE-representation future, given the inputs from that particular time instant. Thus, the summary (4.1–5). The initial condition, which is required to find a solution for the equations, must be at least a part of the state at the initial time instant. As it is defined on Z × T, it is infinite. Evidently equation (4.1) must be sufficiently well behaved so that, with proper initial and boundary conditions, its solution is unique.

A second note concerns the nature of the vector of dependent variables. In most real world problems the dependent variable is a scalar, but the PDE is of a higher order. It is known [176] that, with a proper choice of $\underline{\phi}$, higher order PDESSs may be expressed in the form (4.1–5). On the other hand, systems of first order equations cannot always be expressed as a single higher order PDE. Nevertheless, for modelling purposes, it may be interesting to use a higher order PDE-description.

As PDESS is similar to ODESS the concepts of frame, structure and parameters are useful too. Note that here the boundaries of the field have to be specified explicitly when choosing a frame. For lumped systems (ODESS), setting boundaries could sometimes be done implicitly by just specifying the input and output variables.

In the context of field problems, the model (4.1–5), though it looks formidable, has certain drawbacks from the modelling point of view, in the sense that no provision is made for errors and noise factors. In the literature, there does not seem to exist a well-established procedure to introduce random fields into the equations. There are several options. One can provide:

—*Process noise*: $\underline{w}(\underline{p}, \underline{z}, t)$, which may simply be added at the right side of (4.1) or included into the map $\underline{f} : \underline{f}(\underline{\phi}, \underline{p}, \underline{u}, \underline{w}, \underline{z}, t)$.

—*Boundary noise*: a special additional 'error' component $\underline{w}_b (\underline{z}, t)$ can be inserted into the boundary conditions yielding

$$\underline{b} (\underline{\phi}, \underline{p}, \underline{w}_b, \underline{z}, t)$$

—*Measurement noise*: the sensors may be contaminated with measurement errors $\underline{v} (\underline{p}, \underline{z}, t)$. In (4.4) the noise may be purely additive, or be a part of $\underline{g}$:

$$\underline{g} (\underline{\phi}, \underline{p}, \underline{v}, \underline{z}, t)$$

In order better to compare the similarities and dissimilarities with ODESS, the model properties are discussed first.

4.1.2.2   Model properties

Descriptive power

The descriptive power of the PDESS, is higher than that of the formalism treated in Chapter 3. In many instances its use appears to be more 'natural'. In fact, man's universe comprises space and time, so its properties are likely to change with these variables. In lumped system theory, the real-world system is regarded as being composed of an array of distinct elements interconnected in some specific manner. The lines interconnecting these elements, perhaps linkages in mechanical configurations, wires in electrical circuits, or boundaries in compartmental systems, have no significance other than to indicate the topological relationship of the elements. The physical dimensions and positions of the elements, therefore, are of no direct consequence in the analysis of system behaviour. Lumped models are often approximations, but these may be so accurate that more detailed representation is only a burden.

In other circumstances, the convenient ideas of a lumped element must be relinquished, and the distributed nature of the real-world system has to be recognized. So, though all real systems are distributed, only on particular occasions is a PDESS required. Application areas of the description are plentiful and include:

—parts of electromagnetism: theory with representations for antennas, wave guides, transmission lines, and waves in space;

—structural analysis and design problems, where vibrations and dynamic behaviour are crucial;

—acoustic theory;

—heat and mass transfer: for instance, in chemical and nuclear reactors, in heat exchangers, insulation slabs, etc.;

—geophysical systems like earthquake and seïsmic analysis;

—environmental studies, ranging from underground water and oil exploration to weather forecasting;

—gas and fluid flow systems;

—demographic and agricultural models, etc.

Generally, it is accepted that a distributed representation is preferable as soon as the system response shows significant instantaneous differences along a spatial direction. These differences must have a significant impact on the results taking the modelling goal into consideration. It can be concluded that simply from a descriptive point of view PDEs are preferable to ODEs. Unfortunately, the system representation also has drawbacks.

Analytical tractability

The analytical tractability of PDEs is lower than that of ODEs. Solving partial differential equations with purely mathematical tools is difficult. Some general techniques exist, like separation of variables, the method of characteristics, and the transform approach. An additional problem, however, resides in the irregular system boundaries, which often occur in practical circumstances and often preclude analytical solutions. Whenever a solution is available, it will rarely be in a closed form. Most of the time, an infinite series is obtained. It must be recognized that problems involving distributed systems are often, by an order of magnitude, more difficult than those in the lumped case. In the case of ordinary differential equations, one can get around analytical tractability problems by calling on computational techniques. In the present case, the computational option is far from being so helpful. Numerical techniques are available and diversified. The finite difference technique is one of the oldest. In recent years, "finite element" schemes have been developed. Other approaches are the methods of lines, where the PDE is transformed into a large set of ODEs; modal approximations, where the solution is thought to be built up of an infinite series; approximate transform methods, and numerical integration techniques on integral equation forms. A more esoteric approach relies on Monte-Carlo computations. The computational option, however, is plagued by the "curse of dimensionality". Even modern high-speed computers can need long computation times in order to solve a PDE. A good example is weather forecasting [209]. In order to produce a prediction it is necessary to solve the weather equations over a two-dimensional surface of the earth at a number of altitudes, and at each of many time steps. Halving the approximation grid means four times as many surface points, twice as many steps, and twice as many altitude planes. Consider a hemisphere 24 h forecast with a 270 mile grid. An average of about 10^{11} data operations are required. At a peak speed of 10^8 operations per second, about 15 min are needed for a prediction. Halving the approximation grid would require 4 h of computation. Even one of the fastest present-day computers, Cray I, does not run at the peak speed set forth, so its computation time may stretch towards 24 h, so that prediction itself becomes meaningless. Such a simple example shows how the development of fast computers remains one of the best research areas to enhance the usefulness of the PDESS. This aspect will be looked at in more detail in Chapter 7.

Modelling tractability

A PDESS is, in fact, a complex model. The main theoretical as well as practical difficulty is due to the infinite dimensionality of the state space. The difficulty of the modelling task therefore is, compared with modelling with an ODESS, even more dependent on the structure of the information sources. It is still fair to say that most actual PDEs which model real-world processes, have for a large part been derived from the basis of a priori knowledge and deductive analysis. Simulation is then most useful for solving the equations in order to serve the purpose for which the model was built.

4.1.3 Modelling methodology

Modelling methodology for the PDESS is by no means as extensive as for the ODESS. As in Chapter 3, a classification could be made based on the information that is available to the model-builder. In contrast with the ODE-model, distributed representations have been largely derived from a priori knowledge, by deductive analysis. The frame and the structure followed directly from the laws. Whenever parameter values were not available, they were obtained through carefully planned laboratory experiments. Because the deductive approach is of major importance in building PDE-models, a substantial part of the chapter is dedicated to a unifying overview of the deductive techniques applied to derive the equations.

Not all modelling problems, however, are characterized by the availability of sufficient a priori information. Any required information should then be tapped from the other model-building sources. In a large part of the previous chapter, the methodology for deriving parts of the model from experimental data was presented. Basically, the same subjects can be treated here. Unfortunately, the techniques are not so well developed for the PDESS and some fundamental questions remain. Most often, model-builders have adapted techniques, originally developed for ODEs, to be applicable for PDEs. Such an approach capitalizes on the similarities between the model formalisms. Unfortunately, the infinite dimensionality poses a problem which is very characteristic of the PDE formalism: how are approximations to be made in order to get a tractable problem? Two questions are important in this step: where are the approximations to be made in the course of the solution procedure; and what type of approximation is most suitable for the specific modeling subproblem that is considered? Specialists do not agree yet on these questions. Concerning the approximation time, Athans[13] for instance suggests that any approximation should be made as late as possible in any analysis of a distributed process, in order to retain the distributed nature of the description until numerical results are required. The advice is theoretically sound, but it may lead to computationally untractable cases. It has been experienced that retaining the distributed nature of the process usually results in additional sets of PDEs or integral equations, which must then also be approximated. Polis and Goodson[176] stress a major advantage of early approximations: the knowledge of the process behaviour that follows from a priori knowledge, may be more readily incorporated into the approximation scheme and, in that manner, less insurmountable computational tasks may result.

The typical "field" property of the PDESS is also responsible for the fact that the importance of certain issues in the model-building process differs from when an ODESS has to be assembled. A good example concerns the issue of experimental design. In the lumped case, the choice of the outputs is made on the basis of modelling goals and experimental constrains. For PDEs, sensors often only measure local values. The choice of the sensor locations and their numbers are very important considerations for arriving at a suitable PDE-description. Another consequence of the "field" aspect of PDEs is the need for increased attention towards proper definition of the frame; the boundaries especially have to be suitably specified in order to obtain a solution for the model equation.

The aspects of modelling when the parameters, and eventually small parts of the structure, have to be inferred from the data source, will be presented too, but the discussion, however, will tend to be more superficial.

4.2 DEDUCTIVE FORMULATION OF PDEs FROM A PRIORI KNOWLEDGE

4.2.1 The constituent elements of PDEs in the physical disciplines

The concept of "field" has wide-ranging applications in physics and engineering, including such diverse areas as electrodynamics, fluid mechanics, solid mechanics, heat transfer, acoustics, optics, and many more. In each of these disciplines, the dependent variables (the physical quantities characterizing the excitation and response of the field) are defined as continuous functions in space and time. The intrinsic properties of the medium, which determine the parameters of the governing equations, are likewise defined continuously for every point in the time/space continuum. The partial differential equations characterizing the field can then be derived by applying basic physical laws and, thus, a priori knowledge, and by following a deductive procedure described in the subsequent sections. The formulation of the partial differential equations characterizing distributed parameter systems, is greatly simplified by recognizing certain conceptual similarities in the independent variables, the dependent variables, the parameters, and the basic laws governing the behaviour of systems belonging to the many diverse areas of science. This unified view serves as a convincing explanation for the otherwise surprising observation that three basic partial differential equations and their modified forms serve as the mathematical models for virtually all areas of physics and engineering.

The independent variables in the mathematical models of distributed parameter systems always include space variables, and sometimes the time variable. The space variables identify the location of any point within the field with respect to a reference point: the centre of the coordinate system. Depending upon the dimensionality of the field, one, two, or three space variables may be involved. For convenience in dealing with symmetries within the field and with regularly-shaped field boundaries, one of a variety of different coordinate systems may be employed. The Cartesian coordinate system with its orthogonal x, y and z-axes is by far the most widely-used coordinate system. Where there is symmetry within the field about a straight line, the cylindrical coordinate system has important advantages; where there is symmetry about a point, the spherical coordinate system is the most appropriate. Besides these well-known coordinate systems, others less frequently used ones exist [9,62]. For simplicity, most of the discussion in this text is limited to space variables expressed in the Cartesian or rectangular coordinate system. The time variable appears as an independent variable in mathematical models only for systems in the transient state. Many field problems are concerned only with the static or steady state, in which case the space variables are the only independent variables. However, whenever the time variable appears in mathematical models, a specific instance of time is arbitrarily designated as $t = 0$, and a solution is sought only for times $0 \leqslant t$.

The dependent variables of the mathematical model are the physical quantities, which are measured by instruments and constitute the excitations and responses of the system. These are generally functions of space and/or time. A survey of the diverse areas of physics reveals that these dependent variables fall into two major categories: the potential functions, also referred to as across variables; and the flux functions also referred to as through variables. An across variable relates the condition at one point within the field to that at some other field point or arbitrary reference point. The measuring instrument recording an across field variable must be applied simultaneously to two separated points, and the magnitude specified for this variable usually represents the difference in value between the two points. Thus, for example, temperature, which is always referred to absolute zero or the freezing point of water, is the across variable in heat transfer systems; pressure or, in gravitational systems, the velocity potential, is the across variable in fluid mechanic systems, while electric voltage or potential is the across variable in electrostatic and electrodynamic systems. A through variable on the other hand requires only one point within the field for its specification, and represents a measure of the flux traversing an elemental cross-section of the field. Thus, heat flux in a thermal system, flow rate in a fluid mechanics system, and current density in an electrodynamic system are all through variables. Mathematically, the across variable is generally a scalar, while the through variable is a vector.

The parameters of the mathematical model (the numerical coefficients in the characterizing equations) are derived from the intrinsic physical properties of the material constituting the field, and in the case of linear systems are independent of any specific existing excitations or responses. They may be measured by obtaining a sample of this material, and by performing a laboratory experiment. In such an experiment, an excitation is applied to the sample and the resulting response measured. The nature and magnitude of the field parameter is determined by the relationship between these measured excitations and responses. A survey of the many areas of physics in which partial differential equations arise reveals that the field of parameters invariably fall into one of only three classes:

(i)   dissipators or dampers;

(ii) reservoirs of potential;

(iii) reservoirs of flux.

Where the material comprising a field is a dissipator, the excitation/response relationship between potential and the flux is one of proportionality. Consider a field described by a single space variable oriented in the x direction such as, for example, a thin wire in an electrical system. A potential difference, Δp, is applied across the two ends of a small portion or sample of this system, and the resulting flux, f, is measured. For a dissipative material,

$$\Delta p = - D \Delta x f \qquad (4.6)$$

where D is the dissipativity per unit length, and Δx is the distance between the two ends of the sample. The minus sign indicates that positive flux flows in the direction of decreasing potential, i.e. from a high potential to a low potential. If Δx is made to approach zero, equation (4.6) becomes:

$$\frac{dp}{dx} = - Df \qquad (4.7)$$

In more dimensional cases, one obtains

$$\underline{\nabla p} = - D \underline{f} \qquad (4.8)$$

where the term on the left is termed the potential gradient. The parameter D is a measure of the extent to which the material comprising the field dissipates energy by converting it into heat; or, in the case of heat transfer systems by leading to an increase in entropy). This parameter is termed resistivity in electrical systems, viscosity in fluid flow systems, thermal resistivity in heat transfer systems, and appears in virtually all physical systems.

The material comprising a field acts as a reservoir, if it is capable of storing matter or energy temporarily. In the case of reservoirs of potential, this storage occurs whenever a potential difference is placed across a sample of the material: the greater the potential difference, the more is stored. For example, an electrical capacitor stores electrical energy whenever a voltage difference is applied across its terminals. When a resistor, or a short circuit, is then placed across these terminals, the capacitor produces a current in a direction such as to oppose any change in potential. For a sample of a one-dimensional field with a reservoir of potential property, the relationship between the potential, p, and the flux, f, is

$$\Delta f = - E_p \Delta x \frac{dp}{dt} \tag{4.9}$$

where E_p is the potential reservoir property per unit length, and Δx is the length of the sample. Letting Δx approach zero, leads to

$$\frac{\partial f}{\partial x} = - E_p \frac{\partial p}{\partial t} \tag{4.10}$$

For more dimensional systems, the relationship is

$$\nabla \cdot \underline{f} = - E_p \frac{\partial p}{\partial t} \tag{4.11}$$

Distributed capacitance, or capacitivity, is the reservoir potential parameter in electrical fields; compressibility plays the same role in fluid flow systems; while thermal capacity or specific heat is E_p in heat transfer systems.

In the case of reservoir of flux, the material comprising the field acts to store energy whenever a flux is made to flow through it. For example, in electric circuits an inductor stores energy in its magnetic field whenever a current flows through it; if the terminals of the inductor are short-circuited, a voltage is produced with a polarity tending to oppose any change in current. For a field sample of length Δx, the relationship between flux and potential is

$$\Delta p = - E_f \Delta x \frac{df}{dt} \tag{4.12}$$

where E_f is a measure of the flux reservoir property per unit length. Again letting Δx approach zero,

$$\frac{\partial p}{\partial x} = - E_f \frac{\partial f}{\partial t} \tag{4.13}$$

or in general

$$\underline{\nabla p} = - E_f \frac{\partial \underline{f}}{\partial t} \qquad (4.14)$$

Distributed inductance, or inductivity, is the reservoir of flux parameter in distributed electrical systems, while density or inertia play the same role in fluid flow systems. On the other hand, heat transfer systems never display a reservoir of flux property.

The pertinent across and through variables as they appear in the more important areas of physics are summarized in Table 4.1 together with the parameters or system characteristics necessary to specify completely the properties of the system. It is shown in this chapter that the presence or absence of one or more of the three basic parameter types has a far-reaching importance in determining the behaviour of the system and its mathematical description. Where only one parameter is present (in non-negligible magnitude), the mathematical model takes the form of an elliptic equation, such as Laplace's or Poisson's equations; where dissipation and either reservoir of potential, or reservoir of flux (but not both) is present, the governing equation is parabolic. Where both types of reservoirs are present, the field is characterized by a hyperbolic partial differential equation.

4.2.2 The physical principles and laws

The basic physical principles which account for the analogous nature of field problems in the diverse areas of physics, are known as the principles of conservation and continuity. These principles occur in various forms in all the branches of physics.

The conservation principle applies to that quantity whose transport is measured by the through variable. According to this principle, the total amount of this quantity existing within the field at any time subsequent to an arbitrary initial instant, $t = 0$, must be equal to the algebraic sum of the net amount added (or subtracted) by external excitations, plus the amount initially present within the field at time $t = 0$. For example, in electrical systems, electric charge is conserved; similarly, in dynamic mechanical systems momentum is conserved, and in fluid flow systems, mass is conserved.

The principle of continuity also deals with through variables and specifies that the through variable is continuous and must emanate from a source (internal or external excitation) and return to the same, or some other, source. Generally, the conservation principle implies the continuity principle and vice versa. Usually, it is merely a matter of convention or

TABLE 4.1 Field parameters for different physical areas

Physical area	Across variable p	Through variable f	Parameters		
			Dissipators D	Reservoirs of flux E_f	Reservoirs of potential E_p
Electrodynamics	Voltage	Current	Resistivity	Inductivity	Capacitivity
Electrostatics	Electric potential	Flux	—	—	Dielectric permittivity
Magnetics	Potential, MMf	Flux	Reluctance	Permeability	—
Electromagnetics	Potential, EM	Flux	Conductivity	Permeability	Dielectric permittivity
Statics (mechanical)	Displacement	Force	—	Spring constant	—
Dynamics (mechanical)	Displacement or velocity	Force	Viscous damping	Spring constant	Mass (Inertia)
Elasticity	Strain	Stress	Viscous damping	Young's modulus	Inertia
Fluid mechanics	Velocity potential (pressure)	Flow rate	Viscosity	Inertia (density)	Compressibility
Particle diffusion	Concentration	Mass transfer rate	Diffusivity	Inertial forces	Compressibility
Heat transfer	Temperature	Heat flux	Thermal resistance	—	Thermal capacitance

terminology that has caused one principle to assume a more prominent role in a specific area.

4.2.3 A deductive procedure for deriving the characterizing equations

The structural similarity of the mathematical models characterizing the many different disciplines within physics and engineering, is largely due to the similarity in the methodology employed to derive the characterizing equations. As shown above, regardless of the physical discipline, the characterizing equations involve space and time as the independent variables, potential or flux as the dependent variable, and parameters falling into three distinct classes. Moreover, the basic physical laws governing the diverse disciplines all take the form of conservation principles. The partial differential equations constituting the mathematical model can furthermore be derived, using a procedure which is virtually independent of the physical application area. This procedure takes the following steps.

(1) Identify those field parameters which are present with non-negligible magnitudes. A field may contain all of the three parameter types: dissipation, reservoir of potential, and reservoir of flux; or only one or two of these parameters may be present. Sometimes all three parameters are present, but one or two of these may be of negligible importance in determining the potential and flux distribution. For example, a wire may contain inductance and capacitance, but these may be ignored in determining the voltage distribution along the wire, so that only the resistivity is of significance.

(2) Decide whether the problem should be formulated in one, two, or three space dimensions, and which coordinate system is appropriate. This decision is generally made on the basis of the geometry of the system, and the purposes of the modelling effort. Clearly, all physical systems exist in three space dimensions, and representation in one or two space dimensions therefore inevitably entails approximations. In general, a rectangular coordinate system is preferred, unless there is symmetry about a line or a point.

(3) Select a typical elemental region. The geometry of this element depends upon the number of space dimensions as well as upon the coordinate system selected. In rectangular coordinates, if the system can be characterized adequately in one space dimension, the elemental field portion is a line segment Δx in length; if two space dimensions are required, the elemental portion will be a rectangle of dimensions Δx by Δy; if three dimensions are needed, the elemental portion will be a rectangular solid Δx by Δy by Δz. This is illustrated in Fig. 4.1. A similar approach is employed in other coordinate systems. As examples, elemental field portions in cylindrical and spherical coordinates are shown in Fig. 4.2. These elements

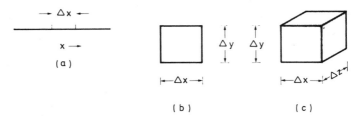

FIG. 4.1   Elemental regions in the rectangular coordinate system

are considered typical of the field as a whole. That is, a description of the potential distribution and flux in an elemental portion of the field, is considered to be representative of all regions within the field boundaries.

(4) Express the flux across each boundary of the typical element in terms of the potential, p, and its derivatives with respect to space and/or time. For fields in one, two, and three space dimensions, this leads to two, four and six equations respectively. These equations are derived from equation (4.8) (4.11) and (4.14) as determined by the types of field parameters existing in the field under study.

(5) Calculate the net flux into the element. Where the field is purely dissipative, this involves only the summation of the flux across all of the boundaries of the element; where reservoir parameters are present, the storage in the reservoir associated with the element must also be taken into account.

(6) Invoke the conservation principle applying to the physical discipline to which the system belongs. This involves account completely for all flux into and out of the element.

(7) Let the dimensions of the element shrink to zero. In rectangular coordinates this means that Δx, Δy and $\Delta z \to 0$.

4.2.4   Types of PDEs: nomenclature

These steps result in a partial differential equation which characterizes the entire field. With the exception of the physical discipline of elasticity, the

FIG. 4.2   Elemental regions in the cylindrical and the spherical coordinate systems

terms appearing in the characterizing differential equations are limited to first and second derivatives, with respect to space and time.

A convenient and frequently used method for classifying the basic partial differential equations which characterize field problems, follows from a consideration of the mathematical character of the solutions. This method of classification is only briefly outlined below to provide a link with more formal mathematical treatments. As demonstrated in the following sections of this chapter, the equations governing physical fields take the general form

$$A\frac{\partial^2 u}{\partial\alpha^2} + 2B\frac{\partial^2 u}{\partial\alpha\partial\beta} + C\frac{\partial^2 u}{\partial\beta^2} = D\frac{\partial u}{\partial\alpha} + E\frac{\partial u}{\partial\beta} + Fu + G \qquad (4.15)$$

By lettering the parameters A to G assume positive, negative or zero magnitudes, all the equations derived in this chapter can be expressed as special cases of the above equation. The two independent variables, α and β, may both be space coordinates, or one may be a space coordinate and the other the time variable. The relative magnitudes of A, B, and C determine the nature of the equation.

If $AC > B^2$, as is the case if $B = 0$ and A and C are both positive, the equation is termed elliptic. This definition applies even if another term $H\,\partial^2 u/\partial\gamma^2$, where H is a positive number, is added to the left side of the above equation, so that three-dimensional fields are included in this definition. If $AC = B^2$, is as the case if B and either A or C are equal to zero, the equation is termed parabolic. The addition of additional second-order derivatives such as $H\partial^2 u/\partial\gamma^2$ does not influence the basic parabolic character of the equation. If $AC < B^2$, as is the case if B is positive or zero and either A or C is negative, the equation is termed hyperbolic.

The classification of partial differential equations into these three categories is valuable, because the basic analytical and numerical methods for treating field problems are inherently different for the three types of equations.

4.2.5 Elliptic partial differential equations

4.2.5.1 *Laplace's equation*

Elliptic partial differential equations characterize those distributed parameter systems in which no more than one of the three parameter types appears with non-negligible magnitude. That is, all fields which are purely dissipative, purely reservoirs of potential or purely reservoirs of flux are characterized by elliptic partial differential equations. In addition, fields containing dissipation, as well as reservoir elements, are characterized by elliptic equations when they have reached the quiescent or steady state. The most important and most often encountered of the elliptic partial differential equations, and indeed of all partial differential equations of applied physics, is known as Laplace's equation. It is the basic equation of potential theory and plays a prominent role in virtually all major areas of physics and engineering. The derivation of this important equation will be illustrated for systems in one, and three space dimensions. As a note, we add that the dependent variable ϕ will often been substituted by the notation p (potential). In Section 4.2, no misunderstanding can entail.

Example I

Consider first the system shown in Fig. 4.3a, in which a thin conductor of flux, assumed to have constant dissipative properties D/unit length, is connected at one end to a source of constant potential p_0, while its other extremity is connected to a source of zero potential, i.e., ground. In accordance with the stepwise procedure outlined in the preceding section, we note that we are dealing with a system containing D but negligible E_p and E_f. We note further that this is a one-dimensional system oriented in the x direction. We now define an elemental line segment as shown in Fig. 4.3b. The element is seen to have two boundaries located at x_1 and x_2. From equation (4.7), the potential/flux relationship at the two boundary points is

$$\left(\frac{dp}{dx}\right)_1 = -Df_1 \qquad \left(\frac{dp}{dx}\right)_2 = -Df_2 \qquad (4.16)$$

Since the field is assumed to be purely dissipative, there can be no storage within the elemental line segment. Therefore, in accordance with the conservation principle

$$f_2 - f_1 = D \qquad (4.17)$$

Solving equations (4.16) for f_1 and f_2 and substituting in equation (4.17),

$$\frac{1}{D}\left(\frac{\partial p}{\partial x}\right)_2 - \frac{1}{D}\left(\frac{\partial p}{\partial x}\right)_1 = 0 \qquad (4.18)$$

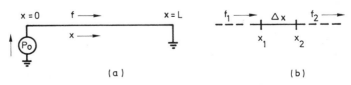

(a)   (b)

FIG. 4.3   A one-dimensional resistive field

By multiplying both sides of equation (4.18) by D and by dividing both sides by Δx, this equation transforms to

$$\frac{\left(\frac{\partial p}{\partial x}\right)_2 - \left(\frac{\partial p}{\partial x}\right)_1}{\Delta x} = 0 \qquad (4.19)$$

We now shrink the size of the elemental line segment of Fig. 4.3b by letting $x \to 0$, which yields

$$\frac{\partial^2 p}{\partial x^2} = 0 \qquad (4.20)$$

This equation is known as Laplace's equation in one dimension. Its solution, either analytically or numerically, provides the function $p(x)$, the potential at all points within the field. Such a solution is only possible if the potential or flux at the boundaries of the field is specified. In the case of Fig. 4.3a, these boundary conditions are

$$\text{at} \begin{cases} x = 0 & p = p_0 \\ x = L & p = p_L = 0 \end{cases} \qquad (4.21)$$

Example II

A three-dimensional field is illustrated in Fig. 4.4a, which shows a rectangular solid composed of a dissipative material having uniform properties. Excitation is in the form of constant potentials applied to three entire sides: the left, right, and top surfaces of the solid. This system might represent an electrically-conductive solid such as graphite, with highly-conductive face plates covering three of its sides. The differential element, shown in Fig. 4.4b, is a small block within this solid. Subscripts 1, 2, 3, 4, 5 and 6 refer to the left, right, bottom, top, front, and rear faces, respectively.

The analysis of this system follows the lines similar to those used above. The potential gradient across each face is first expressed in terms of the flux F across the face and the dissipative parameter D as

$$\left(\frac{\partial p}{\partial x}\right)_1 = -\frac{F_1 D}{\Delta z \Delta y} \qquad \left(\frac{\partial p}{\partial x}\right)_2 = -\frac{F_2 D}{\Delta z \Delta y}$$

$$\left(\frac{\partial p}{\partial y}\right)_3 = -\frac{F_3 D}{\Delta x \Delta z} \qquad \left(\frac{\partial p}{\partial y}\right)_4 = -\frac{F_4 D}{\Delta x \Delta z} \qquad (4.22)$$

$$\left(\frac{\partial p}{\partial z}\right)_5 = -\frac{F_5 D}{\Delta x \Delta y} \qquad \left(\frac{\partial p}{\partial z}\right)_6 = -\frac{F_6 D}{\Delta x \Delta y}$$

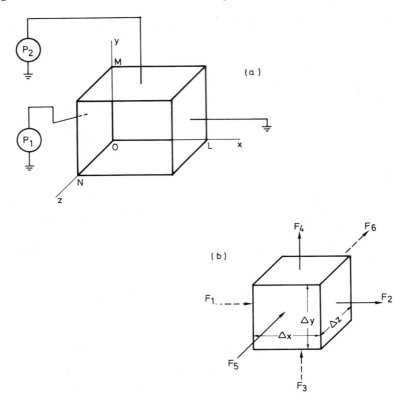

FIG. 4.4   Three-dimensional resistive fields

In this case the flux, F, across each boundary surface of the element is equal to the local flux density (flux/unit area) times the area of the surface. Solving equations (4.22) for $F_1, \ldots, F_6$, and invoking the conservation principle that

$$F_1 - F_2 + F_3 - F_4 + F_5 - F_6 = 0 \tag{4.23}$$

yields upon rearrangement

$$\frac{\Delta x \Delta y \Delta z}{D} \left[\frac{\left(\frac{\partial p}{\partial x}\right)_2 - \left(\frac{\partial p}{\partial x}\right)_1}{\Delta x} + \frac{\left(\frac{\partial p}{\partial y}\right)_4 - \left(\frac{\partial p}{\partial y}\right)_3}{\Delta y} + \frac{\left(\frac{\partial p}{\partial z}\right)_6 - \left(\frac{\partial p}{\partial z}\right)_5}{\Delta z} \right] = 0$$

$$\tag{4.24}$$

When

$$\Delta x \to 0 \qquad \Delta y \to 0 \qquad \Delta z \to 0$$

equation (4.24) becomes

$$\frac{\partial^2 p}{\partial x^2} + \frac{\partial^2 p}{\partial y^2} + \frac{\partial^2 p}{\partial z^2} = 0 \qquad (4.25)$$

This equation is known as Laplace's equation in three dimensions and, together with the boundary conditions applicable to this specific problem, constitutes a complete characterization of the potential distribution within the field. In this case the boundary conditions at the six faces of the solid of Fig. 4.4a are

$$\text{at} \begin{cases} x = 0 \\ 0 < y < M \\ 0 < z < N \end{cases} p = p_1 \qquad \text{at} \begin{cases} 0 < x < L \\ y = M \\ 0 < z < N \end{cases} p = p_2$$

$$\text{at} \begin{cases} 0 < x < L \\ 0 < y < M \\ z = 0 \end{cases} \frac{\partial p}{\partial z} = 0$$

$$\text{at} \begin{cases} x = L \\ 0 < y < M \\ 0 < z < N \end{cases} p = 0 \qquad \text{at} \begin{cases} 0 < x < L \\ y = 0 \\ 0 < z < N \end{cases} \frac{\partial p}{\partial y} = 0$$

$$\text{at} \begin{cases} 0 < x < L \\ 0 < y < M \\ z = N \end{cases} \frac{\partial p}{\partial z} = 0 \qquad (4.26)$$

Laplace's equation, equations (4.20) and (4.25) can be expressed more compactly by introducing the Laplacian operator ∇^2. Regardless of the number of dimensions, Laplace's equation becomes

$$\text{div(grad } p) = \nabla.(\underline{\nabla} p) = 0 \qquad (4.27)$$

$$\nabla^2 p = 0 \qquad (4.28)$$

The boundary excitations in the preceding examples were specified to be sources of potential. Since sources of the flux variable also occur in engineering work, there are actually two types of boundary conditions: a specified potential or a specified flux. It has already been shown that, since no flux flows across an unexcited boundary, the potential gradient normal to this boundary is equal to zero. If a non-zero flux is specified at a boundary, the potential gradient normal to this boundary must be directly proportional to this variable. The boundary conditions may therefore be expressed in a more general form as

$$p = k_1$$

$$\frac{\partial p}{\partial n} = k_2 \qquad\qquad\qquad (4.29)$$

where k_1 and k_2 are specified constants or functions of space variables and may be positive, negative or zero, and where n is the direction normal to the boundary.

4.2.5.2   Modified form

The mathematical model of a distributed parameter system characterized by an elliptic partial differential equation assumes the simple and compact form of equation (4.28) only if a number of assumptions, explicitly or implicitly made in its derivation, are satisfied. In this section, three modified forms of Laplace's equation are considered. Each of these frequently arises in physics and engineering. They include modifications due to non-uniformities in the field parameter, to moving coordinate systems, and to distributed sources of flux.

Non-uniformity

An interesting feature of equations (4.20) and (4.25) is that the dissipative parameter D does not appear explicitly. It follows therefore that the potential distribution within the field is independent of the magnitude of this parameter, which is not unexpected. For example, in Fig. 4.3 it is obvious that the potential at the mid-point of the conductor is exactly equal to half the potential difference between the two end points, and that this is true regardless of the magnitude of the dissipativity, provided of course that D is the same at all points within the system. Implicit in the derivation of equation (4.28) is the assumption that the characteristics of the field are uniform and isotropic. Where D is not independent of the space parameters, some modification in the above derivations must be effected. If the field consists, for example, of two sections of different dissipative properties, these two sections can be treated as two separate fields. In that case, the conservation principle demands that the flux across the junction of the two sections be the same on both sides of the junction and therefore specifies a boundary condition. This really then involves two separate field problems, each governed by equation (4.28).

More generally, the dissipative parameter D can be specified as a function of the space coordinates, either by an analytic expression, or numerically in graphical or tabular form. Referring to the derivation of Laplace's equation in one space dimension, and letting $D = D(x)$, the voltage gradients at the two ends of the line segment of Fig. 4.3b are

$$f_1 = -\frac{1}{D_1}\left(\frac{dp}{dx}\right)_1 \qquad f_2 = -\frac{1}{D_2}\left(\frac{dp}{dx}\right)_2 \qquad (4.30)$$

where D_1 and D_2 are the local dissipativities at x_1 and x_2 respectively. Equation (4.19) therefore becomes

$$\frac{1}{\Delta x}\left[\frac{1}{D_2}\left(\frac{dp}{dx}\right)_2 - \frac{1}{D_1}\left(\frac{dp}{dx}\right)_1\right] = 0 \qquad (4.31)$$

Now when $\Delta x \rightarrow 0$

$$\frac{\partial}{\partial x}\left(\frac{1}{D(x)}\frac{\partial p}{\partial x}\right) = 0 \qquad (4.32)$$

The functional relationship between D and x is therefore embedded within the second derivative. In a similar manner, the derivations for non-uniform fields in three space dimensions can readily be shown to lead to

$$\frac{\partial}{\partial x}\left(\frac{1}{D}\frac{\partial p}{\partial x}\right) + \frac{\partial}{\partial y}\left(\frac{1}{D}\frac{\partial p}{\partial y}\right) + \frac{\partial}{\partial z}\left(\frac{1}{D}\frac{\partial p}{\partial z}\right) = 0 \qquad (4.33)$$

or, in the more compact notation

$$\nabla \cdot \left(\frac{1}{D}\nabla\underline{p}\right) = 0 \qquad (4.34)$$

The above derivations and equation (4.34) apply also to fields in which D is a function of the field potential p. Under these conditions, the field is recognized to be non-linear, and certain convenient analytical techniques (such as the superposition theorem) are inapplicable.

Moving coordinates

A second important modification of Laplace's equation occurs in the characterizations of fields where the medium through which the flux flows is itself moving. This is equivalent to considering that the origin of the co-ordinate system, with respect to which all positions in space are measured, is moving at a specified velocity. Consider, for example, the study of heat transfer in the static or steady state, a phenomenon governed by Laplace's equation. Suppose now that the medium comprising the field is a liquid. While the fluid is at rest, the temperature distribution within this field is governed by the basic Laplace equation, equation (4.28). If now the fluid which comprises the field is made to flow say in the x direction, the transfer of heat is influenced not only by the temperature gradients, as in equation (4.7), but also by the velocity of the fluid particles themselves. Equation (4.28) must therefore be modified to take this phenomenon into account. For problems in one and three space dimensions respectively, it can be shown that this modification takes the form

$$\frac{d^2p}{dx^2} = \alpha v_x \frac{dp}{dx} \tag{4.35}$$

$$\frac{\partial^2 p}{\partial x^2} + \frac{\partial^2 p}{\partial y^2} + \frac{\partial^2 p}{\partial z^2} = \alpha \left(v_x \frac{\partial p}{\partial x} + v_y \frac{\partial p}{\partial y} + v_z \frac{\partial p}{\partial z} \right) \tag{4.36}$$

or, with a short notation

$$\nabla^2 p = \alpha \underline{v} . \nabla p \tag{4.37}$$

where v_x, v_y, and v_z are velocities of the coordinate systems in the x, y and z directions, respectively. These terms may be constant, or they may themselves be functions of the space variables or of the potential p.

Sources and/or sinks
Another important modification of Laplace's equation is required if distributed sources or sinks of flux are active within the field. Consider for example, a conductor made of metal. Under steady-state conditions the temperature distribution within this medium will be governed by Laplace's equation (4.28). However, if an electrical current is made to flow through this material, heat will be generated at every point within the field (the I^2R loss) and will therefore affect the temperature distribution. A similar phenomenon occurs if one considers the steady-state temperature distribution within the core of a nuclear reactor, in which heat is generated by distributed radioactive particles. Under these conditions, the differential elements of Figs 4.3b and 4.4b for one- and three-dimensional fields respectively, must be modified by the inclusion of an additional flux input, representing the distributed internal source. The application of the conservation principle then leads to

$$f_1 - f_2 = - f_i \Delta x$$
$$F_1 - F_2 + F_3 - F_4 + F_5 - F_6 = - f_i \Delta x \, \Delta y \, \Delta z \tag{4.38}$$

where f_i is the additional flux per unit length, or volume respectively, flowing into the element as a result of the distributed source. Laplace's equation then takes the general form

$$\nabla \cdot \left(\frac{1}{D} \underline{\nabla p} \right) = - k f_i \tag{4.39}$$

for D = D(x, y, z). f_i can itself be a function of the space coordinates or of p. This equation is known as Poisson's equation.

The boundary conditions associated with the modified forms of Laplace's equation described in this section are identical to those for the basic form of Laplace's equation as expressed by equation (4.29).

4.2.5.3 *General properties and applications*

A number of general conclusions may be drawn from the foregoing analysis. First of all, it is apparent that Laplace's equation does not contain the independent time variable. This is a direct result of the fact that only one of the three types of parameters (dissipation) was assumed to be present within the system. The direct consequence of the absence of the other two type of parameters (reservoirs of potential and flux), is that if the excitation is a function of time, the response everywhere within the system will have exactly the same transient characteristics, and that steady-state is achieved instantaneously at all points in the field. For example, if the potential applied to one of the boundaries of the field shown in Figs 4.3a and 4.4a is suddenly changed, i.e. a step change, the potential, p, at all points within the field will change at the same instant to new values. This can also be shown to be true if the field contains only potential reservoirs, or only flux reservoirs. The key point is that, if a field is composed entirely of one of the three basic element types, time is not an independent variable. The time variable also disappears and Laplace's equation applies in fields which contain reservoirs, as well as dissipation, provided enough time has elapsed since a previous change in excitation so that steady-state conditions have been reached.

A second important feature of all of the foregoing models, with the exception of those characterized by equation (4.39), is that the excitations are applied only at the boundaries or extremities of the fields. No potential or flux sources appear within the field. According to the conservation principle, therefore, all the energy or matter entering or leaving the field must be accounted for by external sources, and all lines of flux must terminate at boundaries. This implies directly that there can be no maxima or minima of potential within the field. Since the presence of such a potential maximum would imply that some point within the field has a higher potential than all neighbouring points, and since flux always flows from a high potential to the low potential, such a maximum would mean that matter or energy emanates in all directions from this point. In vector analysis such a phenomenon is known as divergence, and fields governed by Laplace's equation must have zero divergence. Likewise a minimum of potential would imply a sink of matter or energy, and again would violate the continuity and conservation principles. This means also that potential gradients cannot change polarity within the field.

The reason for the wide applicability of Laplace's and Poisson's equations is that systems containing only one of the three basic types of elements occur in a great many physical areas, and the conservation and continuity principles are applicable to these systems. A complete review of all the areas of application of these powerful equations would require the inclusion of lengthy and intricate analyses of many highly specialized and esoteric problems. Therefore, only the most often encountered and important applications will be summarized here.

Three basic body force fields are encountered in physics: the fields generated by masses, electric charges, and magnetic poles. All regions of free space which do not contain these field excitations are systems governed by Laplace's equation. Gravitational, electrostatic, and magnetic fields are therefore subject to the same type of analysis as that performed above. The across variable in each of these three areas is termed a potential function and has a significance analogous to that of the potential, p, employed above. Thus the symbol ϕ is frequently used to indicate a general potential function.

The concept of potential functions can also be extended to certain fluid flow systems where ϕ is termed the "velocity potential" and is defined by

$$\frac{\partial \phi}{\partial x} = -v_x \qquad \frac{\partial \phi}{\partial y} = -v_y \qquad \frac{\partial \phi}{\partial z} = -v_z \qquad (4.40)$$

where v_x, v_y and v_z represent the velocity of a fluid particle in the x, y, and z directions, respectively. Since Laplace's equation applies only to systems containing one type of element, a careful examination of the fluid system must precede the application of that equation. If the liquid particles are forced through a medium containing very small pore channels such as compacted sand, the forces upon the fluid due to viscous friction are much larger than the inertial forces; and if, furthermore, the fluid is assumed to be incompressible so there can be no storage of fluid particles, the system is purely dissipative, and Laplace's equation may be applied.

When an incompressible liquid flows in an open channel or a pipe, it is frequently permissible to assume that it is an "ideal" fluid, having negligible viscosity. Under these conditions the inertial (kinetic energy) forces are the only ones that have to be considered, and this system is again governed by Laplace's equation. The through variable in a fluid flow system is the translational velocity of the fluid particles. Since fluid particles may also rotate about their own axes, it is necessary that the flow be irrotational if Laplace's equation is to be applicable.

In mechanics, Laplace's equation is used to describe the static deflection of elastic membranes or sheets having negligible mass. These systems act as pure springs (reservoirs of potential). In problems of heat transfer it is generally not practicable to describe a system entirely by means of one of the three parameter types. Heat flow systems, in which the excitation varies with time, are not therefore governed by Laplace's equation. If steady-state or static conditions have been reached, however, the reservoirs of potential have acquired all the heat that they can store, and therefore exercise no further influence upon the heat-conduction phenomenon. Under these conditions the temperature within the system is a potential function, subject to the same equation and analogous boundary conditions as those described for the preceding systems.

Poisson's equation arises in the above-mentioned disciplines wherever there are distributed sources. The gravitational field within a solid (such as the earth), the magnetic field within a magnet, and the electrostatic field within a vacuum containing a space charge, are all examples of such a situation. The equation also arises in mechanics in the study of torsional stresses and strains, in heat transfer where distributed sources of heat are present, and in many other disciplines.

In the equations derived in this chapter, the potential, p, is the dependent variable. The solutions of these equations yield values of the potential as a function of x, y and z. Digital computers usually generate solutions in tabular form, providing the potentials at discretely-spaced points in the x, y, z domain. On occasion, the solution of problems in two space dimensions and for cross-sections of a three-dimensional field are provided as plots of lines of equal potential, similar to topological contour maps. Sometimes a solution for the flux distribution is preferred to a solution for the field potentials. In accordance with equation (4.7), flux f is proportional to the potential gradient. The flux vector at any point in the field is therefore perpendicular to the line of constant potential, since the potential gradient is zero parallel to such a line. This implies that the lines of constant flux are orthogonal to the lines of equal potential at all points in a field. Once the values for the potential have been determined in a field problem, the solution for the flux at all points in the field can therefore be obtained very easily. Alternatively, flux can be employed as the dependent variable in the derivation of the field equations. This results in partial differential equations which are structurally similar to those already derived for potentials.

4.2.5.4 Analytical solutions

Classical engineering texts [9, 231] which use PDEs as models, often provide analytical solutions for specific problems in order to convey to the reader a feeling concerning the behavioural patterns that can be expected.

In the model-building literature, one often refers to the analytical solution techniques utilized and, therefore, a brief account of some of the methods is presented.

For elliptic equations a useful procedure is based on the principle of the separation of variables. Basically a curvilinear orthogonal coordinate system (ρ, ψ, θ) is chosen so that certain field boundaries can be assimilated with one or more of the surfaces of the coordinate system. Then a solution of the following type is looked for

$$\phi\,(\rho, \psi, \theta) = R(\rho)\,\Psi(\psi)\,\Theta(\theta) \tag{4.41}$$

The functions R, Ψ, Θ, will contain arbitrary constants. The linearity of Laplace's equation ensures that a finite, or infinite, sum of "Laplace" products (4.41) also constitutes an acceptable solution.

$$\phi(\rho, \psi, \theta) = \sum_k \alpha_k R_k(\rho)\Psi_k(\psi)\Theta_k(\theta) \tag{4.42}$$

The nature of the sum and the coefficients then follow from the initial and/or boundary conditions.

As an example the Laplace equation (4.25) is considered for the field shown on Fig. 4.4a, with the boundary conditions (4.26). Due to the geometry of the field, a rectangular coordinate system is adequate. A Laplace product $p(x, y, z) = X(x).Y(y).Z(z)$ is chosen. Equation (4.25) results in (4.43)

$$\frac{1}{X}\frac{\partial^2 X}{\partial x^2} + \frac{1}{Y}\frac{\partial^2 Y}{\partial y^2} + \frac{1}{Z}\frac{\partial^2 Z}{\partial z^2} = 0 \tag{4.43}$$

Note that

$$\left.\frac{\partial p}{\partial z}\right|_{z=0} = \left.\frac{\partial p}{\partial z}\right|_{z=N} = 0.$$

We choose $\partial p/\partial z = 0$ everywhere and take $Z(z) = 1$. The Laplace equation then reduces to:

$$\frac{d^2 X}{dx^2} = -\omega^2 X \tag{4.44}$$

$$\frac{d^2 Y}{dy^2} = \omega^2 Y \tag{4.45}$$

Solutions of the first equation (4.44) are

$$\omega = 0 \qquad X(x) = ax + b$$
$$\omega \neq 0 \qquad X(x) = A\sin(\omega x + B)$$

The constants a, b, A, B are arbitrary, but they can be chosen to fit certain boundary conditions:

$$\omega = 0 \qquad X(0) = p_1, X(L) = 0 : X(x) = \frac{p_1}{L}(L - x)$$

$$\omega \neq 0 \qquad X(0) = 0, X(L) = 0 \qquad X(x) = A_k \sin \frac{k\pi}{L} x$$

Solutions of the second equation (4.45) are

$$\omega = 0 \ Y(y) = a'y + b'$$
$$\omega \neq 0 \ Y(y) = A'_k e^{(k\pi/4)y} + B'_k e^{-(k\pi/L)y}$$

For each of these solutions we require $\left. \dfrac{\partial Y}{\partial y} \right|_{y=0} = 0$

$$\omega = 0 \qquad Y(y) = 1$$

$$\omega \neq 0 \qquad Y(y) = A''_k(e^{(k\pi/L)y} + e^{-(k\pi/L)y}) = A'_k \cosh \frac{k\pi}{L} y$$

Based on superposition a candidate potential p(x, y, z) will have the following form

$$p(x, y, z) = \frac{p_1}{L}(L - x) + \sum_{k=1}^{\infty} \alpha_k \sin \frac{k\pi}{L} x \cosh \frac{k\pi}{L} y \qquad (4.46)$$

The equation is a solution of the PDE and all boundary conditions, except one, are satisfied. If the α_k can be chosen to yield the final boundary condition p(x, M, z) = p_2, (4.46) will be the correct answer.

$$p_2 - \frac{p_1}{L}(L - x) = \sum_{k=1}^{\infty} \alpha_k \sin \frac{k\pi}{L} x \cosh \frac{k\pi}{L} M \qquad (4.47)$$

Fourier theory can be applied on the following function f(x)

$$0 \leqslant x < L \qquad f(x) = p_2 - \frac{p_1}{L}(L - x) \qquad (4.48)$$

$$-L \leqslant x < 0 \quad f(x) = -p_2 + \frac{p_1}{L}(L + x) \qquad (4.49)$$

(4.48) is the left hand side of (4.47) and (4.49) extends the function in a suitable manner in order to make a solution for (4.47) possible. One finds:

$$p(x, y, z) = \frac{p_1}{L}(L - x) +$$

$$+ \sum_{k=1}^{\infty} \left(\frac{4p_2}{k\pi} (1 - (-1)^k) - \frac{2p_1}{k\pi} \right) \sin\left(\frac{k\pi}{L} x \right) \frac{\cosh\left(\frac{k\pi}{L} y \right)}{\cosh\left(\frac{k\pi}{L} M \right)} \qquad (4.50)$$

The example clearly indicates that even very simple field problems yield complex analytical solutions. The solution is available under an infinite sum, as was mentioned in Section 4.1.2.2. So evaluation of the potential in a point x, y, z requires approximation through truncation of (4.50).

For the Poisson equation (4.39), Green's theorem is often applied. The solution is a sum of two components:

$$p(x, y, z) = p_1(x, y, z) + p_2(x, y, z)$$

The first $p_1(x, y, z)$ is a solution of the Laplace equation, while $p_2(x, y, z)$ is known under an integral equation (4.51).

$$p_2(x, y, z) = \int_V \frac{k f_i(x', y', z')}{4\pi[(x - x')^2 + (y - y')^2 + (z - z')^2]^{1/2}} \, dV \qquad (4.51)$$

4.2.6 Parabolic partial differential equations

4.2.6.1 Basic form

Ranking with Laplace's equation as one of the most important and funda-mental equations of applied physics, the parabolic equation is known vari-ously as the diffusion, or conduction equation. This equation is also first derived for a simple one-dimensional system such as that shown in Fig. 4.5a. The field in this case contains distributed dissipation, just as in Fig. 4.3a, but also distributed reservoir properties (potential or flux). Figure 4.5a may describe an electrical resistor (dissipator) coupled to ground by means of a dielectric (potential reservoir), or it may represent a thermal conductor manifesting thermal resistance (dissipation) and heat capacity (potential reservoir). The differential element is shown in Fig. 4.5b.

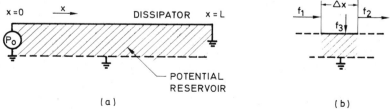

FIG. 4.5   A one-dimensional resistive field with reservoir of potential

In addition to the flux f_1 and f_2 along the conductor, there is now flux f_3 which enters the reservoir. The conservation principle now specifies that

$$f_1 - f_2 - f_3 = 0 \qquad (4.52)$$

If the storage properties per unit length are expressed by E_p, the flux serving to "fill" the reservoir comprised by the differential element can be expressed in accordance with equation (4.9) as

$$f_3 = f_1 - f_2 = E_p \Delta x \frac{\partial p}{\partial t} \qquad (4.53)$$

where p refers to the average potential (with respect to ground) of the differential element, and $E_p \Delta x$ is the total reservoir capacity of this element. The difference between the flux f_1 and f_2 expressed in terms of the rate of change of flux per unit length is

$$f_1 - f_2 = -\frac{\partial f}{\partial x} \Delta x \qquad (4.54)$$

if higher order terms of a Taylor series expansion are neglected. But in accordance with equation (4.7), the flux f can be expressed in terms of the potential gradient as

$$f = -\frac{1}{D} \frac{\partial p}{\partial x} \qquad (4.55)$$

where again D represents the dissipation per unit length. This equation corresponds to the familiar i = e/R in electric circuits. Differentiating equation (4.55) with respect to x yields

$$-\frac{\partial f}{\partial x} = \frac{\partial}{\partial x}\left(\frac{1}{D} \frac{\partial p}{\partial x}\right) \qquad (4.56)$$

Combining equations (4.53), (4.54) and (4.56) yields

$$\frac{\partial}{\partial x}\left(\frac{1}{D} \frac{\partial p}{\partial x}\right) = E_p \frac{\partial p}{\partial t} \qquad (4.57)$$

If the dissipation D is not a function of x, that is if the conductor is uniform,

$$\frac{\partial^2 p}{\partial x^2} = DE_p \frac{\partial p}{\partial t} \qquad (4.58)$$

which is known as the diffusion equation in one dimension. A complete specification of the problem includes the potentials p(0, t) and p(L, t) at the two ends of the field for all time, subsequent to an initial time t = 0, as well as the potential p(x, 0) everywhere along the field at the initial instant.

This type of problem therefore requires more information than the one-dimensional Laplace's equation. Given equation (4.57) or (4.58), along with the necessary boundary and initial conditions, the potential everywhere along the field for all time $t > 0$ can be determined.

The governing equation for a three-dimensional field containing dissipation and one type of reservoir can be derived in a similar fashion. In this case, the differential element is a cube similar to that shown in Fig. 4.4, but containing in addition distributed reservoir properties E_p per unit cube. From the above development it may readily be inferred that in the case of a three-dimensional diffusion field

$$\frac{\partial}{\partial x}\left(\frac{1}{D}\frac{\partial p}{\partial x}\right) + \frac{\partial}{\partial y}\left(\frac{1}{D}\frac{\partial p}{\partial y}\right) + \frac{\partial}{\partial z}\left(\frac{1}{D}\frac{\partial p}{\partial z}\right) = E_p\frac{\partial p}{\partial t} \qquad (4.59)$$

For uniform D,

$$\frac{\partial^2 p}{\partial x^2} + \frac{\partial^2 p}{\partial y^2} + \frac{\partial^2 p}{\partial z^2} = DE_p\frac{\partial p}{\partial t} \qquad (4.60)$$

where, in this case, the boundary conditions are similar to those expressed in equation (4.26) plus the initial condition $p(x, y, z, 0)$ the potentials at all points within the field at the initial instant.

Introducing again the Laplacian operator, equations (4.57), (4.58), (4.59) and (4.60) may be generalized to read

$$\nabla\cdot\left(\frac{1}{D}\nabla p\right) = E_p\frac{\partial p}{\partial t} \qquad \text{or} \qquad \nabla^2 p = k\frac{\partial p}{\partial t} \qquad (4.61)$$

where k is determined by the parameters of the system. The boundary conditions pertinent to this equation are the same as those for Laplace's equation, expressed by equation (4.29). In addition, an initial condition specifying the quantity stored in the field reservoir at the initial time must be furnished. If reservoirs of potential are present, the initial potential distribution $p(x, y, z, 0)$ must be given; if reservoirs of flux are present, the initial potential rate of change of potential $\partial p(x, y, z, 0)/\partial t$ may be furnished instead.

4.2.6.2 *Modified versions*

All of the modifications discussed in Section 4.2.5.2, in connection with elliptic partial differential equations, also apply to parabolic partial differential equations. Where the medium in which diffusion is taking place is itself in motion, i.e. where the coordinate system is moving, the diffusion equation becomes

$$\nabla \cdot \left(\frac{1}{D} \nabla p \right) = E_p \frac{\partial p}{\partial t} + \alpha \underline{v} \cdot \nabla p \tag{4.62}$$

where v is the velocity of the medium. Such fields are said to involve combined mass transfer and diffusion.

The presence of distributed sources of flux, in systems containing dissipation and one type of reservoir parameter, entail the addition of a term proportional to the distributed source to the right-hand side of the diffusion equation. For non-uniform fields, the characterizing equation becomes

$$\nabla \cdot \left(\frac{1}{D} \nabla p \right) = E_p \frac{\partial p}{\partial t} - f_i \tag{4.63}$$

4.2.6.3 *General properties and applications*

In the foregoing derivation the nature of the reservoir, whether it be a reservoir of a potential or of flux, was not specified. It was only assumed that one or the other type of parameter was present. In general terms, the above development leads to the conclusion that the diffusion equation (4.61), is characteristic of systems which are dissipative, and contain one type of reservoir parameter. This parameter may be of the potential or flux variety, but only one type may be present in the system. The presence of the combination of this parameter and the dissipative parameter implies that the response does not achieve its final value instantaneously, as in the case of fields governed by Laplace's equation. The dissipative parameter is sometimes known as a "damping term" and acts in combination with the reservoir parameter to delay the attainment of final values. The constant, k, determined by the system parameters, is a measure of this delay. Time is therefore very definitely an independent variable in such field problems.

The presence of only one rather than both types of storage elements implies that the final values of potential in a field, in response to a sudden change in excitations at the boundaries, is approached monotonically; i.e. there is no change in polarity of potential gradients nor overshooting of the final value of the field potentials. For example, if in Fig. 4.5 the initial condition specifies that the potential is everywhere equal to zero, and if the potential source p_0 takes the form of a step of magnitude Q at time $t = 0$, the final or steady-state potential everywhere along the system $p(x, \infty) = Q(1 - x/L)$, is approached asymptotically at all points along the field. At no time is the potential anywhere in the field higher than the final value, and at no time and at no place is the rate of change of potential negative. For this reason, the diffusion equation is sometimes known as the equalization equation. The rate at which this final value is approached is determined by the dissipative and storage parameters. While Laplace's equation for uniform fields is independent of the field characteristics, the same is therefore not true of the diffusion equation. The parameters of the field must be furnished to permit the prediction of the transient field potentials.

It is apparent that if steady-state conditions exist, i.e. if none of the excitations is a function of time, and if sufficient time has elapsed since any previous change in excitation, the $\partial p/\partial t$ term in the diffusion equation vanishes, and the Laplacian is equal to zero. Laplace's equation may therefore be considered a special, or degenerate, case of the diffusion equation. This implies, as pointed out in the preceding section, that field problems governed by the diffusion equation are described by Laplace's equation if static or steady-state conditions exist.

The diffusion equation finds application in all areas in which problems arise involving two types of elements, only one of which is a reservoir. In heat transfer problems, the system under study is generally a three-dimensional field containing thermal resistance and thermal capacitance, which act respectively as dissipative and reservoir of potential parameters. Thermal resistance is not an energy dissipative parameter in the same sense as an electrical resistor, in that no energy is actually converted. Nevertheless from considerations of entropy it may be reasoned that the two resistances play analogous roles in their respective areas, in that both act to delay or dampen the achievement of final response values. Hence, the diffusion equation permits the determination of the temperature everywhere within the field for all time after the "initial time", provided that the temperature or heat flux at the field boundaries, as well as the temperature distribution within the field at the "initial time", is specified.

As the name implies, the diffusion equation also describes the diffusion of one type of fluid particles in a space occupied by a different fluid. For example, it describes the diffusion of carbon monoxide in motionless air, or of ink in stagnant water. In such problems attention is usually focused on the concentration of one of the two fluids, and this concentration or density denoted by p, comprises the dependent variable of the system. The flux or flow of particles (through variable) is then related to the gradient of the density of the particles (across variable) by the diffusion constant (dissipative or damping term), which is related in turn to the freedom with which molecules are able to move within the field. At the same time there occurs a storage of fluid particles in every volume element of the field. This storage is proportional to the density of the particles. Hence, every volume element of the field comprises a reservoir of potential. The diffusion equation under these conditions is generally expressed as

$$\nabla^2 \rho = \frac{1}{k} \frac{\partial \rho}{\partial t} \tag{4.64}$$

where ρ is the density of the particles and k is termed the diffusivity. These same considerations also apply to the absorption of fluid particles by solids and to the drying of porous solids saturated with liquids.

In Section 4.2.5.3 it is pointed out that, when a fluid flows through an open channel or porous medium, the inertia of the fluid particles corresponds to a reservoir of flux, the viscous forces to dissipation, and the compressibility effects to a potential reservoir. In problems of irrotational incompressible flow, in which viscous forces and inertial forces arise, the diffusion equation can therefore be applied to predict the velocity potential or pressure at points within the flow stream. The same is true for problems involving the analysis of viscous flow of compressible fluids when inertial forces can be neglected, as is the case in gas flow in a porous medium.

An important equation in electromagnetics is the so-called "skin effect" equation, relating the current density J along a conductor to its magnetic permeability μ (reservoir of flux) and its electric conductivity σ (dissipation)

$$\nabla^2 J = \mu\sigma \frac{\partial J}{\partial t} \tag{4.65}$$

This equation evidently has the form of the diffusion equation, as would be expected from a consideration of the types of parameters involved. In general in electromagnetics, Maxwell's equations reduce to the form of the diffusion equation in fields which have conductivity, but in which either the permeability or dielectric constant may be neglected. Some caution is required in the application of these equations, however, since the potential function in this case is a vector having both magnitude and direction, while it is a scalar in the other field problems previously discussed. Dynamic fields containing viscous damping as well as either appreciable mass or springiness, but not both, are also governed by the diffusion equation. The deflection of a spring or drum head of negligible mass, for example, is governed by this equation.

4.2.6.4 Analytical solutions

In the steady state, the parabolic equations reduce to elliptic ones and they can be treated as such. Under unsteady-state conditions the PDE is often analysed with the technique mentioned before separation of variables.

Another technique that is often useful is based on the Laplace transform. The transformation often permits a PDE to convert to an ODE. The usefulness of the method, which is by no means limited to parabolic equations, depends on the analytical tractability of the resulting ODE, and on the ease of obtaining the inverse transform of the solution.

The following example is considered: suppose a one-dimensional heat problem governed by equation (4.61). The boundaries are $x = 0$ and $x = \infty$. At $x = 0$, a step T, in temperature is applied; at $x = \infty$, temperature is finite. At time $t = 0$, the temperature distribution in the field is uniform $(T = 0)$. First the Laplace transform of the potential is defined:

$$P(x, s) = \mathscr{L}[p(x, t)] \tag{4.66}$$

According to transformation rules (4.61) becomes:

$$\frac{\partial^2 P}{\partial x^2} = k \cdot s \cdot P \tag{4.67}$$

A general solution for (4.67) is

$$P = ae^{-\sqrt{ks} \cdot x} + be^{+\sqrt{ks} \cdot x} \tag{4.68}$$

Taking into consideration the boundary conditions one obtains, noting that a step in temperature has Laplace transform T_1/s:

$$P = \frac{T_1}{s} e^{-\sqrt{ks} \cdot x} \tag{4.69}$$

Equation (4.69) is obtained with remarkable ease. The major problem consists in transforming back (4.69). In the present case the solution can be found out from existing tables for transform pairs:

$$\mathscr{L}^{-1}\left[\frac{1}{s} e^{-\alpha\sqrt{s}}\right] = 1 - E\left(\frac{\alpha}{2\sqrt{t}}\right) \tag{4.70}$$

with $E(t) = \dfrac{2}{\sqrt{\pi}}\displaystyle\int_0^t e^{-u^2}\, du$: the error function.

The use of (4.70) yields for the inverse Laplace transform of (4.69):

$$T_1\left[1 - E\left(\frac{\sqrt{k}x}{2\sqrt{t}}\right)\right] \tag{4.71}$$

4.2.7 Hyperbolic partial differential equations

4.2.7.1 The wave equation

The third fundamental equation of physics is termed the wave equation and describes the familiar phenomenon of wave motion. In this case the one-dimensional system, such as that shown in Fig. 4.6a, has distributed parameters which are reservoirs of potential as well as of flux; but no dissipation is present. Such a system may represent an electric transmission line having negligible resistance, but appreciable inductivity and dielectric coupling to ground. Referring to the differential element shown in Fig. 4.6b, in accordance with equation (4.10), the rate of change of flux along the length of the system is expressed as

$$-\frac{\partial f}{\partial x} = E_p \frac{\partial p}{\partial t} \tag{4.72}$$

where E_p is descriptive of the potential reservoir capabilities per unit length. Similarly, the potential gradient is related to the rate of change of flux by a parameter according to

$$-\frac{\partial p}{\partial x} = E_f \frac{\partial f}{\partial t} \tag{4.73}$$

where E_f represents the flux storage capability per unit length. Equations (4.72) and (4.73) are generalizations of the familiar

$$i = C \, de/dt \tag{4.74}$$
$$e = L \, di/dt$$

of electric circuit theory. Differentiating equation (4.72) with respect to

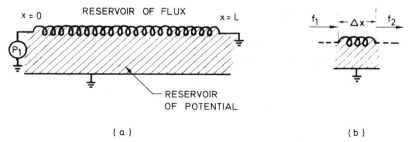

(a)   (b)

FIG. 4.6   One-dimensional field with reservoir of flux and potential

time and equation (4.73) with respect to x yields

$$-\frac{\partial^2 f}{\partial x \partial t} = E_p \frac{\partial^2 p}{\partial t^2}$$

$$-\frac{\partial^2 f}{\partial x \partial t} = \frac{1}{E_f} \frac{\partial^2 p}{\partial x^2} \tag{4.75}$$

Combining these two equations yields

$$\frac{\partial^2 p}{\partial x^2} = E_p E_f \frac{\partial^2 p}{\partial t^2} \tag{4.76}$$

which is known as the wave equation in one dimension. In order to predict the transient potential along the one-dimensional field, the potentials at x = 0 and x = L must be known for all time, as in Laplace's equation and the diffusion equation; and, in addition, two initial conditions are required. These initial conditions correspond to the potential and the flux at every point in the system at the initial instant time, t = 0. This may correspond to a specification of the potential p(x, 0) and the rate of change of potential $\partial p(x, 0)/\partial t$.

Two-dimensional and three-dimensional fields governed by the wave equation, possess distributed potential and flux reservoirs in a plane and in a three-dimensional region, respectively. The above analysis is readily extended to such systems and leads to

$$\nabla^2 p = k \frac{\partial^2 p}{\partial t^2} \tag{4.77}$$

In general, the wave equation is applicable to all those systems which include reservoirs, both of potential and of flux, but do not have dissipative or damping parameters. The presence of these two types of reservoirs implies an interchange of matter or energy. None of the energy applied to the system, or present in the system initially, can be lost. It can only be changed back and forth from kinetic to potential energy. This is what gives rise to the familiar wave or vibration patterns. In the diffusion equation, the constant k is identified with the time constant, the rate at which steady-state conditions or equilibrium conditions are approached. The significance of the constant k in the wave equation is different, since evidently there can be no equilibrium in the same sense in such a system. In the wave equation, the constant k determines rather the velocity with which a disturbance is propagated. For example in Fig. 4.6, the smaller the $E_p E_f$ product, the smaller the constant k, and the more rapidly is the full effect of a sudden change of the excitation p(t) at one end of the system felt at the other end.

In electrical systems, the wave equation arises where inductance and capacitance, but no resistance, are present. This is approximately the case in the study of "ideal" transmission lines. In dynamics, pure wave motion occurs if appreciable inertial mass forces and spring forces are present, and if viscous damping may be neglected. The vibration of a drum head with negligible damping is an example of such motion. Vibrating strings may likewise exhibit these properties. In fluid dynamics, flux storage is associated with the intertia of individual fluid particles, while the storage of potential in a fluid implies compression of the fluid. If the viscous forces within the fluid system are negligible compared to the intertial forces, and if the fluid is compressible, the wave equation can therefore be expected to apply. Wave motion in fluids is frequently observed as in the sound waves in air or in water. The wave equation is therefore of great importance in the field of acoustics. In electromagnetics, the wave equation applies to those systems in which the conductivity is negligible but which contains appreciable permeability and dielectric properties. This is the case in a vacuum, and in most non-metallic materials.

4.2.7.2 The damped wave equation

To this point only systems containing two types of parameters have been considered. Many systems contain both types of energy reservoirs as well as dissipation of appreciable magnitude. To derive the governing equations, the system shown in Fig. 4.6a must be modified to include dissipation. For full generality it is necessary to provide for two types of dissipation: series dissipation D_s which effects a dissipation of energy by virtue of the flow of flux, and parallel dissipation D_p which leads to a loss of system energy by "leakage". In electric transmission, lines have appreciable series resistance, as well as inductance, and appreciable leakage conductance between the two lines as well as dielectric coupling. In this case, in applying the conservation principle to express the change of flux along the x coordinate (for example $f_1 - f_2$ in Fig. 4.6b), it is necessary to include energy flow into the potential energy reservoir, as well as through the parallel dissipative element. Accordingly

$$-\frac{\partial f}{\partial x} = \frac{1}{D_p} p + E_p \frac{\partial p}{\partial t} \qquad (4.78)$$

where E_p is again the potential reservoir capability per unit length and D_p is the parallel dissipation per unit length. Similarly, the potential gradient is expressed as:

$$-\frac{\partial p}{\partial x} = D_s f + E_f \frac{\partial f}{\partial t} \qquad (4.79)$$

where E_f is again the flux reservoir capability per unit length and D_s is the series dissipation per unit length.

Equations (4.78) and (4.79) are generalizations of the electrical transmission line equations

$$i = \frac{e}{R} + C\frac{de}{dt}$$

(4.80)

$$e = iR + L\,di/dt$$

Equations (4.78) and (4.79) have two unknown, p and f. The simultaneous solution of these two equations for p yields

$$\frac{\partial^2 p}{\partial x^2} = E_p E_f \frac{\partial^2 p}{\partial t^2} + (D_p E_p + E_f D_s)\frac{\partial p}{\partial t} + D_p D_s p$$

(4.81)

This is the most general expression for one-dimensional fields. Equation (4.81) is sometimes known as the telegraph equation since it is descriptive of the voltage distribution along telegraph transmission lines. It is apparent that if both D_p and D_s in equation (4.81) are equal to zero, the equation reduces to the wave equation. If, on the other hand, E_f and D_p are zero, the diffusion equation results. If any three of the four types of parameters E_f, E_p, D_p or D_s are equal to zero, equation (4.81) becomes Laplace's equation. In more general terms equation (4.81) can be written as

$$\nabla^2 p = k_1 \frac{\partial^2 p}{\partial t^2} + k_2 \frac{\partial p}{\partial t} + k_3 p$$

(4.82)

and requires the same boundary and initial conditions as the wave equation.

The characteristic response of systems governed by equation (4.82) to step function excitations at a boundary is one of damped oscillation, i.e., an equilibrium condition is gradually approached. This approach is not necessarily monotonic, as in the case of the diffusion equation, but may involve overshooting and oscillation about the equilibrium state. In that respect this equation corresponds to the characterizing ordinary differential equations for lumped systems containing resistance, capacitance and inductance, and exhibiting under-damped, critically-damped or over-damped behaviour.

In addition to electrical transmission lines, the damped wave equation finds application in all those physical systems in which all three types of parameters are present. In dynamic fields containing appreciable mass, spring forces and viscous damping, this equation governs the motion of points within the system. A vibrating string or elastic sheet generally responds to a sudden blow or excitation with sinusoidal oscillations, which gradually die out or reduce to zero. In fluid dynamic systems, where the fluid is compressible and both viscous forces and inertial forces are appreciable, the damped wave equation again applies. Likewise, electromagnetic field problems for systems containing appreciable permeability, dielectric properties, and conductivity are governed by equation (4.82).

4.2.7.3 Analytical solutions

For hyperbolic PDEs, the analytical techniques presented before, can often be applied. The technique of separating the independent variables, for instance, can be applied to the wave equation. For equation (4.77), a solution of type (4.83) can be found.

$$p(x, y, z, t) = e^{j(a/\sqrt{k})t}p'(x, y, z) \tag{4.83}$$

The PDE then reduces to an elliptic equation

$$\nabla^2 p' = -a^2 \tag{4.84}$$

In fact (4.84) is a Poisson equation. Fortunately the source term a^2, is constant throughout the field so that the relationship (4.84) can be handled as a Laplace equation by separation of variables.

Certain simple damped wave equations have been solved with Laplace transform techniques. Typical for field problems of the hyperbolic type is a technique called the method of the characteristics. The concepts apply to a more general class of PDEs and arise when uniqueness problems concerning the solutions of PDEs are considered from a geometrical point of view. For an "informal" introduction of the "characteristics" the following simple equation is considered:

$$a\frac{\partial p}{\partial x} + b\frac{\partial p}{\partial y} = c \quad \text{or} \quad au + bq = c \tag{4.85}$$

Equation (4.85) specifies a family of geometrical surfaces $z = p(x, y)$. Guided by our experience with ODEs, where an initial condition is required to obtain one single solution, it could be expected that here a line C in three-dimensional space is needed. Such a line has a projection C_1 on the x–y plane. The idea of "characteristics" comes from the observation that the PDE itself (4.85) also defines a family of lines described by the equation (4.86), when s is a suitable coordinate on the line:

$$\frac{ds}{dx} = \frac{1}{a} \quad \frac{ds}{dy} = \frac{1}{b} \quad \frac{ds}{dz} = \frac{1}{c} \tag{4.86}$$

These lines are geometrically related to the solution of the PDE (4.85). More specifically, the normal to the surface $p(x, y)$ has direction cosines u, q, -1 and the tangent to the lines defined by (4.86), cosines a, b, c. The partial differential equation is a constraint that makes the normal to the surface $p(x, y)$ in a point normal to the line passing through that point. The projections of the lines defined by (4.86) on the x–y plane are called characteristics and they are defined by $dx/a = dy/b$. The characteristics are useful in specifying conditions for uniqueness, and they may be of help in finding solutions for equation (4.85).

Consider, still for the same PDE, a curve C. Suppose that λ is a coordinate on the curve. Then one can write:

$$\frac{dz}{d\lambda} = \frac{\partial z}{\partial x} \frac{dx}{d\lambda} + \frac{\partial z}{\partial y} \frac{dy}{d\lambda} \tag{4.87}$$

Note that C is required to be on a solution $p(x, y)$ so, the following equations must hold:

$$ua + qb = c \tag{4.88}$$

$$udx + qdy = dp \tag{4.89}$$

where (4.89) follows from (4.87) with $z = p$.
Equations (4.88) and (4.89) can be solved for u, q and one finds:

$$\frac{u}{bdp - cdy} = \frac{q}{cdx - adp} = \frac{1}{bdx - ady} \tag{4.90}$$

For a unique solution the determinant of the set of equations must not be equal to zero.

$$bdx \neq ady$$

or C_1 may not belong to the characteristics.
Besides their role in uniqueness problems, the characteristics may be of help in finding particular solutions of the PDE. Consider again equations (4.85), with $a = 1$, $b = 1$, $c = 1$. The lines defined by (4.86) are

$$z = x + a$$
$$z = y + b$$

Note that the characteristics are given by

$$y = x + a - b$$

Suppose that $p(x, 0)$ is provided—$p(x, 0)$ for $y = 0$ is C here—then $p(x, y)$ can be computed as follows for a point $x_1 y_1$.
The characteristic through $x_1 y_1$ is:

$$y = x + (y_1 - x_1)$$

For $y = 0$, $x_0 = x_1 - y_1$ where $p(x, y) = p(x_0, 0)$

With x_0 and $p(x_0, 0)$ the value of $p(x_1, y_1)$ is

$$p(x_1, y_1) = x + p(x_0, 0) - x_0 \qquad p(x_1, y_1) = y + p(x_0, 0)$$

For second-order equations of type (4.91)

$$a \frac{\partial^2 u}{\partial x^2} + b \frac{\partial^2 u}{\partial x \partial y} + c \frac{\partial^2 u}{\partial y^2} = e \qquad \text{or} \qquad ar + bs + ct = e \qquad (4.91)$$

the characteristics can be found for instance using the conditions for uniqueness. In fact one can write

$$dp = u\,dx + q\,dy$$
$$du = r\,dx + s\,dy$$
$$dq = s\,dx + t\,dy$$
$$e \;= ar + bs + ct$$

Using the last three equations, a unique solution for r, s, t requires a non zero determinant:

$$\begin{vmatrix} dx & dy & 0 \\ 0 & dx & dy \\ a & b & c \end{vmatrix} \neq 0$$

The characteristics are thus given by

$$c(dx)^2 - b(dx)(dy) + a(dy)^2 = 0 \qquad (4.92)$$

The condition which the solution of the PDE must satisfy along the characteristics, can be found by setting another determinant to zero

$$\begin{vmatrix} dp & dx & 0 \\ dq & 0 & dy \\ e & a & c \end{vmatrix} = 0$$

or $e\,dx\,dy - a\,dp\,dy - c\,dq\,dx = 0$ \qquad (4.93)

If the characteristics are real, and the initial line C is not a characteristic, one is able to use (4.92) and (4.93) in a step-by-step process, as in the first-order case, to build up the characteristics and the solution of the PDE. Real characteristics require $b^2 - 4\,ac > 0$, which is, as seen in section 4.2.4, the condition for PDEs of the hyperbolic type. Using lines and characteristics has not only been useful for analytical purposes, but has also been helpful in numerical schemes.

4.2.8 The biharmonic equations

A special class of equations arises in the theory of elasticity. These equations are generally similar to the elliptic, parabolic, and hyperbolic partial differential equations derived above, but contain space derivatives of fourth order instead of second order. This complication arises from the fact that in stress analysis the through variable (the stress) is not a vector quantity as in the preceding examples, but is described by a tensor. To specify completely a vector quantity, such as current or heat flux, it is necessary to know only its magnitude and direction. In the case of a tensor quantity, additional information must be supplied. For the stress tensor six components must be known before the stress is completely defined. Three of these are the same as for vectors, the components in the x, y and z directions. Three other components are necessary to define a plane to which the stress is referred. In stress analysis one is actually concerned with two types of stresses, the normal stress and the shear stress; accordingly, a specification of the total stress contains more information than the specification of current in electrodynamics or heat flux in heat transfer systems.

The basic laws of elasticity corresponding to the general conservation principles are the equations of equilibrium and compatibility. In the general application of these equations to relate the stress and the strain in an elastic body, it is convenient to define a stress function ϕ according to

$$\frac{\partial^2 \phi}{\partial x^2} = \sigma_y,$$

$$\frac{\partial^2 \phi}{\partial y^2} = \sigma_x, \tag{4.94}$$

$$\frac{\partial^2 \phi}{\partial x \partial y} = \rho_{xy}$$

where σ_x and σ_y are the normal stresses in the x and y directions respectively, and ρ_{xy} is the corresponding shear stress. Under static conditions, equilibrium and compatibility then lead to the socalled biharmonic equation, which takes the form

$$\frac{\partial^4 \phi}{\partial x^4} = 0 \tag{4.95}$$

in one dimension, and

$$\frac{\partial^4 \phi}{\partial x^4} + 2 \frac{\partial^4 \phi}{\partial x^2 \partial y^2} + \frac{\partial^4 \phi}{\partial y^4} = 0 \tag{4.96}$$

for two dimensions. These equations are elliptic equations approximately analogous to Laplace's equation in other systems. The left-hand side of equations (4.95) and (4.96) can be abbreviated by the biharmonic operator $\nabla^4\phi$, so that these equations can be expressed compactly as

$$\nabla^4\phi = 0 \tag{4.97}$$

In stress problems, the weight of the beam or elastic plate being studied corresponds to the internal distributed sources as described in Section 4.2.5.2. Where the weight of the elastic member is appreciable, equation (4.97) is modified to read

$$\nabla^4\phi = w \tag{4.98}$$

where w is the weight per unit length or area. This expression is approximately analogous to Poisson's equation.

Under transient conditions spring forces, characterized by Young's modulus, come into play, and vibrations described by

$$\nabla^4\phi = k \frac{\partial^2\phi}{\partial t^2} \tag{4.99}$$

arise. In yet more general formulations, equation (4.99) may be modified by the addition of terms proportional to $\partial\phi/\partial t$ and ϕ.

4.2.9 Summary

The purpose of the preceding discussion is to demonstrate how the partial differential equations characterizing physical systems can be deduced directly from physical considerations. This development is limited to fields governed in some manner by the basic principles of conservation and continuity. The development of the appropriate partial differential equations and boundary conditions then proceeds as follows:

(1) Identify the across and through variables appropriate to the system, recognizing that the across variable is generally the algebraic difference between two scalar quantities, and that the through variable is generally a vector.

(2) Examine the characteristics of the field to determine the types of parameters which are present and which cannot be neglected in the analysis. The possible types of parameters fall into three categories: reservoirs of potential, reservoirs of flux, and dissipators.

(3) Write the pertinent partial differential equation by noting the combination of parameter types present. Here the symbol ∇^2 is useful in specifying compactly that the dependent variable is to be differentiated twice with respect to each pertinent Cartesian space variable, and that the sum of the second derivatives is to be taken.

(4) Modify the basic partial differential equation to take into account any internal distributed sources which may be present.

248

TABLE 4.2 PDEs, their definition, parameters and response

Type	Name	Equation	Response	Sketch
Elliptic	Laplace	$\nabla^2\phi = 0$	D or E_p or E_f	
	Poisson	$\nabla(\sigma\nabla\phi) = 0$	D or E_p or E_f	
		$\nabla^2\phi = k$	D or E_p or E_f	
Parabolic	Diffusion	$\nabla^2\phi = k\dfrac{\partial\phi}{\partial t}$	D + E_p or E_f	
	Moving coord.	$\nabla^2\phi + k_1\dfrac{\partial\phi}{\partial x} = k_2\dfrac{\partial\phi}{\partial t}$	D + E_p or E_f	
Hyperbolic	Wave	$\nabla^2\phi = h\dfrac{\partial^2\phi}{\partial t^2}$	$E_p + E_f$	
	Damped wave	$\nabla^2\phi = k_1\dfrac{\partial^2\phi}{\partial t^2} + k_2\dfrac{\partial\phi}{\partial t} + k_3\phi$	D + E_p + E_f	
Biharmonic	Static beam	$\nabla^4\phi = 0$	E_p	
	Beam vibration	$\nabla^4\phi = k\dfrac{\partial^2\phi}{\partial t^2}$	$E_p + E_f$	
	Loaded beam	$\nabla^4\phi = \omega$	E_p	

B.C.: $\phi = k$ $\dfrac{\partial\phi}{\partial n} = k$

I.C.: $(\phi)_{t=0} = f(x, y, z, 0)$; $\left(\dfrac{\partial\phi}{\partial t}\right)_{t=0} = f(x, y, z, 0)$

(5) Specify the appropraite boundary and initial conditions. The boundary conditions must specify completely and uniquely the potential, or potential gradient, at every extremity or boundary of the field. This specification usually takes the form either of a constant potential, or a constant potential gradient. The initial conditions must specify the energy stored by every energy reservoir element within the field. If in addition to the Laplacian term the partial differential equation includes a first derivative with respect to time, one initial condition is necessary at each point in the field. If the equation includes a second derivative with respect to time, two initial conditions are required.

Table 4.2 constitutes a summary of the concepts introduced in this chapter.

4.2.10 Partial Differential Equations in environmental systems

4.2.10.1 *Environmental systems as a discipline*

The unpleasant and unhealthful effects of air and water pollution, particularly in urban areas, have long been recognized as a serious problem. Not until the early 1970s however, did the continuing and increasing despoiling of the environment come to be regarded as a crisis of national and international proportions.

A large number of physical specialities and disciplines are brought into play in the description of the interaction of human activities and changes in the environment. These include among others: heat transfer, aerodynamics, hydrodynamics, elasticity, and photochemistry. There are, however, marked similarities in the mathematical and computational techniques for treating diverse environmental problems. There are also similarities in motivations for modelling and simulation, and in the ultimate use to which mathematical models are put. It therefore becomes feasible to discuss environmental problems in a unified manner, and to regard the modelling of environmental systems as a distinct discipline. The modelling of environmental systems is concerned with the mathematical description of the depletion, modification, and transient pollution of the water, the land, and the air environment, as a direct result of human activity. The following is a by no means exhaustive list of environmental problems which have been modelled and studied with the aid of computers.

Water

(a) Aquifer depletion: the removal of water from underground reservoirs due to excessive pumping from wells.

(b) Aquifer pollution: the increase of the salt and bacteriological content of ground water as a result of urban and industrial waste.

(c) Stream pollution: the increase in undesirable chemicals and the decrease in dissolved oxygen in rivers and streams, resulting from the disposal of industrial and urban waste products.

(d) Thermal pollution: undesirable increases in temperature of rivers and regions of the ocean due to industrial activity involving the use of large amounts of cooling water.

Land

(a) Subsidence: the sinking of large land areas due to the depletion of underground water or petroleum reservoirs.

(b) Coastline erosion: the modification of coastlines due to changes in coastal currents resulting from channeling, dredging, and harbour development.

(c) Surface erosion: the modification of land topography due to extensive mining activities, e.g. strip mining.

Air

(a) Air pollution: the dispersal into the atmosphere of obnoxious solid particles and gases resulting from industrial, urban or military activity.

(b) Climate modification: changes in temperature, humidity, and sunlight intensity due to industrial and agricultural activities.

If all areas to which the mathematical modelling approach has been applied are placed along a spectrum ranging from so-called "white box" problems to so-called "black box" problems, the environmental systems fall somewhere along the middle of the spectrum. The construction of models of environmental systems involves considerably more recourse to inductive inference and uncertain system observations than do models arising in electric circuits, aerospace engineering, and chemical process control. On the other hand, the basic equations characterizing dynamic phenomena in environmental systems are far better known than in such relatively "dark" areas as biology, economics, sociology, and politics. In fact, most environmental systems are remarkably similar from the mathematical point of view. They are all field problems (distributed parameter system) and are governed by non-linear parabolic partial differential equations. The geometry of the field is irregular, the parameters are time-varying and non-linear, and sources are distributed over large portions of the field. As a class, these problems belong in the area of "large" field problems as distinct from the "small" field problem more frequently analysed using computers. Table 4.3 constitutes a list of the principal features of these two classes of field problems. It can be seen that "large" field problems are characterized by uncertainties as to the geometry of the system, the field parameters (internal characteristics as the medium being

TABLE 4.3   Comparison between "small" and "large" field problems

	"Small" fields	*"Large" fields*
Typical types of problems	Heat transfer Nuclear reactors Vacuum tube fields Elastic structures	Air pollution Ground water dynamics Water pollution Land subsidence
Partial differential equation	Known Elliptic, parabolic hyperbolic, biharmonic	Known $\nabla(\sigma\nabla\phi) = \dfrac{\partial\phi}{\partial t} + u\dfrac{\partial\phi}{\partial x} + Q$
Boundary geometry	Known	Not well known
Parameters	Usually approximately known	Largely unknown
System observations	Good quality Sufficient samples	Low quality Scattered locations Insufficient samples "Noisy"

analysed), and by the relatively low quality of system observation. The modelling of such "large" distributed parameter systems presents problems, which are quite different from those encountered in modelling "small" fields.

It is by no means established that, in view of the quality and quantity of measurements, a PDE-model is required, or even useful, for certain modelling goals, especially those that centre on increased decision-making capability. In the context of the subject of the present chapter, we focus on some of the distributed mathematical models which are most widely used in the modelling of various environmental systems. All of these have been implemented on digital computers, often with the aid of special-purpose digital simulation languages. The objective of this chapter is not to provide an exhaustive survey of all environmental systems, but rather to highlight the similarities that exist in the mathematical models which characterize many important environmental problems.

4.2.10.2   *Environmental problems related to water*

Ground water quantity [174, 184, 213]
In many parts of the world, water for human and industrial use is obtained from wells which extend to underground water reservoirs. The term

"aquifer" is applied to any underground region which has significant hydraulic conductivity, and which is at least partially saturated with water. Geologic formations such as faults, and impermeable horizontal formations, act to restrict the flow of water and form the boundaries of aquifers. In so-called confined aquifers, the underground reservoir is bounded by overlying impermeable formations, so that the ground water is trapped under pressure greater than atmospheric. The water level in a well drilled into such an aquifer rises spontaneously, and may even gush above the surface as in an artesian well. However, most aquifers are unconfined, so an air/water interface exists marking the upper boundary of the water-saturated region. Under these conditions, pumps must be employed to extract water from the aquifer, and such water production results in a lowering of the air/water interface, the water table. Rainfall and underground streams act to replenish the aquifer, compensating in part for the water that is extracted from it.

Underground water is an important resource, one whose utilization must be carefully monitored and controlled. Figure 4.7 shows the horizontal boundaries of the aquifer underlying the San Fernando Valley region of Southern California. Hundreds of wells are scattered throughout this basin, and serious disruptions to agricultural and urban activities would result from a catastrophic lowering of the water table in any part of the valley. In other regions, aquifers are bounded on one side by sea water. Excessive extraction of fresh water from the aquifer results in intrusion of salt water into the freshwater regions. This constitutes a serious pollution of the aquifer. Furthermore, since clay particles, which are contained in underground soils, swell when exposed to salt water, salt water intrusion may cause long-lasting reductions in the hydraulic conductivity of the aquifer, and may therefore have permanent deleterious effects. Quantity models of underground reservoirs are made to facilitate the prediction of the water level throughout an aquifer under various assumed extraction and replenishment conditions. With the aid of such a model, one can determine optimum control strategies, including limitations upon the total number of wells permitted in a region and limitations upon the water that may be extracted from each well.

The basic dependent variable in problems involving the flow of fluids in porous media is the velocity potential, ϕ, which is defined as the sum of the hydrostatic and gravitational potential. At any point in the fluid region, ϕ represents the sum of the local pressure, P, and the head (gρh) above a reference level. For purposes of studying ground water dynamics, the aquifer is regarded as a region manifesting hydraulic conductivity K(x, y, z) and compressibility S_p. The equation characterizing the potential distribution in the water saturated zone can then be obtained based on the con-

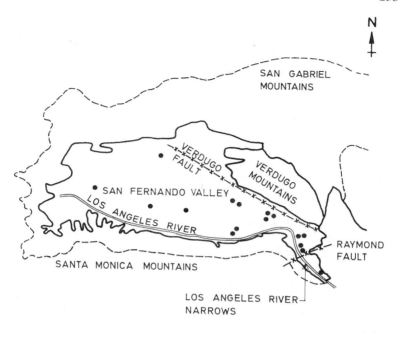

FIG. 4.7 Aquifer underlying the San Fernando Valley region of Southern California

siderations of section 4.2.3. One finds:

$$\frac{\partial}{\partial x}\left(K_x\frac{\partial\phi}{\partial x}\right) + \frac{\partial}{\partial y}\left(K_y\frac{\partial\phi}{\partial y}\right) + \frac{\partial}{\partial z}\left(K_z\frac{\partial\phi}{\partial z}\right) = S_p\frac{\partial\phi}{\partial t} + Q \qquad (4.100)$$

where S Q(x, y, t) represents the fluid input to the aquifer. This input is comprised of rainfall and seepage from surface streams; fluid extracted from wells represents a positive Q. The parameter K(x, y, z) is the hydraulic conductivity, the proportionality constant relating flow rate to potential gradient. The porous medium can be regarded as a network of tiny channels. The smaller the average diameter of the channels and the more tortuous the paths for fluid flow, the smaller the hydraulic conductivity.

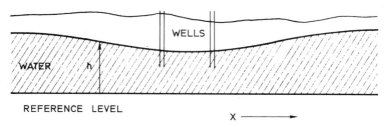

FIG. 4.8   Simplified aquifer: large lateral dimensions

The storage parameter, S_p, is defined by

$$S_p = \rho g(n\beta + \alpha) \tag{4.101}$$

where ρ is the fluid density, n is the porosity of the medium, and α and β are the compressibilities of the soil and the fluid respectively. This parameter may be regarded as being analogous to capacitance in an electrical system.

A very useful approximation can be made by assuming that the water zone is virtually horizontal, and that its thickness h is small compared to the lateral dimensions of the aquifer. This is illustrated in Fig. 4.8. Under these conditions h becomes the dependent problem variable and equation (4.100) can be rewritten as

$$\frac{\partial}{\partial x}\left[T(x, y, h) \frac{\partial h}{\partial x} \right] + \frac{\partial}{\partial y}\left[T(x, y, h) \frac{\partial h}{\partial y} \right] = S(x, y, h) \frac{\partial h}{\partial t} + Q(x, y, t)$$

$$\tag{4.102}$$

In this equation $T(x, y, h) = Kh$, and is termed the transmissibility. Similarly, in place of the storage parameter S_p, we have $S \equiv S(x, y, h) = S_p h$, termed the storage coefficient. S may be viewed as the total fluid capacity of a column $\Delta x . \Delta y$ in cross section and h in height. In place of the three dimensional linear equation (4.100), we now have a non-linear equation with only two space variables. The solution of equation (4.102) provides the height of the water table at all points in the xy domain for all times subsequent to an arbitrary initial time. Often, the results of ground water quantity simulations are presented in the form of topographic maps showing lines of equal elevation, h, of the water table: equi-potential lines at successive periods, usually several months or years apart. Figure 4.9 is an example of such a computer output for the Santa Ana basin south of Los Angeles.

Equation (4.102) constitutes a satisfactory representation of most aquifers. The major difficulty in applying it to practical situations lies in the need to specify the field parameters T and S. These must be inferred from

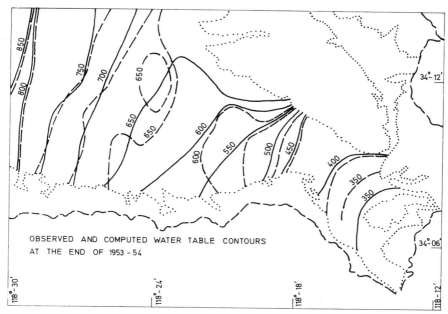

FIG. 4.9   Water table contours for the San Fernando Valley aquifer

geologic observations at the surface supplemented by occasional samples from wells or test borings. The lateral boundaries of the underground reservoir are likewise very difficult to determine from surface observations and are therefore specified primarily from geologic inference. Finally, the term Q in equation (4.102) requires for its complete specification a knowledge of local rainfall, influx and efflux from underground streams, and seepage from a variety of industrial and agricultural sources of waste waters. It is the combination of all of these uncertainties in the specifying of the parameters and the excitations of equation (4.102) that makes it necessary to regard quantity models of underground reservoirs as having a rather "dark shade of grey".

Ground water quality [20, 21]

In controlling and protecting underground water resources, not only the quantity of water contained in an aquifer but also its quality must be carefully considered. In order to be useful for various agricultural purposes, the salinity of water extracted from wells must be below a certain critical level; to be useful for human consumption, not only must the salt content be carefully controlled, but it is also necessary to guard against harmful bacteria. Usually, a large part of the salts dissolved in aquifers are due to natural causes, including the intrusion of sea water at a boundary of an aquifer, minerals carried in underground streams, and salts leached from the surface soil by rain-water. Occasionally industrial and urban waste also find their way into an aquifer. Usually when describing ground water quality, all minerals and salts dissolved in the ground water are lumped together and termed total dissolved salts (TDS). It is the TDS concentration which constitutes the dependent variable in ground water quality models. In characterizing ground water pollution it is usually feasible to consider the aquifer thickness to be small compared to the lateral dimensions of the reservoir, so that the z variable can effectively be eliminated. The movement of a pollutant in an aquifer can then be characterized by

$$\frac{\partial}{\partial x}\left(D_x \frac{\partial c}{\partial x}\right) + \frac{\partial}{\partial y}\left(D_y \frac{\partial c}{\partial y}\right) = \frac{\partial c}{\partial t} + u \frac{\partial c}{\partial x} + v \frac{\partial c}{\partial y} + Q \qquad (4.103)$$

where c is the TDS concentration; D_x and D_y are terms that are combinations of the dispersivities and the diffusivities, and are a measure of the average velocity of pollutant particles due to molecular motion: u and v are respectively the velocity of ground water flow in the x and y directions; $Q = Q(x, y, t)$ represents the source of the pollutant. Where pollutants are created or eliminated by chemical reactions taking place in the aquifer, an additional term $R = R(x, y, t)$ must be added to the right-hand side of the equation (4.103).

An examination of equation (4.103) reveals that ground water quality modelling is at least one level more difficult than ground water quantity modelling. This is because the determination of the parameters u and v in equation (4.103) requires that a solution for a ground water quantity model first be obtained. According to Darcy's law, the velocity of fluids in a porous medium is directly proportional to the potential gradient. The determination of u and v at all points in the xy domain requires the prior determination of h(x, y, t) and the obtaining of the gradient of this function in the x and y directions. Of course, if the water table is quiescent, that is if h is constant everywhere in the aquifer, u and v are zero. Usually, however, there is appreciable ground water movement, so that mass transport due to ground water movement is considerably more effective than diffusion in distributing pollutants.

All the uncertainties involved in identifying the parameters of ground water quantity models, therefore, also come to play in ground water quality modelling. The specification of local diffusivities, of initial pollutant concentration, and of chemical reactions, constitute additional difficulties.

Surface water pollution

The purity of surface waters including streams, rivers, and lakes is important for health as well as aesthetic reasons. In some countries, e.g. Japan,
many people have died as a result of eating fish contaminated by cadmium
and mercury salts that had been discharged into rivers by factories. In
virtually all industrial countries, lakes and rivers have been contaminated
by urban and industrial waste, resulting in the decimation of aquatic wild-
life, and creating unhealthy and unpleasant conditions. The mathematical
models characterizing the pollution of surface waters are structurally very
similar to those characterizing the pollution of aquifers. For example, if a
pollutant is discharged into a river, oriented in the x direction, the concentration, c, of the pollutant downstream from the source is expressed by

$$\frac{\partial}{\partial x}(D_m + D_d)\frac{\partial c}{\partial x} = \frac{\partial c}{\partial t} + u\frac{\partial c}{\partial x} + Q + R \qquad (4.104)$$

where D_m is the molecular diffusion coefficient, D_d is the dispersivity, and u
is the velocity of the stream. $R = R(x, t)$ characterizes the chemical decay
of the pollutant and $Q = Q(x, t)$ is the source term. Molecular diffusion
results from the random motion of the pollutant particles, tending to cause
a net movement of particles from a point of higher concentration to a point
of lower concentration. Dispersion arises from uneven flow due to the fact
that different particles take different tortuous paths. There are actually two
types of dispersions: longitudinal and transverse, and both are proportional
to the velocity of flow, u. Equation (4.104) suffices for streams which are
relatively narrow, and can be used to calculate the transient pollution
developing from a sudden discharge at some point. Typical concentration
profiles showing the downstream progression of the bulk of the pollutant
in the course of time, obtained by solving equation (4.104) are shown in
Fig. 4.10.

A frequent undesired effect of chemical pollution is the result of chemical reactions taking place within the water. These cause a lowering of the
oxygen dissolved in the water; a chemical of critical importance to the
maintenance of animal and vegetable life in the river. As a counter-
measure, artificially generated oxygen may be injected into the river at
various points along its course, thereby maintaining the dissolved oxygen
level above a prescribed limit.

For broad rivers and for lakes, the mathematical model includes two
space dimensions. It is then necessary to specify the parameters u and v
representing the velocity of currents in the x and y directions, which may be
subject to marked variation in time. Occasionally it is necessary to consider
three dimensional pollution models. This is the case, for example, in the

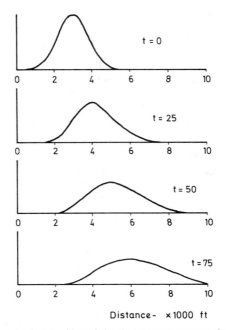

FIG. 4.10   Concentration profiles of the downstream progression of a pollutant

study of the effect of leaks from underwater oil wells, as took place recently in the Santa Barbara channel of California.

Thermal pollution [210]

Many industrial processes entail the generation of considerable amounts of excess heat which must be removed with the aid of heat exchangers. Often a continuous stream of water serves as the cooling medium. Cold water is then pumped into the plant from a nearby river, lake, or shore line, and after absorbing a maximum amount of heat, hot water is returned to the natural environment. Under favourable conditions, this process can result in an appreciable elevation of the temperature of the receiving body of water, a change which is likely to be harmful to aquatic life and to upset the ecological balance. Recent increasing interest in nuclear power generating plants, which require the dissipation of very large amounts of heat, has caused a great deal of concern among environmentalists.

An interesting and frequently studies phenomenon occurs when warm water is injected near the bottom of lakes. The thermal structure of such lakes consists of three distinct layers. Near the surface there is a layer of relatively warm water termed the epilimnion; while there is a relatively cold layer, the hypolimnion, near the bottom of the lake. Separating these two layers is the thermocline, a layer with a sharp thermal gradient. When hot water is discharged into the hypolimnion, a buoyant plume of warming water is produced. When this plume reaches that level in the lake at which the injected water temperature is equal to the ambient water temperature, the injected water spreads rapidly in the horizontal direction as a relatively thin sheet. The effect of the warm injection is therefore to produce an upward shift of the thermocline. This is illustrated in Fig. 4.11. Where the temperature of the injected fluid is higher than the temperature of the surface layer of the lake, the plume rises to the surface, and a source can be assumed to exist at that point. In the absence of horizontal fluid flow, the temperature, T, as a function of depth, z, can be characterized by

$$\frac{\partial}{\partial z}\left(K_h \frac{\partial T}{\partial z}\right) = \frac{\partial T}{\partial t} + w \frac{\partial T}{\partial z} - S \tag{4.105}$$

where K_h is the eddy diffusivity for the transport of heat, and w is the downward vertical velocity of flow which is induced by the discharge. w can be assumed to be volumetric injection rate, Q, divided by the area of the lake. The source termed S is present only where the temperature of the injected fluid is higher than the temperature at the upper surface of the

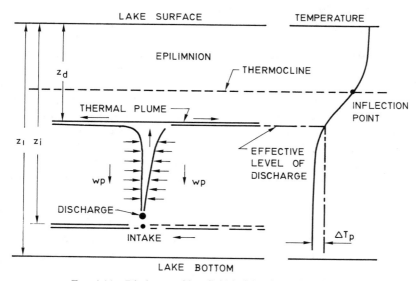

FIG. 4.11   Discharge of hot fluid in lake thermal pollution

lake. S is a rather complicated function given by

$$S(z) = \frac{2w[\,T(z_i) + \Delta T_p - T_s\,]}{a\,\sqrt{\pi}}\,exp\left[\frac{-(z - z_d)^2}{a^2}\right] \qquad (4.106)$$

where ΔT_p represents the effective temperature change produced in the intake water, T_s is the surface temperature, and a is a scale factor.

For hot water injected into rivers or larger bodies of water with appreciable currents, the flow velocities in the horizontal directions must be taken into account. These appear as first derivatives with respect to space variables.

4.2.10.3   *Environmental problems related to air*

Air pollution [71, 135, 211]

Once a serious problem only in a few isolated cities, such as Los Angeles, air pollution has become a major concern in virtually every metropolis throughout the world. Air pollutants such as ozone, hydrocarbons, and oxides of sulphur have become a major health hazard in urban areas; they have become a serious threat to agriculture and plant life; and in some cities such as Venice, Italy, they are gradually eating away and destroying outdoor sculptures and works of art. In many areas, the primary sources of pollutants are industrial plants such as oil refineries and electric power generation units; in other areas the primary culprit is the exhaust from moving automobiles; occasionally smoke from various furnaces, incinerators, and agricultural fires also contributes to the air pollution level.

The control of any of these sources of pollutants entails heavy economic consequences, and therefore involves intense political pressures and conflicts, in which environmentalists are pitted against established industrial, commercial, and agricultural interests. Simulations based on mathematical models are often employed to help clarify the issues and to investigate the long-range effects of various control strategies. Only very rarely are mathematical models used to predict day-to-day pollutant levels. In this section, models describing the mass transport of pollutants are first considered. This is followed by a brief discussion of chemical reactions in the atmosphere.

The atmospheric turbulent diffusion of particles belongs in the area of micrometeorology, and derivations of the equations discussed below may be found in textbooks on that subject. The basic equation governing the concentration, c, of particles in the lower atmosphere is

$$\frac{\partial}{\partial x}\left[K_x\frac{\partial c}{\partial x}\right] + \frac{\partial}{\partial y}\left[K_y\frac{\partial c}{\partial y}\right] + \frac{\partial}{\partial z}\left[K_z\frac{\partial c}{\partial z}\right]$$

$$= \frac{\partial c}{\partial t} + u \frac{\partial c}{\partial x} + v \frac{\partial c}{\partial y} + w \frac{\partial c}{\partial z} + Q \tag{4.107}$$

where Q are the source of pollutants; K_x, K_y and K_z, termed the eddy diffusivities in the x, y and z directions respectively, are a measure of mixing due to local turbulence; u, v and w are the wind velocity components in the three principal directions. In most simulations it is assumed that the wind velocity, w, in the z direction is negligible. The wind velocity in the horizontal directions is generally taken to be a nonlinear function of height, z, according to

$$u = A \left[\log_\varepsilon \frac{(z + z_0)}{z_0} + \frac{1 - \beta}{2} \log_\varepsilon^2 \frac{(z + z_0)}{z_0} + \dots \right] \tag{4.108}$$

In this equation z_0 is termed the roughness length characterizing the quality of the ground surface and represents the height at which the wind velocity is essentially zero. A is a constant. The term β is determined by the thermal gradient in the vertical direction and can be employed to approximate the effect of the inversion layer, which is critical in determining air pollution conditions in many areas. The eddy diffusivity in the z direction is approximated as

$$K_z = B \left[\frac{\partial u}{\partial z} \right]^{-1} \tag{4.109}$$

where B is a constant. If β in equation (4.108) is zero,

$$K_z \simeq \frac{B}{A} z$$

In order to study the distribution of pollutants downwind from a heavily-travelled road such as a freeway, it is assumed that the horizontal wind direction is normal to the freeway, so that if the freeway is oriented along the y axis, $v = 0$. If it is further assumed that transport of pollutants in the x direction due to diffusion is negligible compared to the transport due to the wind, $K_x \simeq 0$, and equation (4.107) becomes

$$\frac{\partial}{\partial y} \left[K_y \frac{\partial c}{\partial y} \right] + \frac{\partial}{\partial z} \left[K_z \frac{\partial c}{\partial z} \right] = \frac{\partial c}{\partial t} + u \frac{\partial c}{\partial x} + Q \tag{4.111}$$

If the roadway can furthermore be assumed to be relatively long, so that the concentration profile is independent of the variable y, parallel to the road, and furthermore that steady-state conditions exist, equation (4.111) can be simplified to read

$$\frac{\partial}{\partial z} \left[K_z \frac{\partial c}{\partial z} \right] = u \frac{\partial c}{\partial x} + Q \tag{4.112}$$

Typical solutions of equation (4.112) are plotted in Fig. 4.12 and show the horizontal concentration profile downwind of the freeway.

As implied by the preceding discussion, the complete modelling of equation (4.107) is so difficult that it is rarely attempted. In order to model the atmosphere in three dimensions, and in order to take into account local terrain conditions such as hills, buildings, etc., it is necessary to define a finite difference net with so many grid points that the obtaining of complete solutions entails an uneconomically large amount of computer time. For this reason simplifying assumptions such as those described above are always necessary.

To date, the most widely-used models for urban air pollution due to emissions from stacks of industrial plants have been based upon the so-called Gaussian plume model. This is a quasi-empirical formula constitut-

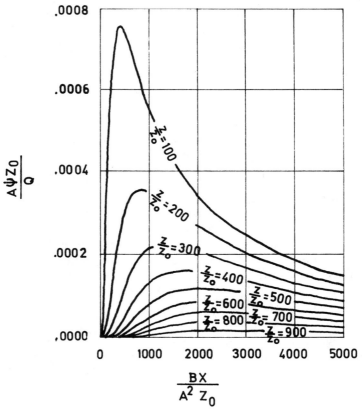

FIG. 4.12   Horizontal pollutant concentration profiles downwind of a freeway

ing a steady-state solution of equation (4.107) subject to a number of simplifying assumptions. According to this approach, the concentration c at ground level due to a source located at a distance H above the ground level is given by

$$c = \frac{Q}{\pi\sigma_y\sigma_z u} \exp\left[1 - \left(\frac{y^2}{2\sigma_y^2} + \frac{H^2}{2\sigma_z^2}\right)\right] \tag{4.113}$$

where Q is the magnitude of the source, assumed to be emitting particles at a constant rate, and u is the wind velocity assumed to be entirely in the x direction. σ_y and σ_z are the standard deviations of the concentrations about the plume axis crosswind and in the vertical direction respectively. Where there are a number of sources of pollutants, their effects can be added by superposition.

The problem of modelling air pollutants becomes more complex if chemical reactions occurring in the atmosphere are taken into account [71]. This is necessary if the effects of automobile exhaust are to be modelled, since the primary irritant, ozone, is not emitted by automobiles but is the result of a photochemical reaction by which sunlight acts to transform oxides of nitrogen emitted by automobiles into ozone. The basic equation relating the concentration of nitrogen dioxide NO_2, which is emitted by automobiles, and ozone O_3 are

$$NO_2 + O_2 \longrightarrow NO + O_3$$
$$NO + O_3 \xrightarrow{h\mu} NO_2 + O_2$$
$$NO + XO \longrightarrow NO_2 + X$$
$$O_3 + X \longrightarrow XO + O_2 \tag{4.114}$$

where $h\mu$ is the solar energy, which varies throughout the day, and X represents other active reactant present in the atmosphere. The rate of formation of the three major constituents, nitrogen dioxide, nitric oxide and ozone can be expressed approximately as

$$-\frac{\partial(NO_2)}{\partial t} = -a\lambda(NO_2) + b(O_3)(NO) + c(NO)(XO)$$

$$\frac{\partial(NO)}{\partial t} = a\lambda(NO_2) - b(O_3)(NO) - c(NO)(XO)$$

$$\frac{\partial(O_3)}{\partial t} = a\lambda(NO_2) - b(O_3)(NO) - d(O_3) \tag{4.115}$$

where the reaction rates a, b, ... d are functions of time, and λ is the ultraviolet light intensity. In order to predict the concentration of ozone

due to automobile traffic, it is therefore necessary to construct at least
three separate models of the type of equation (4.107), or one of its simplified forms, for at least three of the major constituents of air pollution.
Each of these three equations contains a coupling term representing the
distributed sources sinks due to chemical reactions. Equations (4.115)
specify these coupling terms.

4.2.10.4   Environmental problems related to land

Land subsidence [72, 175]

The withdrawal of ground water or petroleum from underground formations causes the appearance of voids between the sand grains comprising
the porous medium. Under the pressure of overlying strata, the reservoir
rock may become more compact, resulting in a sinking or subsidence of the
land surface. This phenomenon is particularly pronounced where there has
been extensive production from water or oil wells for a protracted period,
and where geologic conditions are favourable for this phenomenon. Land
subsidence has long been recognized as a major problem in certain areas of
Tokyo, in Mexico City, and in Long Beach, where subsidence of the order
of several feet has been observed. In Venice, the subsidence is less pronounced, amounting to less than one foot per decade, but nonetheless
constitutes a major long-term threat to the many old buildings perched in
the lagoon. Clearly, the prevention of further land subsidence demands a
sharp curtailment in the fluids which are withdrawn from wells. On occasion, sea water is pumped into the wells to replace fluids that have been
extracted from underground reservoirs.

From the point of view of mathematical modelling, land subsidence
involves two phases: (i) the modelling of the fluid pressures existing in the
reservoir, and (ii) the modelling of the movement of the overlying strata as
a result of compaction within the reservoir. The problem is complicated by
the fact that there may be a number of layers of fluid-bearing formations
separated by impermeable strata. A separate calculation must therefore be
carried out for each one of these layers.

The mathematical model for the pressure or head in each reservoir layer
is similar to equation (4.102), previously discussed in connection with the
modelling of ground water quantity. Using this model, annual changes in
hydraulic head in all fluid reservoirs are calculated. For each layer, the
compaction μ is given by as

$$\mu(t) = \rho\alpha b\Delta h(t) \tag{4.116}$$

where ρ is the density of the fluid, α is the vertical compressibility of the
soil, and b is the thickness of the reservoir layer. The total subsidence is
calculated by adding the compactions of all reservoir layers.

4.3 INDUCTIVE TECHNIQUES FOR PARTIAL DIFFERENTIAL EQUATIONS

4.3.1 Introduction

In the subsequent sections a very general discussion on inductive techniques for partial differential equations will be given. We do not go into details of specific techniques and the sections are only provided to give the reader a flavour of the state of the art in the field as well as of the crucial issues that arise. Many of the concepts and ideas of the previous chapter are applicable for partial differential equations, because their definition or conception is formalism independent. We briefly consider parameter estimation, structure characterization, frame definition, and experiment design.

4.3.2 Parameter estimation

4.3.2.1 Identifiability

In the distributed model case, the identifiability concepts are more important than in the lumped model case. In fact, the state is "infinite" and the sensors are necessarily finite in numbers. In relation to the complexity of the description, the number of measurements is rather limited. Unidentifiability conditions are thus more likely to occur than for ordinary differential equations.

A closer look at the literature shows that people working with PDEs, have been more acutely aware of the fundamental role of identifiability concepts. The first step has been to define observability in the same sense as proposed by Kalman for ordinary differential equations. The recovery of an initial state over the complete spatial domain is required, from measurements of the system dynamical state over some finite time interval. Unfortunately, observability may be neither sufficient nor necessary for identifiability. Parameter identifiability is related, but not identical, to observability.

One could first wonder whether the concepts of identifiability introduced in the previous chapter (Section 3.2.2) carry over to the model representation here. It is not difficult to see that all definitions do not directly require the choice of a specific formalism and thus they could be used here. Unfortunately, it is much more difficult to see how identifiability has to be established. The PDE-equation itself is more complicated, and the role of initial and boundary conditions is more involved. A simple example reveals the heart of the problem. Consider a thin metal plate that is excited by an external driving force. Suppose that displacement sensors have to be located to estimate certain parameters of the plate. There are several locations on the plate, called nodes or nodal lines, where no displacement can be observed. If the sensors are inadvertently placed on these specific locations, unidentifiability will result.

Besides the fact that identifiability is crucial and difficult to check, it is often tied up in practice with the characterizability concept. Recall from Section 4.2 that deduction of PDEs involve field parameters like dampers and reservoirs of potential and flux. The physical parameters are distributed in space. If their distribution is unknown, they result under suitable conditions in an infinite dimensional mathematical parameter vector. The choice of an acceptable description for the field parameter is basically a characterization problem, but it can be reduced to a parameter estimation problem by using a series expansion for the unknown function. Characterizability can eventually be seen here as identifiability of an infinite parameter vector.

Bearing in mind the considerations presented above, it will be clear to the reader why researchers in the field of modelling distributed systems have tended to investigate identifiability for special cases without expending too much effort on general approaches. Chavent [33] provides a guide to the identifiability literature for the transient heat equation, the transport equation, and the wave equation. The survey indicates that, even for special equations, all questions concerning identifiability are far from being resolved. Because the identifiability problem in partial differential equation models is exacerbating, mathematicians have been looking for a mathematical framework in order to be better equipped to attack it. It seems that parameter estimation for the unidentifiable models can be seen as an example of "improperly posed" problems, in the sense that the solution in a certain domain either does not exist, is not unique, or does not depend continuously on the initial data. Due to what now appears to be difficult to explain, the area of applied mathematics that studies improperly posed problems, was left almost untouched until the middle of this century. Nowadays more interest exists for such problems. Colton [39] mentions that, in order to approach a problem that is improperly posed, one must answer at least two questions. What is precisely meant by a solution? How does one find a solution? A basic lack of information cannot be remedied by any mathematical trickery. Hence, in order to determine what is meant by a solution it may be necessary to introduce "non standard" information gained from an intimate knowledge of the physical system. Here again a priori information seems to be important. Whether the newly defined mathematical approach will be helpful remains to be proven.

4.3.2.2 *Generalities*

Just as for ordinary differential equations, the parameter estimation problem in distributed systems can be seen as a problem in optimization and the general discussion of Section 3.2.7 carries over directly. More specifically, one defines:

—an error function $\varepsilon(p, \underline{z}, t)$, which is now a function of space and time;
—a function l from $R \times R_k \times R_{n_p} \times R_{n_\varepsilon} \to r \times r$ symmetric matrices;
—a matrix $Q_{tf}(p)$ defined by (4.117):

$$Q_{tf}(\underline{p}) = \int_{t0}^{tf} \int_{Z} 1(t, \underline{z}, \underline{p}, \underline{\varepsilon}) \, d\underline{z} \, dt \qquad (4.117)$$

—a cost $J(\underline{p})$ which is a scalar function of Q_{tf} (4.118)

$$J(\underline{p}) = h(Q_{tf}) \qquad (4.118)$$

Such general set-up has never been used for PDEs. The cost is directly defined as follows:

$$J(\underline{p}) = \int_{t0}^{tf} \int_{Z} \underline{\varepsilon}^{T}(\underline{p}, \underline{z}, t) H(\underline{z}, t) \underline{\varepsilon}(\underline{p}, \underline{z}, t) \, d\underline{z} \, dt \qquad (4.119)$$

In its most general form the error $\underline{\varepsilon}$ would contain equation, boundary and measurement errors. Chavent [33] mentions that only the equation error and output error have been used in practice, while the latter is by far the most popular. Recalling the discussion in Section 3.2.7.3, it can be concluded that in most cases the system is supposed to be deterministic, and only measurement noise is thought to exist. If in a real problem other noise terms are present, one may expect the output error approach to yield biased results.

4.3.2.3   Off-line parameter estimation schemes

Just as for ODEs, an off-line parameter estimation scheme consists of a suitable error, a cost function, and an optimization scheme. In view of the present day state of the art, one has to add the specification of an approximation procedure. In fact, the fundamental problem with PDEs, is the infinite dimensionality of the representation. Sooner or later, suitable approximations have to be done, and their precise nature is an inherent part of any parameter estimation procedure.

Classification of estimation procedures can be done according to any of their constituent elements. The methods can be discussed according to the choice of the error function: output error, equation error, prediction error; they can be sorted according to the final cost function: least squares, weighted least squares, maximum likelihood or Bayesian; they can be ordered according to the optimization procedures: analytical, gradient, stochastic approximation, quasi-linearization, random search, etc. The

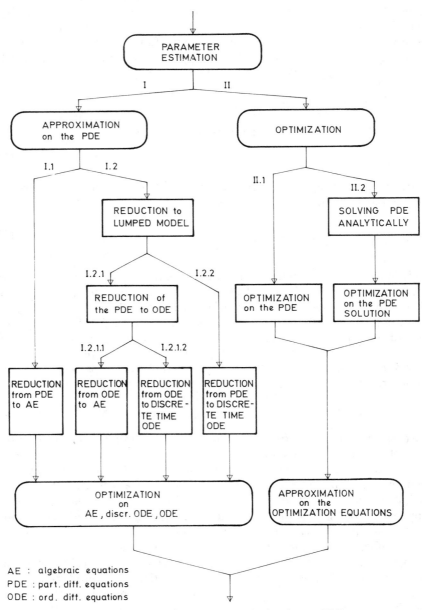

FIG. 4.13   Approaches to parameter estimation on PDEs

most relevant classification from the point of view of this book is a classification according to the approximation approach, because it is this step which distinguishes the distributed case from the lumped one.

There are basically two main groups of techniques (see Fig. 4.13). In the first group one starts with approximating the PDE, either directly to a set of algebraic equations through discretization of the finite field and the finite time period, or to a lumped representation of the PDE. The lumped model may be a set of ordinary difference equations, or a set of ordinary differential equations. In the latter case, the ODESS can be approximated further either by a set of algebraic equations or as a set of difference equations. Then depending on how far the approximation has been carried through, the optimization problem on a set of algebraic, difference or differential equations is considered, and its solution yields the parameters. The second group treats first the optimization problem, either directly on the PDE or on the analytical solution of the PDE. Approximation is done only at the very end of the operation in order to find the numerical values of the parameters. Which are the techniques that are commonly used for approximation? Reduction of the PDE to a set of algebraic equations is often done with the finite difference technique, or with the help of integral transformations. Reduction of the PDE to a set of ordinary differential equations has been achieved with the method of lines or the method of characteristics; Galerkin's method and cubic spline approximations are often used too. The ODEs can be further reduced to algebraic equations by integral transformations. A set of ordinary difference equations can be obtained from the PDE by application of finite difference schemes. For references and more details we refer to survey papers [134, 176].

It is fair to say that the relative merits of the approaches are poorly understood. As mentioned before from a purely mathematical point of view, the second approach may be more adequate. Unfortunately, in view of our analytical and computational capabilities, it may turn out that the first group yields better results in practice. More research is required to clarify the controversy.

A recent survey [33] indicates that the techniques actually used by practitioners are conventional; 75% of the application papers apply the output error criterion. In the off-line case 60% have used a gradient technique for the optimization problem.

4.3.2.4   *On-line parameter estimation schemes*

The most common approach for on-line parameter estimation in distributed systems is based on the extended Kalman filter. Basically, one proceeds as follows:

—the PDE is approximated by an ODE;

—the state of the ODE is expanded in such a manner that the unknown parameters are included in the new state vector;

—the system obtained is non-linear and the extended Kalman filter is used to obtain an on-line estimator of the state which comprises the unknown parameters.

The extended Kalman filter has recently been shown to be occasionally divergent, and a modified scheme is to be applied if convergence in all circumstances is strived at [146]. Even in its modified form, one may wonder how deleterious the approximation phase can be on the parameter estimates.

Once the PDE has been approximated, there is no reason why the extended Kalman filter should be preferred. Any of the on-line parameter estimation procedures discussed in the previous chapter could be taken. In view of the computational requirements it may well be interesting to single out schemes which require a rather limited amount of computations.

4.3.3   Structure characterization and frame definition

Up to now the partial differential equation model has probably never been used for black-box modelling. Usually large parts of the frame and the structure are obtained by deduction from a priori knowledge concerning the system. Even in this special modelling context a number of inductive problems concerning the structure, and even the frame, may arise.

Recall from Section 4.2.1 that a PDE-model contains field parameters, distributed in space. A mathematical description of these parameters requires a function. On the basis of physical insight such function fulfils certain regularity conditions such as continuity. It happens, however, that except for a few regularity conditions, its precise course is unknown and it has to be inferred from measurements.

Concerning the frame it may happen that the precise location of certain boundaries is a matter of uncertainty. The boundary of an aquifer, for instance, which is determined by geological conditions, may not always be known. Is it then possible to find the boundary on the basis of measurements?

Here, again, the concepts and issues concerning structure characterization which have been proposed in the previous chapter can be utilized and many techniques can at least formally be applied.

We have already mentioned that the characterization problem of finding a distributed field parameter description can be seen as an infinite dimensional parameter estimation problem. As the function is subject to certain regularity conditions, an expansion into a infinite sum of weight orthogonal base functions is possible and so, only the weighting coefficients have to be found. It is far from being known whether such an approach is the most adequate. At the contrary Karplus [118] and Simundich [200] have proposed using less conventional characterization techniques. Simple algebraic techniques in a pattern recognition context may be especially useful. The rationale is as follows. Conventional techniques require often optimal parameter estimation. The parameter estimation problem for PDEs is, however, computationally very burdensome. Furthermore, except for certain special cases, approximation is required and thus the "power" of the characterization method may be reduced. Consequently, a real issue concerns a trade-off between power of the method and computational requirements. It is in the light of such trade-off that heuristic approaches in a pattern recognition framework are an alternative to conventional techniques.

Recent research is going on to reveal whether pattern recognition can also be used to locate uncertain boundaries. The technique bears potential for application on this frame definition problem.

4.3.4 Experiment design

The same general considerations as in Chapter 3 can be given for the experiment design problem for PDE-models. The importance of this modelling stage is much more significant here. In the first place, it is much more difficult to choose an experimental set-up properly, due to the usually discrete instead of distributed nature of the sensors. For certain problems it is possible to position them in a very unfortunate manner. A few general guidelines can be given:

(1) Avoid the zeros of the eigenfunctions for processes described by linear PDE's with solutions expressible in the following form:

$$\phi_i(\underline{z}, t) = \sum_{j=0}^{\infty} a_j^i g_j^i(t) E_{gj}^i(\underline{z}) \qquad i = 1, 2, \ldots$$

(2) For hyperbolic equations it is unwise to align measurement patterns along characteristic lines, and the measurement period must be sufficiently long to account for the longest time delays which are inherent in hyperbolic systems.

(3) Investigate whether the data in a measurement location is insensitive to the parameter to be identified.

Another problem consists in positioning the sensors in an optimal way in order to either estimate parameters or discriminate between rival candidate model structures. The optimal sensor location problem has mostly been studied in the filtering context: how do we place the sensors in an optimal manner to estimate the dependent variables? This is not exactly the same problem as measurement system design for model-building purposes. Instead of minimizing the estimation error covariance matrix for the dependent variables, the error covariance matrix for the parameters should be minimized. A recent paper [166] tries to see the optimal sensor location problem for identification as well as for filtering. An optimal control framework is applicable. At present, it is still possible to consider simulation most helpful in assessing the suitability of certain measurement locations. The model is implemented and taken as a data source. Different locations for the sensors are tried out. The sensitivity of the measurements to parameter variation is established through experimentation on the computer model. Due to the computational requirements, however, the approach may be costly.

4.4   CONCLUSION

With this brief survey the topic of modelling with partial differential equations is left. We have intentionally avoided the issue of numerical techniques for solving PDEs on the computer. The reader is referred to standard works on the subject [81, 188]. Analytical procedures for PDEs have only very superficially been addressed. It is, however, the opinion of the authors that even a slightly more thorough discussion of modelling techniques would require a lot of analytical know-how on the PDE-formalisms. In the next chapter attention is shifted to a more simulation oriented topic.

5. Methodology for model information storage and integration

5.1 INTRODUCTION

5.1.1 The purpose of the chapter

In the previous chapters, emphasis has been on mathematical modelling tools for model-building. Application of those tools required computational power. More specifically, the ordinary and partial differential equation formalisms have been treated. Those subjects were thought useful as there is evidence that more advanced modelling methodology could be of major help in improving man's overall capability for tackling scientific and engineering problems (see Section 2.5.4).

Besides advances in methodology, another avenue full of promise seemed to lead towards computer-based general theory. In case of "unstructured" and dubious knowledge on a subject, a more advantageous starting point for modelling and simulation can be obtained by properly storing and integrating known facts and existing models. It was established in Chapter 2, that a priori knowledge concerning the system under investigation is of extreme importance for obtaining a useful mathematical model. Unfortunately, many disciplines contain a body of knowledge that is not sufficiently uniform in exactitude and generality, to derive highly valid mathematical representations easily. The question arises thus, how to feed, train, and use a simulator properly in order to achieve increased modelling capability through intensive interaction between model-builder and machine. Whether such an ambitious goal can be attained, remains a matter of speculation.

The major purpose of the chapter is to develop concepts and procedures to store and integrate available a priori knowledge, here assumed to consist of mathematical relationships and models limited in scope. It will not, however, be possible to present a final and complete answer on the subject under discussion. Only very recently has research started on the topic. It is hoped, however, that the material presented will clarify an approach to the problem, so that further developments become possible. Before proceeding, a motivational and a working example are introduced.

5.1.2 A motivational example: energy models

In response to the energy crisis, a large number of models (in the order of a thousand) have been developed to help governmental and industrial energy planning. Since they were largely developed independently of one another, the set of models does not form a systematic whole and thus is a far from satisfactory basis for decision-making. One faces, clearly, a problem of the kind defined in the prototype. A considerable amount of data has been gathered and a non-negligible amount of modelling effort has been spent. A very striking characteristic is the multifaceted nature of the system, in the sense that it may be approachable from different points of view by different people with different objectives at different times. A more comprehensive theory is certainly lacking. This follows clearly from the fact that a planner/decision maker, who faces a new task, will encounter an unsatisfactory "state of the art". Many of these unsatisfactory features of the field were well brought out in the proceedings of a recent meeting [74]. To be mentioned are certainly the difficulty in choosing a proper model and the uncertainty that arises from discrepancies in the conclusions drawn from different models.

5.1.2.1 The selection problem

For a new application, the systems analyst must know which of the many models potentially at his disposal is suited to the particular issue, he is being faced with. Hudson and Jorgenson [98] discuss this problem by analysing four energy models, chosen to provide a reasonable coverage of methodology and applicability. They find that each model has different strengths and different areas of applicability. This is clearly shown on the "model capability" matrix they provide (Table 5.1). In their discussion, an example is given of an error arising from the application of a model to a task not within its capability.

5.1.2.2 Model comparison

In general, it may well be that different models are able to produce answers on new questions. Here the decision-maker is still faced with a set of models formally capable of dealing with a problem, but potentially differing in the reliability with which they do so. Cherry [34] discusses this difficulty. He reports on the evaluation of ten models available for electric

TABLE 5.1 Model-capability matrix

Application	Model			
	Almon	Pilot	DRI	Hudson–Jorgenson
Economic projections, analyses				
Level of activity, short run			×	
Detailed projections	×		×	
Economic growth				×
Economic structure				×
Energy projections, analyses				
Demand		×		×
Supply and conversion		×		
Conservation				×
Technologies		×		
Energy-economy analyses				
Short run impacts			×	
Full impacts				×

load forecasting (Table 5.2). Consider the following two assignments:

(1) provide a forecast for the energy consumption with time-of-day pricing and appliance efficiency, standard effects removed;
(2) what will be the change in electricity consumption with a 10% price increase relative to the reference case.

For the first question, all models could be used. For the second one, only the first five models were appropriate. As can be seen on the Figs 5.1 and

TABLE 5.2 Name of energy models

Models used in the electric load forecasting study

1. Commonwealth Edison Company, Econometric Model (Comm. Ed.).
2. Oak Ridge National Laboratory, Residential Energy Demand Model (ORNL–REDM).
3. Oak Ridge National Laboratory, State-Level Electricity Demand Forecasting Model (ORNL–SLED).
4. Tennessee Valley Authority, Load Forecasting Model (TVA).
5. Consumers' Power Company, KWh Sales Model (CPC).
6. Florida Power and Light, Simulation Model (FPL).
7. Northeast Utilities, Electric Energy Demand Forecasting Model (NU).
8. University of Texas, Baughman–Joskow Regionalized Electricity Model (Baughman–Joskow).
9. Wisconsin Electric Power Company (WEPCO).
10. General Public Utilities (GPU).

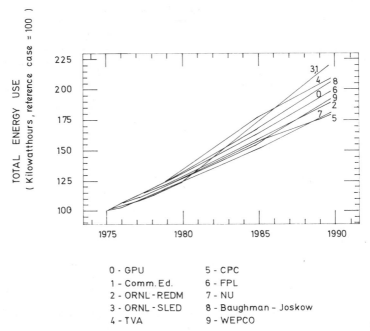

0 - GPU   5 - CPC
1 - Comm. Ed.   6 - FPL
2 - ORNL - REDM   7 - NU
3 - ORNL - SLED   8 - Baughman - Joskow
4 - TVA   9 - WEPCO

FIG. 5.1   Forecasted energy use (from Fig. 5, Cherry [34])

5.2, reproduced from Cherry's Figs 5 and 6 [34] the answers differ; to the extent that models agree one may have more confidence in their common prediction. Conversely, areas of disagreement should signal the necessity for further development, as well as giving rise to uncertainty and caution as a basis for policy-testing. Cross model comparison may also be approached at more structural levels.

The state of the art in modelling energy systems, as briefly discussed here, indicates a pressing need for better integration. It illustrates the arguments presented in Section 2.5.4.2. A classic approach to the present unsatisfactory situation would consist in a search for more general "laws" and "theories" that allow inconsistencies between models to be pinpointed, and then new models to be built by deduction. In fact, composition and integration may be desirable across many lines including:

—methodological, e.g. a linear programming model is coupled to an input-output model [115];
—disciplinary, e.g. an energy supply model is coupled to an econometric model;

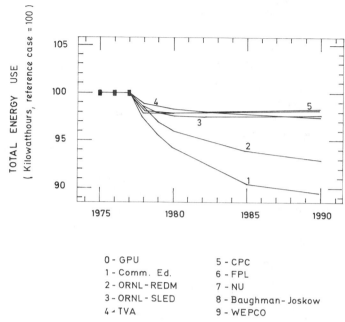

FIG. 5.2   Energy consumption after price increase

—sectorial, e.g. an electricity demand model is coupled to a natural gas demand model;
—spatial, e.g. regional models are coupled to form a national model;
—scope/aggregational e.g. a detailed sectorial model is coupled to a coarser multisectorial model.

As mentioned in Chapter 2, model integration and theory-building along classical lines may be difficult in part, because of the nature of the system itself. Furthermore, due to the rapid changes the world undergoes, it may well be that a more comprehensive theory that supports the data collected, is already outdated at the moment of its maturation. Under such conditions, it is seen that a computer-aided multifaceted methodology can be of enormous help. First of all, through simulation support systems, a much-improved link would be provided between the objectives of a user and the models that can be provided to achieve these objectives. At the same time, all existing knowledge would be available to enhance and speed up the model integration process. Finally, facilities should be available to assist the modeller in new modelling ventures. The example of energy modelling has been useful in illustrating the real needs for more and better modelling support. In developing concepts and design principles for such support, a more simple example will be used.

5.1.3 A working example: university bus service

A simple example is introduced, which, through this chapter, will be used to illustrate and clarify new concepts and procedures.

A university currently provides a transportation service for its students in which a single bus shuttles between a down-town station and a university station. The area surrounding the university has been developing, however, and increasing numbers of non-students are also using the bus service, at least complaints to this effect have been registered by the students who sometimes cannot get on the bus and must wait for it to return from its round trip. The university administration has set up a committee, to review the situation and make recommendations. They are to assess the merits of the following options:

(1) Leave the situation as it is.
(2) Permit only students on the bus.
(3) Permit anyone, but charge non-students.

The administration also foresees the possibility of adding a second bus to the route, but would rather not begin consideration of this until it becomes convinced of its necessity. To help in their deliberations, the committee has asked a team of computer and management science professors to build a model on which they can test the various policies.

Let us analyse the situation in the terms of Sections 2.2 and 2.4. The decision-maker is the university administration. Its primary objective is apparently to guarantee a satisfactory level of bus service for the students. However, it may also see in the bus service a potential for a much-needed source of revenue. The goodwill afforded by providing the community with such a service would not be an unwelcome by-product. Thus a second objective, that of financial gain through expanded service, looms on the horizon. The system boundary implied by these objectives is to encompass the present bus and its route. A second bus may later be added but no further expansion is contemplated; nor have other issues such as acceleration of local development and environmental or safety problems yet been raised, which would require extending the system scope.

Let the term "bus system" designate the system within the above boundaries. The controllable part of the bus system implicit in the above objectives, has to do, firstly, with the identification of potential passengers and, secondly, with the addition of a second bus. In the first case, possibilities for intervention are limited to providing students with identification, and prohibiting entry to or charging non-students. In the second case, these possibilities are expanded somewhat, but most of the system, such as the external demand for service and the capacity of the present bus, is considered uncontrollable.

The kind of intervention being contemplated has management, control, and design aspects. The institution of a new passenger identification policy, or addition of a bus, would be a managerial level decision, here carried out by the administration. Working out the details of the identification policy, and especially of the operation of the expanded bus system, would be a design problem, in this case being handled by the *ad hoc* review committee. Execution of the identification policy would be of a control nature, perhaps assigned to the driver.

Within the objectives and system boundaries given above, different models can be developed. A first model, for instance, may describe the bus system as it is currently. A second one will model the current bus system with passenger identification possibilities. A larger model may take into account city bus transportation issue. Here also, no general principles about bus transportation are available.

5.2   INITIAL AND FUNDAMENTAL CONSIDERATIONS

5.2.1   Initial remarks

In previous chapters, we have made very little reference to the computer itself, though the machine was almost everywhere implicitly present; most techniques are, in fact, much too cumbersome to apply without a computing device. In the context of this chapter, the computer plays a much more crucial role and it has to perform more complicated tasks than simple number-crunching. It is not the intention here to go into implementation details, but it is an inherent part of the subject to present the activities and manipulations involved in a manner that permits computer implementation. We refer to Fig. 1.3 in Chapter 1, concerning different computer software and hardware levels. Within the level of software for modelling and simulation we focus on general principles for storing models and model information, under the assumption that lower level software utilities provide means for the following tasks:

(1) data and information storage through data bases;
(2) easy interaction between user and machine;
(3) standard logical and arithmetic operations.

A second remark concerns the goal of this chapter. As mentioned in the previous section it would be useful if a computer could gather and accumulate knowledge on a more complex modelling problem. With the terminology of Chapter 2, such a "trained" computer would embody structured, a priori knowledge. The very act of "training" will be called "modelling in the large", in contrast to building special purpose models which is referred to by the term "modelling in the small". It is thus hoped that "modelling in the large" will be for a part a substitute for scientific theory construction, or will facilitate the theory construction process.

We finally note that the "modelling in the large" principles are very recent developments, and, as will be seen, still only partly available. It may thus be expected that the material will expand and undergo modifications, even in the near future.

5.2.2   The "feeding ground" for principles concerning "modelling in the large"

In order to find principles for "modelling in the large" one has to rely in part on basic theory concerning mathematical models and modelling methodology. The essential parts have been presented in Chapter 2. Certainly the nature of the model itself will play an important role. Here the "set structure" model is used, but recall that, loosely, state space constructs are meant. Besides the general model itself, the modelling process, or the fundamentals of methodology, will be a "feeding ground" for concepts related to "modelling in the large activities". It is easy to see that, in addition, techniques for comparison, integration, and consistency checking will be needed.

All concepts derived from the items mentioned will have a very general nature, and will be useful as soon as the "set structure" is an adequate description. However, such a degree of generality cannot be maintained for ever. Though the model nature can be specified in general terms, in practice it is utilized in the form of a model formalism. If the formalism dictates procedures, generality is lost, though large classes of modelling problems can still be addressed. Finally, it has to be seen how large the impact of the modelling context will be. Dependent on the discipline of origin, the relative merits of a priori knowledge, data, and model purpose in guiding the modelling process differ. It remains to be investigated how "modelling in the large" principles depend on the precise properties of the information sources. If this is so, generality is in jeopardy, unless a sufficiently wide range of tools are provided. In this case, the model-builder has to indicate which tools are appropriate for his particular case.

The concepts proposed in this chapter have been developed with the discrete-event formalism in mind, while the type of systems that are covered are those which are often studied within that formalism: management and business-related systems. The generality of many findings can easily be assessed, based on the considerations of this paragraph. When it really comes to implementation, it may pay off to build a modular software package, so that some flexibility is available to adapt the program to the application area.

5.2.3 Introductory considerations

The very basic building elements of models are the variables. For a given real-world model many variables can be defined. A model groups different variables into sets. These sets are part of what has been called the static structure of the model. For convenience, a complete model description was thought to be made up of a static structure and a dynamic structure. The distinction is a formal one in that the first group does not contain any reference to the time base, while the second group most certainly does. The static structure provides means for taking snapshots of the system, while the dynamic structure provides the elements for the changes between such "snapshots". Note that if the output function definition is not considered, the static structure relates immediately to the model or system frame.

As soon as models have to be compared for integration purposes, in the hope of discovering similarities and dissimilarities, or recognizing their scope of utility, a comparison of their static structure is of first priority. If such comparisons have to be made in a routine way, a systematic procedure for describing static structures is required. Almost the entire chapter is devoted to principles that derive from the static structure. Clearly a complete "modelling in the large" approach would also consider the dynamic characteristics. The rules of interaction among component models are very important elements for real-world system descriptions. However, the theory has not yet advanced to that level of sophistication. Nevertheless, the contribution that focuses on the static parts of models is by no means without importance. As will be seen in the sequel it is the very base for any further work.

"Modelling in the large" must take the model information sources into account. In this early stage of development, some simple configuration for these sources is proposed. A priori information is stored in the computer in the form of models or model components, and in the form of the processed data of previous experiments. The other sources provide the inputs to the system. A model-builder will interact with the available information with a certain goal in mind, and this goal will guide his activities. Besides the input from the model-builder, new information comes from experiments either on the models, or on the real system. As the nature of the experiments will be influenced by the modelling goal, it seems important to separate the experimental set-up which is a product of the modeller's intentions and the system frame. This consideration has urged specialists to define experimental frames. They are made up of the same variables as the models, but they are distinct from models in the sense that an experimental frame may exist without the existence in the computer of a model that is ready to be the object of the experiment planned by the model-builder. Here provision is made for learning. A systems analyst has a problem in mind concerning a real-world system. The problem may lead him to potential experiments in order to gain insight at least. If he plans to approach the problem with mathematical modelling, he may look for a description of the system. Such descriptions may yet be available or at least there may be candidate descriptions available in the computer. But it may well happen that such candidates are lacking and that model-building is required. If such activities are undertaken, then the global amount of a priori information will increase, and learning will take place.

The experimental frame concept will be discussed in much more detail. It is defined here in rough terms as a set of input conditions and output measurements that specify an experiment useful for a certain modelling purpose.

5.2.4 Outline of the chapter

In Section 5.3 attention is paid to concepts related to the variables that pertain to a real world system. The main objective is to provide a framework that permits the decomposition processes to apply, which are so characteristic for the system concept (see Chapter 2). Here the variables are grouped along a decomposition tree. A number of considerations are made to represent and manipulate such decomposition trees. Procedures are kept simple so as to be executable by a computer, otherwise the whole effort is meaningless. The material directly provides insight. To illustrate this a simulation language SIMSCRIPT is discussed in the light of the new concepts.

In Section 5.4 a general unifying concept is looked for that should have a more direct link with the real-world system, in the sense that it has model integrating power. It turns out that the "entity structure" may do the job. It is shown how the "entity structure" can be used to compare models and "amalgamate" their contribution in order to increase the understanding of the complete system. Here again attention is paid to the requirement for algorithmic implementation.

Section 5.5 deals with experimental frames. It is shown how model objectives generate questions, which in turn point to measurement procedures and experiments. Then it is investigated how the experimental frames relate to models and to each other. In additon, a complete formal description of the experimental frame is given. The effort of formalization is thought worthwhile because of the extreme importance of the concept.

In Section 5.6 we discuss models, parameters, and their relationships with experimental frames. Finally a "state of the art" of "modelling in the large" concepts is presented in Section 5.7.

5.3. CONCEPTS RELATED TO MODEL VARIABLES

5.3.1 Systematic static structure representation

A static structure is for the major part, as the definition shows, a collection of variables, which are assigned the status of input variable, output variable, or state variable. These variables are supposed to represent abstract useful attributes of the real-world system and its parts. As a consequence, their choice is highly influenced by the decomposition of the system. In terms of the concepts introduced in Chapter 2, it is irrelevant here which "information sources" have been used to gain insight into the real-world system.

Based on these considerations, it can be seen that there are two fundamental concepts involved in specifying the static structure of models. These are the concepts of variables and of the decomposition tree.

5.3.1.1 Variables

A variable has a name and a range set. The name is a distinct identifier not possessed by any other variable. The range set is the set of values that the variable can assume. Recall Section 2.3.1.3, where a number of possibilities for such sets were presented. The name and range set play formal roles in specifying the model structure. However, to communicate the significance of the variable, we should also provide meaning and units. The meaning documents what the variable represents, and what each of its range set elements signify. A variable which relates to real-world measurement will also have units of measurement.

5.3.1.2 A decomposition tree

A decomposition tree represents a hierarchical decomposition of a model into components. Formally, a decomposition tree is a finite, uniquely-labelled tree structure. The root node is labelled by the name of the real system the model is intended to represent. The successor nodes of the root are labelled by names of first-level components of the model. Each such first-level component may itself have a decomposition, and these second-level components would be represented by successor nodes in the tree, and so on. Clearly, the decomposition tree is a "trace" of the system decomposition process which was mentioned in Section 2.3.1.2. Since this process must stop, the decomposition tree is a finite one.

Now, the decomposition tree serves as a structure of pigeon-holes for the model's variables. That is, each variable is assigned to one, and only one, node of the tree. An attachment of a variable to a node signifies the fact that this variable represents an attribute of the component named by the node.

5.3.1.3   Examples

Before continuing with a more formal exposition of static structure, let us return to the bus example for illustration. We shall discuss two models of the existing bus system. The first is relatively simple in that it does not keep track of passenger identities as does the second. For the first model, largely based on a priori knowledge about bus systems in general, the following informal description can be given:

—Persons arrive at the ENTRANCE of each STATION. Each arrival at a STATION is recorded by its variable, ARRIVAL, and causes an increment of the # WAITING in that STATION.
—When the BUS arrives at the STATION (recorded by its LOCATION variable) it accepts # WAITING at its time of arrival or the CAPACITY if this is smaller than # WAITING. This loading process lasts a time which is determined by LOADING TIME, a random variable which depends on # NEW PASSENGERS.
—The unloading process goes on simultaneously and lasts a time which is determined by UNLOADING TIME, a random variable which depends on the #-IN-BUS at its time of arrival. Departure of passengers from a station is recorded by its DEPARTURE variable.
—The BUS waits until both processes are completed before starting for the next STATION (a driving process) the time taken to reach it being determined by a random variable TRIP-TIME.

A decomposition tree, with attached variables, is shown in Fig. 5.3, and a list of variables is provided in Table 5.3.

It is immediately clear that, with the model presented, it is not possible to check passenger identity. A more elaborate model has the following informal description:

—Persons arrive at the ENTRANCE of each STATION. Each arrival is

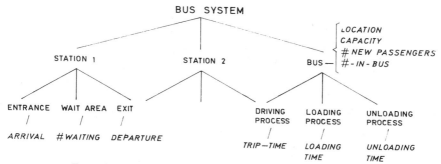

FIG. 5.3 The static structure for the existing bus system model

recorded by the variable HELLO, taking on the person's identification as a value.

—The person immediately joins the queue of those waiting for the bus as is indicated by adding his ID to the end of the list, which is the current value of LINE (short for WAITING. QUEUE).

TABLE 5.3   Variables for the existing bus system

Variable name	Meaning	Range	Units
ARRIVAL	0: no person arriving 1: a person arriving	$\{0, 1\}$	/
# WAITING	persons waiting in waiting area	I_0^+	person
DEPARTURE	0: no person leaves station 1: person leaves station	$\{0, 1\}$	/
LOCATION	bus position	$\{$station 1, station 2$\}$	/
# NEW PASSENGERS	persons who get on the bus	I_0^+	person
#-IN BUS	persons in the bus	I_0^+	person
CAPACITY	maximum number of persons in bus	$\in I^+$	person
TRIP-TIME	driving time period	R^+	min
LOADING TIME	time period for loading persons	R_0^+	min
UNLOADING TIME	time period for un-loading persons	R_0^+	min

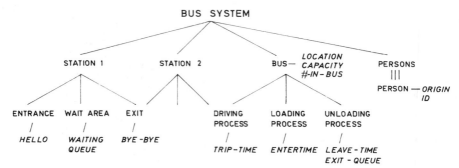

FIG. 5.4   The static structure for the extended bus system model

—When the BUS arrives at the STATION (recorded by its LOCATION variable) the loading and unloading processes begin.

—In the loading process, the first person in LINE enters the bus, taking a time determined by a random variable ENTER-TIME. The second in LINE now becomes the first and the process continues. The loading is completed when the BUS is full (#-IN-BUS = CAPACITY). It pauses when the LINE is empty (LINE = Λ), but in this case it is not completed until the unloading process is finished. This allows late-comers still to get on.

—In the unloading process, the disembarking passengers (all those who entered at the previous STATION) form a LINE and each in term disembarks with a time sampled from LEAVE-TIME, a random variable. Unloading is completed when this LINE is empty.

—The BUS waits until both processes are completed before sampling a time from TRIP-TIME to reach the next STATION.

TABLE 5.4   Additional variables for an extended bus system model

Variable name	Meaning	Range	Units
HELLO/BYE-BYE	identification for arriving/departing persons	$\{\emptyset, a, b, c, \ldots\}$	person name
ID	status of person	{student, non-student}	/
WAITING QUEUE	a list of waiting persons	$\{a, b, c, \ldots\}^*$	{person name}*
EXIT QUEUE	a list of waiting persons	$\{a, b, c, \ldots\}^*$	{person name}*
ORIGIN	station of entrance	{station 1, station 2}	/

$\{.\}^*$ the set of finite sequences of elements of $\{.\}$

The static structure is shown in Fig. 5.4 and additional variables are discussed in Table 5.4.

5.3.2   Conventions for static structures : prestructures

5.3.2.1   *Definitions*

In the previous examples, some conventions were used about static structures which will now be explained. Some new concepts, which will make the development of such structures more convenient, are also introduced. It has been indicated previously that a variable has a unique name, range, meaning, and units; and it is attached to one node exactly in the decomposition tree, which is a finite tree whose nodes are labelled uniquely by component names. It is not convenient that each time we add a new variable or component to the structure, we have to come up with a new name. Moreover, components like STATION 1 and STATION 2 often have the same decomposition and variables except for their names. So, it would be better to have to define a component type like STATION just once, and then have any component of that type, like STATION 1 or STATION 2, automatically have the decomposition and variables of that type. The same idea holds for variables where we would like to be able to define a variable type such as LINE, and then have any variable of that type, such as BUS LINE or STATION LINE, have the same range, meaning, and units of the type. These considerations lead us to define what we call a "prestructure". A prestructure will have the property that it specifies a static structure, i.e. it is a shorthand formalism for static structures of models.

A prestructure consists of a set of variable types attached to a decomposition tree. A variable type has a unique name, range set, meaning, and units. The decomposition tree is a finite labelled tree subject to the following restrictions that, if a label appears more than once, then at most one of the like-labelled nodes can have attached variable types and a successor decomposition. We call the one so honoured the component type node and the other like-labelled nodes are called component nodes of that type. No component node can appear in the subtree under its component type node. The examples in Figs 5.3 and 5.4 are prestructures.

5.3.2.2   *Static structures from prestructures*

To obtain a static structure from a prestructure, one carries out the following filling out procedure:

(1)   Copying.

Copy the variable type names attached to each component type node to all the nodes of its component type. Likewise copy the subtree under the

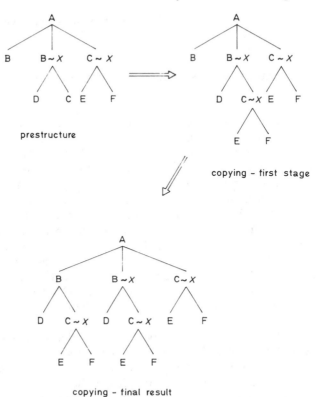

prestructure

copying – first stage

copying – final result

FIG. 5.5 Copying operation for a prestructure

component type node to each of the nodes of the same type. The copying operation is illustrated in Fig. 5.5. One starts at the leaves of the prestructure tree and proceeds towards the root, accumulating new nodes to copy as one goes. Since no component node appears below the component type node, there is no danger of having to reverse direction. Note that the result of the copying is a finite tree with the following properties:

(a) Strict hierarchy: no label appears more than once down any path of the tree. This means that no component can have a decomposition which eventually contains a component of the same type.

(b) Uniformity: any two nodes with the same label have the same attached variable types and isomorphic subtrees (isomorphic here means copies of one another). This just means that any two components of the same type have the same variable types and isomorphic decomposition

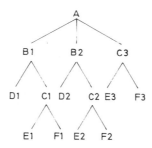

FIG. 5.6   The numerical labelling operation of a decomposition tree

structures. The filled out tree, however, is not uniquely labelled. Indeed all component nodes of the same type must somehow be distinguished from one another. This can be done in many ways. We give two such procedures: a simple one and a more sophisticated one.

(2) Relabelling.

(a) Numerical: go through the labels of the same type in some order and suffix the numbers 1, 2, 3, . . . in turn. This operation is illustrated in Fig. 5.6.

(b) Relative: apply numerical relabelling only to like labelled brother nodes (successors of the same superior node). To distinguish any other pair of like labelled nodes, there are two cases.

(b1) The superior nodes are distinctly labelled: in this case, the nodes can be distinguished by suffixing the string "in" followed by the label of the superior node to each.

(b2) The superior nodes are not distinctly labelled: in this case, return to step (b) in order to label them distinctly, and then return to the present pair to apply (b1).

This is a recursive procedure which must eventually terminate. This is so since any pair of upward paths in a tree must eventually converge so that the re-application of step (b2) must halt, at most when two brother nodes have been reached (and these have already been numerically distinguished). This operation is illustrated in Fig. 5.7.

We now have ways of uniquely labelling the filled-out prestructure tree. At this point, it is not difficult to add variable information. The tree has variable types which may be attached to more than one node. Such multiple appearances of the same variable type represent different variables of the same type. To distinguish these variables, all we need do is prefix the node label to the variable type name. For example, in Fig. 5.6, variable

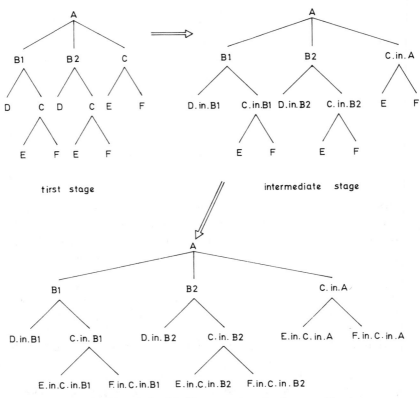

FIG. 5.7   The relative labelling operation of a decomposition tree

type X is attached to components B1, B2, C1, C2 and C3. This represents the attachment of variables B1.X, B2.X, C1.X, C2.X and C3.X to their respective components. Applying this prefixing operation to a relatively labelled decomposition tree, we obtain a variable name of the form, e.g. (F.in.C.in.B1).Y; this reveals that there is a variable of type Y which is attached to a component of type F, which is a subcomponent of a component of type C, which is a subcomponent of B1.

5.3.2.3   *Component types : multiplicities*

We have seen that components of the same type may appear arbitrarily in a decomposition tree, provided strict hierarchy is maintained. So far we have discussed cases where a fixed number of components of the same type occur. For example, STATION 1 and STATION 2 represent two occurrences of the type STATION. There are cases, however, where we would not like to fix the number of occurrences once and for all. For example, Fig. 5.4 represents a model structure in which an arbitrary number of components of type PERSON may appear. In the simulation of such a model, components of type PERSON are created (to represent arriving passengers) and destroyed (once these passengers have reached their destination); so, the actual number of such components varies with time.

Now note how we may represent this possibility while still retaining a decomposition tree with a finite number of nodes. This is done by adding a component of type PERSONS and having a special decomposition of this component, called a multiple decomposition, into components of type PERSON. Notice that PERSONS has a variable type NUMBER with range I^+_0, while PERSON is a distinct component type having other variables types. Figure 5.8a depicts the general definition of multiple decomposition. Let A and B be component types. If B is a multiple decomposition of A, as

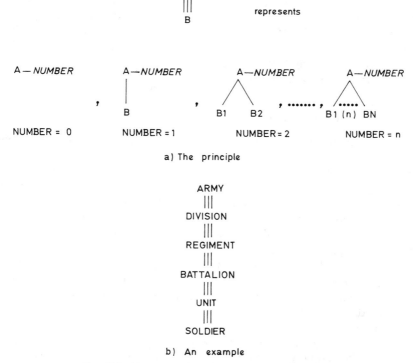

a) The principle

b) An example

FIG. 5.8   Representation of component multiplicities

indicated by the special marking of the vertex joining their occurrences, then this is interpreted to mean that A consists of the number of components of type B, indicated by the current value of A.NUMBER. Often a convenient name for A is the plural form BS (as in PERSONS). Not always, however, since collective noun forms may also be used, e.g. FLOCK has a multiple decomposition into BIRD. And one may have hierarchies of multiple decompositons, e.g. FLOCKS ≡ FLOCK ≡ BIRD.

An example: An army hierarchy consists of divisions, each division consists of regiments, each regiment consists of battalions, etc. Draw a decomposition tree which decomposes an army down to the individual soldier (see Fig. 5.8b). It is important to represent the distinction between a plural component (e.g. PERSONS) and its singular component type (e.g. PERSON) also from the point of view of the variables we may attach to them. We have seen that NUMBER may be attached to the first but should not be attached to the second (unless it is itself a plural, in which case NUMBER indicates the number of its singular components). On the other hand, attributes of the singular may, or may not, also apply to the plural. For example, PERSON has the variable TYPE with range {STUDENT, NON-STUDENT} which does not apply to PERSONS. On the other hand, the variable CAPACITY applies both to a single BUS and to a FLEET of busses. We can see already, though, that the variables of a plural and its singular component may be related (e.g. FLEET.CAPACITY is the sum of BUS.CAPACITY values).

5.3.3 Basic operations on variables

In discrete event modelling (as well as in modelling, more generally) one often wants to treat a group of variables as a single unit. The reason for this is that such a "package" of variables is often the basis for constructing yet more complex variables. For example, in Fig. 5.4 the variable STATION.LINE takes on values which are lists of pairs, each pair being a person's identity and his educational type. It then would be convenient to treat such a pair as a package. Such a packaging mechanism should also clarify the interdependencies in definitions of variables and provide the capability to redefine the variables consistently. This may be necessary, for example, when the range set of some variable is altered, and this change ramifies through variables whose range set definitions are related to the altered one.

To do this, let us recall that a variable has a name and a range set. Let V be its name and R its range set. Then, we may refer to its range as R_V or alternatively as V.range. In other words, V.range = R_V = R. For example, BUS.CONTENTS has range set [O,BUS.CAPACITY] so that BUS.CONTENTS.range and $R_{BUS.CONTENTS}$ both refer to [O,BUS.CAPACITY]. The advantage of this is that we can construct packages of variables without committing ourselves to give them definite ranges sets.

Let $V_1, V_2, \ldots, V_n$ be a listing of variables. The composite of this list is defined as a variable with name $(V_1, V_2, \ldots, V_n)$ and range set $R_{V_1, V_2, \ldots, V_n} = R_{V_1} \times R_{V_2} \times \ldots \times R_{V_n}$. For example, (PERSON.ID,PERSON.TYPE) is the composite of the variables PERSON.ID and PERSON.TYPE, in that order. Moreover, (PERSON.ID, PERSON.TYPE).range = PERSON.ID. range × PERSON.TYPE.range. Thus a typical value of (PERSON,ID PERSON.TYPE) is a pair (i,t), e.g. (GEORGE, STUDENT) where $i \in R_{PERSON.ID}$ and $t \in R_{PERSON.TYPE}$. Now we can use composite variables in combination with other basic set theory operators to construct complex variables. For example, we may define STATION.LINE as a variable having the range set ((PERSON.ID, PERSON.TYPE).range)*. (Recall that A^* is the set of finite sequences of elements of A). And of course, STATION.LINE.range (which refers to this set) may be used to construct other composites.

5.3.4   Analysis of static structure specifications of a simulation language

5.3.4.1   The problem

Up to here, the static structure of models was the theme of the exposition. It is that part of a system description, which provides a framework for taking snap-shots of a system. The static structure can be specified by a hierarchical decomposition tree of components and their attached variables. A more convenient shorthand formalism, the prestructure, enables one to work with component and variable types. Likewise, a simple abstraction mechanism for defining range sets facilitates convenient, understandable, and less error-prone model construction and modification. The concepts introduced, and the systematic procedures developed have many purposes. They can for instance, be used as a tool for understanding and evaluating model descriptive formalisms. After some thought, one can quite rapidly see that a (discrete event) simulation language is a method for model formulation, and its power for defining static structure can be investigated. As an example, the simulation language SIMSCRIPT is discussed. In that language, the entity-attribute set (EAS) formalism is advocated.

5.3.4.2   The entity–attribute set (EAS) formalism

It has been suggested that a good basis for standardizing the description of a static structure is the approach of the widely-used simulation language,

SIMSCRIPT. Without going into a discussion of the merits of this approach it is instructive to present the SIMSCRIPT world view, and formalize it in the terms we have introduced.

In every SIMSCRIPT program there is a preamble which sets up the static structure of a model. This is done by writing a sequence of statements of the following form:

EVERY entity name HAS {attribute names}*, MAY BELONG TO {set names}*, AND OWNS {set names}*.—with for {.}*, the classic interpretation: Section 5.3.3.

Fig. 5.9a shows how a bus system model with many stations and buses might appear in a SIMSCRIPT preamble.

A SIMSCRIPT attribute is a special case of our variable. It is a variable whose range set can be one of a very few types; real, integer, etc. A SIMSCRIPT entity type is a special case of our component type in that it has attached variable types, but there is no direct corresponding notion of decomposition in SIMSCRIPT. As in our concept, a particular entity has attributes of the types attached to its entity type. A set in SIMSCRIPT is what we have called a list. The phrase "EVERY E OWNS $S_1, S_2, \ldots, S_n$," declares in our terms that every entity of type E has attached to it list-valued variables of types $S_1, S_2, \ldots, S_n$ in addition to its attribute type variables. Thus $E.S_1, E.S_2, \ldots, E.S_n$ are variable types with range sets of the form $A^*_1, A^*_2, \ldots, A^*_n$. Now comes the interesting part of the formalization: specifying in our terms what are the sets $A_1, A_2, \ldots, A_n$. The answer lies in the "MAY BELONG TO" phrase. Let S be a set owned by entity type E. Let $E_1, E_2, \ldots, E_m$ be the entities types which may belong to S (as declared in their respective "MAY BELONG TO" phrases).

To capture what SIMSCRIPT does, we now attach the variable type NAME to each entity type. The understanding must now be that each entity is distinctly identified by the value of its name so that this name can be used as a pointer to the entity. Then $E.S.\text{range} = (\cup_{i=1}^{n} E_i.\text{NAME.range})^*$. In other words, the declarations that E OWNS S and that E_i MAY BELONG TO S, $i = 1, \ldots, m$, mean in our terms that attached to component type E there is a variable type with name S and with range A^* where A is the union of the name sets of the E_i, $i = 1, \ldots, m$.

Figure 5.9b shows the formal static structure corresponding to the SIMSCRIPT preamble in Fig. 5.9a. We see that, in our version, a STATION.LINE is essentially a list of PERSON.NAME values. Each such name points uniquely to a PERSON and to the current values of his variables TYPE, ORIGIN, and DESTINATION. Similarly, each BUS.ROUTE is a list of STATION.NAMES. Actually, because of its usual implementation, SIMSCRIPT cannot represent this static structure as easily as indicated

EVERY PERSON HAS AN EDUCATION-TYPE , AN ORIGIN, A DESTINATION
AND MAY BELONG TO A LINE , AN ENTERING-LIST AND A LEAVING-LIST

EVERY STATION MAY BELONG TO A ROUTE
AND OWNS A LINE

EVERY BUS HAS A CAPACITY , A LOCATION , A SENSE
AND OWNS AN ENTERING-LIST , A LEAVING-LIST AND A ROUTE

a) SIMSCRIPT preamble

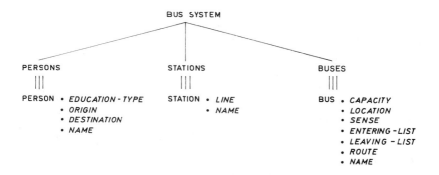

Range definition examples :
STATION. LINE. range = (PERSON. NAME .range)*
BUS. ROUTE. range = (STATION. NAME. range)*
PERSON. ORIGIN. range   = STATION. NAME. range

b) Corresponding static structure

FIG. 5.9   A SIMSCRIPT preamble and its interpretation

here. The reason is that, while an entity may belong to many sets at once, it cannot belong to more than one set of the same type at once. So in the SIMSCRIPT version no STATION can be on more than one BUS.ROUTE, e.g. there cannot be a central station in the model. Of course, our portrayal of the SIMSCRIPT semantics does not represent, nor suffer from, this limitation. By adding new entities to pair up STATIONS and BUSES, one can implement our freer version of the model in SIM-SCRIPT. The merits of such a realization are arguable.

In Fig. 5.9b we also use the abstraction mechanism to define DESTI-NATION and LOCATION ranges. SIMSCRIPT does not have this ability. As we have indicated, only a limited number of range set types are available and one must be specifically chosen for each attribute.

5.3.5 The semantic structure of variables

In the previous sections, attention has been on the static structure of models. Before proceeding to the subject of integrating static structures into a consistent whole, a final consideration concerning the model variables can be made.

Recall that variables also have besides a name, a meaning. This has consequences; in fact there may be variables which have related meanings. The inherent relationships between the meaning of variables is called the semantic structure. In other words, the semantic structure consists in the logical dependence between variables. Such dependence arises because the model-builder may attach a priori meanings to the variables which may be related.

For the bus system under study, an example of a semantic relationship is the connection that exists between the variables: #-WAITING and WAITING.QUEUE. The first variable corresponds with the number of elements in the second variable, which is a list.

A formal definition for a meaning convention is as follows. Consider the variable A with range R_A and the variable B with range R_B. A meaning convention between A and B is defined by a relation $R \subseteq R_A \times R_B$. The effect of such a convention is to make legal those, and only those, assignments of values to the variables A and B, which satisfy the relation. For the example mentioned here the relation between # WAITING and WAITING.QUEUE is given by: # WAITING = # (WAITING.QUEUE). Common forms of semantic relations cause range reduction and coarsening between variables or establish equivalences between names, etc.

Notice that the semantic structure induces structure on the total variable set that can be defined on a real-world system; therefore, it plays a role within the context of "modelling in the large".

5.4 CONCEPTS RELATED TO ENTITIES

Besides being a useful conceptual tool for analysis, the static structure forms the basis for the entity structure concept, which is developed as mentioned in Section 5.2 for model integrating purposes. Suppose that a collection of models for a real-world process are available. How can they be put together in a coherent way? In other words, is it possible to integrate the capabilities of all available models. The basic idea is to construct some all-encompassing "super" static structure, which is called the system entity structure. This structure is made up of entities.

5.4.1 The system entity structure: an example

The idea itself can most easily be explained with an example. Let us think of the labels on the nodes of the decomposition trees as labels for system entities, rather than model components. Now the trees are pasted together so that nodes with the same label become identical; this is illustrated in Fig. 5.10. Each of the trees on the left represents a decomposition of a model and each label therefore represents a component. The amalgamated tree on the right is an entity structure in which each label represents an entity. In this structure, the entity X has a decomposition into entities A and Y, entity A has a decomposition into entities B and C, and so on.

The entity structure at any time thus represents the net result of system decomposition taking into account all the models created at that time. It is thus a template from which the decomposition trees of the existing models can be extracted. More than this, it is a template for constructing models from those already existing. For example, the only extant model for X has components A and Y which are not further decomposed (tree #3). But if the model of A represented by tree #1, was to be composed with Y, one would have a model represented by tree #4, which is also extractable from the entity structure.

The basic idea is simple, but its execution is not and many problems have been glossed over. They arise in performing the amalgamation. The goal, however, should now be clear and we can turn the situation around by taking a top down approach. First, the axioms which an entity structure

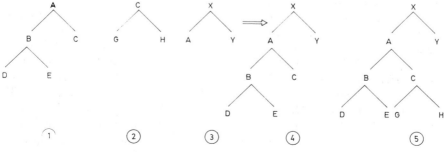

FIG. 5.10   Amalgamation of decomposition trees

should obey, will be laid down. Then it is insisted that models are constructed in conjunction with the development of the entity structure. Of
course, one must also provide as much computer assistance as possible in
maintaining consistency between the model structures and the entity structure. After laying down axioms for the entity structure, we shall return to
reconsider the amalgamation problem (Section 5.4.4.2).

5.4.2 The entity structure: axioms

A system entity structure is a labelled tree with attached variable types
which satisfies the following axioms:

—uniformity: any two nodes which have the same labels have identical
   attached variable types and isomorphic subtrees.
—strict hierarchy: no label appears more than once down any path of the
   tree.
—alternating mode: each node has a mode which is either entity or aspect;
   the mode of a node and the modes of its successors are always opposites.
   The mode of the root is entity.

Except for the last property, an entity structure is formally identical with
the model static structure obtained by filling out a prestructure (without
relabelling, see Section 5.3.2.2). Indeed, the prestructure form will also be
used to specify entity structures as well. There is however, a profound
difference in the entity and model structures brought about by the addition
of the mode concept. Only entity nodes correspond to model components,
as we previously suggested. An aspect node on the other hand, represents a
decomposition. The alternating mode property states that an entity has
zero, or more, decompositions (aspects), and each decomposition consists
of zero, or more, component entities. We need to introduce the aspect
concept since a system entity may correspond to a number of models, each
with its own decomposition structure (amalgamation in the case of multiple
decompositions was one of the problems glossed over earlier).

Figure 5.11 shows an entity prestructure for the university bus system
problem, after the system boundary has been extended to include the
entire city. Note that the CITY is an entity which has currently three
aspects: COMMUTER.ASPECT, DEMOGRAPHIC.ASPECT and
SPATIAL.DECOMPOSITION. SPATIAL.DECOMPOSITION decomposes the CITY into DISTRICTS; the DEMOGRAPHIC.ASPECT
decomposes it into PERSONS while the COMMUTER.ASPECT decomposes it into BUS. and PRIVATE-CAR.SYSTEMS. Models of the CITY
might exist based on each of these three decompositions. For example, a
demographic model might recognize only PERSONS as components of

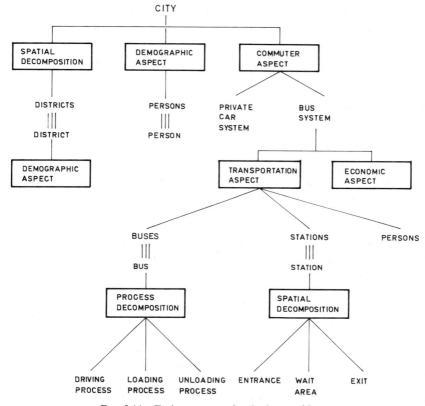

FIG. 5.11   Entity structure for the bus problem

CITY, and proceed to provide dynamic structure to account for population growth or decline.

5.4.3 The system entity structure: remarks

5.4.3.1 *Items and item occurrences*

Note that an entity or aspect may occur in more than one place in the entity structure, so long as the alternating mode and strict hierarchy axioms are obeyed. Using the filling out procedure with relabelling, we can always distinguish the various occurrences if we so wish. We shall refer to an entity or an aspect by the more encompassing term: item. The mode of an item is thus either entity or aspect. Each appearance of an item in the filled out structure is called an item occurrence. For example, the item DEMO-GRAPHIC.ASPECT appears under CITY as well as under DISTRICT in the prestructure. Now DISTRICT itself is a singular component of DISTRICTS. If in a particular city there are three DISTRICTS, there will be a total of four occurrences of DEMOGRAPHIC.ASPECT in the filled-out structure. This facility to represent multiple item occurrences has profound implications, as we now shall see.

5.4.3.2   *Variables: rights of access*

Recall that variable types are attached to nodes in the entity structure. By the uniformity axiom, the same variable types are attached to every occurrence of a particular item. In other words, an item has its own variable types, and carries these with it wherever it is located in the tree. As in the case of model static structure, when a variable type V is attached to an item occurrence I, this signifies that a variable I.V can be used to describe the item occurrence I. We say that the variable I.V belongs to I. For example, the variables BUS 1.LINE and STATION 2.LINE belong to the first and second occurrences of BUS and STATION respectively. Thus, while an unqualified variable type such as LINE may have multiple occurrences, a qualified variable such as STATION 2.LINE belongs to one, and only one, item occurrence.

However, in contrast to a model static structure, the entity structure represents many possible models. As we have seen, a model of an entity may or may not employ all of the substructure of the entity. In other words, there may be many models of the same entity which employ different decompositions and carry these decompositions to different levels of refinement. One thing we do know however, is that these models can employ at most the variables belonging to the entity and to all of the items occurrences in its substructure. In this way we arrive at the relation of a variable pertaining to an item occurrence. A variable pertains to an item occurrence if it belongs to an item occurrence in the tree under it. More formally, let an item occurrence I subordinate an item occurrence J, if there is a path in the tree from I to J (in the direction of root to leaves). We also say that J is in the substructure of I in this case. Then a variable J.V pertains to I if I subordinates J in the tree. Due to the uniformity property, we can also say that a variable type pertains to an item, if it is attached to any item in its substructure. Thus when an item is attached to a node it lends all its pertinent variable types to those of all its new superiors.

An example on Fig. 5.11 should show the power of this concept. Variable types belonging to PERSONS all pertain to DEMO-GRAPHIC.ASPECT and therefore also to CITY. But since DEMO-

GRAPHIC.ASPECT is also subordinate to DISTRICT and ultimately also to CITY, these PERSONS variable types also pertain to DISTRICT, and ultimately to CITY. However, the different sources of PERSONS variable types give rise to distinct variables. To see this, recall that the above occurrences of PERSONS may be distinguished by PERSONS.IN.CITY and PERSONS.IN.DISTRICT (see Section 5.3.2.2). The variable type NUMBER attached to PERSONS thus gives rise to the variables PER-SONS.IN.CITY.NUMBER (in other words the size of the population in the city) and for each i, PERSONS.IN.DISTRICT.i.NUMBER (in other words, the population size of each DISTRICT). Note that all these variables pertain to CITY. Thus the uniformity axiom allows us to talk about PERSONS in the CITY overall and in each DISTRICT, using the same basic characterization of persons.

Equipped with the entity structure concept, it is possible now to discuss its role in model unification and integration.

5.4.4 Entity structure as an organizer of models

5.4.4.1 The role of the entity structure

We can now formally specify how the entity structure is to organize models and experimental frames. A model is always a representation of a particular entity and must employ only variables pertaining to this entity. Thus the entity structure partitions the models into classes associated with entities. Accordingly, an entity is a "key" for retrieving models and frames; knowing the entity which interests us, we can cut down the space of all models and frames to just those which are models of, and concern, it. Of course, since the entity structure itself represents a conceptualization of reality, its structure must be understood by the user in order for it to be an effective aid. This is one place where the interactive software for setting up and querying entity structures can play an important role.

The entity structure also serves to organize the model construction process. Recall the discussion at the beginning of this chapter. It was indicated that all existing models should have static structures, which are extractions of the entity structure. When adding new models, such a compatibility must be retained. However, we have not formally defined what an extraction is, and will now do so. We shall use the term atomic to denote a leaf node in a decomposition tree. Let M_2S_2 be a model static structure and E_2S_2 an entity structure, as shown in Fig. 5.11 for example. Then M_2S_2 is an extraction (or extract for short) of E_2S_2 if the following holds:

—The root component C of M_2S_2 is synonymous with (has the same label as) some entity E in E.S.

—If C is non-atomic, let its first level decomposition components be C_1 $C_2, \ldots, C_m$. Then E must also be non-atomic and have an aspect A with subentities $E_1, E_2, \ldots, E_n$. Moreover, the C_i's must be synonymous with a subset of the E_j's.

—If C is non-atomic, then its variables are synonymous with a subset of variables belonging to E and A. Otherwise, (i.e. when C is atomic) its variables are synonymous with a subset of variables pertaining to E.

—The subdecomposition trees rooted by the C_i's are each extractions of the E_2S_2.

Figure 5.11 displays an entity structure and some of its extractions. Note that it may be convenient to allow an entity or variable to have more than one name. Such names are called synonyms. For example, a long descriptive name, a short abbreviation, and an English equivalent might be synonyms. The classes of such synonyms must all be disjointed, "synonymous with" is an equivalence relation, and may substitute for "has the same label" in the above definition.

Thus, an extraction of an entity structure is obtained by starting with some entity, selecting one of its aspects, and then selecting a subset of the subentities of this aspect to form the first level components of the model structure. One continues in this way, stopping at any entity one wishes. Such an entity becomes an atomic component. One may select any variable for a non-atomic model component from those belonging to the corresponding entity and the selected aspect. For an atomic component, one may select from all the variables pertaining to the corresponding entity. All names given to the extraction must be synonyms of entity structure counterparts.

The set of all extractions of an entity structure characterizes the set of all model static structures with which it is compatible. Conversely, given a set of model structures, one can seek an entity structure of which they are all extractions. Such an entity structure, if it exists, would be called an amalgamation (or amalgam) of the model structures. Indeed the problem of amalgamation was the one we raised originally in Section 5.2 and, in fact, all concepts developed were aimed at this integration process.

5.4.4.2   *Amalgamation: a problem of model unification and integration*

In some domains of large-scale system modelling such as energy, ground water and ecosystems, there are already many models, amounting to hundreds, or even thousands. Efforts are being undertaken to catalogue and document these models to form libraries accessible to interested users. Such efforts come under a rubric "modelling in the large" or "organization of a priori knowledge". They are difficult, not merely for the amount of manual labour involved, just the sheer amount of manpower required to input information about each model would be significant; but, more fundamentally, they are difficult because of the variety of approaches, often idiosyncratic, taken by the various modellers or modelling teams.

With the concepts now available, one can understand and deal with some of the dimensions of this problem of model unification and integration. One can analyse each model, and its builder(s) if possible, by asking questions like:

(1) Of which system entity is this a model (what are the system boundaries implicit in the model)?
(2) What is the decomposition tree of the model (what are its components and subcomponents)?
(3) What are the variables attached to each component (how are its variables organized)?

If, as is to be expected, the models were not built from the top down in the framework, there may be no final answers to the questions. Indeed, one may have to iterate the amalgamation process, which will be described, back to this primary model structuring phase. But let us suppose that the questions 1, 2, and 3 have been answered for each model. Then seeking an amalgamation would be possible and would, if achieved, be a basis for further integration and unification. Also, even if modelling is proceeding "top down" from the entity structure, there are decisions in its development which are analogous to those which must be made in amalgamation. We have to remember that the entity structure is a growing organism, responding to new questions by accommodating new entities, variables, experimental situations, and models. Each modification raises questions like those involved in amalgamation, such as: where should a certain variable be attached? does a new aspect have to be defined?
The phases of the amalgamation are:

—setting down the item information;
—constructing an entity structure from item information;
—testing the entity structure for validity;
—reducing the entity structure to a smaller equivalent.

We shall discuss each phase in turn. Actually, we shall take a more general approach, since similar procedures arise in other contexts.

Setting down the item information

An entity structure is completely specified by giving its set of item names (and their synonyms), and for each item i, the pair $\langle S_i, V_i \rangle$ where S_i is its set of sub-items and V_i is the variable type belonging to it. To satisfy the alternating mode axiom if i is an entity, S_i is a set of aspects and vice versa.

In the case of amalgamation, we are given the set of entities and for each, one or more model static structures. One proceeds as follows. To each entity e we assign a set A_e of aspects such that each aspect a $\in$ A_e corresponds one to one with a model static structure for e; the set V_e of variables belonging to e is empty. To each aspect a $\in$ A_e, we assign the entities E_a, which corresponds to the first level components of the model structure named by a; the variables V_a are the variables attached to the root component (synonymous with e) of this same model structure. The items $\{e\} \cup \{A_e\}$, entity pairs $\langle A_e, V_e \rangle$, and aspect pairs $\langle E_a, V_a \rangle$ constitute item information, which is clearly alternating in mode.

Constructing an entity structure from item information

Call an item maximal if it never appears as a sub-item, i.e. it is in no S_i for any item i in the given set I. In a valid entity structure, there should be exactly one such maximal item, the root item, of mode "entity". However, one can build a structure in any event as follows. Create nodes labelled by the maximal item names. For each of these nodes, i, create successor nodes labelled by its sub-item set S_i. An item i with empty sub-item set S_i is atomic and produces an atomic or leaf node. For each of the nodes i so labelled, create successor nodes labelled by its set S_i. Continue in this way until every newly-created node is atomic. To each node attach the variables V_i of the item i which labels it.

Testing the entity structure for validity

The entity structure created as above from item information satisfies the uniformity axiom. This is because each time a node with the same label i is created it leads to the same attachment of variables V_i and the same labelling of successor nodes S_i. By induction, the uniformity axiom can then be easily shown. The alternating node can be tested directly from the item information as previously indicated (Section 5.4.2). If there is more than one maximal item, then at most three fictitious nodes with no variables can be added, so that an entity rooted tree results.

There remains only the test for strict hierarchy. Since it involves paths, it must be done on the entity structure *per se* (or better still its prestructure). Each time a new node is created, the path to it from the root must be checked for a node labelled by the same item. If this check fails to uncover a superior item occurrence, then the node may be attached and the entity structure remains valid. Otherwise, this item information must be rejected as being inconsistent with the prior information. In the case of amalgamation, assuming strict hierarchy of each model structure, strict hierarchy of the entity can be violated if, and only if, there is a pair of entities, e and f, such that f is subordinate to e in some model structure, and e is subordinate to f in some other structure.

Reducing the entity structure to a smaller equivalent

Two entity structures will be said to be equivalent if they give rise to the same set of extractions. An entity structure is smaller than another if it contains fewer nodes or fewer variable attachments. The following are some size reducing equivalence preserving procedures.

(1) Removing redundant aspects:

Let two aspects a_1 and a_2 be brothers (i.e. sub-aspects of the same (father) entity). If $E_{a_1} \subseteq E_{a_2}$ (sub-entity sets) and $V_{a_1} \subseteq V_{a_2}$ (variables) then a_1 and all its substructures can be eliminated since any extraction employing a_1 can be obtained employing a_2.

(2) Re-assigning variables from aspects to entities:

Let a variable V belong to each aspect a of an entity e. Then V may be removed from each V_a and be added to V_e. Thus, the variables belonging to an entity are common to each of its aspects.

5.4.4.3   *Computer assistance in entity structure manipulation*

The four procedures outlined for amalgamation actually are involved in many entity structure manipulations. Software providing assistance in such manipulation can be developed. An interface to the user (interactive command language) is needed for procedure 1 (entering item information), but the other procedures are largely algorithmic and can be autonomous activities of the computer.

5.4.5   Summary

The concept of entity structure was introduced in order to organize variables, models and experimental frames around the system entities to which they are relevant. The entity structure represents the choices of system boundaries and decompositions implicit in an existing model collection. An amalgamation procedure was given for unifying and integrating such a collection. It constructs an entity structure from which the original model structures are extractable. A basis was laid for computer assistance in formulating and manipulating entity structures.

5.5   THE EXPERIMENTAL FRAME CONCEPT

5.5.1   The modelling goal formalized as an experimental frame

5.5.1.1   Objectives, questions, measurement procedures

In many circumstances, the model purpose can be expressed in a question or a number of questions concerning the real-world system. In order to find an answer for these questions with the help of a mathematical model, it is necessary to translate these questions or, even better, the constituent elements of these questions into model variables. This is then properly and efficiently done by defining an experimental frame. A word of caution is appropriate here. It has not been stated here that the process of translating objectives into questions and questions into variables is the only approach that can be adopted for model-building, or model utilization. It is, however, certainly a frequently occurring approach. Before going into technical details an example is given to clarify these considerations.

Consider again the university bus system introduced in Section 5.1.3, in order to see how experimental frames come into the picture. Recall that the primary objective of the committee, appointed to study the current situation and make recommendations, was to bring about satisfactory bus service for the students. This objective is called here"Passenger Satisfaction". This basic goal engenders a number of questions. When will the passengers, and more specifically the students, be satisfied? Though the answer may be a matter of discourse and debate, a number of related questions can be posed:

How long will it take a student to make a trip?
How long will a student wait in line before getting on the bus?
How many round trips will a bus have made before a student can expect to get on?

Notice that for simplicity here the bus is considered to shuttle between two stations.

It is not so difficult to see that all these questions relate to the modelling goal. The total duration of the journey, or the transit-time, is undoubtedly of direct interest to a student trying to get somewhere on time. As a component of transit-time, the waiting period is certainly relevant as waiting is a definite inconvenience not fully accounted for by increased travel time. The number of missed buses may perhaps, apart from a psychological effect, not be directly related to customer satisfaction, but it is an important variable from the viewpoint of the university as an owner of the bus system.

It is now straightforward to see that variables like TRIP.TIME, WAITING.TIME and #.MISSED.BUSES may play a crucial role in obtaining an answer for the questions posed. In real life, these variables will have a certain variability. During rush hours the trip-time will be different from the trip-time on other moments of the day. Furthermore, the number of potential passengers may vary from day to day, dependent on the weather conditions for instance. The university committee is not supposed to make a decision on the basis of a single case, and some average value, or other statistic, is more adequate.

Finally, it is not difficult for the example here to imagine a measurement procedure for the variables. It suffices to follow particular students and to record the time of arrival and departure from the stations, and those from the queue. In addition to the position of a student in a queue, the location of the bus as a function of time permits the number of missed buses to be computed.

At this point, it can be seen that the modelling goal has guided the model-builder to a set of input and output variables, and in essence to an experimental frame. As input variables one can mention the sequence of arriving passengers at the stations. The output variables are the sequence of leaving passengers and the variables TRIP.TIME, WAITING.TIME and #.MISSED.BUSES. Notice that some a priori knowledge about the system is required: one has to know that a bus shuttles between two stations and that passengers enter a station, enter a waiting line, and eventually board the bus, etc. For this example, such a priori knowledge is trivial. On the other hand, the definition of an experimental frame does not require a complete model of the bus system, it merely points to a part of the system frame (see Section 2.4.5).

5.5.1.2 An experimental frame in the discrete event context

In view of the nature of the real-world system, model-builders will choose a discrete event formalism as a descriptive mathematical tool. Within that formalism, it is now possible to give the variables a more mathematical form. For the variable TRANSIT.TIME, one needs the time of arrival and the time of departure. In the discrete event context it is natural to take input and output variables of the type HELLO and BYE, which simply record a passenger's name and identity (see Fig. 5.12). HELLO will take the value (x, STUDENT) when a student named x arrives at a station. BYE takes the value (x, STUDENT) when a student named x gets off the bus.

For the variable WAITING.TIME one needs an output variable: LINE and then it is possible to see how long a person waits in the queue by his appearance and disappearance from the list of elements in LINE. Finally, for the #.MISSED.BUSES, we need two output variables: LINE and a

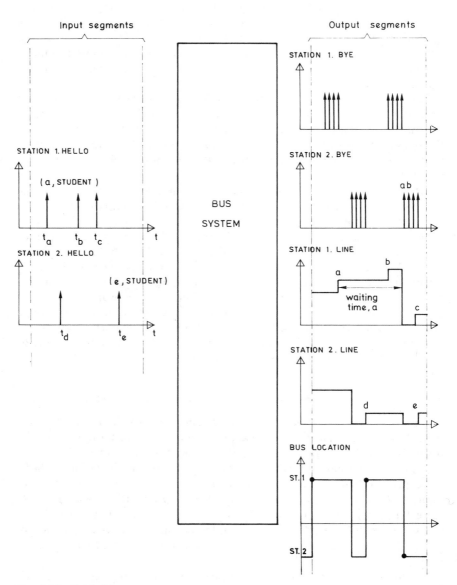

F<small>IG</small>. 5.12   Typical input-output segment pair for passenger satisfaction experimental frame

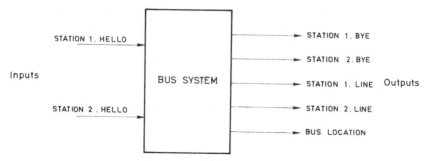

FIG. 5.13 Representation of the passenger satisfaction experimental frame

variable as BUS.LOCATION. The passenger satisfaction objective has inputs and outputs as shown on Fig. 5.13.

5.5.1.3 *Realizability of experimental frames*

In the context of "modelling in the large" it must be possible to investigate a given modelling goal, which has been translated into an experimental frame, and can eventually be attained given a number of existing models. A necessary condition is the applicability of the experimental frame to a given model. A frame is said to be applicable to a model, if the latter is capable of generating the data demanded by the former. This is an informal definition, and one must consider ways in which it can be formalized; two types of applicability can be mentioned.

The strongest definition, called "direct applicability", requires that each variable of the frame appears under the same name in the model. For the example mentioned, a frame involving BUS.LOCATION would be directly applicable to a model which incorporates the variable in its static structure. Requiring direct applicability may be too restrictive since it may happen that a good model has a variable with the same meaning but with another name, or that it has variables which allow the model-builder to deduce the variable of interest from them. In order to capture these situations where a given experimental frame is still valid and useful, a second type of applicability is introduced. A weaker definition, called "indirect applicability", requires that the variables of the frame can be related, or easily deduced from, the variables in the static structure of the model. It may also happen that a frame is not applicable to a model. This happens if considerable modifications have to be included in the model, in order to accommodate the experimental frame.

Consider, for example, the applicability of the passenger satisfaction frame to the bus system models introduced in Section 5.3.1. The frame is not applicable to the simpler model where the passenger identity is not kept track of; the frame is indirectly applicable to the second model. The variables in Fig. 5.12 are indicative of this. TRANSIT.TIME, WAIT-ING.TIME and #.MISSED.BUSES do not directly occur in the model but these variables can be easily deduced from the input-output variables shown on the figure.

Before continuing with a more extensive discussion of the role of experimental frames, their impact on system boundaries is considered.

5.5.1.4 *Objectives and expanding system boundaries*

As mentioned before objectives lead to experimental frames, which select important input and output variables. The modelling goal, however, also provides information about the system boundaries. In all previous examples, the boundaries of the system were clearly specified by the specification of the bus system components: two stations, bus and passengers (see Fig. 5.3). The objective of providing adequate passenger satisfaction could be handled with the simple model provided. It may happen, however, that the university review committee may consider other objectives. The financial burden of maintaining a free bus service for the students may become too high and the committee may envisage expanding the bus system in different ways:

—permit, besides students, other persons who then pay for the bus service;
—add a number of buses and stations in order to attract sufficiently non-students.

The first policy can still be handled within the given system boundaries. A suitable static structure with extra variables added is shown on Fig. 5.14. The second idea requires, however, a considerably extended model. In fact, in order to assess the utility of adding buses and stations, one needs to have a better insight into the distribution of the potential customers. Know-ledge about city districts, about their demographic aspects, and about the population habits of transportation is required. Without going into details, the entity structure of Fig. 5.11 is certainly more adequate, and it clearly shows an expansion compared with previously mentioned structures. Besides the bus system, at least a part of the city is now considered.

It can thus be concluded that in order to make a non-applicable frame applicable, different actions may be required: either a higher descriptive level for a given model has to be looked after, and details are added while boundaries remain unchanged, or instead of adding details the boundaries of the system have to be extended, so that a larger "whole" is to be considered.

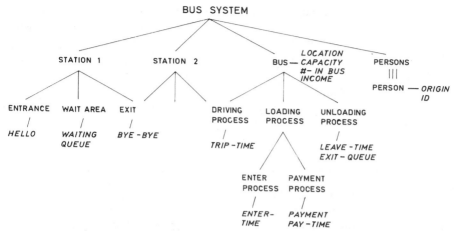

FIG. 5.14   Static structure for bus system with a payment policy for non-students

5.5.1.5   *Final remarks*

It has been shown in previous sections that a modelling goal leads to an experimental frame. A necessary condition to reach the goal eventually with the help of a model is the applicability of an experimental frame, derived from the objective, to the model. The more complex the model, the more experimental frames there are that pertain to the model. Complexity can be the result of higher descriptive detail or larger boundaries. For the purpose of "modelling in the large" it must be possible to extend or modify an experimental frame that is compatible with a given model, so that it becomes compatible in a more complex model which can be considered as an expansion of the simpler one, either in detail or in size.

With the interpretation given here, a fundamental question arises: how detailed or how large has a model to be in order to be retained for a given experimental frame? This is certainly a question related to validity. There is no sense, however in increasing the model complexity beyond a point where the input and output variables do not show marked changes; and so, based on the principle of parsimony, the simplest model is to be retained.

5.5.2   Data acquisition in the light of experimental frames

5.5.2.1   *A more formal definition*

Objectives orient the modelling effort towards a particular system entity. Knowing this entity we have access to any of its existing models; of course, we may also have to construct new models of this entity. Experimental frames also concern such an entity, and capture the questions that we wish to be answered by its models. Section 5.5.1.2 gave a basic introduction to the experimental frame concept, and we want to extend this discussion.

In its complete definition an experimental frame E specifies:

I   – a set of input variables;
O   – a set of output variables;
Ω_I – a set of input segments;
C   – a set of run control variables;
Ω_C – a set of run control segments;
Stt/Spp – a set of statistics or signal processing procedures.

These objects will be explained in due course.

When such a frame is applicable to a model or a real system it selects a set of input-output segment pairs from such pairs potentially obtainable from the model or the real systems. In order to make the experimental frame concept more flexible, especially in the context of data gathering, it is useful if more restricted types of experimental frames can be defined too. Some additional freedom is obtained when it is agreed that only the input and output variable sets are obligatory, i.e. must be specified to define a frame, while the remaining sets are optional. This is because the input and output variables set up the space in which the I/O segment pairs will be collected, so it is absolutely essential to specify these sets. The other sets, when specified, either have the effect of restricting this basic space to one of its subsets, or of specifying output processing to be done on the collected data, e.g. statistical summaries. When one or more of the input segments set, the control variables set, or the control segments set are not specified, we assume that any restriction that could have been placed on the data collection has not been so placed. In other words, the default condition is that of no constraint. Since statistics, for instance are computable from the raw data, they are in fact redundant. Their specification in a frame is a matter of convenience and a statement of interest, but does not change the information content or the derivability relationships of frames (see Section 5.5.3.2).

Since a frame may specify some or all constraints we may write it in the forms:

$$E = \langle I, O \rangle$$
$$\text{or} = \langle I, O, \Omega_I \rangle$$
$$\text{or} = \langle I, O, C, \Omega_C \rangle$$
$$\text{or} = \langle I, O, \Omega_I, C, \Omega_C \rangle$$

We shall now consider how to interpret the specifications of a frame.

5.5.2.2 *The data space of a frame*

Let $E = \langle \{I_i\}, \{O_j\} \rangle$ be an experimental frame with input variable set $I = \{I_i\}$ and output variable set $O = \{O_j\}$. Recall that the range set of the composite input variable $(\{I_i\})$ is $R_{(\{I_i\})}$, the crossproduct of the ranges of the individual input variables. Similarly, $(\{O_j\})$ is the composite output variable with range $R_{(\{O_j\})}$.

We may also speak of the sets $X_E = R_{(\{I_i\})}$ and $Y_E = R_{(\{O_j\})}$ as the input, and output value sets, respectively, of frame E. Now recall from Section 2.3.1.3 that an input segment is a map of the form $\omega \langle t_0, t_1 \rangle \rightarrow X_E$ and (X_E, T) denotes the set of all such segments over a time base T. Similarly (Y_E, T) denotes the set of all output segments of the form $\rho : \langle t_0, t_1 \rangle \rightarrow Y_E$. When dealing with frames here we shall assume that the time base is always the real numbers. In a more flexible treatment we could allow the time base to be specified by the frame as well.

The data space (also called behaviour space) of a frame E, denoted D_E, is the set of all input–output segment pairs set up by its input and output variables. That is,

$$D_E = \{(\omega, \rho) \mid \omega \in (X_E, R), \rho \in (Y_E, R), \mathrm{dom}\,(\omega) = \mathrm{dom}\,(\rho)\}$$

where dom (ω) denotes the domain of ω, i.e. dom $(\omega) = \langle t_0, t_1 \rangle$ if $\omega : \langle t_0, t_1 \rangle \rightarrow X_E$. The restriction dom $(\omega) = $ dom (ρ) means that paired input and output segments represent observations over the same time interval.

Recall the passenger satisfaction frame mentioned in Section 5.5.1.2. Typical I/O segment pairs are given in Fig. 5.12. For ease in discussion, a smaller frame is considered: the transit time frame $E_{transit}$ which has the input variables STATION 1.HELLO and STATION 2.HELLO, both having the same range, PERSON.NAME.range. Then the input value set X_E consists of pairs (name 1, name 2), where name i refers to a PERSON arriving at STATION i, i = 1,2. $E_{transit}$ has as output variables STATION 1.BYE and STATION 2.BYE, both with range PERSON.NAME.range, to record the names of passengers departing at each STATION. In this case, the output value set Y_E has the same form as the input set X_E.

5.5.2.3 *Input segment specification*

Some classes of segments

Some considerations concerning classes of segments, are appropriate. Continuing with $E_{transit}$, note that because the set $X_{E_{transit}}$ is discrete, $D_{E_{transit}}$ cannot have continuous segments. But there is still a wide variety of possibilities. Among them are the step, or piecewise continuous, segments which are typical in $E_{bus\ location}$ (**Fig.** 5.12).

Discrete event segments are often choices for input segment restrictions. Recall from Section 2.3.1.3 that to specify such segments one must distinguish an element in the input value set as denoting the non-event; the rest of the elements are considered to signal external events. When such a non-event element does not already exist it needs to be added. For example, PERSON.NAME.range may be defined as A^* where $A = \{a,b,c, \ldots\}$, so each PERSON would have a textual name such as "John". In this case it would be natural to designate the empty string symbol Λ as the non-event. On the other hand, if PERSON.NAME.range is A (each PERSON has a single letter name) then we would have to add a non-event symbol ϕ.

There is a second consideration in the case of multiple input variables. If we wish to have events occur independently in each component variable, we require that each has a non-event symbol. For example, in $X_{E_{transit}}$ the pairs (Λ, John) means that "John" is arriving at STATION 2, while no one is arriving in STATION 1. Similarly, (Fred, Λ) signals "Fred's" arrival at STATION 1 with no simultaneous event at STATION 2. The non-event symbol in this case is $\phi = (\Lambda,\Lambda)$.

Because it occurs so often, it is worthwhile defining an operation on a variable which adds to its range set a special symbol (or identifies one already existing) as signifying the non-occurrence of the other elements. The operation is called ϕ-closure and it can be formally defined as follows:

ϕ-closure (V, V.range, V.meaning) = (V, V.range′, V.meaning′)
V.range′ = V.range $\cup$ $\{\phi\}$
V.meaning′ = V.meaning $\cup$ [ϕ is the non-occurrence symbol]

The understanding is that ϕ may be some symbol [such as (Λ,Λ)] already existing in the V.range.

Now we can define general classes:

—piecewise constant or step segments:
   STEP (X) = $\{\omega | \omega : \langle t_0, t_1 \rangle \to X,$

there is a subset $\{\tau_1, \ldots, \tau_n\} \subseteq \langle t_0, t_1 \rangle$, such that ω is constant in the intervals $\langle t_0, \tau_1 \rangle, \langle \tau_1, \tau_2 \rangle, \ldots, \langle \tau_n, t_1 \rangle\}$

—discrete event segments:

   DEVS (X) = $\{\omega | \omega : \langle t_0, t_1 \rangle \to X,$

there is a subset $\{\tau_1, \ldots, \tau_n\} \subseteq \langle t_0, t_1 \rangle$, such that ω is constant in the $t \notin \{\tau_1, \ldots, \tau_n\}\}$.

The subset $\{\tau_1, \ldots, \tau_n\}$ in either case is the set of event times (note that it may be empty). At these times a change in value of a ω occurs. We also extend both definitions to apply to lists of variables. We write STEP $(\{V_i\})$

to mean STEP $(({\{V_i\}}).range)$. Similarly DEVS $({\{V_i\}})$ means DEVS $(({\{V_i\}}).range)$ where each of the V_i has been ϕ-closed, as has the composite $({\{V_i\}})$.

Specifying input segments in a frame

We are now in a position to specify frames of the form $E = \langle I, 0, \Omega_I \rangle$. Recall that Ω_I specifies the set of input segments of interest; or, put the input segments admissible within the frame. For example, specifying $\Omega_I = \mathrm{DEVS}(I)$ restricts the admissible input segments to the subset of discrete event segments. This is illustrated in the specification of $E_{transit}$, where a discrete event segment represents a series of arrivals of persons at the two bus stations. Of course further restrictions may be desired.

For example, one may be interested in discrete event segments in which the event times are close together or, alternately, are sparsely distributed. In the case of $E_{transit}$ this would mean a high (respectively, low) rate of passenger arrivals, distinguishing rush hour from normal conditions.

In the context of input segment specification, it is also useful to discuss the different conditions that may occur during experimentation.

Experimentation: generation and acceptance

The experimental frame concept has been formulated in such way that it can be equally interpreted as governing experimentation on a real system or on a model. Let us now look at some implications for this in the case of input segment specifications.

Consider a frame $E = \langle I, 0, \Omega_I \rangle$, for example, $E_{transit}$. Such a frame, for which an admissible input segment set is given, specifies a data space

$$D_E = \{(\omega, \rho) \,|\, \omega \in \Omega_I, \rho \in (Y_E, R), \mathrm{dom}(\omega) = \mathrm{dom}(\rho)\}$$

where, of course, we require that $\Omega_I \subseteq (X_E, R)$.

An experiment in such a frame is a pair $(\omega, \rho) \in D_E$ and can be thought to consist of "applying" an input segment $\omega \in \Omega_I$ and observing an output segment ρ in response. The term "applying" is certainly appropriate in the case of experimentation with a model, i.e. via simulation, but it may not be a good description of experimentation on a real system. Only if all the input variables are controllable (see Section 2.2) can one fully determine the input segment that a real system will receive. More generally, the input segment is determined, at least in part, by the system's environment. For example in $E_{transit}$, normally passenger arrival at the stations is not under experimenter control, although with sufficient effort such control might be arranged. Thus we shall develop a more flexible view of experimentation, in which input segments may be either generated or accepted (in the sense of formal language theory).

It is obvious that, in the case of generated input segments, provisions have to be made for the generation process. If experimentation is done on the real system, devices and materials may be required, and it is up to the model-builder to check the adequacy of the generating mechanisms. In simulation studies, the input generating process is more easy, but it still has to be taken care of. Simulation languages sometimes provide blocks, or commands or subroutines. In GPSS, the GENERATE block is a typical example. Notice that the frame may specify an input segment generator.

Now consider the case of experimentation by acceptance. Here we are in a position where data are available from which we must select those of interest to us. Here the real system is seen as a source of data. Thus the data potentially available are those observations on the input and output variables as considered by the frame. At any time we may have collected a subset of these data. In $E_{transit}$, for example, we may have placed observers at STATION 1 and STATION 2 to record the identity, time of arrival, and time of departure of each passenger. However, this collectable data is not necessarily of interest to us, only a part of it may be admissible in our frame. For example, we specify high rate of arrival input segments, e.g. $E_{transit}^{high}$, then only some parts of the I/0 pairs actually collected may fit this description.

Let us rephrase what we have just said more formally. Suppose we have specified a frame $E = \langle I, 0, \Omega_I \rangle$. The data space for such a frame is D_E as we have defined it at the beginning of this section. However, in the case of experimentation by acceptance, we cannot acquire such data directly. Let $\bar{E} = \langle I, 0 \rangle$, i.e. E without the input segment restriction. Then $D_{\bar{E}}$ represents the space of acquirable real system data and D_E (subset of interest in E) must be extracted from it. The acceptance process is simple conceptually (we accept an observed I/0 pair (ω, ρ) from D_E in $\bar{E}$ only if $\omega \in \Omega_I$) but it may be more difficult to implement automatically, depending on the difficulty in recognizing membership in Ω_I.

The relationship between E and $\bar{E}$ is a special case of a more general one which is called derivability. E is derivable from $\bar{E}$ because any data we can collect within E we can also acquire within $\bar{E}$. We shall return later to this important concept (Section 5.5.3.4).

A final comment concerns the measurement procedures. The output variables and even the input variables if they have to be gathered through acceptance, are not always directly accessible. Very often a sensor or measurement procedure has to be applied. Sometimes these sensors immediately yield the variables under consideration, but it may happen that the sensors have their own dynamics and have to be considered alone as systems. Some authors [47] term the whole of input generators and sensors a co-system. It could be added to an experimental frame or simply included in it.

To summarize: one can engage in experimentation by generation or acceptance. In the generation mode, the input variables of a frame are controllable. Thus, one may couple an input segment generator to a real system or model, and so generate one or more input segments. In the acceptance mode, at least some of the input variables are not controllable, and so the frame can only accept those I/0 segments of interest to it, which the real system in its environment makes available. An important combination of the generation and acceptance modes is what can be called the mixed mode. Here the input variables may be controllable, but instead of obtaining the input segments from a generator we obtain them from available data. For example, arrival pattern data we have collected in $E_{transit}^{high}$ may be used as input segments to drive GPSS simulation instead of the GENERATE block. To do this one has to schedule exogenous events explicitly corresponding to actual arrivals. The mixed mode is important since it allows comparison of model and real system responses to the same input segment, even for uncontrollable input variables.

One may wonder why an experimental frame may need other variables besides the input-output. This is largely due to the existence of a state, the details of which are next discussed.

5.5.2.4   *Run control variables: initiation, termination*

The nature of the set structure means that, in the case of experimentation with a model, specifying the input segment is not sufficient uniquely to determine the output segment, an initial state must be given as well. However, in the case of experimentation on the real system there is no concept of initial state, but we would still like to be able to narrow down the range of possible responses. Since experimental frames must be interpretable both for models and for real systems we must come up with a concept that has the role of restricting the initial state in the case of a model, but is meaningful for real systems too. This concept is that of run control variables (or just "control variables" for short in the proper context).

Run control variables serve not only to initialize experiments, but to terminate them as well. Suppose for example we are interested in experiments starting with an empty BUS at STATION 1 and no one waiting to enter it; and terminating when the BUS arrives at STATION 2. Call such a frame $E_{travel\ time}$ since in it we can ask questions about the bus travel time from STATION 1 to STATION 2 uncorrupted by its standing time at a station. Appropriate control variables for $E_{travel\ time}$ are: BUS.LOCATION, BUS.CONTENTS and STATION 1.#-WAITING.

The conditions under which an experiment is initiated are: BUS.LOCATION =STATION 1, BUS.CONTENTS = 0 and STATION 1.#-WAITING = 0. These are called initialization conditions. The condition under which an experiment is terminated is: BUS.LOCATION = STATION 2. These are called termination conditions.

Note that, even for the simplest model of the bus system, the above control variables do not constitute a set of state variables. For example, the random generator seeds are not included. In general, initialization conditions will not uniquely specify an initial state of a model. Thus, a family of possible experiments, rather than a single one, is what is determined by an experimental frame.

5.5.2.5 Control segments

It turns out that initialization and termination conditions are not the most general or useful way of controlling experiments. To see this, first let us develop those concepts more formally.

Let $C = \{C_i\}$ be a set of control variables specified by a frame E. For example $C = \{\text{BUS.LOCATION, BUS.CONTENTS, STATION 1.\#-WAITING}\}$ in $E_{\text{travel time}}$. The control space thus set up is defined as $R_{(\{C_i\})}$, the range of the composite of the control variables.

A set of initialization conditions has the effect of specifying a subset, call it INITIAL, of the control space. For example, in $E_{\text{travel time}}$, INITIAL = $\{(1. c, n_l) | 1 = \text{STATION } 1, c = 0, n_l = 0\}$, in this case a single point. All experiments must start in INITIAL.

Similarly, the termination conditions specify a subset, TERMINAL, of the control space. An experiment terminates as soon as this TERMINAL subset is entered. Another way of saying the same thing is that an experiment is continued so long as the TERMINAL set is not entered. If we define a set called CONTINUATION as the complement of TERMINAL (all points not in TERMINAL) then an experiment continues while the model or real system remains in the CONTINUATION set. For example in $E_{\text{travel time}}$, TERMINAL = $\{(1, c, n_l) | 1 = \text{STATION } 2\}$ and CONTINUATION = $\{(1, c, n_l) | 1 = \text{STATION } 1\}$.

Clearly, if any experiments are to be possible we must have INITIAL $\subseteq$ CONTINUATION. This is indeed the case in our example. Now consider any experiment allowed by a frame with such INITIAL and CONTINUATION sets. As traced out in the control space, it must originate in INITIAL and remain in CONTINUATION (see Fig. 5.15). Such a trace is called a control segment, or trajectory. The set of all such control segments constitutes Ω_c, the set of control segments permitted by the frame. A formal definition of Ω_c can be given:

$$\Omega_c = \{u \mid u : \langle t_0, t_i \rangle \rightarrow R_{(\{C_i\})}, u(t_i) \in \text{INITIAL},$$

$$u(t) \in \text{CONTINUATION for } t_0 < t < t_1\}$$

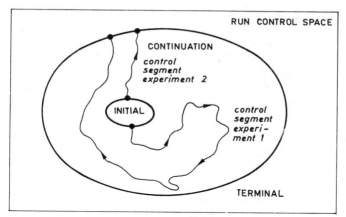

FIG. 5.15   Trace of an experiment in the run control space

Now we come to realize that specification of a set $\Omega_c \subseteq (R_{(\{C_i\})}, R)$ is what a frame wants to do. Specification by means of INITIAL and TERMINAL sets is one convenient, but limited, way of doing this.

For example, suppose we wish to specify a new frame $E_{\text{travel time}}$ in which we can ask questions about the time it takes the BUS to go from any STATION to any other (including itself) provided no passengers ever board on route. Such a frame is simply specified by selecting BUS.CONTENTS as the control variable, and as admissible segments those in which BUS.CONTENTS remains equal to 0. That is, $C = \{BUS.CONTENTS\}$ and $\Omega_C = \{u \mid u : \langle t_0, \ t_1 \rangle \to R_{BUS.CONTENTS}, \ u(t) = 0 \ \text{for all} \ t \in \langle t_0, t_1 \rangle\}$.

Suppose we want to restrict this frame further so that experiments start and end at the same STATION. Then we choose $C = \{BUS.LOCATION, BUS.CONTENTS\}$. A typical segment $u : \langle t_0, t_1 \rangle \to R_{(BUS.LOCATION, BUS.CONTENTS)}$ in Ω_C would be described as follows:

(i) $u(t) = (u_1 (t), u_2 (t)), u_1 (t_0) = u_1 (t_1)$ (start and return to same station);
(ii) $u_2 (t) = 0$ for all $t \in \langle t_0, t_1 \rangle$.

Since the conditions at initialization and termination are the same, we cannot use the INITIAL and CONTINUATION subsets to specify Ω_C, at least not in the chosen control space.

5.5.2.6   Statistics and/or signal processing

As data accumulates within an experimental frame, through real-world experimentation or simulation, it may easily swamp human comprehension. Various kinds of signal processing procedures may be required to reduce the huge amount of data; statistics are well-known types of summaries. Formally, a statistic is a mapping of the data space of a frame into a smaller, usually numerical, space. For example, in $E_{transit}$, an I/O pair can be analysed to obtain the transit times of those passengers who arrived at STATION i and departed from STATION j during the observation interval. Statistics summarizing such an I/O pair include: the average transit time, the maximum transit time, or a histogram of transit times. Similarly statistics can summarize a set of I/O pairs. For example, there are statistics which summarize the results of a statistic applied to each I/O pair, e.g. the average over a number of runs of the maximum transit time observed in each experiment.

Because a statistic provides only a partial view of the primary data, there is always a danger in replacing the data by its statistical summary. Moreover, usually we are interested in inferring what the statistic applied to the whole data space would be like, from the statistic we have computed on a subset of the space. For example, after making 50 runs, each of one day duration, we obtain an average maximum transit time of 25 minutes using our bus system model with identities (Section 5.3.1.3). Can we infer that we would get a similar result were we to make 100 runs, 1000 runs, or 1000 000 runs? Such questions have been extensively studied both within and outside the simulation context. We refer the reader to the literature for an appreciation of the various techniques available for dealing with such issues [27, 129].

5.5.3 The experimental frame derivability relation

5.5.3.1 *Generalities*

The basic structuring principle for experimental frames is the derivability relation which is a partial order. In simple words, a frame E' is said to be derivable from a frame E (written $E' \leq E$) if all questions posable in E' can be posed in E as well, or if all data that can be gathered in E' can be obtained from data gathered in the frame E. A number of requirements must be satisfied in order to establish derivability of E' from E:

(i)   restrictions on data acquisition in E' are over and above those of E;
(ii) data acquired in E can be processed to yield the data acquirable in E'.

The second requirement is pertinent to making the frame relation model independent. An example of the derivability relationship has yet to be given. Remember the relationship between $E = \langle I, O, \Omega_I \rangle$ and $\bar{E} = \langle I, O \rangle$. Instead of all possible input segments, this set is restricted in E by specifying a subset Ω_I of the total set. E is derivable from $\bar{E}$ because the second requirement is fulfilled too. The processing procedure consists in a check for membership to Ω_I of input segments belonging to $\bar{E}$.

If derivability is to be used in the context of software development for "modelling in the large", it might be useful to formalize it further. Hereto, we need the concepts of derivability of variables and induced segment mapping.

5.5.3.2   *Derivability of variables*

Consider a number of variables $V_1, V_2, \ldots, V_n$. A variable V is said to be derivable from $V_1, V_2, \ldots, V_n$, if there is a subset of value assignments to $V_1, V_2, \ldots, V_n$, which uniquely determine via the semantic structure the values of V, and all the values of V are determined in this way. This corresponds with defining a partial function f, where maps $R_{V_1} \times R_{V_2} \times R_{V_3} \ldots R_{V_n}$ ONTO R_V such that $(V_1, V_2, \ldots, V_n, f(V_1, V_2, \ldots, V_n))$ is compatible with the semantic structure for all $(V_1, V_2, \ldots, V_n)$ in the domain of f. If such a function exists, it is expressible as a composition of relations of the semantic structure. An example will clarify the definition: consider the bus system of Fig. 5.14, modified for the payment process. The variable UNLOADING.TIME can be derived from LEAVE.TIME and EXIT.QUEUE. If LEAVE.TIME is random then

$$\text{UNLOADING.TIME} = \sum_{i=1}^{N} (\text{LEAVE.TIME})_i$$

$$N = \#(\text{EXIT.QUEUE})$$

For ease of use, the non-minimality of the source variables is allowed, i.e. if V is derivable from $V_1, V_2, \ldots, V_n$, it may happen to be derivable from a subset of $\{V_i\}$.

5.5.3.3   *Induced segment mapping*

Consider a variable V which can be derived from $V_1, V_2, \ldots, V_N$ through a function f. When looking at dynamic systems, variables will change in time. It is thus possible to define a segment ω in $(R_{V_1} \times R_{V_2} \times \ldots R_{V_N}, T)$. Pointwise the function f can be applied to the variables $V_1, V_2, \ldots, V_N$ to obtain V and so a segment ω' is assembled in (R_V, T), i.e. $\omega'(t) = f(\omega(t))$ for all $t \in \text{dom}(\omega)$. The mapping from ω to ω' is called an induced segment mapping. In the example above, the UNLOADING.TIME can be seen as a step function in time. As passengers leave the bus the exit queue has a shorter length and so the remaining unloading time will decrease.

322 _Computer-aided modelling and simulation_

5.5.3.4   Derivability

A more formal definition of derivability can now be given. E' is said to be derivable from E if:

—the input variables of E' are derivable from the input variables of E;
—the input segments of E' are images of those of E under the induced segment mapping;
—the output variables of E' are derivable from the output variables of E;
—the control variables of E are included in the control variables of E' and the initialization and continuation constraints placed by E' on these variables are identical to those of E; any additional control variables specified by E' are derivable from the input and output variables of E.

The last condition implies the more general condition:

—any experiment that can be initialized in E' can be initialized in E, its being continued in E' implies its being continued in E as well. Whether to terminate or disallow starting an experiment in E' must be able to be checked from data acquired in E.

It is seen that one does not only require that the initialization and continuation spaces of E' are included in the initialization and, respectively, the continuation spaces of E, but also that the relative complements are specified via control variables derived from observable variables in E. This may look awkward, but it is only meant to make the derivability relation independent of the model.

A few examples of derivable frames may be useful. Consider again the passenger satisfaction frame. The input-output variables were provided on Fig. 5.13. A frame which only considers the duration of the trip: $E_{transit}$ is a frame derivable from the former one. As the variables STATION 1.HELLO, STATION 2.HELLO, STATION 1.BYE, STATION 2.BYE required for $E_{transit}$ all appear in the passenger satisfaction frame, the variable derivability function is the identity function on those variables while the other output variables of Fig. 5.13 can simply be dropped. In Section 5.5.2.4, the frame $E_{travel\ time}$ was considered. Is the frame derivable from the passenger satisfaction frame? The answer is no. Though the variables BUS.LOCATION and STATION 1.LINE are available, and thus STATION 1.#-WAITING can be derived, the control variable BUS.CONTENTS cannot be derived from the variables available in the passenger satisfaction frame.

5.5.3.5   Frame-to-frame processing

The derivability relation is known to be transitive. A useful activity related to frame derivability is frame-to-frame processing. Data collected in the

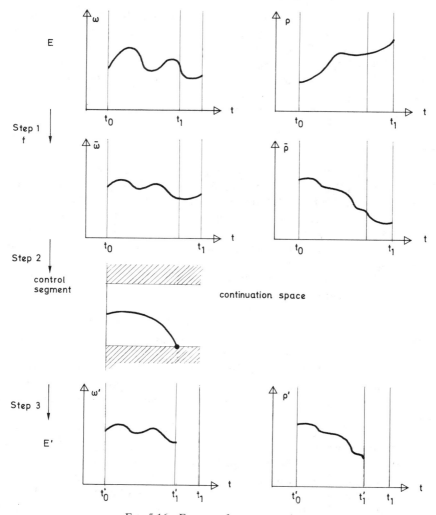

FIG. 5.16   Frame-to-frame processing

most general frame is useful in the derivable frames. Obtaining the data in a derivable frame from a more general frame is called frame-to-frame processing. An example clarifies the operations that may be required. Based on the segments shown on Fig. 5.16, E-to-E′ processing proceeds as follows:

—(ω, ρ) is mapped into (ω', ρ') of E′ by the induced segment mappings known to exist due to the derivability of the input-output variables of E′ from the input-output variables of E;

—(ω, ρ) is mapped into a control segment, r, within the additional control variable space by the induced segment mapping (known to exist due to the derivability of the additional control variables from the observable variables of E);

—(ω', ρ') is the null element if r does not begin within the initialization space of E', otherwise (ω', ρ') is obtained by retaining only that part of (ω', ρ') during which r remains in the continuation space of E'.

5.5.4   Summary and conclusions

Section 5.5 is concluded by summarizing the role of experimental frames. It is recognized that in complex situations models may be inherently intricate and "multifaceted". In such cases, the modelling goal will help tc narrow down a specific aspect of the real-world system. The first purpose of the experimental frame is to formalize the process and to capture given modelling goals. The experimental frame is a sort of early, and limited version of the system frame and, in fact, of parts of the static structure. It still remains independent of specific models. Therefore, the issue of realizability, or applicability, of experimental frames to given models arises.

A second role of the experimental frame follows from the relevance to experimentation. In loose terms one could say that an experimental frame provides a protocol for carrying through experiments on the real system, as well as on the model. When used for this purpose it has to be supplemented with means for exciting the system, controlling it as required for the experiment, and gathering information through measurement procedures and sensors.

A third role could be assigned to experimental frames. They may be useful to structure and condense a data base properly that would contain all data and measurements ever gathered or taken. Such data is a priori knowledge in its most simple and untouched form, and organization of the huge amount of elements may be a very important aspect in order to achieve reasonably easy access. Such access could be regulated through experimental frames. Consider, for instance, a model-builder who intends to approach a given real-world system with a new objective. An experimental frame will be assembled; then the new frame could be checked against others. It may happen that the frame can be derived from another. In that case, all data available to the latter frame can be converted by frame-to-frame processing, and so made available for the new modelling enterprise.

Some thought shows that the concept of experimental frame is at the crossroads of information flow from all information sources: it crystallizes from a given modelling goal, and incorporates a priori knowledge concerning internal workings of the real-world system. At the same time, it provides a frame for gathering data by experiments.

5.6 MODEL AND PARAMETER BASES

In the previous sections, many concepts have been introduced related to the elementary building blocks of models. Another kind of elementary components of models are parameters. These constants however, are usually evaluated in the final stages of the modelling process. In order to discuss the role of the parameter base the model base is first introduced.

5.6.1 The model base

A support system should provide a base for all existing models that have been built in the context of a given real-world system. Due to the multi-faceted nature of many systems, there may be many models expressed in various formalisms and at various levels of specification [253]. Clearly, they will be related to entities. In a more complex case, there are many entities integrated into an entity structure. It may thus happen that certain models are descriptions of a part of the whole real systems, while others provide a more complete picture. The components of a model of an entity are models for the components of the entity. Certain models, however, may stress particular aspects and neglect others. From this viewpoint, models may thus be composed or decomposed, in order to decrease or increase the level of descriptive detail. In addition, models may be coarsened (simplified) or refined (elaborated). The sequence of application of these two classes of operations on model descriptions provides an underlying structure to the set of models resident in the model base. Zeigler [252] has called this structure the operations structure and he gives a good example of relationships between 13 different models for a coin-tossing process (Fig. 5.17). There are two types of relations linking the models. Vertical lines represent composition-decomposition; diagonal lines represent simplification-elaboration. Thus M_{13} is composed of M_{11} and M_{12} which are elaborated versions of M_5 and M_9. M_{13} refines M_{10} which is built up of M_3 and M_7 refining M_1, M_2 en M_6, etc. It can be seen that an intricate "network" structure is obtained.

Notice that for the operations structure, the models are directly compared with each other. A model-builder, or user, with a specific goal in mind may be more interested in the relations between models, seen from his specific viewpoint. It is thus useful if models can be compared within a

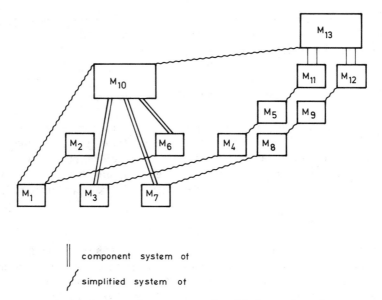

FIG. 5.17   Operations structure of models for a coin-tossing

given frame, which is as mentioned before a formalization of the goal of the modelling exercise. When a model was built, the systems analyst may have had a specific goal in mind. Nevertheless, the model-building process itself, when properly done, provides a certain degree of generality so that its product, the model, is useful in other circumstances too. By its nature it has a system frame and from that frame a general experimental frame could be devised, which is called the scope frame. The scope frame of a model M: E_M can be seen as the most general experimental frame, which represents the most extensive set of questions for which the model is suitable. The scope frame is also useful for checking frame applicability. A frame E, in fact, is applicable to a model M if it is derivable from the scope frame E_M. Recall that direct applicability is a "strong" concept. It may be that weaker versions of the applicability concept are required. Zeigler [252] discusses those weaker versions.

A more general approach of structuring the model base consists in making the relations between the models conditional on an experimental frame. If the latter is taken to be the scope frame, then the models in their most general form are compared with each other. Relations between models have been briefly discussed in Section 2.3.3. A more complete picture of preservation relations or morphisms is available [251]. The usefulness of establishing such relations are manifold:

—it may be checked to what degree given models differ;
—for a given objective, the simplest acceptable model may be identified so that the expense of simulation can be minimized;
—the place a model takes into the whole range of the structure-behaviour relationship can be evaluated.

Once a model base and frame base is available the question of validity can be reconsidered.

5.6.2   Validity of a model in an experimental frame

The validity of a model with respect to another model, or the real system itself, has been discussed in general terms in Section 2.4.4. The inductive aspect is applicable here and, within the context of the concepts introduced in this chapter, the validity concept was presented there under a tacit assumption that the scope frame was generating the relevant data space.

A more elaborate definition concerns the (inductive) validity of a model M in a frame E. The behaviour of M within a frame E, notationally R_M/E, is considered. Note that such behaviour can be obtained by applying frame-to-frame processing on its behaviour in the scope frame. Validity in a frame then means comparable behaviour in the data space, set up by the frame: $R_M/E = R_{\overline{r \cdot s}}(E)$ with $R_{\overline{r \cdot s}}(E)$ the input-output behaviour of the real system, or the system of reference within the data space of E.

It is possible to define weaker and stronger concepts [252]. Partial validity in a frame E means $R_M/E \supseteq R_{\overline{r \cdot s}}(E)$. Partial validity is an interesting property in the context of parameter estimation or calibration. An important result or structuring principle is the following: Let a model M be valid for a real system in a frame E; then for any frame E′ derivable from E, it is the case that M is (partially) valid for R in E′.

5.6.3   The parameter base

Other constituent elements of models are the parameters. Recall from previous sections that parameters can be attributed different roles. In its most basic and representative form, a parameter corresponds with a property of the system or of a subsystem of the real-world object. For the bus example, BUS.CAPACITY is a parameter. However, often the model, or a part of the model only represents an input-output behaviour. Parameters are then not directly related to the real-world system but provide a means to start from a class of models (the model structure), so that more freedom is available to obtain a proper correspondence between model data and system data. It is a pleasing exercise to reformulate the parameter estimation or calibration problem in terms of the model validity concept introduced in the previous paragraph:

$$\text{Find } \underline{p}; \ \underline{p} \in P \text{ and } R_{M(\underline{p})}/E \supseteq R^{\iota}_{\overline{r \cdot s}}(E)$$

If many models related to the same entity structure are available, parameter correspondences may exist between the parameters of different models.

5.6.4 Parameter correspondences

A parameter correspondence is a relation that permits empirical knowledge to be transmitted condensed in the parameter estimate for one model class to another model class. The major problem indeed is to establish the parameter correspondences. It is clear that such activity has the full flavour of "modelling in the large" activities. In a first attempt to establish the meaning of the parameter correspondences, it can be said that they are carried by the operations structure of models as follows:

—whenever one model is a component of another, the parameters of the first constitute a subset of the parameters of the second; in other words "vertical lines in the operations structure" are labelled by identity correspondences in the correspondence structure;
—when a model is a simplified version of another, the parameters of the first may relate in a more complex way to those of the second. Thus, diagonal lines in the operations structure are followed by non-trivial parameter correspondences in the parameter corespondence structure.

A close look at the problem reveals that these types of correspondences are conditional on an experimental frame: in the first case, to specify the isolating conditions for the submodel; in the second case, to specify the condition under which the simplification is valid. Note that carrying over the parameter values identified for a component to the model is justified only to the extent that the conditions under which the component was calibrated in isolation, are compatible with those it experiences within the model. It is worth pondering these considerations more deeply. Especially in environmental and, more generally, in grey box systems, it often occurs that laboratory results are transposed into the field. This is only acceptable if the laboratory experimental frame has sense in the real system, and this is rarely checked or even mentioned.

A more thorough discussion of the role of experimental frames in establishing parameter correspondences is given by Zeigler [252]. To clarify the mechanisms a few examples are given:

—Consider the case of two models M and M'. Suppose that the experimental frame E is applicable to M and M'. It may be that in E, M and M' are equivalent in the sense that $R_M/E \equiv R_{M'}/E$. Under such conditions equivalence encompasses certain relationships between the parameters of M and of M'.

—Consider a second case where E is applicable to M but only partially applicable to M' in the sense that the control variables in E are not checkable in M'. An example is here certainly appropriate. Take the Lotka-Volterra model of prey-predator interaction (5.1) (5.2).

$$\frac{dx}{dt} = ax - \alpha\, xy \tag{5.1}$$

$$\frac{dy}{dt} = -bx + \beta\, xy \tag{5.2}$$

x : prey
y : predator
a, b, α, β : parameters.

If the predators are absent: $y \equiv 0$, then the model reduces to the prey-only form:

$$\frac{dx}{dt} = ax \tag{5.3}$$

Consider a frame E_p with the PREY as variable, control variable predator and initialization/continuation condition PREDATOR $= 0$. It is straightforward to see that E_p is applicable to (5.1–2) but only partially applicable to model (5.3) (which has no PREDATOR variable). A first remark is that validity cannot be ascertained. In the frame $R_M/E_p = R_{M'}/E_p$ for as long as PREDATOR remains zero. Might at a certain point in time PREDATOR deviate from zero, then the output segment is terminated for (5.1–2) but continues for (5.3) and thus validity is in jeopardy. The best that can be strived for is partial validity. M' is partially valid with respect to M if $R_M/E \subseteq R_{M'}/E$, any input-output pair allowed by E in M is also allowed by E in M'. Note that this holds for the example given. At this point the question arises about which kind of parameter correspondence can be established. The "a" parameter in (5.3) carries over directly to the "a" parameter in model (5.1–2), one only has to take care that the data sequence used for parameter estimation fulfils the control conditions mentioned.

—Consider a third case where the frame is applicable to M but not fully applicable to M': E specifies a number of input variables which cannot be found in the model M'. Under such conditions it is still possible that both models generate the same set of output segments. It may happen, for instance, that the inputs are not available in M' because of the fact that the input generating mechanisms belong to the model. Remember that inputs can be seen as the impact of the environment on the part of the real world isolated for modelling. The model M' may have larger boundaries so that some inputs, which had to be provided in M are not required anymore in M'. In these circumstances both models may generate the same set of output segments: for any ρ in M there is a state for M', which generates ρ': $\rho = \rho'$ and vice versa for any ρ' in M' there is a suitable input for M so that ρ is obtained with $\rho = \rho'$. In such cases parameter correspondences can be established.

For "modelling in the large" it might be useful to provide computer support for this type of activity: establishing parameter correspondences. More complete definitions are the following: a parameter correspondence C between M and M', which is a relation defined in $P \times P'$, the product space of the parameter spaces of the individual models, is justified for complete validity in E if $R_{M(p)}/E = R_{M'(p')}/E$ for all $(p, p') \in C$. It is said to be justified for partial validity in E if $R_{M(p)}/E \subseteq R_{M'(p')}/E$ for all $(p, p') \in C$.

The following principle then holds: if a correspondence is justified for (partial, complete) validity in E then the same holds true for any frame E' derivable from E. This is an important result because correspondences established in the scope frame carry over to all derivable frames. It is thus quite clear that the parameter correspondences following the operations structure are crucial. A final remark on parameter correspondences is appropriate. Except when validity can be analytically approached, the validity conditions which underly the parameter correspondences are only justified on a finite sample set. In this case a confidence index which indicates a degree of justification is useful.

This concludes the section on parameter correspondences. We now proceed with a more general view on the results that have been obtained in this chapter.

5.7 "MODELLING IN THE LARGE": THE STATE OF THE ART

5.7.1 An overview

In the course of the discussions of this chapter, many new concepts have been introduced. In this section an overview is given in order to summarize the main ideas. A schematic representation is given in Fig. 5.18. Assembling and integrating a priori knowledge first requires an appropriate form of organized storage called a base. Each of the objects involved in the modelling and simulation enterprise will have its own base. In their simple forms the bases would be almost useless and difficult to use. An analogy with a library is helpful here. Knowledge in a library is structured; the organization will depend on the purpose of the library, but often the books are gathered in groups defined on the basis of subject, year, author, etc. The advantage is that specific search objectives can be easily met and that the individual pieces of information are integrated, at least to a certain level. For the purpose of "modelling in the large", it is highly desirable to provide a suitable organization of the a priori knowledge stored in the

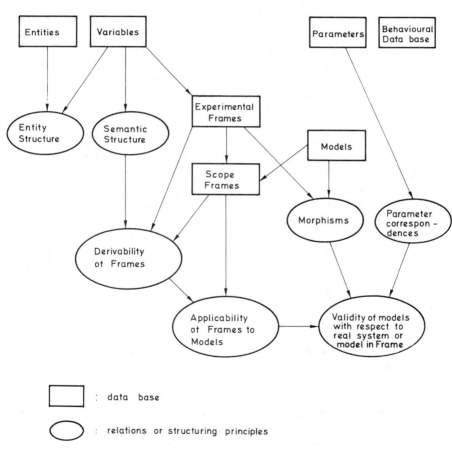

FIG. 5.18 Basic concepts for "modelling in the large"

machine. It is thus useful to discuss the various relations involved in manipulating the "model objects" in terms of structuring principles for the
bases supplied for those objects, and in terms of operations involved in
relating objects of one base to those of others. In Fig. 5.18, the data bases
are distinguished from the relation and structuring principles.

5.7.2   Information bases and structuring principles

The major information bases mentioned up to here are considered.

5.7.2.1   *The variable base*

One of the most basic elements of models are the variables. These variables
are associated with the entities of the real system. They have values which
may change over time. In its basic form the variables' base serves as a
dictionary or lexicon of all variables defined for the real system to date. A
model is constructed by selecting a subset of these variables (to form its
static structure) and adding the rules governing changes in the values of
these variables, the dynamic structures. So the variables belong to groups
which are the elements of models.

A second level of structure is required if the computer is to be capable of
assisting in activities such as relating one model to another, applying
experimental frames to models, etc. We call such a structure the "semantic
structure", since it arises from the intended meanings and logical relations
of the variables. Identities which express aggregation relations, such as the
number of customers being the sum of those in each area, are standard
conventions and they hold across all uses, in models or otherwise, of the
referenced variables, provided the same real system is being referred to. In
general, semantic relations may be much more varied than the
aggregation-disaggregation type just illustrated, although the latter are
common and important.

5.7.2.2   *The entity base*

This base has evolved from being thought of as a third level of structuring
of the variable base to a central organizing structure in its own right. An
entity is a basic part of the real system and it is intended to capture subsystems and system boundaries. The organizing principle here is the entity
structure, which is intended to represent the structure of the real system as
it is conceived at any stage during the modelling process. An entity may
appear as a component in one or more decompositions of other entities.
Variables are attached to an entity either directly or they are indirectly
associated with it via their attachment to its subentities (entities in its

decompositions and their subentities). Thus from this point of view, entities serve as labels for referencing (to a desired degree of specificity) blocks of variables. Such a labelling scheme can be used, for example, to transmit arguments in interfacing component models to construct a composite model. More generally, the entity structure serves as a skeleton on which to organize models and experimental frames of various degrees of specificity and aggregation.

5.7.2.3 The experimental frame base

We have seen that an experimental frame specifies a restricted set of circumstances under which the real system, or a model of it, is to be experimented with and observed. Interesting frames arise from questions raised about the real system, and formalize the data domains required to answer these questions. The frames base is organized by the derivability relation in which one frame may be derivable from another, if any data collectable within the second may be derived via reductions specified in the semantic structure, from data collectable within the first. The frames are thus partially ordered according to the extent of the data they demand and so, roughly, according to the level of detail specified by questions posed on the system.

Easy relation with models is possible if for each of them a scope frame is defined. Every model has an associated scope frame which represents the largest set of questions it is intended to answer. The scope frames form an additional base. Experimental frames relate to variables and model objectives, but can be formulated almost independently of the models themselves. A scope frame, however, is always defined on the basis of a model available in the model base. Of further interest is the applicability of the frame to a model. Applicability can be defined in terms of derivability: an experimental frame is applicable to a model if it is derivable from the model's scope frame. The applicability relation is a formal version of the capability matrix illustrated in Table 5.1.

5.7.2.4 The model base

The model base is an open-ended set of models, i.e. system descriptions at various levels in the behaviour-structure hierarchy for a particular system. As already indicated, the support system should maintain a base of previously developed models. The system should facilitate the free use of appropriate formalisms for model specification. Moreover, the models should be able to be referenced from the entity structure and experimental frames bases. That is, knowing which entity and frame one is interested in, the system should be able to retrieve the existing frames which are similar to it, and the resident models to which these frames apply. Such models, after adaptation and simplification, should serve as components to be interfaced to form a model to which the new frame is applicable. A system appropriately called MBS (model base system) has been developed which maintains econometric and system dynamic models, and allows them to be interfaced to each other and to graphical and analysis programs. The model base should be organized by the morphism relation. A morphism is a means of expressing equivalence of a pair of models within a given frame.

5.7.2.5 *The behavioural data base*

The behavioural data base stores experimentally acquired data from both real system and model. The experimental frame base should provide the key organizing principle for such data storage and retrieval. That is the data should be indexed under the experimental frame in which they were acquired. Of course, when different models are also involved the data must also be categorized according to the model which generated them. A step towards such a data base has been taken by Standridge and Pritsker [208]. Their design of SDL/1 is aimed at integrating a conventional data base management system with a state-of-the-art simulation software system. The relational data base can be defined to hold both simulation generated data, as well as real system data. Simulation programs can store and retrieve data on line by invoking FORTRAN subprograms; statistics and plots can be produced and operations invoked for statistical analyses and validation purposes.

5.7.2.6 *The parameter base*

Parameters are constants in a model specification, which must be determined in order to select a particular model from a class; after a parameter estimation or calibration session, parameters have empirical content. The structuring of models by morphisms induces a structure of correspondences among their parameters as well. When parameter values of a model are estimated, these estimates also constrain the parameter values of other models morphically related to the given model. Thus the parameter base serves to:

—store empirical information about the real system (parameter estimates);
—increase the utility of this information by propagating estimates obtained in model calibration to other models related to it.

Indeed, this base stores and integrates the empirical information gained about the real systems as time proceeds (in contrast to the more definitional information resident in other bases). It thus serves as a key element in the man-machine system considered as a self-organizing system.

Finally there remains to be mentioned the validity relationship between model and system or two models. Validity on inductive grounds is always referenced within a frame.

5.7.3 Interrelation of bases

The bases are not independent but have interbase relations. The central organizer is the entity structure, and its relations to the other bases is illustrated in Fig. 5.19. Such relations are important to implement in order to achieve efficiency, integrity, and consistency in the use of the support system. Concerning consistency, for example, if the entity which a frame concerns is known, then only the frames and models associated with this entity are known to be relevant. This greatly reduces the candidate spaces in derivability and applicability computations. Integrity and consistency are two sides of the same coin. For example, consistency checks arise naturally when the structure of a model under construction is aligned with that prevailing in the entity base. Inconsistencies so uncovered must be resolved (affecting model or entity definitions) to maintain overall integrity.

5.7.4 Activities on the bases

One of the major tasks in completing a useful software package for "modelling in the large" will be the provision of useful activities on the

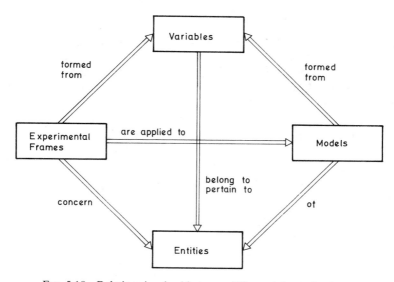

FIG. 5.19   Relations involved between different information bases

TABLE 5.5   Activities on base elements

Objects	Activities
Variables	Definition Association to entities Coarsenino Refining Establishing semantic relations
Entities	Extracting from models Composing Decomposing
Parameters	Reconciling Establishing correspondences Identification Propagation
Experimental frames	Associating with entities Coarsening Refining Testing derivability Testing applicability to models
Models	Associating with entities Coarsening Refining Testing validity in frames

objects defined so far. It remains a task for the future completely to specify and implement all useful activities. A number of such operations has been mentioned throughout the previous sections. As an example we mention the operation of frame-to-frame processing. A certainly not exhaustive list of useful activities is provided in Table 5.5.

In time, new concepts and new activities will be added. A simple observation points in the direction of new work. Recall that a model is made up of a frame, a structure, and parameters. No provisions are made yet for a base that contains structural relationships. Certainly dynamic aspects have to be suitably captured and stored and new developments are thus to be expected.

6. Support languages for model simulation

6.1 INTRODUCTION

It was recognized during the early years of the development of electronic digital computers, that the programming and coding of such computers would be inordinately difficult and error-prone without the availability of programming aids. As a result, there gradually emerged what has come to be known as a hierarchy of languages and software packages, all designed to facilitate the programming effort. At the lowest level of this hierarchy is the machine language, reflecting the command structure and detailed design of the computer. This is in fact the only "language" which a computer can recognize directly, and requires that all instructions be provided as strings of "ones" and "zeros" and that all memory addresses likewise be provided in binary form. At the next level of the language hierarchy we find the so-called assemblers. Assembly languages permit a more compact and easily recognized abbreviation of each command, and are available for virtually every commercial digital computer.

As far as most computer users are concerned, the most important programming aids are found at the third level of the hierarchy, the so-called programming languages. These include the scientific programming languages which facilitate the preparation of a program in a compact manner, using expressions and statements (syntax) that are relatively easy to learn and understand by scientifically-oriented programmers. Languages falling into this category include FORTRAN, PL/1, Algol 60, Algol 68 and PASCAL. Compilers are available for each of these languages to translate the program prepared by the programmer into the assembly or machine language of the digital computer.

An overwhelming majority of all the programs prepared for the solution of mathematical expressions are written in FORTRAN. Although by no means the most suitable language for this application, FORTRAN was the first language to reach maturity so that by the time improved languages became available, a large investment in FORTRAN programs had already been made. Conversion to another language was deemed by many users to be excessively expensive. Furthermore, FORTRAN compilers are available for virtually all large digital computers, while other languages are not nearly as widely disseminated.

A variety of programming packages and programming systems has been prepared to facilitate the programming of mathematical expressions in general-purpose scientific programming languages, such as FORTRAN, or to overcome some of the limitations of these languages. Some of these programming aids take the form of subroutines, or libraries of subroutines, which can be called by the FORTRAN programmer as required. These may include, for example, subroutines for successive over-relaxation, for the solution of tridiagonal linear algebraic systems, or for the Crank–Nicolson method. The availability of such subroutines can save substantial programming time and also avoids the introduction of programming errors. A second class of programming aids is located at the fourth level of the software hierarchy, the higher-level programming languages. A number of such higher-level languages has been developed which permit the user to formulate the problem in a more convenient and direct form than is possible in FORTRAN, and provided a variety of algorithms for the solution of the equations that may be selected by the user or by default. Frequently, such languages are accompanied by translator programs which produce a program in FORTRAN or another third-level language. Higher-level languages utilize syntax and semantics not found in third-level languages such as FORTRAN. They permit the user to make statements which are particularly convenient for the solution of the mathematical expressions in a very compact form. They therefore facilitate programming, particularly by inexperienced programmers, and thereby greatly reduce the time actually spent in programming and debugging. A final category of programming aids is comprised of programming systems prepared for users from a specific application area. Thus there are special software systems to facilitate for instance the solution of the partial differential equations as they arise in structural engineering, fluid mechanics, meteorology, etc.

The structure of the language depends on the form of the model to be implemented. Having to work with a given language may bias or control the form of the model. Therefore, one must be careful in selecting and using computer languages for system simulation. As was explained in Chapter 2, the type of model one selects depends on the degree of aggregation of individual phenomena. One may choose either a continuous or a discrete approach to model development. Continuous models are useful when the behaviour of the system depends more on the aggregate flow of events than upon the occurrence of individual events. Choice of the continuous or discrete event modelling approach depends on the nature of the system, the objectives of the simulation, and the tools available to implement the simulation.

Accordingly, the languages surveyed in this chapter, are partitioned in two groups. Simulation languages designed to represent the continuous event modelling approach to systems characterized by regularly, in fact continuously, occurring events, are discussed first. This group comprises two types of model formalisms depending on the dimensionality of the state: the lumped system description having a finite dimensional state, characterized by a set of ordinary differential equations, and the distributed system description with an infinite dimensional state, and expressed by a set of partial differential equations (Section 2.3.2.2). This fundamental difference entails the development of separate simulation languages. In a second group simulation languages for the discrete event modelling approach are surveyed.

6.2 CONTINUOUS EVENT MODELLING APPROACH

6.2.1 Simulation languages for ordinary differential equations

Historically, continuous-system simulation languages evolved out of attempts at digitally emulating the behaviour of the electronic differential analyser (analog computer) [23]. The need for independent check solutions to analog simulations as well as the potential for increased precision motivated the early digital-analog simulators. Later with the advent of floating-point hardware, the application of digital-analog simulators was expanded to provide information needed to scale the fixed-point analog simulations. Simulation languages started out as an interconnection and control language for a collection of "analog blocks" in the form of subroutines. Thus with DSL/90 (1965) [212], the advent of equation-based simulation languages augmented by a block-oriented capability, began to appear. An excellent historical review of digital-analog simulators, from the initial work by Selfridge in 1953 to the work of Brennan in 1964, is presented in a paper by Brennan and Linebarger [22].

Due to the profusion of digital-analog simulators in the early 1960s, a simulation software committee was formed within Simulation Councils, Inc. (an AFIPS member) to formulate and provide direction for language development in the field of continuous-system simulation. The work of this committee resulted in the publication of a position paper entitled "The SCi Continuous System Simulation Language (CSSL)" [199].

The CSSL report published in 1967 was the first attempt at defining the desirable features of a simulation language. The recommendations

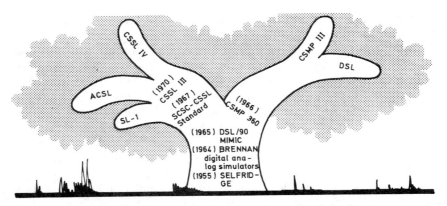

FIG. 6.1   Hierarchy of large-scale digital-continuous simulation languages

presented in this report are in terms of a "communication language" for documenting dynamic system simulations. Using the non-procedural language called MIMIC [41] as a starting point, the first task of the committee was to specify the essentials of an "ideal" simulation language. Next, they posed a collection of design goals and objectives. Finally, the language details were presented along with a structural definition characteristic of most simulation procedures.

The following lists the essentials of an "ideal" simulation language as quoted from the CSSL report.

  (i) applicable areas:
      —all-digital simulation of essentially parallel systems;
      —digital programming for a hybrid problem;
      —check solutions for modern analog and hybrid computers;
      —communication language (documentation).
 (ii) applicable programmer levels:
      —engineer or scientist concerned with a problem, but unfamiliar with
         digital computer techniques;
      —simulation analyst;
      —skilled digital application programmer;
(iii) applicable digital computers:
      —all scientific computers.

Figure 6.1 illustrates the hierarchy of large-scale, digital-continuous simulation languages.

6.2.1.1   *CSMP/360* [102] *and CSMP–III with graphics* [104]

CSMP/360 evolved from the expression-based simulation language DSL/90 [212] with CSMP-III as a vastly improved version of CSMP/360.

These CSMP programs accept a simulation description, including the model definition and run-time instructions, and produce a FORTRAN program as an intermediate result. This allows the user access to all the features (and limitations) of FORTRAN, including extensive library facilities. These CSMP programs are expression-based with the option of handling block-oriented descriptions. They meet or exceed the CSSL report specifications in most instances. They are non-procedural and will sort the user's time dependent equations. Provision is made for user-defined PROCEDURE blocks where the user wishes to define the order of execution. Both system MACROs and user-defined MACROs are provided, along with the ability to handle implicit algebraic equations. Extensive translator directives allow the user to define the structure of his simulation and control the run-time environment of the simulation. Over 50 simulation functions, operators, and MACROs are provided in CSMP/360 and over 60 in CSMP-III. CSMP provides seven different integration schemes including provision for a user specified subroutine. CSMP-III has, in addition, algorithms to handle stiff differential equations and the provision for a double precision arithmetic not found in CSMP. Both CSMP languages provide extensive diagnostic messages as well as special debugging features. Many different input–output options are available including various tabular and plot formats.

The CSMP-III graphics feature using an IBM 2250 display, allows on-line access to the input program, the data set, the translator, the compiler and link editor, and the execution phases of the simulation. Both CSMP/360 and CSMP-III are easy to use and can be learned at various levels. However, they are expensive to run. The use of CSMP requires at least a 360/40 with floating point hardware, a disk, and 102 K bytes of core memory. The convenience offered by CSMP far outweighs the cost, particularly when used by non-computer oriented personnel.

6.2.1.2 *CSSL-III* [42, 179]

CSSL-III is the first attempt to develop a simulation language based solely upon the CSSL report. Originally developed by Programming Sciences Inc., CSSL-III is currently marketed by Control Data Corp. It is also a non-procedural language with a NOSORT option which translates into FORTRAN. Its free-form coding, and extensive function and operator set make it powerful, yet easy to use. CSSL-III has retained the logical control variable feature of MIMIC and provides for convenient structure definition as per the CSSL report. Nine integration algorithms, including two user supplied routines, are provided. Extensive error control aids are incorporated into these algorithms and are available at the discretion of the user. However, double precision is not provided in this system.

A major innovation in CSSL-III is the extensive MACRO definition capability. This provides the sophisticated user with many options for creating and extending the existing language features. A deficiency in CSSL-III, as in CSMP and SL-1, is the lack of a file management system to handle large data sets. CSSL-III like CSMP has extensive user oriented capabilities which reduce programming and debugging time but are paid for in terms of resources and cost per run.

DARE-P [150], being a moderate version, is not as flexible as CSMP-III or CSSL-III, but is entirely written in ANSI-FORTRAN IV and available at a nominal cost.

SL-1 [236] presents additional features for certain sophisticated applications, allows both multiple-rate and multiple-algorithm integration, and accepts multiple independent variables extending the language to the realm of partial differential equations; real-time and hybrid computer features are also included.

6.2.1.3   *ACSL* [164] *versus CSSL-IV* [167]

ACSL basic structure follows the specifications of the CSSL report. An ACSL simulation consists of two sections: a model definition and run-time commands. Using this structure, a continuous system is mathematically modelled with ACSL statements in the model definition section, then the model is analysed under the control of instructions interpreted in the run time command section. The advantage of this structure is that once the model is defined, it can be saved on file and analysed indefinitely with any run-time commands specified interactively and/or in batch mode.

The simulation program is defined in a model definition section consisting of four parts:

(1) Initial
Statements that are performed once at the start of each simulation run. Initial section calculations typically lead to the calculation of initial conditions on the state variable, e.g. launch angles of a missile.

(2) Dynamic
Statements that are performed at every data recording interval. A simple example would be conversion of radians to degrees for recorded data. Efficiency is improved if those calculations relevant to data recording are collected into one block and performed together.

(3) Derivative
Describes the calculations that determine the derivatives of all the state variables. This section allows the selected integration routine to advance the state of the system with respect to its independent variable, usually

time. The statements in this section need not be ordered since they are automatically sorted into the correct sequence.

More than one derivative block may be defined, each with its own independent integration algorithm and step size. If the problem can be appropriately divided, then a section with small time constants can be integrated with a short step size, while the section with longer time constants can be integrated at a more efficient rate with a saving in overall computer time. Integration algorithms are selectable from six, established as part of the basic system: two Euler, two Runge–Kutta and two variable step, variable order algorithms, including Gear's Stiff Integration.

(4) Terminal
Statements that are executed once at the end of a simulation run, e.g. the miss distance of a missile from a target.

ACSL operates on a fully time-shared basis, and provides a truly interactive mode of operation in which simulation commands can be issued one by one, and data displayed and modified on line. Unlike other CSSL type languages, no limits exist for any of the internal tables used by the system translator, since they can all grow to fill available memory. Most simulation languages establish arbitrary limits on such things as the number of symbols, number of state variables, labels, etc. These table sizes are typically built into the translator at system generation time and can only be changed by systems programming personnel. In ACSL, no such artificial limits exist. As a corollary small programs can be executed in a smaller region, since the simulation program does not have to be configured to accommodate the largest conceivable program any user may submit. This cuts both the cost and time involved in running small to medium-sized models, and makes it more attractive to operate than in an interactive mode.

The model definition is translated by ACSL into a FORTRAN program. The translated ACSL model definition is loaded with the run-time library, which reads and interprets the run-time commands. ACSL's graphics system can produce printer and/or line plots at the user's option.

CSSL-IV provides enhancements over CSSL-III, including vector integration, Gear's algorithm for stiff ODEs, fast empirical function generation of families of curves, extended graphic capabilities, and improved performance.

Integration is central to the performance of CSSL-IV. Two new features found in CSSL-IV are the ability to handle vector integration and the addition of Gear's algorithm for integrating stiff differential equations. The CSSL-IV symbol table used both in translation and at run-time has been structured so as to facilitate the use of vector integration without changing any of the CSSL syntax. The major benefit to the user is that vector differential equations of the form

$$\dot{X} = AX$$

can be implemented using a single CSSL-IV statement of the form

X = INTEG (XDOT, XIC)

where X, XDOT and XIC are vector valued variables.

Stiff dynamic systems are ones with widely varying time constants ($>100{:}1$). These systems pose a difficult numerical problem for digital simulations in that numerical stability requires that the step-size be chosen to accommodate the largest time constant (smallest step size). As a result, conventional algorithms applied to stiff systems not only run for long periods of computer time, but exhibit instabilities due to the growth in round-off error. Gear's algorithm, using a variable order implicit predictor corrector scheme, extends the stability region such that step sizes of 100–1000 times larger than normally required for stability can be used, thus saving computer time and increasing solution accuracy.

Many problems in fluid and aerodynamics involve families of curves based upon empirical data. The new fast empirical function generator FTABLE has been added to CSSL-IV to fill this need. An arbitrary number of functions having the same independent variable set (1, 2, 3, or 4 variables) defined over the same break-points can be implemented and invoked using simple CSSL-IV statements. Definition of this family of empirical functions is accomplished using a statement of the form

FTABLE fname, NFUNCT, NVAR, NBREAK, XVAR,
YVAR1,---YVARn

where name labels the family of functions, NFUNCT specifies the number of functions, NVAR specifies the number of independent variables, NBREAK specifies the number of break-points, XVAR specifies the values of the break-points (dim 1, dim 2, dim 3, dim 4), and the list of YVAR specifies the values of each function at each break-point. Evaluation of this empirical function is accomplished using a statement of the form

GENERATE fname (XVAR, ANS1, ANS2,----ANSn)

where fname again specifies which function, XVAR specifies the value(s) of the independent variable(s) and ANSi specifies the variable names in which the results are to be placed.

Finally, the graphics feature of CSSL-IV has been extended and performance improved. Benchmarks, from simple spring mass problems to complex water-hammer simulations, have demonstrated throughout improvements of from 2:1 to 5:1 over CSSL-III depending on the problem. New storage management schemes, coupled with efficient use of operating system functions, have led to these improvement figures. To illustrate the possibilities of CSSL-IV, the coding of the pilot ejection problem is given.

The purpose of the investigation is to calculate the trajectory of a pilot ejected from a fighter aircraft and determine whether he will strike the aircraft's vertical stabilizer. This example is frequently cited in the literature [133].

```
INITIAL
        CONSTANT   M=7.0,        CD=1.0,      S=10.0,     Y1=4.0,        G=32.2,    ...
                   VE=40.0,      VA=0.0,      H=0.0,      THETAD=15.,               ...
                   VSAFE=0.,     HSAFE=0.
        TABLE      RHO           1,           12,                                   ...
                                 0.0,         1.0E3,      2.0E3,         4.0E3,     ...
                                 6.0E3,       10.0E3,     15.E3,         20.E3,     ...
                                 30.E3,       40.E3,      50.E3,         60.E3,     ...
                                 2.377E-3,    2.308E-3,   2.241E-3,      2.117E-3,  ...
                                 1.987E-3,    1.755E-3,   1.497E-3,      1.267E-3,  ...
                                 0.891E-3,    0.587E-3,   0.364E-3,      .2238E-3
                   THETAE=THETAD/57.3
                   VY,V1 = PTR(VE,THETAE)
        L1..  CONTINUE
              VX=VA-V1
              VO=SQRT(VX**2+VY**2)
              THETA0=ATAN2(VY,VX)
              K=0.5*RHO(H)*CD*S
END INITIAL


DYNAMIC
        IF (X.LT.-30.) GO TO L4
        CINTERVAL  CI=.50
              DERIVATIVE EJECT
                   D=K*V**2
                   XDOT=V*COS(THETA)-VA
                   X=INTEG(XDOT,0.)
                   YDOT=V*SIN(THETA)
                   Y=INTEG(YDOT,0.)
                        PROCEDURAL(YGEY1=Y,Y1)
                             YGEY1=1.0
                             DROP
                             IF (Y.LT.Y1) YGEY1=0.
                             PICKUP
                        END PROCEDURAL

                   VDOT=YGEY1*(-D/M-G*SIN(THETA))
                   V=INTEG(VDOT,V0)
```

```
              THEDOT=YGEY1*(-G*COS(THETA)/V)
              THETA=INTEG(THEDOT,THETA0)
       END DERIVATIVE

END DYNAMIC

TERMINAL
L4. .  IF (Y.GT.20.) GO TO L2
       H=H+500.
       IF (H.GT.1.0E+5) GO TO L3
       GO TO L1
L2. .  MISS=Y-12.0
       PREPAR HSAVE,VSAFE
       VSAFE=VA
       HSAVE=H
       PRINT L5,HSAFE,VSAFE,MISS
L5. .  FORMAT(5X,6HHSAFE=,F14.6,6HVSAFE=,F14.6,5HMISS=,F14.6)
L3. .  CONTINUE
       VA=VA+50.
       H=0.
       IF (VA.LE.900.) GO TO L1
END TERMINAL
```

In an evaluation of simulation languages one could look for:
—essential features: like size (large number of variables), flexibility (choice of operators), integration algorithms (variety), modularity, interactiveness, diagnostics, robustness, track record, maintenance.
—desirable features: variable step-size, library and input/output routines, translator and run-time efficiency, documentation, service bureau availability, low acquisition and maintenance cost.
Both languages ACSL and CSSL-IV contain all essential features; favouring ACSL are better diagnostics, more efficient translator, longer track record and lower quoted cost; favouring CSSL-IV are better modularity, more integration algorithms, and more accessibility for help.

6.2.1.4 Structured problem oriented programming languages

A number of languages allow, moreover, an easy set-up of problems of a related or dissimilar nature, such as optimization, incorporation of discrete variables, and even other mathematical procedures intermixed.

DYNAMO [180] is a compiler for translating and executing "system dynamic" simulations.

SLANG [215] and its successor *PROSE* [216] are procedural simulation languages designed to permit the solution of very sophisticated mathematical problems characterized by iterative solution techniques. They handle both continuous and discrete event simulation. Of particular interest to problem-solvers is the ability to perform non-linear optimization. Algorithms are provided to optimize continuous systems through the generation of the Jacobian Matrix at each iteration; included are non-linear programming routines which provide for event-oriented optimization. This language contains specific program commands which are of direct usefulness in parameter identification, like: optimize, maximize, minimize, partials (calculate partial derivatives) as well as step-size optimization. PROSE promises to be a rich and powerful language applicable to a broad range of simulation problems.

GASP IV [178] and FORSIM V [30] are general purpose procedural simulation packages either entirely or partially coded in ANSI-FORTRAN-IV. Simulation of combined continuous and discrete systems can be performed using GASP, while FORSIM allows continuous systems to be described by mixed ordinary and partial differential equations.

Elaborate activity is going on in extending the existing simulation languages to include the occurrence of individual events in system behaviour. Current initiations, however, are still at the research stage and rather diversified. The interested reader is referred to a detailed state-of-the-art review by T. Ören on software for simulation of combined continuous and discrete systems [169].

6.2.2 Simulation packages for partial differential equations

6.2.2.1 General-purpose higher-level languages

The prospect of a single higher-level language, which would be useful for all types of partial differential equations arising in science and engineering, has been a tantalizing one for many years. In the 1960s, a number of such languages were proposed and implemented, and three of these are described below in order to demonstrate their general approach. None of them has stood the test of time. While they were successful in solving relatively simple and straightforward elliptic, parabolic, and hyperbolic partial differential equations, and were therefore useful in an academic or teaching environment, they were too inefficient to compete with specialized program packages for the large "practical" problems. Invariably, in designing a general-purpose programming system, speed in the execution of the programs is sacrificed for programming convenience. The more general a package, the more inefficient is it likely to be for specific problems. For small problems, the loss of efficiency in executing programs is of minor importance, while the ability to permit an inexperienced programmer to obtain meaningful outputs is a great attraction. For the large problems that arise in fluid mechanics, nuclear reactor technology, structural engineering, etc., on the other hand, it is of vital economic importance to make each solution run as brief as possible. Programming ease is therefore necessarily sacrificed, and only experienced programmers are employed.

Furthermore, the various numerical methods available for the solution of ordinary differential equations are quite similar, differing only in the detailed nature of the integration algorithms. It is therefore relatively easy to specify a digital simulation language which is general for all types of ordinary differential equations encountered in practice. By contrast, the partial differential equations arising in physics and engineering fall into a number of distinct classes, each requiring highly specialized numerical methods for their solution. These classes include the elliptic, parabolic, hyperbolic, and biharmonic equations in one, two, and three space dimensions and in a variety of coordinate systems (see Chapter 4).

A number of basic numerical approaches exist to the solution of partial differential equations. These include particularly the following, finite difference methods, the method of characteristics, the Monte Carlo method, and the finite element method [81].

PDEL

One of the first general-purpose languages to be developed in the late 1960s was designed by Cardenas *et al.* [29] at the University of California. It was designed as a fourth-level language and provided with a translator program to translate the source PDEL program into a third-level language. The third-level target language employed was PL/1, so that PDEL can be employed using any digital computer equipped with a PL/1 compiler.

The utilization of PDEL takes the following steps:
—The problem is formulated as a partial differential equation, together with all applicable boundary and initial conditions.
—A finite difference grid is defined for the space as well as the time domains.
—The mathematical model is expressed in PDEL as a sequence of formalized statements, and a separate punched card is prepared for each statement for digital computer input.
—The PDEL translator is employed to convert this program into PL/1.
—The regular PL/1 compiler is employed to translate the resulting program into assembly and, eventually, machine language.
—The program now in machine code is executed, and the required solution is printed out.

PDEL statements are written in PL/1 preprocessor language, i.e. they have the same syntax as PL/1 statements but are preceded by a % sign. There are ten functionally different types of statements: equation, dimension, parameter, geometry, boundary conditions, initial condition, control, output, declare, and comment. These statements are used to specify:

(1) whether the equation being solved is elliptic, parabolic, hyperbolic, or biharmonic;
(2) whether the problem is formulated in one, two, or three space dimensions;
(3) the parameters of the problem, which may be constants, time-varying functions of the space variables, or functions of the dependent variable;
(4) the geometry of the field which may be regular or irregular;
(5) the boundary conditions;
(6) the initial conditions;
(7) the finite difference grid spacings along the space and time coordinates;
(8) the nature of the desired print-out.

A number of different output formats are provided. These include numerical print-outs of the potentials at all node points at the selected time levels, as well as a novel alphabetical print-out. In the latter case, the dynamic range of the dependent variable is divided into 26 equally-spaced levels and a different letter of the alphabet is assigned to each of these levels.

As a simple example of the application of PDEL to a non-linear partial differential equation consider:

$$\frac{\partial}{\partial x}\left(\sigma \frac{\partial \phi}{\partial x}\right) = k \frac{\partial \phi}{\partial t}$$
$$\sigma = 1.0 \qquad k = 0.08\phi \qquad 0 \leqslant x \leqslant 10 \qquad (6.1)$$
$$\phi(0, t) = \phi(10, t) = 0$$
$$\phi(x, 0) = 0.08(5x - x^2/2)$$

The x domain is to be divided into twenty equal intervals, and a time step of 0.125 s is to be used. It is desired to obtain a print-out of the solution at every other point in the x domain for t = 0, 2 and 4, and a plot of ϕ vs. t showing the value of the solution at every grid point for t = 0, 0.125, ..., 4.00. The following is the PDEL program which is prepared by the user.

```
/*PDEL PROGRAM FOR A NONLINEAR DIFFUSION EQUATION*/   0
% INCLUDE $PDEL (INITIAL);                            1
% DIMENSION = '1';                                    2
% DECLARE (SIGMAX, KAPPA1) CHARACTER;                 3
```

```
% EQUATION = 'SIGMAX*PX,PX,PHI = KAPPA1*PT,PHI';          4
% KAPPA1 = '0.08/PHI';                                    5
% SIGMAX = '1.0';                                         6
% SCOND = '(*) = 0.08*((5*X) - (X**2)/(2);               7
% GRIDPOINTSX = '20';                                     8
% GRIDPOINTST = '32';                                     9
% BCOND = '(0) = 0.0; (20) = 0.0';                        10
% DELTAX = '0.5';                                         11
% DELTAT = '0.125';                                       12
% PRINTINTX = '2';                                        13
% PRINTINTT = '16';                                       14
% PLOTINTX = '2';                                         15
% PLOTINTT = '1';                                         16
% INCLUDE $PDEL(HEART);                                   17
```

The statements above play the following role:

0 : a comment
1 : calls from the computer system the initialization part of the translator
2 : defines spatial dimensionality
3 : declares each parameter before being used
4 : defines the equation
5 : defines the parameter k
6 : defines the parameter σ
7 : indicates that the initial conditions at all grid points are defined by the function states
8 : indicates the number of grid points in the x direction
9 : indicates the number of steps in the t direction to be used
10 : indicates that the boundary potentials are 0.0
11 : indicates the spacing between grid points in the x direction
12 : indicates the spacing between grid points in the t direction
13 : indicates that the solution at every other grid point in the x direction is to be printed out
14 : indicates that the solution at every eight time levels (i.e., at t = 0, 2 and 4) is to be printed out
15, 16 : indicate that the solution at every other point in the x direction is to be plotted vs. time at every time step (i.e. at t = 0.125, 0.250, ... 4.00)
17 : calls the part of the PDEL translator which performs the processing of the PDEL program.

For a parabolic equation in two space dimensions such as:

$$\frac{\partial}{\partial x}\left(\sigma_x \frac{\partial \phi}{\partial x}\right) + \frac{\partial}{\partial y}\left(\sigma_y \frac{\partial \phi}{\partial y}\right) = k \frac{\partial \phi}{\partial t} \qquad (6.2)$$

$$k = f(\phi) \qquad 0 \leqslant x \leqslant X \qquad 0 \leqslant y \leqslant Y$$

the applicable equation statement is:

% EQUATION='SIGMAX*PX,PX,PHI+SIGMAY*PY,PY
PHI=K*PT,PHI'

By 1970 the equations shown in Table 6.1 had been implemented. Subsequently the system was expanded to provide for equations formulated in cylindrical and spherical coordinates, as well as biharmonic equations in one space dimension.

LEANS III

This language developed by W. E. Schiesser [197] at Lehigh University is based on FORTRAN, as are virtually all the other simulation packages discussed in this chapter. The system was designed to handle a broad class of partial differential equations as well as the mixed ordinary/partial differential equation models which frequently arise in chemical engineering. For integration in the time domain, the method-of-lines algorithm was implemented.

In order to implement any specific mathematical model, the user of LEANS is required only to specify the parameters of the following partial differential equations:

$$A_3\partial^2 u/\partial t^2 + A_1 \partial u/\partial t = \partial(A_3 u)/\partial x + (1/x^a)\partial(x^a A_4 \partial u/\partial x)/\partial x + A_5 u + A_6$$

$$(6.3)$$

The coefficients $A_1, A_2, \ldots, A_6$ are programmable by the user and may be functions of the independent variables x and t and the dependent variable u; a is a coordinate factor, programmable by the user, which may have the values 0, 1 or 2 for cartesian, cylindrical and spherical coordinates respectively. A few special cases of equation (6.3) indicate the spectrum of equations that it encompasses:

Case I: $A_2 = A_3 = A_5 = A_6 = 0, \quad A_1 = A_4 = 1$

    Case Ia: $a = 0$

    $\partial u/\partial t = \partial^2 u/\partial x^2$

(parabolic heat conduction equation in cartesian coordinates)

    Case Ib: $a = 1$

    $\partial u/\partial t = \partial^2 u/\partial x^2 + (1/x)\partial u/\partial x$

(parabolic heat conduction equation in cylindrical coordinates)

    Case Ic: $a = 2$

    $\partial u/\partial t = \partial^2 u/\partial x^2 + (2/x)\partial u/\partial x$

(parabolic heat conduction equation in spherical coordinates)

TABLE 6.1 Numerical algorithms used in PDEL to solve the basic equations

Type	Partial differential equation	Numerical algorithm
Elliptic 1 dimension	$\dfrac{\partial}{\partial x}\left(\sigma\dfrac{\partial\phi}{\partial x}\right) = K$	Tridiagonal algorithm
Elliptic 2 dimensions	$\dfrac{\partial}{\partial x}\left(\sigma\dfrac{\partial\phi}{\partial x}\right) + \dfrac{\partial}{\partial y}\left(\sigma\dfrac{\partial\phi}{\partial y}\right) = K$	Successive point overrelaxation
Elliptic 3 dimensions	$\dfrac{\partial}{\partial x}\left(\sigma\dfrac{\partial\phi}{\partial x}\right) + \dfrac{\partial}{\partial y}\left(\sigma\dfrac{\partial\phi}{\partial y}\right) + \dfrac{\partial}{\partial z}\left(\sigma\dfrac{\partial\phi}{\partial z}\right) = K$	Successive point overrelaxation
Parabolic 1 dimension	$\dfrac{\partial}{\partial x}\left(\sigma\dfrac{\partial\phi}{\partial x}\right) = K\dfrac{\partial\phi}{\partial t} + F$	Crank-Nicolson, tridiagonal algorithm
Parabolic 2 dimensions	$\dfrac{\partial}{\partial x}\left(\sigma\dfrac{\partial\phi}{\partial x}\right) + \dfrac{\partial}{\partial y}\left(\sigma\dfrac{\partial\phi}{\partial y}\right) = K\dfrac{\partial\phi}{\partial t} + F$	Alternating direction and tridiagonal algorithm
Parabolic 3 dimensions	$\dfrac{\partial}{\partial x}\left(\sigma\dfrac{\partial\phi}{\partial x}\right) + \dfrac{\partial}{\partial y}\left(\sigma\dfrac{\partial\phi}{\partial y}\right) + \dfrac{\partial}{\partial z}\left(\sigma\dfrac{\partial\phi}{\partial z}\right) = K\dfrac{\partial\phi}{\partial t} + F$	Alternating direction and tridiagonal algorithm
Hyperbolic 1 dimension	$\dfrac{\partial}{\partial x}\left(\sigma\dfrac{\partial\phi}{\partial x}\right) = \dfrac{\partial}{\partial t}\left(K\dfrac{\partial\phi}{\partial t}\right) + K\dfrac{\partial\phi}{\partial t} + F$	Von Neuman and tridiagonal algorithm
Hyperbolic 2 dimensions	$\dfrac{\partial}{\partial x}\left(\sigma\dfrac{\partial\phi}{\partial x}\right) + \dfrac{\partial}{\partial y}\left(\sigma\dfrac{\partial\phi}{\partial y}\right) = \dfrac{\partial}{\partial t}\left(K\dfrac{\partial\phi}{\partial t}\right) + K\dfrac{\partial\phi}{\partial t} + F$	Lees algorithm and tridiagonal algorithm

K and F can be functions of x, y, z, t and ϕ. Boundary conditions: Dirichlet and Neuman.

Case II: $A_1 = A_3 = A_5 = A_6 = 0,$ $A_2 = A_4 = 1$

$a = 0$

$\partial^2 u / \partial t^2 = \partial^2 u / \partial x^2$

(hyperbolic wave equation)

Case III: $A_2 = A_4 = A_6 = 0,$ $A_1 = A_3 = A_5 = 1$

$\partial u / \partial t = \partial u / \partial x + u$

(first-order hyperbolic flow equation)

Equation (6.3) has an associated boundary condition:

$$B_1 \partial u / \partial x + B_2 u = B_3 \qquad (6.4)$$

where the coefficients B_1, B_2 and B_3 are programmable by the user and may be a function of the dependent variable u. For example $B_2 = u^3$, $B_3 = u^4$ corresponds to a non-linear, fourth-power radiation boundary condition.

Systems of simultaneous equations of the form of equation (6.3) are allowed along with ordinary differential equations of the initial-value type.

PDELAN

J. Gary *et al*. [73], at the National Center for Atmospheric Research, developed a higher-level language capable of handling more complicated numerical schemes with greater efficiency than is attained in PDEL or LEANS. A preprocessor is employed to convert the source program into a FORTRAN program. Unlike the preceding two languages, PDELAN is procedural in character, so that all statements in the source program must be in the correct order. Moreover, it does not select any finite difference or integration scheme, but rather provides mesh and operator statements to simplify the coding of such schemes.

PDELAN contains three basic declarations MESH, VARIABLE, and OPERAND. The first of these is employed to declare the dimensions of the finite difference grid. The second is employed to declare the dependent variables associated with each finite difference grid point. Since meshes are rectangular, variable statements can be translated directly into FORTRAN DIMENSION statements. The OPERATOR statement is employed to define the domain and the range of dependent variables or functions of such variables. A DOMESH statement is employed to operate upon previously defined meshes, so that these can be translated into FORTRAN DO loops. This is illustrated in the following example taken from the PDELAN User's Manual.

Consider the following simple differential equation with the given initial and boundary conditions

$$\frac{\partial u}{\partial t} + u\frac{\partial u}{\partial x} = 0 \tag{6.5}$$

$$u(x, 0) = f(x) \qquad 0 \leqslant x \leqslant 1$$

$$u(0, t) = g(t) \qquad 0 \leqslant T$$

We may assume a mesh given by $x_i = (i - 1)\Delta x$, $t_n = n\Delta t$ where $1 \leqslant i \leqslant M$, $\Delta x = 1/(M - 1)$, $n \geqslant 0$. We make the definitions

$$U_i^n = u(x_i, t_n)$$

$$\partial(U)_i = (U_i - U_{i-1})/\Delta x \qquad 2 \leqslant i \leqslant M$$

Then we can write a simple finite difference scheme for this problem as follows:

$$\frac{U_i^{n+1} - U_i^n}{\Delta t} + U_i^n \partial(U^n)_i = 0$$

$$U_i^0 = f(x_i) \qquad 1 \leqslant i \leqslant M$$

$$U_1^n = g(t_n) \qquad 1 \leqslant n$$

This can be rewritten as:

$$U_i^{n+1} = U_i^n - \Delta t U_i^n \partial(U^n)_i$$

$$U_i^0 = f(x_i)$$

$$U_1^n = g(t_n)$$

In order to write this in the PDELAN language we must declare the mesh (x_i) and the operator ∂. We represent the values U_i^{n+1} by U2(I) and U_i^n by U1(I). We assume M = 100.

```
C            SIMPLE PDE PROGRAM
         PROGRAM B1A
         MESH MA(100)
         VARIABLE (U1,U2) ON MA
         OPERATOR (MA) TO (MA(2),(100))      IS
      1  DX(W,I)=(W(I)–W(I–1))/DLX
C            INITIALIZE
         M=100 $  DLX=1./(M–1) $  NSTEP=100 $  DLT=.25*DLX
         DOMESH 10 MA(K)
         X=(K – 1)*DLX
     10  U1=F(X)
         N=O
```

```
C                 TIME STEP LOOP
   20   T=N*DLT
        U1(1)=G(T)
        DOMESH 30 MA(K=(2,100))
   30   U2=U1-DLT*U1*DX(U1)
        N=N+1
        DOMESH 40 MA(K)
   40   U1=U2
        IF(N .LE. NSTEP)GOTO 20
        END
```

The equivalent FORTRAN program is:

```
C                 SIMPLE PDE PROGRAM—FORTRAN VERSION
        PROGRAM B1B
        DIMENSION U1(100),U2(100)
        M=100  $  DLX=1./(M–1)  $  NSTEP=100  $  DLT=.25*DLX
C                 INITIALIZE
        DO 10 K=1,M
        X=(K–1)*DLX
   10   U1(K)=F(X)
        N=0
C                 TIME STEP LOOP
   20   T=N*DLT
        U1(1)=G(T)
        DO 30 K=2,M
   30   U2(K)=U1(K)-DLT*U1(K)*(U1(K)-U1(K-1))/DLX
        N=N+1
        DO 40 K=1,M
   40   U1(K)=U2(K)
        IF(N .LE. NSTEP)GOTO 20
        END
```

The MESH and OPERATOR declarations do not result in any output.
The VARIABLE statement produces the following output:

DIMENSION U1(100), U2(100)

The DOMESH 10 statement generates the following DO statement

DO 10 K = 1100

Within the range of this DOMESH, any occurrence of an unsubscripted mesh variable will have the mesh subscript K added to it. Thus U1 becomes U1(K).

The expansion of mesh operators (DX in this example) is central to the language. This is illustrated in the expansion of the range of the DOMESH 30 statement. This statement generates the following DO statement:

DO 30 K = 2100

The statement labelled 30 is expanded by adding the subscript K to any occurrence of the mesh variables U1 and U2. The operator variable DX(U1) is expanded as follows. First DX(U1) is replaced by the defining expression for DX which appears in the OPERATOR statement, namely

(W(I) − W(I − 1))/DLX

In this expression the "marker" W is replaced by the "expression argument" of the operator variable DX(U1), in this case U1. Thus, W is replaced by U1. The subscript for U1 is obtained by substitution of the mesh subscript K (found in the DOMESH statement) for the "subscript argument" I found in the defining expression. Thus, the above defining expression for DX expands to

((U1(K) − U1(K − 1))/DLX)

Note that extra parentheses are added around the defining expression (superfluous in this case). Statement 30 expands to the following

30   U2(K) = U1(K) − DLT*((U(K) − U(K − 1))/DLX)

The expansion of the DOMESH range is the central part of the language.

6.2.2.2   *Software systems for elliptic partial differential equations*

By the late 1970s most efforts to produce general-purpose partial differential equation packages had been abandoned or reduced in scope. Instead, numerous efforts were initiated to provide powerful software systems for specific classes of problems. With very few exceptions, these employed FORTRAN, and are designed to permit the programmer to construct programs by linking suitable FORTRAN subroutines. Some of these subroutines are supplied with the programming system and others must be specified by the user. This makes it necessary for the user to have considerable experience in FORTRAN programming, and an understanding of the algorithms employed in the various subroutines. Sweet and Machura [152] provide an extensive survey of the state of the art of software systems for partial differential equations as of 1979.

Because elliptic partial differential equations occur in most physical and engineering disciplines, a large number of software systems have been designed for this general problem area. Many of these actually consist of subroutine packages for the solution of systems of algebraic equations.

Others are designed to facilitate the formulation of these equations using finite difference or finite element approximations. The following discussion constitutes a sampling of programming systems developed in the late 1970s.

ELLPACK

Under the general coordination and leadership of J. R. Rice [187], the ELLPACK software project is directed towards providing a framework for the development and evaluation of algorithms for the solution of partial differential equations. The emphasis in the late 1970s was on the solution of large, sparse linear systems of algebraic equations, such as arise in the solution of linear elliptic partial differential equations. The general approach is one of modularization. The overall programming task is broken up into five distinct stages, each including a number of programming tasks, and implemented as modules. The interface between these modules is carefully defined and fixed, thus permitting users to design and test individual modules for their requirements and to integrate them into the overall system. All existing modules are available to all users.

As an example of the ELLPACK approach, a program by Houstis and Rice [97] is briefly described. It is designed to employ the method of collocation using bi-cubic piecewise Hermite polynomials for the solution of the linear two-dimensional elliptic equation

$$\alpha u_{xx} + 2\beta u_{xy} + \alpha u_{yy} + \delta u_x + \varepsilon u_y + \zeta u = f \tag{6.6}$$

defined on a general two-dimensional domain and subject to mixed type boundary conditions:

$$au_x + bu_y + cu = g \quad \text{on the boundary}$$

The following are the five major modules.

Input module

The user must specify:

(i) Region boundary definition: user supplied routine

SUBROUTINE BCOORD(P, X, Y)

to define the boundary as parametric curve; the X, Y values are returned corresponding to the parametric value P. Boundaries with an arbitrary number of pieces are allowed.

(ii) A rectangular mesh.

(iii) Problem definition: user supplied FORTRAN functions.

FUNCTION COEF(X, Y, J), J = 1, 2, . . . , 6 for $\alpha, \beta, \ldots, \zeta$
FUNCTION BCOEF(X, Y, J), J = 1, 2, 3 for a, b, c

which evaluate α, β, . . . , ζ, a, b, c and

FUNCTION F(X, Y, J),   J = 1, 2 for f, g

that computes the functions f, g in the differential and boundary operator.

Region module: subroutine REGION

This module locates the region with respect to the grid and provides various information useful in further processing. The output from this module consists of grid specifications and boundary specifications in the form of arrays, which include coordinates of boundary intersection points, their type, and neighbouring grid points, etc.

Equation construction module

This module consists of three components:

(i) SUBROUTINE CLDATA which identifies the type of each grid element, calculates the number of boundary collocation points associated with each element, and calculates the boundary collocation points and the modified nodes of each element.

(ii) SUBROUTINE INDEXING which numbers the nodes of the final mesh to be used later for the approximation of the differential operator, determines the element incidences and estimates the bandwidth.

(iii) SUBROUTINE FORMEQ which generates the system of the collocation equations.

Equation solving module: subroutine BNDSOL

This module solves the system of collocation equations using Gaussian elimination.

Output module

By appropriate commands the user can obtain

(i) the output generated by the REGION module

(ii) the input data to the subroutine FORMEQ

(iii) the values of the approximate solution U and its derivatives U_x, U_y, U_{xy} evaluated at the nodes or at any set of points supplied by the user.

(iv) the execution time of each module.

The paper cited above includes examples of the application of this program to three relatively complicated field problems and includes the computer output obtained by the above procedure.

ITPACK

At the University of Texas, a group of researchers is engaged in the development of programs for the solution of linear, self-adjoint, elliptic partial differential equations of the type:

$$(au_x)_x + (bu_y)_y + cu = f \tag{6.7}$$

where a, b, c may be constants or functions of x and y. One objective of the ITPACK effort is to provide modules to be used within the ELLPACK system described in the preceding paragraph. To this end the ITPACK codes are themselves organized into individual modules having the following functions:

Grid definition.

Generation of nonzero coefficients of the linear system.

Definition of the ordering vector for the grid points.

Initialization of the unknown vector.

Solution by an iterative method.

Output of results.

Grid definition is implemented by a separate subroutine which permits field boundaries which are horizontal, vertical or 45° lines. Within this boundary the mesh spacing must be uniform but holes within the region are permitted. For the solution of the algebraic equations, a variety of adaptive iterative algorithms is provided. These include adaptations of the Jacobi method, the conjugate gradient method and the successive over-relaxation methods. A report by Kincaid and Grimes [126] includes programming details and the results of the application of these algorithms to a variety of problems.

In a paper prepared by Eisenstatt, George, Grimes, Kincaid, and Sherman [58] the effectiveness of software packages for large, sparse, linear systems prepared at four different academic institutions are compared.

LINPACK

Collaboration of researchers at the Argonne National Laboratory, and numerous universities, resulted in 1979 in a very powerful programming system. LINPACK is a collection of FORTRAN subroutines useful for the solution of a wide variety of classes of systems of simultaneous linear algebraic equations. The objective was to provide subroutines which are completely machine independent, fully portable, and which run at near optimum efficiency. Different subroutines are intended to take advantage of different special properties of the linear systems, thereby conserving computer time and memory. As described by Dongarra, Bunch, Moler, and Stewart [53], separate subroutines are provided for each of the following linear systems or problems:

General matrices.

Band matrices.

Positive definite matrices.

Positive definite band matrices.

Symmetric indefinite matrices

Triangular matrices.
Tridiagonal matrices.
Cholesky decomposition.
Q.R. decomposition.
Singular value decomposition.

The scope of LINPACK therefore transcends in large measure the systems arising in the solution of elliptic partial differential equations. Moreover, the entire coefficient matrix is usually stored in the computer memory, although there are provisions for band matrices, and for processing large rectangular matrices row by row. On most large sequential computers, LINPACK can therefore handle full matrices only of an order less than a few hundred, and band matrices of an order less than several thousand. There are no subroutines for general sparse matrices or for iterative methods for large problems. On the other hand, where the size of the field problem is such that it falls within these limits, the LINPACK subroutines prove highly useful. They embody a degree of software engineering not found in most other programming packages.

6.2.2.3 *Software packages for parabolic and hyperbolic partial differential equations*

In the development of software packages for parabolic and hyperbolic partial differential equations, the designer is faced with the dual task of providing for a suitable discretization of the space domain, as well as the time domain. Early software systems tended to favour finite difference methods for approximating the space domain. In recent years, there has been increasing emphasis on finite element methods, most frequently using the Galerkin method and splines. Although numerous methods for approximating the time derivatives of the partial differential equation are available, by the late 1970s virtually all widely disseminated packages made use of the so-called method-of-lines.

In the method-of-lines, the partial differential is first converted to a system of simultaneous ordinary differential equations, one equation for each finite difference or finite grid point in the space domain. Standard subroutines for the integration of ordinary differential equations are then invoked to perform the integration in the time domain. One reason for the overwhelming popularity of the method-of-lines is that very powerful algorithms for ordinary differential equations have been developed over the years. The basic algorithms include Euler's Method, the trapezoidal rule, Runge–Kutta methods, forward integration (Adams–Bashford), and predictor–corrector (Adams–Moulton) methods. Many of the algorithms based on these methods have provision for the automatic control of the step-size in the time domain, so as to keep truncation errors within specified bounds. Of particular use in solving differential equations are the algorithms developed by C. W. Gear, known generally as Gear's methods. These algorithms are particularly useful in the treatment of so-called stiff systems, in which there is a wide spread in the location of the roots or characteristic values, i.e. the solution contains transient terms with widely-ranging time constants. Under these conditions, other algorithms for integration fail to provide correct answers, or make it necessary to take extremely short steps in time so as to avoid instability. Gear's method provide an effective compromise of accuracy, stability, and computer time. A number of useful variations of Gear's method have appeared in the literature and have been implemented in various software packages. Some of these are considered briefly below.

DSS/2

Developed at Lehigh University by W. Schiesser [198] and widely disseminated to universities and government installations, DSS/2 facilitates the solution of ordinary differential equations as well as partial differential equations, via the method-of-lines. The approach is one of linked FORTRAN–IV subroutines with emphasis on transportability and ease of use by students. It consists of a main program to which the user must supply three subroutines. For batch processing, the deck of cards submitted to the computer are organized as follows:

```
JOB OR ACCOUNTING CARD SPECIFYING MEMORY, CPU TIME, ETC
CONTROL CARD(S) TO CALL THE DSS BINARY
CONTROL CARD(S) TO COMPILE THE THREE USER SUBROUTINES
CONTROL CARD(S) TO LOAD AND LINK THE DSS/SUBROUTINE BINARIES
CONTROL CARD(S) TO EXECUTE THE COMPLETE BINARY
TERMINATOR FOR CONTROL CARD SECTION (IF REQUIRED)
        SUBROUTINE INITIAL
            .
            .
            .
        END
        SUBROUTINE DERV
            .
            .
            .
        END
        SUBROUTINE PRINT(NI,NO)
            .
            .
            .
        END
```

TERMINATOR FOR FORTRAN SECTION (IF REQUIRED)
THREE DATA CARDS
END OF RUNS
TERMINATOR FOR DECK (IF REQUIRED)

Four categories of information must be provided by the user:
(1) The DERV subroutine to define the equations being solved.
(2) The INITIAL subroutine to define initial conditions for all the simultaneous ordinary differential equations.
(3) The PRINT subroutine to define the format of the computer output.
(4) Two data cards which specify the numerical parameters of the problem being solved, and which provide control information for the execution of the program.

To illustrate the application of DSS/2 consider the following simple example of a one-dimensional nonlinear parabolic partial differential equation described in the DSS/2 manual.

$$\frac{\partial u}{\partial t} = \frac{\partial^2 u}{\partial x^2} \tag{6.8}$$

which is written as

$$PU/PT = P2U/PX2 \tag{6.9}$$

with boundary conditions

$$PU(0, T)/PX = 0 \tag{6.10}$$

$$PU(L, T)/PX = E*(UA**4) - U(L, T)**4) \tag{6.11}$$

$$U(X,0) = U0 \tag{6.12}$$

where

U	dependent variable
X, T	independent variables
PU/PT	first-order partial derivative of U with respect to T
P2U/PX2	second-order partial derivative of U with respect to X
L	maximum value of X
E, UA, U0	constants

The spatial derivative, P2U/PX2, is approximated at a general point X = I*DX by a finite difference approximation, in this case a second-order, central difference

$$P2U/PX2 = \frac{U(I + 1, T) - 2*U(I, T) + U(I - 1, T)}{DX*DX} \tag{6.13}$$

where

DX Spatial Integration Interval in X
I Index denoting the spatial position of the terms in the finite difference approximation equation (6.13).

Substituting in equation (6.9), a set of simultaneous ordinary differential equations results

$$DU(I, T)/DT = (U(I + 1, T) - 2^*U(I, T) + U(I - 1, T))/(DX^*DX)$$
$$I = 0, 1, 2, 3, \ldots, N \tag{6.14}$$

where DU(I, T)/DT is an ordinary or total derivative of U with respect to T at the point $X = I*DX$ and, N is the total number of increments, each of length DX (i.e., $L = N*DX$). Since for $I = 0$, the point $U(-1, T)$ in equation (6.14) is outside the solution domain $X = 0$ to L, boundary condition (6.10) must be used to handle this point. A second-order, central difference approximation for equation (6.10) is

$$PU(0, T)/PX = (U(1, T)-U(-1, T))/(2^*DX) = 0 \tag{6.15}$$

or

$$U(-1, T) = U(1, T) \tag{6.16}$$

Thus for $I = 0$, equation (6.14) becomes

$$DU(0, T)/DT = 2*(U(1, T) - U(0, T))/(DX*DX) \tag{6.17}$$

Similarly, for $I = N$, $U(N + 1, T)$ in equation (6.14) is outside the solution domain, and boundary condition (6.11) must be used to handle this point. A second order, central difference approximation of equation (6.11) is at $X = L$, with $UA = 500$,

$$U(N + 1, T) = U(N - 1, T) + 2*DX*E*(500**4 - U(N, T**4) \tag{6.18}$$

Equation (6.18) can be used to eliminate the term $U(I + 1, T)$ in equation (6.14) when $I = N$. The initial condition, for $U0 = 600$, becomes

$$U(I, 0) = 600$$
$$I = 0, 1, 2, 3, \ldots, N \tag{6.19}$$

Subroutine DERV to implement equations (6.14) to (6.19) with $L = 1$ is listed below along with the INITIAL and PRINT subroutines and the DATA cards.

The first data card provides the initial and final values of the independent variable, as well as the print interval. The second data card contains the number of first-order differential equations (11 in this case), the maximum ratio of the PRINT interval to the integration interval (in this case 64), the identification number of the integration algorithm to be used (1 in this case), a print option for error messages, relative or absolute error criterions to govern the automatic adjustment of the integration step (REL for relative in this case), and the magnitude of the maximum allowable error at each step in the time domain (0.001 in this case).

The integration algorithm for integrating in the time domain can be chosen from fourteen Runge–Kutta methods of order one through five each with automatic step-size control. Extensions of the above approach to parabolic and hyperbolic differential equations in two and three dimensions in cartesian, cylindrical, and spherical coordinates are straight-forward and well documented.

```
        SUBROUTINE DERV

        COMMON/T/T,NFIN,NRUN/Y/U(11)/F/DUDT(11)/PARM/N,DX,DXS
C. . .
C. . . EVALUATE THE TIME DERIVATIVES FOR 10 SECTIONS (11 GRID
C. . . POINTS)
        DO 1 I=1,N
        IF(I.NE.1)GO TO 2
C. . .
C. . . X=0, EQUATION (5.7) (NOTE – THE SPATIAL INCREMENT, DX,
C. . . AND DX*DX=DXS, ARE SET IN SUBROUTINE INITIAL AND PASSED
C. . . TO DERV THROUGH COMMON/PARM/ TO ACHIEVE COMPUTATIONAL
C. . . EFFICIENCY, I.E., THESE CALCULATIONS ARE DONE ONLY ONCE
C. . . IN SUBROUTINE INITIAL WHICH IS ALL THAT IS REQUIRED SINCE
C. . . DX AND DX*DX ARE CONSTANTS THROUGHOUT THE ENTIRE CAL-
C. . . CULATION)
        DUDT(1)=2./DXS*(U(2)–U(1))
        GO TO 1
2       IF(I.NE.N)GO TO 3
C. . .
C. . . X=1 (NONLINEAR RADIATION BOUNDARY CONDITION), EQUATION
C. . . (6.18)
        DUDT(N)=(1./DXS)*(U(N–1)+2.*DX*1.73E–D9*(500.**4–
     1  U(N)**4)–2.*U(N)+U(N–1))
        GO TO 1
C. . .
C. . . INTERMEDIATE SPATIAL POSITIONS, EQUATION (5.6)
3       DUDT(I)=(1./DXS)*(U(I+1)–2.*U(I)+U(I–1))
1       CONTINUE
        RETURN
        END


        SUBROUTINE INITIAL

        COMMON/T/T,NFIN,NRUN/Y/U(11)/F/DUDT(11)/PARM/N,DX,DXS
C. . .
```

```
C. . .  SET THE NUMBER OF SPATIAL INTERVALS, COMPUTE THE SPATIAL
C. . .  INCREMENT
        N=10
        DX=1./FLCAT(N)
        DXS=DX*DX
C. . .
C. . .  EVALUATE THE INITIAL CONDITION VECTOR FOR 11 GRID
C. . .  POINTS, EQUATION (5.9)
        N=N+1
        DO 1 I=1,N
1       U(I)=600.
        RETURN
        END

        SUBROUTINE PRINT(NI,NO)
        COMMON/T/T,NFIN,NRUN/Y/U(11)/F/DUDT(11)/PARM/N,DX,DXS
        WRITE(NO,1)T
1       FORMAT(/,2X,7HTIME.=,E9.2,/,
     1  11H    X=0     ,11H    X=0.2   ,11H    X=0.4 ,
     2  11H    X=0.6   ,11H    X=0.8   ,11H    X=1.0,
        WRITE(NO,2)(U(I),I=1,N,2)
2       FORMAT(6E11.3)
        RETURN
        END
```

FORSIM VI

This system, which was developed in evolutionary fashion at the Chalk River Nuclear Laboratories by the Atomic Energy of Canada and described by Carver [31] is also based on FORTRAN IV and subroutine oriented. As in DSS/2, the method-of-lines is used and the user can select from a variety of integration algorithms including Gear's method. A wider variety of partial differential equations can readily be handled, however, and there is provision for automatically providing discretization in space, using various types of finite difference approximations, as well as cubic spline approximations. For relatively simple problems, the user is required to prepare only one subroutine – UPDATE. The control card structure of FORSIM then takes the following form.

JOB,BXXX–name/proj.	Job Account Card.
FTN	Compile UPDATE Routine, object code to file LGO.
ATTACH,FORSIM.	Access FORSIM control package.
COPYL,FORSIM,LGO,EXEC.	Merge FORSIM and LGO on file EXEC.
RETURN,FORSIM,LGO	Release FORSIM and LGO
ATTACH,FORSIM,CY=1.	Access FORSIM Library.
LIBRARY(FORSIM)	Declare FORSIM Library
EXEC.	Load and Execute.
7/8/9 (EOR)	
UPDATE Routine	

7/8/9
  FORSIM Data Deck   If Required
7/8/9
6/7/8/9 (EOF)

The update routine specifies the form of the equation to be solved and
is called at each integration step in the time domain to update the current
values of all derivatives. Consider the following example taken from the
FORSIM VI manual.

$$\frac{\partial u}{\partial t} = c\,\frac{\partial^2 u}{\partial x^2} \tag{6.20}$$

spatial range $0 < X < 1.0$, 11 points
initial conditions $U = 1.0$
boundary conditions $U(1) = U(N) = 0$
diffusion coefficient $C = 1.0$

The UPDATE subroutine for this problem is:

```
          SUBROUTINE UPDATE
C
C         SECTION 1 – STORAGE
C
          COMMON/INTEGT/U(11)
          COMMON/DERIVT/UT(11)
          COMMON/DERVX/UX(11)
          COMMON/DERVXX/UXX(11)
          COMMON/RESERV/T/CNTROL/INOUT
C
C         SECTION 2 – INITIAL CONDITIONS AND CONTROLS
C
          IF(T.NE.0)GO TO 100
          C=1.
          NPOINT=11
          NPDE=1
          DO 10 I=1, NPOINT
       10 U(I)=1.0
C
C         SECTION 3 – DYNAMIC SECTION
C
      100 CALL PARSET(NPDE,NPOINT,U,UT,UX,UXX)
C
C         SPECIFY EQUATION AT EACH SPATIAL POINT
C
```

```
      DO 110 I=1,NPOINT
  110 UT(I)=C*UXX(I)
C
      CALL PARFIN(NPDE,NPOINT,U,UT)
C
C     SECTION 4 - PRINTOUT
C
      IF(INOUT.NE.1)RETURN
      PRINT*,T
      PRINT*,U
      CALL FINISH(T,5.0,4HTIME)
      END
```

The routine has four sections; the first containing common block storage with additional blocks /DERVX/ and /DERVXX/ to ensure communication of the spatial derivatives $\partial u/\partial x$ and $\partial^2 u/\partial x^2$ respectively. The first derivative does not appear explicitly, but normally its associated block should be included. The second section sets up the initial values of U, C and two controls NPDE, the number of PDEs, and N, the number of points used. The dynamic section contains the components necessary to solve the PDEs and makes calls to two subroutines PARSET and PARFIN. PARSET establishes the boundary conditions and spatial derivatives. The equations are then stated in a DO loop and followed by a call to PARFIN for end processing. The fourth section prints the array U.

The above subroutine does not specify the integration method, the order of the spatial differentiation formulae, the spatial variable, or the boundary conditions; default values for all these have been used. The solution proceeds with Runge–Kutta–Fehlberg integration, three-point spatial formulae and boundary conditions $U(1) = U(N) = 0$. Any of these may be changed by including further common blocks and common block elements.

Other method of lines packages

Madsen and Sincovec [153] have developed a system called PDECOL. The spatial domain is discretized by the collocation method using B-splines as the basis functions. The user must specify the splines (breakpoints, degree of polynomials, order of continuity), but the collation points are chosen automatically. Gear's method is employed to integrate the system of ordinary differential equations with respect to time.

Hyman [100] at New York University developed a subroutine package which he calls MOL1D. As the name implies, this program is employed to solve parabolic equations in one space dimension using the method-of-lines. A variety of programs are provided for automatically discretizing the space domain using difference equations of various orders, as well as Fast Fourier Transformation approximations for periodic systems. Again, the Gear method is used to effect integration with respect to time.

From the Argonne National Laboratory comes a package called DISPEL described by Leaf *et al.* [136]. The program is intended primarily for the so-called kinetics-diffusion problems in one and two space dimensions which arise in studies of heat and mass transfer. Discretization of the space domain is achieved by using a Galerkin method in conjunction with B-splines of a specified order and smoothness. The resulting system of ordinary differential equations is integrated using a variation of the Gear method.

6.2.2.4   *Special-purpose packages for implementing the finite element method*

Most of the packages discussed in the preceding sections are intended to be general in purpose. That is, they are designed to facilitate the solution of field problems regardless of application area. Usually, a price in computing efficiency is paid for this feature. As a result, there have been intensive efforts in a number of fields of endeavour to develop software packages tailored specifically for users from a specific application discipline. This permits the inclusion of features and terminology that would have no place in a general-purpose package. The development of these packages has been particularly intensive in structural mechanics, most often employing finite element approximations.

Sample listing of finite element computer programs (copies can be obtained from COSMIC Computer Center, Barrow Hall, University of Georgia, Athens, GA 30601) includes:

ANSYS—Swanson Analysis Systems, Inc.

ASKA *(Automatic System for Kinematic Analysis)*—H. Argyris and H. A. Kamel

ASTRA *(Advanced Structural Analyzer)*—The Boeing Co.

BEST 3 *(Bending Evaluation of Structures)*—Structural Dynamics Research Co.

DAISY—H. A. Kamel for Lockheed Missile Space Co.

ELAS and ELAS 8 *(General-Purpose Computer Programs for Equilibrium Problems for Linear Structures)*—Jet Propulsion Lab.

FORMAT *(Fortran Matrix Abstraction Technique)*—McDonnell Douglas Corp.

MAGIC *(Matrix Analysis Via Generative and Interpretive Computations)*—Bell Aerosystems

MARC *(Nonlinear Finite Element Analysis Program)*—Marc Analysis Research Corp.

NASTRAN *(NASA Structural Analysis)*—Computer Science Corp., MacNeal–Schwendler Corp.

SAFE *(Structural Analysis by Finite Elements)*—Gulf General Atomic, Inc.

SAMIS *(Structural Analysis and Matrix Interpretive System)*—Philco Div., Ford Motor Co.

SAP *(A General Structural Analysis Program)*—E. L. Wilson, Univ. of California, Berkeley

SBO-38—Martin Marietta Corp.

SLADE *(A Computer Program for the Static Analysis of Thin Shells)*—Sandia Lab.

STARDYNE—Mechanics Research Inc.

STARS 2 *(Shell Theory Automated for Rotational Structures)*—Grumman Aircraft Engineering Co.

STRESS—M.I.T.

STRUDL (ICES) *(A Structural Design Language in Integrated Civil Engineering System)*—M.I.T.

6.3   DISCRETE EVENT MODELLING APPROACH

6.3.1   General remarks and definitions

A system can be considered as a collection of related entities, each characterized by attributes that may themselves be interrelated [68], e.g. a shop and a customer form a system. The shop-entity has the attributes of the bill, products and costs. The customer-entity has the attributes of budget and needs. The bill of the shop is related to the cost of the products, and these can be related to the needs and the budget of the customer. The relationships can be static or dynamic. For fixed product prices, the relationship between the amount of products and the bill to the customer is static. The bill varies according to his changing needs and budget.

The instantaneous values of the attributes of an entity define its state. A set of independent states of all entities is called the state of a system. The purpose of system simulation is to study its dynamic behaviour, i.e. the change of the output as function of the input changes during a period. This is achieved through the construction of an appropriate model for the system, its entities, attributes, and the interrelationships.

In order to classify the models suited for discrete event simulation, three important model-characteristics can be recognized:

(1) a model can be numerical or analytical;

(2) a model can be static or dynamic: when there are no dynamic relationships between the attributes or entities of a model, then its behaviour is invariant in time for constant inputs and the model is called static;

(3) a model can be stochastic or deterministic. In a deterministic model all relationships are described by fixed mathematical functions. In a stochastic model, entities can have random attributes, which cause probabilistic solutions.

Discrete event simulation essentially deals with numerically treated dynamic models, with a stochastic system definition.

In discrete event simulation, state changes occur only at specific instants of time, called events. Since the states of the entities remain constant between the events, there is no reason to account for this inactivity time in the modelling. Accordingly, the computer simulation programming languages use the "next event" approach to time advance. After all state changes have been made at a time corresponding to a particular event, the simulated time is advanced to the time of the next event, where the required state changes are again made. This process is continuously repeated. In this way, simulation is able to skip over the inactive time.

The concepts of event, process, and activity are especially important in building the model of a system. A process is a sequence of events, ordered in time; an activity is a collection of operations that transform the state of an entity. Discrete event simulation is hence concerned with the representation on a serial machine, of time-consuming activities which take place simultaneously or in parallel in the real world. No attempt is made to monitor continuously the progress of each activity from its inception to its termination; only the transitions from one activity to another are represented explicitly. The irony of the situation is that what consumes time in the real world, the activities, are not explicitly represented in a simulation program and so consume no computer time, whereas the instantaneous (zero time-consuming) transitions between activities, the events, must be represented by sections of a program and so do consume computer time.

6.3.2 World views

6.3.2.1 *Approaches in discrete event simulation*

Three major approaches to discrete modelling underlie the development of languages for discrete event simulation. While it was recognized that these approaches represented distinct decomposition methodologies (so-called "world views"), it was only recently that an attempt was made to set down clearly the underlying formalisms [127]. These formalisms appear under the names "discrete event", "activity scanning" and "process interaction".

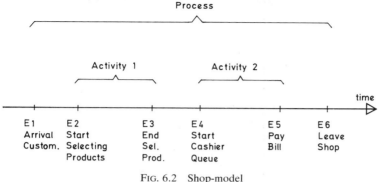

Fig. 6.2   Shop-model

The world views have serious implications towards the model-builder, and also towards the simulation language.

The three concepts are illustrated in Fig. 6.2 for the shop-model. The figure refers to three alternative ways to build-up a discrete event model [127]:

—The event scheduling approach gives the complete description of the steps that occur when an individual event takes place.
—The activity scanning approach emphasizes a review of all activities in a simulation, to determine which can be begun or terminated, each time an event occurs.
—The process-interaction approach is based on the progress of an entity through a system, from its arrival event to its departure event.

The development of discrete event simulation languages is usually based on the implementation of one of these three concepts. SIMSCRIPT [40] and GASP [131] use the event scheduling approach, ECSL [36] is an activity based language. GPSS [103] and SIMULA [223] use the process-interaction approach.

6.3.2.2   Conceptual modelling strategies

The three concepts introduced above give rise to various simulation languages, from which the user has to select the most appropriate one for his purpose. This is illustrated below, where the implementation of the different modelling strategies is considered. As an example, the event-driven, activity scanning, and process-oriented versions of the cashier queue model are used (see Fig. 6.2).

event 1	t1
event 2	t2
event 3	t3
. . .	. . .
event n	tn

FIG. 6.3a   Event approach of the cashier queue

Discrete event formalism

Here events are explicitly scheduled. In the simulation language implemen-tation, event-functions are realized by event routines and the events are scheduled by placing them in accordance with the event-notice, on the future event list. The event approach of the cashier queue is described in Fig. 6.3 There are two events, E4 and E5, corresponding to the arrival and the departure at the cashier queue.

Activity-scanning formalism

In contrast to the previous approach, the activity scanning requires that events be implicitly scheduled. Here the state transition is expressed as a set of functions called activities, each having an activity condition and an action (Fig. 6.4). At every time step the conditions are scanned in some fixed order, and the first condition found to be true causes the immediate execution of its associate action-segment. This scanning, testing, and execution continues until there are no conditions true in the resulting state. Then and only then, the model is advanced to the next time step. The cashier service activity can be represented by Fig. 6.4. The main difference between activity scanning and event-driven simulation appears when there are several activities. Then, whenever time is advanced to the next event, all activities are scanned to determine which activities can be executed. The event-scheduling approach requires that all the operations in an activity that transforms the state of the model, be scheduled as events for

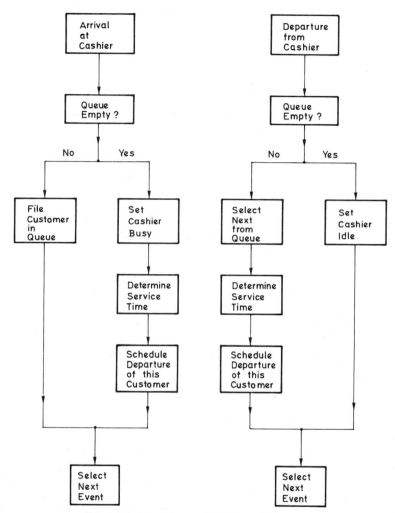

FIG. 6.3b   Event approach of the cashier queue

execution. As the number of activities grows, so does the number of scheduled events and, accordingly, the computer overhead in creating and updating the list of future events. In activity scanning however, the future event list is replaced by a logical checking of each transaction in the model, at each time advance, for the required event-scheduling steps.

Both approaches have their advantages. When there are few activities, but many arrivals, an event scheduling language will be more appealing than

act. 1	c1
act. 2	c2
act. 3	c3
. . .	. . .
act. n	cn

FIG. 6.4a   Activity-scanning approach of the cashier queue

the activity scanning approach, based on the fact that fewer activities call for fewer events, and that the limited information available in the activity-scanning model requires repeated scans to guarantee that all possible state changes occur. On the other hand, when a model can be split up into many activities, the overhead of the future event list can be replaced by a faster scan of all possible activities, at each time step.

Process-interaction formalism

Conceptually this formalism can be looked upon as a combination and a refinement of the above formalisms. A process is a set of activities which are mutually exclusive, at most one can be activated at one time, and connected in the sense that the termination of one activity enables the initialization of another in the set. From Fig. 6.2 it is noted that the process is a collection of events that describes the total history of a customer progress through the shop. Since customers arrive at different times, it is clear that the system behaviour is described by a collection of processes, one for each arrival, some of which may overlap. The process interaction approach modelling stresses the interaction between these processes in describing a system. Again referring to the cashier service facility, the process-interaction of this model is illustrated in Fig. 6.5.

In contrast to the two other approaches, here time may elapse in the model. To solve conflicts between overlapping processes, the process-interaction approach uses wait and delay statements in both conditional and unconditional contexts [68]. In Fig. 6.5 the use of these statements is

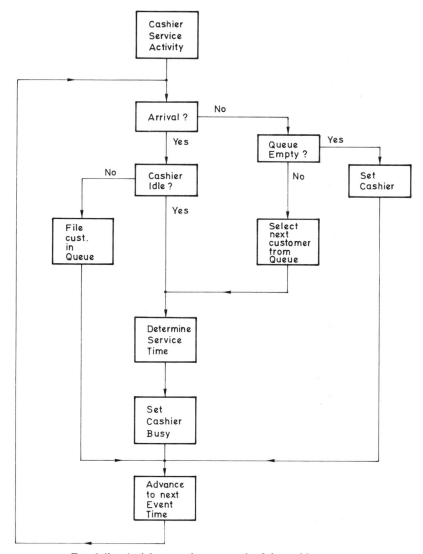

Fig. 6.4b   Activity-scanning approach of the cashier queue

illustrated, "WAIT" being a conditional one and "ADVANCE" an unconditional one. The unconditional "ADVANCE" statement shares a common characteristic with the "SCHEDULE" statement of the event-driven approach. There is a difference, however; each flowchart in the event-scheduling approach represents one event, in contrast to the flow-

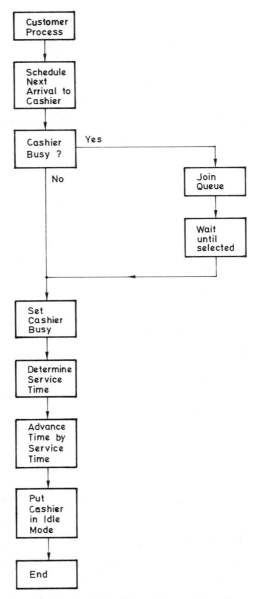

FIG. 6.5   Process-interaction of the cashier queue

charts in the process-interaction approach, which include several events. Therefore, the scheduled event in Fig. 6.5, generated by the "ADVANCE" statement, contains a re-entry or activation point, to which the simulation returns when it selects this event for processing. This point is the location of the statement following the "ADVANCE" statement.

On the other hand, the "WAIT-UNTIL" statement (Fig. 6.5) schedules a re-entry into the flowchart when the job is selected for service. This conditional scheduling procedure, which has to rely on some logical checking, bears much resemblance with the activity scanning approach. GPSS, which uses the process-interaction approach, offers a good example of how conditional and unconditional events are handled. The language has a list of future events (Future Event Chain) and has also a list of conditional events (Current Event Chain). After the execution of all events scheduled at a specific time from the Future Event Chain, it scans the list of current events, executing those tasks which are then possible. This scanning proceeds until no more events can be executed. Then the time is advanced to the next event on the Future Event Chain.

6.3.3 Simulation of system behaviour described by parallel processes

We consider a system of parallel processes which communicate or co-operate with each other. Processes can co-operate to jointly provide a system function, as is the case in distributed systems or in hardware systems consisting of a number of asynchronously operating units. In order to synchronize their activities, co-operating processes must communicate, and there must be some synchronization mechanisms. Cases also exist where processes may communicate without the intention to co-operate, e.g. if they compete for certain resources, as can be found in operating systems.

Inter-process communication necessitates some synchronization mechanism too, usually for the purpose of providing mutual exclusion of shared-data access. Another form of inter-process communication can be given by a mechanism by which a program flow alteration in one process is determined by the state of a global variable (a signal) that is changed by another process.

A typical example of a synchronization mechanism for inter-process co-operation is that a process puts itself into the "wait" state, to wait for another process to reach a certain state. Last but not least, synchronization can simply be achieved via time. "Synchronization via time" means that a "consumer" process, which activates a "producer" process to have a service rendered by the latter, knows the execution time of the producer. In this case, the consumer process may just execute a delay statement in order to allow the producer enough time to render the requested service.

The notion of a process implies a sequence of state changes over time. Thus, synchronization by awaiting a certain state assumed by another process, as well as synchronization via time, both necessitate the state of all processes of the system to be observed over time. Hence, contrasting with the event list driven simulation discussed in the preceding section, in Parallel Process Simulation (PPS) we have the notion of running time. On the other hand, the system states are not observed at equidistant time instants, as is the case in continuous system simulation, but at specific "points of interest". A point of interest is reached whenever a process state must be tested, or an explicit synchronization statement is to be executed in one of the processes.

To allow for the simulation of parallel processes in hardware, firmware, operating system software and distributed system software, an elaborate PPS system called APL∗DS (APL used for Design and Simulation) has been developed and implemented at the Technical University of Berlin [79]. There is hardly any room for interactivity in the classic discrete event simulation systems based on stochastic models (e.g. SIMSCRIPT, GPSS, SIMULA). There is no notion of running time, over which state changes could be observed. Parallel Process Simulation, on the other hand, is somewhere in the middle between the highly interactive CSSLs and the non-interactive discrete event simulation. APL∗DS allows any number of parallel-executable processes to be declared, and it provides a host of mechanisms for inter-process co-operation, communication and synchronization. These mechanisms can be used by the programmer to implement policies of his choosing, e.g. monitors, WAIT-SEND constructs, etc. The only built-in policy is the INITIATE-EVENT-CAUSE construct for inter-process co-operation based on the consumer-producer model (see Section 8.4.3.2). Table 6.2 shows all process declaration and control constructs which APL∗DS provides. These constructs are instrumental

—to introduce co-routine and parallel process behaviour into a language (APL) whose "native" program flow control mechanism is solely that of subroutine calls, and,

—to allow the simulator to schedule the flow of activities of a simulation program properly.

Readers familiar with APL will notice that the "trick" by which this is made possible is to let any declaration or control statement begin with →, i.e., the APL jump command [77].

We call any invocation of one of the constructs listed in Table 6.2 a break point (the break points are identical with the "points of interest" mentioned above).

In order to determine the "process time", that is, the time associated

TABLE 6.2   Process declaration and control constructs of APL*DS

Clause	Purpose
→FUNC	PROCEDURE HEAD
→ENDFUNC	PROCEDURE END
→CALL	PROCEDURE CALL
→RET	PROCEDURE RETURN
→GOTO	UNCONDITIONED JUMP
→IF . . . →DOTO . . . (→ELSE) . . . →FI	CONDITIONED BRANCHING
→CASE . . . →ESAC	ALTERNATIVE BRANCHING
→REPEAT . . . →UNTIL	ITERATION CLAUSE
→FOR . . . FROM . . . TO . . . →ROF	REPETITION CLAUSE
→DECLARE	OPENS DECLARATIVE PART OF PROCESS
→PROCESS	OPENS PROCEDURAL PART OF PROCESS
→FOREVER	REITERATES PROCESS EXECUTION
→END	TERMINATES PROCESS EXECUTION
→PAR	PARALLEL EXECUTION OF OPERATIONS
→ON	SWITCHES SIGNALS AND STATE INDICATORS ON OR OFF,
→OFF	RESPECTIVELY
→WAIT	WAIT FOR SIGNAL TO BECOME TRUE
→LOCK	CRITICAL SECTION LOCK
→FREE	CRITICAL SECTION UNLOCK
→INIT . . . →EVENT . . . →CAUSE	INTER-PROCESS CO-OPERATION CONSTRUCT BASED ON THE CONSUMER-PRODUCER MODEL

with the state of a process, the simulator must do time bookkeeping for each process. This is accomplished by accumulating the execution time of the statements of the process. In APL*DS, process time bookkeeping is based on the scheme the programmer must specify for each program segment between two break points a time estimate for the execution of the segment (the programmer may specify a lower and upper bound, in which case the system generates a random number uniformly distributed between these bounds). A DELAY statement is now an operation which does nothing but add a certain amount to the time bookkeeping of the process. Therefore, a DELAY statement affects scheduling only indirectly (by the time it "consumes"); unlike the event-list-driven simulation, where a DELAY statement causes suspension of the process in which it occurs and, therefore, must explicitly reschedule the reactivation of the process. This example clearly illustrates the difference between parallel process simulation, as discussed in this section, and event-list-driven simulation, namely that only in the former case we have the explicit notion of process time.

Besides the process time, there is a second time associated with each process, called the "breaking time", designating the process time at which the process has reached a break point. Consequently, the clock measuring the breaking time of a process is advanced from break point to break point, whereas the clock measuring the process time is advanced whenever the next execution time specification is encountered in the sequence of process activities (program statements).

During a simulation run, scheduling of activities is performed on the basis of a process-sequencing list which contains activation records that include information identifying a process and its breaking time. The activation records in the process sequencing list are ordered according to the processes' breaking time. In order to fulfil its control function with respect to the piecemeal execution of parallel, interacting processes, the APL∗DS scheduler design is based on what we call the essential precedence principle. This principle stipulates: "No process is permitted to change the value of a state variable, until all other processes of the simulation environment which are lagging behind in their process time have been given the opportunity to examine that value".

The essential precedence principle is guaranteed by a policy according to which, prior to the time a process changes a state variable attribute, all other processes of the simulation lagging behind in their process time are given control first. This policy is implemented by combining the following strategies:

—observation of the simulation time as the minimum of all breaking times;
——"double execution" of the breaking points.

Note that by "state variable" we denote global variables such as signals or semaphores which may affect program flow alteration, or "synchronization by wait" in a process. In the following the mode of operation of the scheduler is discussed in more detail.

The user of the APL∗DS system starts a simulation run by the statement pair:

SIMULATE   '⟨list of names of all processes involved in the simulation⟩'
UPTO   ⟨time limit⟩   COMMENCE   '⟨list of names of processes to be initiated⟩'.

The first statement invokes the simulator and enables it to create the appropriate process-sequencing list. The second statement allows the user to set an upper limit for the simulation time. It also leads to the entry of the first activation records into the process-sequencing list.

At the beginning of a simulation run, the process times and breaking times of the processes listed as argument of the COMMENCE statement are initialized to zero and, consequently, the simulation time is zero too. Whenever from now on the simulation time is set to a new value (including zero), all the processes in the sequencing list whose breaking time equals the (new) simulation time are selected by the scheduler for reactivation. That is, without changing the simulation time, the scheduler reactivates one process after the other, in an order as given by the reactivation precedence rule. Each reactivated process runs uninterruptedly until it reaches its next break point. Whenever a process is reactivated, the scheduler deletes the corresponding record from the process-sequencing list.

In the standard co-routine mechanism, the execution of a suspended co-routine is resumed at the point following the one where it was suspended. This is not so in the case of a "break" of an APL*DS process. Here, a suspended process is reactivated at the same point where it was suspended (the break point). Therefore, it appears as if the break point is executed twice. In fact, however, the "double execution" of break points represents two phases in the execution of a synchronization or program flow alteration statement.

The first phase takes place when the break point is encountered. All that happens in this phase is that the breaking time is updated and a corresponding reactivation record is entered into the process-sequencing list, provided the breaking time does not exceed the time limit specified for the simulation. From the viewpoint of process synchronization this phase has no effect. Thus it may be skipped if the breaking time equals the simulation time.

In the second phase, the control statement associated with the break point is actually executed. As a result, the process involved may
—terminate execution if the control statement is →END;
—suspend execution if the control statement is →WAIT, →EVENT, or →LOCK, in connection with the false attribute of the state variable tested;
—resume execution if the control statement is one of the remaining statements.

The decision which process to reactivate next is made by the scheduler, first of all according to the breaking times in the reactivation records. However, the ordering of the reactivation records is only a partial ordering, as there may be several reactivation records with the same breaking time. In this case the scheduler decides according to the reactivation precedence rule, which states that those processes whose break points correspond with one of the other control constructs that examine signal state attributes are activated last. These control constructs are: →WAIT, →IF, →CASE, →UNTIL, →LOCK, →EVENT. That is, before any of these control statements is executed, other processes awaiting reactivation at the same breaking time, in order to execute one of the state attribute changing constructs, are given precedence over the state attribute examining constructs. State attribute changing control constructs are: →ON, →OFF, →FREE, →CAUSE. The scheduler does not discriminate between the members of each class, that of state changing constructs and that of state examining constructs, respectively.

The following three properties of the scheduling policy ensure that no state variable used in a process for program flow alteration or synchronization can be changed until all other interacting processes have been given a chance to examine it, namely:
—the state of a signal can be modified only by an appropriate control construct or synchronization construct;
—no process can have a process time smaller than the simulation time;
—the execution of any synchronization primitive happens only when the simulation time equals the process time of the process which executes it.

In the course of a simulation, the processes involved can switch between the following six states:

Dormant: a process is dormant before it has been initiated or after it has completed execution. A dormant process is disconnected from the clock. With respect to the simulation it is "unused".

Running: a process under execution is said to be running. A running process is connected to the clock and thus consumes simulation time. With respect to the simulation it is "productive".

Blocked: a blocked process waits for the blocking condition to become true. In that state it is connected to the clock and consumes simulation time. With respect to the simulation it is "idle".

Advanced: a process is advanced when its process time is greater than the simulation time. An advanced process is temporarily disconnected from the clock until the other processes have caught up. With respect to the simulation it is "suspended" and thus consumes no simulation time.

Ready: a process is ready when its process time equals the simulation time. A process in the ready state is waiting for the scheduler to put it into the running state. With respect to the simulation a ready process is "suspended" and consumes no simulation time.

Terminated: a process is terminated when its process time has reached the simulation time limit. With respect to the simulation a terminated process is "suspended" and consumes no simulation time.

Figure 6.6 depicts the possible transitions between the six states as well as the synchronization statements and time conditions that cause the transitions.

In PPS there is the notion of running time over which state changes of the processes could be observed. However, as the simulation time is not represented by a "time count", i.e., a clock which is incremented at equidistant time instants, a diagram showing the state which the processes assume over time can be plotted only after termination of a simulation run. In a PPS one may be interested also in some statistical data, such as the percentage of time during which a process was waiting for another process, was idle for the inavailability of a resource, or was performing a service requested by some other process, etc.

The APL*DS system comprises to this end a report generator which

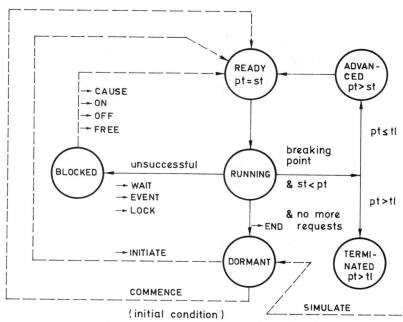

FIG. 6.6 Possible transitions between the six states as caused by the listed synchronization statements and time conditions; pt: process time (breaking time); st: simulation time; tl: time limit; —— transition caused by the process itself; ---- transition caused by other interacting processes

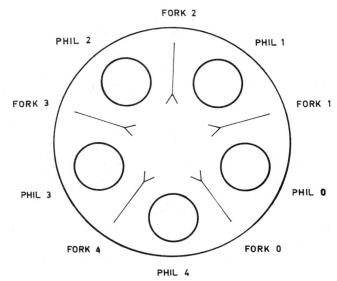

FIG. 6.7   Illustration of the "dining philosophers problem"

automatically collects certain significant data during a simulation run and reports them afterwards, in graphical form of in the form of a table.

As a simple example for a parallel process simulation, we consider the "dining philosophers problem", which is a classical example for resource contention, e.g. in operating systems. Five "philosophers" are sitting

```
                    PHIL0
        [1]     DECLARE
        [2]     SIGNAL'EATP0;THINKP0'
        [3]     SEMAPHORE'FORK0;FORK1'
        [4]     PROCESS
        [5]     ON'THINKP0'
        [6]     DELAY 10 2   PHILO THINKS
        [7]     OFF'THINKP0'
        [8]     LOCK'FORK0'
        [9]     LOCK'FORK1'
       [10]     ON'EATP0'
       [11]     DELAY 20 1   PHILO EATS
       [12]     OFF'EATP0'
       [13]     FREE'FORK1'
       [14]     FREE'FORK0'
       [15]     FOREVER
```

FIG. 6.8   Program text representing one of the five "dining philosophers"

385

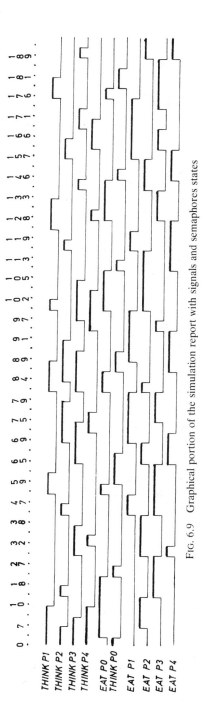

Fig. 6.9 Graphical portion of the simulation report with signals and semaphores states

REPORT
TIME LIMIT IS = 200
SIMULATION TIME IS = 197

*** PROCESS: PHIL0 ⟨=⟩ P.INDEX=1
SIGNALS: EATP0 (S.I=9), THINKP0 (S.I=10),
ACTUAL INVOKING PROCESSINDEX : 1 ⟨=⟩ SIMULATION STARTED
WAITING INVOKING PROCESS INDEX:
P.LINE = 9 , P.STATE = BLOCKED   , FROM TIME =197
P.TOTAL WAITING TIME = 100 , P.TOTAL ACTIVE TIME = 97
PROCESS UTILIZATION : P.UF = 1 , P.WF= 0.5076142132
P.NUMBER OF COMPLETIONS = 6

*** PROCESS: PHIL1 ⟨=⟩ P.INDEX=2
SIGNALS: EATP1 (S.I=11), THINKP1 (S.I=0),
ACTUAL INVOKING PROCESS INDEX : 1 ⟨=⟩ SIMULATION STARTED
WAITING INVOKING PROCESS INDEX :
P.LINE = 9 , P.STATE = BLOCKED   , FROM TIME =181
P.TOTAL WAITING TIME = 98 , P.TOTAL ACTIVE TIME = 99
PROCESS UTILIZATION : P.UF = 1 , P.WF=0.4974619289
P.NUMBER OF COMPLETIONS = 5

*** PROCESS: PHIL2 ⟨=⟩ P.INDEX=3
SIGNALS: EATP2 (S.I=12), THINKP2 (S.I=1),
ACTUAL INVOKING PROCESS INDEX : 1 ⟨=⟩ SIMULATION STARTED
WAITING INVOKING PROCESS INDEX :
P.LINE = 12 , P.STATE = BEYOND LIM. , AT TIME = 204
P.TOTAL WAITING TIME = 78 , P.TOTAL ACTIVE TIME = 126
PROCESS UTILIZATION : P.UF = 1 , P.WF= 0.3823529412
P.NUMBER OF COMPLETIONS = 6

*** PROCESS: PHIL3 ⟨=⟩ P.INDEX=4
SIGNALS: EATP3 (S.I=13), THINKP3 (S.I=2),
P.LINE = 8 , P.STATE = BLOCKED   , FROM TIME=192
P.TOTAL WAITING TIME = 60 , P.TOTAL ACTIVE TIME = 137
PROCESS UTILIZATION : P.UF = 1 , P.WF= 0.3045635279
P.NUMBER OF COMPLETIONS = 7

*** PROCESS: PHIL4 ⟨=⟩ P.INDEX=5
SIGNALS: EATP4 (S.I=14), THINKP4 (S.I=3),
ACTUAL INVOKING PROCESS INDEX : 1 ⟨=⟩ SIMULATION STARTED
WAITING INVOKING PROCESS INDEX :
P.LINE = 7 , P.STATE = BEYOND LIM. , AT TIME = 207
P.TOTAL WAITING TIME = 99 , P.TOTAL ACTIVE TIME = 103
PROCESS UTILIZATION : P.UF = 1 , P.WF= 0.4732608596
P.NUMBER OF COMPLETIONS = 6

FIG. 6.10   Textual portion of the simulation report on statistical summaries

around a table, each one alternating between thinking and eating. In front of each philosopher, there is a plate of spaghetti. There are, however, only five forks on the table, one between every two plates (Fig. 6.7). For a philosopher to eat his spaghetti he must use both forks that are adjacent to his plate. No forks are needed for a philosopher to pursue his main occupation, which is to think.

In our simulation, we have five processes, PHIL0 through PHIL4, that are synchronized by pairs of semaphores (FORKi, FORKj), $j = (i + 1)$ mod 5, $0 \leqslant i \leqslant 4$. Associated with each philosopher is also a pair of signals, (EATPi, THINKPi), $0 \leqslant i \leqslant 4$, to indicate the length of time when PHILi is thinking or eating, respectively. APL$*$DS provides the capability for the user to write a "generic process" and then have any desired number of instances of this process created by the system (with different names and different parameter values). This feature is exploited to generate the five processes, PHIL0 through PHIL4.

The program text of one of the five processes is listed in Fig. 6.8. Figure 6.10 gives an example of a report generated by the report generator on a simulation run. Note that deadlocks are avoided by the "randomization" of access time and access duration to the resources (the forks). This is a common measure employed quite often to mitigate the effects of resource contention, e.g. bus contention in a distributed system.

As Fig. 6.9 demonstrates, the "philosophers" are not only concurrent but truly parallel processes (more than one process can be running at a given time) and it is left to the user's judgement of a philosopher's endeavour whether he considers eating or thinking to be the "productive phase".

Note that the user writes only one "generic process", of which the system then generates the five instances.

In Chapter 6, support languages for the simulation of systems governed by ordinary and partial differential equations, as well as discrete events, have been discussed. The state of the art is in continuous evolution. This is not only the case for the software aspects, but also for the hardware. The latter aspect will be discussed in the next chapter.

7. Hardware trends and their impact on simulation

7.1 INTRODUCTION

Prior to World War II numerical treatment of problems was done with the aid of mechanical calculators or using a variety of analog techniques. Stimulated by military requirements during World War II, the first modern electronic digital computers began to make their appearance in the late 1940s and early 1950s. During that pioneering period a number of different approaches to digital computer organization and digital computing were investigated. Primarily as a result of the constraints imposed by the then-available electronics technology, the designers of digital computers soon focused upon the concept of computer system architecture championed by Dr John von Neumann and first implemented in the computer constructed for the Institute of Advanced Studies at Princeton. Because of the pervasiveness of the von Neumann architecture in digital computers during the 1950s and 1960s, most numerical analysts and other computer users concentrated their efforts on developing algorithms and software packages suitable for computers of that type. Virtually all the algorithms and numerical techniques discussed in this text are an outgrowth of that era of the computer field.

The large and powerful digital computers, which came into use in the late 1960s and 1970s, included numerous modifications and improvements over the computers of the earlier generation. However, most of these were relatively "transparent" to the programmer, affecting the speed and sometimes the precision of the computations without demanding any serious re-evaluation or restructuring of the algorithms or programs. It was not until the mid 1970s that there appeared classes of digital computers which differed from the von Neumann architecture so radically that the need for new algorithmic approaches became apparent. Of particular importance in this connection was the introduction of the techniques of multiprocessing and of pipelining in digital computer system design. It is the purpose of this chapter to provide a perspective on the potential impact of these major innovations in digital computer system design upon the development of simulators.

7.2 THE VON NEUMANN ARCHITECTURE

Though differing in some details, the digital computers manifesting the by-now classic von Neumann architecture are generally organized along the lines shown in Fig. 7.1 and are well described in standard textbooks [92, 214].

A key feature of the von Neumann organization is the "bottle-neck" represented by the memory buffer. In effect, only one item of information at a time may be read out of memory, and only one arithmetic operation may be performed at any one time. All algorithms and programs must therefore specify a sequence of operations to be performed one at a time. For that reason, computers using a von Neumann organization perform sequential computation.

The overwhelming acceptance of the von Neumann architecture also had a profound affect upon the design of programming languages and programming systems. Starting with the development of FORTRAN in the 1950s and continuing with ALGOL and PL/1 in the 1960s, all major programming languages intended to facilitate the solution of numerical problems, were designed for procedural or sequential operation. That is, each of these languages is designed so as to carry out only a single arithmetic or logical operation at any one time, and it is up to the programmer to specify the appropriate sequence. The overwhelming majority of programs for the solution of partial differential equations are written in FORTRAN. This makes it relatively easy to transplant a program from one digital computer system to another, provided, however, that both computers manifest the von Neumann architecture.

7.3 MULTIPLE PROCESSING ELEMENTS

The term parallelism in automatic computation refers in its most general sense to the simultaneous execution of two or more operations by a computer system, something not possible in the von Neumann architecture. The present section is concerned with one approach to the attainment of parallelism, through the replication of one or more of the basic major functional units of the computer. Conventional digital processors contain a single control unit, a single arithmetic unit, and a single memory unit. Some recently-introduced computers, on the other hand, have two or more of

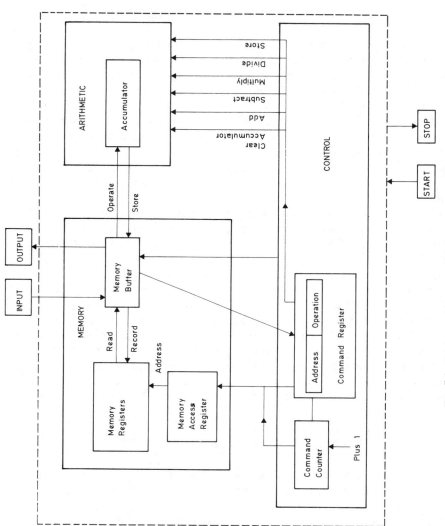

FIG. 7.1 Basic von Neumann digital computer architecture

these basic architectural units, which are arranged so that they can operate simultaneously, thereby increasing the system's computational speed and power.

In the past, parallel data processing was realized exclusively by means of a continuous-time data processor. For many years only the analog processor has been available as a parallel data processor. Because it has some basic properties which make it particularly suited to parallel data processing, it has been applied successfully, although analog computation has some well-known drawbacks. Examples of these basic properties are:

—parallel data transfer can be easily realized, because there is only one time set for both data transfer and data processing;
—the ratio between physical time and data processing time (time scale factor β) is fixed in the sense that this ratio is not influenced by the data processing so β can be easily changed;
—parallel, direct display of variables can easily be implemented because all variables are continuously available in parallel;
—the processor is very fast;
—there is one algorithm for the basic mapping "integration with respect to time" (state mapping);
—an instantaneous mapping is realized as a damped first-order state mapping with small time constant;
—the length of the propagation delay time depends on the kind of mapping.

Combining both analog and digital computer gave an even more powerful tool: the hybrid computer. There have been many attempts to digitize the analog part of the hybrid computer, resulting in a variety of so-called digital differential analysers (DDAs) [90, 201]. The DDA was not a real success because often its nature was too specialized. Many DDAs used incremental representation of the variables, which has the following disadvantages:

—no explicit variables available;
—the multiplication process has been transformed to addition;
—the architecture is too much directed to hardware savings;
—the approach is not simulation oriented.

Hybrid computers are still improving, as shown in Chapter 8, by the arrival of autopatch computers and microprocessor control of the analog and logic components (the Electronic Associates EAI 2000 computer).

The term multiprocessor on the contrary, is usually reserved for computer systems in which there are two or more processing elements, each with individual memory, arithmetic, and control. Moreover, all of these processing elements must have access to a large central memory so that they can all be working simultaneously on the same problem. The term "array of processing elements" is sometimes used to identify systems in which there is replication of memory and arithmetic, but not of control. Flynn [69] provides a widely-used technique for classifying such systems, while Enslow [61] presents a detailed survey of the many different implementations of this concept.

In a von Neumann type computer, at any instant there can be just a single command in the command register, and this command can effect an arithmetic or logical operation only upon the single word then resident in the accumulator. Such a machine organization is termed "single instruction stream–single data stream" (SISD).

An important class of digital computer systems is organized as shown in Fig. 7.2, where there are a number of processing elements each consisting of an arithmetic unit and a memory unit. The arithmetic and memory units are interconnected to form an array; hence, a structure of this type is sometimes termed an "array of processors" or an "array of processing elements". The control unit can activate any, or all, of the arithmetic units. Each active element of the array performs the same arithmetic or logic operation under command of the single control unit. Of course, each arithmetic element may be operating on different data in executing the

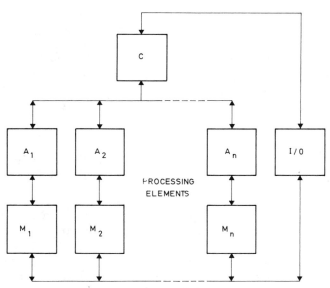

FIG. 7.2   SIMD parallel structure

instruction resident in the control unit. For this reason, this type of structure is termed "single instruction stream–multiple data stream" (SIMD).

SIMD computing systems were designed in the 1960s and early 1970s. The intent was to achieve high computing speeds, particularly in the treatment of partial differential equations by finite difference methods, without the need to replicate the relatively expensive control unit. The ILLIAC IV computer described in Section 7.5 is an example of this approach. With the advent of low-cost minicomputers and microcomputers, and the declining cost of digital hardware in general, replication of the control unit has become more and more feasible from the economic point of view. As a result, a wide variety of multiprocessor systems of the type shown in Fig. 7.3 have been constructed or proposed. Each element of the array of processors now includes a control unit, as well as an arithmetic and a memory unit. The elements of the array can therefore be fully-fledged independent digital computers, and the processing element can carry out a different arithmetic or logic operation. For this reason, systems of this type are termed "multiple instruction stream–multiple data stream" (MIMD). Systems of this type are discussed in Section 7.9.

The replication of the memory units in SIMD and MIMD computers is an important step towards overcoming the "bottle-neck" in von Neumann architectures. In many respects, each processing element can proceed

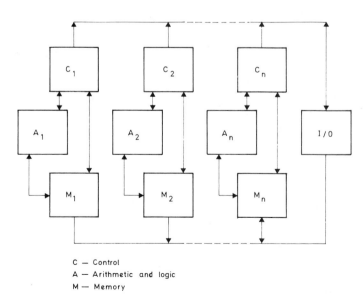

C — Control
A — Arithmetic and logic
M — Memory

FIG. 7.3   MIMD architecture

independently, thereby potentially effecting an appreciable increase in computing speed. Under these conditions, the major impediment to the realizing of the potential advantages of parallelism arises when it is necessary to exchange information between the various processing elements. The connectors, switching elements, and control circuits, which are employed to transfer data from one processing element to another, then act as effective constraints upon the computing speed. For this reason, multiprocessor systems are often classified in accordance with the manner in which the individual processing elements are interconnected. As discussed in detail by Enslow [61], three different approaches to interconnection can be recognized:

  (i) common bus;
 (ii) cross-bar switch;
(iii) multi-port memory.

In common bus multiprocessors, such as those shown in Figs. 7.2 and 7.3, the processing elements time-share common electrical connection paths. A

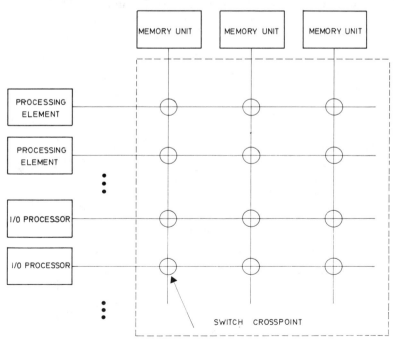

FIG. 7.4   Crossbar switch method for interconnecting processing elements and memory units

number of these may be provided to facilitate higher throughput rates, and to increase system reliability. Elaborate algorithms and hardware controllers must be provided to assure the achievement of the desired information flow.

In a cross-bar switching system, each arithmetic unit may be granted access to each memory unit through a switching matrix as shown in Fig. 7.4. Numerous transfers can therefore occur simultaneously. This provides greater flexibility in system design and utilization albeit at a considerably increased cost.

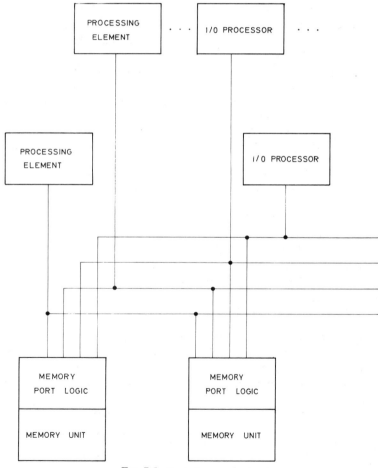

FIG. 7.5 Ported memory structure

Multi-port memory multiprocessors achieve an effect similar to that attained using a crossbar switching matrix. In this case the memory units themselves are equipped with hardware units to control all switching functions, so that each memory module can communicate directly with each of the arithmetic units, as shown in Fig. 7.5.

7.4 PIPELINING

The term "pipeline" is employed to designate parallelism of a different sort. A sequential computational procedure is broken down into stages, and separate hardware units are provided for carrying out the computations of each stage. When the pipeline is full, each hardware unit is engaged in processing different data, and as each completes its task, it passes the results of its computation to the next unit.

As an example of a typical pipelining application, consider the performance of floating-point addition. Assume that numbers are represented in floating-point form as shown in Fig. 7.6 and that it is desired to add the numbers 987 and 65.4. The floating point representation of these numbers is $(+0.9870 + 03)$ and $(+0.6540 + 02)$.

The sequential addition of these numbers involves four distinct operations:

(1) Modify one of the exponents so that the two numbers will have the same exponent.
$$(+.6540 + 02) \rightarrow (+.0654 + 03)$$
(2) Add the mantissas:
$$(+.9870) + (+.0654) \rightarrow + 1.0524$$
(3) Normalize:
$$(+1.0524 + 03) \rightarrow (+.10524 + 04)$$
(4) Round off the result:
$$(+.10524 + 04) \rightarrow (+.1052 + 04)$$

Each of these operations can be regarded as a separate stage and so can be performed by a separate hardware unit. Assume that the characteristics of the electronic circuits are such that the slowest of these operations requires less than 50 ns. It is then possible to pass data from one unit to the next and

FORMAT:	$\pm$	.	× × × ×	$\pm$	× ×
	SIGN OF MANTISSA	RADIX POINT	MANTISSA	SIGN OF EXPONENT	EXPONENT

FIG. 7.6   Format for floating-point number representation

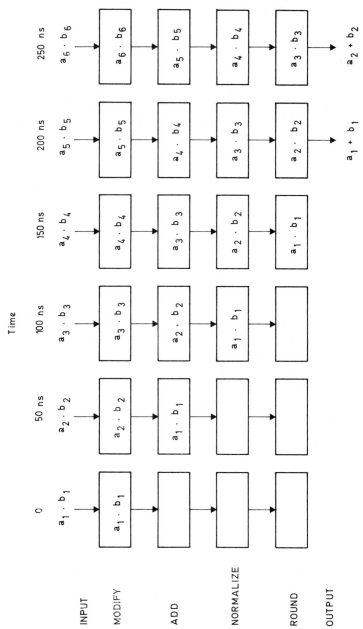

Time

FIG. 7.7   Operation of a pipeline adder

to commence work on a new pair of inputs every 50 ns. Once the pipeline is full, a new sum will appear at the output of the pipeline every 50 ns. This is illustrated in Fig. 7.7 where summations are to be performed on two streams of numbers $a_1, a_2, a_3, \ldots$ and $b_1, b_2, b_3, \ldots$. At time t = 0, the first pair of numbers to be added, a_1 and b_1, enter the pipeline. 200 ns later, the sum $a_1 + b_1$ emerges from the pipeline adder. At that time each element in the pipeline is simultaneously operating on a different pair of numbers. Provided that the streams a and b are sufficiently long to keep the pipeline filled for a substantial length of time, the pipeline adder provides the same throughput as a single adder with a 50 ns addition time, or four times as rapidly as a conventional adder.

Pipelining techniques are particularly effective in enhancing execution speeds when processing loops. In FORTRAN, the DO command is employed to perform identical computations on arrays of numbers. For example, the two statements

$$\text{DO } 100 \text{ I} = 1, 75$$
$$100 \text{ A(I)} = \text{B(I)} + 5$$

are employed in FORTRAN to define an elementary loop operation. Two arrays A and B are involved. In this example, the index I ranges from 1 to 75 in steps of 1. The effect is to add the number 5 to each element of array B and to store the result in array A. In carrying out such an operation using a von Neumann architecture, it is necessary to update the index after each computation and to expend an appreciable amount of computer time in loop control. By employing a pipelining approach, this "overhead" can be eliminated. The pipelining concept has been extensively implemented, and a wide variety of computing systems utilizing pipelines are described in a detailed survey by Ramamoorthy and Li [183]. Several so-called "supercomputer" systems employ several parallel pipeline processors. These include the STAR, the ASC, and the CRAY-1 computers discussed in Section 7.6. In matrix terminology, streams of numbers are termed vectors, and these pipeline computers are therefore referred to as vector processors.

7.5 ARRAYS OF PROCESSING ELEMENTS

One of the most widely heralded of the supercomputers to be proposed in the 1960s was intended primarily to help in solving the massive field problems arising in meteorology, seismology, and fluid dynamics. Evolving from the earlier Solomon computers, ILLIAC IV was developed at the University of Illinois and is now installed at the NASA-Ames Research

Center in California. Since becoming fully operational in 1975, it has served as the chief testing ground for the SIMD architectural concept. At the same time it has provided computer engineers with an insight into the formidable difficulties inherent in achieving adequate performance as described by Economidis [57], and by Thurber and Wald [219].

Initial plans for ILLIAC IV called for 256 parallel processing elements

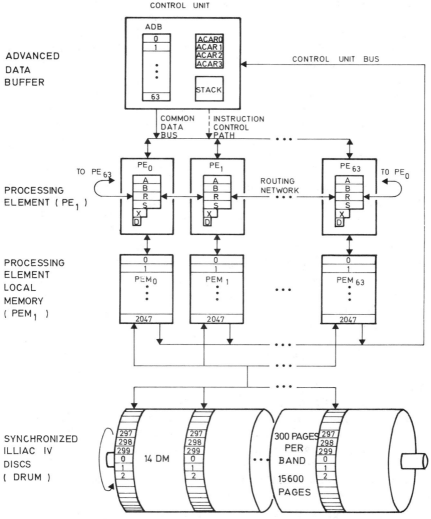

FIG. 7.8   Organization of ILLIAC IV

and four control units. The machine, as finally delivered by Burroughs Corporation, actually contains only one control unit and 64 processing elements. Figure 7.8 is a simplified diagram of the ILLIAC IV organization. In line with the SIMD concept, each parallel processing element has an arithmetic unit including the registers and logic necessary to execute a full set of instructions. In addition, each processing element has a separate fast semiconductor memory with 2048 64-bit registers.

The control unit is capable of executing some serial instructions, but most commands are transmitted to the processing elements. In the parallel mode, all processing elements are either executing a given instruction, or they are temporarily disabled by the control unit. The control unit also supervises the transfer of data between the various processing elements. The main memory of the system is a magnetic drum with a capacity of 16 million words, which can be accessed by all the processing elements. A number of other memory devices, including magnetic disks and a laser memory, provide back-up and establish a memory hierarchy. Distributed around the central memory is an array of mini- and midicomputers to facilitate communication with the external world and to perform other input–output operations. By means of the ARPA Network, the computer can be accessed via telephone lines by a large number of computer installations throughout the United States and the world. Unlike serial or sequential computer operation, parallel processing makes it indispensable that the programmer comprehend the architectural features of the machine, and takes these into account in designing his algorithms and programs. In most current applications, the 64 processing elements can be considered to comprise an 8×8 array, as shown in Fig. 7.9. Each processing element is connected only to its four nearest neighbours. Processing elements on the boundary of the array are connected to corresponding elements at the opposite boundary. Thus processing element 1 is connected to processing elements 57 and 64, as well as to elements 2 and 9. Data transfer between the processing elements and the magnetic drum memory is carried out in blocks of data, termed pages, each consisting of 1024 64-bit words. Walkden *et al.* [228] consider how some commonly-used algorithms for solving partial differential equations, can be advantageously modified for parallel processing, and provide a performance evaluation of ILLIAC IV including comparisons with large serial computers. They conclude that for problems of significant size, the speed advantage of ILLIAC IV compared to large serial computers, such as the IBM 360/195 or the CDC 7600, is three to four at best. Reasons for this disappointingly small speed ratio (considering the size and cost of ILLIAC IV) include:

—The time required to move blocks of data from the disk to the processing elements.

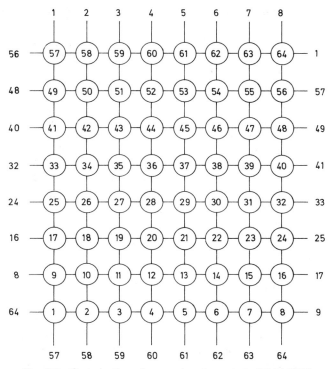

FIG. 7.9   Organization of processing elements in ILLIAC IV

—The need in many algorithms to pass data among processing elements which are not nearest neighbours (see Fig. 7.9).

—Difficulties in structuring data for storage and transfer, where the array of finite difference net points does not readily conform to the structure shown in Fig. 7.9. This includes situations in which nets substantially larger than 8 × 8 are to be handled, so that each processing element is required to carry out the calculations for a number of net points and situations, in which the finite difference net is not a square array of points.

—Shortcomings in the processing elements in carrying out arithmetic operations.

Hopkins [94] describes the application of ILLIAC IV to a complicated seismology problem, involving the solution of a hyperbolic partial differential equation in three dimensions. He reports attaining a speed-up of approximately 60 when comparing the ILLIAC IV solution to one obtained on a Univac 1108. The key to attaining this speed advantage lies in very careful database design and in the adoption of a sophisticated data management scheme, so as to minimize time lost in data transfers. Moreover, the finite difference grid selected was structured so as to conform as closely as possible to the organization of the ILLIAC IV processing elements.

Sameh and Cook [192] present a comprehensive survey of the use of parallel computers to treat systems of linear algebraic equations, updating an earlier comprehensive survey of all published numerical algorithms for vector and parallel computers up to 1974 compiled by Poole and Voight [177]. Particularly intensive efforts have been devoted to solving tridiagonal systems of algebraic equations using parallel processors. This work has particular application in treating partial differential equations in one-space dimensions, as well as in two- and three-dimensional systems using alternating direction algorithms.

7.6   VECTOR PROCESSORS

The technique of pipelining, briefly described in Section 7.4, has been used to a limited extent in a variety of sequential computers, e.g. such as the IBM 360/91, in a way that does not substantially modify the basic von Neumann architecture of these machines. In the mid 1970s, however, there appeared three "supercomputer" systems, which employed pipelines as major architectural elements and which therefore differed radically from classical architectural approaches. They are directed toward optimizing the processing of one-dimensional arrays of numbers, such as frequently arise in the solution of partial differential equations, and are therefore referred to as vector processors.

The general structure of the STAR-100 computer, manufactured by Control Data Corporation, is shown in Fig. 7.10, and described in considerable detail by Thurber [220]. This system is seen to be designed around two pipelined processors. Each of these contains a floating-point addition unit; one of them contains a multiply unit, while the other contains a divide unit. Buffering is the process of storing the results of a computation temporarily before passing them on to another structural element. Since the various elements in a pipeline may require different lengths of time to carry out their tasks, buffering is one of the principal problems encountered in the design of vector processors. In the STAR-100 system, the Write and Read buffers are employed to align the two vectors treated by the parallel pipeline processing units. There is also an instruction buffer which is replenished from memory. The memory banks of the STAR-100 contain 32 interleaved units of 2048 512-bit words, with expansion possible to

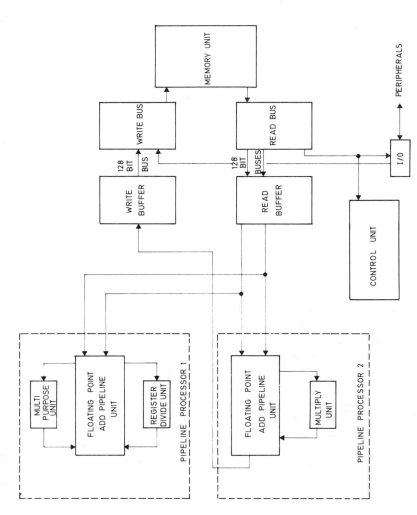

FIG. 7.10   Organization of the Control Data Corporation STAR-100

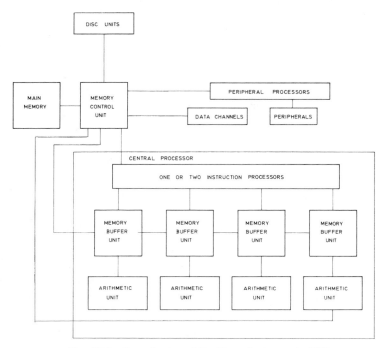

FIG. 7.11   Organization of the Texas Instruments ASC

twice that size. Considerable effort has gone into the preparation of software systems to facilitate the utilization of the STAR-100. These include a variety of FORTRAN extensions, making it possible to specify vector operations in a compact and efficient manner.

The design of the ASC (for Advanced Scientific Computer) manufactured by Texas Instruments, Inc. and also described by Thurber [220] is similar in many respects to the STAR-100. However, as shown in Fig. 7.11, the ASC system contains four identical parallel pipeline units. Each of these pipeline units contains pipeline hardware for floating-point and fixed-point addition and multiplication. When functioning in an optimum manner, these pipelines can produce a new result every 10 ns, corresponding to 100 million results per second. As in the STAR-100, an extended FORTRAN package has been developed to facilitate programming.

Unlike the STAR-100 and the ASC, which were designed principally for vector operation and which rely upon peripheral processors for sequential computing, the Cray-I system manufactured by Cray Research Inc. is designed for both scalar and vector operations. As described by Johnson [114] and shown in Fig. 7.12, CRAY-I contains both vector and scalar

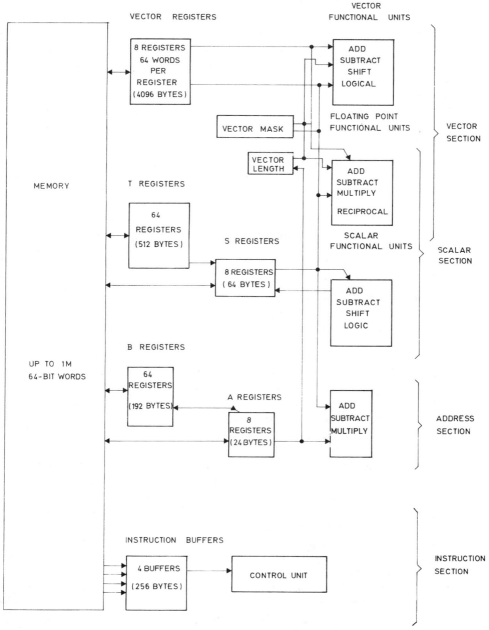

FIG. 7.12   Organization of the Cray research CRAY-1

sections, the latter serving for sequential computations. As in the case of the other vector processors, CRAY-I is highly effective in minimizing the "overhead" computations inherent in processing loops. In addition to its facility for non-vector processing, CRAY-I also has improved channels for communicating with memory, thereby avoiding so-called memory conflicts which arise in other vector processors. Vector processing is carried out with the aid of the eight vector registers, each containing 64 words. Fixed- or floating-point arithmetic operations are carried out using the pipeline ADD, MULTIPLY, and RECIPROCAL (divide) units. A new pair of operands can be accepted every 2.5 ns. The memory contains up to one million 64-bit words arranged in sixteen banks.

Although vector processors have been in use since the mid 1970s, at the time of writing no comprehensive theory for the design of algorithms for such computers has emerged. In fact, there are only very few reports of the solution of large and practical problems on such machines, and these usually employ adaptation of algorithms developed for serial processors. In constructing algorithms for vector processing, a basic aim is to perform the bulk of the computational task on one-dimensional arrays, i.e. on vectors. When the length of these vectors is relatively short, the overhead involved in initiating vector instructions and in waiting for the pipeline to become full, may well outweigh any advantages gained from vector processing, so that vector processor computers may actually be slower than competing serial computers. As the pipeline becomes longer (say 100 to 1000 elements), vector processors become more and more effective. Ortega and Voight [172] present a detailed review of various approaches to the solution of partial differential equations on vector computers. The discussion in the rest of this section is based upon their paper.

In the solution of elliptic partial differential equations, on serial computers, there is a great advantage in dealing with tridiagonal matrices, which have non-zero terms only on the main diagonal, and on the elements immediately adjacent to the main diagonal. This permits the utilization of the so-called tridiagonal algorithm to provide solutions for one-dimensional problems without iterations, and suggests the use of alternating direction methods for problems in two and three space dimensions. In the case of vector processors, on the other hand, no effective algorithms have as yet appeared to take full advantage of the special structure of tridiagonal matrices. For one-dimensional elliptic equations, so-called cyclic reduction techniques appear to be most effective. For problems in two and three dimensions, Jacobi iteration is often preferred to the Gauss-Seidel and the successive over-relaxation methods. By careful ordering of grid points and by clever programming techniques, alternating direction and successive over-relaxation methods can be successfully

implemented on vector processors, albeit without achieving any spectacu-
lar increase in speed. With regard to parabolic partial differential equations, comparisons of the relative effectiveness of various algorithmic
approaches to simple problems exist. Consider the one-dimensional diffusion equation.

$$\frac{\partial^2 u}{\partial x^2} = \frac{1}{\alpha} \frac{\partial u}{\partial t} \quad 0 < s < 1 \tag{7.1}$$

with initial and boundary conditions

$$u(0, x) = g(x) \tag{7.2}$$
$$u(t, o) = \beta \qquad u(t, 1) = \gamma$$

where α, β, and γ are constants. The simplest explicit solution method
characterized by

$$u_{j+1,l} = u_{j,l} + a(u_{j,l+1} - 2u_{j,l} + u_{j,l-1}) \, l = 1, \ldots N$$

where

$$a = \alpha \frac{\Delta t}{\Delta x^2} \tag{7.3}$$

and $u_{j,l}$ and $u_{j+1,l}$ refer to the current and succeeding time levels respectively, are most easily and directly handled on vector computers. The
length of the vector in this case is equal to the number of interior grid
points in the x domain, and five arithmetic operations are carried out on
each element of the vector. By contrast, vector computers are not nearly as
efficient for implicit schemes such as the Crank-Nicolson method.

$$u_{j+1,l} = u_{j,l} + a/2(u_{j+1,l+1} - 2u_{j+1,l} + u_{j+1,l-1}$$
$$+ u_{j,l+1} - 2u_{j,l} + u_{j,l-1}) \tag{7.4}$$

In this case, a tridiagonal system of algebraic equations must be solved at
each time level, which is not particularly easy using a vector processor. On
the other hand, equation (7.4) is computationally stable regardless of how
large Δt is, whereas stringent limits on Δt are imposed by stability considerations in the case of equation (7.3). Depending upon the desired accuracy and the parameter α, it may be necessary to take an uneconomically
large number of steps if the explicit method is used. The Dufort-Frankel
method

$$u_{j+1,l} = u_{j-1,l} + 2a(u_{j,l+1} - u_{j+1,l} - u_{j-1,l} + u_{j,l-1}) \tag{7.5}$$

is explicit, requiring only four vector operations per time step, and is also
unconditionally stable. Unfortunately, equation (7.5) is not computation-

TABLE 7.1   (Ortega and Voight [172])

	STAR-100 μs	CYBER 175 μs
Explicit (equation (7.3))		
N = 50	43	150
N = 1000	194	2500
Implicit (equation (7.4))		
N = 50	600	560
N = 1000	3900	11700
Dufort–Frankel (equation (7.5))		
N = 50	42	165
N = 1000	196	2800

ally consistent, so that the solution of the finite difference system does not necessarily approach the solution of equation (7.1) as Δx and Δt approach zero. Unless care is taken with the net spacings in the x and t directions, error terms proportional to $\partial^2 u/\partial t^2$ may appear in the solution. A comparison of the effectiveness of the CDC STAR-100 vector processor and the CYBER 175 serial computer in solving equation (7.1) using Equations (7.3), (7.4) and (7.5) is presented in Table 7.1. It is readily seen in all three cases, that the relative effectiveness of the vector processor is far greater for 1000 interior net points, than it is for 50 net points. In the case of 50 net points, almost 75% of the time for each vector operation is consumed by start-up, while start-up time drops to approximately 12% for 1000 interior points in the x domain. It can be seen that the times required for the two explicit methods characterized by equations (7.3) and (7.5) are very nearly identical, and far shorter than the times required by the implicit equation (7.4).

7.7 PERIPHERAL ARRAY PROCESSORS

In the late 1970s a number of manufacturers introduced a class of devices which they identified as "array processors". This designation is misleading, since the units are neither designed for the processing of multidimensional arrays of numbers, nor are they composed of arrays of processing elements as is the case in the ILLIAC-IV. As a class, they are intended to function as peripheral devices for conventional serial computers and, with the aid of internal parallelism, greatly to accelerate the solution of certain problems.

Array processors are generally structured as shown in Fig. 7.13. They employ a multipath bus structure which permits the simultaneous performance of fetches from a data memory, multiplication, and addition. Data to be processed are read into the peripheral processor by a host computer and subjected to a very rapid sequence of operations. Through the use of the latest solid-state circuitry, compact design, and extensive pipelining,

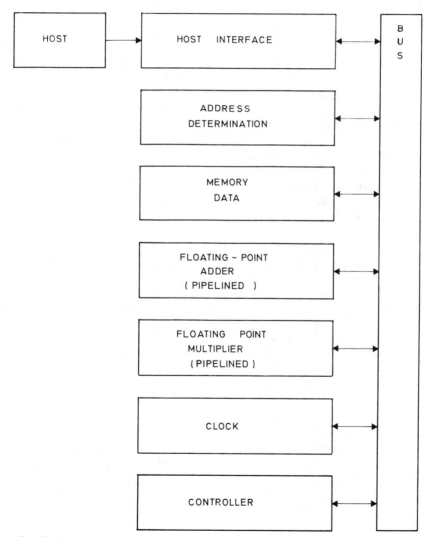

FIG. 7.13   General structure of array processors functioning as peripheral elements

these peripheral processors are able to exceed the speed of even the most powerful general purpose digital computers at a relatively modest cost. Manufacturers who market such array processors include IBM, Control Data Corporation, Data General Corporation, CSP Inc., Applied Dynamics Inc., and many others. Floating Point Systems Inc., which produces units designated as AP-120B and AP-190, delivered well over 500 such units prior to 1980, and thereby assumed a leadership position in this specialized field.

Figure 7.14 shows a block diagram of Floating Point Systems AP-120B, described by Wittmayer [233]. The system elements are interconnected by multiple paths so that transfers can occur in parallel. All internal floating-point data are 38 bits in width (10-bit exponent and 28-bit mantissa). The interface unit is designed especially for the host computer, which is usually a minicomputer, and is organized so that either I/O or direct memory access channels can be utilized for data transfer. Instruction and data transfers take place at a 6 MHz rate, corresponding to a cycle time of 167 ns. The operation of the unit is controlled by the execution of 64-bit instruction words which reside in the program memory. Additional control functions are provided by the S-PAD unit which performs integer address indexing, loop counting and other tasks required by specific algorithms. Addition is performed in two pipelined stages, each of which takes 167 ns. Multiplication is performed in three pipelined stages, each requiring 167 ns. The data memory unit is the primary data store for the AP-120B and has a cycle time of 333 ns, so that a new memory operation may be initiated every other machine cycle. To optimize the operation of the processor, it is necessary for the programmer to "look ahead" and initiate memory fetches prior to the actual time that arguments from the data memory are to be used in the calculations. The table memory unit employs more rapid and therefore more expensive circuitry, and as the name implies, is used to store data for table look-up. The DATA-PAD unit consists of two fast accumulator blocks, each with 32 floating-point locations. This unit serves primarily for the storage of intermediate results of computations.

During the 1970s the AP-120B and other peripheral array processors were used almost entirely for signal processing applications, particularly those arising in medical tomography and seismic data handling. Algorithms for the solution of partial differential equations remained to be developed. One possible approach to this problem has been reported by Dawson *et al.* [45] in the use of the AP-120B for the simulation of physical phenomena in plasma systems.

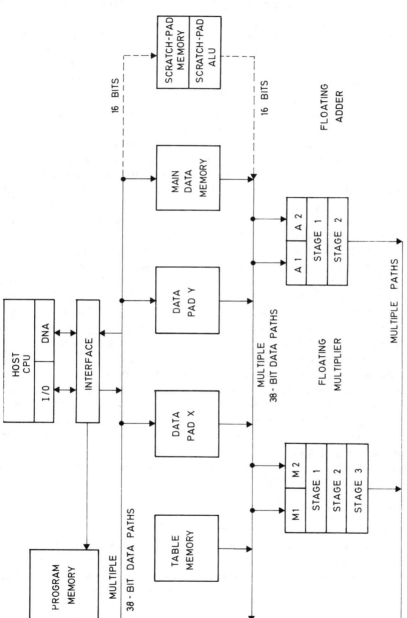

FIG. 7.14 Organization of the Floating Point Systems AP-120B

7.8   SIMULATION-ORIENTED PERIPHERAL ARRAY PROCESSORS

The AP-120B was designed primarily for signal processing. By contrast, the AD-10 manufactured by Applied Dynamics Inc. is a simulation-oriented peripheral processor intended primarily for the solution of systems of ordinary differential equations. As shown in Fig. 7.15 and described by Gilbert and Howe [76], this unit has a structure similar in many respects to that of other array processors. The multi-bus is a parallel high-speed bus composed of 16 data lines, 18 address lines, and several control lines, and supports 20 data and address transfers per microsecond. All transfers as well as all memory processor functions are synchronously controlled by 40 MHz master clock. In addition to the data memory and the pipelined arithmetic processors, the AD-10 also contains separate hardware units to permit memory mapping, break-point determinations in non-linear function generation by table look-up, and a number of other functions of importance in solving non-linear equations.

The AD-10 is unique among available peripheral processors in that it has a distributed program-control memory. Each functional unit has a separate instruction memory which controls its action during each clock cycle. Prior to a computer run, the host computer loads each of these program memories. The host interface controller couples the host computer to the AD-10, distributes the instructions to the appropriate processors, and loads data into the multi-port data memory. The memory is organized in pages of 4096 16-bit words, and each page is ported separately so that it may be addressed independently. The arithmetic processor contains two adders and one multiplier, as well as a number of temporary storage registers (Fig. 7.16). With the aid of the pipelining, this unit can perform 20 additions and 10 multiplications per microsecond. The speed of this unit results from the use of pipelining techniques, overlapped move and arithmetic operations, and the inclusion of a very fast 128-word temporary register file. The arithmetic processor unit, shown in Fig. 7.16, is designed to execute an arithmetic instruction of the form

$$R = + (A + B) * (C + D)$$

in 175 ns. Unlike other array processors, the AD-10 is a fixed-point machine, making it necessary to scale all variables to assure that no register overflow or underflow occurs. In all functional units the data are presented as 16-bit integers; the integrator module employs 48-bit words. An extension towards floating-point is currently under investigation.

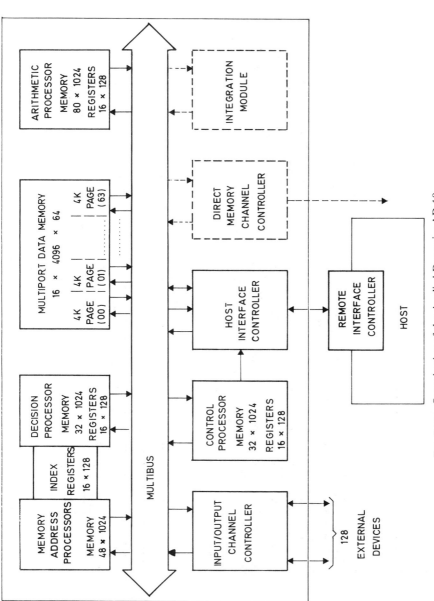

Fig. 7.15 Organization of the Applied Dynamics AD-10

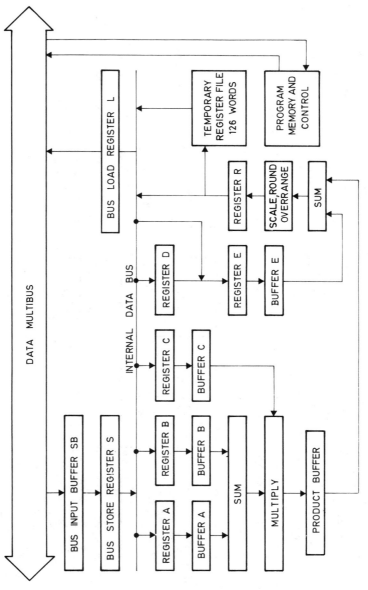

Fig. 7.16 The arithmetic processor of the AD-10

7.9   NETWORKS OF MICROPROCESSORS

The prospect of fashioning networks of general-purpose computers so as to obtain greater speed through parallelism has been a tantalizing prospect for many years. G. A. Korn [132] has for some time championed the fashioning of inexpensive high-speed digital simulators by interconnecting general-purpose minicomputers. He showed that a system consisting of three DEC PDP-11/45's could outperform analog computers in most applications. As pointed out above, ILLIAC IV is a prominent example of a large simulation-oriented parallel computer.

With the increasing availability of very fast and inexpensive LSI units, it becomes feasible to contemplate the construction of special-purpose simulation-oriented multiple-instruction/multiple-data (MIMD) peripheral processors. Each element of the array of processors would contain an arithmetic and logic unit (ALU), memory, and its own control. A favourable cost/speed tradeoff can be achieved by limiting the instruction repertoire to those commands which are required for the solution of differential equations. The HEP (Heterogeneous Element Processor) proposed by Denelcor Inc., and the G-471 from W. W. Gaertner Research Inc., are examples of this approach.

The G-471 is an array of processors providing a high degree of multiprocessing and pipelining. No complete versions of this unit have as yet been built. The proposed system appears, however, to be well within the state of the art, since it employs only off-the-shelf modules and circuit techniques. Figure 7.17 is a block diagram of the proposed G-471. The host computer can be any standard general-purpose computer such as a PDP-11. The host controls the operation of the processing elements (PE) and the array of data-routeing elements. The processing elements in the PE array are standard microcomputer boards, each of which processes 16 or 32 bits in parallel. The local memory associated with each PE is expandable to at least 56K bytes. This storage area can be assigned to data or program in any mix.

PEs can be readily operated in parallel arrays of up to 1024 elements. Each PE can directly address up to 16 megabytes of semiconductor, random-access, central working storage. This working storage is partitioned into at least as many memory banks as there are PEs so as to permit parallel access. The array of data-routeing elements performs the communication functions among the PEs, the real-time I/O channels, the central working storage memory banks, and the mass memory modules. It is basically a programmable cross-point switch, whose switch settings are determined dynamically. The G-471 operates on a clock which provides a 90 ns cycle time.

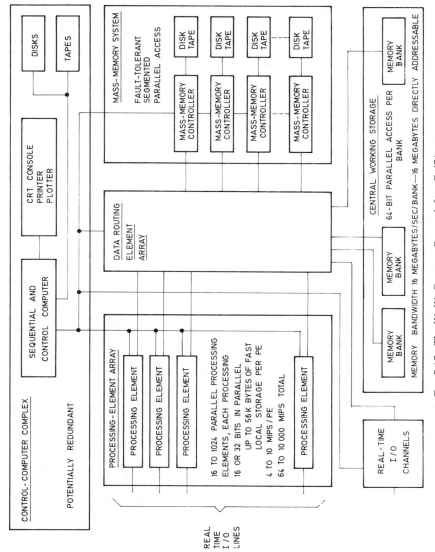

FIG. 7.17 The W. W. Gaertner Research Inc. G-471

Notwithstanding the many potentially attractive features of microprocessor networks, the development of actual prototype systems of this kind has been frustratingly slow. Probably a major handicap in the development of this type of simulator system has been the fact that most manufacturers have not seen a financial stake in the development of such systems. Indeed, there are formidable hardware and software problems to be resolved. On the hardware side, it is necessary to select one of a number of ways of interconnecting the individual microprocessor units, and different simulation applications appear to demand different connection strategies. Also, substantially different algorithmic approaches seem to be indicated. For these and other reasons, large-scale simulation-oriented microprocessor networks remained in the proposal rather than the implementation stage throughout the 1970s.

Weissberger [229] presented a detailed analysis of the various considerations involved in the specification of a microprocessor network. He lists well over fifty commercially-available microprocessor units which could be candidates for network applications. He then describes alternative ways of allocating tasks, and of interconnecting and synchronizing the microprocessors comprising the network. The ability to identify and isolate component failures is an important attribute of multiprocessor systems. As the number of microprocessors in a network is increased, the probability that any one of them will be malfunctioning at any given time increases, and careful design techniques are required to maintain system reliability.

In 1977, a workshop sponsored by the Rand Corporation considered the feasibility of a special-purpose microprocessor network designed to solve the Navier-Stokes equations describing fluid flow. The report [87] produced by this workshop focused on a network simulator consisting of an array of 10 000 identical microprocessor units arranged in a 100×100 matrix. To minimize interconnection costs, each processor is limited to communicate only with its nearest neighbours. The proposed topology is therefore essentially similar to that shown in Fig. 7.9, albeit much larger. For problems in three space dimensions, each processing element represents a point in a two-dimensional plane, data in the third dimension being carried along by the memory associated with each processing elements. In this way, a three-dimensional finite difference grid containing approximately one million grid points can fit on this computer at one time, making it unnecessary to communicate with a back-up memory in the course of a computation. Each processing element would be capable of storing 256 64-bit words and of carrying out a 64-bit fixed-point multiplication in 5 μs. Inter-processor transfers are assumed to require 9 microseconds per word. The system would be much more powerful than ILLIAC IV and would far surpass the processing capability of any competitive system. Grosch [88] has made detailed studies of algorithms suitable for the proposed simulator. In particular he considered the solution of Poisson's equation in three-dimensions

$$\frac{\partial^2 u}{\partial x^2} + \frac{\partial^2 u}{\partial y^2} + \frac{\partial^2 u}{\partial z^2} = u(x, y, z)$$

with various boundary conditions. A number of alternative algorithms were evaluated from the point of view of operations count and overhead, including the time expended for data transfers between processing elements.

Many other proposals for microprocessor networks have appeared in the literature. Most of these contain some novel architectural features. For example, the sytem proposed by Cyre *et et*. [44] is composed of a three-dimensional array of microprocessor units arranged to permit rapid nearest-neighbour data transfer and featuring a special "pass-through" scheme to facilitate transfers to other than nearest-neighbour processing elements.

7.10   A BENCHMARK PROBLEM

Two types of aircraft whose real-time simulation requirements even now exceed the capability of available computer systems and which will become more complex in years to come, are lift-fan vehicles and helicopters. A preliminary study showed that a simulation system capable of satisfactorily representing helicopter aircraft would also be capable of representing lift-fan vehicles. This led to the selection of an advanced helicopter—the Rotor Systems Research Aircraft (RSRA) operating in the helicopter mode—as a benchmark vehicle. A variety of engineering models of the helicopters exists, notably the C-81 model prepared by Bell Helicopter Company and the REXOR program developed by Lockheed Aircraft Company. These are immensely complex programs consisting of over 30 000 punched cards and running orders of magnitude slower than real time. These models are therefore unsuitable for real-time experiments involving cockpit simulators and other kinds of man-in-the-loop simulation experiments. Such experiments require greatly simplified models, like the model developed by Sikorsky Aircraft Corporation and subsequently implemented at NASA/ Langley and NASA/Ames. Figure 7.18 is a simplified block diagram of the simulation system built around that model. The general equations of helicopter motion which are transmitted to the cockpit are affected by five major subsystems: the main rotor, the fuselage and wing, the empennage, the tail rotor, and auxiliary propulsion engines.

In representing these units mathematically, the representation of the

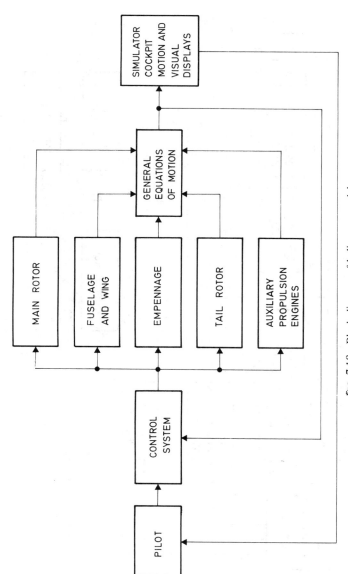

Fig. 7.18   Block diagram of helicopter model

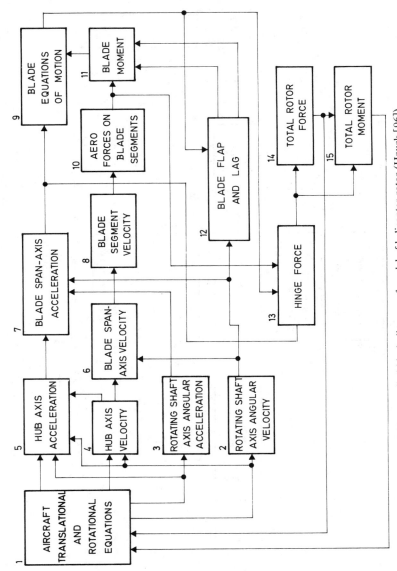

Fig. 7.19   Detailed block diagram of model of helicopter rotor (Houck [96])

main rotor is by far the most complex task, usually accounting for well over 90 % of the overall computational load. This complexity arises from the multiplicity of flexible rotor blades used by modern helicopters. Each of these blades must be subdivided into a number of elements, and each of which acts as a separate dynamic body generating lift and drag. If the rotor system contains N rotor blades, and if each blade is divided into s finite elements, the simulation involves the modelling of an aircraft with Ns separate wing surfaces.

Figure 7.19 is a detailed block diagram of the rotor system of the helicopter: the portion of the overall model which largely determines the computational load. J. A. Houck [96] and Robert M. Howe of the University of Michigan have made detailed analyses of the Sikorsky/NASA implementation of this model. In integrating the aircraft differential equations it is assumed that the integration algorithm requires but a single function evaluation during each time frame (in distinction to a fourth-order Runge-Kutta formula, which requires four function evaluations). Table 7.2 lists the arithmetic operations required during a single time frame for each of the 15 blocks in Fig. 7.19. Some computations are independent of the number of rotor blades, some are proportional only to the number N of rotor blades, while others must be performed for each wing segment and are therefore proportional to Ns. As part of his analysis, Houck determined that for a five-blade system, each blade must be represented by at least five segments. He also demonstrated that, in order to provide reasonably satisfactory dynamic accuracy, the digital frame time can be no longer than 5 ms. At the Langley Research Center using a FORTRAN program implemented on a CYBER 175, a rotor model consisting of five blades of five segments required a minimum of 10 ms, i.e., twice the maximum allowable time. A Sigma 7 implementation at NASA/Ames had a frame time of approximately 40 ms. The need for faster computing is clear.

The benchmark mathematical model ignores many potentially interesting and important physical effects, such as aeroelasticity, downwash, and air turbulence. More ambitious real-time simulations will therefore require even greater computational speeds than does our benchmark problem. Implementation results of the proposed helicopter aircraft problem on the AP-120B, the AD-10 and the G-471 will be compared.

If the control system of the helicopter is to be represented in the host computer while all differential equations governing rotor dynamics are solved in the AP-120B, the inputs to the peripheral processor at the beginning of each time frame include rotor control signals, deflection angles for the stabilizing surfaces, and changes in the magnitude of the thrust vector. Environmental effects, failure modes, and other changes in the simulation will also be transmitted from the host computer. These

TABLE 7.2 Operations count for a single time frame of the benchmark problem (times in microseconds)

Block #	Multiply/divide	Add	Trigonometric functions	One-variable functions	Two-variable functions	Square roots
1	59	38	6			
2	$8 + 11 N$	$6 + 5 N$	$6 N$			
3	$8 + 2 N$	$5 + 2 N$				
4	14	11				
5	20	19				
6	$6 N$	$4 N$				
7	$11 N$	$8 N$				
8	$10 N + 2 Ns$	$5 N + 2 Ns$				
9	$14 N$	$9 N$				
10	$6 N + 26 Ns$	$5 N + 6 Ns$	$2 N + 2 Ns$		$3 Ns$	$3 Ns$
11	$4 N + 2 Ns$	$2 N + 2 Ns$		N		
12	N	$2 N$				
13	$10 N$	$6 N + 3 Ns$				
14	$8 + 12 N$	$5 + 10 N$				
15	$14 + 5 N$	$11 + 5 N$				
Total	$131 + 92 N$ $+ 30 Ns$	$95 + 63 N$ $+ 13 Ns$	$6 + 8 N$ $+ 2 Ns$	N	$3 Ns$	$3 Ns$
Total for $N = 5, s = 5$	1341	735	96	5	75	75

N = number of blades; s = number of segments per blade.

terms may be read from the host computer via the DMA channel, and placed in the data memory or in the data scratch-pads. The program resident in the program memory is then executed without further communications from the host computer.

At the end of each time frame all the quantities needed for cockpit instrumentation displays and for control-system computations are transmitted to the host computer via the interface and the DMA channel. In essence, therefore, from the point of view of the host computer the AP-120B acts as a subroutine which is called once during each time frame.

The estimate of the frame time required for the benchmark problem rests on the assumptions that all the calculations listed in Table 7.2 will be performed in the AP-120B, and that the integration algorithm requires but a single function evaluation during each time frame. The results of the frame-time computation for the benchmark problem are shown in Table 7.3. If N represents the number of rotor blades and s is the number of elements per blade, the total time T required for a time frame is

$$T = 148.8 + 144.6\,N + 107.5\,Ns\ \mu s$$

For a helicopter with five rotor blades and five segments per blade, the estimated frame time becomes 3.56 ms, well within Houck's limit of 5 ms. Frame times for the AD-10 and the HEP are, respectively, 0.630 and 0.460 ms. Note that a special purpose hybrid computer manufactured by Paragon Pacific Inc., the SPURS (Special Purpose Helicopter Simulator) designed specifically for real time simulation of rotorcraft, requires a total frame time of 5 ms.

The principal shortcoming of the AP-120B, as far as the benchmark problem is concerned, arise from its having been developed for applications other than simulation. The AP-120B is in fact intended primarily for problems requiring the transfer of large blocks of data from the host computer to the data memory, and subjecting the elements of these blocks to a relatively compact series of arithmetic operations and manipulations. This is the situation, for example, in signal analysis using the Fast Fourier transform.

Aerospace simulation problems, on the other hand, require reading relatively small sequences of numbers from the host computer at the beginning of each time frame and subjecting them to extremely lengthy and elaborate computations. For example, for the helicopter problem the input vector would contain only twelve elements. The FORTRAN program describing the manipulations of this vector during each time frame requires over 450 statements. The translation of this program into AP-120B assembly language results in a program which exceeds 2000 statements. The treatment of problems substantially larger than the benchmark problem using the existing AP-120B configuration is therefore not practical. Another disadvantage of the AP-120B is the absence of facilities for direct access to the processor from external communication lines. All data must enter and leave the peripheral processor via the interface module and the host computer, which creates an intolerable bottle-neck under certain conditions.

All differential equations governing the dynamics of the helicopter can be solved in the AD-10 during each time frame. As in the case of the AP-120B, it is assumed that the integration algorithm selected requires but a single function evaluation during each time frame and that suboptimal programming methods are employed. Under these conditions the computer time required for the various steps involved in the solution of the benchmark problem are as shown in Table 7.3. If N is the number of rotor blades and s is the number of elements per blade, the total time T for a single time frame on the AD-10 is

$$T = 51.1 + 33.3\,N + 16.5\,Ns \ \mu s$$

For a helicopter with five rotor blades and five segments per blade, the frame time becomes 0.63 ms, very much shorter than Houck's limit.

TABLE 7.3   Estimates of the benchmark problem frame time using three peripheral processors (times in microseconds)

	Required frame times (μs)		
	AP-120B	AD-10	G-471 5 PE's
Computations independent of N and s			
131 multiplications	65.5	33.9	7.1
95 additions	31.6		3.4
6 functions of one variable	51.7	17.2	0.7
Computations proportional to N			
92 multiplications	$46.0\,N$	$23.3\,N$	$5.0\,N$
63 additions	$21.0\,N$		$2.3\,N$
9 functions of one variable	$77.6\,N$	$9.9\,N$	$1.0\,N$
Computations proportional to N and s			
30 multiplications	$15\,Ns$	$6.5\,Ns$	$1.62\,Ns$
13 additions	$4.3\,Ns$		$0.46\,Ns$
2 functions of one variable	$17.2\,Ns$	$2.2\,Ns$	$0.22\,Ns$
6 functions of two variables	$71.0\,Ns$	$7.8\,Ns$	$4.21\,Ns$
Total for $N = 5, s = 5$	3560	630	140

In implementing the benchmark problem on the G-471, it is assumed that the entire program would be executed by the G-471. This program would be read into the memories of the processing elements at the beginning of the computer run. For the helicopter problem, a separate processor might be dedicated to each rotor blade, since the blades do not interact during a time frame. Table 7.3 lists the estimated times which would be required for a single time frame of the benchmark problem. If five processing elements are employed, the total time T required for a time frame is

$$T = 11.2 + 8.3\,N + 3.59\,Ns \; \mu s$$

For a helicopter including five rotor blades with five finite elements per blade, the total frame time required is 0.14 ms less than 1/30th of Houck's limit.

It has been the purpose of Chapters 6 and 7 to give an overview of both software and hardware evolutions for simulation. The final chapter will develop trends in designing tools for simulation based on methodological issues.

8. Simulation systems and architectures arising from methodological research

8.1 INTRODUCTION

The von Neumann architecture may be characterized as a computer architecture satisfying the postulate of hardware minimality. It is a common feature of "innovative" (or "non von Neumann") architectures that they comprise additional hardware resources, as compared to the classical von Neumann architecture, to attain certain "design objectives". A major design objective for simulators is to enhance the support of system-modelling and model use. A systematic attempt to devise an innovative computer architecture should be conceived as a top-down process. Such a process starts with the specification of the design objective. The next step is to devise an operational principle of the computer hardware by which the desired aim can be attained. Such a principle must promise not only to eliminate the constraints of the von Neumann architecture with respect to the design objectives, but also to offer a cost-effective solution. The established principle will provide a blueprint for a functional definition of the tool organization.

What so far is rather vaguel characterized as the "establishment of an operational principle" is in reality the act of defining the components and the structure of the information representation in the machine. In the case of special purpose architectures, the information components and structures are readily defined by the class of algorithms which are to be performed on certain data objects. The situation is much more complicated in the case of general-purpose architectures, which must satisfy the requirements of a comprehensive, extremely variant "universe" of possible algorithms. Here, the lack of an identifiable homogeneous class of algorithms necessitates a search for other, more general, principles. One such principle may be, for instance, the selection of an appropriate general-purpose, high-level programming language, and the utilization of the control structure and/or the data structure of that language as a blue-print for the information representation in the machine [35]. Another well-known principle is that of "tagged" architecture [67], i.e. of self-descriptive data. At the Technical University of Berlin the operational principle of data structure architectures is considered and implemented in the STARLET computer structure. This class of architectures is designed for the processing of appropriately structured data entities [80]. In reality, many existing architectural concepts were developed in a bottom-up approach, rather than in the systematic top-down fashion epitomized above.

The concepts and theories developed through methodological research dealt with in the previous chapters (essential for the above top-down approach) suggest, and indeed make possible to contemplate, greatly expanded software and hardware systems for modelling and simulation. Such systems aim to provide computer assistance in many aspects of the modelling process either not supported, or only rudimentarily supported, by the contemporary languages, packages, and systems.

The architectural scheme outlined in Fig. 8.1 can be used as an orientation framework for considering methodologically based systems. In such a scheme, users interact with the computer system through interfaces which enable them to initiate or engage in activities. The sequencing of activities

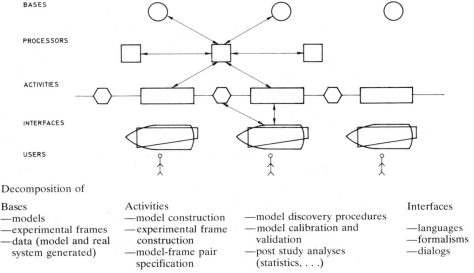

Decomposition of			
Bases	Activities		Interfaces
—models	—model construction	—model discovery procedures	
—experimental frames	—experimental frame	—model calibration and	—languages
—data (model and real	construction	validation	—formalisms
system generated)	—model-frame pair	—post study analyses	—dialogs
	specification	(statistics, . . .)	

FIG. 8.1   Architectural scheme for computer support systems

may be partly fixed and partly open to users' control. An activity is executed by one or more processors (in conjunction with the user) and acts upon one or more data bases (where the "data" may be of various kinds to be described). In executing an activity, information is stored in the bases. The information so generated is accessible to the user through the interfaces. This scheme is a rather broad framework which is interpretable, on the one hand, to the most primitive computer, and on the other, to all varieties of ambitious computer systems for design, information, control, etc.

A number of methodologically based systems are under development in this framework.

GEST78

GEST78 (General System Theory Language) is a simulation language being designed to support the fundamental distinction between model construction and model experimentation. It recognizes the following activities:
—model related: model specification, model composition;
—experimentation related: experimental frame specification;
—simulation related: application of a frame to a model, simulation run specification, post study analysis.

GEST78 provides linguistic elements required by these activities. A GEST78 program is highly structured, consisting of blocks for models, experimental frames, model-frame pairs, run control, and post-study analysis. The reader is referred to [59] for further exposition of the language elements.

A primary goal in the structure-oriented design of GEST78 is to improve man–machine and man–man communication. In terms of our framework, it attempts to provide an effective interface between users and the above-mentioned activities. Moreover, the modularity it encourages in model and experimental frame definitions makes possible the design of bases to store such descriptions.

GSPS

GSPS (General Systems Problem Solver) is a software system for assisting in the solution of systems problems. It accepts as fundamental a hierarchical taxonomy of systems descriptions (evolved over the past several years in systems research) which ascend upwards from purely observational to behavioural and increasingly structural levels. Problems, as formulated within this taxonomy are of two kinds:
—given a particular system determine another system of a given taxonomical type satisfying given requirements;
—given two particular systems determine some property, satisfying given requirements, of the relation between the two.

In terms of our framework, GSPS provides an interface through which such problems may be formulated and communicated to the software system. The activities it supports are those connected with finding solutions to the given problems. Such activities include:

(i)   Associating a lower level system with a higher level one.
(ii) Discovery of a higher level system which associates to a lower level one. This involves such subactivities as:
      —searching through candidate model spaces
      —evaluation of candidates (this involves type 1 activities).

Type 1 activities are generalizations of the structure-to-behaviour computation process, and include for example, simulation of models as a special case. Type 2 activities are generalizations of the behaviour-to-structure inference process, and include, for example, model identification as a special case.

In the problem subdomain in which it has been implemented, GSPS has standardized activity sequences which enable it automatically to produce solutions to given problems. However, human intervention is needed in the selection and execution of activities once a certain problem size is reached. For this reason, GSPS provides a set of tools appropriate to each problem type. In terms of our framework, it contains a tool base and an interface able to suggest the tools appropriate to the activity currently undertaken [130].

PARALLEL SIMULATION SYSTEMS

The role of simulator architecture in greatly facilitating interactive simulation experimentation is emphasized in Section 8.3 further on. In relation to GEST78 and GSPS, large, spatially disaggregated, highly parallel models are focused on. The dimension most clearly brought out in our framework by such a focus is that of the processors, but it impacts on the other dimensions (interfaces, activities and bases) as well.

In this chapter, operational principles for simulators are derived related to all previously mentioned dimension levels (Fig. 8.1). They should characterize simulators in order to satisfy their design objective: system-modelling support. Implementations under development will illustrate the statements.

8.2   PROPOSAL OF OPERATIONAL PRINCIPLES FOR SIMULATORS

A future simulator must be designed based upon the general characteristics of system and simulation studies, and the practical needs of the experimenter. Simulation should be both system-oriented and experimenter-oriented, but it will be clear that both orientations are not fully disjunct.

For a certain level of descriptive detail, a *one-to-one analogy in space and in time* between the system under study and the implemented model is a condition for both. Experimenter-oriented simulation further demands that the time-set of the simulation system is compatible with the time-set of human observation capabilities of simulation results, as well as with the time-set of the experimenter's decision process. This can be called: *human-time simulation*. (in contrast to real-time simulation). Human-time simulation can imply that the implemented model runs (much) faster or (much) slower than real time. Experimenter-oriented simulation also requires that an experimenter can perform the execution of model experiments in an interactive way: *interactive simulation*. In interactive human-time simulation an attractive property of one-to-one structural analogy is that the time-set of the simulation system can be independent of the complexity. Accessibility through a *transparent simulation system* is important for experimenter- as well as system-oriented simulation.

Modelling methodology must be available for in-line operational use in simulation studies. It should provide procedures and algorithms for activities like: frame definition, structure characterization, parameter estimation, experimental design, validation. Modelling methodology support is still missing for a great deal. So in order to be able to exploit the power of future processing tools for modelling and simulation purposes, it is obligatory to pay much attention to its development and implementation.

For the purpose of both interactive simulation and transparency, a simulator must have the capability to implement relevant mathematical models of a system on the basis of *computation modelling by exception* and *programming by exception* to an ultimate extent, meaning that the experimenter has to take part only in very special situations in specifying computational, e.g. numerical, aspects and their implementation. "Computation modelling by exception" requires that the state transition, input and output operators of the mathematical model can normally be mapped autonomously and in a direct way to the set of admissible algorithms of a simulator. "Programming by exception" implies the same for the mapping of algorithms to hardware/software implementations. For interactive simulation, it is important that a simulator can offer an experimenter the feature of so-called *system modelling by exception*. It implies that a simulator must be able, not only to implement and up-date the information to be stored in a data-base, but also to utilize this data-base for interactive modelling in a methodology supported way.

Methodology has to be incorporated in a simulator for in-line operational use for other purposes. As an example, *background modelling* can be mentioned (i.e. modelling without previous specification by the experi-

menter), and *background experimentation* on a model (like parallel sensitivity analysis). Results of background activities are accessible in an interactive way.

A future simulator should contain a powerful data-processing system
consisting of four functional blocks for specific tasks (Fig. 8.2):

Simulation executor:
"computation modelling by exception" and "programming by exception"
(modelling phase), implementation and execution of validation and other
simulation experiments in an interactive way (experimenting phase): a
simulation executor must have the capability to perform *adaptive
experimentation*. During the running of a simulation experiment in the
foreground under control of the experimenter, in the background an experiment can run under control of the robot experimenter hereafter described.
Of course background experimentation should not influence noticeably
foreground experimentation.

Model-base handler:
in the modelling phase the mode-base handler takes care of utilizing and
updating model data bases, as well as corresponding significant information
designed for "modelling in the large" activities (see, e.g. Chapter 5).
Modelling can be performed in the way as described in previous chapters,
as well as by searching in the model-base an appropriate specimen. If the
modelling is done by means of a data-base search, the model-base handler
should perform this search in an interactive way under support of both
the methodology executor and the robot experimenter (both described
below).

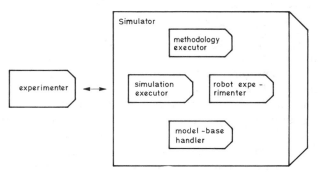

FIG. 8.2   Global set-up of simulator

Robot experimenter:
performing activities for support to observation and decision-making by the experimenter.

Methodology executor:
supporting previous simulation tasks, and the experimenter as well, by simulation and modelling methodology (e.g. in designing relevant models), available for in-line operational use. Examples of methodologies can be found in Chapters 3 to 5.

The simulation tasks assigned to the above-mentioned functional blocks are strongly autonomous, and it must be possible to perform them in parallel. It will be clear that the tasks assigned to the simulation executor: "execution of experiments" in the foreground (under control of the experimenter) and in the background (under control of the robot experimenter), require *true parallel* data-processing capability. All of the mentioned tasks require *advanced sequential* data-processing capabilities. Note that for performing adequately background activities, implementation of artificial intelligence techniques is required. From the above, it is clear that data base management is of great importance. Because of the demand of human-time interactivity, the data base management task has to be performed based on parallellism (*parallel data base management*). Current research activities in this domain are noteworthy [10]. Finally all decision-making processes in a simulation study must be supported by adequate graphical and alpha-numerical display of information.

8.3   IMPACT OF OPERATIONAL PRINCIPLES ON SIMULATOR ARCHITECTURE

8.3.1   Hierarchies in systems and system models

If "simulation" is considered as experimentation on a mathematical model of an actual system, a close relationship between the system and the model is important for the success of simulation.

A system is some form of composition of interacting subsystems. This notion is accepted as axiomatic across the methodological spectrum of systems thinking, from heuristic (systems approach) to formal (systems theory). Yet, until recently, there were no aids to help the systems thinker rigorously to work with this fundamental concept. In the last few years, projects have begun to provide tools which will help a user to find useful decompositions of a system and their hierarchical relations (see Sections 5.3 and 5.4).

Mostly, these subsystems behave in parallel. All system variables are functions of time, and they are constantly exchanged in a parallel way between the subsystems. Hence it is necessary for a data-processing system, in order to be a "true" simulator, to approximate these important features enclosed in the nature of parallelism. In the following the concept "hierarchies" will be dealt with in relation to both structures in space (Section 8.3.1.1) and structures in time (Section 8.3.1.2) of systems and models.

8.3.1.1   *Structure in space of systems and models*

A system belongs to some spatial region. Normally spatial regions of different systems can be taken disjunct. Since physical spatial size and location of a system are normally of no importance for the time behaviour of a system, spatial dependence is not incorporated in the usual system definitions. But for systems decomposed in simultaneously operating or parallel subsys-

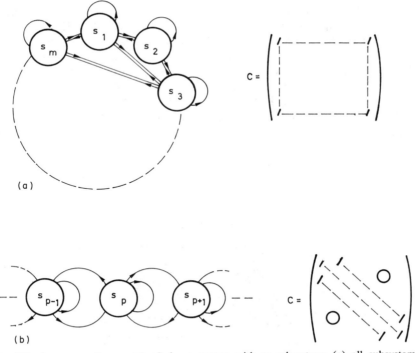

FIG. 8.3   Interconnection matrix C for a system with m subsystems (a) all subsystems mutually interconnected; (b) only neighbour subsystems mutually interconnected

tems, there exists some ordering of these subsystems in space. The parallel subsystems operate in a spatial structure. As to the interactions between the subsystems there is no need to formulate the spatial structure in much detail. For so-called ill-defined systems, it can already be difficult to make conclusions about the existence of interactions between subsystems. Still more difficult is the question whether the interaction between subsystems is direct, or via other subsystems. Figure 8.3 shows for two typical classes of systems the interconnections between the subsystems, expressed by means of the interconnection matrix C.

In practice, often a system can be decomposed in a natural way, once or successively, in smaller systems. Normally, decomposition will be based on the properties of the interaction structure as is present inside the system. By successive decomposition a system becomes ordered in a *spatial hierarchy*. Successive decomposition results in systems which can either be decomposed further on (*intermediate systems*) or not (*bottom systems*). The original not yet decomposed system can be denoted as the *top system*. Large systems usually have a more or less sparse interaction structure. Thus a spatial hierarchy can be meaningfully recognized in large systems.

A system can be ordered in a spatial hierarchy in different ways, depending on how the properties of the interaction structure are judged. This can be illustrated for a so-called fixed-four hierarchy in the administration-optimizing case in economic geography as shown in Fig. 8.4. At a first glance this figure suggests that a natural decomposition rule could be to decompose each time a system in four subsystems, yielding the spatial hierarchy of Fig. 8.5 with decomposition levels l, l = 0, 1, 2 and a level dimension L, L = 2. This spatial hierarchy belongs to the class of recursive spatial hierarchies where recursive means that each decomposition results in

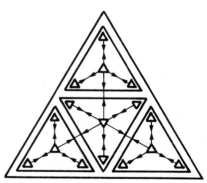

FIG. 8.4   Schematic spatial configuration of a fixed-four hierarchy in the administration-optimizing case in economic geography ($\triangle$ = system)

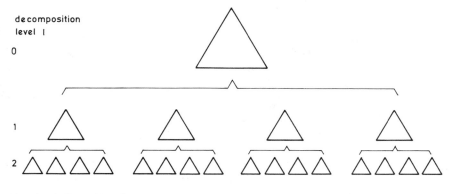

decomposition
level l

0

1

2

L = level dimension = 2

FIG. 8.5   Spatial hierarchy of the fixed-four hierarchy of Fig. 8.4, obtained by applying twice the decomposition rule "decompose each system in four subsystems"

the same number of subsystems with a constant ratio between intermediate and bottom systems. A decomposition rule, where each system is decomposed in k subsystems results in a *recursive spatial hierarchy of order k* (binary spatial hierarchy k = 2 and ternary spatial hierarchy k = 3 are common). If for each level l, l = 0, . . ., L-1 all systems are decomposed, then we have a *full spatial hierarchy*. So a full spatial hierarchy only contains bottom systems at level L, but in general a spatial hierarchy will contain bottom systems at each level. The spatial hierarchy of Fig. 8.5 is a full recursive spatial hierarchy of order 4. A non-full recursive spatial hierarchy will be called a *truncated recursive spatial hierarchy* if the same truncation rule is applied to all occurring decompositions in the different decomposition paths.

The decomposition rule as shown in Fig. 8.5 results in a great unbalance between the central subsystem and the other three subsystems. For this reason, another natural way of successive decomposition may be preferred (Fig. 8.6). There are two types of systems: "full systems f and aggregate systems a" with decomposition rules f $\Rightarrow$ (f, a) and a $\Rightarrow$ (f, f, f). Resulting systems f become finally bottom systems. In analogy, this spatial hierarchy can be called a truncated recursive spatial hierarchy of order (2.3).

As for systems, successive decomposition can also often be applied to system models, based upon natural decomposition guidelines. The hierarchical system model definition of the spatial hierarchy of Fig. 8.6 can be described in a recurrent way using 'spatial structure operators':

$$s = h(s_0, s_1)$$
$$s_0 = h_0(s_{00}, s_{01})$$

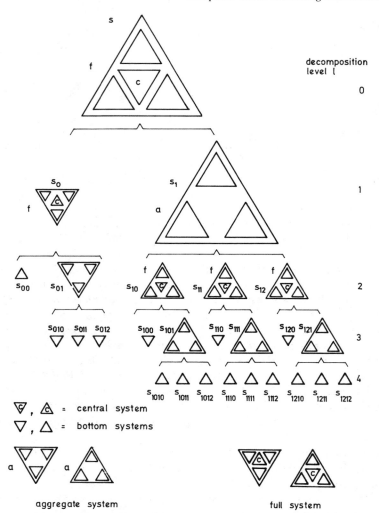

FIG. 8.6   Spatial hierarchy of the fixed-four hierarchy of Fig. 8.4 obtained by applying different decomposition rules to a full system and an "aggregate" system

$$s_1 = h_1(s_{10}, s_{11}, s_{12})$$
$$s_{01} = h_{01}(s_{010}, s_{011}, s_{012})$$
$$s_{10} = h_{10}(s_{100}, s_{101})$$
$$s_{11} = h_{11}(s_{110}, s_{111})$$
$$s_{12} = h_{12}(s_{120}, s_{121})$$

$$s_{101} = h_{101}(s_{1010}, s_{1011}, s_{1012})$$
$$s_{111} = h_{111}(s_{1110}, s_{1111}, s_{1112})$$
$$s_{121} = h_{121}(s_{1210}, s_{1211}, s_{1212})$$

with $h = h_0 = h_{10} = h_{11} = h_{12}$

and $h_1 = h_{01} = h_{101} = h_{111} = h_{121}$.

Through so-called interaction kernels k_j (Fig. 8.7) the subsystem models s_j, $j = 0, \ldots$, m (intermediate system models decomposed again in s_{jk},

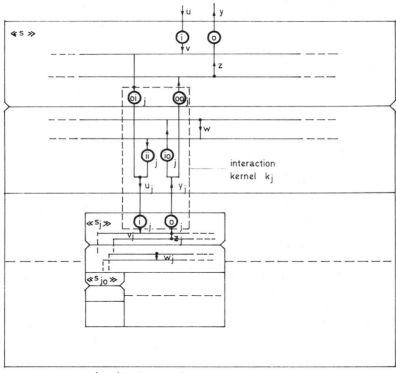

i = input operator
o = output operator
oi = outer input operator
ii = inner input operator
io = inner output operator
oo = outer output operator

FIG. 8.7 Interaction kernel k_j: the contribution of intermediate system s_j to the interaction structure of the spatial hierarchy of system s

$k = 0, \ldots, m_j$) interact with each other. For practical reasons input mappings have been introduced to the system model definition from Chapter 2. In this way often arising system properties, like internal feedback and dimension reduction from input vector to state vector, can be modelled in a more flexible way.

8.3.1.2   *Structure in time of systems and models*

The input-output relation of a system can be constant in time or time-dependent. This time-dependency can occur in different ways. Either the inter-connection structure of a system remains constant but the intensity of existing interactions changes in time, or the interconnection structure changes in time. In the latter case, at a certain time only one of the potential subsystems can be an actual subsystem. In the course of time, however, several of the potential subsystems can become the actual subsystem, one after another in some sequence. The time order of actuality of these sequential sub-systems can be distinguished: the initial subsystem, successor subsystems, the actual subsystems, predecessor subsystems, the terminal subsystem. Obviously there will be "decision-making" causal rules to realize the transition from the actual subsystem to its successor subsystem at the right time.

As an illustration, a game with several players will be considered. There is no doubt that a player is a system. During a game, "player" systems (forming together the game system) operate according to general and individual properties of a "human being", and have mutual interactions according to the rules of the game. There is a start at some time, normally defined from the environment of the "game" system, as well as a finish, defined either from the "game" system itself, or also from its environment. A game of touch, with only three players p_j, $j = 0$, 1, 2, is considered. Among the "player" systems p_j there is always one "hunter" system and several "prey" systems. One can say that the successive spatial structures of the "game" system can be identified by the value of the index j of the "hunter" system. It will take some time before the actual "hunter" system succeeds in touching one of the actual "prey" systems. As soon as this happens the two systems change their roles and the game goes on in the same way. A time of touch is the time of a transition discrete event. The condition of touch is a common transition condition for all possible successor systems. The value of the index j of the touched prey system is the pointing value of the selection operator.

A system consisting of a number of such sequential subsystems can be modelled as follows. Some restrictions are put on the modelling of a time-dependent spatial structure of a system: at each time there exists a uniquely defined spatial structure of subsystem models; in a finite time interval only a finite number of spatial structures of models can appear. Hence a transition from an actual spatial structure to one of its possible successors must be modelled as a discontinuous transition. A spatial structure transition is accordingly a discrete event. This discrete event occurs at the time that the condition of transition from the actual spatial structure to the corresponding successor becomes fulfilled. There are as many transition conditions as there are possible successors. One selection operator can be distinguished. At the occurrence of a transition discrete event it selects the corresponding successor from the possible successors. Transition conditions are based on the behaviour of the state of the system model in past and present, and eventually also on a prognosis of this behaviour in the future. The possible sequences of spatial structures of subsystem models with corresponding transition conditions can be represented as a *time-order hierarchy*. Figure 8.8 shows such a time-order hierarchy representation of the game of touch. Because the number of players has been taken equal to three, there are two possible successors for each decomposition; in other words, a binary time-order hierarchy is obtained. The rules of the game of touch result in special properties of the time-order hierarchy. The transition structure is not only constant, but it is even a recursive one. Here recursive means that for all decompositions the same structural transition rule is applied, i.e. for each actual system the number and the way of allocation of possible successors is the same. In other words, the game of touch can be described by means of a "recursive time-order hierarchy." Another property of the structural transition rule, namely that the possible successor spatial structures are the potential spatial structures of the game of touch minus the actual one, implies that the game of touch can be formulated as a "cyclic time-order hierarchy" (Fig. 8.8).

Note that this choice of cyclic representation is an attractive one, because it has a constant ordering of the possible successors.

The description of the time-order hierarchy of Fig. 8.8, based upon the time structure operator t, results in

$$(s^0, s^1, s^2) = t(\emptyset)$$
$$(s^{00}, s^{01}) = t^0(s^0)$$
$$(s^{10}, s^{11}) = t^1(s^1)$$
$$(s^{20}, s^{21}) = t^2(s^2)$$
$$(s^{000}, s^{001}) = t^{00}(s^{00})$$
$$(s^{010}, s^{011}) = t^{01}(s^{01})$$
$$(s^{100}, s^{101}) = t^{10}(s^{10})$$

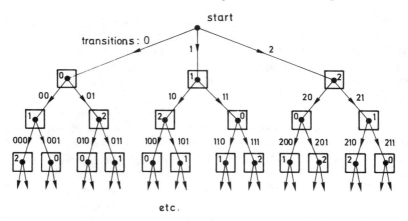

etc.

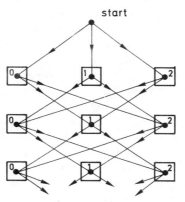

$\boxed{j_{\bullet}}$ ≡ 'game' system with player p_j as the 'hunter' system

FIG. 8.8 Some "time-order hierarchy" representations of the "game of touch" with three
players: full binary time-order hierarchy; cyclic binary time-order hierarchy.

$$(s^{110}, s^{111}) = t^{11} (s^{11})$$
$$(s^{200}. s^{201}) = t^{20} (s^{20})$$
$$(s^{210}, s^{211}) = t^{21} (s^{21})$$
etc.,

where $\emptyset$ stands for a null system model, i.e. a system with a vanishing
length of its time interval T. Note that the description of the cyclic binary
time-order hierarchy turns out to be very simple:

$$(s_0, s_1, s_2) = t(\emptyset)$$

$$(s_1, s_2) = t_0 (s_0)$$
$$(s_2, s_0) = t_1 (s_1)$$
$$(s_0, s_1) = t_2 (s_2)$$

8.3.2 Current simulators vs. some operational principles

Transparency is one of the operational principles of a simulator. A necessary condition for transparency in simulation is "one-to-one analogy in space and in time". A system model has to be transformed in a computational version implementable on a simulator. In a simulation run, experimental results are delivered by the model implemented on the simulator. Adequate simulation requires that a simulator allows the experimenter to perform computation modelling by exception and programming by exception. The demand of "one-to-one analogy in space and in time" determines, as a consequence, the architecture of a parallel data processor, in order to be able to implement as closely as possible the spatial hierarchies and time-order hierarchies present in the system model. A criterion for the architecture of a parallel data processor is also that the degree and way of implementation of the interconnectibility of the data processing subsystems is appropriate for the majority of subsystem models. In this section it will be seen that quite often it is impossible to implement a model on existing data-processing systems in such a way that the structure in space and in time of the model is preserved. The demand for automated and interactive programming has been so strong in the recent past that, nowadays, it overshadows the demand for one-to-one analogy of the structure in space and in time. Tools are being built gradually approaching the operational principles.

A conventional digital computer can handle a spatial hierarchy by transforming it into a time-order hierarchy, after reformulation of the spatial hierarchy in a spatial hierarchy of level dimension 1 (loss of one-to-one analogy in space). This reformulation and transformation actually means that the user has to perform extra computation modelling. Because the transformation in a time-order hierarchy is not unique, it is not possible to automate much of that part of the computation modelling, prohibiting a high degree of computation modelling by exception. Both reformulation and transformation imply that even small changes in the system description might require a significant "computation modelling overhead". As a consequence, the implemented system will have bad transparency and a restricted degree of interactivity.

An analog computer can handle a time-order hierarchy of spatial structures by transformation into a spatial structure. This transformation forces the user to extra computation modelling (although to a lesser extent than previously). Because this transformation is unique, the extra computation modelling can be automated (through digital support). A complication may arise with respect to the required number of data-processing subsystems (analog and boolean components), because all subsystem models of the spatial structures in the time-order hierarchy have to be implemented in parallel.

An advanced hybrid computer, with automatic patching, can easily handle a time-order hierarchy by repatching within a user's program by means of parallel overlays. For a system implemented on an advanced hybrid computer, transparency and interactivity could be made adequate for parallel simulation. Since up to now the parallel data-processing power in a hybrid computer implies continuous-time parallel data-processing, realized in the analog part and as such for many systems too limited with respect to the class of parallel algorithms (see Chapter 7), the applicability of an advanced hybrid computer is too much restricted with respect to parallel simulation. Moreover, it would require a new architecture of the parallel data-processing power.

A *time-shared hybrid system* project was started some years ago at the Delft University of Technology [46] based on demands for full automation of programming, time-shared operation, and direct experimenting capability (in an advanced interactive way). A global block-scheme of the architecture of the system is given in Fig. 8.9.

The "central parallel processor" contains an arithmetical parallel subprocessor (the automated analog computer) and a boolean parallel subprocessor. Both subprocessors have a modular design structure; submodules

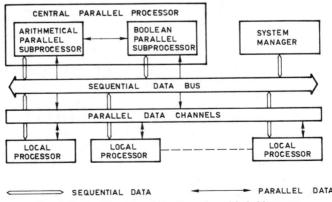

FIG. 8.9   Architecture of the time-shared hybrid system

within a module can be programmed to realize specimens from a set of possible (arithmetical or logic) operations, and can be arbitrarily interconnected via programmable switch matrices (selectors); the interconnectibility between modules is subject to restrictions. The central parallel processor is time-shared over the users. The parallel load module (containing the system definition, i.e. the interconnection scheme, the coefficient values, and the state of the parallel processing system) is stored in a distributed memory, consisting of a number of layers (multiple buffered) in order to have a minimal overhead in loading and storing user's programs. The inputs to the boolean parallel module are selected from the arithmetical module (comparator signals), the other boolean modules and the sequential processor (control lines). The outputs can be routed to the arithmetical module (integrator mode control and switches), to the other boolean modules and to the sequential processor (sense lines). Within the boolean parallel module there exists full interconnectability. At each input of a submodule inversion, differentiation, stretching, or delay operations can be performed. The submodules can be programmed to perform boolean functions on their input variables.

The "local processor" provides the user with access to the system. The local processor contains (compared to the time-shared central processor) a small amount of parallel data processing power (definition is compatible with the central parallel processor) as well as a sequential processor (see Fig. 8.10). The local sequential processor has two main tasks: it provides

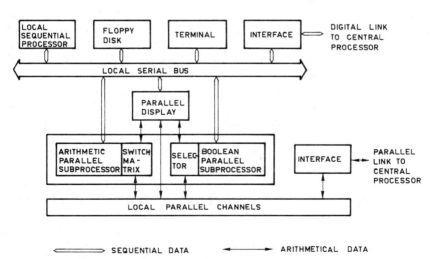

FIG. 8.10   Architecture of a local processor of the time-shared hybrid system

the sequential power for tasks like editing, compiling, and file manipulation, while it also executes the sequential part of the user's hybrid program.

The "system manager" is a sequential processor which coordinates all time-sharing aspects of the system. This processor determines, for instance, the system definition of the central parallel processor.

The automation of a hybrid computer, as studied in this project, has given hybrid computation a new degree of freedom: application of the principle of extension in time by means of parallel overlays. When for a simulation problem, the capacity of the parallel processor is not sufficient, the user can split up the system model in different parts, and execute them sequentially (assuming the model structure allows such a decomposition without the need for an extensive iteration process).

In the following section some important aspects, which can result in potential bottle-necks, of the architecture of a parallel data processor as part of a simulator, are discussed without going in details as to component hardware/software restrictions (a more elaborate version can be found in [47]).

8.3.3   Proposed architecture of a parallel data processor

8.3.3.1   *Spatial and time-order hierarchy implementability*

Because of the demand of a modular architecture with a strong regularity for hardware and software, only recursive sptial hierarchies of data-processing modules can be considered to be relevant for a parallel data processor. As seen above, modelling a system will often not naturally result in a recursive spatial hierarchy, but can easily be transformed into a recursive one (see example in Figs. 8.5 and 8.6). When successive decomposition results in bottom system models at many decomposition levels, transformation in a full-recursive spatial hierarchy will result in a large percentage of unused subsystem models, as well as an increase of the percentage of dummies (both introduced to satisfy the regularity in the decomposition rules).

In a similar way, because of the demand of a modular architecture, for the realization of an appropriate "time-order hierarchy" implementability, the time-order hierarchy to be incorporated in a parallel data processor by hardware and software must be a recursive one. In a time-order hierarchy of a system model, in principle each potential submodel can be reached via different transition paths. Consequently, in contrast with a full spatial hierarchy, a full time-order hierarchy can have either an increasing or a decreasing number of potential subsystem models for increasing transition level. The occurrence of identical subsystem models can have considerable influence on the hardware/software implementation in a parallel data processor. Transformation in a recursive time-order hierarchy is only possible if a given system model time-order hierarchy has a maximum number of possible successors smaller than, or equal to, the number of possible transitions in the recursive time-order hierarchy. In this respect it looks acceptable to restrict the class of transparently implementable time-order hierarchies by limitation of the number of different system model definitions (also restricted by "storage capacity"), as well as the number of possible successors per transition level.

As for "spatial hierarchy implementability" it is necessary to analyse typical time-order hierarchies practical system models in order to be able to design the implementability in more detail.

8.3.3.2 *Interconnectability*

In a spatial hierarchy representation, the mappings in the interaction kernels (Fig. 8.7) are instantaneous ones. Implementation of an instantaneous mapping on a data-processing module always requires computation modelling, resulting in a transformation of the mapping in an algorithm. Algorithms are inherently state-transition mappings. It is assumed, therefore, that the design of algorithms for instantaneous mappings is such that they can be considered to be quasi-instantaneous, compared with the algorithms for the state transition mappings occurring in the bottom system models.

Successive decomposition of a system model in a natural way might, but not necessarily, lead to bottom system models of the first order. Uniformity in the architecture of a parallel data processor implies that the submodules of a data processor bottom module are first order, but showing full interconnectability among each other within the module. This implies that the submodules must be able to handle a vectorial input variable of a dimension equal to the number of submodules in the data processor bottom module. For the same reason the submodules of the interaction kernels will also have to represent first-order models with a vectorial input variable.

As was discussed earlier, for large systems and models the interconnection matrix is sparse. Hence, interconnectability reduction can be allowed in the spatial hierarchy of the data processor. The interconnectability reduction is considered in Fig. 8.11 in the case of a parallel data processor with a truncated ternary spatial hierarchy.

There are systems (the majority of distributed parameter systems) showing an interaction structure which does not allow interconnectability reduction in its spatial hierarchy, if one-to-one analogy in space has to be pre-

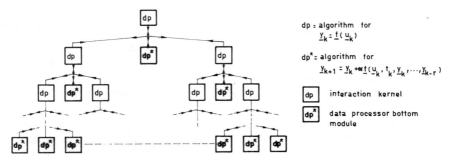

FIG. 8.11   Spatial interconnection structure of a parallel data processor in the case its spatial hierarchy is truncated ternary

served. Simulation of such systems by means of only extension in space will not be possible. The advanced sequential data processing power of the simulator has to be used, allowing extension in time in an efficient way, by applying parallel overlays in for example block-iterative procedures.

8.3.3.3   *Parallel data processing and algorithms*

Taking into account the current hardware technology, the hardware/software design of the parallel data processor can primarily be based on methodology in terms of data processing algorithms and methods. Much effort has to be spent on the design and development of algorithms (because they will influence the parallel data processor) based upon true parallel as well as advanced sequential data processing in the future. True parallel data processing concerns handling of continuously conflicting tasks in parallel.

In each data processing module of any level in Fig. 8.11, implementation of a certain mapping has to be performed using compound algorithms designed through the extension in space and in time principle from the set of basic algorithms operating in the discrete time set T_p (with processing cycle time τ_p). A basic algorithm is preprogrammed in a spatial configuration of arithmetic components operating parallel in time in the discrete time set T_b (with basic cycle time $\tau_b \ll \tau_p$) and is therefore called a *parallel algorithm*.

Consider an example of the use of a parallel algorithm in advanced sequential data processing: a multipoint compound algorithm for a set of n homogeneous first-order differential equations:

$$\frac{d(\underline{x}(t))}{dt} = \underline{f}(\underline{x}(t)), \qquad\qquad t_0 < t < t_1;\ \underline{x}(t_0) = \underline{x}_0 \qquad\qquad (8.1)$$

where "multipoint" means that a point algorithm (mapping in one point of the argument space) has to be executed for a sequence of values of the input variable. Continuously interacting parallel interval mappings (like the ones representing the n continuous-time models of first order in (8.1)) and ditto algorithms are called, respectively, true parallel interval mappings and *true parallel algorithms*.

The recursive interval mapping (8.1) is realized by a multipoint algorithm $x_k = F(x_{k-1})$, $k = 1, 2, \ldots$, with $t_k - t_{k-1} = \tau$. This algorithm "a" is a compound one and composed of n algorithms a_j, $j = 1, \ldots, n$. The parallel algorithms a_j are composed of arithmetic components of delay type with delay τ_b. It implies that the parallel algorithm a_j is a delay algorithm of delay τ_j, $\tau_j \gg \tau_b$. Delay algorithms are algorithms which evaluate a certain function with a delay between input and output, dependent on the complexity of the function. Hence the value of τ_j depends on the function f_j. Also the algorithm "a" becomes a delay algorithm of delay τ, $\tau \gg \tau_b$. Therefore algorithm "a" is not a true parallel algorithm in T_b, but a true parallel algorithm in T_a, $T_a = \{t_k\}$. The values of τ and τ_j, $j = 1, \ldots, n$ satisfy the unequality:

$$\tau \geq \max_j \tau_j \qquad\qquad (8.2)$$

Realization of the interval mapping (8.1) in this way as a *parallel delay algorithm* yields much profit only in the case of balanced complexity. In the best case, the extension in space of delay algorithm "a" in n parallel delay algorithms a_j results in an increase of processing speed by a factor n. In the worst case there is hardly an improvement; then implementation of interval mapping (8.1) as a sequential delay algorithm is a good alternative.

This example is illustrative for some bottle-necks which occur in practice. Realization of a complex point algorithm as a parallel delay algorithm often requires optimization of the decomposition in smaller parallel operating delay algorithms, in order to obtain an acceptable balance of complexity. This makes it more difficult to realize "computation modelling by exception". But implementation of recursive interval mappings as a multipoint parallel delay algorithm also raises the problem that the time scale factor is dependent, in a nontransparent way, on the complexity of the interval mappings. In interactive simulation studies these bottle-necks can be great disadvantages.

A better approximation of the natural approach taken in the continuous-time parallel data processor will be obtained when, instead of parallel delay algorithms, discrete-time *true parallel algorithms* (also called continuous-time algorithms) are utilized. Such algorithms allow the exchange of "usable" data, usable a.o. with respect to accuracy at all discrete times of the basic time set T_b. This way of parallel processing is a discrete-time version of continuous-time true parallel data processing (the way of data processing in analog computation). Whether the produced data of such true parallel operating algorithms can be considered to be usable or not, depends on the further properties of the algorithms.

Consider the design of true parallel algorithms in more detail. A mapping $y = f(u)$ cannot be realized instantaneously, so $y_{k+1} = f(u_k)$. The function value at time t_k can be approximated by a mapping f^*, a function of a finite number of preceding argument values:

$$y_k \approx f^* (u_{k-1}, u_{k-2}, u_{k-3}, \ldots, u_{k-L-1})$$

where:

—the preceding argument values have a decreasing influence on the function value when time increases;
—for a constant argument, f^* will be equal to f.

Suppose now that the mapping f^* can be decomposed into simple mappings f_i (possible to generate within a time τ_b) which can be nested hierarchically:

$$y_k = f_0 (u_{k-1}, f_1 (u_{k-2}, f_2 (u_{k-3}, \ldots, f_L (u_{k-L-1}) \ldots), t_k \ \varepsilon \ T_b, k \geqslant L + 1$$
$$(8.3)$$

where f_j, $j = 0, \ldots,$ L represent the mapping of the algorithm as implemented in block j, and where t_0 is the initial time. If the time indices in equation (8.3) are all equal to k-L-l, the reader will recognize the classical "sequential pipeline". If the indices are different, a "hybrid pipeline" is obtained (Fig. 8.12). The term hybrid is used because the blocks operate not only sequentially in space, but also parallel in space, with respect to the input variable. The output of a hybrid pipeline has a delay of only τ_b. The initial value of a hybrid pipeline algorithm is a nxL matrix for $u \in R^n$. Note that (8.3) also represents the description of a non-recursive, non-linear digital filter in time set T_b.

The generation of trigonometric functions, for example, can be done using
– a sequential pipeline algorithm:

$$(\sin u)_{k+5} = \left(u_k \cdot \left(\frac{1}{1!} + u_k^2 \left(\frac{-1}{3!} + u_k^2 \left(\frac{1}{5!} + u_k^2 \left(\frac{-1}{7!} + u_k^2 \cdot \frac{1}{9!} \right) \right) \right) \right) \right)$$

–a hybrid pipeline algorithm:

$$(\sin u)_{k+1} = \left(u_k \cdot \left(\frac{1}{1!} + u_{k-2}^2 \left(-\frac{1}{3!} + u_{k-3}^2 \left(\frac{1}{5!} + u_{k-4}^2 \left(-\frac{1}{7!} + u_{k-5}^2 \cdot \frac{1}{9!} \right) \right) \right) \right) \right)$$

In this case all pipeline segments, except for the last one, have to execute similar arithmetics.

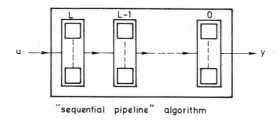

"sequential pipeline" algorithm

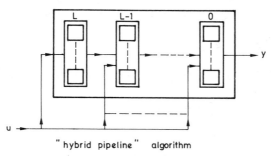

" hybrid pipeline " algorithm

FIG. 8.12   Spatial configurations in general form of a "sequential pipeline" and a "hybrid pipeline" algorithm

Several examples of hybrid pipeline algorithms are discussed in [8]. Note that in some cases the pipeline may become too long, e.g. when the truncation in the above example includes too many terms. In such cases, a combination of table look-up methods and hybrid pipeline arithmetic [47] must be used.

In designing a compound algorithm there is often need for one or more closed loops. A stability study made in [64] concludes that in a parallel data processor compound algorithms should be implemented in different time sets T_{pj}, $j = 1, 2, \ldots$ when true parallel algorithms are used. Hence, input and output buffers in the arithmetic components will be necessary in order to "transform" these different time sets in the time set of data transfer T_d (with $\tau_d \leqslant \min \tau_{pj}$).

Stability conditions of true parallel algorithms are not only dependent on the mathematical properties of the topology of the spatial structure of its parallel operating arithmetic components, but also on the stability intervals of these components. So is the stability interval of the linear open loop hybrid pipeline

$$y_k = \alpha_1 u_{k-1} + \alpha_2 u_{k-2} + \ldots + \alpha_m u_{k-m} \quad \text{with} \quad \sum_{j=1}^{m} \alpha_j = 1$$

evaluated using Z-transform analysis, and results for the special case α_j = $1/m$ for $j = 1, \ldots , m$ in $-m <$ feedback gain < 1.

In case internal feedback from the output of a hybrid pipeline to the inputs of all blocks is utilized, a closed loop hybrid pipeline algorithm is obtained, described by:

$$y_k = f_0(u_{k-1}, y_{k-1}, f_1(u_{k-2}, y_{k-2}, f_2(u_{k-3}, y_{k-3}, \ldots, f_L(u_{k-L-l}, y_{k-L-l}) \ldots)$$

$$(8.4)$$

Note that this description is identical to a recursive non-linear digital filter in time set T_b. A special case of the linearized version,

$$y_k = \sum_{j=1}^{m} (\beta_j y_{k-j} + \alpha_j u_{k-j})$$

the true parallel algorithm (so-called single step algorithm)

$$y_k = y_{k-1} + \frac{\tau_b}{\tau} (u_{k-1} - y_{k-1})$$

shows a stability interval

$$-\frac{2\tau}{\tau_b} + 1 < \text{feedback gain} < 1$$

Hence a large stability interval requires $\tau \gg \tau_b$.

Note that the single step algorithm is a discretized version of the unconditionally stable continuous-time algorithm

$$\tau \frac{dy(t)}{dt} + y(t) = u(t)$$

For constant $u(t)$ the algorithms have the same equilibrium state.

For a more extensive treatment on design criteria of a parallel data processor based on stability aspects, the reader is referred to [64].

A final consideration concerns the integration of ordinary differential equations. Various numerical methods exist to perform the integration of

$$\frac{d\underline{x}(t)}{dt} = \underline{f}(\underline{x}(t), \underline{u}(t)), t \in [t_0, t_e) ; \underline{x}(t_0) = \underline{x}_0$$

but nearly all are unsuited for parallel data processing; application of methods with local truncation errors of order higher than $0(\Delta t_k)^2$ is useless [64]. When integration is realized by means of discrete-time integration algorithms which are continuous in T_b, the method of Euler (first order) is attractive. An important objection to this method although is that the stepsize has to be rather small, which increases the accumulation of round-off errors.

From the numerical integration method of Euler

$$\underline{x}_k = \underline{x}_{k-1} + \Delta t_k \, \underline{f}(\underline{x}_{k-1}, \underline{u}_{k-1})$$

an attractive parallel algorithm in T_b can be derived. With the smallest Δt_k equal to τ_b:

$$\underline{x}_k = \underline{x}_{k-1} + \tau_b \, \underline{v}_{k-1}$$
$$\underline{v}_k = \underline{f}(\underline{x}_{k-1}, \underline{u}_{k-1}) \tag{8.5}$$

As arithmetic components of the parallel algorithm, a "linear combination" delay algorithm of dimension two and a "function generation" algorithm, are needed. The function will be in general too complex to be implemented within τ_b. "Quasi-continuous-time table look-up" algorithms have to be applied [47]. Data transfer between arithmetic components requires, however, that all data are transferred in the same word length. Consequently, each output variable has to be rounded off before transfer. On the other hand, in true parallel data processing, because of the small time step τ_b, the term $\tau_b \, \underline{v}_{k-1}$ should be taken into account in such a way that the resulting cumulative contribution is in agreement with the required accuracy. Hence a *round-off correction* should be introduced in the next processing cycle.
With

$$\underline{x}_k = \underline{x}_{l,k} + \underline{x}_{r,k} \tag{8.6}$$

where $\underline{x}_{l,k}$ is the round-off value of $\underline{x}_k$ and $\underline{x}_{r,k}$ the local round-off error, round-off correction applied to (8.5) results in:

$$\underline{x}_k = \underline{x}_{k-1} + \underline{x}_{r,k-1} + \tau_b \underline{v}_{k-1} \tag{8.7}$$
$$\underline{v}_k = \underline{f}(\underline{x}_{l,k-1}, \underline{u}_{k-1})$$

In a parallel data processor all arithmetic components have to be internally provided with such a round-off procedure.

8.3.3.4 *An experimental parallel data processor*

In order to be able to experiment with parallel algorithms and the extension in space and in time principle, an experimental parallel data processor has been built at the Delft University of Technology, consisting of data processing elements which can be ordered in time and in space in a flexible way.

The basic building-block of the experimental parallel processor is the data-processing element (DPE). Each element is able to perform a parallel/sequential data-processing task autonomously, according to a programmable system definition. The set of possible arithmetical operations is quite large and is comparable with the set of operations in calculator-type microprocessors. The operations can be performed in a single DPE or a group of DPEs. In order to do this, the DPEs can be hierarchically ordered to form a data processing module (DPM). Compound algorithms can be formed in such a way.

In the experimental parallel processor the DPEs operate in parallel and have to be interconnected in some way. The interconnections are made via a data transfer system (Fig. 8.13), via which arithmetical and boolean variables are transmitted between the system components. As was described earlier, the discrete-time sets of the DPEs must not necessarily be the same. This means that the data transfer system has to be an intermedium between the different time sets of the DPEs and between the DPEs and the environment such as a sequential processor. In the experimental parallel processor each output is connected to each input. It is obvious that this cannot be extended to an unlimited number of DPMs. Above a certain number of DPMs modularization is necessary.

The system definition can be changed at an implicitly or explicitly given time. The DPEs have a restricted boolean processing capability. The result-

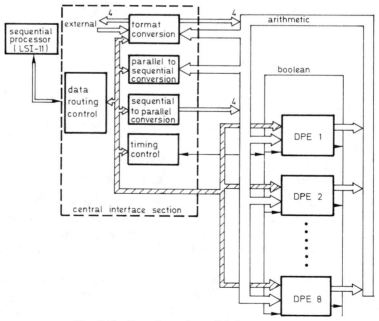

FIG. 8.13   Experimental parallel data processor

ing boolean variables can be connected to an external boolean parallel processor, as in the Time Shared Hybrid System (see Section 8.3.2).

The sequential processor is an LSI-11. Program preparation, loading of the system definition of the DPEs, and the implementation of the hierarchical structure is done via this processor. For the transfer of variables between the sequential processor and the parallel processor, a sequential to parallel conversion unit is included. For coupling external devices a format conversion unit is needed.

In the experimental parallel processor there are eight DPEs. Each DPE has one arithmetical and a number of boolean outputs. A DPE autonomously controls the selection of 16 arithmetical variables. The time-set of a DPE is determined by a timing control block, and can be chosen independently from the time-sets of the other DPEs. The arithmetical variables are represented in 16 or 32-bit integers, or 32-bit floating-point format. All output variables are transmitted in parallel via the data transfer system in a 4-bit parallel/byte serial format. The transfer is periodic, each transfer cycle time a parallel data transfer takes place. The structure of a data processing element is outlined in Fig. 8.14. The processing power of the DPE is formed by an arithmetical processor (Am 9511). For the temporary storage of variables a data memory is included (max. 64 variables).

The functioning of the DPE components is controlled by a microprogrammable control section. The desired algorithm is programmed in a specially developed assembly language. A cross assembler in the sequential processor translates the parallel program into the machine code of the DPEs. In the execution phase each DPE autonomously executes the programmed algorithms. The program determines the transfer of variables within the DPE, the modes of the input and output buffers and the operations performed on variable in the arithmetical processor. The program-

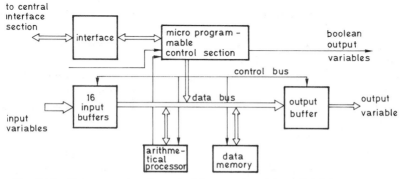

FIG. 8.14   Data-processing element of the experimental parallel data processor

mer can use boolean input variables to control the flow of his program and boolean output variables can be programmed for external use. The sequential processor initializes and controls the parallel process via a sequential program. This program is written in FORTRAN extended with a set of routines for the communication with the parallel processor. For more details the reader is referred to [7].

8.4 ARCHITECTURE OF INTERACTIVE SOFTWARE

8.4.1 Characterization of interactive systems

A program architecture is needed enabling the user to control interactively to a certain extent the flow of activities during program execution. Normally, the user can exercise influence on a program's control flow only at points where the program is ready for it. The means which the program provides the user with to exercise influence on the flow of control during execution shall be called the "user interface of the program". The user interface consists of certain media for man-machine interaction, and a language in which the user formulates commands and other messages to the system, [78].

Man-computer interaction takes place in the form of a dialog with the following properties:

—Dialogs may be non-sequential and non-procedural processes. A dialog may consist of concurrent processes that need be synchronized for communication at certain points. They are non-procedural in the sense that, unlike the activities of the computer, the activities of the human operator are not determined in procedural form (by a program).

—The relationship between the dialog partners is asymmetric. One of them usually has the initiative and gives orders; the other one is obliged to respond to the orders and perform specified tasks.

—Dialogs are state-dependent. Certain messages may not be processed directly, but may be stored in memory and affect the processing of ensuing messages, which may be differently interpreted depending on the course of actions taken so far.

In the future, one may find an increasing use of speech as communication medium in interactive systems; be it in the form of an output of synthesized speech by the system, or in the form of an input of spoken user commands into the system. Speech synthesizers mostly work with a set of "phonems" (the primitive sound elements of which spoken words consist). The wave-form of each phonem has been digitized and stored in a memory. The synthesis of spoken words or phrases is then accomplished by reading the appropriate phonems in the right order form memory, and reconverting them into the sounds they represent. A speech output of this type with a capacity of several hundred words fits on a single VLSI chip. Speech input is more complicated than speech output, as it requires a speech recognition system. Despite tremendous efforts invested over the years into research in this area, it has not been possible to devise economical systems which would recognize, with a high rate of success, a large vocabulary of words spoken by arbitrary speakers. The systems that exist either must be calibrated to a particular speaker and then are able to recognize a vocabulary of 100 words or less with a success rate of 99%, or they can recognize a very restricted vocabulary of not more than ten carefully selected words which now may be spoken by various speakers. At the time being, the general application of either type of speech recognition system as communication medium in a terminal, however, is prohibited by the fact that they still are much too expensive for this purpose.

8.4.2 The use of abstractions in interactive systems design

In abstract descriptions of interactive systems we need models and descriptive tools for:
—communication abstraction,
—program and data abstraction.

8.4.2.1 *Communication abstraction*

It certainly is very useful to have an abstract model for the user interface. Such a model was developed by Parnas [173] and is called the transition diagram model. A basic notion of the transition diagram model is that the medium by which the system communicates messages to the user, and the user issues commands to the system, is provided by a terminal of some sort. At any point in time, that terminal is in some specific terminal state. A terminal state is a state of the automaton

$$UI = (TS, IM, OM, \delta, \lambda)$$

where TS is the set of all terminal states;
  IM is the set of all possible input messages;
  OM is the set of all possible output messages;
  $\delta : TS \times IM \rightarrow TS$ is the state transition function;
  $\lambda : TS \times IM \rightarrow OM$ is the output function.

Hence, we have a finite state machine which performs a transition whenever it receives an input. On each transition it produces an output, i.e. a message for the user. The transition performed is a function of the input received and the current state.

It is a specific feature of the terminal state model that, in any given state, only a small fraction of the set of all possible input messages will be meaningful. All other possible input messages will be rejected by the system. There are two possible ways in which the rejection may take place:

—The input message is simply ignored, i.e., no state-transition occurs.

—The user is informed by an appropriate error message that the input message received is invalid. In this case, a transition takes place from the current state to itself, thus producing the error message.

Meaningful input messages are interpreted by the system appropriately, e.g., as a procedure call, a parameter value, etc.

It is one of the advantages of the terminal state diagram model that it makes design errors apparent.

Error 1: almost alike states. A system may have a number of different terminal states which are very similar in the sense that most of the input messages have the same interpretation. Such a situation may cause considerable difficulties for a user who must:

(1) be aware that there are several distinct states,

(2) learn the conditions under which each of these states is reached,

(3) remember the difference between them as well as which input message is appropriate in which state,

(4) occasionally respond in two different ways to apparently identical stimuli.

Error 2: inconsistent ways of reaching an individual state. A user who takes some action to reach a new state may later decide to return to the old state. In some cases this may be possible simply by pressing a single button. In other cases he may have to press the button more than once. In still other cases he may have to give a sequence of specific command to the system in order to get to the desired state; and in some cases he may not be able to make the return at all.

Error 3: terminal or almost terminal submachines. A terminal submachine of a finite state machine is a set of states which, once entered, cannot be exited. There may be such states in the user interface which it may be impossible to leave by other than the general escape mechanism, e.g., provided through a "break" button. For example, in the case of a file manipulation system the user may be informed by the system at some point that the file name he has used is not associated with a defined file, and that he must supply the name of a defined file. The user has either forgotten to define his file or assumed that the system would do it for him when he first used the name. In any event he has no appropriate file name that he can use. Any name of message that he gives is rejected as not being the name of a defined file, and there is no way out of the state.

Error 4: inability to correct errors in long strings of parameters. Sometimes, a system provides no way after inputting a parameter to go back and correct a previously inputted parameter.

Parnas, who pointed out the possible errors listed above, also lists some general guidelines for the design of a user interface.

Guideline 1: The user interface must make it simple for the user to use the system in the manner of a desk tool. That means that the user should not be expected to work on a single task in a predictable fashion until he can go no further with that task. Rather, the user of a desk tool expects to be interrupted at one task and to switch to another with little effort. He expects to be able to switch in the middle of a task to another task, which may provide data to be used on a return to the first task. He does not wish to be subjected to any particular discipline (e.g., last suspended—first resumed) in resuming a suspended task. If his suspended task has a data base, he would like to have access to it in a simple way while working on some other task.

Guideline 2: The user interface should be elaborate for users who implement subsystems for the "end users". For example, to this end restricted access to certain system functions and system tables must be provided. Examples are:
—access to absolute memory space,
—cursor control on the CRT terminal,
—access to certain internal representations,
—access to system variables (e.g., subroutine return stack),
—capability to define access rights.
A programming system which probably excels all others in that respect is APL. The long term usefulness of a system depends on its flexibility and the ease with which it expands by the addition of subsystems, or even of new syntactic constructs.

8.4.2.2 *Program and data abstraction (description of control flow and data flow)*

The behaviour of a software module in general can be described by a functional specification, defining the input-output behaviour of the module. In principle, this also holds true for the description of interactive

programs. However, in the latter case we also need a behavioural description of the human operator in the system. In software engineering, we distinguish three different approaches toward a formal specification of software behaviour, namely:
—the algebraic method,
—the state-machine method,
—the abstract model method.
Each of these methods describes the semantics of software modules on the basis of underlying abstractions (representations); i.e. the specifications are abstract in the sense that they are given independently of any possible implementation. In the cases of the "algebraic method" and the "state-machine method", the underlying abstractions are part of the method and thus given. In the case of the "abstract model method", however, it is left to the user of the method arbitrarily to choose the abstractions that should be introduced as representations of the functions and data objects under consideration.

The algebraic method is hardly suitable for describing the behaviour of the human operator in an interactive system. The state-machine method, on the other hand, is quite appropriate to model the cause-and-effect behaviour of the human operator by the input-output relation of a finite state machine; provided it is safe to assume that the human operator behaves in a deterministic fashion.

A recently developed, general approach to the finite state machine, is to model an interactive system by an interconnection of "channels" and "agencies", called a channel/agency net. The two component types of such a net can be characterized as follows:

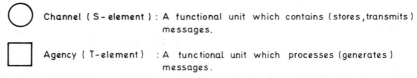

Channel (S - element) : A functional unit which contains (stores, transmits) messages.

Agency (T-element) : A functional unit which processes (generates) messages.

The functions performed by either human operators or processors are modelled by agencies; whereas the channels represent the transmission or storage of messages, the supply of an argument to a function, or the storage of a result produced by a function. In a channel/agency net (CA-net), channels and agencies are connected by unidirectional (or bidirectional) links. These links may connect a channel with an agency and vice versa, but never a channel with a channel or an agency with an agency. Channel-/agency nets may be considered as generalization of data flow nets. The possible relationships between a channel and an agency are illustrated in Fig. 8.15. Figure 8.16 depicts a very coarse model of an interactive system.

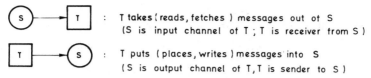

FIG. 8.15   Relationships between a channel and an agency

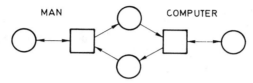

FIG. 8.16   A very coarse model of an interactive system

Models given in the form of channel/agency nets may be refined into more elaborate and detailed channel/agency nets. Figure 8.17 is an example of a refinement of the model of Fig. 8.16.

The channel/agency model is general enough to allow for agencies which are non-procedural and non-deterministic. On the other hand, this seeming advantage reduces its expressive power and thus its usefulness. It would be more straightforward and more simple if we could model a dialog system by the inter-action of several concurrent processes, one of them representing the user's activities and the others representing the activities of the system.

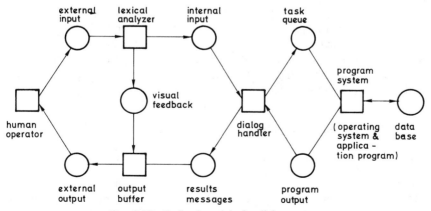

FIG. 8.17   Refined model of a dialog system

For systems of concurrent processes we have well-known and well-understood abstract models and descriptive tools such as Petri Nets, path expressions, and computational schemata. An abstract data type represents the entirety of all data objects of a certain type, together with the set of functions which can be applied to the data objects. The notion of abstract data types has come to play a central role in modern software engineering, and will probably play a central role in future programming languages. Therefore, it is justified to consider here the notion of abstract data types in more detail.

The essential feature of an abstract data type is that its objects cannot be accessed through simple referencing (as is the case for the data objects of the conventional high-level programming languages) but only through the functions defined on them. Therefore, an abstract data type encapsulates its data objects.

The functions (operations) of an abstract data type come in three categories:
—state-changing functions (O-functions),
—value-rendering functions (V-functions),
—combined state-changing and value-rendering functions (OV-functions).
O-functions allow for changes of the state (the value) of the data objects to which they are applied. Usually, there are functions to create or destroy a data object, to insert a new data item into an object or remove an existing data item from it, or replace the value of a data item in a data object by a new value. V-functions yield copies of the values of the data objects, or certain substructures of them, including the elementary data item. That is, V-functions render values but do not affect the state of an object. OV-functions combine the effect of both the V-function and the O-function.

Of course, it depends on the structure of the data objects how the data items of an object can be accessed (remember that such common data structures as stacks, queues, arrays, trees, lists, etc. all differ in their access mode). By the same token, however, one may say that, once the access mode has been specified as part of the function definitions of an abstract data type, the structure of the data objects of this type is implied (whichever view one prefers).

8.4.3   Design considerations for interactive software

8.4.3.1   *Design methodology in general*

Modern software design is envisaged as a top-down process as depicted in Fig. 8.18. It begins with requirement engineering, i.e. the definition of the required functionality of the system, as well as certain attributes such as

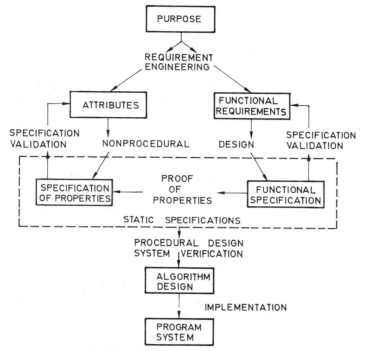

Fɪɢ. 8.18   Hierarchical software design methodology

performance, reliability, portability, etc. that the system is supposed to meet. In the case of interactive systems, an important attribute may be the maximum response time of the system to a user's message. Hence, the result of requirement engineering is some information about the functional requirements and the attributes the system will have to meet.

Based on the result of "requirement engineering", the next step consists in the non-procedural design, the result being a complete set of static specifications of the functions the system must be able to perform, and the properties the system must have, in order to exhibit the required attributes. The specifications obtained should be validated, i.e. it should be demonstrated, either by formal deductions or by examples (testing), that the specifications cover all functional requirements and attributes.

Based on the static specifications obtained, the next step consists in a procedural design. In this step the algorithms are designed which realize the functional behaviour of the system as set forth by the functional specifications.

The procedural design is to be refined until an implementation has been obtained. Each refinement step should include a validation phase in which it is shown, either by formal correctness proof or by testing, that the procedural design obtained meets the given static specifications. However, formal correctness proving of complex "real-world" programs is at least very tedious, if not too difficult to be practically feasible, and, consequently, the usual approach to validation is through testing. This may change in the future if automated verification systems (verification condition generators and theorem provers) become available [14].

8.4.3.2 Design methodology for interactive software

In general, the hierarchical software design methodology outlined in Section 8.4.3.1 may of course also be applied to interactive software. What makes interactive software specific, however, is the fact that we may find attributes which are quite idiosyncratic, and we certainly will find functional requirements which are unique for interactive systems, namely the functions required to provide the user interface and carry out the man–computer dialog. Because of its specific nature, specific tools are needed to describe the man–computer dialog. Such a descriptive tool may be the channel/agency net model discussed in Section 8.4.2.2. Because of its specific nature and the specific descriptive tools required, the process of interactive software design does not differ in methodology from the process of software design in general but in the techniques used.

Strictly sequential dialog handling

DEFINITION: Strictly sequential dialog.
A total sequentialization of the man–computer dialog is accomplished by introducing the following two rules:
—the user cannot take any action unless being prompted by the system accordingly;
—the system, immediately after having sent a "prompt" (an appropriate message) to the user, puts itself into the "wait" state until the user's response to the "prompt" has been received.
Naturally, the strictly sequential execution leaves no room for any spontaneity whatsoever on the side of the user. Its biggest disadvantage, however, is the fact that it may lead to a considerable amount of unnecessary waiting. Therefore, such a simple organizational scheme is usually affordable only in dedicated systems.

In this simple scheme the man–computer interaction can be modelled by a simple finite-state automaton model, in lieu of the more general channel/agency model of Section 8.4.2.2. In the state-machine model, the states now are the "wait" states of the system, when it waits for an input message from the user. An input received stimulates a transition into a new state. On each transition, the system executes a certain procedure and generates an output which is a message to prompt the next action of the user. In principle, one could incorporate into these procedures all the polling loops, case selection constructs, etc. by which the inputs of the user are handled. However, this would be poor programming style, as such an approach would make it very difficult to modify the dialog as well as the system procedures.

Logically, the dialog handling, (which results in system procedure calls) and the procedure themselves should be separated. Therefore, we define a special software module, called a "dialog handler", to handle communication with the user and the execution of his commands. It is now the dialog handler who sends out messages to the user, receives input messages from the user, interprets them, and converts them into procedure calls.

This separation makes the dialog system readily modifiable and extensible, e.g. by adding new menus or new commands to a menu, changing the wording of commands or messages, augmenting the system accordingly if new communication media are to be added, etc. All this can be carried out without having to change any of the "service modules" of the system, i.e. the procedures which perform computations, handle data bases, etc.

Attempts have been made to define a dialog description language, i.e. a meta-language for describing the nature of the dialog, the communication media involved, and the commands and messages to be used. If such a syntactically consistent and complete formal language existed, then it would be no major problem to implement a compiler which would automatically generate a corresponding dialog handler from the description. As yet we have not seen any such system really being used. The problem here, however, is more a problem of language definition than implementation. It hardly seems possible to define a universal dialog description language, but languages of that kind will necessarily be rather application-oriented.

Concurrent dialog handling

In the case of the system providing a processor separate from the central processing unit (CPU) to run the dialog handler (e.g., an input-output processor), then the user's activities and the activities of the system may to some extent take place concurrently. This creates the situation where two (or more) concurrent processes share common data objects. This immediately raises the question of mutual exclusion of accesses to the shared objects: since a simultaneous access of two processes to the same data object may lead to undefined or incorrect states, it must be prevented. Therefore, it is a task of the programmer to prohibit such access overlapping. Sections of a process whose execution must not overlap with the execution of other processes, are called critical sections or critical regions. A collection of critical regions of a number of concurrent processes under execution is called a class of critical regions. The principle of mutual exclusion requires that, once a critical region of the class has been entered, all other critical regions of the class cannot be entered.

A number of mechanisms exist for the implementation of the mutual exclusion principle. These are primarily:
—use of monitors,
—explicit use of semaphores (WAIT, SIGNAL).

Monitor concept

High-level constructs for mutual exclusion, synchronization, etc. have a built-in policy that is visible, whereas the mechanisms used to implement the policy are not visible from the outside. One such high-level construct for the mutual exclusion policy is the monitor.

A monitor may be viewed as an abstract data type (Section 8.4.2.2) plus certain synchronization rules. That is, a monitor defines a (sharable) data object and all the operations the users (other processes) can potentially perform on it. The basic policy of a monitor is the principle of mutual exclusion; therefore, a monitor comprises appropriate synchronization mechanisms called monitor procedures. These procedures may be written so that, in addition to the mutual exclusion policy, the monitor will control the order in which several processes competing for access to the object can use the shared resource. However, this latter feature is not part of the basic policy but must be explicitly provided for by the implementor of the monitor. A monitor also defines an initial operation which is executed when its data object is created.

In the monitor concept, processes cannot directly reference (and thus operate on) shared data. They can only call monitor procedures that have access to the object. A monitor procedure is executed as part of the calling process (just like any other procedure). If concurrent processes simultaneously call monitor procedures which operate on the same (shared) object, these procedures can only be executed one at a time. Otherwise, processes might find the data object in some (unknown) intermediate state, which would make the results of monitor calls unpredictable. Therefore, a monitor must also take care of the mutual exclusion requirements.

To illustrate the operation of a monitor, we consider a monitor called line buffer. If defines a shared object: content (which is of type line); and some internal variables: full (which is of type boolean), sender, and receiver (both of type queue). "Line" is a user-defined type representing a text string. By calling the monitor procedure "receive (text)", the buffer "content" is assigned to "text", and the buffer is left empty; by calling the

```
type  linebuffer =
monitor
var content : line ; full : boolean ; sender ; receiver : queue
procedure entry receive ( var text : line ) ;
begin
   if not full then  delay ( receiver )
   text : = content ; full : = false ; continue ( sender ) ;
end ;
procedure entry   send ( text : line) ;
begin
   if full then  delay ( sender )
   content : = text ; full : = true  ;  continue ( receiver ) ;
end
begin full  : = false  end
```

FIG. 8.19   Example of a monitor implementation based on a queuing mechanism

monitor procedure "send (text)", "text" is filled into the buffer. However, "receive" can be executed only if the buffer is full, and "send" can be executed only if the buffer is empty. The monitor implementation based on the desired queuing mechanism is depicted in Fig. 8.19 [24].

The monitor procedure "receive" delays its calling process until the buffer is full. It then returns a text line to the process and, subsequently, the procedure continues the execution of a sending process (if there is one waiting in the sender queue). The monitor procedure "send" delays its calling process until the buffer is empty. It then puts a text line into the buffer and continues the process waiting in the receiver queue (if existent). Whether or not the buffer is empty is indicated by the boolean variable "full". Initially, the buffer is marked empty.

Semaphores
Concurrent processes may not only communicate via shared data objects but may co-operate in a joint effort to perform a certain function of the system. In this case it may be required that a process can send a message to another process. This is called inter-process communication (IPC).

The simplest possible construct for inter-process communication is provided by the pair of statements WAIT(EVENT) and SIGNAL(EVENT) (sometimes, the word SEND is used instead of SIGNAL). EVENT hereby is a (global) boolean variable, and the effect of the WAIT-SIGNAL mechanism is as follows. WAIT(EVENT): for EVENT = 0 the executing process goes into the 'wait' state until another process sets EVENT = 1 by executing the function SIGNAL(EVENT);
for EVENT = 1 the executing process sets EVENT = 0 and continues execution without further delay.

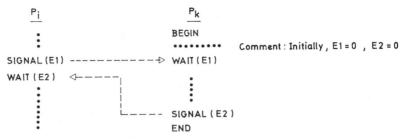

FIG. 8.20   Inter-process communication with the WAIT-SIGNAL mechanism

As an example, the WAIT-SIGNAL construct could be used by a process, P_i, to start execution of another process, P_k, and subsequently, go into the "wait" state. Process P_k is already initialized but suspended on a WAIT. When P_k is done, it signals completion to P_i, who was waiting for that event and can now go on.

In interactive programming, for instance, the WAIT-SIGNAL mechanism could be utilized for organizing the man–computer dialog in the "prompt/response" fashion. In general, it can be shown that the WAIT-SIGNAL mechanism is sufficient to handle all possible process synchronization tasks. However, it is a low-level construct which is error-prone and may have dangerous side effects. An especial argument against WAIT-SIGNAL mechanism is that the event variables are global and thus can be changed from anywhere in the program, i.e., from outside the processes involved.

For the conscientious system programmer, the WAIT-SIGNAL mechanism may be an indispensable tool; for the application programmer, it should be hidden inside the appropriate high-level constructs. The WAIT-SIGNAL mechanism can be used, for example, as a mechanism for the implementation of monitors. However, it is also possible to modify it so that it becomes a safe construct for inter-process communication.

We devised such a modification which works as follows: we introduced a construct consisting of three operations: INITIATE, EVENT, CAUSE; the effect of which is the following:

INITIATE (<process name>): allows a process to initiate another process; more precisely, send an initiation request to the scheduler to have another process initiated on his behalf; simultaneously, a unique internal system variable called "event notice" is created and initialized to "false".

EVENT (< process name >): tests the value of the event notice received from the named process; if the value is "false", then the executing process must wait for it to become true; if the value is "true", then the WAIT statement is executed and the event notice is "consumed" (destroyed).

CAUSE: signals an event to the waiting process by setting the appropriate event notice to "true".

This policy falls into the "no-wait send" category of inter-process cooperation protocols, i.e. the initiator can send an initiation request, and then continue with his work until he cannot proceed any further without the requested service having been completed. The event notices are local variables, shared only between initiator and initiated, and invisible from the outside. Thus a unique communication path is established between an initiating process and an initiated process, totally transparent to the programmer. Because of the unique communication path set up by the "guardian" (the scheduler) of the processes, the CAUSE operation needs no argument (the guardian knows who the initiator is). Consequently, a service process can be written without the need to know the names of the initiators (Fig. 8.21).

Interactive system as a distributed system

Probably the most important development in computer architecture currently under way is distributed computing. Distributed computing systems (or distributed systems) are the only computer architecture offering the potential to fulfil simultaneously all major requirements that can be postulated for a computer system, namely:

—high performance achieved through parallel processing, taking advantage of inexpensive LSI components (e.g., microprocessors);

—modular extensibility of the system;

—fault-tolerance of the system;

—increased economy achieved through a simplification of software.

A general definition of distributed computing systems is as follows.

DEFINITION: distributed computing system

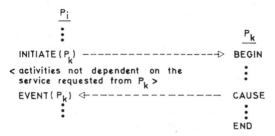

FIG. 8.21   High-level inter-process communication mechanism

A distributed system is a computing system, consisting of several 'processing nodes', which satisfies the following conditions:

—The overall functions of the system are provided through the cooperation of several processes.

—There are no two processes who have the same view of the global state of the system.

—There exists no unique process in the system who could make sure that the other processes have a consistent and identical view of the global state of the system.

From this definition it becomes obvious that it is primarily the system control which is distributed throughout the system. Moreover, the processing nodes of the system itself may be "spatially" or "geographically" distributed over a building, a complex of buildings, a region, a country, or even over some continents. The geographical dispersion of the nodes of the system implies that they can be only loosely coupled. By definition, a loosely coupled system of processing nodes is a system in which the nodes communicate solely through the exchange of messages. It should be mentioned that there is also a great interest in multiprocessor systems in which the processors are not dispersed but locally concentrated, yet in which control is nevertheless distributed (decentralized).

One of the basic requirements a distributed system must satisfy is that it can operate under the condition that the exchange of messages between nodes is subjected to a rather large, and possibly variable, propagation delay. Under such a condition, it is hard if not impossible to maintain a common time reference among the nodes. In other words, if a process in node i communicates its state to another process residing in node j, the state of the process in node i may already have changed again when the message finally arrives at node j. In locally dispersed systems, this is the reason why the nodes cannot have a consistent and identical view of the global state of the system.

In the conventional, locally concentrated computer systems there exists, of course, propagation delay as well. The difference to the locally dispersed systems, however, is that in the former case the delay times are so small that it becomes affordable to perform a "synchronization through waiting". That is, if a hardware resource in a conventional computer has activated another hardware resource to perform a service on its behalf, it goes into the wait state until it receives a message informing it that the other resource has reached a definite state, e.g. has performed the required service. In "local networks", where the processing nodes of a system are dispersed over a building or a complex of buildings (as is the case in office automation systems and certain transactional systems), or even in the case of (geographically distributed) computer networks, the delays are of such a magnitude that it is simply not economic to perform a synchronization through waiting.

There is another reason for systems with distributed control, and that is fault-tolerance. A system is said to be fault-tolerant with respect to failures of its components, if the failure of a component does not necessarily lead to a breakdown of the total system. Rather, a fault-tolerant system will under almost all circumstances maintain a certain residual functionality. This implies that there be no centralized components in the system, and this postulate includes centralized control. This may be the reason for applying the principle of distributed control, even in the case of locally concentrated multiprocessor systems. The processing nodes of such systems which consist basically of a processor-memory configuration plus some peripherals, are to a large extent autonomous in their activities. However, since they must co-operate in their endeavour to provide the required overall functionality of the system, they are obliged to obey certain co-operation rules (principle of co-operative autonomy). One such co-operation rule, for example, may be that a node has the freedom to decide when to honour a request for a service received from another node, but does not have the freedom arbitrarily to turn down such a request in the first place.

From our discussion we recognize that there are the following similarities between an interactive system and a distributed system:

—An interactive system consists of at least two "processing nodes", namely, the computer itself and its user.
—The two nodes (system and user) are only loosely coupled (through the exchange of messages).
—No authority exists in the system that would know at any given time instant the global state of the system.
—Consequently, control is distributed among the system and its user; both operate to a high extent autonomously, yet must obey certain co-operation rules.

This similarity implies that many of the principles and techniques developed for the organization of distributed computer systems may as well be used for the organization of interactive systems. Moreover, distributed systems, one they have reached a certain maturity, may become the favourite architectural solution for a wide range of interactive application systems.

As a concluding comment, the significance of Chapter 8 has been its multitude of suggestions for further research. The chapter reports to a certain extent on currently accomplished trial pieces, with the aim of providing the modelling process "computer-aided" features.

REFERENCES

1. AKAIKE, H. (1969), Statistical predictor identification. *Ann. Inst. Statist. Math.*, **21**, pp. 203–217, Tokyo.
2. AKAIKE, H. (1971), Information theory and an extension of the maximum likelihood principle. Proc. of the 2nd Intern. Symp. on Information Theory, Budapest.
3. AKAIKE, H. (1976), Canonical correlation analysis of time series and the use of an information criterion. *In* "System Identification: Advances and Case Studies", R. K. Mehra, D. G. Lainiotis (eds), Academic Press, New York and London.
4. AKISHIN, B. A., IVAKHNENKO, A. G. (1975), Extrapolation using monotonically varying noisy data. *Soviet Automatic Control* (June).
5. ANDERSON, T. W. (1958), "Introduction to Multivariate Statistical Analysis", John Wiley & Sons, New York.
6. ANDERSON, T. W. (1971), "The Statistical Analysis of Time Series", John Wiley & Sons, New York.
7. ANDRIESSEN, J. H. M., SIPS, H. J. and DE SWAAN ARONS, H. (1979), An experimental study of parallel data-processing structures. Proc. of the IMACS Congress on Simulation of Systems, Sorrento, North Holland Publishing Co.
8. ANDRIESSEN, J. H. M. (1980), Discrete-time parallel algorithms with continuous-time response. Proc. Simulation 80, Interlaken, Acta Press.
9. ANGOT, A. (1965), "Compléments de Mathématiques", Masson & Cie, Paris.
10. ASTROM, K. J., BOHLIN, T. (1965), Theory of self-adaptive control systems. Proc. of the IFAC Symp. Teddington, P. H. Hammond (ed.), Plenum Press, New York.
11. ASTROM, K. J. (1970), "Introduction to stochastic control theory", Academic Press, New York and London.
12. ASTROM, K. J., WITTENMARK, B. (1973), On Self-tuning regulators. *Automatica*, **9**.
13. ATHANS, M. (1970), Towards a practical theory for distributed parameter systems. *IEEE Trans. Autom. Contr.*, **AC-15**, pp. 245–247.
14. BALZER, R. M. (1974), A Language-independent programmers interface. Proc. AFIPS 1974 National Computer Conf., pp. 365–370.
15. BECK, M. B. (1980), Model structure identification from experimental data. *In* "Theoretical Systems Ecology: Advances and Case Studies", E. Halfon (ed.), Academic Press, New York and London.
16. BEER, J. T. (1963), "Cybernetics and Management", New York.

17. BELLMAN, R., ASTROM, K. J. (1970), On structural identifiability. *Math. Biosciences*, **7**.
18. BOX, G. E. P., HILL, W. J. (1967), *Technometrics*, **9**, p. 57.
19. BOX, G. E. P., JENKINS, G. M. (1970), "Time Series Analysis Forecasting and Control", Holden Day, San Francisco.
20. BREDEHOEFT, J. D., PINDER, G. F. (1970), Digital analysis of a real flow in multi-aquifer groundwater systems: a quasi three dimensional model, *Water Resources Research*, **6**, nr. 3, pp. 883–888.
21. BREDEHOEFT, J. D., PINDER, G. F. (1973), Mass transport in flowing ground-water, *Water Resources Research*, **9**, nr. 1, pp. 194–210.
22. BRENNAN, R. D., LINEBARGER, R. N. (1964), A survey of digital simulation: digital analog simulator programs, *Simulation*, **3**, nr. 6, pp. 22–36.
23. BRENNAN, R. D. (1968), "Continuous System Modeling Programs: State of the Art and Prospectives for Development", Simulation Programming Languages, North Holland Publishing Co.
24. BRINCH HANSEN, P. (1977), "The Architecture of Concurrent Programs". Prentice Hall, Englewood Cliffs, New Jersey.
25. BROWNLEE, K. A. (1965), "Statistical Theory and Methodology", John Wiley & Sons, New York.
26. BRYSON, A. E., HO, Y. C. (1969), "Applied Optimal Control", Mass. Ginn & Co.
27. BENDAT, J. S., PIERSOL, A. G. (1971), "Random Data Analysis and Measurement Procedures", Wiley–Interscience, New York.
28. CALVERT, T. W., YOUNG, T. Y. (1974), "Classification, Estimation and Pattern Recognition", American Elsevier, New York.
29. CARDENAS, A. F., KARPLUS, W. J. (1970), PDEL—a language for partial differential equations, *Communications of ACM*, **13**, pp. 184–191.
30. CARVER, M. B. (1974), FORSIM—a FORTRAN package for the automated solution of coupled partial and/or ordinary differential equation systems. User's Manual, Atomic Energy of Canada Ltd., Chalk River, Nuclear Laboratories, Chalk River, Ontario, Canada.
31. CARVER, M. B., STEWART, G. D., BLAIR, J. M. and SELANDER, W. N. (1978), The FORSIM VI simulation package for the automated solution of arbitrarily defined and partial and/or ordinary differential equation systems. Report No. AECL-5821, Atomic Energy of Canada Ltd., Chalk River, Ontario, Canada.
32. CASTI, J. L. (1977). "Dynamical Systems and their Applications, Linear Theory", Academic Press, New York and London.
33. CHAVENT, G. (1979), On the identification of distributed parameter systems. *In* "Identification and System Parameter Estimation", R. Iserman (ed.), Pergamon Press, Oxford.
34. CHERRY, B. H. (1980), Electric load forecasting: probing the issues with models. *In* "Gass, S. I., 1980".
35. CHU, Y. (1975), Concepts of high-level language computer architectures. Proc. ACM 1975 Annual Conf., pp. 6–13.
36. CLEMENTSON, A. T. (1977), Extended control and simulation language. Computer-aided Programming System, Lucas Institute for Engineering Production, University of Birmingham.
37. CLOSE, C. M., FREDERICK, D. K. (1978). "Modeling and Analysis of Dynamic Systems", Houghton Mufflin, New York.

38. COBELLI, C., ROMANIN-JACUR, G. (1976), On the structural identifiability of biological compartmental systems in a general input-output configuration. *Math. Biosciences*, **30**.
39. COLTON, D. L. (1980), "Analytic Theory of Partial Differential Equations", Pitman Advanced Publishing Program, Boston.
40. CONSOLIDATED ANALYSIS CENTERS, Inc. (1971), *SIMSCRIPT II.5 Reference Handbook*, Santa Monica, California.
41. CONTROL DATA CORPORATION (1968), *MIMIC Digital Simulation Language Reference Manual*, Sunnyvale, California.
42. CONTROL DATA CORPORATION (1971), *Continuous System Simulation Language Version 3, User's Guide*, Sunnyvale, California.
43. COVER, T. HART, P. (1976), "Nearest Neighbour Pattern Classification in Machine Recognition of Patterns", Aslok, Agrawala (eds), IEEE Press, New York.
44. CYRE, W. R., DAVIS, C. J., FRANK, A. A., JEDYNAK, L., REDMOND, M. J. and RIDEOUT, V. C. (1977), WISPAC: a parallel array computer for large-scale system simulation. *Simulation*, **29**, pp. 165–172.
45. DAWSON, J. M., HUFF, R. W. and WU, C. C. (1978), Plasma simulation on the UCLA CHI computer system. Proc. AFIPS National Computer Conf., 47, pp. 395–407.
46. DEKKER, L., ZUIDERVAART, J. C. (1977), A time-shared hybrid minisystem. Proc. Simulation 77, Montreux, pp. 192–197, Acta Press.
47. DEKKER, L., KERCKHOFFS, E. J. H., VANSTEENKISTE, G. C. and ZUIDERVAART, J. C. (1979), Outline of a future parallel simulator. Proc. of the IMACS Congress on Simulation of Systems, Sorrento, North Holland Publishing Co., pp. 837–864.
48. DENHAM, M. J. (1974), Canonical forms for the identification of multivariable linear systems. *IEEE Trans. Autom. Contr.*, **AC-19**, pp. 646–656.
49. DERTOUZOS, M., ATHANS, M., SPANN, R. and MASON, S. (1972), "Systems, Networks and Computations, Basic Concepts", McGraw Hill, New York.
50. DEUTSCH, R. (1969), "Estimation Theory", Prentice Hall, Englewood Cliffs, New Jersey.
51. DI STEFANO, J. J. (1979), Identifiability on linear systems. Lecture Notes on Cybernetics, U.C.L.A. .
52. DI STEFANO III, J. (1980), Identifiability concepts for dynamical systems. *IEEE Trans. Automatic Control*, **AC-25**.
53. DONGARRA, J. J., BUNCH, J. R., MOLER, C. B. and STEWART, C. W. (1979), "LINPACK User's Guide", to be published by Society for Industrial and Applied Mathematics.
54. DOOB, J. L. (1953), "Stochastic Processes'", John Wiley & Sons, New York.
55. DURBIN, J. (1954), *Rev. Int. Stat. Inst.*, **22**, p. 23.
56. DVORETSKY, A. (1956), On stochastic approximation. Proc. third Berkeley Symp. on Mathematical Statistics and Probability, 1, pp. 39–56.
57. ECONOMIDIS, T. (1977), Computing in the range of 100 megaflops. Wescon 77 Convention Record, San Francisco, (September).
58. EISENSTAT, S., GEORGE, A., GRIMES, R., KINCAID, D. and SHERMAN, S. (1979), Some comparisons of software packages for large sparse linear systems. *In* "Advances in Computer Methods for Partial Differential Equations III", R. Vichnevetsky (ed.).

59. ELZAS, M. S. (1979), What is needed for robust simulation? *In* "Methodology in Systems Modelling and Simulation", B. P. Zeigler, M. S. Elzas, G. J. Klir, T. I. Ören (eds), North Holland Publishing Co., Amsterdam.
60. EINSTEIN, A. (1956), "Uber die spezielle und die allgemeine Relativitätstheorie", Friedr. Viewig & Sohn, Braunschweig.
61. ENSLOW, P. H. (1977), Multiprocessor organization—a survey. *ACM Computing Surveys*, **9**, pp. 103–129.
62. EPSTEIN, B. (1962), "Partial Differential Equations—An Introduction", McGraw Hill, New York.
63. ESCHENROEDER, A., BELMAN, C. (1973), Mathematical models of smog. *Simulation*, **20**, nr. 3, pp. 41–44.
64. EUROPEAN SIMULATION MEETING (1979), Algorithms in parallel data processing and simulation. Delft, The Netherlands.
65. EYKHOFF, P. (1974), "System Identification—parameter and state estimation", John Wiley & Sons, New York.
66. FEUER, A., MORSE, S. (1978), Adaptive control of single-input, single-output linear systems. *IEEE, T.A.C.*, **AC-23**.
67. FEUSTEL, E. A. (1973), On the advantages of tagged architectures. *IEEE, TC, C-22*, **7**, pp. 644–656.
68. FISHMAN, G. S. (1973), "Concepts and Methods in Discrete Event Digital Simulation", John Wiley & Sons, New York.
69. FLYNN, M. J. (1972), Some computer organizations and their effectiveness. *IEEE Trans. on Computers*, **C-21**, pp. 948–960.
70. FREDRICKSON, A. G., MEGEE III, R. D. and TSUCHIYA, H. M. (1970), Mathematical Models of fermentation processes. *In* "Advances in Applied Microbiology", Perlman (ed.), 13, Academic Press, New York and London.
71. FRIEDLANDER, S. K., SEINFIELD, J. H. (1969), A dynamic model of photo-chemical smog. *Environ. Sci. Technol.*, **3**, nr. 3, pp. 1175–1181.
72. GAMBOLATI, G., FREEZE, R. A. (1973), Mathematical simulation of the subsidence of Venice, 1. Theory. *Water Resources Research*, **9**, nr. 3, pp. 721–733.
73. GARY, J., HELGERSON, R. (1972), An extension of FORTRAN containing finite difference operators. Software Practice and Experience, **2**, pp. 321–336.
74. GASS, S. I. (1977), Evaluation of complex models. Comp. & O.R., 4.
75. GENESIO, R., MILANESE, M. (1979), Methods for the selection of approximating classes of models. *In* "Identification and System Parameter Estimation", R. Iserman (ed.), Pergamon Press, Oxford.
76. GILBERT, E. O., HOWE, R. M. (1978), Design considerations in a multiprocessor computer for continuous system simulation. Proc. AFIPS National Computer Conf., 47, pp. 385–393.
77. GILOI, W. K., HOFFMANN, R. (1976), Adding a modern control structure to APL without changing its syntax. Proc. APL 76 Congress, North Holland Publishing Co.
78. GILOI, W. K. (1977), "Interactive Computer Graphics", Prentice Hall, Englewood Cliffs, New Jersey.
79. GILOI, W. K., BALACI, R. and BEHR, P. (1978), APL∗DS—a powerful portable programming system for RT-level hardware description and simulation, microprogram specification and the simulation of parallel processing

concepts. Technical University of Berlin, BF Informatik, Tech. Report 78–21.

80. GILOI, W. K., BERG, H. (1975), STARLET—a contribution to the computer architecture of the post von Neumann era. University of Minnesota, Dept. of Computer Science, Tech. Report 75–21.

81. GLADWELL, I. WAIT, R. (ed.) (1979), "A survey of numerical methods for partial differential equations", Clarendon Press, Oxford.

82. GLOVER, K, WILLEMS, J. C. (1974), Parametrizations of linear dynamical systems—canonical forms and identifiability. *IEEE Trans. on Autom. Contr.*, **AC-19**, nr. 6, pp. 640–645.

83. GOODWIN, G. and PAYNE, R. (1977), "Dynamic System Identification: Experiment Design and Data Analysis", Academic Press, New York and London.

84. GOODWIN, G. C., RAMADGE, P. J. and CAINES, P. E. (1979), Ultimate objectives and prior knowledge in system identification. *In* "Identification and System Parameter Estimation", R. Iserman (ed.), Pergamon Press, Oxford.

85. GRAYBILL, F. A. (1961), "An Introduction to Linear Statistical Models, 1", McGraw Hill, New York.

86. GREWAL, M. S., GLOVER, K. (1976), Identifiability of linear and non-linear dynamical systems, *IEEE Trans. on Autom. Contr.*, **AC-21**, pp. 833–837.

87. GRITTON, E. C., KING, W. S., SUTHERLAND, I., GAINES, R. S., GAZLEY, Jr., C., GROSCH, C., JUNCOSA, M. and PETERSEN, H. (1977), Feasibility of a special-purpose computer to solve the Navier-Stokes equations. Rand Corporation, Report No. R-2183-RC (June).

88. GROSCH, C. E. (1978), Poisson solvers on a large array computer. Dept. of Mathematical and Computing Sciences, Old Dominion University, TR78-4 (October).

89. GUIDORZI, R. (1975), Canonical structures in the identification of multivariable systems. *Automatica*, **11**, p. 361.

90. HANNINGTON, C., WHITEHEAD, D. G. (1976), A floating point multiplexed DDA system. *IEEE Trans. on Computers*, **C-25**, nr. 11, (November).

91. HASSEL, H. *et al.* (1976), Patterns of dynamical behaviour in single species populations. *J. Anim. Ecol.*, **45**, pp. 471–486.

92. HAYES, J. P. (1978), "Computer Architecture and Organization", McGraw Hill, New York.

93. HOLST, J. (1977), Report LUTFD 2/(TRFT-1013)/1-206/, Lund Institute of Technology, Division of Automatic Control.

94. HOPKINS, A. S. (1977), A three-dimensional finite difference code for seismic analysis on the ILLIAC IV parallel processor. Society of Automotive Engineers, Aerospace Meeting, Paper No. 770956, Los Angeles, CA, (November).

95. HOSTEN, L. (1978), Mathematische modelbouw in de chemische reaktietechniek. Proefschrift tot het verkrijgen van de graad van geaggregeerde voor het hoger onderwijs, R.U.G.

96. HOUCK, J. A. (1976), Computational aspects of real-time simulation of rotary-wing aircraft. MS thesis, School of Engineering and Applied Science, George Washington University, Washington, D.C. (May).

97. HOUSTIS, E. N., RICE., J. R. (1977), Software for linear elliptic problems on general two-dimensional domains. *In* "Advances in Computer Methods

for Partial Differential Equations II", R. Vichnevetsky (ed.), IMACS, pp. 7–12.

98. HUDSON, E. A., JORGENSON, D. W. (1980), Assessment and selection of models for energy and economic analysis. *In* "Gass, S. I., 1980".

99. HUNTER, W. G., REINER, A. M. (1965), *Technometrics*, **7**, p. 307.

100. HYMAN, J. M. (1976), The method of lines solution of partial differential equations. Report nr. COO-3077-139, ERDA Mathematics and Computing Lab., New York University.

101. IEEE TRANSACTION ON COMPUTERS (1979), Issue on data-base machines. **C-12**, nr. 3.

102. IBM (1968), System/360 – Continuous system modeling program (CSMP) User's Manual. A type II program number 360A-CX-16X, Manual number GH 20-0367, available from IBM, White Plains, New York.

103. IBM (1969), General purpose simulation system/360 OS and DO 5 version 2, user's manual. SH20-0694-0, White Plains, New York.

104. IBM (1971), Continuous system modeling program III (CSMP-III) and graphic feature, general information manual. A program product number 5734-X59, Manual number GH 19-7000, White Plains, New York.

105. IVAKHNENKO, A. G. (1970), Heuristic self organization in problems of engineering cybernetics. *Automatica*.

106. IVAKHNENKO, A. G., IVAKHNENKO, N. A. (1974), Long term prediction of random processes by GMDH algorithm using unbiasedness criterion and balance-of-variables criterion, *Soviet Automatic Control*.

107. IVAKHNENKO, A. G. *et al.* (1975), Simulation of the dynamics of the environment plankton ecological system of the white sea and analysis of its stability. *Soviet Automatic Control*.

108. IVAKHNENKO, A. G., KROTOV, G. I. and VISOTSKY, V. N. (1979), Identification of the mathematical model, *In* "Theoretical Systems Ecology", E. Halfon (ed.), Academic Press, New York and London.

109. JACOBY, S., KOWALIK, J. and PIZZO, J. (1972), "Iterative methods for non-linear optimization problems", Prentice Hall, Englewood Cliffs. New Jersey.

110. JACQUEZ, J. (1972), "Compartmental Analysis in Biology and Medicine," Elsevier Publishing Company, Amsterdam.

111. JAKEMAN, A. J., YOUNG, P. C. (1979), Refined instrumental variable methods of recursive time series analysis, Part II: multivariable systems. *Int. J. of Control*, **29**, p. 621.

112. JAYNES, E. T. (1957), Information theory and statistical mechanics. *Phys. Rev.*, **106**, pp. 620–630.

113. JOHNSON, J. (1963), "Econometric Methods", McGraw Hill, New York.

114. JOHNSON, P. M. (1978), An introduction to vector processing. *Computer Design*, **17**, pp. 89–97.

115. JONES, W. T. (1979), Integrated modelling systems: application to energy systems. *In* "Gass, S. I., 1980".

116. JURY, E. I. (1964), Proc. of the 2nd IFAC Congress, Butterworth, London.

117. KALMAN, R., FALB, P. and ARBIB, M. (1969), "Topics in Mathematical System Theory", McGraw Hill, New York.

118. KARPLUS, W. J. (1972), System identification and simulation – a pattern recognition approach. Proc. of the AFIPS Fall Joint Computer Conf., Montvale, pp. 385–392.

119. KARPLUS, W. J. (1976), The future of mathematical models of water

resources systems. *In* "System Simulation in Water Resources", G. C. Vans-teenkiste (ed.), North Holland Publishing Co., Amsterdam, pp. 11–18.

120. KARPLUS, W. J. (1976), The spectrum of mathematical modeling. *In* "Simulation of Systems", L. Dekker (ed.), North Holland Publishing Co., Amsterdam, pp. 5–13.

121. KASHYAP, R. L., RAO, A. R. (1976), Dynamic stochastic models from empirica; data. *Math. in Sci. and Eng.*, **122**, pp. 182–183, Academic Press, New York and London.

122. KASHYAP, R. L. (1977), A Bayesian comparison of different classes of dynamic models using empirical data. *IEEE, T.A.C.*, **AC-22**.

123. KASHYAP, R. L. (1980), Inconsistency of the AIC rule for estimating the order of autoregressive models, *IEEE Trans. on Autom. Contr.*, **AC-25**, nr. 5, pp. 996.

124. KANAL, L. (1974), Patterns in pattern recognition, 1968–1974. *IEEE Trans. on Inform. Theory*, **IT-20**, nr. 6.

125. KENDAL, M. G., STUART, A. (1961), "Advanced Theory of Statistics", Griffin, London.

126. KINCAID, D. R., GRIMES, R. C. (1977), Numerical studies of several adaptive iterative algorithms. Report CNA-126, Center for Numerical Analysis, University of Texas at Austin, (August).

127. KIVIAT, P. J. (1967), Digital computer simulation: Modeling concepts. The Rand Corporation, RM-5378-PR, Santa Monica, California.

128. KIVIAT, P. J. (1969), Digital computer simulation: computer programming languages. The Rand Corporation, RM-5883-PR, Santa Monica, California (January).

129. KLEYNEN, J. P. C. (1974/75), "Statistical Techniques in Simulation", Marcel Dekker Inc., New York.

130. KLIR, G. J. (1979), General systems problem solving methodology. *In* "Methodology in systems modelling and simulation", B. P. Zeigler et al. (eds.), North Holland Publishing Co., Amsterdam.

131. KNUTH, D. C., McNELEY, J. L. (1964), SOL – a symbolic language for general-purpose system simulation, *IEEE Trans. on Electronic Computers*, (August).

132. KORN, G. A. (1972), Back to parallel computation: proposal for a completely new on-line simulation system using standard minicomputers for low-cost multiprocessing, *Simulation*, **19**, nr. 2, pp. 37–45.

133. KORN, G. A., WAIT, J. V. (1978), "Digital Continuous System Simulation", Prentice Hall, Englewood Cliffs, New Jersey.

134. KUBRUSLY, C. S. (1977), Distributed parameter system identification, a survey. *Int. J. of Control*, **26**, nr. 4, pp. 509–535.

135. LAMB, R. G., NEIBURGER, M. (1971), An interim version of a generalized urban air pollution model. *Atmospheric Environment*, **5**, pp. 239–264.

136. LEAF, C. K., MINKOFF, M., BYRNE, C. D., SORENSEN, D., BLEAK-NEY, T. and SALTZMAN, J. (1977), DISPEL: a software package for one and two spatially dimensioned kinetics-diffusion problems. Report No. ANL-77-12, Argonne National Laboratory.

137. LEVIN, M. J. (1963), Proc. of the Joint Automatic Control Conference, 452.

138. JOSEPH, P., LEWIS, J. and TOU, J. (1961), *Trans. A.I.E.E.*, (March).

139. LJUNG, L. (1974), On consistency for prediction error identification methods. Div. Autom. Contr., Lund Inst. of Techn., Lund, Sweden, Rep. 7405.

140. LJUNG, L., RISSANEN, J. (1976), On canonical forms, parameter identifiability and the concepts of complexity. Proc. of the 4th IFAC Symp. on Identification and System Parameter Estimation, Tbilisi, N. S. Rajbman (ed.), Pergamon Press, Oxford.

141. LJUNG, L. (1976), Consistency of the least-squares identification method. *IEEE Trans. on Autom. Contr.*, **AC-21**.

142. LJUNG, L. (1976), On the consistency of prediction error identification methods. *In* "System Identification: Advances and Case Studies", R. K. Mehra, D. G. Lainiotis (eds), Academic Press, New York and London.

143. LJUNG, L. (1977), Analysis of recursive stochastic algorithms. *IEEE Trans. on Autom. Contr.*, **AC-22**, pp. 551–575.

144. LJUNG, L. (1978), Convergence analysis of parametric identification methods. *IEEE Trans. on Autom. Contr.*, **AC-23**, nr. 5, pp. 770–782.

145. LJUNG, L., GLOVER, K. (1979), Frequency domain versus time domain methods in system identification – a brief discussion. *In* "Identification and System Parameter Estimation", R. Iserman (ed.), Pergamon Press, Oxford.

146. LJUNG, L. (1979), Asymptotic behaviour of the extended Kalman filter as a parameter estimator for linear systems. *IEEE Trans. on Autom. Contr.*, **AC-24**, nr. 1, pp. 36–50.

147. LJUNG, L. (1979), Convergence of recursive estimators. *In* "Identification and System Parameter Estimation", R. Iserman (ed.), Pergamon Press, Oxford, pp. 131–144.

148. LJUNG, L. (1977). On positive real functions and the convergence of some recursive schemes. *IEEE Trans. on Autom. Contr.*, **AC-22**, pp. 539–551.

149. LEE, C. K. (1964), "Optimal estimation identification and control", M.I.T. Press, Cambridge.

150. LUCAS, J. J., WAIT, J. V. (1974), DARE-P User's Manual – CSRL Report 255. University of Arizona, College of Engineering, Dept. of Electrical Eng., Computer Science Research Lab., Tucson, AR., U.S.A.

151. LUENBERGER, D. (1973). "Introduction to linear and non-linear programming", Addison & Wesley.

152. MACHURA, M., SWEET, R. A. (1980), A survey of software for partial equations. *ACM Trans. Mathematical Software* **6**, 4, pp. 461–488.

153. MADSEN, N. and SINCOVEC, R. (1976), General software for partial differential equations *In* "Numerical Methods for Differential Equations", Academic Press, London and New York, pp. 229–242.

154. MANN, H. B., WALD, A. (1943), *Econometrica*, **11**, nrs. 3 and 4.

155. MAY, M. (1974), Biological populations with non-overlapping generation of stable points, stable cycles and chaos. *Science*, **186**, pp. 645–647.

156. MEDITCH, J. (1969), "Stochastic optimal linear estimation and control", McGraw Hill, New York.

157. MEHRA, R. K. (1974), Optimal input signals for parameter estimation in dynamic systems – survey and new results. *IEEE Trans. on Autom. Contr.*, **AC-19**, nr. 6, pp. 754.

158. MEHRA, R. K. (1976), Synthesis of optimal inputs for multi-input–multi-output systems with process noise. *In* "System Identification: Advances and Case Studies", R. K. Mehra, D. G. Lainiotis (eds), Academic Press, New York and London.

159. MEHRA, R. K., WANG, J. Y. (1977). Input design for non-linear system identification using catastrophe theory. Personal communication (to appear IFAC Monograph on Identification).

160. MEHRA, R. K. (1978), Group method of data handling, review and experience. Proc. of the Joint Automatic Control Conference.
161. MEHRA, R. K. (1979), Non-linear system identification. *In* "Identification and system Parameter Estimation", R. Iserman (ed.), Pergamon Press, Oxford, pp. 77–84.
162. MELSA, J. L., SAGE, A. P. (1973), "An Introduction to Probability and Stochastic Processes", Prentice Hall, Englewood Cliffs, New Jersey.
163. MESAROVIC, M. D., TAKAHARA, Y. (1975), "General Systems Theory: Mathematical Foundations", Academic Press, New York and London.
164. MITCHELL, E. E., GAUTHIER, J. S. (1976), ACSL: advanced continuous simulation language–Elser/guide reference manual. To be ordered from: Mitchell and Gauthier Assoc., 1337 Old Marlboro Road, Concord. MA 1742, U.S.A.
165. MONOD, J. (1942), "Recherches sur la croissance des cultures bacteriennes", Hermann et Cie, Paris.
166. NAKAMORI, Y., MIYAMOTO, S., IKEDA, S. and SAWARAGI, Y. (1980), Measurement optimization with sensitivity criteria for distributed parameter systems. *IEEE Trans. on Autom. Contr.*, **AC-25**, nr. 5, pp. 889.
167. NILSEN, R. N. (1976), CSSL-IV: the successor to CSSL-III. To be ordered from: Young Lee and Assoc., 2710 W. 233rd street, Torrance, CA, U.S.A.
168. OGATA, K. (1967), "State Space Analysis of Control Systems", Prentice Hall, Englewood Cliffs, New Jersey.
169a. OREN, T. I. (1977a), Software for simulation of combined continuous and discrete systems: a state-of-the-art Review, *Simulation*, Febr., pp. 33–45.
169b. OREN, T. I. (1977b), Software additions. *Simulation*, Oct., pp. 125–126.
170. OREN, T. I. (1979), Concepts for advanced computer assisted modelling. *In* "Methodology in Systems Modelling and Simulation", B.P. Zeigler, M. S. Elzas, G. J. Klir, T. I. Oren (eds), North Holland Publishing Co., Amsterdam.
171. OREN, T. I. ZEIGLER, B. P. (1979), Concepts for advanced simulation methodologies. *Simulation*, **32**, nr.3.
172. ORTEGA, J. M., VOIGHT, R. G. (1977), Solution of partial differential equations on vector computers. Report nr. 77-7, ICASE, March 30.
173. PARNAS, D. L. (1969), On the use of transition diagrams in the design of a user interface for an interactive computer system. Proc. of the ACM Nat. Conf., pp. 379–386.
174. PINDER, G. F., BREDEHOEFT, J. D. (1968), Application of the digital computer for aquifer evaluation. *Water Resources Research*, **4**, nr. 5, pp. 1069–1093.
175. POLAND, J. F. (1969), Status of present knowledge and needs for additional research on compactness of aquifer systems in land subsidence. *Int. Ass. Sci. Hydrol.*, Tokyo, pp. 11–21.
176. POLIS, M. P., GOODSON, R. E. (1976), Parameter identification in distributed systems: a synthesizing overview. *IEEE Trans.*, **64**, nr. 1.
177. POOLE, W., VOIGHT, R. (1974), Numerical algorithms for parallel and vector computers: an annotated bibliography. *ACM Computing Reviews*, **15**, pp. 379–388.
178. PRITSKER, A. A. B. (1974), The GASP-IV simulation language, John Wiley & Sons, New York.
179. PROGRAMMING SCIENCES CORPORATION (1970), CSSL-III user's guide and reference manual, Los Angeles, California.

180. PUGH, A. L. (1970), DYNAMO II user's manual, M.I.T. Press, Cambridge, Massachusetts.
181. PIERCE, D. A. (1972), Least squares estimation in dynamic-disturbance time series models. *Biometrika*, **59**, nr. 1, p. 73.
182. RAO, R. (1973), "Linear Statistical Inference and its Application", John Wiley & Sons, New York.
183. RAMAMOORTHY, C. V., LI, H. F. (1977), Pipeline architecture. *ACM Computing Surveys*, **9**, pp. 61–103.
184. REMSON, I., HORNBERGER, G. M. and MOLZ, F. J. (1971), "Numerical Methods in Subsurface Hydrology", Wiley – Interscience, New York.
185. REID, J. C. (1977), Structural identifiability in linear time-invariant systems. IEEE, *Trans. on Autom. Contr.*
186. REILLY, P. M. (1970), *Canadian Journ. of Chem. Eng.*, **48**, pp. 168.
187. RICE, J. (1977), ELLPACK: a research tool for elliptic partial differential equation software. *Mathematical Software III*, Academic Press, London and New York, pp. 319–341.
188. RICHTMEYER, R. D., MORTON, K. W. (1967), "Difference Methods for Initial Value Problems", Wiley – Interscience, New York.
189. RISSANEN, J. (1976), Parameter estimation by shortest description of data. Proc. of JACC, Lafayette, (July).
190. RISSANEN, J. (1976). Minimax entropy estimation for models for vector processes. *In* "System Identification: Advances and Case Studies", R. K. Mehra, D. G. Lainiotis (eds.), Academic Press, New York and London.
191. RISSANEN, J. (1973), Basis of invariants and canonical forms for linear dynamic systems. *Automatica*, **10**, pp. 175–182.
192. SAMEH, A. H., KUCK, E. J. (1977), Parallel direct linear system solvers–a survey. *Trans. IMACS, Mathematics and Computers in Simulation*, **19**, pp. 272–277.
193. SARIDIS, G., HOFSTADTER, R. (1974), A pattern recognition approach to the classification of nonlinear systems. *IEEE Trans. on Systems, Man and Cybernetics*, **4**, pp. 362–371.
194. SCHWARZ, G. (1978), Estimating the dimension of a model. *Ann. Statist.*, **6**.
195. SHANNON, C. E., WEAVER, W. (1949). "The mathematical theory of communication", University of Illinois Press, Urbana.
196. SHIBATA, R. (1976), Selection of an autoregressive model by Akaike's information criterion. *Biometrika*, **68**, pp. 117.
197. SCHIESSER, W. E. (1972), A digital simulation system for higher-dimensional partial differential equation. Proc. of the 1972 Summer Computer Simulation Conference, San Diego, CA, pp. 62–72.
198. SCHIESSER, W. (1976), "DSS/2–An Introduction to the Numerical Solution of Lines Integration of Partial Differential Equations", 2 volumes, Lehigh University.
199. SIMULATION (1967), "The SCI Continuous System Simulation Language (CSSL)", Vol. 9, nr. 6, pp. 281–303.
200. SIMUNDICH, T. (1975), Systems characterization, a pattern recognition approach. PhD dissertation, U.C.L.A.
201. SIZER, T. R. H. (1968), "The digital differential analyzer", Chapman and Hall, London.
202. SÖDERSTRÖM, T., STOICA, P. (1979), Comparison of some instrumental variables methods–consistency and accuracy aspects. *In* "Identification and

system parameter estimation", R. Iserman (ed.), Pergamon Press, Oxford, pp. 297–306.

203. SÖDERSTRÖM, T. (1977), Model structure testing in system identification, *Internat. Journ. of Control*, **26**, nr. 1, pp. 4–18.
204. SOLO, V. (1978), Time series recursions and stochastic approximation, PhD thesis, Australian National University.
205. SOLO, V. (1978), Report No. AS/R20. Centre for Resource and Environmental Studies, Australian National University.
206. SPRIET, J. A., VANSTEENKISTE, G. C. (1978), New approach towards measurement and identification for control of fermentation systems. *In* "Simulation of Control Systems", I. Troch (ed.), North Holland Publishing Co., Amsterdam, pp. 240–245.
207. SPRIET, J. A. (1980), Struktuurkarakterisatie in het Raam van Patroonherkenning. PhD Thesis, University of Ghent.
208. STANDRIDGE, C. R., PRITSKER, A. A. B. (1980). Using data base capabilities in simulation. Proceedings of Simulation '80, Interlaken, Switzerland.
209. SUGARMAN, R. (1980), Superpower computers. *IEEE Spectrum,* **17**, nr. 4.
210. SUNDARAM, T. R., REHM, R. G., RUDINGER, G. and MERRITT, G. E. (1971), Research on the physical aspects of thermal pollution. Environmental Protection Agency.
211. SUTTON, O. G. (1953), "Micrometeorology", McGraw-Hill, New York.
212. SYN, W. M., LINEBARGER, R. L. (1966), DSL/90–a digital simulation program for continuous system modeling. Proc. of the SJCC.
213. TAM, W. C., KARPLUS, W. J. (1973), The use of the digital simulation language PDEL in hydrological studies. *Water Resources Bulletin,* **9**, nr. 6, pp. 1100–1111.
214. TANENBAUM, A. S. (1976), "Structured Computer Organization", Prentice Hall, Englewood Cliffs, New Jersey.
215. THAMES, J. M. (1969), SLANG, a problem solving language for continuous model simulation and optimization. Proc. of the 24th ACM National Conference, San Francisco, pp. 23.
216. THAMES, J. M. (1973), PROSE, a problem-level programming system. Solveware Associates, San Pedro, California.
217. THIGA, R., GOUGH, N. (1974), Artificial intelligence applied to the discrimination of the order of multivariable linear systems. *Int. Journ. of Control.*
218. THOM, R. (1975), Structural stability and morphogenesis, Benjamin/ Cummings, Reading, MA.
219. THURBER, T. J., WALD, L. D. (1975), Associative and parallel processors. *ACM Computing Surveys*, **7**, pp. 215–255.
220. THURBER, K. J. (1979), Parallel processor architectures, part 1: general purpose systems. *Computer Design*, **18**, pp. 89–97.
221. TOUSSAINT, G. T. (1974), Bibliography on estimation of misclassification. *IEEE Trans. Inform. Theory,* **IT-20**, pp. 472–479.
222. TSUCHIYA, H. M., FREDRICKSON, A. G. and ARIS, R. (1966), *Advances in Chemical Engineering*, **6**, pp. 125.
223. UNIVAC, 1106/1108 (1971), SIMULA programmer reference. UP-7556.
224. VAN OVERBEEK, A. J., LJUNG, L. (1979), On-line structure selection for multivariable state space models. *In* "Identification and system parameter estimation", R. Iserman (ed.), Pergamon Press, Oxford.

225. VANSTEENKISTE, G. C. (1976), System simulation in the testing role. *In* "System Simulation in Water Resources", G. C. Vansteenkiste (ed.), North Holland Publishing Co., Amsterdam.
226. VON NEUMANN, J. (1966), "Theory of Self-Reproducing Automata," Univ. of Illinois Press, Urbana.
227. WADDINGTON, C. H. (ed.) (1970), "Towards a Theoretical Biology", Edinburgh.
228. WALKDEN, F., McINTYRE, H. A. J. and LAWS, G. T. (1977), A user's view of parallel processors. Inst. for Advanced Computation, *Newsletter*, **1**, nr. 8, pp. 1–14.
229. WEISSBERGER, A. J. (1977), Analysis of multiple-microprocessor system architectures. *Computer Design*, **16**, pp. 151–163.
230. WELLSTEAD, P. E. (1978), An instrumental product moment test for model order estimation. *Automatica*, **14**, pp. 89–91.
231. WELTY, J. R., WICKS, C. E. and WILSON, R. E. (1969), "Fundamentals of Momentum, Heat and Mass Transfer", John Wiley & Sons, New York.
232. WHITEHEAD, P. G., YOUNG, P. C. (1975), A dynamic stochastic model for water quality in part of Bedford-Ouse river system. *In* "Computer Simulation of Water Resources", G. C. Vansteenkiste (ed.), North Holland Publishing Co., Amsterdam.
233. WITTMAYER, W. R. (1978), Array processor provides high throughput rates. *Computer Design*, **17**, pp. 93– 100.
234. WOLOVICH, W. A. (1974), "Linear Multivariable Systems", Springer Verlag, New York.
235. WOODSIDE, C. (1971), Estimation of the order of linear systems, *Automatica*, **7**, pp. 727–733.
236. XEROX DATA SYSTEMS (1970), SL-1 reference manual. El Secundo, California.
237. YOUNG, P. C. (1966), "Theory of self-adaptive control Systems", P. H. Hammond (ed.) Plenum Press, New York.
238. YOUNG, P. C. (1969), PhD thesis, Dept. of Eng., Univ. of Cambridge.
239. YOUNG, P. C. (1972), *Trans. I.E.E.E.*, **AC-17**, nr. 2.
240. YOUNG, P. C. (1972), Lectures on recursive approaches to parameter estimation and time series analysis. *In* "Theory and Practice of Systems Modeling and Identification", Ecole Nationale Supérieure de L'Aeronautique et de l'espace.
241. YOUNG, P. C. (1976), Some observations on instrumental variable methods of time series analysis. *Int. J. of Control*, **23**, nr. 5, pp. 593–612.
242. YOUNG, P. C. (1978), General theory of modeling for badly defined systems. *In* "Modelling Identification and Control in Environmental Systems" G. C. Vansteenkiste (ed.). pp. 103–136, North Holland Publishing Co., Amsterdam.
243. YOUNG, P. C., JAKEMAN, A. J. (1978), Reports No. AS/R16, AS/R27, AS/R17, Centre of Resource and Environmental Studies, Australian National University.
244. YOUNG, P. C., JAKEMAN, A. J. (1979), Refined instrumental variable methods of recursive time series analysis, part I: single input, single output systems. *Int. Journal of Control*, **29**, pp. 1–30.
245. YOUNG, P. C. (1979), Parameter estimation for continuous time models–A SURVEY, *In* "Identification and system parameter estimation", R. Iserman (ed.), Pergamon Press, Oxford.

246. YOUNG, P. C., JAKEMAN, A. J. (1980), Refined instrumental variable methods of recursive time series analysis, part III: extensions. *Int. J. of Control* (May).

247. YOUNG, P. C., JAKEMAN, A. J. and McMURTRIE, R. (1980), An instrumental variable method for model order identification. *Automatica*, **16**, pp. 281–294.

248. ZAZWORSKY, R. M., KNUDSEN, H. K. (1977), Comments on controllability, observability and structural identifiability of multi-input and multi-output biological compartmental systems, *IEEE Trans. Biomed. Eng.*, **24**.

249 ZEEMAN, E. C. (1978), "Catastrophe Theory: Selected Papers 1972–77", Addison-Wesley.

250. ZEIGLER, B. P. (1979), Modelling and simulation methodology: state of the art and promising directions. *In* "Simulation of Systems", L. Dekker (ed.), North Holland Publishing Co., Amsterdam.

251. ZEIGLER, B. P. (1976), "Theory of Modelling and Simulation", John Wiley & Sons, New York.

252. ZEIGLER, B. P. (1979), Structuring principles for multifacetted system modeling, *In* "Methodology in Systems Modeling and Simulation", B. Zeigler, M. Elzas, G. Klir, T. Oren (eds), North Holland Publishing Co., Amsterdam.

253. ZEIGLER, B. P. (1979), Multilevel, multiformalism modelling–an ecosystem example. *In* "Theoretical Systems Ecology", E. Halfon (ed.), Academic Press, New York and London.

INDEX